21 世纪英语专业系列教材
北京大学优秀教材

SELECTED READINGS IN AMERICAN LITERATURE

美国文学选读

（第二版）

主编　陶　洁
编者　陶　洁　程朝翔　刘建华　刘树森　张世耘
　　　沈建青　李　晋　陈法春　林　斌　崔鲜泉

北京大学出版社
PEKING UNIVERSITY PRESS

图书在版编目(CIP)数据

美国文学选读/陶洁主编.—2版.—北京：北京大学出版社，2017.4
(21世纪英语专业系列教材)
ISBN 978-7-301-28223-6

Ⅰ.①美… Ⅱ.①陶… Ⅲ.①英语—阅读教学—高等学校—教材 ②文学—作品—介绍—美国 Ⅳ.H319.4:I

中国版本图书馆CIP数据核字(2017)第057672号

书　　　名	美国文学选读(第二版) MEIGUO WENXUE XUANDU
著作责任者	陶　洁　主编
责任编辑	李　娜
标准书号	ISBN 978-7-301-28223-6
出版发行	北京大学出版社
地　　　址	北京市海淀区成府路205号　100871
网　　　址	http://www.pup.cn　　新浪微博:@北京大学出版社
电子信箱	345014015@qq.com
电　　　话	邮购部 62752015　发行部 62750672　编辑部 62754149
印　刷　者	涿州市星河印刷有限公司
经　销　者	新华书店
	787毫米×1092毫米　16开本　20印张　590千字 2012年6月第1版　2017年4月第2版　2023年1月第6次印刷
定　　　价	46.00元

未经许可，不得以任何方式复制或抄袭本书之部分或全部内容。
版权所有，侵权必究
举报电话：010-62752024　电子信箱：fd@pup.pku.edu.cn
图书如有印装质量问题，请与出版部联系，电话：010-62756370

21世纪英语专业系列教材
编写委员会

（以姓氏笔画排序）

王立非	王守仁	王克非
王俊菊	文秋芳	石　坚
申　丹	朱　刚	仲伟合
刘世生	刘意青	孙有中
李　力	李正栓	杨俊峰
张旭春	张庆宗	张绍杰
陈法春	金　莉	封一函
胡壮麟	查明建	袁洪庚
桂诗春	殷企平	黄国文
梅德明	董洪川	蒋洪新
程幼强	程朝翔	虞建华

第二版前言

以前常说，美国文学没有很长的历史。这指的是白人的文学史。首先因为从1640第一批殖民者到达新大陆到1778年美国立国到今天还没有超过500年。其次因为其中没有包括原来生活在美洲大陆的土著居民（又叫印第安人）。不过，这种情况在20世纪70年代的民权运动以后有所改变。现在美国强调多元文化，不再认为美国是个大熔炉，大家都融入白人文化。这一认识充分表现在美国大学的文学选读教材里。2007年出版的美国大学经典教材《诺顿美国文学选读》第七版不仅把白人文学追溯到哥伦布在1493年写给西班牙国王财务大臣的信，还增加了大约公元1000年后土著居民各部族口口相传的故事、歌谣和讲话，甚至还有白人批判当年殖民者对待土著居民残酷行为的文章。在现当代部分不仅增加了土著居民的歌谣，还扩大了黑人作家和妇女作家的数量，甚至还有华裔、墨西哥裔等少数族裔作家。

当然，这样做的结果是教材篇幅越来越大，动辄两三千页。作为外国学生，我们是不可能在一个学期或一个学年内读完这类教材。我们只能选择经典中的经典，最有代表性的作家和作品，为学生提供一个了解美国文学发展的概貌。这就是我们编写这本教材的目的。

在编写过程中我们遵循以下几条原则：

首先，在作家的取舍方面，凡是已经成为经典的我们仍然收入，如海明威、福克纳和菲茨杰拉德等小说家和庞德、威廉斯、史蒂文斯等诗人。但我们增加了比较多的当代作家，帮助学生了解美国文学的新发展和新动态。

其次，考虑到美国文学的多元化发展，我们所选的作家不仅在文学史上占有一定的地位，而且在主题、手法、文体风格或种族、性别等方面有一定的代表性。所选篇目必须是该作家的经典作品。例如，我们不仅有白人、黑人和犹太裔作家，还增加了华裔和墨西哥裔作家；不仅有现实主义作家，也有采用试验手法的诗人和小说家。在选材上，除了戏剧和个别小说家如托妮·莫里森外，我们还尽量使用独立完整的文本，并且尽量选用既有代表性又不是大家已经十分熟悉的材料。

第三，我们认为一本好的教科书不能面面俱到，包办一切，而是应该起引导作用，给教师和学生留有充分的思考空间和余地。因此，我们只有简明扼要的作者简介和作品赏析，却提供了进一步阅读的篇目和一些参考书。另一方面，虽然此选读供一学期18周使用，但我们提供了22个单元，为了使有限的篇幅能包含更多的内容，我们把爱默生和梭罗合成一个单元，诗歌方面介绍的诗人就更多一些。在选材方面，我们也在可能的情况下提供一些既是作家的代表作但又并不一定跟其他《美国文学选读》雷同的选文。我们甚至没有收入米勒的戏剧，而是选了当代剧作家马麦特，因为米勒的作品比较容易寻找。总之，我们的目的是希望让教师和学生有更多的选择余地，更能发挥自己的主观能动性。

1

这本书还是集体合作的成果。每个篇目后署名的编写人员均为大学英语系的骨干教授或副教授，对所编对象有比较深入的研究。本次新版教材除了改正一些错误之外，我们还根据授课教师和学生的意见对部分章节的选文进行了调整，旨在提供更丰富的选读文章供教师选取和供学生自学，提高教材的适用性和灵活性。

　　尽管我们努力了，但仍不免挂一漏万。我们真心希望使用这本教材的教师和学生能提出意见和建议，以便我们的教材能够不断改进和完善。

陶　洁

目录

绪　论	1
第一单元	1
Benjamin Franklin（1706—1790）本杰明·富兰克林	1
Autobiography	1
第二单元	10
Ralph Waldo Emerson（1803—1882）拉尔夫·华尔多·爱默生	10
Self-Reliance	10
Henry David Thoreau（1817—1862）亨利·大卫·梭罗	21
Walden	21
第三单元	28
Nathaniel Hawthorne（1804—1864）纳撒尼尔·霍桑	28
Ethan Brand	28
第四单元	40
Herman Melville（1819—1891）赫尔曼·梅尔维尔	40
Moby-Dick	40
第五单元	45
Walt Whitman（1819—1892）沃尔特·惠特曼	45
Song of Myself（I, II, VI & LII）	46
Emily Dickinson（1830—1886）埃米莉·狄金森	53
Hope	54
Because I Could Not Stop for Death	55
Edgar Allan Poe（1809—1849）埃德加·爱伦·坡	58
The Raven	59
第六单元	64
Mark Twain（1835—1910）马克·吐温	64
The £1,000,000 Bank-Note	64
第七单元	78
Henry James（1843—1916）亨利·詹姆斯	78
The Real Thing	78
Sherwood Anderson（1876—1941）舍伍德·安德森	95
A Story Teller's Story	95
第八单元	105
Ezra Pound（1885—1972）艾兹拉·庞德	105
A Girl	105

1

Wallace Stevens（1879—1955）华莱士·史蒂文斯 ·················· 107
   The Snow Man ·················· 107
Robert Frost（1874—1963）罗伯特·弗罗斯特 ·················· 109
   Love and a Question ·················· 109
William Carlos Williams（1883—1963）威廉·卡洛斯·威廉斯 ·················· 112
   The Uses of Poetry ·················· 112
Langston Hughes（1902—1967）兰斯顿·休斯 ·················· 114
   The Weary Blues ·················· 114

第九单元 ·················· 117
Eugene Gladstone O'Neill（1888—1953）尤金·格拉斯通·奥尼尔 ·················· 117
   Long Day's Journey into Night ·················· 117

第十单元 ·················· 135
F. Scott Fitzgerald（1896—1940）弗·斯科特·菲茨杰拉德 ·················· 135
   Winter Dreams ·················· 135

第十一单元 ·················· 150
William Faulkner（1897—1962）威廉·福克纳 ·················· 150
   Barn Burning ·················· 150

第十二单元 ·················· 163
Ernest Hemingway（1899—1961）厄内斯特·海明威 ·················· 163
   Hills Like White Elephants ·················· 163

第十三单元 ·················· 168
Ralph（Waldo）Ellison（1914—1994）拉尔夫·埃里森 ·················· 168
   King of the Bingo Game ·················· 168

第十四单元 ·················· 177
John Updike（1932—2009）约翰·厄普代克 ·················· 177
   Separating ·················· 178

第十五单元 ·················· 186
Saul Bellow（1915—2005）索尔·贝娄 ·················· 186
   A Silver Dish ·················· 186

第十六单元 ·················· 206
Robert Hayden（1913—1980）罗伯特·海登 ·················· 206
   Those Winter Sundays ·················· 206
Robert Lowell（1917—1977）罗伯特·洛威尔 ·················· 209
   Man and Wife ·················· 209
Allen Ginsberg（1926—1997）艾伦·金斯堡 ·················· 212
   Howl ·················· 212
Robert Creeley（1926—2005）罗伯特·克里莱 ·················· 216
   Water Music ·················· 216
Sylvia Plath（1932—1963）西尔维娅·普拉斯 ·················· 218

Last Words	218

第十七单元 · 221

Edward Franklin Albee（1928—2016）爱德华·富兰克林·阿尔比 · 221
Who's Afraid of Virginia Woolf? · 221

第十八单元 · 231

Toni Morrison（1931—   ）托妮·莫里森 · 231
Beloved · 231

第十九单元 · 238

Maxine Hong Kingston（1940—   ）汤亭亭 · 238
The Woman Warrior · 238

第二十单元 · 250

Leslie Marmon Silko（1948—   ）莱丝莉·摩门·西尔柯 · 250
Lullaby · 250

第二十一单元 · 257

Robert Bly（1926—   ）罗伯特·布莱 · 257
The Buried Train · 257
John Ashbery（1927—   ）约翰·阿什贝利 · 259
And Ut Pictura Poesis Is Her Name · 259
Adrienne Rich（1929—2012）艾德里安娜·里奇 · 262
Diving into the Wreck · 262
Robert Pinsky（1940—   ）罗伯特·平斯基 · 267
To Television · 267
Rita Dove（1952—   ）丽塔·达夫 · 270
My Mother Enters the Work Force · 270
Gary Soto（1952—   ）加里·索托 · 273
Mexicans Begin Jogging · 273
How Things Work · 274

第二十二单元 · 276

David Alan Mamet（1947—   ）大卫·艾伦·马麦特 · 276
Oleanna · 276

绪 论

美国文学的历史不长,但发展较快。20世纪以来,美国作家的探索试验和变革创新的精神一直激励着世界各国的作家不断革新,超越前人。改革开放以来,美国文学对我国新时期的作家也产生了巨大的吸引力。盛行一时的朦胧诗恐怕就是在美国及西方现代派诗歌的影响下产生的。海明威、福克纳及塞林格等人几乎成为我们年轻一代作家文学创作的楷模。因此,在我们加强与美国的交往的时候,有必要学一点美国文学,了解他们的文化,以促进与美国人民的交流、沟通和理解,同时也借以丰富我们的知识,充实我们的文化修养,提高我们的精神素质。

下面按不同的历史时期简单介绍一下美国文学的历史。

(一) 殖民时期

在讨论这个问题以前必须指出,美国是个移民国家,但在英法等欧洲殖民者来到以前,美洲大陆上原来就有被新大陆发现者称为"印第安人"的土著居民。他们满腔热情地欢迎那些外来的殖民者,帮助他们学会在当地生活和种植作物。然而,白人殖民者以怨报德,站住脚跟后对他们大肆屠杀,使他们的文化和民间口头文学的传统受到致命的摧残,直到20世纪后期才有所发掘,从而使文学选读教材里有了他们的一席之地。

过去认为殖民时期大约涵盖从1607年约翰·史密斯船长领导第一批移民在北美大陆建立第一个英国殖民地詹姆斯敦到1765年殖民地人民愤怒抗议英国政府颁布的印花税法的这一段时间。但现在的做法是向前推至哥伦布发现新大陆的1492年。这一时期的文学并不繁荣,模仿性很强,主要形式是叙述文。然而,它对日后的美国文学还是有很大影响的。当年来美洲大陆移民的人基本上属于两种人:一种是为了逃避国内政治迫害、追求宗教自由的英国清教徒;另一种是谋求发财致富的欧洲老百姓,包括野心勃勃的冒险家。不论哪一种人都相信在新大陆可以得到自由平等,有机会实现自己的理想。这种观点使"美国梦"成为日后美国文学的一个永恒的主题。清教主义有关人生来有罪及上帝主宰一切等思想也影响美国作家不断思考人性与原罪、人与上帝的关系。此外,作为一个由移民组成的国家,美国受各种文化的影响,这决定了美国文学要比其他西方文学更具有多样性。

这一时期,由于人们忙于生存,无暇吟诗作曲,加上清教主义反对虚构的小说戏剧,因此多半的文学采用叙事文体,如当时的宗教领袖和殖民区领导人物布雷德福(William Bradford, 1590—1657)、温思罗普(John Winthrop, 1588—1649)等人撰写的书籍多半是讲经布道等有关神学的材料或日记。此外还有一些探险家和已经定居的殖民者为欧洲读者或亲人甚至上级领导所撰写的介绍新大陆的山水风貌和日常生活的小册子或游记书信,最著名的是约翰·史密斯船长(Captain John Smith, 1580—1631)关于新英格兰地区和弗吉尼亚的文章。他大力渲染新大陆土地肥沃,物产丰富,只要勤劳,不怕艰难,一定能够发财致富。他的文章对推动殖民化起到了很大的作用。

这时期的诗歌也摆脱不了宗教色彩和描述殖民经历的特点。比较出色的诗人有安妮·布雷特兹里特(Anne Bradstreet, 约1612—1672)和爱德华·泰勒(Edward Taylor, 约1642—1729)。前者是北美第一位在英国出版诗集的女诗人,她的诗歌虽然宗教气息较浓,但她描写夫妻恩爱、家庭美满等日常生活题材的诗歌感情真挚,富有感染力。她偶尔流露的女性意识也值得肯定。泰勒是位牧师,虔诚的清教徒,诗歌创作也是为上帝服务,有些跟他的讲道有密切关系。他的作品在生前并未发表,直到20世纪30年代才被发现并整理出版。两位诗人的一个共同特点是都受英国玄学派诗人的影响,诗歌有较大的模仿性。

(二) 革命与建国时期(1765—18世纪末)

这时期的文学仍然以理性的叙述文为主,但宗教色彩不那么浓厚了。因为经济发展了,殖民者的注意力开始转向世俗生活,在欧洲启蒙主义和自然神论等哲学思潮的影响下,上帝的作用被大大削弱,清教主义的统治逐渐衰落。只有在18世纪30年代,清教徒们掀起一场"大觉醒"运动,企图恢复清教主义的统治。领导人爱德华兹(Jonathan Edwards, 1703—1758)是个杰出的神学家,他吸收当时先进的心理学理论,从打动听众的感情入手,宣传上帝之万能和地狱之恐怖,人如想得到拯救必须皈依上帝。然而,"大觉醒"运动未能阻挡历史的潮流,未能使清教主义免于衰亡。

这一时期涌现出大量论证独立之必要的文章。从1765年新大陆来自英国的殖民者第一次反对英国政府的印花税到1789年美国联邦政府成立的二十多年里,北美大陆的政治形势发展很快。1775年独立战争爆发,1776年宣布独立,1783年对英战争胜利,1789年新宪法生效,华盛顿当选第一任总统。各派政治力量对于革命的必要性、革命的前途与方向、政府的形式与性质等重大问题展开激烈争论,产生了大批论点鲜明、充满战斗力和说服力的杂文、政论文和演讲词,如潘恩(Thomas Paine, 1737—1809)的《常识》(*Common Sense*, 1776)、杰斐逊(Thomas

Jefferson, 1743—1826)参与写成的《独立宣言》(The Declaration of Independence, 1776)和汉密尔顿(Alexander Hamilton, 1757—1804)、麦迪逊(James Madison, 1751—1836)及杰伊(John Jay, 1745—1829)三人的《论联邦》(The Federalist Papers, 1788)等。即便诗歌也常常以政治为内容。

1789年,美利坚合众国正式成立,革命的成功为文学发展提供了机会。1783年,词典学家韦伯斯特(Noah Webster, 1758—1843)强调"美国在政治上独立了,在文学方面也必须独立;美国以军事著称,也必须以艺术著称世界"。虽然小说还处于起步阶段,还深受英国以及整个欧洲的影响,但从1789年威廉·希尔·布朗(William Hill Brown, 1765—1793)发表第一部美国小说《同情的力量》(The Power of Sympathy)开始,美国文坛很快出现查尔斯·布罗克丹·布朗(Charles Brockden Brown, 1771—1810)、休·亨利·布拉肯里奇(Hugh Henry Brackenridge, 1748—1816)等一批有上乘之作的小说家。尽管诗歌仍不景气,但弗瑞诺(Philip Freneau,1752—1832)赞美北美花草、歌颂印第安人的诗歌已经具有浪漫主义的萌芽。

18世纪美国一个极为重要的作家是启蒙运动的代表人物富兰克林(Benjamin Franklin, 1706—1790)。他是爱德华兹的同时代人,但两人的生活道路截然不同。富兰克林是个人文主义者,相信人性善良,主张人权天赋、政治平等,认为行善是忠于上帝的最好表示。他出身贫苦,但意志坚定,顽强奋斗,从商、参政、写文章、研究科学,终于成为文学家、科学家和在美国立国过程中起重大作用的政治家。他的《格言历书》(Poor Richard's Almanac, 1732—1758)通过大量的格言警句宣传创业持家、待人处世的道德原则和勤奋致富的生活道路。他在独立革命期间撰写的《自传》(Autobiography, 1771—1788)以亲身经历再次说明,美国有的是机会,只要勤奋便能成功。富兰克林的成功经验对美国人的人生观、事业观和道德观产生过深远的影响。他的《自传》还开创了美国名人写传记的风气,建立了传记文学的传统。

(三)浪漫主义时期(1800—1865)

19世纪初,美国开始以独立国家的身份进入世界政治舞台。民族文学开始全面繁荣,逐渐打破英国文学在美国的垄断局面。这一时期的作家跟英国浪漫主义作家一样,强调文学的想象力和感情色彩,反对古典主义的形式与观点,歌颂大自然,崇尚个人和普通人的思想感情,并且寻根问祖,发幽古之思情。尽管他们仍然模仿英国作家,素材却完全取自美国现实,如西部开发与拓荒经历。他们赞美美国山水、讴歌美国生活、反映美国人民的乐观与热情。早期浪漫主义的主要代表作家是欧文(Washington Irving, 1783—1859)、库柏(James Fenimore Cooper, 1789—1851)和布赖恩特(William Cullen Bryant, 1794—1878)。欧文以短篇小说见长,他的《见闻札记》(The Sketch Book, 1819—1820)开创了美国短篇小说的传统,使他成为第一个享有国际声誉的美国作家。其中《睡谷的传说》("The Legend of Sleepy Hollow")和《瑞普·凡·温克尔》("Rip Van Winkle")虽取材于德国民间故事,却以纽约哈德逊河谷为背景,充满美国式的浪漫气息和传奇色彩,尤其那长不大的反英雄小人物凡·温克尔至今仍脍炙人口。库柏主要写长篇小说,而且有三种不同类型的小说:历史小说、细节准确详尽的冒险小说和对后来西部文学影响甚大的边疆小说——《皮袜子故事集》(The Leather Stocking Tales, 1827—1841)五部曲。在这五本小说里,库柏开创了美国文学的一个重要主题——文明的发展对大自然和它所代表的崇高品德的摧残与破坏。他还塑造了美国文学的一个重要的原型人物——独立不羁、逃避社会、在大自然中寻求完美精神世界的班波。在诗歌方面,威廉·科伦·布赖恩特是美国第一个浪漫主义诗人,也是第一个受到英国诗坛赞赏的美国诗人。《致水鸟》("To a Waterfowl", 1818)、《黄色的堇香花》("The Yellow Violet", 1815)等代表作描写美国的山水花鸟、讴歌大自然的精神启示、满腔热情地歌颂美国的生活现实、表现乐观向上的精神面貌,不仅在形式上开始摆脱英国新古典主义的影响,在内容上也不再宣传清教主义的来世思想,转而强调现世生活。

1829年,出身贫寒的安德鲁·杰克逊成为美国总统。他推行民主路线,使美国民主气氛大大高涨。随着工业的发展和西部边疆的开拓,美国开始成为一个充满民族自信、繁荣兴旺的国家。但是,对印第安人的迫害和南方的蓄奴制日益成为尖锐的社会矛盾焦点。从杰克逊上台到南北战争(1860—1865)是浪漫主义文学的全盛时期,常被称为美国文学史上的"第一次大繁荣"。此时,文学不再是为宗教和政治服务的工具,而是作家抒发个人胸怀、探讨人性、人与自然、科学与进步等哲理问题以及评论时政、批评不良现象的手段。在欧洲浪漫主义运动的影响下,作家们试验各种创作形式与表现手法,开始重视对人物心理的分析,注意运用象征手段。无论散文、诗歌还是小说都有了较大的发展,涌现出了一大批风格迥异的作家和诗人。19世纪浪漫主义运动的中心在新英格兰地区,主要表现形式为超验主义(Transcendentalism)。超验主义理论崇尚直觉,反对理性和权威,强调人有能力凭直觉直接认识真理,人能超越感觉获得知识。因此,人的存在就是神的存在的一部分,人在一定范围内就是上帝,自然界是神对人的启示,人可以从自然界认识真理,了解物质发展规律,得到精神道德原则方面的启示。超验主义理论的奠基人是爱默生(Ralph Waldo Emerson, 1803—1882)。他和志同道合的朋友们组成一个非正式的"超验主义俱乐部",还创办过一个杂志《日晷》(The Dial)。爱默生的《论自然》("Nature", 1836)、《论自立》("Self-Reliance", 1841)等著作对打破神学统治、摒弃以神为中心的清教教义、强调人在宇宙万物中的地位、号召人们摆脱英国的影响以及确立民主思想和发展民族文化起了极大的作用。《论自然》曾被称为超验主义理论的"圣经"。另一位超验主义作家梭罗

（Henry David Thoreau,1817—1862）是爱默生的朋友和门徒。他接受爱默生关于认识自我和研究自然的思想,并且身体力行,独自在家乡森林沃尔登湖畔生活了两年,把超验主义的原则和自己的哲理信念付诸实践。《沃尔登湖》(Walden, 1854)详细描写他在湖畔的生活,宣传自然的美好,批判资本主义文明的消极影响,呼吁人们返璞归真,到自然中去寻找生活的意义和丰富的精神世界。梭罗富有正义感,反对美国对墨西哥的战争,谴责蓄奴制。他的《论公民的不服从》("Civil Disobedience", 1849)主张用和平斗争的方式反对战争和奴隶制,对印度的甘地、20世纪60年代的美国黑人领袖马丁·路德·金等人起过积极的影响。

在诗歌方面,新英格兰地区比较出名的诗人有朗费罗（Henry Wadsworth Longfellow, 1807—1882)、霍姆斯（Oliver Wendell Holmes, 1809—1894)和洛威尔（James Russell Lowell, 1801—1891)等。他们大都出身世家、有地位有名望、文化修养比较高,但又都比较守旧、缺乏创新精神,对社会问题虽有批评却比较温和。因此他们常被称为波士顿的"婆罗门"（Brahmins)。朗费罗常以民间传说为题材,创作长篇叙事诗,较为著名的有《海华莎之歌》（The Song of Hiawatha, 1855)。他的《人生颂》("A Psalm of Life", 1838)曾在19世纪70年代被翻译成中文。霍姆斯写过不少适合社交界口味的轻松风趣的诗歌,运用古典主义的文体,在遣词造句上很下功夫。洛威尔不仅是诗人还是散文家,早年热心社会改革,晚年日趋保守。在波士顿附近的另一位诗人惠蒂埃（John Greenleaf Whittier, 1807—1892)却以迥然不同的风格,不加雕琢的语言描写新英格兰农村的美丽景色、淳朴的劳动人民和他们的日常生活。长诗《大雪封门》（Snow-Bound, 1866)曾被誉为"一部优美的新英格兰田园诗"。惠蒂埃还是一位坚定的废奴运动诗人,写过大量的斗争性很强的诗歌和政论文,揭露奴隶主的暴行和黑奴的悲惨命运。

19世纪美国最伟大的浪漫主义诗人是惠特曼（Walt Whitman, 1819—1892）。他在1855年出版的《草叶集》(Leaves of Grass)标志着美国文学进入了一个崭新的时代。他在前言里明确宣称他要建立美国式的独立自主的文学,用以反映美国的社会、历史和各个种族。《草叶集》第一版只有12首诗,但惠特曼不断增加新内容,到1892年他逝世时,已经收入近400首诗歌。惠特曼是一位伟大的民主诗人。他的诗篇涉及从死亡、爱情到民主、革命,从草叶、芦笛到宇宙、灵魂等众多内容,歌颂普通的人与事及人与人之间同志般的友好关系,强调灵与肉的统一,精神与肉体同等重要。惠特曼的诗歌粗犷奔放、气魄雄壮,反映美国人民在民主革命时期乐观向上的精神,充满对生活、人类和大自然的热爱。《草叶集》中的《自己的歌》概括了惠特曼一生的主要思想,是他最重要的作品。为了更好地表现美国生活的多样化,他对诗歌形式进行大胆的改革,摒弃传统的诗歌技巧,采用自由体,诗行较长,比较接近散文诗。他采用日常口语,比喻、意象也取自生活,比较粗糙。但这种粗犷奔放的诗歌语言和形式十分恰当地表达了诗人的激情和胸怀。可以说,惠特曼是美国诗歌革命的先驱。另一位革新诗歌的诗人是狄金森（Emily Dickinson, 1830—1886)。她一生几乎从未离开过她出生的小镇,晚年更是足不出户,不见生人,与外界完全隔绝。她的诗歌有很大的局限性,不像惠特曼那样包罗万象。但她在摆脱旧诗体的束缚、创造新诗形式方面却与惠特曼不谋而合。她的诗歌诗行不多,口语色彩浓厚,不强调韵律,常常押半韵或完全不押韵,没有标点符号,也不受语法限制,但意象鲜明活泼,来自生活却又富有新意。狄金森一生写过1700余首诗歌,生前仅发表过5首。虽然她的诗歌以描写日常生活的普通事物为主,但内容深邃,别具一格。她对现代派诗歌影响较大,被誉为美国20世纪新诗的先驱,因为她经常探讨的有关死亡、爱情、自然、永恒、人的自我本质和宗教信仰等主题也是20世纪诗人关心的问题。1955年出版的《艾米莉·狄金森诗集》确立了狄金森在美国文学史上的重要地位。

浪漫主义时期两位重要的小说家是霍桑和梅尔维尔。霍桑（Nathaniel Hawthorne, 1804—1864)不赞成超验主义,尤其是"人即是神"的说法。他对社会改革、生产发展和科学进步也表示疑虑与不安,反对清教主义对人的压抑,但常用清教主义关于人的罪恶天性、人生来有罪等观念去看待社会中的现实问题。在《福谷传奇》（The Blithedale Romance, 1852)中以自己在超验主义者开办的布鲁克农场的生活为基础,讽刺嘲笑超验主义的改革措施。他的作品大都取材于新英格兰地区的历史或现实生活,中心主题往往是人的内心深处隐蔽的罪恶和过于自信的个人主义的种种缺陷。《红字》（The Scarlet Letter, 1850)描写罪恶对人精神面貌的作用,《带有七个尖阁楼的房子》（The House of the Seven Gables, 1851)表现祖上的罪孽对后代的报应。短篇小说《教长的黑纱》（"The Minister's Black Veil", 1836)、《好小伙子布朗》("Young Goodman Brown", 1835)等力图证明邪恶是人的共性;《胎记》（"The Birthmark", 1843)和《拉伯西尼医生的女儿》("Rappaccini's Daughter", 1844)等强调理性和科学技术的破坏作用。霍桑善于借用哥特式小说的手法塑造魔鬼似的恶人,把灵魂出卖给魔鬼的人等人物形象,并把这种手法和传统的寓言故事的特点相结合。他偏爱渲染背景和剖析人物心理,对后世作家影响颇大。

梅尔维尔（Herman Melville, 1819—1891)深受霍桑的影响,关心人类命运,承认邪恶的普遍性,怀疑超验主义的乐观主义理论,对社会进步持悲观态度。但是梅尔维尔不像霍桑那样安于命运、接受现实。他进行更为深刻的钻研,探讨上帝的本质、人类的天性和邪恶战胜一切的原因。代表作《白鲸》（Moby-Dick, 1851)对此作了深刻的反映。他通过亚哈船长一心捕杀曾咬断他一条腿的白鲸,最后与鲸鱼同归于尽的故事说明人的悲惨在于他不能了解自己,不能掌握自己的命运,他向宇宙和自然规律的挑战必然走向灭亡。梅尔维尔跟霍桑一样,认为小说中最重要的是主题,作家应充分利用意象、象征手段、人物和情节来表达中心思想。他与霍桑的不同之处在于他在作品中大量提供以事实和生活经历为基础的生动具体的细节,使故事带有极大的现实性和可靠性。不仅如此,他还巧妙地安排这些细节和故事结构,使之含有非同一般的象征意义。因此,他的作品往往比霍桑的作品更为深刻、更发人深思。《白鲸》既是一个捕鲸故事,又是一则寓意深刻的寓言,还是一首扣人心弦的史诗。

在浪漫派作家中,埃德加·爱伦·坡(Edgar Allan Poe,1809—1849)比较独特。他在南方生长,深受南方贵族阶级思想的影响,反对民主,赞成蓄奴制。他一生清贫、命运坎坷,因而思想悲观,作品色彩阴暗、情调低沉。坡是美国第一位主张为艺术而艺术的作家。他的作品脱离现实生活,从不涉及自由、民主、边疆、改革等国家大事。他强调诗歌应当通过音乐节奏给人以美感,最能打动人的主题是对死去恋人的哀悼。他的诗歌如《乌鸦》("The Raven",1845)等充满古怪、奇特,甚至病态的形象,对法国波德莱尔等象征派诗人产生了极大的影响。坡创作了一百多篇短篇小说,大致分恐怖小说和推理小说两种。恐怖小说深受英国哥特式小说的影响,以异国他乡为背景,以混乱、死亡、怪诞和变态心理为主要内容。比较著名的有《丽盖亚》("Ligeia",1838)和《厄舍大厦的倒塌》("The Fall of the House of Usher",1839)等。坡还因为写了大量推理小说而被推崇为西方侦探小说的鼻祖。《莫根街的凶杀案》("Murders in the Rue Morgue",1841)、《失窃的信件》("The Purloined Letter",1844)等小说所创造的模式至今仍为西方侦探小说家所沿袭。坡还是美国第一位文艺理论家,著有《创作哲学》(*Philosophy of Composition*,1846)和《诗歌原理》(*The Poetic Principle*,1848)等论著。坡并不受同时代作家的重视,但他反对文学以说教为目的,强调创造美感和激情的理论对后世作家产生了较大的影响。坡至今仍是世界上最受欢迎的作家之一。

浪漫主义时期还值得一提的现象是废奴文学的兴起。18世纪30年代开始,蓄奴制成为南北作家共同关心的问题。新英格兰地区的学者、诗人和作家无不发表对蓄奴制的看法。爱默生和梭罗公开抨击南方蓄奴制,支持废奴运动领袖约翰·布朗(John Brown)。诗人惠蒂埃写过大量诗歌杂文抗议蓄奴制。但是,影响最大的是斯托夫人(Harriet Beecher Stowe,1811—1896)的被林肯总统称之为"发动了一场大战"的小说——《汤姆叔叔的小屋》(*Uncle Tom's Cabin*,1852)。这时期还出现了大量的黑奴自述,多半描写他们在南方的悲惨生活和争取自由的奋斗经历。最为著名的是弗莱德雷克·道格拉斯(Frederic Douglass,约1818—1895)的《弗莱德雷克·道格拉斯,一个美国奴隶的自述》(*Narrative of the Life of Frederic Douglass, an American Slave*,1845)。

(四)现实主义时期(1865—1918)

从南北战争结束到第一次世界大战爆发,美国完成了从农业社会到工业社会的转化,社会面貌和经济生活开始发生急剧的变化。铁路的建设、资源的开发、移民带来的廉价劳动力等都促进了工业的发展。但是工业化造就了靠剥削致富的资本家的同时也带来劳资纠纷,贫富差距日益扩大,罢工斗争时有发生。工业化的另一个后果是政治日趋腐败,政界丑闻屡见不鲜。所有这些变化迫使人们要求发现和认识新的生活和新开发的土地。于是乡土文学的出现成为南北战争以后美国文学的一大发展。乡土文学在新英格兰地区的代表是女作家朱厄特(Sarah Orne Jewett,1849—1909)。她的短篇小说集《迪普黑文》(*Deep Haven and Other Stories*,1877)和长篇小说《尖枞树之乡》(*The Country of Pointed Firs*,1896)描绘了新英格兰农村的宁静生活、勤奋的人民和战后的衰落。南方乡土文学作家有哈里斯(Joel Chandler Harris,1848—1908)。他的《雷莫斯大叔:他的歌与话》(*Uncle Remus: His Songs and Sayings*,1880)通过黑奴雷默斯大叔介绍了大量起源于非洲的幽默诙谐的民间故事和神话,对马克·吐温产生了一定的影响。另一位南方乡土作家肖邦(Kate Chopin,1850—1904)写过一百多篇反映南方城乡的法国和西班牙殖民者后裔同黑人与印第安人之间关系的作品。她描写一位女性自我意识觉醒过程的长篇小说《觉醒》(*The Awakening*,1899)已成为女性文学的经典作品。西部的乡土文学作家是哈特(Bret Harte,1836—1902)。他的作品主要反映西部的边疆生活,最著名的是《咆哮营的幸运儿》(*The Luck of Roaring Camp*,1868)。

19世纪70年代,随着梭罗、霍桑等人的去世,浪漫主义文学运动衰落。纽约取代了波士顿成为美国文学的中心。各地区风格独特的乡土文学促进了现实主义文学的发展。这时期的作家不再写生死之奥秘或歌颂英勇的个人,也不满足于充满幻想与激情的浪漫主义。他们着眼于现实生活,努力表现这个充满活力与矛盾、自由竞争和崇尚物质享受的新时代,同时也开始批判社会现实,揭露美国社会的阴暗面。现实主义文学时期三位最重要的作家是豪威尔斯(William Dean Howells,1837—1920)、马克·吐温(Mark Twain,1835—1910)和亨利·詹姆斯(Henry James,1843—1916)。豪威尔斯在美国文学史上的作用在于他为现实主义文学提出了一系列的理论原则和指导方针;向美国人民介绍了国外名作家,尤其是屠格涅夫的现实主义理论和方法以及托尔斯泰关于作家要关心社会的主张;大力扶植有才能的青年作家。这些理论和观点集中在论文集《批评与小说》(*Criticism and Fiction*,1891)。由于他强调作家应该表现"微笑的现实主义",他的理论有很大的局限性。豪威尔斯写过一百多部作品,笔调温和,解决办法往往是乌托邦式的改良主义,比较出色的是长篇小说《赛拉斯·拉帕姆的发迹》(*The Rise of Silas Lapham*,1885)。

马克·吐温是塞缪尔·朗荷恩·克莱门斯(Samuel Langhorne Clemens)的笔名。他在1865年发表的第一篇幽默小说《卡拉维拉斯县驰名的跳蛙》("The Celebrated Jumping Frog of Calaveras Country")使他一举成名。幽默游记《傻子国外旅行记》(*Innocents Abroad*,1869)等进一步奠定了他幽默作家的声誉。但是,马克·吐温实际上是一位严肃的作家,对政治、社会矛盾和道德风尚十分关心。他与人合作的《镀金时代》(*The Gilded Age*,1873)尖锐地批评了南北战争后美国国内政治腐败、投机盛行的恶劣风尚。他写过两部关于儿童的小说《汤姆·索耶历险记》(The Adventures of Tom Sawyer, 1876)和《哈克贝里·费恩历险记》(The Adventures of Huckleberry Finn, 1885)。后者超出了儿童文学的范畴,是马克·吐温的代表作,也是美国文学的一部经典之作。马克·吐温通过野孩子哈克和逃亡黑奴吉姆在密西西比河上的流浪生活揭露了社会矛盾,批判美国这个所谓文明世界的残暴,寄托他对理想世界的向往。马克·吐温晚年对美国社会感到失望,他的作品越来越从幽默和宽容转向尖刻的讽刺和激烈的抨击。19世纪90年代以后,他创作了一系列谴责美帝国主义的作品,如《赤道旅行记》(Following the Equator, 1897)、《败坏了哈德莱堡的人》(The Man That Corrupted Hadleyburg, 1899)和《神秘的来客》(The Mysterious Stranger, 1916)等,反映他对贪婪自私、残暴虚伪的人类的失望情绪。马克·吐温吸收乡土文学和西部幽默的长处,并加以发展,形成自己别具一格的文体。他擅长人物刻画,精于表现富有戏剧性的情节,尤其善于运用生动的口语和地方方言。他对美国现实主义文学的贡献极大。海明威曾说过:"全部现代美国文学起源于马克·吐温写的一本叫《哈克贝里·费恩历险记》的书。"

19世纪后期,和马克·吐温并驾齐驱的另一位著名作家是詹姆斯。他的作品属于世态小说,主人公基本上都是上流社会人士和有产阶级,代表作有《一位女士的画像》(The Portrait of a Lady, 1881)、《鸽翼》(The Wings of the Dove, 1902)、《专使》(The Ambassadors, 1903)、《金碗》(The Golden Bowl, 1904)等。基本主题是三方面:纯真而粗俗的美国人和虚伪但有教养的欧洲人之间的矛盾与对比,现实生活同艺术的矛盾以及艺术家的孤独,物质与精神的矛盾和人生的道德抉择。在小说技巧方面,詹姆斯一反通常以作者为中心的叙述角度,创造了"有限视角"的叙述方法,以某个人物为"意识中心",从他的"角度"叙述故事、铺展情节。他后期的小说大量采用内心独白。为了细腻地表现人物心理和潜意识活动,詹姆斯常用冗长的句子、堆砌的副词与形容词、隐晦的比喻和象征,因此常被称为心理分析小说家。他那晦涩的文体、开放性结局和内心独白等手法大大影响了后世的现代派,尤其是意识流文学。

19世纪末,美国垄断资本逐步形成,国内矛盾日益尖锐。作家们对美国的扩张政策和国内贫富不均等社会现象深感忧虑。一批青年作家受法国自然主义的影响,用悲观主义宿命论的观点看待事物,认为人受环境和遗传因素的支配,不能把握自己的命运。他们比现实主义作家更为激进,关心社会底层的人民,以他们的悲惨生活说明世界上没有道德原则、人没有自由意志、宗教是荒唐的。有代表性的作家是克莱恩(Stephen Crane, 1871—1900)、诺里斯(Frank Norris, 1870—1902)和伦敦(Jack London, 1876—1916)。克莱恩反映大城市贫民窟生活的《街头女郎梅季》(Maggie: A Girl of the Streets, 1893)和描写战争中恐怖心理的《红色英勇勋章》(The Red Badge of Courage, 1895)都描写外界环境对人物心理的影响,对第一次世界大战后"迷惘的一代"的作家有一定的影响。克莱恩的诗歌短小精悍、意象鲜明,对20世纪的意象派诗人颇有影响。在欧洲自然主义文学运动的影响下,还出现了一批黑幕揭发者(muckrakers),主要是新闻界人士。他们专门揭发大企业的贪婪和残暴以及政界触目惊心的腐败行径。最著名的作品是辛克莱(Upton Sinclair, 1878—1968)反映芝加哥屠宰场残酷剥削工人的《屠场》(The Jungle, 1906)。现实主义和自然主义文学运动中成就最大的是德莱塞(Theodore Dreiser, 1871—1945)。他出身贫苦,自幼过着颠沛流离的艰难生活,饱尝失业和贫穷的痛苦,对下层人民有深刻的了解和深厚的同情。德莱塞早年受尼采和社会达尔文主义思想的影响,但自20世纪20年代以后转向社会现实主义,甚至自然主义,具有鲜明的进步倾向。《嘉莉妹妹》(Sister Carrie, 1900)由于描写乡村姑娘为生活所迫而沦落但最后成为名演员的故事被指责为伤风败俗,曾一度遭到禁止。然而,德莱塞并未退却,又以同样的主题写了《珍妮姑娘》(Jennie Gerhardt, 1911)。代表作《美国的悲剧》(An American Tragedy, 1925)被评论界称颂为"美国最伟大的小说",以感人的故事深刻阐明主人公克莱德是美国社会制度的受害者,他的堕落应由社会负责。

(五) 现代主义时期(1918—1945)

美国文学在20世纪初,尤其是第一次世界大战以后到20世纪20年代进一步发展成熟,开始对欧洲文化产生影响,并被称为"第二次文艺复兴"。

1917年美国参战,1918年大战结束。美国进入经济繁荣时期。科技革新加速了钢铁、建筑工业、玻璃制造业,尤其是汽车制造业的发展。无线电、电话和电影的发明,家用电器的出现,迅速改变了人民的生活方式。广播、电影等大众媒介开始在人们生活中起着越来越重要的作用。1928年美国人达到世界上最高的生活水平,1929年美国的产品已经占世界总产量的1/3以上。生产、消费、娱乐和享受成了20世纪20年代的一大特点。因此,这个时代有"喧嚣咆哮的时代"(The Roaring Age)的雅名,也因为对黑人文化,尤其黑人音乐的兴趣而获得了"爵士时代"(The Jazz Age)的称号。

然而,歌舞升平、繁荣昌盛的景象背后是重重矛盾。整个社会右倾保守。人们,尤其是敏感的知识分子和曾经怀着"为民主而战"的理想报名参军的文学青年,对自由民主的信念开始动摇,对国家、社会、个人前途悲观失望,对历史传统和价值观念,包括宗教失去信念。于是在20世纪20年代初,大批年轻人涌向欧洲,特别是巴黎,在流浪漂泊和寻欢作乐中消磨时光,有些人用文学形式来描写战争带来的痛苦与烦恼,表现他们的失落与绝望,形成了斯泰因(Gertrude Stein, 1874—1946)称之为"迷惘的一代"的文学流派。他们几乎都以自己的经历为素材,如海明威

(Ernest Hemingway，1899—1961)的《太阳照样升起》(The Sun Also Rises, 1926)、《永别了，武器》(A Farewell to Arms, 1929)和以尼克·亚当斯为主人公的短篇小说，菲茨杰拉德(F. Scott Fitzgerald, 1896—1940)的《人间天堂》(This Side of Paradise, 1920)和《了不起的盖茨比》(The Great Gatsby, 1925)等。这些自传性作品悲天悯人，对当代世界悲观失望，甚至厌恶愤慨。但它们的作者却成为20世纪20年代美国文学的"第二次文艺复兴"的中坚力量。许多优秀作品都是在美国国外写成的，这也许是这个时期美国文学的一个奇怪的特点。

1929年美国股票市场暴跌，引起了持续10年的经济萧条，加深了社会普遍性的悲观与绝望。精神方面的危机导致文学的繁荣，众多的历史事件，工业化和城市化带来的社会矛盾等都要求作家以新的手法、形式和体裁加以表现。因此，这又是一个大胆创新、大胆试验的时代，各种技巧、流派、文艺理论相继出现。与此同时，欧洲的文艺思潮，如弗洛伊德的精神分析学说、尼采的超人哲学和悲剧理论、弗雷泽的神话、柏格森关于"持续时间"和直觉的观点以及马克思的阶级论等都对美国文学产生了积极的作用。作家们开始注意探索人物的内心世界，发扬惠特曼等人改革诗歌形式的革新精神。不完整的片断和不连贯发展的情节成为作品形式上的主要特点。故事往往在突厄中开始，发展进程没有一定的逻辑和说明，结尾也不提供解决问题的方式，叙述角度、声音、语气也不断变换。描述方面最大的变化是从外部世界转向内心，从客观转向主观。这类现代主义作品为阅读制造困难，对读者提出很高的要求。

现代主义文学是从诗歌开始的。20世纪初，芝加哥成为诗人们反对传统的诗歌技巧、创作目的和主题的革命中心。一本小杂志《诗刊》(Poetry)起了重要作用。已在英国参与领导意象派新诗歌运动的庞德(Ezra Pound, 1885—1972)是杂志的驻外编辑，经常提供有关英国、法国和其他任何地方的文学变革信息，后来有成就的诗人如林赛、桑德堡、洛威尔，以至庞德、艾略特、斯蒂文斯等人都曾在这个刊物上发表过作品。

当时的诗人大致可分为三类：

(1) 芝加哥诗人。他们无论在诗歌形式上还是题材上都坚持惠特曼的传统，反映劳动人民的思想感情。林赛(Vachel Lindsay, 1879—1931)有意识地吸收民歌和爵士音乐的成分，使诗歌更具有美国特色。马斯特斯(Edgar Lee Masters, 1869—1950)采用短小精悍、自由韵体和日常口语的诗歌反映小城镇平庸保守的生活给人带来的磨难。桑德堡(Carl Sandburg, 1878—1967)是最有成就的芝加哥派诗人。他继承惠特曼的传统，诗歌接近散文，没有格律韵脚和规则重音，也没有复杂的形象或比喻。桑德堡还吸收民间歌谣、民间谚语的优良传统，语言朴素而幽默。《芝加哥诗集》(Chicago Poems, 1916)、《人民，是的》(The People, Yes, 1936)是他最有代表性的诗集。这些诗歌表现了他对土地、人民和社会的无限热爱。还有一位诗人克莱恩(Hart Crane, 1899—1932)，早年追随艾略特，后来接受惠特曼和桑德堡的影响。长诗《桥》(The Bridge, 1930)描写20世纪的机器文明和"美国神话"，既模仿艾略特，又有惠特曼的影响。

(2) 以庞德和当时在伦敦居住尚未加入英国籍的艾略特(T. S. Eliot, 1888—1965)为首的身居海外的诗人。他们是诗歌革命的主要力量。1908年庞德初到伦敦便和英国诗人休姆创立意象派(Imagism)诗歌，强调诗要具体，避免抽象，意象比喻要十分明确，语言要精练，删除一切与意象无关的词语，诗歌形式可以采用自由体，格律可以根据口语节奏等。接受他思想的美国意象派诗人有洛威尔(Amy Lowell, 1874—1925)、希尔达·杜利特尔(Hilda Doolittle, 1886—1961)和威廉斯(William Carlos Williams, 1883—1963)等。庞德虽然后来脱离意象派，但他的诗歌理论冲击了陈旧的诗歌传统，为美国诗歌的发展开辟了道路。庞德最著名的诗歌是讽刺英国文化和表明献身艺术的决心的《休·赛尔温·毛伯莱》(Hugh Selwyn Mauberley, 1920)和长篇史诗《诗章》(The Cantos, 1915—1962)。《诗章》的第一部分在1917年出版，以后陆续增加，到1959年时共有109篇。《诗章》的内容庞杂，从诗歌理论到道德哲学以至名人评价、经济政策，几乎无所不包。意象派诗歌在第一次世界大战以后开始衰落，但是这一流派对美国诗歌在采用自由体、口语和铸造意象方面影响颇大。艾略特是新诗运动的主要人物，他的《荒原》(The Waste Land, 1922)借用大量的欧洲文学典故、神话、历史、暗示和联想，运用多种语言，以不连贯的结构、有节奏的自由体，构成一部思想和情调和谐一致的诗篇，一时成为诗人们模仿的典范。主要的追随者有斯蒂文斯(Wallace Stevens, 1879—1955)。他的诗歌热情活泼，却又深奥、富有哲理。代表作有《带蓝吉他的人》(The Man with a Blue Guitar, 1937)等。他的诗歌的主题往往表现想象力如何使混乱的世界获得秩序以及艺术表面上歪曲现实、实际上更深刻地揭示现实等理论。但是扎根美国生活的诗人并不完全接受艾略特的诗歌理论。威廉斯就曾说过："《荒原》的发表好像爆炸了一个原子弹，把我们的世界给毁灭了。"威廉斯既摒弃诗歌传统，又反对艾略特大量运用博学典故、过分强调修辞的主张。他的诗歌如《佩特森》(Paterson, 1946—1958)等深受惠特曼的影响，朴素简洁、不拘形式，摆脱传统韵律的束缚。

(3) 新英格兰诗人弗洛斯特(Robert Frost, 1874—1963)和罗宾逊(Edward Arlington Robinson, 1869—1935)属于第三类诗人，介乎上述两派之间，受到新诗歌运动的感染，却并不全盘接受它的原则和主张。弗洛斯特基本上采用传统的诗歌形式，但排斥其中矫揉造作等消极因素。他的诗歌多半以新英格兰地区为背景，运用当地普通人民的语言，描写乡间普通人民和日常生活。他的诗歌简洁朴素、易于上口，然而朴素中寓有深意，往往从自然景色、凡人俗事开始，以深刻的哲理思想结束。代表诗集有《少年的意志》(A Boy's Will, 1913)、《西去的溪流》(West-Running Brook, 1928)和《又一片牧场》(A Further Range, 1936)等。《修墙》("Mending Wall", 1914)、《摘苹果之后》("After Apple-Picking", 1914)和《白杨树》("Birches", 1916)等诗歌把细腻的观察、深刻的象征意义和优美的格律音韵十分恰当地综合在一起,已经成为20世纪脍炙人口的诗篇。另一位诗人罗宾逊也以新英格兰的小镇生活作为创作的主要内容。代表作《夜之子》(*The Children of the Night*, 1897)表现新英格兰人民勇敢勤劳的美德。他的诗歌语言朴素、立意新奇,富有含蓄的冷嘲和幽默。

美国的戏剧由于清教主义的影响一向不很发达,但第一次世界大战后情况却有了很大的变化。德国的表现主义戏剧、瑞典表现主义戏剧家斯特林堡(August Strindberg)、挪威的易卜生(Henrik Ibsen)、意大利的皮兰德娄(Luigi Pirandello)、英国的萧伯纳(Bernard Shaw)等开始影响美国戏剧界。另一方面,由戏剧艺术爱好者组成的试验性的小剧院开始出现,对百老汇等商业剧院进行了有力的挑战。最为著名的是"华盛顿广场剧院"(战后1919年改名为"剧院协会")、普罗文斯敦剧社和以哈佛大学的47号工作室为代表的学员剧团。这些小剧场或戏剧团体几乎都有自己的剧作家。他们努力避免俗套,大胆试验,用不同的手法进行创作,甚至在一个剧本中使用两种不同的手法,最常见的是现实主义手法和浪漫主义或象征主义手法相结合。这种幻想与现实相交织的表现主义手法推动了第二次世界大战以后的荒诞派戏剧。这个时期戏剧的另一个特点是以社会问题为题材,目的在于批评时政,揭露社会的阴暗面。如赖斯(Elmer Rice, 1892—1967)的《加算器》(*The Adding Machine*, 1923)反映资本主义社会把人变成机器的奴隶。20世纪30年代以后,左翼文学兴起,戏剧的批判作用更为明显。代表人物奥德兹(Clifford Odets, 1906—1963)的《等待老左》(*Waiting for Lefty*, 1935)便以罢工斗争为题材,揭露和批判资本主义社会。

新剧运动中成就最大的剧作家是奥尼尔(Eugene O'Neill, 1888—1953)。他综合各家之长,既采用传统的手法,又大胆革新,充分吸取自然主义、象征主义和表现主义的长处。第一部多幕剧《天边外》(*Beyond the Horizon*, 1920)采用传统的手法,是美国第一部严肃的反浪漫主义的戏剧。但是同年发表的《琼斯皇帝》(*Emperor Jones*, 1920)却采用表现主义手法,用非剧中人的对话、布景及不停顿的击鼓声表现剧中人物由不安到恐惧最后发展到歇斯底里的心理状态。《毛猿》(*The Hairy Ape*, 1922)是一部兼有现实主义、表现主义和象征主义手法的戏剧。《伟大之神布朗》(*The Great God Brown*, 1926)则运用象征主义手法,用面具表现人物的双重性格,用独白表现人物的内心冲突。《奇妙的插曲》(*Strange Interlude*, 1928)采用弗洛伊德的心理分析方法,以独白和旁白来表现意识流手法。奥尼尔十分关心美国的社会问题,作品大多有深刻的现实意义。《天边外》反映现实对人们理想生活的摧残。《毛猿》描写在冷酷无情的资本主义社会里,工人被当成动物来对待。《榆树下的欲望》(*Desire under the Elm*, 1925)表现资产阶级家庭争夺财产和由此引起的后果。《卖冰的人来了》(*The Iceman Cometh*, 1940)揭示30年代经济危机时期人们的空虚和绝望。奥尼尔还不断探索个人理想与现实的矛盾冲突,他认为在神秘而有敌意的宇宙里,个人寻求自我的努力总是不能实现,事物的发展总是与个人愿望相违背。奥尼尔勤于探索、勇于实践,创立了独特的风格,使美国戏剧在20世纪20年代和30年代达到前所未有的繁荣,真正成为美国文学的一个组成部分。他是美国戏剧史上一个十分重要的人物。

这时期的小说也在不断革新。无论是斯泰因、凯瑟(Willa Cather, 1873—1947)、安德森(Sherwood Anderson, 1876—1941)和德莱塞等老一代作家还是战后成长起来的年轻一代作家,如多斯·帕索斯(John Dos Passos, 1896—1970)、菲茨杰拉德、海明威、福克纳(William Faulkner, 1897—1962)以及黑人作家吉因·图默(Jean Toomer, 1894—1967)等人都在技巧方面做各种试验:海明威在故事里穿插新闻报道,多斯·帕索斯在小说中插入电影、新闻片、报纸,甚至流行歌曲的片段。总之,作家们不断破坏故事的叙述线索以表现世界的混乱和社会的失控。当然,这时期传统的手法并没有消失。德莱塞、刘易斯(Sinclair Lewis, 1885—1951)采用文献式描写和细节堆砌等自然主义手法;凯瑟、菲茨杰拉德却十分注意对细节的取舍,更看重故事的氛围,因而使他们的作品富有诗意。海明威试验用小词、短句,多对话,少描述,他的"冰山理论"确实开创了新的文风。跟他相反,福克纳用繁复的长句和晦涩的语言来表现世界的复杂。在故事情节的处理上,刘易斯等人采用传统的手法,从时序出发,分开端、发展、高潮、结局四个步骤。但更多的作家对传统手法进行改革。有些作品没有贯穿全书的主人公,众多的人物之间也没有一定的联系;有的小说时序颠倒,正叙和倒叙穿插进行。有的小说情节错综复杂,但又彼此之间仿佛毫无联系;还有的小说采用多角度多人称叙述法,角度不断变化。总之,作家们力图通过叙述手法表现社会和人的精神世界的混乱场面。在人物的刻画方面,这时期的小说家几乎都摒弃作家出场发表评论的手法。他们强调通过对话和行动来表现人物的个性和内心世界。海明威总是以细致的动作描写和大量对话来提示人物的心理。安德森不注重人物形象的刻画,而着意于他们的内心活动和精神状态。弗洛伊德的心理学给作家开辟了探索人物心理的广阔天地。他们认识到表现人物复杂的心理活动和似乎毫无逻辑的潜意识状态的重要性,开始大量采用意识流等表现手法。

20世纪20年代对美国作家影响最大的是身居海外的斯泰因,代表作《三个女人的一生》(*Three Lives*, 1909)对传统的小说技巧进行大胆的改革。她吸收电影以画面表现景象的手法,以重复基本相同而略有不同的句子和文字来表现中心思想。她主张遣词造句力求简单,以重复突出主题。她的创作思想和实践对安德森以及第一次世界大战后崛起的年轻作家产生了很大的影响。第一次世界大战前后其他比较著名的女作家有华顿(Edith Wharton, 1862—1937)、格拉斯哥(Ellen Glasgow, 1874—1945)和凯瑟。她们基本上都是坚持现实主义传统的乡土作家,都关心新富和物质主义对传统道德观念的影响。华顿的《快乐之家》(*The House of Mirth*, 1905)和《天真时代》(*The*

Age of Innocence, 1920）既讽刺暴发户的庸俗和私利，又批判上流社会狭隘的文化和传统的道德观念。格拉斯哥反映南方贵族文化的没落和庄园主的败落。《荒芜的土地》(The Barren Ground, 1925)和《浪漫主义喜剧演员》(The Romantic Comedians, 1926)都涉及在注重物质享受的世界里人们如何保持精神理想的问题。凯瑟早期的作品《哦，拓荒者》(Oh Pioneers, 1913)和《我的安东尼亚》(My Antonia, 1918)歌颂第一代移民在开发西部边疆过程中所表现的英勇品质。《一个沉沦的妇女》(A Lost Lady, 1923)和《教授的住宅》(The Professor's House, 1925)揭露物质享受和拜金主义思想对优良传统和道德品质的腐蚀。她最优秀的作品《死神迎接大主教》(Death Comes for the Archbishop, 1927)歌颂早年在新墨西哥州印第安人中传教的天主教神父的献身精神，企图以这种对精神世界的追求作为解决问题的方法。

随着大工业、大城市的兴起，一些美国作家开始揭露小镇平庸闭塞的生活和狭隘庸俗的传统观念对人们精神生活的扼杀。刘易斯和安德森是比较有代表性的两位作家。刘易斯采用传统的现实主义手法。《大街》(Main Street, 1920)描写小镇居民安于现状，固守旧俗，拒绝一切新的思想和变革。《巴比特》(Babbitt, 1922)塑造了一位无力摆脱工业社会拜金主义思想束缚的小人物，为英语词汇增加了一个"庸俗的市侩"的同义词。1930年，刘易斯成为第一个接受诺贝尔文学奖的美国作家。安德森和刘易斯在创作手法上大不相同。他深受斯泰因的影响，抛弃以情节为主的传统格局，强调刻画人物的内心世界，通过人物一瞬间爆发出来的感情来表现他们的个性和内心深处的隐秘。在题材方面，他也描写小市镇生活，但侧重表现普通人的彷徨和苦闷。代表作《俄亥俄州的温斯堡镇》(Winesburg, Ohio, 1919)就描写这样一群畸零人。他们追求理想、探索生活的真理、渴望爱与同情，可是狭隘的社会观念、枯燥乏味的平庸生活压抑了他们个性的发展，使他们成为心理变态的怪人。他还对小说形式进行试验，在《俄亥俄州的温斯堡镇》中用具有同一个背景、同一个主人公和同一种气氛的一系列短篇故事来加强这些故事作为整体的总主题。这一切使他成为美国现代派作家的先驱，对海明威、福克纳等青年作家有很大的影响。

"迷惘的一代"（the Lost Generation）。主要代表作家有多斯·帕索斯、菲茨杰拉德和海明威等。多斯·帕索斯是最早表现年轻人反抗社会的作家。《三个士兵》(Three Soldiers, 1920)描述第一次世界大战对艺术和艺术家的摧残。《美国》(U.S.A.)三部曲——即《北纬四十二度》(The 42nd Parallel, 1930)、《一九一九年》(Nineteen Nineteen, 1932)和《赚大钱》(Big Money, 1936)——是他最主要的作品，曾被誉为"一部伟大的民族史诗"。菲茨杰拉德虽然没有去过前线，却是典型的"迷惘的一代"的作家。第一部长篇小说《人间天堂》和一百多篇短篇小说真实地反映爵士时代人们醉生梦死的空虚的精神面貌，生动地再现了20年代美国青年认为"一切上帝都死亡了，一切战争都打完了和一切对人的信念都动摇了"的绝望心理。《了不起的盖茨比》和《夜色温柔》(Tender Is the Night, 1934)从内容到技巧都更为成熟，进一步揭露"美国梦"和"美国精神"的迷惑性和空虚。他是继德莱塞以后又一个抨击腐蚀人们灵魂的美国梦的作家。海明威是"迷惘的一代"作家的主要人物。《太阳照样升起》反映第一次世界大战后在欧洲彷徨游荡的美国青年绝望和幻灭的情绪。《永别了，武器》表现战争如何粉碎人们的理想和生活目的。《丧钟为谁而鸣》(For Whom the Bell Tolls, 1940)描写西班牙的内战。海明威小说的主人公常常是位心灵受过创伤、敏感而玩世不恭的年轻人，但他作品里往往又有一位勇敢正直的英雄。海明威笔下的英雄可能是名不见经传的猎人、士兵、斗牛士、拳击家，但他们都具有"硬汉"性格，百折不挠、视死如归。他们给海明威的主人公以启示，教育他们在困难面前不低头、在压力之下不弯腰。《老人与海》(The Old Man and the Sea, 1951)中的老渔民集中体现了海明威大力推崇的在失败中保持尊严从而取得精神胜利的生活原则。海明威不仅为美国文学创造了"硬汉"形象，他那含蓄简练、清新有力的文体对美国文学也产生了极大的影响。

1929年，纽约股票市场崩溃，引发了美国历史上前所未有的经济危机。与此同时，1930年开始的持续干旱使大萧条雪上加霜，沙尘暴几乎横扫美国中部和东部地区，破坏了大量农田，迫使农民背井离乡，向西部迁移去寻找生路。这场危机波及面广，延续时间很长，几乎使整个国家都处于风雨飘摇之中。到1933年罗斯福就任总统时全国几乎所有的银行都已关闭，三千多万家庭没有正常收入，数以百万计的人生活在极度的贫困之中，更有成千上万的人失去家园，在铁路线上颠沛流离，妄图找到可以糊口的工作。工矿企业中罢工运动四起，劳资矛盾十分尖锐。

在这种形势下，"左翼"文学或"无产阶级文学"一度成为20世纪30年代颇有影响的主流文学，使它有"红色十年"之称。在《震撼世界的十日》(Ten Days That Shook the World, 1919)的作者约翰·里德（John Reed, 1887—1920）的帮助下，1919年美国共产党成立了。左翼作家如迈克尔·高尔德（Michael Gold, 1894—1967）、约瑟夫·弗里曼（Joseph Freeman, 1897—1965）、麦克斯·伊斯特曼（Max Eastman, 1883—1969）等人还创办了一些进步刊物，比较重要的有《群众》(The Masses, 1913—1926)、《解放者》(The Liberator, 1918—1924)，尤其是标志美国激进文学重要里程碑的、后来成为共产党喉舌的《新群众》(The New Masses, 1926—1948)等杂志。它们介绍十月革命后的苏联，研究马克思主义理论，讨论作家的责任和文艺的方向。作家们把社会主义的苏联看成是希望的曙光，从老一代的德莱塞、新闻记者麦克斯·伊斯特曼到年轻的黑人诗人兰斯顿·休斯（Langston Hughes, 1902—1967）和评论家埃德蒙·威尔逊（Edmund Wilson, 1895—1972）等都前往苏联进行访问，公开提出社会主义才是美国的出路。1935年在"约翰·里德俱乐部"的倡议下，作家们在纽约召开了第一次美国作家代表大会，成立"美国作家同盟"并且接受总部设在苏联的国际革命作家联盟的领导。

同年，罗斯福为了对付经济衰退实行新政，设立公共事业振兴署，为失业者提供就业机会，也为困难的作家、艺术家们设立了联邦艺术、联邦作家、联邦戏剧等项目。其中，联邦作家项目资助了已经成名的作家，如诗人康拉德·艾肯(Conrad Aiken, 1889—1973)、剧作家埃尔默·赖斯、黑人诗人克劳德·麦克凯(Claude McKay, 1889—1948)等以及日后成为名家的犹太小说家索尔·贝娄(Saul Bellow, 1915—2005)、剧作家阿瑟·米勒(Arthur Miller, 1915—2005)、女作家尤多拉·韦尔蒂(Eudora Welty, 1909—2001)、黑人作家理查德·赖特(Richard Wright, 1908—1960)和拉尔夫·埃里森(Ralph Waldo Ellison, 1914—1994)、黑人女作家佐拉·尼尔·赫斯顿(Zora Neale Hurston, 1891—1960)等。对政府来说，这些项目是要保持与提高人民对国家的信心，树立美国是一个包容所有人的多元文化国家的形象。他们组织作家们编写各州旅游指南，同时也资助赖特、赫斯顿、埃里森等黑人作家发掘黑人文化，撰写黑人历史，反映他们的苦难生活。当然，由于是政府资助的项目，作家们不可避免地受到一定的限制，但他们还是发表了一些比较进步的作品，如在编写指南时把重点放在普通劳动人民而不是知名人士上。赖特在芝加哥、埃里森在纽约收集的有关黑人的材料对他们后来写《土生子》(Native Son, 1940)和《看不见的人》(Invisible Man, 1952)都起了一定的作用。赫斯顿收集整理的民间故事集《骡与人》(Mules and Men, 1935)就是联邦作家项目的一个课题。当时联邦戏剧项目创造了一种特殊的戏剧形式——"活报剧"，中心人物总是一个对当前某个问题不明白的普通老百姓，通过他对问题的探究把全剧串起来，把作家的意图向观众进行交代。根据辛克莱·刘易斯小说改编的反法西斯剧作《它不可能在这里发生》(It Can't Happen Here, 1935)同时在全国22个城市上演，造成很大的声势。但正是由于他们演出的思想内容都比较进步，国会怀疑他们是由共产党控制的，终于在1939年停止资助该项目。

有些作家并未积极参加左翼活动，但也有意识地关心社会现实。如福克纳的《圣殿》(Sanctuary, 1931)、《八月之光》(Light in August, 1932)都直接反映当时的社会问题。另一位南方作家凯瑟琳·安·波特(Katherine Anne Porter, 1890—1980)虽然主要描写南方社会与家族问题，但也为《民族》《新共和》等左翼杂志撰稿。尽管奥尼尔的《卖冰的人来了》(The Iceman Cometh, 1934)在1946年才上演，但这个剧本还是多少折射出他在30年代的心态。然而，最著名的作品还是斯坦贝克(John Steinbeck, 1902—1968)反映30年代大萧条时期的小说《愤怒的葡萄》(The Grapes of Wrath, 1939)。小说通过俄克拉荷马州佃农乔德一家被迫背井离乡去西部另谋生路的故事，深刻揭露美国严重的社会问题。斯坦贝克还写过描写加利福尼亚摘水果的流动工人罢工斗争的《胜负未决的战斗》(In Dubious Battle, 1936)。

这时期美国南方作家开始联合起来，出版小型刊物，对文艺思想和评论各抒己见。1925年《弗吉尼亚评论》(The Virginia Review)杂志创刊，南方终于有了一个堪与北方优秀刊物相媲美的文学刊物。南方文艺中心的一支中坚力量是"逃亡者派"(the Fugitives)。这个松散的文化团体聚集了一批杰出的作家和诗人，如兰塞姆(John Crowe Ransom, 1888—1974)、华伦(Robert Penn Warren, 1905—1989)、泰特(Allen Tate, 1899—1979)等，并出版颇有影响的文艺杂志《逃亡者》。他们思想比较保守，提倡维护南方传统的文学地方主义，反对工业化社会，鼓吹南方继续保持农业传统，因此又被称为"重农学派"。30年代美国经济萧条时期，重农思想在南方影响极大。他们的杂志《南方评论》(Southern Review)和《肯庸评论》(Kenyon Review)对"新批评派"文艺理论的形成起过很大的作用。南方文艺复兴时期最主要的作家是福克纳。他一生写了19部长篇小说和一百来个短篇故事，大部分故事发生在南方密西西比州一个虚构的叫约克纳帕塔法的地方。福克纳以他神妙的想象力把这片土地、人民和历史构成一个神秘的王国。这些作品探索从南北战争到20世纪30年代的历史和庄园主贵族、新富、穷白人和黑人，甚至印第安人组成的阶级社会，表现南方大家族的兴衰、黑奴制的后果、种族矛盾、敏感而理想主义的年轻主人公与现代社会的冲突等等。他的主人公，如《喧哗与骚动》(The Sound and the Fury, 1929)中的昆丁，常常是悲剧性的，因为他们背负沉重的历史负担和社会传统习俗的枷锁，无法面对现实生活。与他们相反，福克纳还塑造了一群乐天知命、不受生活体系和习俗束缚的，因而有力量有勇气能处危不惊的"自然人"，如《喧哗与骚动》中的黑女佣迪尔西、《熊》("The Bear")中的山姆·法泽斯等。在他的笔下，那些适应现代社会的人，如《喧哗与骚动》中的杰生和《斯诺普斯》三部曲——由《村子》(The Hamlet, 1940)、《小镇》(The Town, 1957)、《大宅》(The Mansion, 1959)组成中的弗莱姆·斯诺普斯，则冷酷无情，没有人性。在福克纳的世系小说中，最有代表性的是《喧哗与骚动》《八月之光》《押沙龙，押沙龙！》(Absalom, Absalom!, 1936)与《去吧，摩西》(Go Down, Moses, 1942)等。《喧哗与骚动》通过康普生贵族家庭的衰落反映传统价值体系的破产和道德法则的消亡。《八月之光》表现一个不知自己是白人还是黑人的年轻人与社会观念与习俗的冲突以及人的异化和孤寂。《押沙龙，押沙龙！》讲述白手起家、一心创建自己家园的塞德潘及他的失败。福克纳采用侦探小说的形式，让几位不完全知道内情的人来分析塞德潘的命运并进一步企图解释历史。《去吧，摩西》是一部由一系列关于基本上是同一个主人公的故事组成的小说，主旨在于表现南方社会中黑人与白人的种族关系。福克纳不仅以他丰富的想象力著称，而且还以他出色的技巧和试验手法获得世人的赞赏。他在众多的作品中几乎不用雷同的手法。他的作品语言艰涩、句子冗长，加上意识流、内心独白、多视角叙述、时序颠倒、象征隐喻等手法，给读者造成很大的困难。然而，他正是运用这种扑朔迷离、纷乱复杂的文体表明世间事物和人心的复杂性。福克纳认为作家的责任在于表现人的内心冲突，描写包括爱、荣誉感、自豪感、同情心和牺牲精神等古老的真理，以便提醒人们铭记曾经造就他们光荣历史的品质，帮助他们得以永存。评论家们一致认为，他不仅仅是一个南方作家，而且是在美国文学史、甚至世界文坛上举足轻重的一位大师。

两次世界大战期间,文艺批评开始在美国文学上起主导作用。影响最大的文艺理论流派是新批评派。新批评派接受艾略特的理论,反对介绍作品的背景知识、作者生平、创作过程和发挥个人印象的批评方式,认为文学作品是艺术并主张对作品本身进行精密的分析。新批评派虽然常常忽略作品的社会意义,割裂作品与历史的关系,但它提出的一系列理论原则,对推动美国文艺理论的发展起过极大的作用。它的主要代表人物有布莱克默(R.P. Blackmur, 1904—1965)、兰塞姆(John Crowe Ransom, 1888—1974)、伯克(Kenneth Burke, 1897—1993)、布鲁克斯(Cleanth Brooks, 1906—1994)等。另外一些批评家如考利(Malcolm Cowley, 1898—1989)和威尔逊等则吸收各家之长。考利的著名作品《流放者归来》(*Exiles Return*, 1934)深入分析并评价20世纪20年代"迷惘的一代"的各位作家。威尔逊写过不少文章,研究文学的社会意义和政治意义。

第一次世界大战以后,随着白人知识分子对旧习惯、旧传统和旧的生活感到厌倦,对黑人文化和音乐日益产生浓厚的兴趣,黑人文化有了较大的发展。图默的《甘蔗》(*Cane*, 1923)是第一本采用意识流手法的黑人作品。20世纪20年代后期到20世纪30年代初,居住在纽约哈莱姆贫民区的黑人作家以大量作品表现黑人的悲惨生活,形成哈莱姆文艺复兴。麦克凯(Claude McKay, 1890—1948)、卡伦(Countee Cullen, 1903—1946)和图默(Jean Toomer, 1894—1967)等人都是在这一时期崛起的黑人作家。但最著名最有成就的是休斯(Langston Hughes, 1902—1967)。诗集《萎靡的布鲁斯》(*The Weary Blues*, 1926)中的诗歌采用爵士音乐的节奏和韵律,热情奔放。休斯的出色诗歌使他获得"哈莱姆桂冠诗人"的称号。休斯是位多才多艺的作家,除了诗歌以外,还写小说和戏剧。很多以黑人辛波儿为主人公的小说——如《辛波儿谈自己的想法》(*Simple Speaks His Mind*, 1950)——和《黑白混血儿》(*Muletto*, 1935)等戏剧用幽默揶揄的手法描写黑人眼中的白人,对他们的虚伪行径进行讽刺和挖苦。休斯在文艺思想和各种文学体裁方面的成就不仅对黑人文学,也对白人文学产生过不小的影响。20世纪30年代的经济危机妨碍了哈莱姆文艺复兴运动的发展。但以赖特为首的一群黑人作家仍然发表了很多战斗性很强的抗议文学。赖特的《土生子》常跟德莱塞的《美国的悲剧》相提并论,因为赖特也在小说中证明黑人别格并非天性凶暴,而是社会逼他走上杀人的绝路。赖特的故事生动紧凑,文笔精练而富有激情。比较重要的作品还有《汤姆大叔的孩子们》(*Uncle Tom's Children*, 1938)和自传《黑孩子》(*Black Boy: A Record of Childhood*, 1945)等。

(六)第二次世界大战后的美国文学

1945年8月美国在日本广岛和长崎投下的原子弹,结束了第二次世界大战,也震惊了全世界。从此,美国以头号强国的面目出现于世界。

作为在大战中获益最大而损失最小的国家,战后美国进入了空前的繁荣、发达和扩张的时期。然而,美国的政治和社会却趋向保守。苏联、中国等社会主义国家与共产党都被认为是"红色恐怖",是美国的敌人。1950年2月,参议员麦卡锡(Joseph McCarthy)声称共产主义分子已经渗入美国国务院,后来又不断强调他们甚至打入了军队和政府的高层机构,从而开始了一场全国性的政治迫害运动。同时,这也是两极分化十分严重的时期,在中产阶级收入不断提高、人们乐观向上的同时,处于社会底层的20%的人民看不到希望。贫富之间、白人与少数族裔之间、郊区居民与城市贫民区居民之间的差距日益扩大,为20世纪60年代的社会动荡埋下了不安定因素。

第二次世界大战以后,在小说方面,老一代作家如福克纳、海明威和斯坦贝克等仍在继续写作,但功力已经不如以前。海明威的《过河入林》(*Across the River and into the Trees*, 1950)刚出版就受到评论家的严厉批评,虽然第二年发表的《老人与海》证明他不愧大师的称号。福克纳的情况好一些,但他常常怀疑自己是否已经江郎才尽。老作家基本延续过去的主题,但参加过战争的年轻一代作家开始在40年代末发表关于第二次世界大战的作品。他们的作品同第一次世界大战以后海明威等人的作品有相似之处,都描写军队生活的贫乏和战争的可憎,质疑军事组织的权力和军官阶层的残酷与没有人性,但不再充满自怨自艾的情绪,涉及的面比较广。如欧文·肖(Irwin Shaw, 1913—1984)的《幼狮》(*The Young Lions*, 1948)用多角度的手法描写纳粹分子和美国士兵的心理活动;梅勒(Norman Mailer, 1923—2007)的《裸者与死者》(*The Naked and the Dead*, 1948)反映士兵和军官之间的矛盾,曾连续62周上了《纽约时报》的畅销小说榜,被称为最为出色的美国战争小说之一;琼斯(James Jones, 1921—1977)的《从这里到永恒》(*From Here to Eternity*, 1951)表现单调乏味的军营生活和军事机构对个人尊严的践踏。然而,约瑟夫·海勒(Joseph Heller)在1961年发表的《第22条军规》(*Catch-22*)不仅跟其他战争小说一样,揭露战争的恐怖、军队的官僚主义以及军事与工业组织如何左右人们的生活、摧残人的精神,还在技巧上有新的发展,大量采用象征手段和超现实主义手法,使整个故事荒诞不经却又寓意深刻,开创了"黑色幽默"的先河。

随着冷战与麦卡锡主义的加剧,美国作家开始反思美国价值的真实内涵、考虑个人是否应该顺应时势和社会规范。20世纪50年代作家普遍批评郊区中产阶级对物质生活的追求以及企业和公司对人的个性的压抑。影响最大的著作可能是塞林格(J. D. Salinger, 1919—2010)的《麦田的守望者》(*The Catcher in the Rye*, 1951)和金斯堡(Allen Ginsberg, 1926—1997)的长诗《嚎叫》(*Howl*, 1956)。前者讲述中学生霍尔顿的苦闷、寂寞和最终的精神崩溃。他出身富裕家庭,因弟弟的去世而深受打击。他渴望人间关爱,但父亲忙于赚钱,母亲忙于应酬享乐,只要求他按照社会要求按部就班地上学过日子。他开始质疑成人世界,认为那里充满虚假、浅薄和虚荣,只有童年世界才有纯真。他一心想当个守望者,保护儿童不受成人世界的腐蚀。由于小说反映了50年代美国青少年的心态与精神世界,对读者起了振聋发聩的作用,其魅力经久不衰,多年来一直是大中学生心爱的读物。评论界还常常把它和马克·吐温的《哈克贝里·费恩历险记》相提并论。不同之处在于主人公霍尔顿已经不像哈克那样可以离开虚伪的社会,到大自然中去寻求安慰。

至于金斯堡,他和凯鲁亚克(Jack Kerouac,1922—1969)、巴勒斯(William Burroughs,1914—1997)、劳伦斯·佛林盖谧(Lawrence Ferlinghetti,1919—)等人形成了50年代声势浩大的反文化运动,常常被称为"垮掉的一代"。他在《嚎叫》中强烈抗议美国的军事主义,大声疾呼美国社会对物质主义的追求和对性欲的压抑正在扼杀有才华的年轻人。金斯堡还对诗歌形式进行试验和改革,从惠特曼的自由诗和史诗形式中吸取灵感。他那直抒胸臆而又激情澎湃的长句一反艾略特的非个性诗歌理论,冲破新批评派为诗歌规定的种种束缚,掀起一场新诗歌革命。当时已经成名的老诗人威廉斯把金斯堡给他的信件收入长诗《佩特森》。金斯堡1955年在旧金山朗诵他的代表作《嚎叫》,震撼了比他年长许多的罗伯特·洛威尔(Robert Lowell,1917—1977)——一位紧跟新批评规范的诗人,迫使他改变诗风,采用个人化的话语,写出自传性诗篇《人生写照》(Life Studies,1959),反映他个人的生活经历和情感与心态的变化,开创了"自白诗歌"的先例,也在年轻人中间造就了自白派诗人,如写了大量关于人工流产、妇女的性生活和她在精神病院中的经历的塞克斯顿(Anne Sexton,1928—1974),描写自己酗酒和精神失常等事实的贝里曼(John Berryman,1914—1972)和反映想自杀的女人心理的普拉斯(Sylvia Plath,1932—1963)等。这一时期的诗歌还带有强烈的政治色彩。洛威尔愤怒抗议对越战争,里奇(Adrienne Rich,1929—2012)拥护女权运动,黑人女诗人布鲁克斯(Gwendolyn Brooks,1917—2000)支持黑人解放运动,黑人诗人勒鲁伊·琼斯(Leroi Jones,1934—2014)则更进一步提出"黑人权力"的口号。此外,以奥尔逊(Charles Olson,1910—1970)为首的黑山派诗人坚持摈弃一切正规的诗行长度和规范的诗歌格律,甚至连诗行左端的页边行距都不需要整齐划一。阿什贝里(John Ashberry,1927—)和奥哈拉(Frank O'Hara,1926—1966)等纽约派诗人认为诗歌不过是即兴之作,写完以后便失去了任何意义。第二次世界大战以后,美国诗歌派别众多、风格迥异,但却具有一个共同的特点:即它们摆脱了艾略特的"非个性化"诗歌的影响,摆脱了过去的超脱客观、含蓄诙谐的诗风,而是在内容上直抒个人胸怀,以个人的经历和感受表现机械化和现代物质文明对人的精神世界的摧残;在形式上公开反对以英国诗歌为中心,进一步强调诗歌的美国特色。

"垮掉的一代"小说家凯鲁亚克一气呵成的《在路上》(On the Road,1957)综合多种文学体裁和表现手法。它既是游记小说又是一个青少年成长的故事,既刻画人物流动的心理意识又描述具体的游历过程。它通过主人公一路追寻而又始终未能实现梦想的经历嘲弄了美国梦和西部理想天堂等美国神话。凯鲁亚克的"自发散文"把写作过程和游历过程高度统一,迫使读者分享他的经验和感受。这种试验文体虽然模仿者不多,却启发作家在手法和技巧方面进行多种探索和实验。巴勒斯的作品,如他的名著《赤裸的午餐》(Naked Lunch,1959)采用半自白半自传的形式描写自己的吸毒经历和同性恋问题,结构松散,由21个片段组成,情节发展非线性,时空和场景不断变换,但地点都是巴勒斯去过的地方,情节很难归纳或概括,然而用意却很鲜明,以尖刻激烈的嘲讽抨击社会和现实。佛林盖谧是诗人但他还是出版家。他在宣传推动"垮掉的一代"文学中起了十分重要的作用。他听了金斯堡朗诵以后马上决定出版这首长诗。1957年,他因印刷出版"淫秽作品"受到控告。但最后法官判决《嚎叫》虽然用了粗俗的语言,提出了并不正统和有争议的观点,但它并非没有社会意义,因此不能认定是淫秽诗歌。这场诉讼的胜利大大鼓舞了年轻作家,也使旧金山成为新文学的中心。"垮掉的一代"作家常常抽大麻,过放荡不羁的生活,以持不同政见的文化战士自居,通过诗歌和小说来揭露中产阶级的美国和官方政治,冲击传统的观念、习俗,甚至生活方式。他们的出现受到欢迎,也引起恐惧和攻击。经过几乎半个世纪的争论,现在的共识是:"垮掉的一代"的诗人和作家在嬉笑怒骂的背后是对生存危机的严肃关注。他们企图通过嘲弄调侃来颠覆已有的秩序,惊醒读者,解放受各种压抑,包括性压抑的年轻人,使他们考虑建立新秩序和重建一个新的美国。

这时期的南方文学在小说方面发展很快。除福克纳以外还有波特、麦卡勒斯(Carson McCullers,1917—1967)、奥康诺(Flannery O'Connor,1925—1964)、韦尔蒂(Eudora Welty,1909—2001)和华伦(R.P. Warren,1905—)等。波特是美国极有成就的短篇小说家之一。她的作品主要描写人的孤独失意的罪恶感,现代人空虚贫乏的精神世界,文笔细腻、用字严谨、风格优美。代表作有短篇小说集《斜塔》(The Leaning Tower and Other Stories,1934)和长篇小说《愚人船》(Ship of Fools,1962)等。奥康诺的小说以怪诞阴暗著称。在她的笔下,世界总是充满暴力和邪恶,勤奋正直等传统美德无法得到继承和发扬,奥康诺的文体简略诙谐,善于运用日常口语。代表作有《慧血》(Wise Blood,又译《智血》,1952)和短篇小说集《好人难寻》(A Good Man Is Hard to Find,1955)等。韦尔蒂是又一位擅长短篇小说的南方女作家。她的作品和福克纳一样充满浓郁的乡土气息。但她不像福克纳那样对世风日下持忧患态度,而是以冷静的眼光客观地表现人的愚蠢和生活中的可笑现象。《金苹果》(The Golden Apples,1949)、《英尼斯佛伦的新娘》(The Bride of Innisfallen,1955)等都是比较出色的短篇小说集。麦卡勒斯擅长用哥特式故事形式描写人的孤独和对无望的爱的渴求。代表作有《心灵是孤独的猎手》(The Heart Is a Lonely Hunter,1946)和短篇小说集《伤心咖啡馆之歌》(The Ballad of the Sad Café,1951)等。评论家们普遍认为华伦是南方继福克纳之后最重要的作家,他不仅在小说方面颇有建树,而且还是个杰出的诗人和文艺理论家。他是新批评理论的创始人之一,还与人合作编写了《理解诗歌》(Understanding Poetry, 1939)等作品。他的诗歌《允诺》(Promises: Poems 1954—1956, 1957)和《今与昔》(Now and Then: Poems 1976—1978, 1978)曾两度获得普利策诗歌奖。小说方面的代表作《国王的人马》(All the King's Men, 1946)集中表现华伦作品的中心主题:人只有通过认识自我才能实现自我以及物质世界,如权力对人的腐蚀作用。

美国作家中犹太裔比较多。第二次世界大战后,他们发表的作品日益增多,形成了影响很大的犹太人文学这个流派。最为著名的犹太裔作家是贝娄(Saul Bellow, 1915—2005)、马拉默德(Bernard Malamud, 1914—1986)和罗斯(Philip Roth, 1933—   )。贝娄的处女作《晃来晃去的人》(Dangling Man, 1944)和《赛姆勒先生的行星》(Mr. Sammler's Planet, 1970)表现大屠杀给犹太人造成难以消除的恐惧和伤害,法西斯的迫害使他们失去信念。其他几部小说,如《雨王汉德逊》(Henderson the Rain King, 1959)、《赫尔索格》(Herzog, 1964)、《洪堡的礼物》(Humboldt's Gift, 1975)等,都描写富裕社会中敏感的犹太知识分子的迷惘、空虚和绝望。这一主题其实已经并不局限于犹太人。贝娄探索的是西方世界的精神危机,关注的是人道主义的危机以及个人在社会中的地位。他的作品具有深刻的社会意义。1976年,贝娄获得诺贝尔文学奖。马拉默德专门描写大城市里的下层犹太裔居民,如小店主、杂役、鞋匠、裁缝等。他以现实主义手法、简洁隽永的文笔,刻画这些小人物的善良品质和所受的磨难,尤其是社会和排犹太主义者对犹太人的歧视与迫害。他的故事幽默诙谐,既富有戏剧性,又寓意深远,探索生活在孤独中的犹太人与犹太传统的关系。比较出色的有长篇小说《店员》(The Assistant, 1957)、《装配工》(The Fixer, 1966)、《房客》(The Tenant, 1971)和短篇小说集《魔桶》(The Magic Barrel, 1958)等。罗斯是年轻一代犹太裔作家的代表人物,擅长描写已经彻底美国化了的犹太中产阶级的生活、肤浅的拜金主义思想和年轻人的迷惘与反抗。《再见吧,哥伦布》(Goodbye, Columbus, 1959)和《波特诺伊的抱怨》(Portnoy's Complaint, 1969)描写年轻一代的犹太人对传统和家庭的反抗。

在戏剧方面,第二次世界大战以后美国戏剧家跟小说家一样,也表现战争及其后果,如托马斯·赫根(Thomas Heggen)和乔西亚·洛根(Joshua Logan)根据小说改编的喜剧《罗伯茨先生》(Mister Roberts, 小说1946, 戏剧1948)讽刺一位暴君般的海军指挥官。但影响更大的恐怕是根据《安妮·弗兰克的日记》改编的戏剧。此剧1956年开始上演,反映法西斯对犹太人的迫害。虽然当时社会日趋保守,但剧作家还是用戏剧表现政治权力的腐败作用,如1956年根据罗伯特·潘·沃伦的《国王的人马》改编的戏剧和戈尔·维达尔(Gore Vidal, 1925—2012)的《最佳人选》(The Best Man, 1960)等。这时期奥尼尔虽已去世,但1956年上演的《漫长的一天到黑夜》使他重新引起人们的注意,证明他不愧为一位出色的有创新戏剧家。第二次世界大战以后,美国出现了四位优秀的剧作家:英奇(William Inge, 1913—1973)、威廉斯(Tennessee Williams, 1914—1983)、米勒(Arthur Miller, 1915—2005)和阿尔比(Edward Albee, 1928—2016)。英奇擅长描写小人物的失意,作品采用颇多象征手段,但深度不够。代表作有《回来吧,小希巴》(Come Back, Little Sheba, 1950)和《野餐》(Picnic, 1953)等。威廉斯主要描写南方的没落、普通人的失意和痛苦、追求幸福之艰难。他一生创作很多,最著名的是《欲望号街车》(A Street Car Named Desire, 1947)、《玻璃动物园》(The Glass Menagerie, 1944)和《热铁皮屋顶上的猫》(Cat on a Hot Tin Roof, 1955)。米勒是战后最著名的美国戏剧家,成名作是一部社会道德剧《全是我的儿子》(All My Sons, 1947)。但《推销员之死》(Death of a Salesman, 1949)被一致公认为第二次世界大战后最优秀的剧本之一。主人公洛曼一生追求成名成家,但始终未能如愿。米勒不仅以一首失败者的挽歌迫使千百万普通美国人从主人公的悲剧联想到自己的命运,还通过洛曼和他的美国梦的幻灭证明普通人也可以成为悲剧式人物。另一部名作是无情地揭露与讽刺迫害左翼人士的麦卡锡主义的《炼狱》(The Crucible, 1953)。此外,涉及他跟大明星梦露婚姻的《堕落之后》(After the Fall, 1964)和探讨家庭关系的《代价》(The Price, 1968)等剧本则表明米勒无论在主题还是技巧方面都是个多面手。另一个杰出的剧作家阿尔比对荒诞派戏剧的兴起有很大的功劳。

50年代后期,剧作家不满越来越商业化的百老汇剧院,认为那里上演的剧目并没有真正反映美国现实,因此外百老汇等小剧场开始兴起。在这里上演的剧目无论在主题内容还是手法技巧方面都可以说是百老汇的对立面。60年代影响最大的戏剧家爱德华·阿尔比认为所谓的"荒诞派戏剧"才是真正的、可以迫使观众"面对真实的人类景况"的戏剧。他身体力行,不断在作品中揭露人们忍受现实的幻想。为此,他大胆革新,运用象征、暗喻、夸张等近乎超现实主义的手法并且采用不完整的阐述、模棱两可的结局和语言游戏等荒诞派手法。他的著名作品有《动物园的故事》(The Zoo Story, 1958)、《美国梦》(The American Dream, 1960)、《谁怕弗吉尼亚·伍尔夫?》(Who's Afraid of Virginia Woolf?, 1961—1962)等。阿尔比所刻画的主题往往是美国梦的破灭、人的孤独和追求自我本质的困难。

美国乐观自信的时代精神随着1963年11月22日肯尼迪总统的遇刺事件而烟消云散,开始了动荡不安的多事之秋。紧接着它又加剧冷战,很快在1965年卷入对越南的战争。美国的冷战政策及扩张行动在国内受到人民的反对。20世纪60年代,争取自由平等的黑人民权运动,反对校园内政治压制、争取言论自由的学生运动以及反对越南战争的罢课示威、贫民区的骚动等事件此起彼伏,加上自20世纪50年代末期开始的嬉皮士反文化运动,对美国社会和政治产生了深刻的影响。黑人运动促使印第安人看到自己面临的困境,也开始了他们的抗议和示威。妇女领袖如贝蒂·弗里丹(Betty Friedan, 1921—2006)等人开始质疑妇女的不平等地位。人们对政府普遍失望与不信任,抛弃旧的信念和追求,对一切权威体系和价值观念进行挑战,强调个人在追求幸福时有采取自己方式的自由,在性观念、性行为,甚至毒品观念等方面都产生了激烈的变化。这一切有其积极的效果,如民权运动结束了种族隔离的制度,改变了美国的种族关系和南方的面貌。但反文化生活方式造成的性自由及吸毒等负面影响也为社会带来了很多后遗症。所有这一切政治和社会等领域中发生的问题都在这一时期的美国文学中有比较真实的反映。

在动荡不安的20世纪60年代里,作家们积极投身政治,参加反对越南战争、支持民权运动等政治活动并在文学作品中加以反映。例如,梅勒的《黑夜的军队》(*The Armies of the Night*, 1967又译《夜幕下的大军》, 1968)就是描写1967年向华盛顿的五角大楼进军的示威活动。哈伯·李(Harper Lee, 1926—   )的《杀死一只模仿鸟》(*To Kill a Mockingbird*, 又译《杀死一只知更鸟》, 1960)描写南方一个小镇中的种族矛盾。小说出版后引起空前的轰动,一年之内发行250万册,第二年获普利策奖并被改编成电影。这一事实说明不仅作家关心社会问题,读者的阅读兴趣也转向政治题材。同时,贝蒂·弗里丹(Betty Friedan, 1921—2006)的《女性的奥秘》(1963)、蒂莉·奥尔逊(Tillie Olsen, 1912—2007)探讨女作家缘何为数极少的讲演稿和文集《沉默》(*Silences*, 1978)拉开了妇女解放运动的序幕。肯·凯西(Ken Kesey, 1935—2001)不仅在小说《飞越疯人院》(*One Flew over the Cuckoo's Nest*, 1962)里揭露冷酷无情的社会对自由的束缚和对人的个性的压抑,而且身体力行地推动反对社会体制的反文化运动。1964年6月他和一群志同道合的朋友自称为"快乐的捣蛋鬼",驾驶一辆油漆得五颜六色的公共汽车,一边抽大麻、吸麻醉药品,一边发表演说、进行演唱,从西向东漫游全国,到纽约跟"垮掉的一代"作家金斯堡与凯鲁亚克会晤,又继续东上去联系其他的嬉皮士,从而把一场反文化运动推向整个美国。

这时期文学的一个重要特点是作家们在越来越关注社会政治问题的同时也不断在手法技巧方面加以创新。20世纪60年代出现一种新型的"非虚构小说",又称"新新闻体小说",或"新新闻主义"。这种小说把事实和猜测糅合在一起,以社会上轰动一时的事件为基础,掺杂作家自己的观察和想象。它们既不同于一般的报告文学,因为其中包含作者的观点,又不同于虚构小说,因为是以真实事件为依据的。梅勒的《黑夜的军队》和他早在1960年就运用这种方式所写关于肯尼迪的《超人来到超级市场》("Superman Comes to the Supermarket")是这方面的典型作品。杜鲁门·卡波特(Truman Capote, 1924—1984)在1966年发表的《残杀》(*In Cold Blood*, 又译《冷血》)也是既报道了一场残酷的谋杀案,又仿佛在撰写侦探小说,把虚构成分和事实相结合。另一位20世纪60和70年代流行的"新新闻主义"创始人是汤姆·沃尔夫(Tom Wolfe, 1931—   )。他在对肯·凯西反文化的全国漫游的报道《电动冷饮剂酸性试验》(*The Electric Kool-Aid Acid Test*, 1968)中把新闻报道的手法和小说技巧相结合,把事实重新安排并加上作者的主观想象使之更富有戏剧性。他还编辑过一本《新新闻主义》(*The New Journalism*, 1973),收入了梅勒、卡波特和琼·迪狄恩(Joan Didion, 1934—   )等人的文章,证明新闻可以写得像小说一样。这时期还出现了一些年轻作家,如用黑色幽默的手法表现荒诞的、没有理性的世界的约瑟夫·海勒、喜好在小说中加入科学和数学概念的托马斯·品钦(Thomas Pynchon, 1937—   ),还有以极其精炼短小的短篇小说见长的唐纳德·巴塞尔姆(Donald Barthelme, 1931—1989)等,他们常常被称为"后现代主义"作家。

第二次世界大战以后涌现出一批黑人新作家。最出色的是拉尔夫·埃里森(Ralph Ellison, 1914—1994)。他的《看不见的人》(*Invisible Man*, 1952)描写了一个黑人少年的成长和寻求自我的过程,反映了黑人与白人之间的种族矛盾,但并不局限于对种族歧视和压迫的抗议。小说的主人公无论在南方还是在北方都发现人们用固定的眼光看待他,他在别人的眼里是个没有个性的人,因此是别人"视而不见的人"。许多评论家认为这是西方现代人具有共性的命运问题。埃里森在小说中运用各种象征手段、历史典故和神话以及现实主义、表现主义、超现实主义等手法,甚至还吸收黑人爵士音乐和布鲁斯的一些手法,是一部从内容到技巧都极为出色的作品。20世纪50年代并不重视黑人作家,但《看不见的人》使埃里森在1953年成为第一个获得国家图书奖的黑人作家。到了20世纪60年代,随着民权运动和女权运动的兴起,黑人作家变得更加活跃。黑人作家詹姆斯·鲍德温(James Baldwin, 1924—1987)从多年居住的法国回到美国参加民权运动,并在20世纪60年代发表了批评美国种族歧视的散文集《没有人知道我的名字》(*Nobody Knows My Name*, 1961)和《下一次将是烈火》(*The Fire Next Time*, 1963)。他最优秀的作品是描写青少年生活的《向苍天呼吁》(*Go Tell It on the Mountain*, 1953)。他的小说《告诉我火车开走多久了》(*Tell Me How Long the Train's Been Gone*, 1968)也是一本战斗性很强的作品,他甚至还撰写戏剧,但成就不如小说与散文。黑人诗人、剧作家勒鲁伊·琼斯原本是"垮掉的一代"作家,后来为了表示决心献身黑人解放事业,1965年改信伊斯兰教,放弃原来的名字,改为伊玛穆·阿米利·巴拉卡(Imamui Amiri Baraka),跟白人妻子离婚,并且搬到黑人贫民窟去居住。他企图创作一种只有黑人能使用也只有黑人才理解的文体和语言,用以排斥传统的语言、意象和思想,即他所谓的"白人"的诗歌特色。他的《蓝调民族:白人美国中的黑人音乐》(*Blues People: Negro Music in White America*, 1963)赞扬黑人艺术和文化,诗歌如《黑人艺术》("Black Art", 1966)呼吁以暴力建立黑人世界,他反映种族冲突的剧本《荷兰人》(*Dutchman*, 1964)在外百老汇小剧院演出时大受欢迎。他还在纽约黑人居住区哈莱姆建立"黑人艺术宝库剧院",为发扬黑人文化而努力。黑人作家中有些人不用小说的形式,而是用大量的事实和个人经历来反映他们所受的压迫与痛苦,如著名的和平主义者马丁·路德·金(Martin Luther King, Jr., 1929—1968)的《我有一个梦想》("I Have a Dream", 1963)就是一篇激情澎湃的演说词。另一位黑人活动家马尔科姆·爱克斯(Malcolm X,

1925—1965)也是以演讲著称,他的《自传》(*The Autobiography of Malcolm X,* 1965)在1998年被《时代周刊》评为"十大必读非虚构作品之一"。

另一方面,女作家(无论白人还是黑人)也开始在文坛上占有一席之地。例如,普拉斯的小说《钟瓮》(*The Bell Jar*, 1963)和诗歌《爹爹》("Daddy", 1962)、《拉扎罗斯夫人》("Lady Lazarus", 1962)等以及女诗人阿德里安·里奇的诗集《一个儿媳妇的快照》(*Snapshots of a Daughter-in-Law: Poems*, 1963)都有明显的女性意识。黑人女作家玛格丽特·沃克·亚历山大(Margaret Walker Alexander, 1915—1998)的小说《欢乐》(*Jubilee*, 1966)和诗集《新日子的预言家》(*Prophets for a New Day*, 1970)、诗人玛雅·安吉罗(Maya Angelou, 1928—   )的自传《我知道笼中鸟为什么会唱歌》(*I Know Why the Caged Bird Sings*, 1968)、洛兰·汉斯贝里(Lorraine Hansberry, 1930—1965)歌颂一个黑人家庭敢于反抗命运的戏剧《阳光下的葡萄干》(*A Raisin in the Sun*, 1959)等把种族与性别元素纳入文学题材的范围之中,使黑人文学登上了美国文坛,成为美国文学的一个引人注目的分支。所有这一切预示着在70年代会出现一个新的文学繁荣时期。

(七) 20世纪70年代以来的美国文学

20世纪70年代开始,美国和世界的形势都有很大的变化。在世界方面,70年代的大事是尼克松访华,中美恢复邦交;80年代是东西德统一,柏林墙被拆除;90年代则是苏联的瓦解。世界不再是两个超级大国对峙的局面。冷战似乎结束了,但美国却越来越多地扮演世界警察的角色,不断干预第三世界的政治,甚至出动武力,尽管它总是争取联合国或欧洲国家的支持。

20世纪70年代延续了20世纪60年代的学生运动和民权运动,社会仍然动荡不安,游行示威成了家常便饭。人们上街可以是为了抗议越南战争或争取种族与男女平等,也可以是反对试验核武器;可以是批评政府腐败,也可以是抗议警察的暴虐。当时影响最大的是妇女解放运动。尽管她们争取宪法增加平等法案的努力始终没有成功,但妇女的地位确实有所提高。她们开始到过去只收男生的高等院校就读,在过去属于男人的领域里工作,甚至进入高校和企事业机构的领导阶层。1975年全国有175个妇女研究中心,学校课程开始注意将妇女问题包括在内。总的来说,美国社会的混乱局面一直到1975年美国从越南撤军以后才有所缓和。但是,1972年尼克松卷入水门事件,1973年副总统因受贿而被迫辞职,1974年尼克松辞职和福特上台后对他无条件宽恕,这一切使得人们对政府和政治更加失望。20世纪80年代表共和党极右势力的里根当选总统,整个美国社会再度趋向保守。20世纪80年代被称为"我,我,我"的时代,至今并未有太多变化。人们一心向往的是金钱和地位,对政治不再关心。1996年克林顿竞选连任时,只有不到一半的选民投票。虽然美国在海湾战争(1990—1991)、瓦解海地军事政变(1993)和轰炸南斯拉夫(1999)等国际事件中都扮演重要角色,但都没有引起美国人民的太多关注。

然而,所有这一切都在文学与文化中有所反映,甚至人们的语言也受到影响。过去美国被称为"大熔炉",因为移民都希望被同化,但现在强调多元文化,人们更强调美国像"马赛克",更看重如何保持各自的民族文化及传统特色。为了尊重妇女地位的变化,人们注意用不突出性别的中性名词,所谓"政治准确"的语言,尽管这受到思想保守人士的反对。

20世纪70年代以来美国社会的一大特点是很多过去壁垒分明的界限变得模糊。比如20世纪60年代嬉皮士的服装与发式是为了表示他们对社会的不满而有意跟传统不一样,它们一直被视为"另类"的文化现象,但现在被社会接受了。同样,在文学方面,主流文学与边缘文学的区别也渐渐地不太明显。一些过去处于边缘的少数族裔文学,如黑人文学、亚裔文学、妇女文学开始进入文学主流。其中,黑人文学的成就最大。七八十年代,黑人文学作品,如阿历克斯·哈利(Alex Haley, 1921—1992)的《根》(*Roots: the Saga of an American Family*, 1976)、艾丽斯·沃克(Alice Walker, 1944—   )的《紫颜色》(*The Color Purple*, 1982)、托妮·莫里森(Tony Morrison, 1931—   )的《宝贝儿》(*Beloved*, 又译《爱娃》《娇女》《宠儿》, 1987)等不仅登上畅销书名单而且被改编成电影。20世纪80年代以来,沃克和莫里森在美国文坛上声望日高。沃克关心妇女运动,尤其是黑人妇女的问题和斗争。《紫颜色》突破了传统黑人文学的题材,正面描写黑人男女之间的矛盾和冲突以及黑人男人大男子主义对黑人女人的摧残,提出黑人女人如何互相关心、建立女性意识、成为具有独立个性的新人的办法。这本小说已经成为美国妇女文学的经典著作。莫里森的成就更大,她关心黑人女性的心灵世界,也表现黑人男人的新问题,但她更注意的是黑人和白人两种文化的冲突对黑人的影响,更强调黑人忘却自己的祖先和自己本民族的传统文化的严重后果。她的技巧也比沃克更胜一筹,既吸收现代派的意识流、多视角等技巧,又充分运用黑人民间文学中诸如人会飞,树木、鱼、鸟能思维有感情,死人能还魂的传说,使她的作品,如《所罗门之歌》(*Song of Solomon*, 1977)、《宝贝儿》等别具一格,回味无穷。1993年,莫里森被授予诺贝尔文学奖,成为得此殊荣的第一个也是迄今为止唯一的黑人女作家。此举也进一步提高了黑人文学在美国文坛的地位。更值得注意的是,现在的黑人文学不再以抗议为主要主题、以现实主义为主要手法、以白人读者为主要受众,而是在语言、技巧、主题方面都有了新的突破。例如莫里森对意识流、多视角、象征等手法的运用,她对黑人文化、民族神话和传说的借鉴使她继承并超越了黑人文学和白人文学的优秀传统。其他出色的黑人作家还有1993—1995年担任美国桂冠诗人的丽塔·达夫(Rita Dove, 1952—   )、曾在克林顿就职仪式上朗诵诗歌的玛雅·安吉罗、得过两次普利策奖的剧作家奥古斯特·威尔逊(August Wilson, 1925—2005)以及诗人、小说家伊什梅尔·里德(Ishmael Reed, 1938—)、约翰·埃德加·韦德曼(John Edgar Wideman, 1941—)和格罗莉亚·内勒(Gloria Naylor, 1950—)等。有意思的是他们中间很多人是大学英语系的教授。这体现了黑人文学在美国的影响,预示着黑人文学更加光明的未来。

在美国,亚裔人口占总人口的2.9%,其中绝大部分是华裔。但长期以来,他们没有形成自己的文学,即使有亚裔作家,他们也并未受到重视。这种情形一直到20世纪70年代后期才有所改变。1974年赵健秀(Frank Chin, 1940—)与人合作编撰的包括华裔、日裔和菲裔美国作家文选《哎——咿!》(Aiiieeeeee! An Anthology of Asian-American Writers, 1974)出版,被评论家称作"亚裔美国文艺复兴的宣言",是亚裔美国人"思想和语言的独立宣言"。1976年汤亭亭(Maxine Hong Kingston, 1940—)发表《女勇士》(The Woman Warrior),引起轰动。1982年韩裔美国作家和大学教授金惠经(Elaine H. Kim)发表了第一本关于亚裔美国文学的专著《亚裔美国文学:有关作品和社会背景的介绍》(Asian-American Literature: An Introduction to the Writings and Their Social Context)。从此,亚裔(主要是华裔)美国文学作品走进美国大学课堂,成为大学教材,例如强调多元文化的《希思美国文学选读》(The Heath Anthology of American Literature,初版1989年)就收有10位亚裔美国作家的作品。这些作家基本上是在美国出生的。他们的写作有明确的目的,要回忆过去,诉说长期受忽略的族群的历史和心声,更要纠正主流社会对他们的误解和陈腐的看法,肯定他们自己是美国社会中合法的一部分。他们表现自己族裔特殊的种族、文化、性别、阶级等问题,也反映如越南战争、民权运动和妇女解放运动以及环保等美国作家所共同关心的问题。现在美国文坛上比较著名的亚裔作家有华裔小说家汤亭亭、谭恩美(Amy Tan, 1952—)、任碧莲(Gish Jen, 1955—),诗人、剧作家、小说家赵健秀,剧作家黄哲伦(David Henry Hwang, 1957—)等,以及兼有韩裔和华裔血统的诗人宋凯蒂(Cathy Song, 1955—)等。他们采用的如超现实主义的时空换位、现代拼贴、多视角多叙述者以及模棱两可的开放性结局等手法也说明他们在艺术技巧方面已经相当成熟了。

早在美国立国以前,印第安人就是美洲大陆的土著居民。但他们的早期文学(主要是部落口头文学)长期以来一直被忽视。然而,1968年印第安诗人、小说家斯科特·莫马迪(N. Scott Momaday, 1934—)发表小说《黎明之屋》(House Made of Dawn)并在第二年获普利策文学奖,从而改变了印第安文学默默无闻的状况。此后,年轻的印第安作家和他们的优秀作品不断涌现,如詹姆斯·威尔契(James Welch, 1940—2003)的《血中冬季》(Winter in the Blood, 1974)和《富尔斯克鲁》(Fools Crow, 1986)、莱斯莉·马蒙·西尔科(Leslie Marmon Silko, 1948—)的《仪典》(Ceremony, 1977)和诗集《雨》(Rain, 1996)、路易丝·厄德里奇(Louise Erdrich, 1954—)的《春药》(Love Medicine, 1984)和诗集《欲望的洗礼》(Baptism of Desire, 1989)等。这些作家和作品构成了20世纪70年代以来的"印第安文学复兴",证明了印第安文学进入主流文坛的可能性。

即便是以白人作家为主的主流文学在这几十年内也产生了很大的变化。在小说方面,贝娄、马拉默德等老作家继续用现实主义手法探索美国社会和美国价值观念,表现那些失去精神支柱、对现代社会并不满足的人的痛苦与困惑。罗斯连续写了好几部关于一位叫朱克曼的主人公的小说,如《鬼作家》(The Ghost Writer, 1979)、《解放了的朱克曼》(Zuckerman Unbound, 1981)和《解剖学课》(The Anatomy Lesson, 1983)等,描写一个颇有事业心的年轻作家的成名与失落,有一定的自传成分。罗斯后来还写了好几部关于朱克曼或以他为叙述者的小说。罗斯的小说以幽默见长,但性描写过多。此外,约翰·厄普代克(John Updike, 1932—2009)是位多才多艺的作家,不仅写小说,而且作诗编剧本,散文和评论也很出色。他还是位多产作家,几乎年年都有作品问世。他的作品涉及的面很广,有关于少年如何努力摆脱小市镇生活的束缚企图走向更广阔天地的经历,有描写家庭生活、婚姻问题、人和人之间关系的。但最著名的是从1960年开始每隔10年出一本的《兔子》四部曲《兔子,跑吧》(Rabbit Run, 1960)、《兔子回来了》(Rabbit Redux, 1971)和《兔子富了》(Rabbit Is Rich, 1981)及《兔子歇了》(Rabbit at Rest, 1990)。这四部曲通过主人公哈里的变化,深刻反映从20世纪50年代到20世纪80年代末的时代特征和人的精神面貌的变化。但厄普代克意犹未尽,在2001年又发表了一个短篇《怀念兔子》(Rabbit Remembered),通过哈里的私生女在1999年突然要求认祖归宗和家人的回忆总结了兔子的一生。另一方面,他仍然在故事中穿插描写了那时期美国发生的如希拉里竞选纽约参议员等真实事件,甚至这时期流行的歌曲和电影,再度把一个小人物的生活跟时代大背景联系在一起,把前四部曲的历史画面延伸到了20世纪末。

还有相当一部分作家认为面对已经变得光怪陆离、充满暴力、犹如梦魇的现实生活,传统的手法已经不能发挥作用,文学也已经不可能起到教育的作用,作家不可能也没有责任为读者指出生活的道路或前进的方向。于是他们下功夫在语言文字和手法技巧等方面进行试验。库特·冯纳古特(Kurt Vonnegut, 1922—2007)延续并发展了60年代海勒式的黑色幽默。埃·劳·道克托罗(E. L. Doctorow, 1931—2015)和罗伯特·库佛(Robert Coover, 1932—)等利用历史"事实"来创造新的小说形式,把历史上的真人真事和虚构的人物与匪夷所思的情节巧妙地糅合在一起,从而在嬉笑之余无情地揭露美国政治的虚伪性,迫使读者或者怀疑美国"光辉"历史的真实性,或者明白过去的不光彩的历史在今天也还是有可能重复的。在语言与形式的试验方面最为成功的作家是托马斯·品钦,他运用混乱而不相关的事物、不知所终的故事情节以及语言上的重复、不关联等手法说明科技进步造成的信息过剩正在形成对现代生活的威胁。他的故事犹如枝叶蔓生的大树,情节难以分出主次,线索杂乱交错。代表作有《拍卖第49批》(*The Crying of Lot 49*, 1966)、《万有引力之虹》(*Gravity's Rainbow*, 1973)和《梅森和迪克森》(*Mason and Dixon*, 1997)等。

在品钦等作家倾心于构建规模庞杂的寓言式元小说的时候,另外一些作家却在试验完全不同的小说形式。20世纪80年代出现了"简约派"小说,代表作家为诗人、小说家雷蒙德·卡佛(Raymond Carver, 1938—1988)。这类作家常常描写普通人日常生活中发生的小事情以及他们的失意与绝望。他们对文字很吝啬,绝对不使用多余的话或可能影响读者的文字,只是用最简单的语言把生活中一个个特定的时刻或事件告诉读者。作品中没有一个全能的、无所不知的、起主宰作用的叙述者,一切均由读者自己来做各种层次的分析。

由于试验小说的文体和结构比故事更重要,由于作家们力图扩大读者与情节或人物之间的距离,他们的作品常常给读者造成阅读上的困难,因此也就常常失去读者。20世纪80年代以后,随着整个社会渐趋保守,作家们也逐渐放弃试验,回归到现实主义手法。当然,这并非传统的现实主义,而是有所变革、有所不同。尽管冯纳古特在《囚鸟》(*Jailbird*, 1979)和《神枪手迪克》(*Deadeye Dick*, 1982)中并没有放弃黑色幽默,但他不再使用试验手法,也不如过去尖刻激烈。曾经极力主张革新的巴思(John Barth, 1930—)在《信件》(*LETTERS*, 1979)和《休假》(*Sabbatica: A Romance*, 1982)中也改用了比较传统的写作手法。

在戏剧方面,由于电视、电影和录像机的发展,也由于剧院票价的不断上涨,去剧院的人少了,戏剧失去越来越多的观众,但它作为叙述的一种方式,仍然被人们阅读。另一方面,自60年代开始,演员扮演角色而观众被动地观看的传统戏剧方式受到质疑,一些打破生活与艺术、演员与剧作家、演员与观众界限的试验剧场,如外百老汇、外外百老汇剧场和一些地方小剧场迅速兴起并且发展得很快。1998年,戏剧发展基金会和剧院与制作人联盟对纽约所有剧院观众的调查报告说明,去外百老汇或外外百老汇剧场看戏的观众是百老汇剧院观众人数的两倍,前者平均一年要看10次以上的演出,而后者只看5次。由此可以看出小剧场的旺盛的生命力。这些剧场上演的剧目往往是电视电影为了票房价值所不愿意触及的颠覆性很强的试验题材,因此是表现美国社会现实问题的先锋和主力军。这时期戏剧的总体情况正如华裔戏剧家黄哲伦(David Henry Hwang, 1957—)所说:"美国戏剧正在开始发现美国人。(有了)黑人戏剧、妇女戏剧、同性恋戏剧、亚裔美国人戏剧、西班牙裔美国人戏剧"。确实,女性戏剧家的出现可能是个典型的例子。70年代,在美国上演的所有剧目中,只有7%是妇女写的,6%是妇女导演的。1978年,女导演朱莉亚·迈尔斯创办了"妇女戏剧与演出工程"来帮助女作家撰写剧本并协助她们找机会演出。1986年,这一工程成为美国最大也是历史最悠久的、专门上演妇女写的剧本的独立妇女剧院和剧团。这工程每年举行活动,奖励有卓越成就的妇女,从朗诵活动、研究小组和大众读者寄来的500到800部稿子里选出三到四个剧本,请著名的演员、导演和舞台设计家组织演出,还把优秀剧作结集出版了11卷妇女戏剧选,为国内外演出提供方便。为了后继有人,她们甚至在全国两千多所学校进行妇女写作戏剧的教育项目。所有这一切大大促进了妇女戏剧的发展。

20世纪的最后几十年内涌现出一大批出色的戏剧家,如以《蝴蝶君》(*M. Butterfly*, 1988)引起轰动的华裔作家黄哲伦,以《晚安,母亲》('*night Mother*, 1982)而一举成名并连连获奖的女作家玛莎·诺曼(Marsha Norman, 1947—),连续获得两个普利策戏剧奖的黑人作家奥古斯特·威尔逊(August Wilson, 1945—2005)以及既是戏剧家又是导演、既在舞台上又在银幕上获得成功、由于专写男人世界而不断引起争议的大卫·马麦特(David Mammet, 1947—)等。更有意思的是,美国现代语言学会的会刊PMLA和颇具权威性的《美国文学》杂志开始改变以往不刊登有关戏剧的文章的做法,出版《美国文学》的杜克大学还决定推出一本新的杂志《戏剧》。也许临近世纪末年,人们开始怀旧,纽约剧院重新上演了米勒的《推销员之死》、威廉斯的《并非关于夜莺》(*Not About Nightingales*, 1938)和奥尼尔的《卖冰的人来了》,并且大获成功。这一切都说明,戏剧已经是美国文学不可忽略的一部分。

诗歌跟戏剧、小说一样,20世纪70年代一方面继续60年代的反叛及在诗行长短、节奏、遣词造句方面的试验与革新,另一方面由于大学的写作课程和各种诗歌朗诵活动的兴起而变得大众化。诗人们根据他们对诗歌的看法而分成了各种派别。金斯堡与里奇相信诗歌可以改变现实,约翰·阿什贝利则认为人们生活在一个荒诞的世界里,他们的思想和感情跟外部现实只有一种任意的、非逻辑性的联系。查尔斯·奥尔森认为诗歌是认识和感觉的过程;罗伯特·布莱(Robert Bly, 1926—)却相信诗歌表现诗人刚开始想的,甚至还没有开始想的思想。但无论他们的见解如何不同,他们都企图寻找能够直接表现个人经历的最佳方式。20世纪80年代,自白派诗歌和超现实主义的"深层意象"派诗歌开始受到读者和诗人的质疑,影响有所减弱。与此同时,新现实主义诗歌开始兴起,并渐渐成为主流。诗人们从自身经历出发既反映个人与社会问题也探讨历史、思想观念、个人与社会责任等哲理问题。另一方面,20世纪60年代一些激进的左派诗人,尤其是"深层意象"派诗人在突破诗歌传统中起了很大的作用。今天他们继续对诗歌形式进行各种试验,一心解构和颠覆"官方诗歌文化",可惜他们把试验、语言、理论看得比生活和诗歌本身更重要,结果他们的"语言诗歌"不免有些曲高和寡。在诗歌走向大众化时,还有些比较保守的诗人却努力想恢复它过去高雅的、为少数人所掌握或欣赏的文化。他们模仿20世纪四五十年代后期现代主义诗歌,强调严谨的格律和反讽、象征等技巧,追求完美的形式,因而他们的作品被称为新形式主义诗歌。20世纪80年代语言诗派和新形式主义派曾互相攻击，前者说后者是"落伍的造句者"，以"填满平庸杂志的空白和奖项"为目的，而后者说前者"不过是在填补学院论文之空白而已……"进入20世纪90年代以后，诗歌发展仍然是多元化，或者按思想体系（如女性主义、同性恋、族裔），或者按地区（纽约派、爱荷华市超现实主义等）分门别类。正是各种不同的流派和各种不同族裔的诗人使20世纪后期的诗歌变得十分丰富多彩。1985年美国国会通过一个法案，把过去的国会图书馆"诗歌顾问"正式改名为"桂冠诗人"，充分说明从政府到公众社会对诗歌发展的重视。

　　20世纪最后的几十年中还有一个值得注意的现象是文学批评理论的兴起。由于几乎主宰20世纪60年代整个社会的反传统反主流的思想行为，在文学批评方面曾经占主导地位的新批评开始衰落，20世纪70年代以后欧洲大陆，尤其是法国的各种新思潮新观念大量涌入美国，学者们在接受这些理论之余还努力用它们来审视自己的文学，构建可以应用于美国文学的批评理论。跟其他文学现象一样，这时期的理论也是百花齐放，有多元化的特点。不仅如此，文学批评理论已经发展成为一个独立的学科，成为一种独立的专业。

　　另外一个变化是严肃文学和通俗文学的界限越来越模糊。严肃文学也可以上畅销书榜，也可以被拍成电影，成为大众文化的一部分。例如，尤多拉·韦尔蒂、托尼·莫里森，甚至以复杂难懂著称的托马斯·品钦等严肃作家的作品都上过畅销榜，凯西的《飞越疯人院》、沃克的《紫颜色》、埃·劳·道克托罗的《雷格泰姆音乐》都曾被拍成电影。另一方面严肃作家也喜欢采用通俗小说的格局，冯纳古特在很长的时间里一直被认为是科幻小说家，品钦的作品就像侦探小说，主人公千方百计想要破解奥秘，只是永远不得所求。其实，通俗文学并不是完全没有政治含义的。如汤姆·克兰西（Tom Clancy，1947—　）的间谍小说就跟苏联没有解体以前的冷战有关。迈克尔·克莱顿（Michael Crichton，1942—2008）的高科技惊险小说跟科技的突飞猛进有着密切的联系。当人们为高离婚率带来的后果所困扰、对爱情的追求产生疑惑时，他们希望从西德尼·谢尔顿（Sidney Sheldon，1917—2007）或埃里克·西格尔（Erich Segal，1937—2010）等人的爱情小说中得到安慰。暴露小说一直在美国有市场，20世纪初就有过"专门报道丑事"的作品。20世纪70年代以来，腐败事件层出不穷，这方面的作品就成为最受欢迎的通俗小说类别之一。最著名的作家是20世纪90年代崛起的、专写司法界腐败的约翰·格里森姆（John Grisham，1955—　）。通俗小说家中间有些人的作品发行量常常在100万册以上。当前，美国学术界和思想界对通俗文学日益重视的现象应该引起我们的注意。

　　这三十年还是电视、录像机、手机、个人电脑迅速发展的时代。20世纪90年代更是电子时代。1992年万维网的诞生改变了人们的生活方式，人们可以在网上进行通讯、购物、做生意、寻找信息，甚至阅读电子书籍。据统计，1998年美国有一亿以上的人使用互联网。这一切正在改变人们的生活和思维方式，也一定会在文学中有所表现，但恐怕要到21世纪中期才能看清眉目和结果。

（陶　洁）

第一单元
Benjamin Franklin (1706—1790)
本杰明·富兰克林

 作者简介

  本杰明·富兰克林(Benjamin Franklin, 1706—1790),企业家、政治家、科学家、作家,出生于波士顿一个笃信清教的小商人家庭。富兰克林上学读书只有短短两年,辍学后帮父亲打理生意,但并不喜欢他的蜡烛生意,一心想着出海远游。父亲知道,儿子是个书迷,印刷这一行可能适合他,因此决定让他在哥哥的印刷所做契约学徒。他12岁就发表了两首叙事诗。16岁时,他开始在报刊上发表讽刺文章,评论时事。17岁时,他只身来到费城,这时他还是一文不名的穷小子,到22岁时,他与人合伙开办印刷所,后来又拥有了一家报纸。他24岁结婚,26岁开始发表广受欢迎的《格言历书》(*Poor Richard's Almanack*, 1732)。他的印刷出版生意也日渐红火,到了1748年,他就不再参与经营,但每年都可以获得经营收益。此后,他更多参与和承担起公共服务。1751年,他作为费城代表当选宾夕法尼亚议会议员,后担任过议会议长。英国与殖民地之间爆发危机前后,他曾作为议会代理人出使英国。尽管他赞赏英国政制并反对殖民地脱离英国,但是随着双方冲突的发展,他意识到英国和殖民地之间存在难以调和的利益冲突。回到北美后,他参加了大陆会议(Continental Congress),其后与约翰·亚当斯等人协助杰弗逊撰写《独立宣言》。随后,他又代表美国出使法国,任全权公使,为美国独立争取道义和物质上的支持。随着战事的进展,他和亚当斯等人一起与英国谈判达成停战协定,使英国最终承认了美国的独立。除了政治上的卓越成就以外,他还是一个科学家,发明了后来广泛使用的富兰克林火炉和避雷针,他用风筝做雷电实验,还提出热量吸收理论等。同时,他也是公益活动家,先后推动、建立了公共图书馆、消防公司、"美洲哲学会"、费城学院(后为宾夕法尼亚大学)、宾夕法尼亚医院等。1771年,他开始撰写《自传》(*The Autobiography*),历时18年。纵观富兰克林传奇的一生,他通过勤奋自学和个人努力,摆脱了贫穷和卑微,获得了财富和崇高国际声望,不但实践了从普通人到伟人的成功故事,而且诠释了新教传统的个人道德完善和公共责任。苏格兰哲学家大卫·休谟称他为来自美洲的"第一个哲学家和第一个伟大作家"。

Autobiography
(*Excerpt*)

  We have an English proverb that says, "*He that would thrive, must ask his wife.*" It was lucky for me that I had one as much dispos'd① to industry and frugality as myself. She assisted me cheerfully in my business, folding and stitching pamphlets, tending shop, purchasing old linen rags for the papermakers, etc., etc. We kept no idle servants, our table was plain and simple, our furniture of the cheapest. For instance, my breakfast was a long time bread and milk (no tea), and I ate it out of a two penny earthen porringer, with a pewter spoon. But mark how luxury will enter families, and make a progress, in spite of principle: being call'd one morning to breakfast, I found it in a China bowl, with a spoon of silver! They had been bought for me without my knowledge by my wife, and had cost her the enormous sum of three-and-twenty shillings, for which she had no other excuse or apology to make, but that she thought her husband deserv'd a silver spoon and China bowl as well as any of his

---

① dispos'd: disposed.

neighbors. This was the first appearance of plate and China in our house, which afterward, in a course of years, as our wealth increas'd, augmented gradually to several hundred pounds in value.

 I had been religiously educated as a Presbyterian; and tho'[①] some of the dogmas of that persuasion, such as *the eternal decrees of God, election, reprobation, etc.*, appeared to me unintelligible, others doubtful, and I early absented myself from the public assemblies of the sect, Sunday being my studying day, I never was without some religious principles. I never doubted, for instance, the existence of the Deity; that he made the world, and govern'd it by his Providence; that the most acceptable service of God was the doing good to man; that our souls are immortal; and that all crime will be punished, and virtue rewarded, either here or hereafter. These I esteem'd the essentials of every religion; and, being to be found in all the religions we had in our country, I respected them all, tho' with different degrees of respect, as I found them more or less mix'd with other articles, which, without any tendency to inspire, promote, or confirm morality, serv'd principally to divide us, and make us unfriendly to one another. This respect to all, with an opinion that the worst had some good effects, induc'd me to avoid all discourse that might tend to lessen the good opinion another might have of his own religion; and as our province increas'd in people, and new places of worship were continually wanted, and generally erected by voluntary contributions, my mite for such purpose, whatever might be the sect, was never refused.

 Tho' I seldom attended any public worship, I had still an opinion of its propriety, and of its utility when rightly conducted, and I regularly paid my annual subscription for the support of the only Presbyterian minister or meeting we had in Philadelphia. He us'd to visit me sometimes as a friend, and admonish me to attend his administrations, and I was now and then prevail'd on to do so, once for five Sundays successively. Had he been in my opinion a good preacher, perhaps I might have continued, notwithstanding the occasion I had for the Sunday's leisure in my course of study; but his discourses were chiefly either polemic arguments, or explications of the peculiar doctrines of our sect, and were all to me very dry, uninteresting, and unedifying, since not a single moral principle was inculcated or enforc'd, their aim seeming to be rather to make us Presbyterians than good citizens.

 At length he took for his text that verse of the fourth chapter of Philippians, "*Finally, brethren*[②], *whatsoever things are true, honest, just, pure, lovely, or of good report, if there be any virtue, or any praise, think on these things.*"[③] And I imagin'd, in a sermon on such a text, we could not miss of having some morality. But he confin'd himself to five points only, as meant by the apostle, viz.: 1. Keeping holy the Sabbath day. 2. Being diligent in reading the holy Scriptures. 3. Attending duly the publick[④] worship. 4. Partaking of the Sacrament. 5. Paying a due respect to God's ministers. These might be all good things; but, as they were not the kind of good things that I expected from that text, I despaired of ever meeting with them from any other, was disgusted, and attended his preaching no more. I had some years before compos'd a little Liturgy, or form of prayer, for my own private use (viz., in 1728), entitled, *Articles of Belief and Acts of Religion*. I return'd to the use of this, and went no more to the public assemblies. My conduct might be blameable, but I leave it, without attempting further to excuse it; my present purpose being to relate facts, and not to make apologies for them.

 It was about this time I conceiv'd the bold and arduous project of arriving at moral perfection. I wish'd to live without committing any fault at any time; I would conquer all that either natural inclination, custom, or company might lead me into. As I knew, or thought I knew, what was right and

---

① tho': though.
② brethren: brothers.
③ "*Finally, brethren, whatsoever things are true, honest, just, pure, lovely, or of good report, if there be any virtue, or any praise, think on these things.*": 引自圣经《新约—腓立比书》(Philippians 4: 8),可能是保罗(Saint Paul the Apostle)在罗马被囚时所作,这句话是保罗对信众的劝勉之词。
④ publick: public.

wrong, I did not see why I might not always do the one and avoid the other. But I soon found I had undertaken a task of more difficulty than I had imagined. While my care was employ'd in guarding against one fault, I was often surprised by another; habit took the advantage of inattention; inclination was sometimes too strong for reason. I concluded, at length, that the mere speculative conviction that it was our interest to be completely virtuous, was not sufficient to prevent our slipping; and that the contrary habits must be broken, and good ones acquired and established, before we can have any dependence on a steady, uniform rectitude of conduct. For this purpose I therefore contrived the following method.

In the various enumerations of the moral virtues I had met with in my reading, I found the catalogue more or less numerous, as different writers included more or fewer ideas under the same name. Temperance, for example, was by some confined to eating and drinking, while by others it was extended to mean the moderating every other pleasure, appetite, inclination, or passion, bodily or mental, even to our avarice and ambition. I propos'd to myself, for the sake of clearness, to use rather more names, with fewer ideas annex'd to each, than a few names with more ideas; and I included under thirteen names of virtues all that at that time occurr'd to me as necessary or desirable, and annexed to each a short precept, which fully express'd the extent I gave to its meaning.

These names of virtues, with their precepts, were:

1. TEMPERANCE.

Eat not to dullness; drink not to elevation.

2. SILENCE.

Speak not but what may benefit others or yourself; avoid trifling conversation.

3. ORDER.

Let all your things have their places; let each part of your business have its time.

4. RESOLUTION.

Resolve to perform what you ought; perform without fail what you resolve.

5. FRUGALITY.

Make no expense but to do good to others or yourself; i.e., waste nothing.

6. INDUSTRY.

Lose no time; be always employ'd in something useful; cut off all unnecessary actions.

7. SINCERITY.

Use no hurtful deceit; think innocently and justly, and, if you speak, speak accordingly.

8. JUSTICE.

Wrong none by doing injuries, or omitting the benefits that are your duty.

9. MODERATION.

Avoid extreams[①]; forbear resenting injuries so much as you think they deserve.

10. CLEANLINESS.

Tolerate no uncleanliness in body, cloaths[②], or habitation.

11. TRANQUILLITY.

Be not disturbed at trifles, or at accidents common or unavoidable.

12. CHASTITY.

Rarely use venery but for health or offspring, never to dulness, weakness, or the injury of your own or another's peace or reputation.

---

① extreams: extremes.
② cloaths: clothes.

13. HUMILITY.

Imitate Jesus and Socrates.

My intention being to acquire the *habitude* of all these virtues, I judg'd it would be well not to distract my attention by attempting the whole at once, but to fix it on one of them at a time; and, when I should be master of that, then to proceed to another, and so on, till I should have gone thro'[①] the thirteen; and, as the previous acquisition of some might facilitate the acquisition of certain others, I arrang'd them with that view, as they stand above. Temperance first, as it tends to procure that coolness and clearness of head, which is so necessary where constant vigilance was to be kept up, and guard maintained against the unremitting attraction of ancient habits, and the force of perpetual temptations. This being acquir'd and establish'd, Silence would be more easy; and my desire being to gain knowledge at the same time that I improv'd in virtue, and considering that in conversation it was obtain'd rather by the use of the ears than of the tongue, and therefore wishing to break a habit I was getting into of prattling, punning, and joking, which only made me acceptable to trifling company, I gave *Silence* the second place. This and the next, *Order*, I expected would allow me more time for attending to my project and my studies. *Resolution*, once become habitual, would keep me firm in my endeavors to obtain all the subsequent virtues; *Frugality* and *Industry* freeing me from my remaining debt, and producing affluence and independence, would make more easy the practice of Sincerity and Justice, etc., etc. Conceiving then, that, agreeably to the advice of Pythagoras[②] in his Golden Verses[③], daily examination would be necessary, I contrived the following method for conducting that examination.

I made a little book, in which I allotted a page for each of the virtues. I rul'd each page with red ink, so as to have seven columns, one for each day of the week, marking each column with a letter for the day. I cross'd these columns with thirteen red lines, marking the beginning of each line with the first letter of one of the virtues, on which line, and in its proper column, I might mark, by a little black spot, every fault I found upon examination to have been committed respecting that virtue upon that day.

Form of the Pages

TEMPERANCE.						
EAT NOT TO DULNESS; DRINK NOT TO ELEVATION.						
S.	M.	T.	W.	T.	F.	S.
T.						
S.	*	*		*		*	
O.	**	*	*		*	*	*
R.			*		*		
F.		*			*		
I.			*				
S.							
J.							
M.							
C.							
T.							
C.							
H.							

---

① thro': through.
② Pythagoras: 毕达哥拉斯(580—500 B.C.),古希腊数学家和哲学家。
③ Golden Verses: *The Golden Verses of Pythagoras*. 道德劝诫诗篇,共71行诗句,一般认为是毕达哥拉斯所作。

I determined to give a week's strict attention to each of the virtues successively. Thus, in the first week, my great guard was to avoid every the least offence against *Temperance*, leaving the other virtues to their ordinary chance, only marking every evening the faults of the day. Thus, if in the first week I could keep my first line, marked T, clear of spots, I suppos'd the habit of that virtue so much strengthen'd and its opposite weaken'd, that I might venture extending my attention to include the next, and for the following week keep both lines clear of spots. Proceeding thus to the last, I could go thro' a course compleat① in thirteen weeks, and four courses in a year. And like him who, having a garden to weed, does not attempt to eradicate all the bad herbs at once, which would exceed his reach and his strength, but works on one of the beds at a time, and, having accomplish'd the first, proceeds to a second, so I should have, I hoped, the encouraging pleasure of seeing on my pages the progress I made in virtue, by clearing successively my lines of their spots, till in the end, by a number of courses, I should he happy in viewing a clean book, after a thirteen weeks' daily examination。

This my little book had for its motto these lines from Addison's *Cato*②: "Here will I hold.

> If there's a power above us
> (And that there is all nature cries aloud
> Thro' all her works), He must delight in virtue;
> And that which he delights in must be happy."

Another from Cicero③:

"O vitae Philosophia dux! O virtutum indagatrix expultrixque vitiorum! Unus dies, bene et ex praeceptis tuis actus, peccanti immortalitati est anteponendus."④

Another from the Proverbs of Solomon, speaking of wisdom or virtue:

"Length of days is in her right hand, and in her left hand riches and honour. Her ways are ways of pleasantness, and all her paths are peace."

And conceiving God to be the fountain of wisdom, I thought it right and necessary to solicit his assistance for obtaining it; to this end I formed the following little prayer,which was prefix'd to my tables of examination, for daily use.

"*O powerful Goodness! bountiful Father! merciful Guide! increase in me that wisdom which discovers my truest interest. strengthen my resolutions to perform what that wisdom dictates. Accept my kind offices to thy other children as the only return in my power for thy continual favors to me.*"

I used also sometimes a little prayer which I took from Thomson's Poems⑤, viz.:

> "Father of light and life, thou Good Supreme!
> O teach me what is good; teach me Thyself!

---

① compleat: complete.
② Addison: 约瑟夫·艾迪生(Joseph Addison, 1672—1719),英国散文家,诗人,剧作家。*Cato*:《卡托》为艾迪生创作的悲剧作品。
③ Cicero: 西塞罗(Marcus Tullius Cicero, 106—43 B.C.),古罗马政治家、演说家。
④ "O vitae Philosophia dux! O virtutum indagatrix expultrixque vitiorum! Unus dies, bene et ex praeceptis tuis actus, peccanti immortalitati est anteponendus.":(拉丁文)意为:"啊! 哲学,人生的指南! 啊,你是美德的导师,你消除罪恶。拥有美德的一天胜于罪恶中的永生。"出自《图斯库卢姆谈话录》(*Tusculum Disputations*)。
⑤ Thomson: 詹姆斯·汤姆逊(James Thomson, 1700—1748),英国诗人,诗句出自《冬季》("Winter," 1726)。

Save me from folly, vanity, and vice,
From every low pursuit; and fill my soul
With knowledge, conscious peace, and virtue pure;
Sacred, substantial, never-fading bliss!"

The precept of Order requiring that *every part of my business should have its allotted time*, one page in my little book contain'd the following scheme of employment for the twenty-four hours of a natural day:

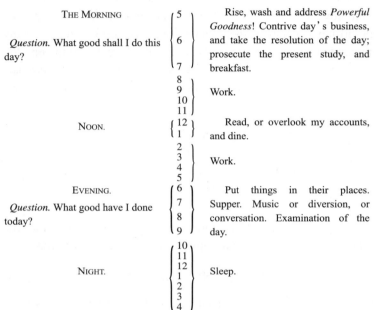

THE MORNING		5	Rise, wash and address *Powerful Goodness*! Contrive day's business, and take the resolution of the day; prosecute the present study, and breakfast.
Question. What good shall I do this day?		6	
		7	
		8	Work.
		9	
		10	
		11	
NOON.		12	Read, or overlook my accounts, and dine.
		1	
		2	Work.
		3	
		4	
		5	
EVENING.		6	Put things in their places. Supper. Music or diversion, or conversation. Examination of the day.
Question. What good have I done today?		7	
		8	
		9	
NIGHT.		10	Sleep.
		11	
		12	
		1	
		2	
		3	
		4	

I enter'd upon the execution of this plan for self-examination, and continu'd it with occasional intermissions for some time. I was surpris'd to find myself so much fuller of faults than I had imagined; but I had the satisfaction of seeing them diminish. To avoid the trouble of renewing now and then my little book, which, by scraping out the marks on the paper of old faults to make room for new ones in a new course, became full of holes, I transferr'd my tables and precepts to the ivory leaves[①] of a memorandum book, on which the lines were drawn with red ink, that made a durable stain, and on those lines I mark'd my faults with a black-lead pencil, which marks I could easily wipe out with a wet sponge. After a while I went thro' one course only in a year, and afterward only one in several years, till at length I omitted them entirely, being employ'd in voyages and business abroad, with a multiplicity of affairs that interfered; but I always carried my little book with me.

My scheme of ORDER gave me the most trouble; and I found that, tho' it might be practicable where a man's business was such as to leave him the disposition of his time, that of a journeyman printer, for instance, it was not possible to be exactly observed by a master, who must mix with the world, and often receive people of business at their own hours. *Order*, too, with regard to places for things, papers, etc., I found extreamly[②] difficult to acquire. I had not been early accustomed to it, and, having an exceeding good memory, I was not so sensible of the inconvenience attending want of method. This article, therefore, cost me so much painful attention, and my faults in it vexed me so much, and I made so little progress in amendment, and had such frequent relapses, that I was almost

---

① ivory leaves：厚质纸张。
② extreamly: extremely.

ready to give up the attempt, and content myself with a faulty character in that respect, like the man who, in buying an ax of a smith, my neighbour, desired to have the whole of its surface as bright as the edge. The smith consented to grind it bright for him if he would turn the wheel; he turn'd, while the smith press'd the broad face of the ax hard and heavily on the stone, which made the turning of it very fatiguing. The man came every now and then from the wheel to see how the work went on, and at length would take his ax as it was, without farther grinding. "No," said the smith, "turn on, turn on; we shall have it bright by-and-by; as yet, it is only speckled." "Yes," said the man, *but I think I like a speckled ax best.*" And I believe this may have been the case with many, who, having, for want of some such means as I employ'd, found the difficulty of obtaining good and breaking bad habits in other points of vice and virtue, have given up the struggle, and concluded that "*a speckled ax was best*"; for something, that pretended to be reason, was every now and then suggesting to me that such extreme nicety as I exacted of myself might be a kind of foppery in morals, which, if it were known, would make me ridiculous; that a perfect character might be attended with the inconvenience of being envied and hated; and that a benevolent man should allow a few faults in himself, to keep his friends in countenance.

In truth, I found myself incorrigible with respect to Order; and now I am grown old, and my memory bad, I feel very sensibly the want of it. But, on the whole, tho' I never arrived at the perfection I had been so ambitious of obtaining, but fell far short of it, yet I was, by the endeavour, a better and a happier man than I otherwise should have been if I had not attempted it; as those who aim at perfect writing by imitating the engraved copies, tho' they never reach the wish'd-for excellence of those copies, their hand is mended by the endeavor, and is tolerable while it continues fair and legible.

It may be well my posterity should be informed that to this little artifice, with the blessing of God, their ancestor ow'd the constant felicity of his life, down to his 79th year, in which this is written. What reverses may attend the remainder is in the hand of Providence; but, if they arrive, the reflection on past happiness enjoy'd ought to help his bearing them with more resignation. To Temperance he ascribes his long-continued health, and what is still left to him of a good constitution; to Industry and Frugality, the early easiness of his circumstances and acquisition of his fortune, with all that knowledge that enabled him to be a useful citizen, and obtained for him some degree of reputation among the learned; to Sincerity and Justice, the confidence of his country, and the honorable employs it conferred upon him; and to the joint influence of the whole mass of the virtues, even in the imperfect state he was able to acquire them, all that evenness of temper, and that cheerfulness in conversation, which makes his company still sought for, and agreeable even to his younger acquaintance. I hope, therefore, that some of my descendants may follow the example and reap the benefit.

It will be remark'd that, tho' my scheme was not wholly without religion, there was in it no mark of any of the distingishing[①] tenets of any particular sect. I had purposely avoided them; for, being fully persuaded of the utility and excellency of my method, and that it might be serviceable to people in all religions, and intending some time or other to publish it, I would not have any thing in it that should prejudice any one, of any sect, against it. I purposed writing a little comment on each virtue, in which I would have shown the advantages of possessing it, and the mischiefs attending its opposite vice; and I should have called my book THE ART OF VIRTUE, because it would have shown the means and manner of obtaining virtue, which would have distinguished it from the mere exhortation to be good, that does not instruct and indicate the means, but is like the apostle's man of verbal charity, who only without showing to the naked and hungry how or where they might get clothes or victuals, exhorted them to be fed and clothed.

---

① distingishing: distinguishing.

But it so happened that my intention of writing and publishing this comment was never fulfilled. I did, indeed, from time to time, put down short hints of the sentiments, reasonings, etc., to be made use of in it, some of which I have still by me; but the necessary close attention to private business in the earlier part of life, and public business since, have occasioned my postponing it; for, it being connected in my mind with *a great and extensive project*, that required the whole man to execute, and which an unforeseen succession of employs prevented my attending to, it has hitherto remain'd unfinish'd.

In this piece it was my design to explain and enforce this doctrine, that vicious actions are not hurtful because they are forbidden, but forbidden because they are hurtful, the nature of man alone considered; that it was, therefore, every one's interest to be virtuous who wish'd to be happy even in this world; and I should, from this circumstance (there being always in the world a number of rich merchants, nobility, states, and princes, who have need of honest instruments for the management of their affairs, and such being so rare), have endeavored to convince young persons that no qualities were so likely to make a poor man's fortune as those of probity and integrity.

My list of virtues contain'd at first but twelve; but a Quaker friend having kindly informed me that I was generally thought proud; that my pride show'd itself frequently in conversation; that I was not content with being in the right when discussing any point, but was overbearing, and rather insolent, of which he convinc'd me by mentioning several instances; I determined endeavouring to cure myself, if I could, of this vice or folly among the rest, and I added Humility to my list giving an extensive meaning to the word.

I cannot boast of much success in acquiring the *reality* of this virtue, but I had a good deal with regard to the *appearance* of it. I made it a rule to forbear all direct contradiction to the sentiments of others, and all positive assertion of my own. I even forbid myself, agreeably to the old laws of our Junto, the use of every word or expression in the language that imported a fix'd opinion, such as *certainly*, *undoubtedly*, etc., and I adopted, instead of them, *I conceive, I apprehend*, or *I imagine* a thing to be so or so; or it *so appears to me at present*. When another asserted something that I thought an error, I deny'd myself the pleasure of contradicting him abruptly, and of showing immediately some absurdity in his proposition; and in answering I began by observing that in certain cases or circumstances his opinion would be right, but in the present case there *appear'd* or *seem'd* to me some difference, etc. I soon found the advantage of this change in my manner; the conversations I engag'd in went on more pleasantly. The modest way in which I propos'd my opinions procur'd them a readier reception and less contradiction; I had less mortification when I was found to be in the wrong, and I more easily prevail'd with others to give up their mistakes and join with me when I happened to be in the right.

And this mode, which I at first put on with some violence to natural inclination, became at length so easy, and so habitual to me, that perhaps for these fifty years past no one has ever heard a dogmatical expression escape me. And to this habit (after my character of integrity) I think it principally owing that I had early so much weight with my fellow-citizens when I proposed new institutions, or alterations in the old, and so much influence in public councils when I became a member; for I was but a bad speaker, never eloquent, subject to much hesitation in my choice of words, hardly correct in language, and yet I generally carried my points.

In reality, there is, perhaps, no one of our natural passions so hard to subdue as *pride*. Disguise it, struggle with it, beat it down, stifle it, mortify it as much as one pleases, it is still alive, and will every now and then peep out and show itself; you will see it, perhaps, often in this history; for, even if I could conceive that I had compleatly① overcome it, I should probably be proud of my humility.

---

① compleatly: completely.

富兰克林在英国担任宾夕法尼亚议会代理人期间开始撰写《自传》第一部分,时年65岁。《自传》开篇以父亲的口吻讲述自己的经历,向"后人"细说自己如何从出身贫寒、默默无闻的小人物,通过勤奋获得财富,成为世界名人的历程,以及成功的"手段"。接下来发生的美国革命打断了《自传》的写作,直到1784年才得以继续,这时的写作对象已经是公众读者,而后他的公职又打断了他的写作,直到他去世,他仍有30多年的人生经历未能记录在《自传》中。《自传》的结构虽然显得较为松散,但其清新、质朴无华的文笔生动展示了作者前半生的经历。《自传》面世后一直深受读者欢迎,先后译成多种文字,成为公认的经典自传作品。《自传》主人公身处的时代,适逢美洲新世界作为自由庇护所开始崛起(当然,在当时美洲人的自由概念中并没有包括奴隶),一个小人物的成就和自身品格塑造,凸显了美国资本主义社会典型的个人主义价值取向,也创造出一个经典人物形象,其影响力因作品自身的艺术价值及其思想意义而历久不衰。

　　18世纪英属北美殖民地在英国自由主义共和思想影响下,旧世界的封建王权势力在这里没有市场,在政治上,殖民地享有高度自治,经济阶层分化相对不发达,大多数农民都拥有土地,也没有欧洲社会中的极端贫困阶层。相对于当时其他国家,殖民地居民享有更多自由,因而崇尚独立自主,他们更少受到封建和社会等级的压迫,因而也少有身份区分观念。在宗教观念上,清教徒们虽然相信得救预定论(Predestination),但他们认为,自己的生活方式能显示他们是否能够得救,因此圣洁、勤奋和成功的生活可以是上帝恩典的表现。在这样的文化土壤里,《自传》讲述的就不仅仅是一个贫穷后生发家致富的经济成功故事,而且传达了更加广义的自由主义和个人主义理念:只要通过个人努力,就可以完善自身,塑造自己的命运,改变贫寒卑微的地位,从而拥有参与和影响政治和社会的能力,而这其中所表现的乐观向上的自信和活力也是这片新大陆的时代精神写照。韦伯(Max Weber)运用了马克思主义上层建筑和经济基础的分析进路,把富兰克林看成是新教伦理和美国资本主义精神的典型(富兰克林本人是一个自然神论者)。在资本主义秩序中,合法获得财富本身,而不是通过财富获得快乐,成了生活的最终目的。"我……把勤奋看成获得财富和声望的手段"。从富兰克林这句话中可以看出勤奋等美德与获得名利之间的功利主义关系,这或许也能佐证他的心态所表现的所谓"资本主义精神"。

　　富兰克林的《自传》文体朴实亲切,毫无矫饰雕琢,其娓娓道来的叙事风格将个人独特经历的诸多细节展现得活灵活现;常常短短数行描写,使一个活脱形象跃然纸上,例证之一是富兰克林对自己初到费城时的自我描绘,这几乎成了其后人们心中穷小子进城的经典形象。富兰克林文中对自己成功经历背后的价值信念虽多有着墨,但其表达方式与自传叙事相辅相成,自然合一。无疑,富兰克林的《自传》无论其思想和历史价值还是自传文体风格都无愧于其傲立美国乃至世界自传文学之林的经典地位。

 思考题

1. What is the author's view on religion?
2. How did Franklin try to achieve moral perfection?
3. What does the author mean, when he says, "vicious actions are not hurtful because they are forbidden, but forbidden because they are hurtful"?

"The Way to Wealth" (1758)
The Autobiography(1818)

参考资料

Baida, Peter. *Poor Richard's Legacy: American Business Values from Benjamin Franklin to Donald Trump*. New York: W. Morrow, 1990.

Lemay, Joseph. A. Leo and Paul. M. Zall, eds. *Benjamin Franklin's Autobiography: An Authoritative Text, Backgrounds, Criticism*. New York: W. W. Norton & Company, Inc., 1986.

Levin, David. ed. *The Puritan in the Enlightenment: Franklin and Edwards*. Chicago: Rand McNally, 1963.

(张世耘)

第二单元
Ralph Waldo Emerson (1803—1882)
拉尔夫·华尔多·爱默生

 作者简介

　　拉尔夫·华尔多·爱默生(Ralph Waldo Emerson, 1803—1882), 散文家、诗人、哲学家。他出生于波士顿一个牧师家庭, 14岁入读哈佛(这在当时是正常入学年龄), 4年后毕业。此后几年, 他在不同学校教书, 但心中理想是成为诗人, 演说家或牧师。1829年, 他受聘担任牧师, 但三年后辞职, 主要原因是他接受了哥白尼宇宙观, 也无法认同神学赎罪说以及相关教会仪式, 同时他坚信, 宗教信仰绝不是轻信, 实践宗教也不需要任何附加的外在形式。他渴望摆脱羁绊, 自主探求真理。同年, 他首次出行欧洲, 拜访了兰德、柯勒律治、卡莱尔、华兹华斯等作家。他们之中尤其值得一提的是柯勒律治和卡莱尔, 他们摒弃洛克、休谟所代表的英国经验主义传统, 采用康德、费希特等人的德国唯心主义进路, 不是通过感官现象途径, 从经验对象出发达至真理, 而是从心灵出发, 通过直觉感悟真理, 进而向外达至对经验对象的统摄。这对爱默生的超验主义哲学(Transcendentalism)或所谓"直觉哲学"(intuitional philosophy)产生了重要影响。回国后, 他开始了演讲和写作生涯。1836年, 他匿名发表了《论自然》("Nature"), 探讨自然与人、精神与世界的关系, 主张以全新的眼光看待世界, "建造你自己的世界"。翌年, 他在哈佛演讲, 题目为《美国学者》("The American Scholar")。该演讲对美国文化产生了深远影响, 诗人霍姆斯称之为美国"思想的独立宣言"("intellectual Declaration of Independence")。演讲中, 他把"学者"定义为"思考的人", 不因他人书籍、传统、习俗、教会、社会、时空等影响而偏离自己的"运行轨道", 不会从一个完整的宇宙沦为一颗"卫星", 而学者的自由除自身束缚外, 别无障碍。爱默生通过演讲和散文宣扬个人就是整个宇宙, 他的思想成了美国个人主义意识形态的重要基石。

　　爱默生的其他主要著作包括:《散文集:第一辑》(*Essays: First Series*, 1841),《散文集:第二辑》(*Essays: Second Series*, 1844),《代表人物》(*Representative Men*, 1850),《英国特色》(*English Traits*, 1856),《生活的准则》(*The Conduct of Life*, 1860), 诗集《五月节》(*May-Day and Other Pieces*, 1867)等。

Self-Reliance
(*Excerpt*)

　　I read the other day some verses written by an eminent painter① which were original and not conventional. The soul always hears an admonition in such lines, let the subject be what it may. The sentiment they instil is of more value than any thought they may contain. To believe your own thought, to believe that what is true for you in your private heart is true for all men, —that is genius. Speak your latent conviction, and it shall be the universal sense; for the inmost in due time becomes the outmost, —and our first thought is rendered back to us by the trumpets of the Last Judgment. Familiar as the voice of the mind is to each, the highest merit we ascribe to Moses, Plato, and Milton is, that they set at naught books and traditions, and spoke not what men but what they thought. A man should learn to detect and watch that gleam of light which flashes across his mind from within, more than the lustre of the firmament of bards and sages. Yet he dismisses without notice his thought, because it is his. In

---

① an eminent painter: 指华盛顿·奥尔斯顿(Washington Allston, 1779—1943), 美国诗人、画家。

every work of genius we recognize our own rejected thoughts: they come back to us with a certain alienated majesty. Great works of art have no more affecting lesson for us than this. They teach us to abide by our spontaneous impression with good-humored inflexibility then most when the whole cry of voices is on the other side. Else, to-morrow a stranger will say with masterly good sense precisely what we have thought and felt all the time, and we shall be forced to take with shame our own opinion from another.

There is a time in every man's education when he arrives at the conviction that envy is ignorance; that imitation is suicide; that he must take himself for better, for worse, as his portion; that though the wide universe is full of good, no kernel of nourishing corn can come to him but through his toil bestowed on that plot of ground which is given to him to till. The power which resides in him is new in nature, and none but he knows what that is which he can do, nor does he know until he has tried. Not for nothing one face, one character, one fact, makes much impression on him, and another none. This sculpture in the memory is not without preestablished harmony①. The eye was placed where one ray should fall, that it might testify of that particular ray. We but half express ourselves, and are ashamed of that divine idea which each of us represents. It may be safely trusted as proportionate and of good issues, so it be faithfully imparted, but God will not have his work made manifest by cowards. A man is relieved and gay when he has put his heart into his work and done his best; but what he has said or done otherwise, shall give him no peace. It is a deliverance which does not deliver. In the attempt his genius deserts him; no muse befriends; no invention, no hope.

Trust thyself: every heart vibrates to that iron string. Accept the place the divine providence has found for you, the society of your contemporaries, the connection of events. Great men have always done so, and confided themselves childlike to the genius of their age, betraying their perception that the absolutely trustworthy was seated at their heart, working through their hands, predominating in all their being. And we are now men, and must accept in the highest mind the same transcendent② destiny; and not minors and invalids in a protected corner, not cowards fleeing before a revolution, but guides, redeemers, and benefactors, obeying the Almighty effort, and advancing on Chaos and the Dark.

What pretty oracles nature yields us on this text, in the face and behaviour of children, babes, and even brutes! That divided and rebel mind, that distrust of a sentiment because our arithmetic has computed the strength and means opposed to our purpose, these have not. Their mind being whole, their eye is as yet unconquered, and when we look in their faces, we are disconcerted. Infancy conforms to nobody: all conform to it, so that one babe commonly makes four or five out of the adults③ who prattle and play to it. So God has armed youth and puberty and manhood no less with its own piquancy and charm, and made it enviable and gracious and its claims not to be put by, if it will stand by itself. Do not think the youth has no force, because he cannot speak to you and me. Hark! in the next room his voice is sufficiently clear and emphatic. It seems he knows how to speak to his contemporaries. Bashful or bold, then, he will know how to make us seniors very unnecessary.

The nonchalance of boys who are sure of a dinner, and would disdain as much as a lord to do or say aught to conciliate one, is the healthy attitude of human nature. A boy is in the parlour what the pit④

---

① preestablished harmony:前定的和谐。这一概念来源于德国哲学家莱布尼兹(Gottfried Wilhelm Leibniz, 1646—1716)的单子论(Monadology)。根据单子论,每一个单子(monad)是具有精神活动(从简单知觉到理性灵魂)的不可分割的统一体,它完全依照自身内在本性而行动和发展,与任何其他单子毫无关联,也不受影响。但经验世界并不因此而产生混乱,因为上帝在创造单子时就已经确保了各个单子互不相关的发展既可以互不相通,又能相互和谐。
② transcendent:这里指内心直觉领悟。这一术语来源于康德哲学,意为"超验",指经验范围之外、不能成为知识的领域,与此相关的"先验"(transcendental)一词指知识形成的必要条件。尽管爱默生使用了康德的哲学术语,并将超验主义的名称归因于康德的"先验"一词,但我们不能对他使用的术语严格按照康德的原意理解。
③ one babe commonly makes four or five out of adults... :一个婴孩通常使一些成年人变成了4个或5个婴孩……
④ 早期剧院中廉价座位区,这里的观众较为喧闹,也较少约束。

is in the playhouse; independent, irresponsible, looking out from his corner on such people and facts as pass by, he tries and sentences them on their merits, in the swift, summary way of boys, as good, bad, interesting, silly, eloquent, troublesome. He cumbers himself never about consequences, about interests: he gives an independent, genuine verdict. You must court him: he does not court you. But the man is, as it were, clapped into jail by his consciousness. As soon as he has once acted or spoken with éclat①, he is a committed person, watched by the sympathy or the hatred of hundreds, whose affections must now enter into his account. There is no Lethe for this. Ah, that he could pass again into his neutrality! Who can thus avoid all pledges, and having observed, observe again from the same unaffected, unbiased, unbribable, unaffrighted innocence, must always be formidable. He would utter opinions on all passing affairs, which being seen to be not private, but necessary, would sink like darts into the ear of men, and put them in fear.

  These are the voices which we hear in solitude, but they grow faint and inaudible as we enter into the world. Society everywhere is in conspiracy against the manhood of every one of its members. Society is a joint-stock company, in which the members agree, for the better securing of his bread to each shareholder, to surrender the liberty and culture of the eater. The virtue in most request② is conformity. Self-reliance is its aversion. It loves not realities and creators, but names and customs.

  Whoso would be a man must be a nonconformist. He who would gather immortal palms③ must not be hindered by the name of goodness, but must explore if it be goodness. Nothing is at last sacred but the integrity of your own mind. Absolve you to yourself, and you shall have the suffrage④ of the world. I remember an answer which when quite young I was prompted to make to a valued adviser, who was wont to importune me with the dear old doctrines of the church. On my saying, What have I to do with the sacredness of traditions, if I live wholly from within? my friend suggested, —"But these impulses may be from below, not from above."⑤ I replied, "They do not seem to me to be such; but if I am the Devil's child, I will live then from the Devil." No law can be sacred to me but that of my nature. Good and bad are but names very readily transferable to that or this; the only right is what is after my constitution, the only wrong what is against it. A man is to carry himself in the presence of all opposition, as if every thing were titular and ephemeral but he. I am ashamed to think how easily we capitulate to badges and names, to large societies and dead institutions. Every decent and well-spoken individual affects and sways me more than is right. I ought to go upright and vital, and speak the rude truth in all ways. If malice and vanity wear the coat of philanthropy, shall that pass? If an angry bigot assumes this bountiful cause of Abolition⑥, and comes to me with his last news from Barbadoes⑦, why should I not say to him, 'Go love thy infant; love thy wood-chopper: be good-natured and modest: have that grace; and never varnish your hard, uncharitable ambition with this incredible tenderness for black folk a thousand miles off. Thy love afar is spite at home.' Rough and graceless would be such greeting, but truth is handsomer than the affectation of love. Your goodness must have some edge to it, —else it is none. The doctrine of hatred must be preached as the counteraction of the doctrine of love when that pules and whines. I shun father and mother and wife and brother, when my genius calls me. I

---

① éclat：(法语)炫目的展现出来。
② The virtue in most request...：最需要的美德……
③ palms：棕榈叶，象征胜利和成功。
④ suffrage：指支持、赞同。
⑤ "But these impulses may be from below, not from above."：基督教传统将世界看成一个上帝创造的等级秩序系统，上帝位于顶端，人的灵魂从精神和感情上必须追求上帝，而不应该沉迷于下、导致邪恶的对象。
⑥ Abolition：美国历史上的废奴运动。
⑦ Barbadoes：巴巴多斯，位于西印度群岛最东部的独立岛国，人口大部分为非洲裔黑人。巴巴多斯于1627年成为英国殖民地，于1691年获得完全自治，英国通过立法于1834年在西印度群岛废除了奴隶制。

would write on the lintels of the door-post, *Whim*.① I hope it is somewhat② better than whim at last, but we cannot spend the day in explanation. Expect me not to show cause why I seek or why I exclude company. Then, again, do not tell me, as a good man did to-day, of my obligation to put all poor men in good situations. Are they *my* poor? I tell thee, thou foolish philanthropist, that I grudge the dollar, the dime, the cent, I give to such men as do not belong to me and to whom I do not belong. There is a class of persons to whom by all spiritual affinity I am bought and sold; for them I will go to prison, if need be; but your miscellaneous popular charities; the education at college of fools; the building of meeting-houses to the vain end to which many now stand; alms to sots; and the thousandfold Relief Societies; —though I confess with shame I sometimes succumb and give the dollar, it is a wicked dollar which by and by I shall have the manhood to withhold.

Virtues are, in the popular estimate, rather the exception than the rule. There is the man and his virtues. Men do what is called a good action, as some piece of courage or charity, much as they would pay a fine in expiation of daily non-appearance on parade. Their works③ are done as an apology or extenuation of their living in the world, —as invalids and the insane pay a high board. Their virtues are penances. I do not wish to expiate, but to live. My life is for itself and not for a spectacle. I much prefer that it should be of a lower strain, so it be genuine and equal, than that it should be glittering and unsteady. I wish it to be sound and sweet, and not to need diet and bleeding④. I ask primary evidence that you are a man, and refuse this appeal from the man to his actions. I know that for myself it makes no difference whether I do or forbear those actions which are reckoned excellent. I cannot consent to pay for a privilege where I have intrinsic right. Few and mean as my gifts may be, I actually am, and do not need for my own assurance or the assurance of my fellows any secondary testimony.

What I must do is all that concerns me, not what the people think. This rule, equally arduous in actual and in intellectual life, may serve for the whole distinction between greatness and meanness. It is the harder, because you will always find those who think they know what is your duty better than you know it. It is easy in the world to live after the world's opinion; it is easy in solitude to live after our own; but the great man is he who in the midst of the crowd keeps with perfect sweetness the independence of solitude.

The objection to conforming to usages that have become dead to you is, that it scatters your force. It loses your time and blurs the impression of your character. If you maintain a dead church, contribute to a dead Bible-society⑤, vote with a great party either for the government or against it, spread your table like base housekeepers, —under all these screens I have difficulty to detect the precise man you are. And, of course, so much force is withdrawn from your proper life. But do your work, and I shall know you. Do your work, and you shall reinforce yourself. A man must consider what a blindman's-buff is this game of conformity. If I know your sect, I anticipate your argument. I hear a preacher announce for his text and topic the expediency of one of the institutions of his church. Do I not know beforehand that not possibly can he say a new and spontaneous word? Do I not know that, with all this ostentation of examining the grounds of the institution, he will do no such thing? Do I not know that he is pledged to himself not to look but at one side, —the permitted side, not as a man, but as a parish minister? He is

---

① lintels：源于圣经《旧约—申命记》(Deuteronomy 6: 6-9)，摩西嘱咐以色列人将耶和华的诫命记在心上，写在门楣和城门上。I would write on the lintels of the door-post, *Whim*.：这个比喻的背景来源是圣经《旧约—出埃及记》(Exodus 12: 7-13)，上帝让摩西告诉所有犹太人将羊血涂在自己住房的门楣上作为标记，这样，当上帝巡行埃及，杀掉其他所有生灵的第一胎后代、惩罚埃及诸神时，不会伤及他们。爱默生在此用相似方法对人做出区分标记。
② somewhat: something，爱默生通常使用"somewhat"表示"something"。
③ works：善行，善举。
④ bleeding：放血疗法。
⑤ Bible-society：圣经会。

a retained attorney, and these airs of the bench① are the emptiest affectation. Well, most men have bound their eyes with one or another handkerchief, and attached themselves to some one of these communities of opinion. This conformity makes them not false in a few particulars, authors of a few lies, but false in all particulars. Their every truth is not quite true. Their two is not the real two, their four not the real four; so that every word they say chagrins us, and we know not where to begin to set them right. Meantime nature is not slow to equip us in the prison-uniform of the party to which we adhere. We come to wear one cut of face and figure, and acquire by degrees the gentlest asinine expression. There is a mortifying experience in particular, which does not fail to wreak itself also in the general history; I mean "the foolish face of praise,"② the forced smile which we put on in company where we do not feel at ease in answer to conversation which does not interest us. The muscles, not spontaneously moved, but moved by a low usurping wilfulness, grow tight about the outline of the face with the most disagreeable sensation.

For nonconformity the world whips you with its displeasure. And therefore a man must know how to estimate a sour face. The by-standers look askance on him in the public street or in the friend's parlour. If this aversation had its origin in contempt and resistance like his own, he might well go home with a sad countenance; but the sour faces of the multitude, like their sweet faces, have no deep cause, but are put on and off as the wind blows and a newspaper directs. Yet is the discontent of the multitude more formidable than that of the senate and the college. It is easy enough for a firm man who knows the world to brook the rage of the cultivated classes. Their rage is decorous and prudent, for they are timid as being very vulnerable themselves. But when to their feminine rage the indignation of the people is added, when the ignorant and the poor are aroused, when the unintelligent brute force that lies at the bottom of society is made to growl and mow③, it needs the habit of magnanimity and religion to treat it godlike as a trifle of no concernment.

The other terror that scares us from self-trust is our consistency; a reverence for our past act or word, because the eyes of others have no other data for computing our orbit than our past acts, and we are loath to disappoint them.

But why should you keep your head over your shoulder? Why drag about this corpse of your memory, lest you contradict somewhat you have stated in this or that public place? Suppose you should contradict yourself; what then? It seems to be a rule of wisdom never to rely on your memory alone, scarcely even in acts of pure memory, but to bring the past for judgment into the thousand-eyed present, and live ever in a new day. In your metaphysics you have denied personality to the Deity: yet when the devout motions of the soul come, yield to them heart and life, though they should clothe God with shape and color. Leave your theory, as Joseph his coat in the hand of the harlot, and flee.④

A foolish consistency is the hobgoblin of little minds, adored by little statesmen and philosophers and divines. With consistency a great soul has simply nothing to do. He may as well concern himself with his shadow on the wall⑤. Speak what you think now in hard words, and to-morrow speak what to-morrow thinks in hard words again, though it contradict every thing you said to-day. —'Ah, so you shall be sure to be misunderstood.' —Is it so bad, then, to be misunderstood? Pythagoras was

---

① the bench: 指法官的座位,引申指法官。
② "the foolish face of praise,": 引自英国诗人亚历山大·蒲柏(Alexander Pope, 1688—1744)的著名自传式讽刺诗《致阿巴斯诺特医生书》("Epistle to Dr. Arbuthnot", Line 212)(1735)。
③ mow: grimace.
④ as Joseph his coat in the hand of the harlot, and flee.: 就像约瑟那样摆脱荡妇纠缠,只把他的外衣留在她手中,自己逃开。比喻出自圣经《旧约—创世纪》(Genesis 39:12)。
⑤ shadow on the wall: 比喻可能源于柏拉图《理想国》中的洞穴说:世人就像身处洞穴的囚徒,由于从未走出洞穴,自然误将洞壁上看到的影像当真,喻指世人被虚假现象蒙蔽了双眼,无法看到事物的真实面目。

misunderstood, and Socrates, and Jesus, and Luther, and Copernicus, and Galileo, and Newton, and every pure and wise spirit that ever took flesh. To be great is to be misunderstood.

  I suppose no man can violate his nature. All the sallies of his will are rounded in by the law of his being, as the inequalities of Andes and Himmaleh① are insignificant in the curve of the sphere. Nor does it matter how you gauge and try him. A character is like an acrostic or Alexandrian stanza②; — read it forward, backward, or across, it still spells the same thing. In this pleasing, contrite wood-life③ which God allows me, let me record day by day my honest thought without prospect or retrospect, and, I cannot doubt, it will be found symmetrical, though I mean it not, and see it not. My book should smell of pines and resound with the hum of insects. The swallow over my window should interweave that thread or straw he carries in his bill into my web also. We pass for what we are. Character teaches above our wills. Men imagine that they communicate their virtue or vice only by overt actions, and do not see that virtue or vice emit a breath every moment.

  There will be an agreement in whatever variety of actions, so they be each honest and natural in their hour. For of one will, the actions will be harmonious, however unlike they seem. These varieties are lost sight of at a little distance, at a little height of thought. One tendency unites them all. The voyage of the best ship is a zigzag line of a hundred tacks. See the line from a sufficient distance, and it straightens itself to the average tendency. Your genuine action will explain itself, and will explain your other genuine actions. Your conformity explains nothing. Act singly, and what you have already done singly will justify you now. Greatness appeals to the future. If I can be firm enough to-day to do right, and scorn eyes, I must have done so much right before as to defend me now. Be it how it will, do right now. Always scorn appearances, and you always may. The force of character is cumulative. All the foregone days of virtue work their health into this. What makes the majesty of the heroes of the senate and the field④, which so fills the imagination? The consciousness of a train of great days and victories behind. They shed an united light on the advancing actor. He is attended as by a visible escort of angels. That is it which throws thunder into Chatham's⑤ voice, and dignity into Washington's port⑥, and America into Adams's⑦ eye. Honor is venerable to us because it is no ephemeris. It is always ancient virtue. We worship it to-day because it is not of to-day. We love it and pay it homage, because it is not a trap for our love and homage, but is self-dependent, self-derived, and therefore of an old immaculate pedigree, even if shown in a young person.

  I hope in these days we have heard the last of conformity and consistency. Let the words be gazetted⑧ and ridiculous henceforward. Instead of the gong for dinner, let us hear a whistle from the Spartan fife. Let us never bow and apologize more. A great man is coming to eat at my house. I do not wish to please him; I wish that he should wish to please me. I will stand here for humanity, and though I would make it kind, I would make it true. Let us affront and reprimand the smooth mediocrity and squalid contentment of the times, and hurl in the face of custom, and trade, and office⑨, the fact which

---

① Himmaleh: the Himalayas.
② Alexandrian stanza: 回文, 顺读, 倒读都一样。
③ wood-life: 林中生活。
④ the field: 这里指战场。
⑤ Chatham: 查塔姆伯爵(Earl of Chatham), 即老威廉·皮特(William Pitt the Elder, 1708—1778), 18世纪英国伟大政治家, 他主张英国与美洲殖民地和解。
⑥ port: 举止, 气质。
⑦ Adams: 可能指萨缪尔·亚当斯(Samuel Adams, 1722—1803), 美国独立战争革命家, 政治家, 或指约翰·亚当斯(John Adams, 1735—1826), 曾与本杰明·富兰克林等人协助托马斯·杰弗逊起草《独立宣言》, 并参加起草了《美国宪法》, 是美国"建国之父"之一, 他曾当选第一任美国副总统, 后当选第二任美国总统, 或指约翰·昆西·亚当斯(John Quincy Adams, 1767—1848), 第六任美国总统。
⑧ gazette: 抛弃。
⑨ office: 职责。

is the upshot of all history, that there is a great responsible Thinker and Actor working wherever a man works; that a true man belongs to no other time or place, but is the centre of things. Where he is, there is nature. He measures you, and all men, and all events. Ordinarily, every body in society reminds us of somewhat else, or of some other person. Character, reality, reminds you of nothing else; it takes place of the whole creation. The man must be so much, that he must make all circumstances indifferent. Every true man is a cause, a country, and an age; requires infinite spaces and numbers and time fully to accomplish his design; —and posterity seem to follow his steps as a train of clients. A man Caesar is born, and for ages after we have a Roman Empire. Christ is born, and millions of minds so grow and cleave to his genius, that he is confounded with virtue and the possible of man. An institution is the lengthened shadow of one man; as, Monachism①, of the Hermit Antony②; the Reformation, of Luther③; Quakerism, of Fox④; Methodism, of Wesley⑤; Abolition, of Clarkson⑥. Scipio⑦, Milton called "the height of Rome"; and all history resolves itself very easily into the biography of a few stout and earnest persons.

Let a man then know his worth, and keep things under his feet. Let him not peep or steal, or skulk up and down with the air of a charity-boy, a bastard, or an interloper, in the world which exists for him. But the man in the street, finding no worth in himself which corresponds to the force which built a tower or sculptured a marble god, feels poor when he looks on these. To him a palace, a statue, or a costly book have an alien and forbidding air, much like a gay equipage, and seem to say like that, 'Who are you, Sir?' Yet they all are his, suitors for his notice, petitioners to his faculties that they will come out and take possession. The picture waits for my verdict: it is not to command me, but I am to settle its claims to praise. That popular fable of the sot who was picked up dead drunk in the street, carried to the duke's house, washed and dressed and laid in the duke's bed, and, on his waking, treated with all obsequious ceremony like the duke, and assured that he had been insane,⑧ owes its popularity to the fact, that it symbolizes so well the state of man, who is in the world a sort of sot, but now and then wakes up, exercises his reason, and finds himself a true prince.

Our reading is mendicant and sycophantic. In history, our imagination plays us false. Kingdom and lordship, power and estate, are a gaudier vocabulary than private John and Edward in a small house and common day's work; but the things of life are the same to both; the sum total of both is the same. Why all this deference to Alfred⑨, and Scanderbeg⑩, and Gustavus⑪? Suppose they were virtuous; did they wear out virtue? As great a stake depends on your private act to-day, as followed their public and renowned steps. When private men shall act with original views, the lustre will be transferred from the actions of kings to those of gentlemen.

The world has been instructed by its kings, who have so magnetized the eyes of nations. It has been taught by this colossal symbol the mutual reverence that is due from man to man. The joyful loyalty with which men have everywhere suffered the king, the noble, or the great proprietor to walk

---

① Monachim:修行,寺院制度。
② the Hermit Anthony:(埃及的)圣安东尼(Saint Anthony of Egypt, c. 251—356),基督教早期修士,曾隐居山中,禁欲修行,据传创立隐修制度。
③ Luther:马丁·路德(Martin Luther, 1483—1546),宗教改革的德国倡导者。
④ Fox:乔治·福克斯(George Fox, 1624—1691),基督教公谊会(Quakerism)(又称贵格派或教友派)创始人。
⑤ Wesley:约翰·卫斯理(John Wesley, 1703—1791),基督教卫理工会(Methodism)的创始人。
⑥ Clarkson:托马斯·克拉克森(Thomas Clarkson, 1760—1846),英国废奴主义者。
⑦ Scipio:大西庇阿(Scipio Africanus, 237—183 B.C.),罗马执政官,罗马将领,在扎马一战打败迦太基统帅汉尼拔,最终罗马赢得了第二次布诺战争。弥尔顿在《失乐园》中对他赞赏有加(*Paradise Lost*, Book IX, Line 510)。
⑧ 莎士比亚在《驯悍记》中使用这个寓言(*The Taming of the Shrew*, Introduction, Scene i, Lines 34-68)。
⑨ Alfred:阿尔弗烈德大王(Alfred the Great, 849—899),英国韦塞克斯王朝国王。
⑩ Scanderbeg:乔治·卡斯特里塔·斯坎德培(George Castriota Scanderbeg, 1404—1468),阿尔巴尼亚民族英雄。
⑪ Gustavus:古斯塔夫二世(Gustavus II Adolphus, 1594—1632),瑞典国王。

among them by a law of his own, make his own scale of men and things, and reverse theirs, pay for benefits not with money but with honor, and represent the law in his person, was the hieroglyphic by which they obscurely signified their consciousness of their own right and comeliness, the right of every man.

  The magnetism which all original action exerts is explained when we inquire the reason of self-trust. Who is the Trustee? What is the aboriginal Self, on which a universal reliance may be grounded? What is the nature and power of that science-baffling star, without parallax, without calculable elements, which shoots a ray of beauty even into trivial and impure actions, if the least mark of independence appear? The inquiry leads us to that source, at once the essence of genius, of virtue, and of life, which we call Spontaneity or Instinct. We denote this primary wisdom as Intuition, whilst all later teachings are tuitions. In that deep force, the last fact behind which analysis cannot go, all things find their common origin. For, the sense of being which in calm hours rises, we know not how, in the soul, is not diverse from things, from space, from light, from time, from man, but one with them, and proceeds obviously from the same source whence their life and being also proceed. We first share the life by which things exist, and afterwards see them as appearances in nature, and forget that we have shared their cause. Here is the fountain of action and of thought. Here are the lungs of that inspiration which giveth man wisdom, and which cannot be denied without impiety and atheism. We lie in the lap of immense intelligence, which makes us receivers of its truth and organs of its activity. When we discern justice, when we discern truth, we do nothing of ourselves, but allow a passage to its beams. If we ask whence this comes, if we seek to pry into the soul that causes, all philosophy is at fault. Its presence or its absence is all we can affirm. Every man discriminates between the voluntary acts of his mind, and his involuntary perceptions, and knows that to his involuntary perceptions a perfect faith is due. He may err in the expression of them, but he knows that these things are so, like day and night, not to be disputed. My wilful actions and acquisitions are but roving; —the idlest reverie, the faintest native emotion, command my curiosity and respect. Thoughtless people contradict as readily the statement of perceptions as of opinions, or rather much more readily; for, they do not distinguish between perception and notion. They fancy that I choose to see this or that thing. But perception is not whimsical, but fatal. If I see a trait, my children will see it after me, and in course of time, all mankind, —although it may chance that no one has seen it before me. For my perception of it is as much a fact as the sun.

  The relations of the soul to the divine spirit are so pure, that it is profane to seek to interpose helps. It must be that when God speaketh he should communicate, not one thing, but all things; should fill the world with his voice; should scatter forth light, nature, time, souls, from the centre of the present thought; and new date and new create the whole. Whenever a mind is simple, and receives a divine wisdom, old things pass away, —means, teachers, texts, temples fall; it lives now, and absorbs past and future into the present hour. All things are made sacred by relation to it, —one as much as another. All things are dissolved to their centre by their cause, and, in the universal miracle, petty and particular miracles disappear. If, therefore, a man claims to know and speak of God, and carries you backward to the phraseology of some old mouldered nation in another country, in another world, believe him not. Is the acorn better than the oak which is its fulness and completion? Is the parent better than the child into whom he has cast his ripened being? Whence, then, this worship of the past? The centuries are conspirators against the sanity and authority of the soul. Time and space are but physiological colors which the eye makes, but the soul is light; where it is, is day; where it was, is night; and history is an impertinence and an injury, if it be any thing more than a cheerful apologue or parable of my being and becoming.

  Man is timid and apologetic; he is no longer upright; he dares not say 'I think,' 'I am,' but quotes some saint or sage. He is ashamed before the blade of grass or the blowing rose. These roses under my window make no reference to former roses or to better ones; they are for what they are; they exist with God to-day. There is no time to them. There is simply the rose; it is perfect in every moment of its existence. Before a leaf-bud has burst, its whole life acts; in the full-blown flower there is no more; in the leafless root there is no less. Its nature is satisfied, and it satisfies nature, in all moments alike. But man postpones or remembers; he does not live in the present, but with reverted eye laments the past, or, heedless of the riches that surround him, stands on tiptoe to foresee the future. He cannot be happy and strong until he too lives with nature in the present, above time.

  This should be plain enough. Yet see what strong intellects dare not yet hear God himself, unless he speak the phraseology of I know not what David①, or Jeremiah②, or Paul③. We shall not always set so great a price on a few texts, on a few lives. We are like children who repeat by rote the sentences of grandames and tutors, and, as they grow older, of the men of talents and character they chance to see, — painfully recollecting the exact words they spoke; afterwards, when they come into the point of view which those had who uttered these sayings, they understand them, and are willing to let the words go; for, at any time, they can use words as good when occasion comes. If we live truly, we shall see truly. It is as easy for the strong man to be strong, as it is for the weak to be weak. When we have new perception, we shall gladly disburden the memory of its hoarded treasures as old rubbish. When a man lives with God, his voice shall be as sweet as the murmur of the brook and the rustle of the corn.

  And now at last the highest truth on this subject remains unsaid; probably cannot be said; for all that we say is the far-off remembering of the intuition. That thought, by what I can now nearest approach to say it, is this. When good is near you, when you have life in yourself, it is not by any known or accustomed way; you shall not discern the foot-prints of any other; you shall not see the face of man; you shall not hear any name;—the way, the thought, the good, shall be wholly strange and new. It shall exclude example and experience. You take the way from man, not to man. All persons that ever existed are its forgotten ministers. Fear and hope are alike beneath it. There is somewhat low even in hope. In the hour of vision, there is nothing that can be called gratitude, nor properly joy. The soul raised over passion beholds identity and eternal causation, perceives the self-existence of Truth and Right, and calms itself with knowing that all things go well. Vast spaces of nature, the Atlantic Ocean, the South Sea, —long intervals of time, years, centuries, —are of no account. This which I think and feel underlay every former state of life and circumstances, as it does underlie my present, and what is called life, and what is called death.

  Life only avails, not the having lived. Power ceases in the instant of repose; it resides in the moment of transition from a past to a new state, in the shooting④ of the gulf, in the darting to an aim. This one fact the world hates, that the soul *becomes*; for that for ever degrades the past, turns all riches to poverty, all reputation to a shame, confounds the saint with the rogue, shoves Jesus and Judas⑤ equally aside. Why, then, do we prate of self-reliance? Inasmuch as the soul is present, there will be power not confident but agent. To talk of reliance is a poor external way of speaking. Speak rather of that which relies, because it works and is. Who has more obedience than I masters me, though he should not raise his finger.⑥ Round him I must revolve by the gravitation of spirits. We fancy it rhetoric, when we speak of eminent virtue. We do not yet see that virtue is Height, and that a man or a company

---

① David: 大卫（公元前11世纪—公元前962），古以色列第二代国王。
② Jeremiah: 耶利米，公元前7世纪晚期到公元前6世纪早期犹太国的重要先知。
③ Paul: 保罗（Saint Paul the Apostle，公元1世纪），基督教传教士，基督教神学家。
④ shooting: 奔流。
⑤ Judas: 犹大（加略人）（Judas Iscariot），基督的12门徒之一，后出卖基督。
⑥ he should not raise his finger: 他不费举手之劳。

of men, plastic and permeable to principles, by the law of nature must overpower and ride all cities, nations, kings, rich men, poets, who are not.

This is the ultimate fact which we so quickly reach on this, as on every topic, the resolution of all into the ever-blessed ONE. Self-existence is the attribute of the Supreme Cause, and it constitutes the measure of good by the degree in which it enters into all lower forms. All things real are so by so much virtue as they contain. Commerce, husbandry, hunting, whaling, war, eloquence, personal weight, are somewhat, and engage my respect as examples of its presence and impure action. I see the same law working in nature for conservation and growth. Power is in nature the essential measure of right. Nature suffers nothing to remain in her kingdoms which cannot help itself. The genesis and maturation of a planet, its poise and orbit, the bended tree recovering itself from the strong wind, the vital resources of every animal and vegetable, are demonstrations of the self-sufficing, and therefore self-relying soul....

　　散文《论自助》("Self-Reliance")选自《论文集:第一辑》,发表于1841年。该篇散文概述了爱默生此前8年演讲和日记所表达的"自助"思想。当然,这一思想与他的超验主义观念密不可分。爱默生的超验主义思想基于柯勒律治对所谓"理性"(the Reason)(特指直觉)和"知性"(the Understanding)所做的区分。"理性"不依赖经验知识,通过直觉领悟普遍真理,而"知性"则指经验观察和归纳性概括。个人的"理性"能力则是个人自助的前提。个人必须遵从"理性"的直觉领悟,摆脱社会传统习俗和观念的羁绊,相信自我,从而达到超越经验世界的道德和理性自由境界。出于他的宗教情怀,与上帝同一的神秘直觉与源于柯勒律治的"理性"相结合,形成了他的"内在上帝"(God within)观念,即真理和力量的源泉来自于存在于个人内心中的上帝,或者说"我中之我"(me of me),从而"个人不再被看成一个部分,而被看成一个整体,他就是世界"。这意味着个人一方面自主主宰思想和行动乃至外部环境,具有自身独立性,但另一方面,个人心灵神性又与统摄宇宙和人类的上帝神性融为一体,而武断、随机、个别性则与神性本质格格不入,从而心灵或内在上帝同样具有普遍性。爱默生的所谓"理性"或道德本性并非心灵所创造,而是被心灵领悟、察觉或辨识,因而众人心灵又被整体心灵(the One Mind)、"超灵"(Over-Soul)或上帝所统一。不难看出,爱默生的"自助"思想涵盖了个体自我、超越个别的同一(the One)或上帝、自主与服从(服从"理性"、道德本性、普遍法则和上帝)等多重关联。布鲁姆(Harold Bloom)称爱默生的"自助"为"上帝之助"(God-reliance)。纽菲尔德(Christopher Newfield)则认为,爱默生的个人主义隐含对权威的屈从,其效果是,美国资本主义现实中形成了所谓"团体个人主义"(corporate individualism)。当然,爱默生的"自助"论点有其宗教色彩和内在矛盾,但他肯定和颂扬个人自然本性,与传统加尔文教义压抑人性本能形成了鲜明反差。他主张完全释放并发挥个人天赋,抛弃社会、传统、习俗、教会等外在权威和相应制度及其强加于个人的虚假观念和准则,但这并非利己主义或自我中心主义(egoism),不是无所约束的随心所欲或肆无忌惮,而是"私人的无限性"(the infinitude of the private man),"每一个人都是崭新的、无法计量的力量",个人没有固定不变的本质,只有不断塑造自我的无限空间,通过内在"理性"或直觉领悟普遍法则,突破时空的局限,自主判断寻求真理,达到思想和行为的"自助"。爱默生正是以这样的"自助"精神,主张个人与社会的对立,绝不盲从,做自己的事,自立自强,同时包容对立观念,避免偏执于一端。不难看出,爱默生的个人主义基石是所谓独立于他人的原子化个人,而19世纪中期美国出现了形形色色改革运动和团体性改革社群,对此,爱默生则抱持怀疑态度,他坚持以个人为基础自我完善。对于个人主义,19世纪欧洲不乏反对之声。梅斯特尔(Joseph de Maistre)认为新的个人主义行为模式将个人置于社会公益之上,会导致社会共同体逐渐瓦解,托克维尔(Alexis de Tocqueville)在评论美国民主时,也提到个人主义的根源在于"理智的缺失和道德情怀的堕落",最终会沦为"彻头彻尾的自私自利"。与之针锋相对,《论自助》则旗帜鲜明的弘扬个人主义及其道德价值。如果说《美国学者》是美国思想的独立宣言,《论自助》也可以说是爱默生毕生追求"私人无限性"的个人主义宣言。

　　爱默生的文笔清新活泼,语气如同朋友之间的攀谈,文中"你""我""我们"等口语化称谓更使读者不觉之中参与对话思索。爱默生的文字挥洒自如,奇言妙语随处可见,哲思遐想更是举重若轻。作为著名演说家,其精妙的修辞手法可略见一斑。行文中,比喻、典故、随想、先贤哲人的名言洞见信手拈来,尽管论点和思路略显庞杂松散,但广博的视野、丰富的想象力,使其思想表达独具魅力。也许正如爱默生在《诗人》一文中所说,一本富于想象的书,首先要通过运用比喻激发我们,我们由此获益要胜于作者的精确用意。而书籍的唯一价值就在于其超验脱俗。由此唤起我们的领悟。爱默生眼中的"诗人"就是如此自由,也使他人自由,这让我们从陈词老调中摆脱出来。"这也就是最成功的会话,是自由的魔法,能够将世界变得像一个球,置于我们的掌心。"

思考题

1. Why does the author call consistency "foolish"? And why does he celebrate "Whim"?
2. Why is a character like an acrostic or Alexandrian stanza?
3. Why should a man keep things under his feet?
4. When the author says, "You take the way from man, not to man," what does he means?
5. Can "the popular code" be dispensed with? Why or why not?
6. When the author says, "To talk of reliance is a poor external way of speaking. Speak rather of that which relies, because it works and is," what does he mean?

推荐作品

"Nature"(1836)
"The American Scholar"(1837)
"The Poet"(1844)
Representative Men(1850)

参考资料

Emerson, Ralph Waldo. *Essays & Lectures,* Ed. Joe Porte. New York: Literary Classics of the United States, Inc., 1983.

Kateb, George. *Emerson and Self-Reliance*. Thousand Oaks, California: Sage Publications, Inc., 1995.

Richardson, Robert D. *The Mind on* Fire. Berkeley: University of California Press, 1995.

Whicher, Stephen E. *Freedom and Fate: An Inner Life of Ralph Waldo Emerson*. 2nd ed. Philadelphia: University of Pennsylvania Press, 1971.

(张世耘)

Henry David Thoreau (1817—1862)

亨利·大卫·梭罗

 作者简介

  亨利·大卫·梭罗,散文家,诗人,哲学家,超验主义运动主要成员,出生于马萨诸塞州康科德镇。1833年至1837年间,梭罗就读于哈佛大学,毕业后做过教师,后在爱默生家中住过一段时间。1840年,梭罗在超验主义杂志《日晷》(Dial)上发表诗歌和文章。1845年,他在沃尔登湖畔结庐独居,实践他的超验主义理念,通过探索大自然点滴细节中蕴含的深刻意义,感悟道德真谛。梭罗将这段经历写成其代表作《沃尔登湖》(Walden or, Life in the Woods),后于1854年发表。1849年,梭罗发表了著名的《论公民的不服从》(On the Duty of Civil Disobedience)一文,提出公民个人有责任不服从非正义的法律,阻碍政府机器的运转。杰弗逊曾有名言:"最少治权的政府是最好的政府。"梭罗文中更进一步,期望好的政府不治而治。在美国,宪法严格限制政府权力,禁止国会立法侵犯公民宪法权利,立法也必须经民主多数同意,但是梭罗认为,法律必须建立在良知之上,仅仅依靠政治制度程序并不足以阻止立法者滥权,制定非正义的法令。而面对法律的强制,公民个人行为应遵从内心良知,即便因此触犯法律而受到惩罚。梭罗此前因为拒交人头税而被拘禁,但第二天,有人代他补交税款使他获释,对此,他十分愤怒,他本希望通过坐牢引起社会关注,以此抗议不公正的奴隶制和政府行为。如果说梭罗如此行为是反体制的政治叛逆,他在沃尔登湖畔融入大自然的实验则是反世俗传统、反商业化的文化叛逆。当然,这样的个人叛逆或个人主义"革命"并没有持续下去,但何尝不是引发人们更多思考的大胆尝试呢。至少在政治层面,非暴力抵抗的传承者甘地、马丁·路德·金等成功引领了制度变革。尽管梭罗并没有像爱默生那样,系统阐释超验主义和个人自由,但他以自己的方式实践超验个人主义:个人可以由内及外,超越物质追求,独立于流俗和传统体制,回归心灵、大自然和上帝的神性同一。

  梭罗的其他主要作品包括:《康科德河和梅里马克河一周记》(A Week on the Concord and Merrimack Rivers, 1849),《漫步》(Walking, 1862),《郊游》(Excursions, 1863),《缺少原则的生活》(Life Without Principle, 1863),《缅因森林》(The Main Woods, 1864),《科德角》(Cape Cod, 1865),《在加拿大的新英格兰人》(A Yankee in Canada, 1866)。

Walden
*Economy*①
(*Excerpts*)

  Near the end of March, 1845, I borrowed an axe and went down to the woods by Walden Pond, nearest to where I intended to build my house, and began to cut down some tall, arrowy white pines, still in their youth, for timber. It is difficult to begin without borrowing, but perhaps it is the most generous course thus to permit your fellow-men to have an interest in your enterprise. The owner of the axe②, as he released his hold on it, said that it was the apple of his eye; but I returned it sharper than I received it. It was a pleasant hillside where I worked, covered with pine woods, through which I looked

---

① 该篇为《沃尔登湖》的第一章,也是最长的一章。该章在梭罗最早的手稿中曾使用和其他各章不同的页码,可能作者原打算以此作为全书的开场白。
② The owner of the axe:一种说法认为,这把斧子是梭罗从阿尔科特(Bronson Alcott)那里借来的,但也有人认为是爱默生借给他的,而钱宁(William Ellery Channing)说,是他借给梭罗这把斧子。阿尔科特是超验俱乐部的成员;钱宁是梭罗的朋友,超验主义诗人。

out on the pond, and a small open field in the woods where pines and hickories were springing up. The ice in the pond was not yet dissolved, though there were some open spaces, and it was all dark-colored and saturated with water. There were some slight flurries of snow during the days that I worked there; but for the most part when I came out on to the railroad, on my way home①, its yellow sand heap stretched away gleaming in the hazy atmosphere, and the rails shone in the spring sun, and I heard the lark and pewee and other birds already come to commence another year with us. They were pleasant spring days, in which the winter of man's discontent② was thawing as well as the earth, and the life that had lain torpid began to stretch itself. One day, when my axe had come off and I had cut a green hickory for a wedge, driving it with a stone, and had placed the whole to soak in a pond-hole in order to swell the wood, I saw a striped snake run into the water, and he lay on the bottom, apparently without inconvenience, as long as I stayed there, or more than a quarter of an hour; perhaps because he had not yet fairly come out of the torpid state. It appeared to me that for a like reason men remain in their present low and primitive condition; but if they should feel the influence of the spring of springs arousing them, they would of necessity rise to a higher and more ethereal life. I had previously seen the snakes in frosty mornings in my path with portions of their bodies still numb and inflexible, waiting for the sun to thaw them. On the 1st of April it rained and melted the ice, and in the early part of the day, which was very foggy, I heard a stray goose groping about over the pond and cackling as if lost, or like the spirit of the fog.

So I went on for some days cutting and hewing timber, and also studs and rafters, all with my narrow axe, not having many communicable or scholar-like thoughts, singing to myself, —

Men say they know many things;
But lo! they have taken wings —
The arts and sciences,
And a thousand appliances;
The wind that blows
Is all that any body knows.③...

It would be worth the while to build still more deliberately than I did, considering, for instance, what foundation a door, a window, a cellar, a garret, have in the nature of man, and perchance never raising any superstructure until we found a better reason for it than our temporal necessities even. There is some of the same fitness in a man's building his own house that there is in a bird's building its own nest. Who knows but if men constructed their dwellings with their own hands, and provided food for themselves and families simply and honestly enough, the poetic faculty would be universally developed, as birds universally sing when they are so engaged? But alas! we do like cowbirds and cuckoos, which lay their eggs in nests which other birds have built, and cheer no traveller with their chattering and unmusical notes. Shall we forever resign the pleasure of construction to the carpenter? What does architecture amount to in the experience of the mass of men? I never in all my walks came across a man engaged in so simple and natural an occupation as building his house. We belong to the community. It is not the tailor alone who is the ninth part of a man;④ it is as much the preacher, and the merchant, and the farmer. Where is this division of labor to end? and what object does it finally serve? No doubt another may also think for me; but it is not therefore desirable that he should do so to the

---

① home: 指梭罗一家当时在火车站西面的居所,是一座两层建筑物。
② the winter of man's discontent: 源自莎士比亚戏剧《理查三世》: "Now is the winter of our discontent"。
③ 此诗乃梭罗自己创作。梭罗引用他人诗句时通常加引号,以示引用。
④ ninth part of a man: 在当时指裁缝。英语成语 "Nine tailors make but one man" 曾有不同释义,裁缝曾被认为懦弱、胆小怕事,因此在18、19世纪有一种说法是: "It took nine tailors to make a real man." 莎士比亚戏剧《亨利四世》中裁缝的名字就是 "Feeble"(懦弱),到19世纪初,这一成语的意义是:要找九个裁缝,才能做出一套上好服装。

exclusion of my thinking for myself.

True, there are architects so called in this country, and I have heard of one at least possessed with the idea of making architectural ornaments have a core of truth, a necessity, and hence a beauty, as if it were a revelation to him①. All very well perhaps from his point of view, but only a little better than the common dilettantism. A sentimental reformer in architecture, he began at the cornice, not at the foundation. It was only how to put a core of truth within the ornaments, that every sugarplum, in fact, might have an almond or caraway seed in it — though I hold that almonds are most wholesome without the sugar — and not how the inhabitant, the indweller, might build truly within and without, and let the ornaments take care of themselves. What reasonable man ever supposed that ornaments were something outward and in the skin merely — that the tortoise got his spotted shell, or the shell-fish its mother-o'-pearl② tints, by such a contract as the inhabitants of Broadway their Trinity Church③? But a man has no more to do with the style of architecture of his house than a tortoise with that of its shell: nor need the soldier be so idle as to try to paint the precise *color* of his virtue on his standard.④ The enemy will find it out. He may turn pale when the trial comes. This man seemed to me to lean over the cornice, and timidly whisper his half truth to the rude occupants who really knew it better than he. What of architectural beauty I now see, I know has gradually grown from within outward, out of the necessities and character of the indweller, who is the only builder-out of some unconscious truthfulness, and nobleness, without ever a thought for the appearance and whatever additional beauty of this kind is destined to be produced will be preceded by a like unconscious beauty of life. The most interesting dwellings in this country, as the painter knows, are the most unpretending, humble log huts and cottages of the poor commonly; it is the life of the inhabitants whose shells they are, and not any peculiarity in their surfaces merely, which makes them *picturesque*⑤; and equally interesting will be the citizen's suburban box⑥, when his life shall be as simple and as agreeable to the imagination, and there is as little straining after effect in the style of his dwelling. A great proportion of *architectural* ornaments are literally hollow, and a September gale⑦ would strip them off, like borrowed plumes,⑧ without injury to the substantials. They can do without architecture who have no olives nor wines in the cellar.⑨ What if an equal ado were made about the ornaments of style in literature, and the architects of our bibles spent as much time about their cornices as the architects of our churches do? So are made the *belles-lettres*⑩ and the *beaux-arts*⑪ and their professors. Much it concerns a man, forsooth, how a few sticks are slanted over him or under him, and what colors are daubed upon his box. It would signify somewhat, if, in any earnest sense, *he* slanted them and daubed it; but the spirit having departed out of the tenant, it is of a piece with constructing his own coffin — the architecture of the grave — and "carpenter" is but another name for "coffin-maker." One man says, in his despair or indifference to life,

---

① him:指美国雕塑家格林诺(Horatio Greenough,1805—1852),他强调,建筑的功能决定建筑的形式,主张所谓功能性建筑装饰。
② mother-o'-pearl:mother-of-pearl。
③ Trinity Church:著名教堂,位于纽约,梭罗在沃尔登湖独居期间,曾被大火烧毁,后于1846年重建。
④ paint the precise color of his virtue on his standard:梭罗这里似乎是指古时士兵在旗帜上着色,以此象征自身优越特质。
⑤ picturesque:指景观建筑设计领域中"如画景观流派",偏好模仿原始状态自然景观,其理念在19世纪初十分流行。
⑥ box:指居所,简陋如木箱。
⑦ September gale:在康科德地区,九月是一年中风力最强的季节。
⑧ like borrowed plumes:源于伊索寓言《松鸦和孔雀》。一只松鸦捡拾起孔雀掉落的羽毛,绑在自己的尾巴上,但很快被孔雀发现,将这些"借来的羽毛"啄掉,松鸦被打回原形。松鸦伙伴告诉它:鸟儿可爱并只是羽毛亮丽。
⑨ who have no olives nor wines in the cellar:指无力消费昂贵食物的家庭。
⑩ belles-lettres(法语):artistic literature.
⑪ beaux-arts(法语):the fine arts.

take up a handful of the earth at your feet, and paint your house that color.① Is he thinking of his last and narrow house②? Toss up a copper for it as well.③ What an abundance of leisure he must have! Why do you take up a handful of dirt? Better paint your house your own complexion; let it turn pale or blush for you. An enterprise to improve the style of cottage architecture! When you have got my ornaments ready, I will wear them.

Before winter I built a chimney, and shingled the sides of my house, which were already impervious to rain, with imperfect and sappy shingles made of the first slice of the log, whose edges I was obliged to straighten with a plane.

I have thus a tight shingled and plastered house, ten feet wide by fifteen long, and eight-feet posts, with a garret and a closet, a large window on each side, two trap doors, one door at the end, and a brick fireplace opposite. The exact cost of my house, paying the usual price for such materials as I used, but not counting the work, all of which was done by myself, was as follows; and I give the details because very few are able to tell exactly what their houses cost, and fewer still, if any, the separate cost of the various materials which compose them: —

Boards, ... $8.03½④, mostly shanty boards.
Refuse shingles for roof and sides, ... 4.00
Laths, ... 1.25
Two second-hand windows with glass, ... 2.43
One thousand old brick, ... 4.00
Two casks of lime, ... 2.40   That was high.
Hair⑤, ... 0.31   More than I needed.
Mantle-tree iron, ... 0.15
Nails, ... 3.90
Hinges and screws, ... 0.14
Latch, ... 0.10
Chalk, ... 0.01
Transportation, ... 1.40   I carried a good
                                              part on my back.
In all, ... $28.12½⑥

These are all the materials, excepting the timber, stones, and sand, which I claimed by squatter's right⑦. I have also a small woodshed adjoining, made chiefly of the stuff which was left after building the house.

I intend to build me a house which will surpass any on the main street in Concord in grandeur and luxury,⑧ as soon as it pleases me as much and will cost me no more than my present one.

---

① 英国诗人华兹华斯(William Wordsworth)在《湖区指南》(*Guide to the Lakes*, 1810)第三部分有一段谈到建筑着色：The principle that ought to determine the position, apparent size, and architecture of a house, viz. that it should be so constructed, and (if large) so much of it hidden, as to admit of its being gently incorporated into the scenery of nature — should also determine its colour. Sir Joshua Reynolds used to say, "if you would fix upon the best colour for your house, turn up a stone, or pluck up a handful of grass by the roots, and see what is the colour of the soil where the house is to stand, and let that be your choice."
② last and narrow house：指墓穴。
③ Toss up a copper for it as well：指抛掷一美分铜币，做出选择。另外，古希腊神话中，冥河(Styx)摆渡者卡隆(Charon)将亡灵送入冥界。传说须将钱币置于死者口中，酬谢其劳。
④ $8.03½：8美元3.5美分。半美分硬币当时仍光流通。
⑤ Hair：指马匹鬃毛，混入灰泥后可增加灰泥强度。
⑥ In all, ... $28.12½：梭罗在"经济篇"前文提到，当地居民建造居所的平均费用大约800美元。
⑦ squatter's right：指通过擅自占有土地获得其产权，美国开拓边疆时期，边民常依此理定居一地。其实，梭罗建屋，并非强占土地，这块林地由爱默生购买，并同意梭罗使用。
⑧ 梭罗告别沃尔登湖小屋后不久，他的父母就购买了康科德镇大街上一座高档房屋，梭罗在此居住直至离世。对梭罗这样的文化叛逆者来说，这多少有些悖论意味。

I thus found that the student who wishes for a shelter can obtain one for a lifetime at an expense not greater than the rent which he now pays annually. If I seem to boast more than is becoming, my excuse is that I brag for humanity rather than for myself; and my shortcomings and inconsistencies do not affect the truth of my statement. Notwithstanding much cant and hypocrisy — chaff which I find it difficult to separate from my wheat, but for which I am as sorry as any man — I will breathe freely and stretch myself in this respect, it is such a relief to both the moral and physical system; and I am resolved that I will not through humility become the devil's attorney①. I will endeavor to speak a good word for the truth. At Cambridge College② the mere rent of a student's room, which is only a little larger than my own, is thirty dollars each year, though the corporation had the advantage of building thirty-two side by side and under one roof, and the occupant suffers the inconvenience of many and noisy neighbors, and perhaps a residence in the fourth story.③ I cannot but think that if we had more true wisdom in these respects, not only less education would be needed, because, forsooth, more would already have been acquired, but the pecuniary expense of getting an education would in a great measure vanish. Those conveniences which the student requires at Cambridge or elsewhere cost him or somebody else ten times as great a sacrifice of life as they would with proper management on both sides. Those things for which the most money is demanded are never the things which the student most wants. Tuition, for instance, is an important item in the term bill, while for the far more valuable education which he gets by associating with the most cultivated of his contemporaries no charge is made. The mode of founding a college is, commonly, to get up a subscription of dollars and cents, and then, following blindly the principles of a division of labor to its extreme — a principle which should never be followed but with circumspection — to call in a contractor who makes this a subject of speculation, and he employs Irishmen④ or other operatives actually to lay the foundations, while the students that are to be are said to be fitting themselves for it; and for these oversights successive generations have to pay. I think that it would be *better than this*, for the students, or those who desire to be benefited by it, even to lay the foundation themselves. The student who secures his coveted leisure and retirement by systematically shirking any labor necessary to man obtains but an ignoble and unprofitable leisure, defrauding himself of the experience which alone can make leisure fruitful. "But," says one, "you do not mean that the students should go to work with their hands instead of their heads?" I do not mean that exactly, but I mean something which he might think a good deal like that; I mean that they should not *play* life, or *study* it merely, while the community supports them at this expensive game, but earnestly *live* it from beginning to end. How could youths better learn to live than by at once trying the experiment of living? Methinks this would exercise their minds as much as mathematics. If I wished a boy to know something about the arts and sciences, for instance, I would not pursue the common course, which is merely to send him into the neighborhood of some professor, where anything is professed and practised but the art of life; — to survey the world through a telescope or a microscope, and never with his natural eye; to study chemistry, and not learn how his bread is made, or mechanics, and not learn how it is earned; to discover new satellites to Neptune,⑤ and not

---

① the devil's attorney：根据罗马天主教封圣程序要求，教会任命一位教会法规专家为列圣审查官(the devil's advocate)，专门对候选人资格提出种种质疑。
② Cambridge College：Harvard College in Cambridge, Mass.
③ a residence in the fourth story：梭罗在哈佛求学时，曾住在宿舍楼(Hollis Hall)四层。
④ he employs Irishmen：当时爱尔兰移民大多从事体力劳动。
⑤ to discover new satellites to Neptune：1846年，英国天文学拉塞尔(William Lassell)发现了海王星的第一颗卫星，而海王星的其他卫星直到一个世纪后之后才被陆续发现。

detect the motes in his eyes,① or to what vagabond he is a satellite himself; or to be devoured by the monsters that swarm all around him, while contemplating the monsters in a drop of vinegar. Which would have advanced the most at the end of a month — the boy who had made his own jackknife from the ore which he had dug and smelted, reading as much as would be necessary for this — or the boy who had attended the lectures on metallurgy at the Institute② in the meanwhile, and had received a Rodgers' penknife③ from his father? Which would be most likely to cut his fingers?... To my astonishment I was informed on leaving college that I had studied navigation! — why, if I had taken one turn down the harbor I should have known more about it. Even the *poor* student studies and is taught only *political* economy, while that economy of living which is synonymous with philosophy is not even sincerely professed in our colleges. The consequence is, that while he is reading Adam Smith, Ricardo④, and Say⑤, he runs his father in debt irretrievably.

作品赏析

1845年3月末，梭罗开始在沃尔登湖畔林地上为自己建造小屋，7月4日入住，这一天恰是美国独立日，自此他离群索居两年，并将这段经历写成《沃尔登湖》一书。选文摘自《沃尔登湖》第一章"经济篇"。作者开篇立论，质疑现代人的生存方式。19世纪初，美国传统小农自足经济向市场化资本主义转变，在梭罗看来，人们终日奔忙，为生计、为财富，无暇他顾，不觉之中已成自己的"奴隶"。世俗观念的无形权威占据了个人独立思想的空间，芸芸众生皆为物所累，崇高精神则已丧失应有的家园。如此生活，代价是"绝望"，是社会和心灵的疾患。

超验主义者相信，心灵直觉可以超越经验知识，洞悉普遍法则，不是依赖逻辑分析，而是通过体验真实的大自然，从中获得启示，升华精神生活。梭罗的导师爱默生曾说过，"精神就在大自然背后，在大自然中无所不在"。上帝、大自然和人因共同的神性而相通。同样作为超验主义思想家，梭罗将信念付诸他的实验性实践，在沃尔登湖畔结庐而居，目的是尝试另一种可能的生活方式，寻求大自然对自己的教诲，要"活得深入，吸吮生活的全部精髓"。

选文开始部分，梭罗思考建造房屋和现代工商业社会分工问题。建房这种"简单""自然"的工作往往交给他人去做。一方面，分工可能使人们丧失了原本自然的劳动所带来的快乐，甚至可能失去"自然"劳动所需的个人独立思考。另一方面，大多同时代人迫于"必需"的物质需求，无心自主精神追求。而如果文明只是一味改进住房而不关注空虚的心灵，如果人们一生大多时间只是为了获取粗俗的必需物品和舒适享受，则无论住房如何完美，文明也无法进步。梭罗使用形容词"短暂""一时"或"世俗"（temporal）修饰所谓必需物品，启发读者重新寻求真实、永恒的精神自我完善。

简朴生活是梭罗超验主义实验的一个重要观念。他从房屋外在装饰说开去，进而谈到建筑者和建筑物、内在和外表、精神和物质的关系。梭罗坚信，只要生活得简朴、智慧，生存并非难事，他可以每年只工作大约六个星期，靠自己的双手养活自己，有大量的闲暇学习、思考。新英格兰的加尔文宗清教徒相信，尽管不知道他们之中谁是上帝的选民，但通过勤奋工作赎罪，获得更多的财富和商业成功，可看作得救、得到上帝恩典的证明。加之富兰克林（Benjamin Franklin）等人宣扬、传播清教工作伦理，财富的追求更是永无止境。显然，梭罗对工作和财富的观点与主流传统价值截然不同。用梭罗的形象比喻来说，应该是放牧人掌控牧群而不是牧群掌控放牧人。当然，梭罗并没有否定勤劳和工作的价值；选文中区分了"不光彩的、无益的闲暇"（ignoble and unprofitable leisure）和"富有成果的闲暇"（fruitful leisure）。他崇尚"人生必要的劳动"，在闲暇中学习、思考，融入大自然，与大自然互动、神交。

当然，即便我们接受梭罗的生活哲学，恐怕很难想象自己能够照猫画虎，像梭罗那样，实验个人乌托邦生活。事实上，梭罗也并不希望别人盲目模仿他的做法，他希望，每个人都可以是与众不同的独立个体。能够慎重找寻属于自己的生活目的。梭罗的实验也绝不是为了远离他眼中的"绝望"生活和盲

---

① 源于圣经《新约—路加福音》(Luke 6: 41) "Why beholdest thou the mote that is in thy brother's eye, but perceivest not the beam that is in thine own?"《新约—马太福音》(Matthew 7: 3)中也有类似词句。
② the Institute：梭罗可能是指波士顿的洛厄尔学院（Lowell Institute），创建于1836年，为波士顿地区居民举办免费讲座。
③ a Rodgers' penknife：高品质英国刀具，品牌始创于1682年。
④ Ricardo：David Ricardo (1772—1823)，李嘉图，英国经济学家，提出比较优势理论。
⑤ Say：Jean-Baptiste Say (1767—1832)，萨伊，法国经济学家，提出"萨伊定理"。

从他人的社会大众，而是为了破除既有制度和思维的禁锢，自主思考，践行内心的信念，尝试简朴的、自然的生活。

从今天的角度重新审视《沃尔登湖》，思考我们面临的问题：自然，现实环境，工业化消费社会，近乎遗忘的精神境界和贴近自然的生活方式，我们或许可以以我们各自的方式体验、感悟更加广义的"自然"。的确，如拉巴斯蒂尔（Anne Labastille）所说，梭罗集自然主义者、生态主义者、哲学家、生态保护主义者、木匠、农夫、环保主义者和《沃尔登湖》作者于一身，他已经做得相当出色，他让我们明白一个道理：如果尝试实践自己的梦想，努力以自己的方式生活，尽管身在庸碌之中，也会体验意想不到的"成功"。

阅读梭罗的文字，我们可以看到写实风格的客观描述，翔实记录事物和个人体验，随机而发的哲理思考，甚至还有财务收支记录，同时，我们感动于文字间的诗情画意，任意驰骋的想象，对大自然的浪漫情怀。梭罗的文字自然、简练，但看似寻常的字词常常蕴含丰富的意义，引人联想、回味和反思。比如，梭罗谈论的"经济"既有世人常用之意，是他描述财务成本效益的基础概念，但同时也特指梭罗所说的"简朴"（simplicity）。梭罗常把"简朴"等同于"贫困"（poverty），而"贫困"对于梭罗却是真正的财富，是道德重生的必要条件。同样，文中"必需之物"（necessities）有时是"必要需求"之意，有时却转而暗示，人们以为必需之物，其实是不必要的外在装饰，是群体文化中必须求得的物质符号，商品原本是人们满足需要的工具，而现在人们为获得商品，不得不终日劳作，沦为"工具的工具"。梭罗文中随处可见的双关语、典故、格言、比喻，启发读者跟随他的视角，一道探究大自然，重新审视生活和传统价值，寻求"完全的自由"。

思考题

1. To what extent do you agree with the author's contention that there is some of the same fitness in a man's building his own house that there is in a bird's building its own nest?
2. How do you interpret the author's call for the indweller to build truly within and without and let the ornaments take care of themselves?
3. When the author says, "If I seem to boast more than is becoming, my excuse is that I brag for humanity rather than for myself; and my shortcomings and inconsistencies do not affect the truth of my statement," can he justify his brag, and is his statement true from today's point of view? Why or why not?
4. What do you make of the author's statement: "I mean that they should not *play* life, or *study* it merely, while the community supports them at this expensive game, but earnestly *live* it from beginning to end"?

推荐作品

A Week on the Concord and Merrimack Rivers（1849）
On the Duty of Civil Disobedience（1849）
Walking（1862）
Life Without Principle（1863）

参考资料

Cain, William E., ed. *A Historical Guide to Henry David Thoreau.* Oxford: Oxford University Press, 2000.
Myerson, Joel, ed. *The Cambridge Companion to Henry David Thoreau.* Shanghai: Shanghai Foreign Language Education Press, 2000.
Sayre, Robert F., ed. *New Essays on Walden.* Beijing: Peking University Press, 2007.
Thoreau, Henry D. *Walden: A Fully Annotated Edition.* Ed. Jeffrey S. Cramer. New Haven: Yale University Press, 2004.

（张世耘）

第三单元
Nathaniel Hawthorne (1804—1864)

纳撒尼尔·霍桑

 作者简介

  霍桑出生于马萨诸塞州塞勒姆镇,家庭曾为当地望族,祖上有人参与过1692年的塞勒姆女巫审判。霍桑四岁丧父,后随母迁往缅因州,1821—1824年在博多因学院(Bowdoin College)学习。

  霍桑大学毕业后开始文学创作,初以短篇故事为主。1828年匿名发表第一部长篇小说《范肖》(Fanshawe),但未引起关注。1837年,署名出版短篇小说集《重讲一遍的故事》(Twice-Told Tales),反映出其对社会和人性阴暗面的关注以及对清教主义传统既反叛又受制的矛盾思想,受到爱伦·坡等人的称赞。

  1836—1844年,以波士顿为中心的超验主义运动如火如荼,受其女友索菲亚的影响,霍桑于1841年投资参与超验主义者创办的布鲁克农场,与爱默生、梭罗等人成为朋友。次年,霍桑完婚,之后三年,霍桑夫妇住在康科德。其间霍桑完成短篇小说集《古宅青苔》(Mosses from an Old Manse, 1846)。

  1848年,霍桑因政见不同再度失去在海关的工作岗位后,专心创作,于1850年发表长篇小说《红字》(The Scarlet Letter),抨击清教思想的狂热、狭隘、虚伪和教条,在心理揭示和道德探究,特别是罪恶对人的影响等方面颇具深度,大获成功。随后,霍桑又连续发表《带有七个尖角阁的房子》(The House of the Seven Gables, 1851)和《福谷传奇》(The Blithedale Romance, 1852)等作品。

  1853年,霍桑的大学同学皮尔斯(Franklin Pierce)当选为美国总统,任命霍桑为驻英国利物浦的领事。1857年皮尔斯届满离任,霍桑侨居意大利。1860年,霍桑发表另一部讨论善恶问题的长篇小说《玉石雕像》(The Marble Faun)。同年回国,在康科德定居,继续撰文投稿。1864年,卒于赴新罕布什尔州朴次茅斯旅途中。

  霍桑的作品以其丰富的想象、精巧的构思、严谨的结构、洗练而准确的语言、深刻的心理分析和象征主义手法经受了时间的检验,一百多年来长盛不衰,使霍桑稳居美国一流作家之列。除长篇小说《红字》外,最能代表其思想和艺术特色的非其广为流传的短篇小说莫属,特别是《小伙子布朗》("Young Goodman Brown")、《教长的黑纱》("The Minister's Black Veil")、《拉伯西尼医生的女儿》("Rappaccini's Daughter")、《胎记》("The Birthmark")、《伊桑·布兰德》("Ethan Brand")、《美艺术家》("The Artist of the Beautiful")等。这些短篇小说着重探讨人性之恶、"原罪"之深、科学和理性之极端,心理描写细腻,人物内心冲突激烈,对伦理道德的揭示意义深刻,多带有浓厚的宗教气氛和神秘色彩。

Ethan Brand
A Chapter from an Abortive Romance [①]

  Bartram the lime-burner, a rough, heavy-looking man, begrimed[②] with charcoal, sat watching his

---

[①] 故事的题目 Ethan Brand 为人物名字,同时具有意义。作为名词的"brand"是个多义词,可以指"燃烧(或烧焦)的木头""耻辱的标记、污名""(家畜、奴隶或罪犯身上的)烙印""商标、牌子"等。作为人物的 Ethan Brand 被追寻"不可饶恕之罪"的邪火燃烧18年,最后又投身窑炉把自己烧焦,显然是邪念的奴隶、道德的罪犯。Ethan是《圣经》人物——以斯拉人以探(Ethan the Ezrahite),以聪明智慧著称,却与所罗门相形见绌。故事中的 Ethan 也自认为聪明无比,而村民们却不以为然,德国犹太人显然更胜一筹:他让 Ethan 在西洋镜里看"不可饶恕之罪",Ethan 却一无所见。
  故事的副标题暗示 Ethan Brand 和汉弗莱(Humphrey)之女的浪漫关系,随着他对"不可饶恕之罪"越来越着魔,他放弃爱情,并在自己女友身上做起罪恶的实验来,两人的爱情未果。另一说,"abortive"指主人公自绝于人类,无法得到拯救。之所以用"A Chapter"是因为霍桑原计划把 Brand 的一生及其追寻"不可饶恕之罪"的路程写成长篇。
[②] begrime: (煤灰等)沾污;弄脏。

kiln, at nightfall, while his little son played at building houses with the scattered fragments of marble, when, on the hill-side below them, they heard a roar of laughter, not mirthful, but slow, and even solemn, like a wind shaking the boughs of the forest.

"Father, what is that?" asked the little boy, leaving his play, and pressing betwixt his father's knees.

"O, some drunken man, I suppose," answered the lime-burner; "some merry fellow from the bar-room in the village, who dared not laugh loud enough within doors, lest he should blow the roof of the house off. So here he is, shaking his jolly sides at the foot of Gray-lock①."

"But, father," said the child, more sensitive than the obtuse, middle-aged clown, "he does not laugh like a man that is glad. So the noise frightens me!"

"Don't be a fool, child!" cried his father, gruffly. "You will never make a man, I do believe; there is too much of your mother in you. I have known the rustling of a leaf startle you. Hark! Here comes the merry fellow, now. You shall see that there is no harm in him."

Bartram and his little son, while they were talking thus, sat watching the same lime-kiln that had been the scene of Ethan Brand's solitary and meditative life, before he began his search for the Unpardonable Sin. Many years, as we have seen, had now elapsed, since that portentous night when the IDEA was first developed. The kiln, however, on the mountain-side, stood unimpaired, and was in nothing changed since he had thrown his dark thoughts into the intense glow of its furnace, and melted them, as it were, into the one thought that took possession of his life. It was a rude, round, tower-like structure, about twenty feet high, heavily built of rough stones, and with a hillock of earth heaped about the larger part of its circumference; so that the blocks and fragments of marble might be drawn by cart-loads, and thrown in at the top. There was an opening at the bottom of the tower, like an oven-mouth, but large enough to admit a man in a stooping posture, and provided with a massive iron door. With the smoke and jets of flame issuing from the chinks and crevices of this door, which seemed to give admittance into the hill-side, it resembled nothing so much as the private entrance to the infernal regions, which the shepherds of the Delectable Mountains② were accustomed to show to pilgrims.

There are many such lime-kilns in that tract of country, for the purpose of burning the white marble which composes a large part of the substance of the hills. Some of them, built years ago, and long deserted, with weeds growing in the vacant round of the interior, which is open to the sky, and grass and wild-flowers rooting themselves into the chinks of the stones, look already like relics of antiquity, and may yet be overspread with the lichens of centuries to come. Others, where the lime-burner still feeds his daily and nightlong fire, afford points of interest to the wanderer among the hills, who seats himself on a log of wood or a fragment of marble, to hold a chat with the solitary man. It is a lonesome, and, when the character is inclined to thought, may be an intensely thoughtful occupation; as it proved in the case of Ethan Brand, who had mused to such strange purpose, in days gone by, while the fire in this very kiln was burning.

The man who now watched the fire was of a different order, and troubled himself with no thoughts save the very few that were requisite to his business. At frequent intervals, he flung back the clashing weight of the iron door, and, turning his face from the insufferable glare, thrust in huge logs of oak, or

---

① Gray-lock:指马萨诸塞州最高的山 Mount Greylock,海拔1,063米。1838年夏,霍桑访问北亚当斯镇时曾几度登此山,其中一次半夜在山上散步时看见一个正在燃烧的窑炉,给了他创作本篇的灵感。
② the Delectable Mountains:英国作家约翰·班扬的寓言小说《天路历程》中的"愉悦山"。《天路历程》讲述了一个坚韧的基督徒为寻求永生而踏上荆棘遍布的漫漫长旅,逃离"毁灭城",背负种种罪孽跌入"失望壑",在"帮助"的协助下,通过小"便门"开始通往"天国"之旅。他在"蒙辱谷"大战恶魔,在"死亡谷"备受惊吓,在"名利场"饱受煎熬,在"怀疑城堡"几乎被"绝望巨人"战败,但最终得以到达"愉悦山",并渡过"死亡河",进入"天国"。

stirred the immense brands with a long pole. Within the furnace were seen the curling and riotous flames, and the burning marble, almost molten with the intensity of heat; while without, the reflection of the fire quivered on the dark intricacy of the surrounding forest, and showed in the foreground a bright and ruddy little picture of the hut, the spring beside its door, the athletic and coal-begrimed figure of the lime-burner, and the half-frightened child, shrinking into the protection of his father's shadow. And when again the iron door was closed, then reappeared the tender light of the half-full moon, which vainly strove to trace out the indistinct shapes of the neighboring mountains; and, in the upper sky, there was a flitting congregation of clouds, still faintly tinged with the rosy sunset, though thus far down into the valley the sunshine had vanished long and long ago.

The little boy now crept still closer to his father, as footsteps were heard ascending the hill-side, and a human form thrust aside the bushes that clustered beneath the trees.

"Halloo! who is it?" cried the lime-burner, vexed at his son's timidity, yet half infected by it. "Come forward, and show yourself, like a man, or I'll fling this chunk of marble at your head!"

"You offer me a rough welcome," said a gloomy voice, as the unknown man drew nigh. "Yet I neither claim nor desire a kinder one, even at my own fireside."

To obtain a distincter view, Bartram threw open the iron door of the kiln, whence immediately issued a gush of fierce light, that smote full upon the stranger's face and figure. To a careless eye there appeared nothing very remarkable in his aspect, which was that of a man in a coarse, brown, country-made suit of clothes, tall and thin, with the staff and heavy shoes of a wayfarer. As he advanced, he fixed his eyes—which were very bright—intently upon the brightness of the furnace, as if he beheld, or expected to behold, some object worthy of note within it.

"Good evening, stranger," said the lime-burner; "whence come you, so late in the day?"

"I come from my search," answered the wayfarer; "for, at last, it is finished."

"Drunk!—or crazy!" muttered Bartram to himself. "I shall have trouble with the fellow. The sooner I drive him away, the better."

The little boy, all in a tremble, whispered to his father, and begged him to shut the door of the kiln, so that there might not be so much light; for that there was something in the man's face which he was afraid to look at, yet could not look away from. And, indeed, even the lime-burner's dull and torpid sense began to be impressed by an indescribable something in that thin, rugged, thoughtful visage, with the grizzled hair hanging wildly about it, and those deeply-sunken eyes, which gleamed like fires within the entrance of a mysterious cavern. But, as he closed the door, the stranger turned towards him, and spoke in a quiet, familiar way, that made Bartram feel as if he were a sane and sensible man, after all.

"Your task draws to an end, I see," said he. "This marble has already been burning three days. A few hours more will convert the stone to lime."

"Why, who are you?" exclaimed the lime-burner. "You seem as well acquainted with my business as I am myself."

"And well I may be," said the stranger; "for I followed the same craft many a long year, and here, too, on this very spot. But you are a newcomer in these parts. Did you never hear of Ethan Brand?"

"The man that went in search of the Unpardonable Sin?" asked Bartram, with a laugh.

"The same," answered the stranger. "He has found what he sought, and therefore he comes back again."

"What! then you are Ethan Brand himself?" cried the lime-burner, in amazement. "I am a newcomer here, as you say, and they call it eighteen years since you left the foot of Gray-lock. But, I can tell you, the good folks still talk about Ethan Brand, in the village yonder, and what a strange errand took him away from his lime-kiln. Well, and so you have found the Unpardonable Sin?"

"Even so!" said the stranger, calmly.

"If the question is a fair one," proceeded Bartram, "where might it be?"

Ethan Brand laid his finger on his own heart.

"Here!" replied he.

And then, without mirth in his countenance, but as if moved by an involuntary recognition of the infinite absurdity of seeking throughout the world for what was the closest of all things to himself, and looking into every heart, save his own, for what was hidden in no other breast, he broke into a laugh of scorn. It was the same slow, heavy laugh, that had almost appalled the lime-burner when it heralded the wayfarer's approach.

The solitary mountain-side was made dismal by it. Laughter, when out of place, mistimed, or bursting forth from a disordered state of feeling, may be the most terrible modulation of the human voice. The laughter of one asleep, even if it be a little child—the madman's laugh—the wild, screaming laugh of a born idiot—are sounds that we sometimes tremble to hear, and would always willingly forget. Poets have imagined no utterance of fiends or hobgoblins so fearfully appropriate as a laugh. And even the obtuse lime-burner felt his nerves shaken, as this strange man looked inward at his own heart, and burst into laughter that rolled away into the night, and was indistinctly reverberated among the hills.

"Joe," said he to his little son, "scamper down to the tavern in the village, and tell the jolly fellows there that Ethan Brand has come back, and that he has found the Unpardonable Sin!"

The boy darted away on his errand, to which Ethan Brand made no objection, nor seemed hardly to notice it. He sat on a log of wood, looking steadfastly at the iron door of the kiln. When the child was out of sight, and his swift and light footsteps ceased to be heard treading first on the fallen leaves and then on the rocky mountain path, the lime-burner began to regret his departure. He felt that the little fellow's presence had been a barrier between his guest and himself, and that he must now deal, heart to heart, with a man who, on his own confession, had committed the one only crime for which Heaven could afford no mercy. That crime, in its indistinct blackness, seemed to overshadow him. The lime-burner's own sins rose up within him, and made his memory riotous with a throng of evil shapes that asserted their kindred with the Master Sin, whatever it might be, which it was within the scope of man's corrupted nature to conceive and cherish. They were all of one family; they went to and fro between his breast and Ethan Brand's, and carried dark greetings from one to the other.

Then Bartram remembered the stories which had grown traditionary in reference to this strange man, who had come upon him like a shadow of the night, and was making himself at home in his old place, after so long absence that the dead people, dead and buried for years, would have had more right to be at home, in any familiar spot, than he. Ethan Brand, it was said, had conversed with Satan[①] himself in the lurid blaze of this very kiln. The legend had been matter of mirth heretofore but looked grisly now. According to this tale, before Ethan Brand departed on his search, he had been accustomed to evoke a fiend from the hot furnace of the lime-kiln, night after night, in order to confer with him about the Unpardonable Sin; the man and the fiend each laboring to frame the image of some mode of guilt which could neither be atoned for nor forgiven. And, with the first gleam of light upon the mountain-top, the fiend crept in at the iron door, there to abide the intensest element of fire, until again summoned forth to share in the dreadful task of extending man's possible guilt beyond the scope of Heaven's else infinite mercy.

While the lime-burner was struggling with the horror of these thoughts, Ethan Brand rose from the

---

① Satan: 撒旦，《圣经》里与上帝作对的魔鬼。

log, and flung open the door of the kiln. The action was in such accordance with the idea in Bartram's mind, that he almost expected to see the Evil One issue forth, red-hot from the raging furnace.

"Hold! hold!" cried he, with a tremulous attempt to laugh; for he was ashamed of his fears, although they overmastered him. "Don't, for mercy's sake, bring out your devil now!"

"Man!" sternly replied Ethan Brand, "what need have I of the devil? I have left him behind me, on my track. It is with such halfway sinners as you that he busies himself. Fear not because I open the door. I do but act by old custom, and am going to trim your fire, like a lime-burner, as I was once."

He stirred the vast coals, thrust in more wood, and bent forward to gaze into the hollow prison-house of the fire, regardless of the fierce glow that reddened upon his face. The lime-burner sat watching him, and half suspected his strange guest of a purpose, if not to evoke a fiend, at least to plunge bodily into the flames, and thus vanish from the sight of man. Ethan Brand, however, drew quietly back, and closed the door of the kiln.

"I have looked," said he, "into many a human heart that was seven times hotter with sinful passions than yonder furnace is with fire. But I found not there what I sought. No, not the Unpardonable Sin!"

"What is the Unpardonable Sin?" asked the lime-burner; and then he shrank further from his companion, trembling lest his question should be answered.

"It is a sin that grew within my own breast," replied Ethan Brand, standing erect, with a pride that distinguishes all enthusiasts of his stamp. "A sin that grew nowhere else! The sin of an intellect that triumphed over the sense of brotherhood with man and reverence for God, and sacrificed everything to its own mighty claims! The only sin that deserves a recompense of immortal agony! Freely, were it to do again, would I incur the guilt. Unshrinkingly I accept the retribution!"

"The man's head is turned," muttered the lime-burner to himself. "He may be a sinner, like the rest of us—nothing more likely—but, I'll be sworn, he is a madman too."

Nevertheless he felt uncomfortable at his situation, alone with Ethan Brand on the wild mountain-side, and was right glad to hear the rough murmur of tongues, and the footsteps of what seemed a pretty numerous party, stumbling over the stones and rustling through the underbrush. Soon appeared the whole lazy regiment that was wont to infest the village tavern comprehending three or four individuals who had drunk flip beside the bar-room fire through all the winters, and smoked their pipes beneath the stoop through all the summers, since Ethan Brand's departure. Laughing boisterously, and mingling all their voices together in unceremonious talk, they now burst into the moonshine and narrow streaks of fire-light that illuminated the open space before the lime-kiln. Bartram set the door ajar again, flooding the spot with light, that the whole company might get a fair view of Ethan Brand, and he of them.

There, among other old acquaintances, was a once ubiquitous man, now almost extinct, but whom we were formerly sure to encounter at the hotel of every thriving village throughout the country. It was the stage-agent. The present specimen of the genus was a wilted and smoke-dried man, wrinkled and red-nosed, in a smartly cut, brown, bob-tailed coat, with brass buttons, who, for a length of time unknown, had kept his desk and corner in the bar-room, and was still puffing what seemed to be the same cigar that he had lighted twenty years before. He had great fame as a dry joker, though, perhaps, less on account of any intrinsic humor than from a certain flavor of brandy-toddy[①] and tobacco-smoke, which impregnated all his ideas and expressions, as well as his person. Another well-remembered though strangely altered face was that of Lawyer Giles, as people still called him in courtesy; an elderly

---

① brandy-toddy: 用温水调并加糖的香甜热威士忌酒。

ragamuffin, in his soiled shirt-sleeves and tow-cloth trousers. This poor fellow had been an attorney, in what he called his better days, a sharp practitioner, and in great vogue among the village litigants; but flip①, and sling, and toddy, and cocktails, imbibed at all hours, morning, noon, and night, had caused him to slide from intellectual to various kinds and degrees of bodily labor, till, at last, to adopt his own phrase, he slid into a soap-vat. In other words, Giles was now a soap-boiler, in a small way. He had come to be but the fragment of a human being, a part of one foot having been chopped off by an axe, and an entire hand torn away by the devilish grip of a steam-engine. Yet, though the corporeal hand was gone, a spiritual member remained; for, stretching forth the stump, Giles steadfastly averred that he felt an invisible thumb and fingers with as vivid a sensation as before the real ones were amputated. A maimed and miserable wretch he was②; but one, nevertheless, whom the world could not trample on, and had no right to scorn, either in this or any previous stage of his misfortunes, since he had still kept up the courage and spirit of a man, asked nothing in charity, and with his one hand—and that the left one—fought a stern battle against want③ and hostile circumstances.

Among the throng, too, came another personage, who, with certain points of similarity to Lawyer Giles, had many more of difference. It was the village doctor; a man of some fifty years, whom, at an earlier period of his life, we introduced as paying a professional visit to Ethan Brand during the latter's supposed insanity. He was now a purple-visaged, rude, and brutal, yet half-gentlemanly figure, with something wild, ruined, and desperate in his talk, and in all the details of his gesture and manners. Brandy possessed this man like an evil spirit, and made him as surly and savage as a wild beast, and as miserable as a lost soul; but there was supposed to be in him such wonderful skill, such native gifts of healing, beyond any which medical science could impart, that society caught hold of him, and would not let him sink out of its reach. So, swaying to and fro upon his horse, and grumbling thick accents at the bedside, he visited all the sick chambers for miles about among the mountain towns, and sometimes raised a dying man, as it were, by miracle, or quite as often, no doubt, sent his patient to a grave that was dug many a year too soon④. The doctor had an everlasting pipe in his mouth, and, as somebody said, in allusion to his habit of swearing, it was always alight with hell-fire.

These three worthies pressed forward, and greeted Ethan Brand each after his own fashion, earnestly inviting him to partake of the contents of a certain black bottle⑤, in which, as they averred, he would find something far better worth seeking for than the Unpardonable Sin. No mind, which has wrought itself by intense and solitary meditation into a high state of enthusiasm, can endure the kind of contact with low and vulgar modes of thought and feeling to which Ethan Brand was now subjected. It made him doubt—and, strange to say, it was a painful doubt—whether he had indeed found the Unpardonable Sin, and found it within himself. The whole question on which he had exhausted life, and more than life, looked like a delusion.

"Leave me," he said, bitterly, "ye brute beasts, that have made yourselves so, shrivelling up your souls with fiery liquors! I have done with you. Years and years ago, I groped into your hearts, and found nothing there for my purpose. Get ye gone!"

"Why, you uncivil scoundrel," cried the fierce doctor, "is that the way you respond to the kindness of your best friends? Then let me tell you the truth. You have no more found the Unpardonable Sin than yonder boy Joe has. You are but a crazy fellow—I told you so twenty years ago—neither better nor

---

① flip: 失控、狂热。
② 尽管他残缺不全、痛苦不堪。
③ want: 贫困、需要。
④ 过早地把人送入坟墓。
⑤ 酒瓶,内装烈酒(布兰德称之为"fiery liquor")。

worse than a crazy fellow, and the fit companion of old Humphrey, here!"

He pointed to an old man, shabbily dressed, with long white hair, thin visage, and unsteady eyes. For some years past this aged person had been wandering about among the hills, inquiring of all travellers whom he met for his daughter. The girl, it seemed, had gone off with a company of circus-performers; and occasionally tidings of her came to the village, and fine stories were told of her glittering appearance as she rode on horse-back in the ring, or performed marvellous feats on the tight-rope.

The white-haired father now approached Ethan Brand, and gazed unsteadily into his face.

"They tell me you have been all over the earth," said he, wringing his hands with earnestness. "You must have seen my daughter, for she makes a grand figure in the world, and everybody goes to see her. Did she send any word to her old father, or say when she was coming back?"

Ethan Brand's eye quailed beneath the old man's. That daughter, from whom he so earnestly desired a word of greeting, was the Esther of our tale, the very girl whom, with such cold and remorseless purpose, Ethan Brand had made the subject of a psychological experiment, and wasted, absorbed, and perhaps annihilated her soul, in the process.

"Yes," murmured he, turning away from the hoary wanderer; "it is no delusion. There is an Unpardonable Sin!"

While these things were passing, a merry scene was going forward in the area of cheerful light, beside the spring and before the door of the hut. A number of the youth of the village, young men and girls, had hurried up the hill-side, impelled by curiosity to see Ethan Brand, the hero of so many a legend familiar to their childhood. Finding nothing, however, very remarkable in his aspect—nothing but a sun-burnt wayfarer, in plain garb and dusty shoes, who sat looking into the fire, as if he fancied pictures among the coals—these young people speedily grew tired of observing him. As it happened, there was other amusement at hand. An old German Jew, travelling with a diorama on his back, was passing down the mountain-road towards the village just as the party turned aside from it, and, in hopes of eking out the profits of the day, the showman had kept them company to the lime-kiln.

"Come, old Dutchman," cried one of the young men, "let us see your pictures, if you can swear they are worth looking at!"

"O, yes, Captain," answered the Jew—whether as a matter of courtesy or craft, he styled everybody Captain—"I shall show you, indeed, some very superb pictures!"

So, placing his box in a proper position, he invited the young men and girls to look through the glass orifices of the machine, and proceeded to exhibit a series of the most outrageous scratchings and daubings, as specimens of the fine arts, that ever an itinerant showman had the face to impose upon his circle of spectators. The pictures were worn out, moreover, tattered, full of cracks and wrinkles, dingy with tobacco-smoke, and otherwise in a most pitiable condition. Some purported to be cities, public edifices, and ruined castles in Europe; others represented Napoleon's battles and Nelson's sea-fights[①]; and in the midst of these would be seen a gigantic, brown, hairy hand—which might have been mistaken for the Hand of Destiny, though, in truth, it was only the showman's—pointing its forefinger to various scenes of the conflict, while its owner gave historical illustrations. When, with much merriment at its abominable deficiency of merit, the exhibition was concluded, the German bade little Joe put his

---

① Horatio Nelson(1758—1805)：英国海军上将，在其长达35年的海军生涯中，身经大小战斗不下百余次，他作战英勇顽强，不因循守旧，善于在战斗中发挥独创和主动精神，被誉为"英国皇家海军之魂"。他12岁参加海军，20岁任舰长，39岁参加著名的英西圣文森特海战(Battle of Cape St Vincent)，抗命舰出列，插入西班牙战舰编队，使其大乱，英国舰队趁机打败了西班牙海军，战后被封为爵士，晋升为海军少将。40岁，在阿布基尔(Aboukir Bay)海战(又称Battle of the Nile)打败拿破仑的法国舰队，从此名震天下。1805年10月，在19世纪规模最大的一场海战——特拉法尔加海战(Battle of Trafalgar)中指挥27艘战舰组成的英国舰队大败33艘战舰组成的法西联合舰队，而他本人却因其耀眼的将军礼服被法国枪手击中身亡，年仅47岁。

head into the box. Viewed through the magnifying glasses, the boy's round, rosy visage assumed the strangest imaginable aspect of an immense Titanic① child, the mouth grinning broadly, and the eyes and every other feature overflowing with fun at the joke. Suddenly, however, that merry face turned pale, and its expression changed to horror, for this easily impressed and excitable child had become sensible that the eye of Ethan Brand was fixed upon him through the glass.

"You make the little man to be afraid, Captain," said the German Jew, turning up the dark and strong outline of his visage, from his stooping posture. "But look again, and, by chance, I shall cause you to see somewhat that is very fine, upon my word!"

Ethan Brand gazed into the box for an instant, and then starting back, looked fixedly at the German. What had he seen? Nothing, apparently; for a curious youth, who had peeped in almost at the same moment, beheld only a vacant space of canvas.

"I remember you now," muttered Ethan Brand to the showman.

"Ah, Captain," whispered the Jew of Nuremberg②, with a dark smile, "I find it to be a heavy matter in my show-box—this Unpardonable Sin! By my faith, Captain, it has wearied my shoulders, this long day, to carry it over the mountain."

"Peace," answered Ethan Brand, sternly, "or get thee into the furnace yonder!"

The Jew's exhibition had scarcely concluded, when a great, elderly dog—who seemed to be his own master③, as no person in the company laid claim to him—saw fit to render himself the object of public notice. Hitherto, he had shown himself a very quiet, well disposed old dog, going round from one to another, and, by way of being sociable, offering his rough head to be patted by any kindly hand that would take so much trouble. But now, all of a sudden, this grave and venerable quadruped, of his own mere motion, and without the slightest suggestion from anybody else, began to run round after his tail, which, to heighten the absurdity of the proceeding, was a great deal shorter than it should have been. Never was seen such headlong eagerness in pursuit of an object that could not possibly be attained; never was heard such a tremendous outbreak of growling, snarling, barking, and snapping—as if one end of the ridiculous brute's body were at deadly and most unforgivable enmity with the other. Faster and faster, round about went the cur; and faster and still faster fled the unapproachable brevity of his tail; and louder and fiercer grew his yells of rage and animosity; until, utterly exhausted, and as far from the goal as ever, the foolish old dog ceased his performance as suddenly as he had begun it. The next moment he was as mild, quiet, sensible, and respectable in his deportment, as when he first scraped acquaintance with the company.

As may be supposed, the exhibition was greeted with universal laughter, clapping of hands, and shouts of encore, to which the canine performer responded by wagging all that there was to wag of his tail, but appeared totally unable to repeat his very successful effort to amuse the spectators.

Meanwhile, Ethan Brand had resumed his seat upon the log, and moved, it might be, by a perception of some remote analogy between his own case and that of this self-pursuing cur, he broke into the awful laugh, which, more than any other token, expressed the condition of his inward being. From that moment, the merriment of the party was at an end; they stood aghast, dreading lest the inauspicious sound should be reverberated around the horizon, and that mountain would thunder it to mountain, and so the horror be prolonged upon their ears. Then, whispering one to another that it was late—that the moon was almost down—that the August night was growing chill—they hurried homewards leaving the lime-burner and little Joe to deal as they might with their unwelcome guest.

---

① Titanic: 泰坦神的；巨大的。
② Nuremberg: 德国城市纽伦堡。
③ 无主野狗。

Save for these three human beings, the open space on the hill-side was a solitude, set in a vast gloom of forest. Beyond that darksome verge, the fire-light glimmered on the stately trunks and almost black foliage of pines, intermixed with the lighter verdure of sapling oaks, maples, and poplars, while here and there lay the gigantic corpses of dead trees, decaying on the leaf-strewn soil. And it seemed to little Joe—a timorous and imaginative child—that the silent forest was holding its breath, until some fearful thing should happen.

Ethan Brand thrust more wood into the fire, and closed the door of the kiln; then looking over his shoulder at the lime-burner and his son, he bade, rather than advised, them to retire to rest.

"For myself, I cannot sleep," said he. "I have matters that it concerns me to meditate upon. I will watch the fire, as I used to do in the old time."

"And call the devil out of the furnace to keep you company, I suppose," muttered Bartram, who had been making intimate acquaintance with the black bottle above-mentioned. "But watch, if you like, and call as many devils as you like! For my part, I shall be all the better for a snooze. Come, Joe!"

As the boy followed his father into the hut, he looked back at the wayfarer, and the tears came into his eyes, for his tender spirit had an intuition of the bleak and terrible loneliness in which this man had enveloped himself.

When they had gone, Ethan Brand sat listening to the crackling of the kindled wood, and looking at the little spirts of fire that issued through the chinks of the door. These trifles, however, once so familiar, had but the slightest hold of his attention, while deep within his mind he was reviewing the gradual but marvellous change that had been wrought upon him by the search to which he had devoted himself. He remembered how the night dew had fallen upon him—how the dark forest had whispered to him—how the stars had gleamed upon him—a simple and loving man, watching his fire in the years gone by, and ever musing as it burned. He remembered with what tenderness, with what love and sympathy for mankind, and what pity for human guilt and woe, he had first begun to contemplate those ideas which afterwards became the inspiration of his life; with what reverence he had then looked into the heart of man, viewing it as a temple originally divine, and, however desecrated, still to be held sacred by a brother; with what awful fear he had deprecated the success of his pursuit, and prayed that the Unpardonable Sin might never be revealed to him. Then ensued that vast intellectual development, which, in its progress, disturbed the counterpoise between his mind and heart. The Idea that possessed his life had operated as a means of education; it had gone on cultivating his powers to the highest point of which they were susceptible; it had raised him from the level of an unlettered laborer to stand on a star-lit eminence, whither the philosophers of the earth, laden with the lore of universities, might vainly strive to clamber after him. So much for the intellect! But where was the heart? That, indeed, had withered—had contracted—had hardened—had perished! It had ceased to partake of the universal throb. He had lost his hold of the magnetic chain of humanity. He was no longer a brother-man, opening the chambers or the dungeons of our common nature by the key of holy sympathy, which gave him a right to share in all its secrets; he was now a cold observer, looking on mankind as the subject of his experiment, and, at length, converting man and woman to be his puppets, and pulling the wires that moved them to such degrees of crime as were demanded for his study.

Thus Ethan Brand became a fiend. He began to be so from the moment that his moral nature had ceased to keep the pace of improvement with his intellect. And now, as his highest effort and inevitable development—as the bright and gorgeous flower, and rich, delicious fruit of his life's labor—he had produced the Unpardonable Sin!

"What more have I to seek? What more to achieve?" said Ethan Brand to himself. "My task is done, and well done!"

Starting from the log with a certain alacrity in his gait, and ascending the hillock of earth that was raised against the stone circumference of the lime-kiln, he thus reached the top of the structure. It was a space of perhaps ten feet across, from edge to edge, presenting a view of the upper surface of the immense mass of broken marble with which the kiln was heaped. All these innumerable blocks and fragments of marble were red-hot and vividly on fire, sending up great spouts of blue flame, which quivered aloft and danced madly, as within a magic circle, and sank and rose again, with continual and multitudinous activity. As the lonely man bent forward over this terrible body of fire, the blasting heat smote up against his person with a breath that, it might be scorched and shrivelled him up in a moment.

Ethan Brand stood erect, and raised his arms on high. The blue flames played upon his face, and imparted the wild and ghastly light which alone could have suited its expression; it was that of a fiend on the verge of plunging into his gulf of intensest torment.

"O Mother Earth," cried he, "who art① no more my Mother, and into whose bosom this frame shall never be resolved! O mankind, whose brotherhood I have cast off, and trampled thy② great heart beneath my feet! O stars of heaven, that shone on me of old, as if to light me onward and upward!—farewell all, and forever. Come, deadly element of Fire—henceforth my familiar friend! Embrace me, as I do thee!"

That night the sound of a fearful peal of laughter rolled heavily through the sleep of the lime-burner and his little son; dim shapes of horror and anguish haunted their dreams, and seemed still present in the rude hovel, when they opened their eyes to the daylight.

"Up, boy, up!" cried the lime-burner, staring about him. "Thank Heaven, the night is gone, at last; and rather than pass such another, I would watch my lime-kiln, wide awake, for a twelvemonth. This Ethan Brand, with his humbug of an Unpardonable Sin, has done me no such mighty favor, in taking my place!"

He issued from the hut, followed by little Joe, who kept fast hold of his father's hand. The early sunshine was already pouring its gold upon the mountain-tops; and though the valleys were still in shadow, they smiled cheerfully in the promise of the bright day that was hastening onward. The village, completely shut in by hills, which swelled away gently about it, looked as if it had rested peacefully in the hollow of the great hand of Providence③. Every dwelling was distinctly visible; the little spires of the two churches pointed upwards, and caught a fore-glimmering of brightness from the sun-gilt skies upon their gilded weather-cocks. The tavern was astir, and the figure of the old, smoke-dried stage-agent, cigar in mouth, was seen beneath the stoop. Old Graylock was glorified with a golden cloud upon his head. Scattered likewise over the breasts of the surrounding mountains, there were heaps of hoary mist, in fantastic shapes, some of them far down into the valley, others high up towards the summits and still others, of the same family of mist or cloud, hovering in the gold radiance of the upper atmosphere. Stepping from one to another of the clouds that rested on the hills, and thence to the loftier brotherhood that sailed in air, it seemed almost as if a mortal man might thus ascend into the heavenly regions. Earth was so mingled with sky that it was a day-dream to look at it.

To supply that charm of the familiar and homely, which Nature so readily adopts into a scene like this, the stage-coach was rattling down the mountain-road, and the driver sounded his horn, while echo caught up the notes, and intertwined them into a rich and varied and elaborate harmony, of which the original performer could lay claim to little share. The great hills played a concert among themselves, each contributing a strain of airy sweetness.

Little Joe's face brightened at once.

---

① art: Be 的古英语形式。
② thou, thy, thee: 古英语中第二人称代词作主语、定语和宾语的不同形式。
③ Providence: 上帝；神。

"Dear father," cried he, skipping cheerily to and fro, "that strange man is gone, and the sky and the mountains all seem glad of it!"

"Yes," growled the lime-burner, with an oath, "but he has let the fire go down, and no thanks to him if five hundred bushels of lime are not spoiled. If I catch the fellow hereabouts again, I shall feel like tossing him into the furnace!"

With his long pole in his hand, he ascended to the top of the kiln. After a moment's pause, he called to his son.

"Come up here, Joe!" said he.

So little Joe ran up the hillock, and stood by his father's side. The marble was all burnt into perfect, snow-white lime. But on its surface, in the midst of the circle—snow-white too, and thoroughly converted into lime—lay a human skeleton, in the attitude of a person who, after long toil, lies down to long repose. Within the ribs—strange to say—was the shape of a human heart.

"Was the fellow's heart made of marble?" cried Bartram, in some perplexity at this phenomenon. "At any rate, it is burnt into what looks like special good lime; and, taking all the bones together, my kiln is half a bushel the richer for him."

So saying, the rude lime-burner lifted his pole, and, letting it fall upon the skeleton, the relics of Ethan Brand were crumbled into fragments.

《伊桑·布兰德》创作于1848年底，原副标题为"不可饶恕的罪恶"（The Unpardonable Sin），几经周折，最终于1851年，以"不可饶恕的罪恶"为标题发表在《霍尔顿美元杂志》（Holden's Dollar Magazine）上，同年又收录在霍桑的最后一个故事集《雪人及其他复述故事》（The Snow-Image, and Other Twice-Told Tales）中，副标题改成"摘自一部未完成的罗曼史"（A Chapter from an Abortive Romance）。

同《拉帕西尼的女儿》《胎记》等故事一样，《伊桑·布兰德》通过描述主人公因为追求知识而变态来表现对理性和科学的怀疑。伊桑·布兰德孑然一人在荒山野岭烧石灰窑，长期的寂寞和孤独使原本善良、通情达理、"对人类富有爱心和同情"的他变得偏执，陷入探索人类不可饶恕之罪的执迷中，继而离开石灰窑，周游世界18年寻找该罪。在此过程中，他完全被偏执的求知欲所控制，不再敬仰上帝，不再关心他人，而是强迫他人屈服于诱惑，希望借此发现人们心中的大恶。渐渐地，他失去人性，变得冷酷无情，铁石心肠，成为疏离同类的"冷酷旁观者"、"把人类视为试验对象"的恶魔。追寻"不可饶恕之罪"的欲望吞噬了他的灵魂，而他又毁灭别人的灵魂。18年后，布兰德重返故里，高傲地宣布找到了"不可饶恕之罪"。颇具讽刺意义的是，尽管他声称曾见过许多人的心因为邪念比燃烧的窑炉"还滚烫七倍"，却最终发现"不可饶恕之罪"原来存于自己的胸膛里！于是，他决定葬身于他开始这一念头的窑炉的火海。

"不可饶恕之罪"出自《圣经》。《新约》中，犹太教派中的一个分支——法利赛教派（the Pharisees）曾多次与耶稣发生冲突，他们不承认耶稣是救世主，自以为是，以律法阻挡神恩的降临。耶稣称之为"伪善者"（Matt. 23:15-27），并对其屡加斥责。法利赛教派曾铁石心肠地暗地指责耶稣借助魔鬼的力量制造奇迹，耶稣警告他们有犯"不可饶恕之罪"的危险。本故事中的布兰德同受耶稣斥责的法利赛教派有相像之处。然而，对"不可饶恕之罪"和布兰德之死还有几种不同的解释：一说他虽然得所求，满足了求知欲，却发现自己多年来为了一个念头，摒弃人之天性，把理智和情感完全割裂，苦思冥想、损人害己的做法是"不可饶恕之罪"，他以死谢罪。第二种说法是，自杀本身才是不可饶恕之罪，因为布兰德通过自杀彻底切断同世界和人类的联系，刻意拒绝悔恨和拯救的机会，是一种变相的人类灭绝行为。如果说《拉帕西尼的女儿》《胎记》揭示了变态的研究对他人的毁坏，那么《伊桑·布兰德》主要表现了疯狂求知者自灭的悲剧。第三种说法是，布兰德根本没有找到"不可饶恕之罪"，重返故里表明他还在意他人的看法，尚未完全割裂同他人的联系，因此，他18年的追寻以失败告终，其在村民心目中的传奇色彩也荡然无存，他无法接受这一现实而自尽。第四种看法认为，布兰德的高傲是"不可饶恕之罪"。也有人认为，霍桑以同时代作家赫尔曼·梅尔维尔为原型创造出布兰德的形象，尽管本篇发表时两人尚未谋面。

这些解释进一步证明霍桑作品道德审视之冷峻和心理探究之深刻。此外，本篇的主要情节发生在故事开始之前,主人公故事的圆形结构、三次发笑,一系列象征物,如火(欲望、邪念)、幼儿(纯真、同情)、狗(常识)、大理石(铁石心肠)的运用等,都体现出霍桑的写作特色。

 思考题

1. How does Hawthorne create an eerie atmosphere and evoke a sense of mystery at the beginning of the story?
2. Does Ethan Brand come back to Mount Greylock to announce the fulfillment of his pursuit or to renew his bond with humanity? Why?
3. Compare Hawthorne's description of the night and morning.
4. How does the old dog's pursuit of his tail parallel or mock Ethan Brand's search for the Unpardonable Sin? Why does Ethan Brand break into an "awful laugh" at the scene?
5. Why does the German Jew ask Ethan Brand to look at the Unpardonable Sin in the diorama?
6. What sin do you think Ethan Brand has committed?

"Young Goodman Brown" (1835)
"The Birthmark" (1843)
The Scarlet Letter (1850)

 参考资料

Bloom, Harold, ed. *Nathaniel Hawthorne*. New York: Chelsea House, 1986.
Dunne, Michael. *Hawthorne's Narrative Strategies*. Jackson: University Press of Mississippi, 1995.
Harris, Mark. "A new reading of 'Ethan Brand': The failed quest." *Studies in Short Fiction*, Winter 94, Vol. 31 Issue 1.
Klingel, Joan E. "'Ethan Brand' as Hawthorne's Faust." *Studies in Short Fiction*, Winter 82, Vol. 19 Issue 1.
Wagenknecht, Edward. *Nathaniel Hawthorne: The Man, His Tales and Romances*. New York: Continuum, 1989.

(陈法春)

第四单元
Herman Melville (1819—1891)
赫尔曼·梅尔维尔

 作者简介

  赫尔曼·梅尔维尔,小说家、诗人、散文家,其文学创作为美国民族文学的发展做出了重要贡献。生于纽约市,父亲经商,受过四年学校教育,后因父亲破产家道中落而辍学。1837年开始工作,曾任中学教师、农夫、职员和水手,数年间在太平洋航行,历尽艰辛,阅历丰富,谙悉捕鲸等海上行业。1847年婚后,梅尔维尔告别航海生涯,定居马萨诸塞州西部匹兹菲尔德市,经营农场,同时开始涉足文学创作,展露出其艺术才华。梅尔维尔自学成才,创作艺术日臻完善,但在世时可谓穷困潦倒,作品出版后无人问津,版税收入每况愈下,难以养家糊口。1866年至1885年,他曾在纽约海关任职,后因病去世。20世纪20年代之后,他的作品逐渐得到美国学术界和文学界的青睐和认同,被誉为美国文学的经典。

  梅尔维尔的早期作品以散文和游记为主,包括《泰皮》(Typee: A Peep at Polynesian Life,1846)和《欧穆》(Omoo: A Narrative of Adventures in the South Seas,1847)。他步入而立之年以后开始创作小说,包括《玛地》(Mardi: And a Voyage Thither,1849)、《白外套》(White-Jacket: or, The World in a Man-of-War,1850)和《白鲸》(Moby-Dick,1851)等,大多是依托其航海经历而创作的各种探险故事,题材别致,情节不落俗套,叙事风格清新脱俗。无奈曲高和寡,梅尔维尔在世时呕心沥血创作的代表作《白鲸》也仅仅售出3000册。他还著有短篇小说集《广场故事》(The Piazza Tales,1856),其中包括《皮埃尔》("Pierre: or, The Ambiguities",1852)和《代笔者巴特贝》("Bartleby the Scrivener",1853)等脍炙人口的佳作。他去世前未及完成的长篇小说《毕利·伯德》(Billy Budd, Sailor: An Inside Narrative)于1924年出版。

  1857年之后,梅尔维尔主要致力于诗歌创作,诗作包括以美国内战为题的《战事集》(Battle Pieces: And Aspects of the War,1866),描写宗教朝圣的长诗《克拉瑞尔》(Clarel: A Poem and Pilgrimage in the Holy Land,1876)等。

Moby-Dick
Chapter 135
The Chase – Third Day

  Almost simultaneously, with a mighty volition of ungraduated[①], instantaneous swiftness, the White Whale[②] darted through the weltering sea. But when Ahab[③] cried out to the steersman to take new turns with the line, and hold it so; and commanded the crew to turn round on their seats, and tow the boat up to the mark; the moment the treacherous line felt that double strain and tug, it snapped in the empty air!

  "What breaks in me? Some sinew cracks!—tis whole again; oars! oars! Burst in upon him!"

  Hearing the tremendous rush of the sea-crashing boat, the whale wheeled round to present his blank forehead at bay; but in that evolution, catching sight of the nearing black hull of the ship;

---

① ungraduated:不分等级的,指迅猛而爆发的方式。
② the White Whale:指小说中作为裴廓德(Pequod)号捕鲸船船长的仇敌的白鲸,名叫莫比·迪克(Moby Dick)。
③ Ahab:亚哈,裴廓德号捕鲸船船长。

seemingly seeing in it the source of all his persecutions; bethinking it—it may be—a larger and nobler foe; of a sudden, he bore down upon its advancing prow, smiting his jaws amid fiery showers of foam.

Ahab staggered; his hand smote his forehead. "I grow blind; hands! Stretch out before me that I may yet grope my way. Isn't night?"

"The whale! The ship!" cried the cringing oarsmen.

"Oars! oars! Slope downwards to thy depths, O sea, that ere① it be for ever too late, Ahab may slide this last, last time upon his mark! I see: the ship! the ship! Dash on, my men! Will ye not save my ship?"

But as the oarsmen violently forced their boat through the sledge-hammering seas, the before whale-smitten bow-ends of two planks burst through, and in an instant almost, the temporarily disabled boat lay nearly level with the waves; its half-wading, splashing crew, trying hard to stop the gap and bale out the pouring water.

Meantime, for that one beholding instant, Tashtego's② mast-head hammer remained suspended in his hand; and the red flag, half-wrapping him as with a plaid, then streamed itself straight out from him, as his own forward-flowing heart; while Starbuck and Stubb③, standing upon the bowsprit beneath, caught sight of the down-coming monster just as soon as he.

"The whale, the whale! Up helm④, up helm! Oh, all ye sweet powers of air, now hug me close! Let not Starbuck die, if die he must, in a woman's fainting fit. Up helm, I say-ye fools, the jaw! the jaw! Is this the end of all my bursting prayers? all my life-long fidelities? Oh, Ahab, Ahab, lo, thy work. Steady! helmsman, steady. Nay, nay! Up helm again! He turns to meet us! Oh, his unappeasable⑤ brow drives on towards one, whose duty tells him he cannot depart. My God, stand by me now!"

"Stand not by me, but stand under me, whoever you are that will now help Stubb; for Stubb, too, sticks here. I grin at thee, thou grinning whale! Who ever helped Stubb, or kept Stubb awake, but Stubb's own unwinking eye? And now poor Stubb goes to bed upon a mattress that is all too soft; would it were stuffed with brushwood⑥! I grin at thee, thou grinning whale! Look ye, sun, moon, and stars! I call ye assassins of as good a fellow as ever spouted up his ghost. For all that, I would yet ring glasses with thee, would ye but hand the cup! Oh, oh! oh, oh! thou grinning whale, but there'll be plenty of gulping⑦ soon! Why fly ye not, O Ahab! For me, off shoes and jacket to it; let Stubb die in his drawers! A most mouldy⑧ and over salted death, though; -cherries! cherries! cherries! Oh, Flask, for one red cherry ere we die!"

"Cherries? I only wish that we were where they grow. Oh, Stubb, I hope my poor mother's drawn my part-pay ere this; if not, few coppers will now come to her, for the voyage is up."

From the ship's bows, nearly all the seamen now hung inactive; hammers, bits of plank⑨, lances, and harpoons, mechanically retained in their hands, just as they had darted from their various employments; all their enchanted eyes intent upon the whale, which from side to side strangely vibrating his predestinating head, sent a broad band of overspreading semicircular foam before him as he rushed. Retribution, swift vengeance⑩, eternal malice were in his whole aspect, and spite of all that

---

① ere: 在……之前。
② Tashtego: 塔斯蒂哥是小说中的一个人物,生于南美的印第安人,体格硕壮,捕鱼技术独特。
③ Starbuck and Stubb: 斯达巴克与斯塔布是小说中的两个人物。
④ helm: 舵。
⑤ unappeasable: 无法平息的;压制不住的;忍受不住的。
⑥ brushwood: 砍下或断落的树枝。
⑦ gulping: 吞食;狼吞虎咽。
⑧ mouldy: 霉烂的;陈腐的。
⑨ plank: 厚木板。
⑩ vengeance: 复仇;报仇。

mortal man could do, the solid white buttress of his forehead smote the ship's starboard① bow, till men and timbers reeled. Some fell flat upon their faces. Like dislodged trucks, the heads of the harpooneers aloft shook on their bull-like necks. Through the breach, they heard the waters pour, as mountain torrents down a flume②.

"The ship! The hearse③! —the second hearse!" cried Ahab from the boat; "its wood could only be American!"

Diving beneath the settling ship, the whale ran quivering along its keel; but turning under water, swiftly shot to the surface again, far off the other bow, but within a few yards of Ahab's boat, where, for a time, he lay quiescent④.

"I turn my body from the sun. What ho, Tashtego! let me hear thy hammer. Oh! ye three unsurrendered⑤ spires of mine; thou uncracked keel⑥; and only god-bullied hull; thou firm deck, and haughty helm, and Pole-pointed prow, -death-glorious ship! must ye then perish, and without me? Am I cut off from the last fond pride of meanest shipwrecked captains? Oh, lonely death on lonely life! Oh, now I feel my topmost greatness lies in my topmost grief. Ho, ho! from all your furthest bounds, pour ye now in, ye bold billows of my whole foregone life, and top this one piled comber of my death! Towards thee I roll, thou all-destroying but unconquering whale; to the last I grapple⑦ with thee; from hell's heart I stab at thee; for hate's sake I spit my last breath at thee. Sink all coffins and all hearses to one common pool! and since neither can be mine, let me then tow to pieces, while still chasing thee, though tied to thee, thou damned whale! Thus, I give up the spear!"

The harpoon was darted; the stricken whale flew forward; with igniting velocity⑧ the line ran through the grooves; -ran foul. Ahab stooped⑨ to clear it; he did clear it; but the flying turn caught him round the neck, and voicelessly as Turkish mutes bowstring⑩ their victim, he was shot out of the boat, ere the crew knew he was gone. Next instant, the heavy eye-splice⑪ in the rope's final end flew out of the stark-empty tub, knocked down an oarsman, and smiting⑫ the sea, disappeared in its depths.

For an instant, the tranced boat's crew stood still; then turned. "The ship? Great God, where is the ship?" Soon they through dim, bewildering mediums saw her sidelong fading phantom⑬, as in the gaseous Fata Morgana⑭; only the uppermost masts out of water; while fixed by infatuation, or fidelity, or fate, to their once lofty perches, the pagan harpooneers still maintained their sinking look-outs on the sea. And now, concentric circles seized the lone boat itself, and all its crew, and each floating oar, and every lancepole, and spinning, animate and inanimate, all round and round in one vortex, carried the smallest chip of the Pequod out of sight.

But as the last whelmings⑮ intermixingly poured themselves over the sunken head of the Indian at

---

① starboard: 右舷。
② flume: 水槽;水道。
③ hearse: 棺架;棺台;灵车。
④ quiescent: 安静的;休止的。
⑤ unsurrendered: 不屈服的;不放弃的。
⑥ keel: (船的)龙骨。
⑦ grapple: 扭打;格斗。
⑧ velocity: 速度。
⑨ stoop: 弯腰。
⑩ bowstring: 绞索。
⑪ eye-splice: 索眼;眼圈形接头。
⑫ smiting: 重击。
⑬ phantom: 鬼怪;幽灵;幻象。
⑭ Fata Morgana: 海市蜃楼。
⑮ whelmings: 涡流;涡旋。

the mainmast①, leaving a few inches of the erect spar yet visible, together with long streaming yards of the flag, which calmly undulated, with ironical coincidings, over the destroying billows they almost touched; —at that instant, a red arm and a hammer hovered② backwardly uplifted in the open air, in the act of nailing the flag faster and yet faster to the subsiding spar. A sky-hawk that tauntingly③ had followed the main-truck downwards from its natural home among the stars, pecking at the flag, and incommoding Tashtego there; this bird now chanced to intercept its broad fluttering wing between the hammer and the wood; and simultaneously feeling that ethereal④ thrill, the submerged savage beneath, in his death-gasp, kept his hammer frozen there; and so the bird of heaven, with archangelic shrieks, and his imperial beak thrust upwards, and his whole captive form folded in the flag of Ahab, went down with his ship, which, like Satan, would not sink to hell till she had dragged a living part of heaven along with her, and helmeted herself with it.

Now small fowls flew screaming over the yet yawning⑤ gulf; a sullen white surf beat against its steep sides; then all collapsed, and the great shroud of the sea rolled on as it rolled five thousand years ago.

作为小说家,梅尔维尔人生阅历丰富,思想深邃,感觉敏锐,才华横溢,尤其擅长描写非同寻常的题材和令人刻骨铭心的人物形象,文笔隽永,意象清新,风格犀利,无论是与其同时代的小说家相比,还是就整个美国小说史和西方小说而言,其作品都别具一格。《白鲸》充分体现了梅尔维尔的上述创作特征,被公认为是其代表作品,也历来被誉为西方小说中的奇葩。

梅尔维尔的重要创作特征之一是以自身的生活经历和人生体验为基础,从中提炼情节和构思人物,选择真实的背景,由此创作具有深刻哲理和艺术内涵以及富有人性魅力的故事,而并非像爱伦·坡等同时代的作家那样依赖纯粹的想象力和艺术灵感,淡化故事背景,突出刻画复杂缠绵的故事情节,凸显人物个性的丰富性与张力。从其早期小说《泰皮》和《欧穆》等作品开始,他创作了以自己航海捕鱼的生活经历为题材的作品,通过描写惊心动魄的海洋历险故事和海岛上的风土人情来反映社会现实,就此而言,《白鲸》也是其中的典范。《白鲸》中所描写的捕鲸的故事,真实而栩栩如生地向读者展示了鲜为人知的捕鲸行业,以及水手、捕鲸者等远离社会的群体的生活和工作,被誉为"捕鲸业的百科全书"。

《白鲸》采用第一人称叙事,与19世纪中叶广为流行的第三人称叙事相比,显然更能让读者感到故事的真实性。小说的故事情节并非复杂,但跌宕起伏,动人心魄,尤其是具有强烈悲剧色彩的结尾令人心绪纠结,充满遐想。"裴廓德"号是当时最为先进的商业捕鲸船,船上拥有系统化的捕杀鲸鱼的设施装备,堪称一座在海上流动的现代化工厂,长年在浩瀚无际、波澜起伏的海洋中追逐、捕捉和加工鲸鱼。船长亚哈具有丰富的捕鲸经验,深谙各种鲸鱼的习性,多年的捕鲸生涯塑造了他不畏艰险、深沉、狡诈、孤独和冷酷的性格。在一次捕鲸过程中,亚哈遇到了躯体硕大而充满野性的白鲸莫比·迪克,由于他低估了莫比·迪克的智慧,在试图捕杀它的时候,反被凶狠反击的白鲸咬掉了一条腿。莫比·迪克逃之夭夭,消失在苍茫的大海之中,侥幸逃生的亚哈此后一直期待复仇的机会。他数年如一日,驾驶"裴廓德"号捕鲸船漂洋过海,唯一的动机和目的就是寻找莫比·迪克复仇,将其杀害,报仇雪恨。他长时间忍受的折磨,不仅仅是失去一条腿对身体所造成的创伤,更在于白鲸的攻击让他蒙受了耻辱,由此而带来的心理伤害让他无地自容。亚哈终于遇见了莫比·迪克,经过历时三天三夜的追踪和搏斗,双方都累得筋疲力尽,此时亚哈用尽全身的气力巧妙地将鱼叉刺入白鲸的身躯。这是致命的一击,莫比·迪克疼痛无比,疯狂地摇动自己的身躯,不仅将"裴廓德"号捕鲸船的船体撞毁,而且体内鱼叉上的绳索还猝不及防地把亚哈拖入了大海。白鲸体力不支,逐渐沉入水中,全船人也落海遇难,唯一的幸存者是船上的水手

---

① mainmast: 主桅杆;主桅。
② hover: 盘旋;翱翔。
③ tauntingly: 嘲弄似地;讥讽似地。
④ ethereal: 轻飘的;虚空的;太空的。
⑤ yawning: 裂开豁口的;敞开的;多洞穴的。

以实玛利。故事便由劫后余生的以实玛利叙述。

《白鲸》是一部具有史诗般内涵和意义的作品,问世一个多世纪以来颇受大众读者和批评家的青睐。在主题方面,小说涉及人性、社会、宗教、伦理、生态、复仇等诸多方面的问题,因此可以有各种解读。就小说与社会现实的关系而言,19世纪中叶随着资本主义的蓬勃发展,捕鲸已经成为一个能够带来丰厚利润的行业,捕鲸在创造财富的同时也暴露和刺激了人类的贪婪,由此也使得人类与鲸鱼、海洋乃至整个自然界产生了矛盾和冲突,对人类与自然之间和谐共处造成了威胁。梅尔维尔通过讲述亚哈与莫比·迪克之间的故事,艺术地呈现出上述问题,并以小说中两位主人公两败俱亡的悲剧提出警示。

在创作特征方面,梅尔维尔卓越地运用了多种象征手法,包括大量使用典故、引文、景物、情节和具有象征意义的人物名称等,以此委婉地表达各种思想情怀,启发读者的联想。小说中大约一半以上人物的名字均取自《圣经》,其人物品性和行为的特征也都与《圣经》中的同名人物相仿,因此人物名称具有显而易见的寓意。船长亚哈的名字取自《圣经》中以色列第七代王亚哈,意为"恶毒",如将二者相对比,可以发现其性格和命运如出一辙。换言之,梅尔维尔在刻画亚哈的人物形象时复制了《圣经》中同名的历史人物,折射出船长亚哈所代表的人性中的各种邪恶。白鲸莫比·迪克也具有典型的寓意,它庞大的身躯洁白如玉,象征着超凡而神圣的纯洁和质朴,巨大的力量和顽强的意志体现了大自然的神秘、深邃而令人敬畏的品格,它与亚哈之间的纠葛、冲突和势不两立的斗争则是处于工业化进程中的人类与自然之间关系的一个缩影。

 思考题

1. What are the differences between the first-person narrative in *Moby-Dick* and the traditional third-person narrative that was popular in Melville's age?
2. What do you think of the symbolism Melville uses in Moby-Dick?
3. Can you find some biblical allusions in Moby-Dick and interpret their significance?

 "Bartleby, the Scrivener: A Story of Wall Street" (1853)
Typee (1846)

 参考资料

Bloom, Harolded. *Herman Melville's Moby-Dick.* Broomall: Chelsea House Publications, 1996.
Fruscione, Joseph. "'What Is Called Savagery': Race, Visual Perception, and Bodily Contact in Moby-Dick." *Leviathan: A Journal of Melville Studies* 10.1 (2008): 3-24.
Kelley, Wyn. *Herman Melville: An Introduction.*(Blackwell Introductions to Literature). Malden, MA: Blackwell, 2008.

(刘树森)

第五单元
Walt Whitman (1819—1892)
沃尔特·惠特曼

 作者简介

以《草叶集》(*Leaves of Grass*, 1855—1881)闻名于世的沃尔特·惠特曼是美国历史上最伟大、最具影响力的诗人之一,19世纪在世时因诗歌创作主题和技巧上的大胆创新而引来颇多争议,尤其是对性的大胆描述和同性恋倾向使其一度被当作淫秽诗人封杀,而后获得公众广泛认可,被誉为"美国民主诗人"、"自由诗之父";他创作了《自我之歌》《我听见美国在歌唱》《当紫丁香最近在庭院开放时》《哦!船长,我的船长》等广为流传的诗篇佳作,同时也是散文家、小说家,著有中篇小说《富兰克林·伊凡斯》(*Franklin Evans*, 1842)、长篇政论散文《民主的远景》(*Democratic Vistas*, 1871)等。

惠特曼生于纽约州长岛的一个劳动阶层家庭,母亲是具有民主主义倾向的贵格会牧师希克斯(Elias Hicks, 1748—1830)的热心追随者,父亲是一名木匠,由于接受了著名资产阶级启蒙家托马斯·潘恩(Thomas Paine, 1737—1809)所宣扬的激进自由主义理念和民主共和思想,给膝下八名子女中的三兄弟分别命名以美国开国元勋安德鲁·杰克逊、乔治·华盛顿、托马斯·杰斐逊之名。幼年时的惠特曼在1825至1830年间上过学堂,但多半还是自学成才,一生中做过印刷厂学徒工、新闻记者、教师、杂志社编辑、政府部门职员等。从事文学创作之初,他先是写一些零散短诗,1842年发表唯一一部小说作品——以戒酒为题材的《富兰克林·伊凡斯》,40年代先后在《纽约曙光》《布洛克林每日鹰报》《自由民报》担任编辑,后于1855年自费出版《草叶集》第一版,在英美文坛异军突起,几十年间不断对这部诗集进行扩充、修改,直到1892年过世为止总共推出九版,收录的诗作数量也从最初的12首发展到383首。此外,美国内战期间,惠特曼还曾作为林肯解放黑奴主张的积极支持者自愿到华盛顿的战地医院做过护理和心理疏导工作,随即创作战争诗《鼓声集》和《鼓声集续编》(*Drum-Taps and Sequel*, 1865—1866)以及散文集《战争备忘录》(*Memoranda During the War*, 1875—1876),这些作品代表了他关注于历史的现实主义转向,为克莱恩、海明威、梅勒等人的自然主义战争文学做了很好的铺垫。1873年,惠特曼不幸中风并半身不遂,遂迁居新泽西州卡姆登养病,于1892年病重辞世。

19世纪中叶的美国作家在欧陆文风影响下深受清教主义束缚,而作为一名土生土长的美国诗人,惠特曼一反当时美国文坛脱离人民、脱离生活的陈腐贵族倾向,第一次把目光投向普通人和日常生活,讴歌民主自由,倡导人类平等,赞美大自然和创造性劳动,谴责奴隶制,由此被公认为美国首位"民主诗人"。一方面,其诗歌创作总体上呈现出一种个性分明的美国特性和民族意识;另一方面,民主思想构成了贯穿其全部作品的一条主线。这不仅表现在诗人的废奴主义立场和种族平等观念以及为普通劳动大众代言的姿态上,而且表现在他打破"男性与女性、农民与工人、妓女与奴隶、美国公民与世界公民"等社会身份界限并"自由穿梭于过去、现在和未来"的气魄上①。同时,其诗歌艺术风格也是民主精神的体现:他所创造的自由体诗(free verse)不受格律、韵脚的限制,文体上十分接近口语和散文,使语言冲破传统诗歌形式的束缚,自由洒脱地表达思想,激情奔放地表露情感,由此开创了一种全新的美国诗风。值得一提的是,惠特曼的诗歌在很大程度上是通过声音来传达讯息和力量的,适合通过大声诵读来体验其精髓。

尽管发表伊始备受冷遇和抨击②,美国当代著名评论家哈罗德·布鲁姆在惠特曼150周年诞辰纪念版《草叶集》的"序言"中将这部诗集初版与梅尔维尔的《白鲸》、马克·吐温的《哈克贝里·费恩历险记》、

---

① Paul Lauter, et al., eds. *The Heath Anthology of American Literature*, Vol. 1, 4th ed. Boston, MA: Houghton Mifflin, 2002, p. 2846.
② 《草叶集》初版印了1000册,一本都没能卖掉,只好全部送人。惠蒂埃(John Greenleaf Whittier, 1807—1892)干脆将其付之一炬,而朗费罗(Henry Wadsworth Longfellow, 1807—1882)、洛威尔(James Russell Lowell, 1819—1891)、霍姆斯(Oliver Wendell Holmes, 1809—1894)等功成名就的诗人们也都对它不屑一顾。公众则认为这些诗作太过大胆的性描写有伤风化,甚至提出删节要求。唯爱默生(Ralph Waldo Emerson, 1803—1882)独具慧眼,他敏锐地意识到新大陆已"诞生了一个伟人",并在给惠特曼的回信里盛赞《草叶集》,后来他与惠特曼的交往成了美国文学史上的一段佳话,惠特曼在1856年9月推出《草叶集》增订版时特意将那封如今已成为美国文学史上一篇重要文献的回信全文刊在封底。

爱默生的两个散文系列及《生活的准则》一并称为"美国的世俗圣经",并且强调它对美国民族性格的塑造作用无与伦比:无论你写诗与否,"如果你是美国人,那么沃尔特·惠特曼就是你的精神父母"。① 评论界普遍认为《草叶集》从语言和题材上奠定了美国诗歌的基础,豪放粗犷、不拘一格的惠特曼诗风对后世美国文坛的影响是显而易见的;借用布鲁姆的话来说,"惠特曼之后的美国诗人无一能够宣称完全不受他的影响。一代又一代作家的诗歌作品里都传出惠特曼的回声——从第一次世界大战后那些心灰意冷到极点的现代主义作家,到20世纪20年代哈莱姆文艺复兴中脱颖而出的明星人物,再到五六十年代'垮掉派'和自白派诗人中的最玩世不恭者"。其中最耳熟能详的一例当属"垮掉派"核心人物之一艾伦·金斯堡(Allen Ginsberg, 1926—1997),惠特曼的影子在他身上清晰可见。事实上,惠特曼的影响力不仅仅局限于美国,而且是世界性的,对其他国家的诗歌艺术也同样产生了深远的影响;比如,现代诗人郭沫若是我国最早接触惠特曼自由体诗的诗人之一,五四时期的新体诗《女神》直接从《草叶集》中吸取了精华,《匪徒颂》更是将惠特曼誉为文艺革命家。

Song of Myself (I, II, VI & LII)②

I

I Celebrate myself, and sing myself,
And what I assume you shall assume,
For every atom belonging to me as good③ belongs to you.

I loafe④ and invite my soul,
I lean and loafe at my ease observing a spear of summer grass.

My tongue, every atom of my blood, form'd from this soil, this air,
Born here of parents born here from parents the same, and their parents the same,
I, now thirty-seven years old in perfect health begin,
Hoping to cease not till death.⑤
Creeds and schools in abeyance⑥,
Retiring back a while sufficed⑦ at what they are, but never forgotten,
I harbor for good or bad,⑧ I permit to speak at every hazard,⑨
Nature without check with original energy.

---

① Harold Bloom. "Introduction to Leaves of Grass", in Harold Bloom, ed., *Leaves of Grass*. New York: Penguin Classics, 2005, pp. xxi-xxx.
② 该诗自1855年作为《草叶集》的开篇诗章面世以来,历经修改,存在多个不同版本;初版未分诗节,后来的版本则划分为52个诗节。这里选取的版本录自美国诗人学会(Academy of American Poets)官方网站"poets.org"(http://www.poets.org/viewmedia.php/prmMID/15755),与《希思文选》(*Heath Anthology*)中收录的版本有所不同。
③ as good: as well, also.
④ loafe. =loaf,[口] 虚度光阴。
⑤ begin后面省略了动词不定式to sing;Hoping to cease not 正常语序应为Hoping not to cease,意为"希望不停地唱下去"。
⑥ in abeyance:处于暂时搁置(或中止)状态。
⑦ sufficed:此处相当于satisfied。
⑧ harbor在句中为动词,表示"拥抱",其宾语nature被挪至下一行开头,该句意为"我一味怀抱自然"。
⑨ at every hazard意为"无所顾忌",与下一行的without check意思相近。

II

Houses and rooms are full of perfumes... the shelves
    are crowded with perfumes,
I breathe the fragrance myself, and know it and like it,
The distillation would intoxicate me also, but I shall not let it.

The atmosphere is not a perfume... it has no taste
    of the distillation... it is odorless,
It is for my mouth forever... I am in love with it,
I will go to the bank by the wood and become undisguised and naked,
I am mad for it to be in contact with me.

The smoke of my own breath,
Echoes, ripples, and buzzed whispers... loveroot, silkthread,
    crotch and vine,①
My respiration and inspiration②... the beating of my heart...
    the passing of blood and air through my lungs,
The sniff of green leaves and dry leaves, and of the shore
    and darkcolored sea-rocks, and of hay in the barn,
The sound of the belched words of my voice... words loosed
    to the eddies of the wind,

A few light kisses... a few embraces... reaching around of arms,
The play of shine and shade on the trees as the supple boughs wag,
The delight alone or in the rush of the streets, or along
    the fields and hill-sides,
The feeling of health... the full-noon trill③... the song of me
    rising from bed and meeting the sun.

Have you reckoned a thousand acres much? Have you reckoned
    the earth much?
Have you practiced so long to learn to read?
Have you felt so proud to get at the meaning of poems?

Stop this day and night with me and you shall possess the origin
    of all poems,
You shall possess the good of the earth and sun... there are
    millions of suns left,
You shall no longer take things at second or third hand... nor
    look through the eyes of the dead, nor feed on the spectres in books,
You shall not look through my eyes either, nor take things from me,
You shall listen to all sides and filter them from yourself.

---

① loveroot, silkthread, / crotch and vine: 爱根、丝线、桠枝和藤蔓。
② respiration and inspiration: 呼与吸。
③ the full-noon trill: 正午时的颤音。

VI

A child said *What is the grass?* fetching it to me with full
    hands;
How could I answer the child? I do not know what it is any
    more than he.
I guess it must be the flag of my disposition[①], out of hopeful
    green stuff woven.

Or I guess it is the handkerchief of the Lord,
A scented gift and remembrancer designedly dropt,[②]
Bearing the owner's name someway in the corners, that we
    may see and remark, and say *Whose*?
Or I guess the grass is itself a child, the produced babe of
    the vegetation.

Or I guess it is a uniform hieroglyphic,[③]
And it means, Sprouting alike in broad zones and narrow
    zones,
Growing among black folks as among white,
Kanuck, Tuckahoe, Congressman, Cuff,[④] I give them the
    same, I receive then the same.

And now it seems to me the beautiful uncut hair of graves.

Tenderly will I use you curling grass,
It may be you transpire[⑤] from the breasts of young men,
It may be you are from old people, or from offspring taken,
It may be if I had known them I would have loved them,
    soon out of their mother's laps,
And here you are the mothers' laps.

This grass is very dark to be from the white heads of old
    mothers,[⑥]
Darker than the colorless beards of old men,
Dark to come from under the faint red roofs of mouths.

O I perceive after all so many uttering tongues,
And I perceive they do not come from the roofs of mouths
    for nothing[⑦].

---

① the flag of my disposition: 我性情的旗帜, 由充满希望的绿色物质构成。
② remembrancer designedly dropt: 特意留下的纪念品。remembrancer 是指 something to remember one by; dropt 应为 dropped。
③ a uniform hieroglyphic: 一种统一的象形文字。hieroglyphic 是指有象征意义的东西。
④ Kanuck, Tuckahoe, Congressman, Cuff: 法裔加拿大人, 弗吉尼亚人, 议会会员, 黑人。Cuff 一词来自非洲, 拼法原为 Cuffee。
⑤ transpire: 原意为"出现、发生", 此处为"生长"。
⑥ 这片草叶颜色暗黑, 不会是从年老的母亲的白头上长出来的。
⑦ for nothing: 无端, 没有缘由。

I wish I could translate the hints about the dead young men and women,
And the hints about old men and mothers, and the offspring taken soon out of their laps.
What do you think has become of the young and old men?
And what do you think has become of the women and children?

They are alive and well somewhere,
The smallest sprout shows there is really no death,
And if ever there was it led forward life,① and does not wait at the end to arrest it,
And ceas'd the moment life appear'd.

All goes onward and outward, nothing collapses,
And to die is different from what any one supposed, and luckier.

LII

The spotted hawk swoops by and accuses me, he complains of my gab and my loitering.②

I too am not a bit tamed, I too am untranslatable,③
I sound my barbaric yawp④ over the roofs of the world.

The last scud of day holds back for me,⑤
It flings my likeness after the rest and true as any on the shadow'd wilds,
It coaxes me to the vapor and the dusk.⑥

I depart as air, I shake my white locks⑦ at the runaway sun,
I effuse my flesh in eddies, and drift it in lacy jags⑧.

I bequeath myself to the dirt to grow from the grass I love,
If you want me again look for me under your boot-soles.

You will hardly know who I am or what I mean,
But I shall be good health to you nevertheless,

---

① if ever there was 后面省略名词death, 主句中的代词it均指death, 动词arrest在此意为"阻挡, 抑制"。
② spotted hawk是"花斑雄鹰", my gab and my loitering译为"我的饶舌和游荡"。
③ untranslatable: 难以理解的, 无法解释的。
④ barbaric yawp: 粗野的呼声。
⑤ scud: [主诗/文] 飘飞的云雾。此句可转译为"白天的最后步履为我停留"。
⑥ 这两行诗句可译为"它把我的形象投掷在其他一切形象的后面, 如同它们一样确实, 把我/丢在暗影重重的野地, 它诱劝我走近雾霭和暮色。"
⑦ locks: [诗] 头发。
⑧ jag: a sharp projection, 意为"突出的尖角"。lacy jags是指花边状的尖突, 用来形容汹涌翻滚的波涛。

And filter and fibre your blood.①

Failing to fetch me at first keep encouraged,
Missing me one place search another,
I stop somewhere waiting for you.

1855年7月4日，惠特曼自费出版了《草叶集》，这一天刚好是美国的独立日。惠特曼在自序里以先知的口吻指出"一个诗人必须和他的民族相称"，"他的精神应该和他的国家的精神相呼应"。此外，他还曾多次宣称，之所以把诗集取名为"草叶集"，是因为草叶是最普通、最有生命力的东西，象征着当时正在蓬勃发展的美国。诗集通过"自我"感受的抒发和"自我"形象的塑造，热情歌颂了资本主义上升时期的美国时代精神。《自我之歌》②是《草叶集》中最长的一首诗，长达1,336行，内容几乎包括了作者毕生的主要思想；作为惠特曼最重要的诗歌之一，它集中反映了纽约和长岛各劳动阶层的生活：船夫、挖蛤蜊者、屠夫的小伙计、铁匠、赶马车的黑人、木匠、纺纱女、排字工、筑路者、拉纤者，应有尽有；这些人物代表了美国人的整体形象，被平等地赋予了高贵品质。这首诗通常被认为是惠特曼最优秀的代表作，最为充分地体现出诗人颂扬劳动和普通劳动者、讴歌人类平等、高唱自由新世界的民主精神。

在惠特曼的诗歌世界里，"自我"是一个重要概念。③1881年版《草叶集》的开篇短诗《我歌唱一个人的自身》便对此有所界定：

> 我歌唱一个人的自身，一个单一的个别的人，
> 不过要用民主的这个词、全体这个词的声音。
>
> 我歌唱从头到脚的生理学，
> 我说不单止外貌和脑子，整个形体更值得歌吟，
> 而且，与男性平等，我也歌唱女性。
>
> 我歌唱现代的人，
> 那情感、意向和能力上的巨大生命，
> 他愉快，能采取合乎神圣法则的最自由的行动。④

显然，诗中勾勒出的"现代人"自我形象具有多重性：既强调个性，又涵盖整体；不仅赞美灵魂，而且歌颂肉体；无论身份贵贱，不分男女性别，全都富于乐观向上的激情、律动的活力和强大的生命力，在神

---

① filter and fibre your blood：滤净和充实你的血液。
② 诗题最初由徐志摩译为《我自己的歌》，后来楚图南改译《自己之歌》，赵萝蕤又译作《我自己的歌》，另外还有《我自己之歌》的译法。
③ 库克、梅森、米勒等评论家曾分别从不同角度指出"自我"概念的阐释对于理解全诗至关重要，详见Cook, Alice L. "A Note on Whitman's Symbolism in 'Song of Myself.'" *Modern Language Notes* 65.4 (1950): 228-32; Mason, John B. "Walt Whitman's Catalogues: Rhetorical Means for Two Journeys in 'Song of Myself.'" *American Literature* 45.1 (1973): 34-49; Miller, James E. *Walt Whitman*. New York: Twayne Publishers, 1962.
④ 本章引用的惠特曼诗句均出自楚图南、李野光译《草叶集》（人民文学出版社，1994年）。英文原文如下：
One's-Self I sing—a simple, separate Person;
Yet utter the word Democratic, the word En-masse.

Of Physiology from top to toe I sing;
Not physiognomy alone, nor brain alone, is worthy for the muse—
I say the Form complete is worthier far;
The Female equally with the male I sing.

Of Life immense in passion, pulse, and power,
Cheerful—for freest action form'd, under the laws divine,
The Modern Man I sing.

圣法则的约束下享有"最自由的行动"。①值得注意的是,诗人用了"一个人的自身"(One's Self)而不是"自我"(Myself)这样的字眼,有效地建立起作者与读者之间的纽带。同样,《自我之歌》的"自我"也并非局限于诗人的自我,第一人称叙述颇有助于获得读者的认同;正如诗歌开篇所称,"我赞美我自己,歌唱我自己,/我所讲的一切,将对你们也一样适合"。事实上,这首诗在《草叶集》初版发表时并无标题,也未分小节,次年推出的第二版中加上标题"沃尔特·惠特曼,一个美国人的诗歌",1860年第三版将其简化为"沃尔特·惠特曼",1867年第四版被划分为52个小节,直到1881年终版才采用了"自我之歌"这一标题;在这个过程中,诗人的"自我"也超越了传统的个体身份界限,获得了更为宽泛的意义和普适价值,由"小我"走向"大我"。②

当代文学史家将惠特曼对自我身份的深切关注和智性思考归因于19世纪下半叶美国的政治气候③:由奴隶制、妇女权利、宗教复兴等问题引发的争端乃至内战使这个新兴的国家陷入危机,诗人正是在这种语境下提出"教条和学派且暂时搁开,……不论是善是恶,我将随意之所及,/毫无顾忌,以一种原始的活力述说自然"的诗歌创作主张,发出破除传统束缚、提倡民主平等的呼声,并力图从大自然中寻求佐证。诗人坦言"我愿意走到林边的河岸上,去掉一切人为的虚饰,赤裸了全身,/我疯狂地渴望能这样接触到我自己";而与大自然亲密接触并融合后的"自我"便具有了自然的属性和神性:"和我在一处呆过一日一夜,你就会有了一切诗歌的泉源,/你将会得到大地和太阳的一切美善,(还有千万个太阳留在那里,)/你将不再会间接又间接地去认识事物,也不会通过死人的眼睛去观看一切,也不会以书本里的假象和鬼影作为你的粮食,/你也不会通过我的眼睛观察,从我去获得一切,/你将静静地向各方面倾听,经过你自己而滤取它们。"具体说来,诗中的"草叶"便充当了感知主体和客体的双重角色,诗人将自我融于大自然,声称"我将我自己遗赠给泥土,然后再从我所爱的草叶中生长出来"。这一意象还浓缩了普通人的自我特质,拉近了不同身份人群之间、人与自然以及生与死之间的距离:对于一个孩子提出的"草是什么"的问题,诗人给予了多重答案——它代表了希望,是神的赠礼;它"自身便是一个孩子",也是书写平等的"一种统一的象形文字";它是从坟墓上长出来的,也是从青年人、老年人、婴孩身上长出来的,象征着永生。

美国批评家理查德·蔡斯认为,这首长诗是一种包括"意象派似的小诗、现实主义城乡风俗画、各式各样的目录、说教、哲理探讨、滑稽插曲、自由漫谈和抒情沉思"的特殊组合。④总体上看,诗作内容丰富,结构松散,文体多样,观点驳杂;这里节选的第一、三、六和五十二小节不仅在主题,而且在形式上也很好地体现出惠特曼诗歌的主要特色。每个诗节都由一组松散的句子构成,不仅没有严格的韵脚,而且打破了传统的诗歌形式,开创了一种散文化的自由诗体,其特征包括:句子的排列长短交替,短则十几字,长则多达近三十个字。另外,诗人尽管使用了近乎口语的语言,散文化风格却暗藏着一种特殊的节奏感,很大程度上来自诗人个性化的遣词造句,比如词汇重复、句式递进等。如最后一节所吟,"苍鹰在附近飞翔着,他斥责我,怪我不该饶舌和游荡。/我也一点没有被驯服,我也是不可解说的。/我在世界的屋脊上发出我的粗野的呼声";可以说,《自我之歌》以其独特的语言形式最大限度地释放了诗人的"自我",放飞了美国的民族个性,因此堪称诗歌版的美国独立宣言。

 思考题

1. Walt Whitman is often considered to be a larger-than-life poet, writing expansive lines and embracing the whole of America as his inspiration. How does Whitman call attention to small objects in this poem? Why do you think he called his life's work *Leaves of Grass*? What does "a leaf of

---

① 这里包含了惠特曼与美国超验主义的分歧,尽管超验主义思想最初也是他的一个灵感源泉。超验主义者强调的是精神(或超灵)、个人(或自立)和自然(或神性象征),有摒弃肉体和物质的倾向;此外,作为浪漫主义的一个分支,超验主义带有脱离现实的乌托邦色彩,但惠特曼却在庸常生活的细节铺陈中亦表现出现实主义的一面。
② Greenspan, Ezra, ed. *Walt Whitman's "Song of Myself": A Sourcebook and Critical Edition*. New York: Routledge, 2005.
③ Erkkila, Betsy. *Whitman the Political Poet*. New York: Oxford University Press, 1989.
④ Chase, Richard. "Walt Whitman, 1819—1892." In *American Writers: A Collection of Literary Biographies*. Vol. 4. Ed. Leonard Unger. New York: Charles Scribner's Sons, 1974.

grass" mean to Whitman? To you?
2. Describe Whitman's conceptions of self. What is the relationship between the soul and the body, and which is more important, in his view? How do you account for the eroticism in Whitman's poetry?
3. How does this poem represent Whitman as a romanticist? How does Whitman contribute to the ongoing evolution of such concepts as self-reliance, individual freedom, and democracy respectively?
4. Two of the most important structures in Whitman's poetry are the list and the anecdote. What functions do they serve respectively? Why might he be using these rather than traditional structures like rhyme?
5. Describe Whitman's diction. What kind of language does he use? Does this have implications politically? Poetically?
6. What is uniquely American about Whitman's poetry? Consider both substance and style.

Leaves of Grass (1855—1881)
"Crossing Brooklyn Ferry"
"I Hear America Singing"
"O Captain! My Captain!"
"Out of the Cradle Endlessly Rocking"
"To You"
"Spontaneous Me"
"When Lilacs Last in the Door-yard Bloom'd"
Democratic Vistas (1871)

Callow, Philip. *From Noon to Starry Night: A Life of Walt Whitman*. Chicago: Ivan R. Dee, 1992.
Reynolds, David S. *Walt Whitman's America: A Cultural Biography*. New York: Vintage Books, 1995.
Stacy, Jason. *Walt Whitman's Multitudes: Labor Reform and Persona in Whitman's Journalism and the First Leaves of Grass, 1840—1855*. New York: Peter Lang Publishing, 2008.

（林　斌）

Emily Dickinson (1830—1886)

埃米莉·狄金森

 作者简介

埃米莉·狄金森与惠特曼一起被誉为19世纪美国文学史上两位划时代的民族诗人、独立"美国诗风"的创始人。狄金森在世时过着一种深居简出、特立独行的生活,大约只有不到十首诗歌面世。然而,她身后却留下1800首诗,其中包括定本的1775首与新近随狄金森秘密日记《孤独是迷人的》曝光的25首。这些诗作以突破传统的多样题材和个性化多变诗风被公认为美国现代诗发轫之作,而诗人独坐世界一隅品评人生百味的非凡勇气、细腻情感和哲学思考则被看作现代女性写作典范。

这位天才女诗人出生于马萨诸塞州阿默斯特的一个富足中产阶级家庭,其家族成员在当地享有较高的社会地位和威望,与爱默生等文化名流都有过交往。祖父塞缪尔·福勒·狄金森毕业于达特茅斯大学,是一名律师,也是阿默斯特学院创办人之一;父亲爱德华笃信卡尔文宗,是耶鲁大学校友、知名律师,曾在州议会、众议院担任职务,并在阿默斯特学院主持财务工作多年。自1840年起,狄金森在阿默斯特学院就读七年,师从科学家兼神学家爱德华·希契科克,后到南哈德利女子神学院(现为曼荷莲学院)求学,但仅一年就以健康状况不佳为由退学回家。她在阿默斯特学院研修过拉丁语、英国文学等多门科目,涉猎范围很广,早年便显露出超群的智力与才华。随后她逐渐淡出公众视线,几乎足不出户,并且谢绝会客,被当地人称为"阿默斯特的修女",1886年5月患肾病去世。

狄金森大约二十岁开始写诗,其诗歌创作是在几乎不为人知的情况下进行的,直到其妹拉维尼娅整理她的遗物时才吃惊地发现了写有八百多首诗歌的四十册手稿。这些尘封的诗作一经面世便轰动一时。狄金森诗歌遗作的出版过程经历了收集改写、形式还原、恢复顺序等三个关键环节。最早版本是狄金森去世后不久由希金森与托德共同编辑的诗集,于1890、1891和1896年分别推出三个分册。1914年,另一部诗集《孤犬》(*The Single Hound*)由狄金森的侄女玛莎·狄金森·比安奇(Martha Dickinson Bianchi)编辑出版。然而,这些诗集的共同特点是,为了迎合当时公众的诗歌欣赏趣味,编者均对狄金森的诗作进行了不同程度的改动,擅自修改了诗中不合乎传统规范的标点符号、措辞和韵律,同时也打乱了这些诗歌的排列顺序。1955年,托马斯·H.约翰逊(Thomas H. Johnson)出版了按时序排列的三卷本《狄金森诗歌全集》,从形式上还原了狄金森遗作的原貌,使其个性化诗风首次完全呈现在世人面前。1981年,哈佛大学出版社推出《艾米莉·狄金森手稿诗集》(*The Manuscript Books of Emily Dickinson*),编者拉尔夫·W.富兰克林(R.W. Franklin)在对狄金森诗歌手稿上的物理痕迹(如污迹、针孔等)进行研究的基础上,进一步还原了诗稿的排列顺序,诗人亲手结集成册的原初意图得以彰显。至此,狄金森对英语诗歌的创新贡献一览无余。

狄金森是一位直觉型诗人,跃动在诗行中的生命激情和思想火花与其生前那独具神秘色彩的封闭生活状态形成了鲜明对照。她没有抽象的诗歌理论,却在1862年给希金森的信中给诗歌下过一个颇为感性的定义:"如果我读一本书,它使我浑身发冷,以至于火都无法使我暖和过来,我知道这就是诗歌。如果我身体的感觉仿佛天灵盖被掀开一样,我知道这就是诗歌。这些就是我感知它的唯一方式。还有其他方式吗?"狄金森的诗歌既有日常家庭生活题材,又有抽象深奥命题思考;不仅具有很强的抒情性,而且还富于哲性内涵。评论家往往会在她的诗作中找到17世纪玄学派与19世纪浪漫主义诗风及创作理念的明显印记;超验主义代表人物爱默生的个人主义和自助精神、梭罗的自然观和反物质主义都直接影响了她的诗歌主题;新英格兰文学的地方色彩,如内敛、节制、精练等特征,在她的诗作里也有体现。狄金森善于在最平凡的事物和经历中发现美、恐怖以及包含反讽、悖论等的不平凡意义,在创作中摆脱了当时盛行的华而不实的浪漫诗风影响,以大胆直白的诗性语言、简单明快的诗歌意象表现了她对人类境遇的敏锐洞察力。其诗作形式多变,颇具独创性和个性化特点,如:无标题、押半韵、改变字母大小写和飘忽不定的断句分行策略等。标点符号的运用更是与众不同,她在诗句中使用许多倾斜角度不同、长短不一的破折号,使抑扬格、音步、节奏等诗歌元素的搭配产生突兀的起伏跳动,以拓展诗句的特殊意义层面,从而有效地再现了她对物质、意识和精神世界之复杂性的个性化认识。

Hope

"Hope" is the thing with feathers—
That perches① in the soul—
And sings the tune without the words—
And never stops — at all—

And sweetest — in the Gale② — is heard;
And sore must be the storm—
That could abash③ the little Bird
That kept so many warm—

I've heard it in the chillest land—
And on the strangest Sea—
Yet, never, in Extremity,④
It asked a crumb⑤ — of Me.

　　这首小诗是狄金森的早期作品,原为《生命》(*Life*)的第六部分。在这首诗里,"希望"这个抽象概念被比作鸟儿,赋予了栩栩如生的自然意象:这只小鸟长着羽毛,高栖在枝头,在大风中不间断地唱着无言的歌曲;它现身于最寒冷的土地和最偏远的海洋,哪怕身处绝境也无欲无求地甜美高歌。与之相似,希望栖息于灵魂,无条件地给人带来温暖和慰藉;它无处不在,历经磨难却永不消亡,困境之中愈发彰显可贵。如同猛烈的暴风雨使鸟儿局促不安一样,强烈的负面情绪也会毁灭自身的希望,造成他人的痛苦;所以说,只要不去折断它的翅膀,这希望之鸟就会振翅高飞,一直自由歌唱。

　　该诗体现了狄金森诗歌常见的布道体风格,源自于《圣经·诗篇》和宗教赞美诗。诗歌一开篇便推出全诗的一个主导性隐喻(希望被比作小鸟),随后层层展开论述,通过描写鸟儿的所作所为(无休止地歌唱、暴风雨中无所畏惧、险恶环境下无欲无求)歌颂其美好品性,从而揭示出希望的本质特征:它拥有顽强的生命力,并且无条件地给予。作为狄金森的早期作品,该诗在主题和语言上均未达到后期成熟诗作的复杂性和爆发力,但诗人高超的语言驾驭能力仍可窥见一斑,比如第二小节中出现的"abash"(使尴尬,使局促不安)一词便被评论界看作神来之笔——这个词一举粉碎了前几行诗句构建的美好意境,有效地推出了严酷现实对理想的暴力侵扰,即艰难困苦给希望带来的打击和重创并不亚于暴风雨对柔弱小鸟造成的威胁和摧残。

　　从形式上看,这首诗采用的是狄金森诗歌惯常使用的三步抑扬格,有时会在诗句末尾附加上第四个重音(如:"And sings the tune without the words—"),而且韵流常会被女诗人标志性的长破折号调节或打断(如:"And never stops—at all—")。此外,一如狄金森的多数抒情诗,该作品的韵脚并不严格,大致遵循"ABCB"模式,但在这首诗中由于出现了"words"与"heard"和"Bird","Extremity"与"Sea""Me"的隔行押韵现象,韵脚总体上表现为松散的"ABBB"模式。

---

① perch:(鸟)飞落,栖息。
② gale:大风,狂风。
③ abash:使局促,使窘迫。
④ in Extremity:极窘迫的境地,绝境。
⑤ crumb:点滴,少许。这两句的意思是:但它纵然身处绝境,也不向我索取分毫。

思考题

1. Dickinson's poems often introduce an idea, and then develop it with a sequence of metaphoric images. What images does the poet present in this poem? How do they work as metaphors?
2. In this poem, the speaker describes hope as a bird ("the thing with feathers") that perches in the soul. How does the poet render this nature image consistent throughout the work?
3. Compare this early Dickinson poem to a later one (such as "My Life Closed Twice Before Its Close"). How has her work changed? How has it remained the same? Did Dickinson experience much development as a poet as she grew older, or did her work largely remain the same?

Because I Could Not Stop for Death

Because I could not stop for Death—
He kindly stopped for me—
The Carriage held but just Ourselves—
And Immortality.

We slowly drove—He knew no haste①
And I had put away
My labor and my leisure too,
For His Civility—②

We passed the School, where Children strove③
At Recess—in the Ring—
We passed the Fields of Gazing Grain—
We passed the Setting Sun—

Or rather—He④ passed us—
The Dews drew⑤ quivering and chill—
For only Gossamer, my Gown—⑥
My Tippet—only Tulle—

We paused before a House that seemed
A Swelling of the Ground—

---

① He knew no haste: 他(死神)不慌不忙。其中 knew 与 no 押头韵,类似例子还有: Because I could not stop for Death (line 1); My labor and my leisure too (line 7); At Recess—in the Ring—(line 10); Gazing Grain (line 11); Setting Sun (line 12); For only Gossamer, my Gown (line 15); My Tippet—only Tulle (line 16); toward Eternity (line 24)。
② For His Civility: 因为他彬彬有礼,为了他的礼让。
③ strove: 动词原形为"strive",这里是指孩子们你推我操的动作。下一行是时间和地点: 课间休息时间,在圆形广场。此行中的"We passed"句式重复三次,在修辞上称作"首语重复法"(anaphora)。
④ 这里的 He 是指落日。
⑤ drew 在此意为"引起"。
⑥ 这两行诗句在语法上不完整,应为: For my gown is only gossamer and my tippet is only tulle.(因为我的外衣轻若游丝,我的披肩薄如轻纱。)此处的描述确立了叙述者的女性身份,这种衣着扮装暗指新娘的婚纱礼服,与死神的绅士形象共同营造了一个婚礼场景。

55

The Roof was scarcely visible—
The Cornice—in the Ground—

Since then—'tis① Centuries—and yet
Feels shorter than the Day
I first surmised② the Horses' Heads
Were toward Eternity—

  《因为我不能停下来等待死神》是一首抒情诗，首次发表于诗人身后结集出版的诗集《诗歌：第一系列》(*Poems: Series* 1)，该系列三个分册分别于1890、1891和1896年推出，在狄金森去世后不久由希金森(Thomas Wentworth Higginson)与托德(Mabel Loomis Todd)二位友人共同编辑而成。这首诗最初被编辑命名为《敞篷马车》("Chariot")，其主题涉及时间、死亡和永生，主要通过拟人手法表达了诗人对待死亡的达观态度：死神被比作一位风度翩翩的绅士，不慌不忙地赶着一辆四轮敞篷马车，彬彬有礼地前来迎娶未婚妻；由生到死的整个过程被比作一段从容而悠闲的旅途，乘客经过了分别代表人生三个不同阶段的学校(童年)、麦田(壮年)和落日(老年)，一路看尽沿途风景，感受到"寒露透薄衫"的清冷凄凉，于傍晚时分抵达坟墓，最终获得永生。

  值得注意的是，尽管该诗围绕死亡展开，但叙述者自始至终表现出一种积极向上的生活态度：这位女性一生忙于劳作和休闲，根本无暇顾及死亡，当死亡来临时坦然面对，欣然接受命运的安排，死后则体悟到来世与永生的奥秘。事实上，诗歌首尾呼应，揭开了永生之谜：原来死神的马车上从一开始就载有第三位乘客——永生；不仅如此，这架马车虽驶向坟墓，但马头却朝向永恒。此外，叙述者的新娘装扮代表了新生活的开始，并非生命的终结；来世的不同时间体验将几个世纪压缩为"不到一天"，也从侧面暗示着新生活的愉悦，而非困苦。可以说，这些细节共同构建了诗人个性化的死亡观：既是自然之无尽轮回的一个组成部分，死亡何所惧？

  20世纪美国批评家、诗人艾伦·塔特(Allen Tate, 1899—1979)曾经给予这首诗极高的评价，认为它不仅代表了狄金森诗歌的最高艺术成就，而且称得上"英语诗歌中最伟大的作品之一；就连细枝末节也无可挑剔"。在他看来，这首诗的韵律充满动感，精准的意象之间相互帮衬，实现了与主旨的完美结合。从形式上讲，该诗由六个四行诗节组成，诗句交替出现四步抑扬格和三步抑扬格；除第三节以外的各个诗节在第二、四行上押尾韵，只是其中一部分是相似韵或视觉韵，而第三节二、三、四行中的"Ring""Gazing""Setting"等词分别押中间韵，"held"与"Ourselves"(第3行)、"slowly""drove"与"no"(第5行)、"Dews"与"drew"(第14行)都是行中韵。从修辞上讲，除拟人以外，诗人还运用了象征、头韵、首语重复、悖论等手法。正如塔特所说，各种诗歌元素的巧妙运用展现了诗人"以深邃文化为创作源泉的深刻头脑"。

 思考题

1. Do you believe the speaker's relaxed attitude toward death? Sometimes we pretend to be confident when we're nervous and brave when we're scared. Is this an example of that? Which lines of the poem support your opinion?
2. The speaker seems to speak fondly and clearly of her memory of death. Why might the speaker not fear death? What do you think that means about the afterlife?
3. If Dickinson were writing this today, do you think she could still illustrate the journey to death with as a carriage ride, or would that be silly? What would be a good present-day equivalent?

---

① 'tis：同it is。此句暗示叙述者已死去多时，长达几个世纪。其中的Centuries与shorter than the Day构成悖论修辞法。
② first surmised：第一次猜测到。

Try reading the poem out loudly. How does the sound of the poem affect your reading of it? Think about the action in the poem (the driving, the stopping). When does the sound mimic the action?

 The Poems of Emily Dickinson (1999)
The Complete Poems of Emily Dickinson (1960)

Bloom, Harold. *Emily Dickinson*. Broomall, PA: Chelsea House Publishers, 1999.
Farr, Judith, ed. *Emily Dickinson: A Collection of Critical Essays*. Upper Saddle River, New Jersey: Prentice Hall International Paperback Editions, 1996.
Martin, Wendy, ed. *The Cambridge Companion to Emily Dickinson*. Cambridge: Cambridge University Press, 2002.

（林　斌）

Edgar Allan Poe (1809—1849)
埃德加·爱伦·坡

 作者简介

埃德加·爱伦·坡,19世纪美国著名小说家、诗人、文学评论家,以神秘惊悚的题材、诡异空灵的文风和瑰丽唯美的想象著称。作为美国首位卖文为生的知名作家,坡开创了美国大众文化传统的先河,被视为西方侦探小说鼻祖、哥特式恐怖小说大师、科幻小说先驱;他也是首位将注意力引向文学作品的文体效果和结构特征的评论家,故被看作西方唯美主义运动的先行者;他亦给象征主义诗歌和现代派文学带来了深远的影响,波德莱尔、马拉美等作家均公开承认继承了他的衣钵,因此他被认为是美国文学史上最早获得国际声誉并产生世界影响的作家之一。评论界普遍认为,其作品风格在任何时代都是"独一无二"的,代表作有诗歌《乌鸦》("The Raven")、短篇小说《厄舍古屋的倒塌》("The Fall of the House of Usher")等。

由于爱伦·坡的生平自述多有夸大和不实之处,也由于读者常将作家本人与其笔下的病态叙述者混为一谈,并难以理解他所倡导的创作美学自律原则与他那散漫、放荡的生活作风之间表现出的巨大反差,他的个人生活始终是公众争议的焦点,与他的创作生涯密不可分。事实上,坡一生命运多舛。他于1809年出生在波士顿,父母均为演员,父亲在他出生后不久离家出走,母亲在他不到三岁时去世,里士满烟草富商约翰·爱伦将他收养,送他去读最好的寄宿学校,后于1826年资助他上弗吉尼亚大学。大学期间,坡一开始便显示出高超的语言天分,却沉迷于赌博、酗酒,在养父拒绝代为偿还赌债之后被迫辍学,到波士顿出版了他的首部诗集《帖木儿及其他诗》(Tamerlane and Other Poems, 1827),并改名换姓加入了美国陆军。他于1829年离开军队,在养母去世后与养父有过短暂和解,养父通过关系将他送入西点军校学习,同年他推出诗集《阿尔·阿拉夫、帖木儿及小诗》(Al Aaraaf, Tamerlane and Minor Poems)。不料,养父拒绝继续为他提供资助并于1830年再婚,使得坡继承遗产的希望破灭;他很快便因故意违纪而被军校开除,1831年靠军校同学筹款出版了《诗集》("Poems")。

随后,继早年的诗歌创作热情之后,坡将写作重心转向随笔和小说。他辗转于巴尔的摩、里士满、费城、纽约等地,担任过《南方文学信使》(Southern Literary Messenger)等多家文学刊物的编辑,以他犀利的批判眼光和独到的文学见解成为小有名气的文学评论家。这期间,坡主要以写作为生,重要作品不断问世:1833年短篇小说《瓶中手稿》("Found in a Bottle")获巴尔的摩《星期六游客报》(Saturday Visitor)举办的征文比赛一等奖;1838年以连载方式发表唯一一部中长篇小说《阿瑟·戈登·皮姆的故事》(The Narrative of Arthur Gordon Pym);1839年出版《怪异故事集》(Tales of the Grotesque and Arabesque);1843年因短篇小说《金甲虫》("The Gold Bug")在费城获奖而获得一定的文学声誉;1845年诗作《乌鸦》在纽约的发表轰动一时。尽管坡在文坛声名鹊起,但他一直过着颠沛流离、穷困潦倒的生活,1836年同十三岁的表妹弗吉尼亚结婚,引起诸多非议,弗吉尼亚1847年死于肺结核;坡本人也贫病交加,1849年酗酒后倒在巴尔的摩街头昏迷不醒,几天后去世,评论界对他的死因仍存在争议。

尽管爱伦·坡主要以短篇小说闻名于世,其诗歌成就同样举足轻重,《乌鸦》《安娜贝尔·李》("Annabel Lee")、《丽诺》("Lenore")、《钟声》("The Bells")等被奉为文学史上的经典名篇,确立了坡作为诗人的声名和地位。如前所述,坡的早期作品以诗歌为主,毕生不断对这些诗作进行修改润色,晚期又推出《尤拉路姆》("Ulalume")、《征服者蠕虫》("The Conqueror Worm")、《梦中梦》("A Dream within a Dream")、《海之城》("The City in the Sea")等佳作。坡的诗歌在主题和风格上与其小说创作一脉相承,充满怪诞意象、感伤情调和唯美韵律。在主题方面,坡的诗歌涉及爱与死亡、人生的宿命与无常、内在的自我矛盾、自然的美好、人类想象的创造与破坏力等。在风格方面,坡最著名的文艺理论是"效果论",他在《创作哲学》("The Philosophy of Composition", 1846)中指出"在短篇小说这种文艺形式当中,每一个事件,每一个描写的细节,甚至每一个字句,都应该收到某种统一的效果,某种预想的效果,或某种印象主义的效果"。对坡来说,文学创作中最重要的莫过于完整思想的美学再现;他运用重复以及头韵、内韵和谐韵等文学技法，力图将各种诗歌元素整合为一个旨在达到预期效果的有机整体，对现代英语诗歌的发展做出了独特的贡献。

The Raven

Once upon a midnight dreary, while I pondered, weak and weary,①
Over many a quaint and curious volume of forgotten lore—
While I nodded, nearly napping, suddenly there came a tapping,
As of some one gently rapping, rapping at my chamber② door—
"'Tis some visitor," I muttered, "tapping at my chamber door—
　　Only this and nothing more."

Ah, distinctly I remember it was in the bleak December;
And each separate dying ember wrought③ its ghost upon the floor.
Eagerly I wished the morrow④;—vainly I had sought to borrow
From my books surcease⑤ of sorrow—sorrow for the lost Lenore—
For the rare and radiant maiden whom the angels name Lenore—
　　Nameless here for evermore.

And the silken, sad, uncertain rustling of each purple curtain
Thrilled me—filled me with fantastic terrors never felt before;
So that now, to still the beating of my heart, I stood repeating,
"'Tis some visitor entreating entrance at my chamber door—
Some late visitor entreating entrance at my chamber door;—
　　This it is⑥ and nothing more."

Presently my soul grew stronger; hesitating then no longer,
"Sir," said I, "or Madam, truly your forgiveness I implore;
But the fact is I was napping, and so gently you came rapping,
And so faintly you came tapping, tapping at my chamber door,
That I scarce⑦ was sure I heard you"—here I opened wide the door;—
　　Darkness there and nothing more.

Deep into that darkness peering, long I stood there wondering, fearing,
Doubting, dreaming dreams no mortal ever dared to dream before;
But the silence was unbroken, and the stillness gave no token,
And the only word there spoken was the whispered word, "Lenore?"

---

① weak and weary（虚弱疲乏，或慵懒疲竭）与下一行的 quaint and curious（古怪离奇）都是押头韵（alliteration）。
② chamber：[诗／文，或古] 私室（尤指卧室），比同义词 bedroom 更具阴郁的神秘色彩。
③ wrought：[古，诗，方] work 的过去式和过去分词。每一团奄奄一息的余烬都形成阴影伏在地板。
④ morrow：[诗] 翌日，次日，第二天。[古] 早晨。
⑤ surcease：[古] 停止，终止。我竭力读书，想以此排遣心中的哀伤。
⑥ 该句倒装表示强调，应为 It is this。
⑦ scarce：adv. [古，诗] 同 scarcely。

This I whispered, and an echo murmured back the word, "Lenore!"—
 Merely this and nothing more.
Back into the chamber turning, all my soul within me burning,
Soon again I heard a tapping somewhat louder than before.
"Surely," said I, "surely that is something at my window lattice;
Let me see, then, what thereat① is, and this mystery explore—
Let my heart be still a moment and this mystery explore;—
 'Tis the wind and nothing more!"

Open here I flung the shutter, when, with many a flirt and flutter②,
In there stepped a stately Raven of the saintly days of yore;③
Not the least obeisance made he; not a minute stopped or stayed he;
But, with mien of lord or lady,④ perched above my chamber door—
Perched upon a bust of Pallas⑤ just above my chamber door—
 Perched, and sat, and nothing more.

Then this ebony bird beguiling my sad fancy into smiling,
By the grave and stern decorum⑥ of the countenance it wore,
"Though thy crest be shorn and shaven⑦, thou," I said, "art sure no craven,⑧
Ghastly grim and ancient Raven wandering from the Nightly shore—
Tell me what thy lordly name is on the Night's Plutonian⑨ shore!"
 Quoth⑩ the Raven "Nevermore."

Much I marvelled this ungainly fowl to hear discourse so plainly,
Though its answer little meaning—little relevancy bore;
For we cannot help agreeing that no living human being
Ever yet was blest with seeing bird above his chamber door—
Bird or beast upon the sculptured bust above his chamber door,
 With such name as "Nevermore."

But the Raven, sitting lonely on the placid bust, spoke only
That one word, as if his soul in that one word he did outpour.
Nothing further then he uttered—not a feather then he fluttered—
Till I scarcely more than muttered⑪ "Other friends have flown before—
On the morrow he will leave me, as my hopes have flown before."
 Then the bird said "Nevermore."

---

① thereat: adv. 在那里。
② flirt and flutter: 摆动，颤动。这两个词押头韵，意为：心儿扑扑直跳。
③ 此句和接下来的两句均为倒装。stately 指仪表堂堂，saintly 意为神圣、圣洁，of yore 是从前、往昔。make obeisance: 鞠躬，致礼。
④ 以绅士淑女的风度。mien: 风度，风采。
⑤ a bust of Pallas: 帕拉斯女神的胸像，帕拉斯即希腊神话中的雅典娜（Athena）。
⑥ decorum: 端庄，正派。
⑦ 你的冠毛被剪除。shorn and shaven 又是一例头韵，动词 shorn 的原形是 shear。
⑧ 此行的 thy, thou 和 art 都是古英语说法，分别是 your, you 和 are。下文出现的 thee 为 thou 的宾格。
⑨ Plutonian: 阴间的，地府的。
⑩ Quoth: [古，谑] 说。
⑪ scarcely more than muttered: 几乎是喃喃自语。

Startled at the stillness broken by reply so aptly spoken,
"Doubtless," said I, "what it utters is its only stock and store①
Caught from some unhappy master whom unmerciful Disaster
Followed fast and followed faster till his songs one burden bore—
Till the dirges of his Hope that melancholy burden bore
    Of 'Never—nevermore.'"

But the Raven still beguiling my sad fancy into smiling,
Straight I wheeled a cushioned seat in front of bird, and bust and door;
Then, upon the velvet sinking②, I betook myself to linking③
Fancy unto fancy, thinking what this ominous bird of yore—
What this grim, ungainly, ghastly, gaunt and ominous bird of yore
    Meant in croaking "Nevermore."

This I sat engaged in guessing, but no syllable expressing
To the fowl whose fiery eyes now burned into my bosom's core;
This and more I sat divining④, with my head at ease reclining
On the cushion's velvet lining that the lamp-light gloated o'er,⑤
But whose velvet violet lining with the lamp-light gloating o'er,
    She shall press, ah, nevermore!⑥

Then, methought,⑦ the air grew denser, perfumed from an unseen censer
Swung by Seraphim⑧ whose foot-falls tinkled on the tufted floor.
"Wretch," I cried, "thy God hath lent thee—by these angels he hath sent thee
Respite—respite and nepenthe⑨, from thy memories of Lenore;
Quaff, oh quaff this kind nepenthe and forget this lost Lenore!"
    Quoth the Raven "Nevermore."

"Prophet!" said I, "thing of evil!—prophet still, if bird or devil!—
Whether Tempter⑩ sent, or whether tempest tossed thee here ashore,
Desolate yet all undaunted, on this desert land enchanted—
On this home by Horror haunted—tell me truly, I implore—
Is there—is there balm in Gilead?—tell me—tell me, I implore!"
    Quoth the Raven "Nevermore."

"Prophet!" said I, "thing of evil—prophet still, if bird or devil!
By that Heaven that bends above us—by that God we both adore—

---

① stock and store:押头韵,译为"存货,本钱"。
② sink 此指"坐下"。
③ betake oneself to doing sth.:[古] 去,往,投身于,专心于,致力于。
④ divine:v. 猜测。
⑤ 即 gloat over:爱慕地凝视。
⑥ 动词 press 的宾语应为 velvet violet lining,意为:用熨斗熨平紫色天鹅绒衬垫。
⑦ methought:[古] 我想,在我看来。
⑧ Seraphim:《圣经》旧约)撒拉弗,六翼天使。这里勾勒的形象是六翼天使手提着晃动的隐形香炉,脚步响在铺着簇绒地毯的地板上。
⑨ respite 意为"休养,休息";nepenthe 是古希腊传说中的忘忧药。
⑩ Tempter:魔鬼。

Tell this soul with sorrow laden if, within the distant Aidenn①,
It shall clasp a sainted maiden whom the angels name Lenore—
Clasp a rare and radiant maiden whom the angels name Lenore."
  Quoth the Raven "Nevermore."

"Be that word our sign in parting,② bird or fiend!" I shrieked, upstarting—
"Get thee back into the tempest and the Night's Plutonian shore!③
Leave no black plume as a token of that lie thy soul hath spoken!
Leave my loneliness unbroken!—quit the bust above my door!
Take thy beak from out my heart, and take thy form from off my door!"
  Quoth the Raven "Nevermore."

And the Raven, never flitting, still is sitting, still is sitting
On the pallid bust of Pallas just above my chamber door;
And his eyes have all the seeming of a demon's that is dreaming,
And the lamp-light o'er him streaming throws his shadow on the floor;
And my soul from out that shadow that lies floating on the floor
  Shall be lifted—nevermore!

  《乌鸦》是爱伦·坡的诗作里最著名的一首。创作于1844年的这首叙事诗讲述的是一位痛失爱人的男子在孤苦伶仃、心神恍惚的深夜里与一只乌鸦邂逅并交谈的故事；其灵感据说来自于狄更斯1841年出版的历史小说《巴纳比·拉奇》(*Barnaby Rudge*)，小说主人公拥有一只会讲话的宠物乌鸦，第五章出现乌鸦敲打百叶窗的情节。诗中描述的"幽灵般可怕"而"狰狞丑陋"的乌鸦实为一种以小动物、腐肉、果实和种子为食的体型较大的渡鸦，在民间传说和文学作品中它的出场本身往往就是一个不祥之兆乃至死亡的象征。与之呼应，坡将乌鸦现身的场景设定在12月的一个寒冷萧瑟的午夜，这个颇具超自然色彩的不速之客枯立在智慧女神的塑像上，沙哑刺耳的"永不复还"声声传达着令人毛骨悚然的冥界讯息，与诗歌开篇描述的窗外飒飒阴风、屋内重重暗影和突兀的敲门声共同营造出一派神秘与恐怖的哥特氛围。事实上，"永不复还"这句话一共重复了11次，既是乌鸦的名字，也是它对叙述者每次质询做出的一成不变的应答，将一场貌似荒诞不经的对话推向了对生与死、爱与永恒、希望与未知、真实与虚幻等人类生存价值的终极追问和哲理探寻。如评论界所称，全诗基调悲怆凄凉，源于不可逆转的绝望，随着一声声"永不复还"而加深，直至绝望到无以复加的终行。

  爱伦·坡最著名的文艺理论是"效果论"(unity of effect)：他力图在创作伊始先确立某种预期效果，再将主题、场景、基调、人物、冲突、情节设置等所有文学要素整合起来追求这种效果。他在《怪异故事集》序言中称"自己的作品绝大部分都是深思熟虑的苦心经营"。《乌鸦》这首诗堪称这种文学创作理念的完美体现：诗作在遣词造句方面极其考究，weary、dreary、bleak、dying、sorrow、sad、darkness、stillness、mystery、ebony、grave、stern、lonely、grim、ghastly、gaunt 等一系列词语的巧妙运用取得了一种阴郁、惊悚的整体效果；在音韵的处理上独具匠心，头韵、内韵和谐韵的大量使用以及近似音的超常排列、重读音节和非重读音节的规则交错（八步扬抑格）使诗行富于哀伤沉重的乐感，且每一节中都有一系列的短句构成长行，只在行间换气，真实地表现了叙述者低回哀婉的语调。《创作哲学》是爱伦·坡就其《乌鸦》一诗的创作谈，如将此文与他发表于1850年的《诗歌原理》("The Poetic Principle")对照阅读，即可更加全面清晰地了解坡的诗歌理念。

---

① Aidenn：坡虚拟的一个地名，暗指伊甸园(Eden)。
② Be that word our sign in parting：让这话做我们的道别之辞吧。此指上文的"永不复还"(Nevermore)。
③ 回你的暴风雨中去，回你那阴森的冥府彼岸！祈使句，thee 仅表示强调。

思考题

1. What is the setting of the poem? How does the setting contribute to the mood of the poem? How essential is the setting? Could the poem have taken place in another place or time?
2. Give a physical description of the raven. What might it represent? In the last stanza of the poem, the narrator is trapped in the raven's shadow. What does the shadow symbolize?
3. What are the conflicts in the poem? What types of conflict (physical, moral, intellectual, or emotional) do you read?
4. List five things you know about the narrator of the poem. Do you trust him/her? What six things does the narrator say/ask to which the raven responds "Nevermore"? How do the narrator's emotions change throughout the poem?
5. In what way(s) does the work relate to Poe's other works of supernatural and horror literature?

 推荐作品

"Lenore" (1843)
"Annabel Lee" (1849)
"Ligeia" (1838)
"The Fall of the House of Usher" (1839)
"The Cask of Amontillado" (1846)

 参考资料

Carlson, Eric Walter. *A Companion to Poe Studies*. Westport, CT: Greenwood Press, 1996.
Frank, Frederick S., and Anthony Magistrale. *The Poe Encyclopedia*. Westport, CT: Greenwood Press, 1997.
Hayes, Kevin J. *The Cambridge Companion to Edgar Allan Poe*. Cambridge: Cambridge University Press, 2002.
Quinn, Arthur Hobson. *Edgar Allan Poe: A Critical Biography*. Baltimore: Johns Hopkins University Press, 1998.
Sova, Dawn B. *Edgar Allan Poe A to Z: The Essential Reference to His Life and Work*. New York: Checkmark Books, 2001.

（林　斌）

第六单元
Mark Twain (1835—1910)
马克·吐温

 作者简介

马克·吐温是萨缪尔·克莱门斯(Samuel Clemens)的笔名,生于密苏里州,12岁丧父,后与兄弟共同经营出版社。1853—1856年间去圣路易、纽约、费城等地旅行,期间做印刷工以挣取路费。做过密西西比河上的汽船的领航员,美国内战期间为联邦军队服过短役。早年为众多报纸撰写文章,形成幽默风趣、短小精悍的文体特征。

成名作《加拉维拉县驰名的跳蛙》(*The Celebrated Jumping Frog of Calaveras Country*,1865)发表后,陆续出版了游记《傻瓜出国记》(*The Innocents Abroad*,1869)、《镀金时代》(*The Gilded Age*,与查尔斯·华纳合著,1873),回忆童年趣事的《汤姆·索耶历险记》(*The Adventures of Tom Sawyer*,1876),批判奴隶制的《哈克贝里·费恩历险记》(*The Adventures of Huckleberry Finn*,1883),记录密西西比河上经历的《密西西比河上》(*Life on the Mississippi*,1883),讽刺作品《亚瑟王朝廷上的康涅狄格州美国佬》(*A Connecticut Yankee in King Arthur's Court*,1889),揭露奴隶制弊端的《傻瓜威尔逊》(*The Tragedy of Pudd'nhead Wilson*,1894)以及批判人性贪婪的《败坏哈德莱堡的人》(*The Man That Corrupted Hadleyburg*,1900)。晚年,女儿生病与生意破产等一系列打击迫使他四处演讲,挣钱还债,所做的演讲收在《赤道旅行记》(*Following the Equator*,1897)。马克·吐温认为,任何作者都无法在自传中再现真实的自我,因此在撰写自传时他与出版社达成协议,去世百年后才允许出版其自传(*The Autobiography of Mark Twain*,2010—2013)。

马克·吐温以其独特的语言创作观和价值观开创了美国的文学传统,他的幽默笔触和口语体散文影响了安德森、海明威、艾略特、福克纳、塞林格等美国作家。马克·吐温的知己豪威尔斯这样评价他:"克莱门斯独一无二,无与伦比,是我国文学界的林肯。"

The £1,000,000 Bank-Note

When I was twenty-seven years old, I was a mining-broker's clerk in San Francisco, and an expert in all the details of stock traffic. I was alone in the world, and had nothing to depend upon but my wits and a clean reputation; but these were setting my feet in the road to eventual fortune, and I was content with the prospect.

My time was my own after the afternoon board, Saturdays, and I was accustomed to put it in on a little sail-boat on the bay. One day I ventured too far, and was carried out to sea. Just at nightfall, when hope was about gone, I was picked up by a small brig which was bound for London. It was a long and stormy voyage, and they made me work my passage without pay, as a common sailor. When I stepped ashore in London my clothes were ragged and shabby, and I had only a dollar in my pocket. This money fed and sheltered me twenty-four hours. During the next twenty-four I went without food and shelter.

About ten o'clock on the following morning, seedy and hungry, I was dragging myself along Portland Place, when a child that was passing, towed by a nurse-maid, tossed a luscious big pear—minus one bite—into the gutter. I stopped, of course, and fastened my desiring eye on that muddy treasure. My mouth watered for it, my stomach craved it, my whole being begged for it. But every time I made a move to get it some passing eye detected my purpose, and of course I straightened up then, and looked indifferent, and pretended that I hadn't been thinking about the pear at all. This same thing kept happening and happening, and I couldn't get the pear. I was just getting desperate enough to brave all the shame, and to seize it, when a window behind me was raised, and a gentleman spoke out of it, saying:

"Step in here, please."

I was admitted by a gorgeous flunkey, and shown into a sumptuous room where a couple of elderly gentlemen were sitting. They sent away the servant, and made me sit down. They had just finished their breakfast, and the sight of the remains of it almost overpowered me. I could hardly keep my wits together in the presence of that food, but as I was not asked to sample it, I had to bear my trouble as best I could.

Now, something had been happening there a little before, which I did not know anything about until a good many days afterwards, but I will tell you about it now. Those two old brothers had been having a pretty hot argument a couple of days before, and had ended by agreeing to decide it by a bet, which is the English way of settling everything.

You will remember that the Bank of England once issued two notes of a million pounds each, to be used for a special purpose connected with some public transaction with a foreign country. For some reason or other only one of these had been used and canceled; the other still lay in the vaults of the Bank. Well, the brothers, chatting along, happened to get to wondering what might be the fate of a perfectly honest and intelligent stranger who should be turned adrift in London without a friend, and with no money but that million-pound bank-note, and no way to account for his being in possession of it. Brother A said he would starve to death; Brother B said he wouldn't. Brother A said he couldn't offer it at a bank or anywhere else, because he would be arrested on the spot. So they went on disputing till Brother B said he would bet twenty thousand pounds that the man would live thirty days, anyway, on that million, and keep out of jail, too. Brother A took him up. Brother B went down to the Bank and bought that note. Just like an Englishman, you see; pluck to the backbone. Then he dictated a letter, which one of his clerks wrote out in a beautiful round hand, and then the two brothers sat at the window a whole day watching for the right man to give it to.

They saw many honest faces go by that were not intelligent enough; many that were intelligent, but not honest enough; many that were both, but the possessors were not poor enough, or, if poor enough, were not strangers. There was always a defect, until I came along; but they agreed that I filled the bill all around; so they elected me unanimously, and there I was now waiting to know why I was called in. They began to ask me questions about myself, and pretty soon they had my story. Finally they told me I would answer their purpose. I said I was sincerely glad, and asked what it was. Then one of them handed me an envelope, and said I would find the explanation inside. I was going to open it, but he said no; take it to my lodgings, and look it over carefully, and not be hasty or rash. I was puzzled, and wanted to discuss the matter a little further, but they didn't; so I took my leave, feeling hurt and insulted to be made the butt of what was apparently some kind of a practical joke, and yet obliged to put up with it, not being in circumstances to resent affronts from rich and strong folk.

I would have picked up the pear now and eaten it before all the world, but it was gone; so I had lost that by this unlucky business, and the thought of it did not soften my feeling towards those men. As soon as I was out of sight of that house I opened my envelope, and saw that it contained money! My opinion of those people changed, I can tell you! I lost not a moment, but shoved note and money into my vest pocket, and broke for the nearest cheap eating house. Well, how I did eat! When at last I couldn't hold any more, I took out my money and unfolded it, took one glimpse and nearly fainted. Five millions of dollars! Why, it made my head swim.

I must have sat there stunned and blinking at the note as much as a minute before I came rightly to myself again. The first thing I noticed, then, was the landlord. His eye was on the note, and he was petrified. He was worshiping, with all his body and soul, but he looked as if he couldn't stir hand or foot. I took my cue in a moment, and did the only rational thing there was to do. I reached the note towards him, and said, carelessly:

"Give me the change, please."

Then he was restored to his normal condition, and made a thousand apologies for not being able to break the bill, and I couldn't get him to touch it. He wanted to look at it, and keep on looking at it; he couldn't seem to get enough of it to quench the thirst of his eye, but he shrank from touching it as if it had been something too sacred for poor common clay to handle. I said:

"I am sorry if it is an inconvenience, but I must insist. Please change it; I haven't anything else."

But he said that wasn't any matter; he was quite willing to let the trifle stand over till another time. I said I might not be in his neighborhood again for a good while; but he said it was of no consequence, he could wait, and, moreover, I could have anything I wanted, any time I chose, and let the account run as long as I pleased. He said he hoped he wasn't afraid to trust as rich a gentleman as I was, merely because I was of a merry disposition, and chose to play larks on the public in the matter of dress. By this time another customer was entering, and the landlord hinted to me to put the monster① out of sight; then he bowed me all the way to the door, and I started straight for that house and those brothers, to correct the mistake which had been made before the police should hunt me up, and help me do it. I was pretty nervous; in fact, pretty badly frightened, though, of course, I was no way in fault; but I knew men well enough to know that when they find they've given a tramp a million-pound bill when they thought it was a one-pounder, they are in a frantic rage against him instead of quarreling with their own near-sightedness, as they ought. As I approached the house my excitement began to abate, for all was quiet there, which made me feel pretty sure the blunder was not discovered yet. I rang. The same servant appeared. I asked for those gentlemen.

"They are gone." This in the lofty, cold way of that fellow's tribe.

"Gone? Gone where?"

"On a journey."

"But whereabouts?"

"To the Continent, I think."

"The Continent?"

"Yes, sir."

"Which way—by what route?"

"I can't say, sir."

"When will they be back?"

"In a month, they said."

"A month! Oh, this is awful! Give me some sort of idea of how to get a word to them. It's of the last importance."

"I can't, indeed. I've no idea where they've gone, sir."

"Then I must see some member of the family."

"Family's away, too; been abroad months—in Egypt and India, I think."

"Man, there's been an immense mistake made. They'll be back before night. Will you tell them I've been here, and that I will keep coming till it's all made right, and they needn't be afraid?"

"I'll tell them, if they come back, but I am not expecting them. They said you would be here in an

---

① the monster: 指百万英镑。

hour to make inquiries, but I must tell you it's all right, they'll be here on time and expect you."

So I had to give it up and go away. What a riddle it all was! I was like to lose my mind. They would be here "on time." What could that mean? Oh, the letter would explain, maybe. I had forgotten the letter; I got it out and read it. This is what it said:

"You are an intelligent and honest man, as one may see by your face. We conceive you to be poor and a stranger. Enclosed you will find a sum of money. It is lent to you for thirty days, without interest. Report at this house at the end of that time. I have a bet on you. If I win it you shall have any situation that is in my gift—any, that is, that you shall be able to prove yourself familiar with and competent to fill."

No signature, no address, no date.

Well, here was a coil to be in! You are posted on what had preceded all this, but I was not. It was just a deep, dark puzzle to me. I hadn't the least idea what the game was, nor whether harm was meant me or a kindness. I went into a park, and sat down to try to think it out, and to consider what I had best do.

At the end of an hour my reasonings had crystallized into this verdict.

Maybe those men mean me well, maybe they mean me ill; no way to decide that—let it go. They've got a game, or a scheme, or an experiment, of some kind on hand; no way to determine what it is—let it go. There's a bet on me; no way to find out what it is—let it go. That disposes of the indeterminable quantities; the remainder of the matter is tangible, solid, and may be classed and labeled with certainty. If I ask the Bank of England to place this bill to the credit of the man it belongs to, they'll do it, for they know him, although I don't; but they will ask me how I came in possession of it, and if I tell the truth, they'll put me in the asylum, naturally, and a lie will land me in jail. The same result would follow if I tried to bank the bill anywhere or to borrow money on it. I have got to carry this immense burden around until those men come back, whether I want to or not. It is useless to me, as useless as a handful of ashes, and yet I must take care of it, and watch over it, while I beg my living. I couldn't give it away, if I should try, for neither honest citizen nor highwayman would accept it or meddle with it for anything. Those brothers are safe. Even if I lose their bill, or burn it, they are still safe, because they can stop payment, and the Bank will make them whole; but meantime I've got to do a month's suffering without wages or profit—unless I help win that bet, whatever it may be, and get that situation that I am promised. I should like to get that; men of their sort have situations in their gift that are worth having.

I got to thinking a good deal about that situation. My hopes began to rise high. Without doubt the salary would be large. It would begin in a month; after that I should be all right. Pretty soon I was feeling first-rate. By this time I was tramping the streets again. The sight of a tailor-shop gave me a sharp longing to shed my rags, and to clothe myself decently once more. Could I afford it? No; I had nothing in the world but a million pounds. So I forced myself to go on by. But soon I was drifting back again. The temptation persecuted me cruelly. I must have passed that shop back and forth six times during that manful struggle. At last I gave in; I had to. I asked if they had a misfit suit that had been thrown on their hands. The fellow I spoke to nodded his head towards another fellow, and gave me no answer. I went to the indicated fellow, and he indicated another fellow with his head, and no words. I went to him, and he said:

" 'Tend to you presently."

I waited till he was done with what he was at, then he took me into a back room, and overhauled a pile of rejected suits, and selected the rattiest one for me. I put it on. It didn't fit, and wasn't in any way attractive, but it was new, and I was anxious to have it; so I didn't find any fault, but said, with some diffidence:

"It would be an accommodation to me if you could wait some days for the money. I haven't any small change about me."

The fellow worked up a most sarcastic expression of countenance, and said:

"Oh, you haven't? Well, of course, I didn't expect it. I'd only expect gentlemen like you to carry large change."

I was nettled, and said:

"My friend, you shouldn't judge a stranger always by the clothes he wears. I am quite able to pay for this suit; I simply didn't wish to put you to the trouble of changing a large note."

He modified his style a little at that, and said, though still with something of an air:

"I didn't mean any particular harm, but as long as rebukes are going, I might say it wasn't quite your affair to jump to the conclusion that we couldn't change any note that you might happen to be carrying around. On the contrary, we can."

I handed the note to him, and said:

"Oh, very well; I apologize."

He received it with a smile, one of those large smiles which goes all around over, and has folds in it, and wrinkles, and spirals, and looks like the place where you have thrown a brick in a pond; and then in the act of his taking a glimpse of the bill this smile froze solid, and turned yellow, and looked like those wavy, wormy spreads of lava which you find hardened on little levels on the side of Vesuvius. I never before saw a smile caught like that, and perpetuated. The man stood there holding the bill, and looking like that, and the proprietor hustled up to see what was the matter, and said, briskly:

"Well, what's up? what's the trouble? what's wanting?"

I said: "There isn't any trouble. I'm waiting for my change."

"Come, come; get him his change, Tod; get him his change."

Tod retorted: "Get him his change! It's easy to say, sir; but look at the bill yourself."

The proprietor took a look, gave a low, eloquent whistle, then made a dive for the pile of rejected clothing, and began to snatch it this way and that, talking all the time excitedly, and as if to himself:

"Sell an eccentric millionaire such an unspeakable suit as that! Tod's a fool—a born fool. Always doing something like this. Drives every millionaire away from this place, because he can't tell a millionaire from a tramp, and never could. Ah, here's the thing I am after. Please get those things off, sir, and throw them in the fire. Do me the favor to put on this shirt and this suit; it's just the thing, the very thing—plain, rich, modest, and just ducally nobby; made to order for a foreign prince—you may know him, sir, his Serene Highness the Hospodar of Halifax; had to leave it with us and take a mourning-suit because his mother was going to die—which she didn't. But that's all right; we can't always have things the way we—that is, the way they—there! trousers all right, they fit you to a charm, sir; now the waistcoat; aha, right again! now the coat—Lord! look at that, now! Perfect—the whole thing! I never saw such a triumph in all my experience."

I expressed my satisfaction.

"Quite right, sir, quite right; it'll do for a makeshift, I'm bound to say. But wait till you see what we'll get up for you on your own measure. Come, Tod, book and pen; get at it. Length of leg, 32″"—and so on. Before I could get in a word he had measured me, and was giving orders for dress-suits, morning suits, shirts, and all sorts of things. When I got a chance I said:

"But, my dear sir, I can't give these orders, unless you can wait indefinitely, or change the bill."

"Indefinitely! It's a weak word, sir, a weak word. Eternally—that's the word, sir. Tod, rush these things through, and send them to the gentleman's address without any waste of time. Let the minor customers wait. Set down the gentleman's address and—"

"I'm changing my quarters. I will drop in and leave the new address."

"Quite right, sir, quite right. One moment—let me show you out, sir. There—good day, sir, good day."

Well, don't you see what was bound to happen? I drifted naturally into buying whatever I wanted, and asking for change. Within a week I was sumptuously equipped with all needful comforts and luxuries, and was housed in an expensive private hotel in Hanover Square. I took my dinners there, but for breakfast I stuck by Harris's humble feeding house, where I had got my first meal on my million-pound bill. I was the making of Harris[①]. The fact had gone all abroad that the foreign crank who carried million-pound bills in his vest pocket was the patron saint of the place. That was enough. From being a poor, struggling, little hand-to-mouth enterprise, it had become celebrated, and overcrowded with customers. Harris was so grateful that he forced loans upon me, and would not be denied; and so, pauper as I was, I had money to spend, and was living like the rich and the great. I judged that there was going to be a crash by and by, but I was in now and must swim across or drown. You see there was just that element of impending disaster to give a serious side, a sober side, yes, a tragic side, to a state of things which would otherwise have been purely ridiculous. In the night, in the dark, the tragedy part was always to the front, and always warning, always threatening; and so I moaned and tossed, and sleep was hard to find. But in the cheerful daylight the tragedy element faded out and disappeared, and I walked on air, and was happy to giddiness, to intoxication, you may say.

And it was natural; for I had become one of the notorieties of the metropolis of the world, and it turned my head, not just a little, but a good deal. You could not take up a newspaper, English, Scotch, or Irish, without finding in it one or more references to the "vest-pocket million-pounder" and his latest doings and saying. At first, in these mentions, I was at the bottom of the personal-gossip column; next, I was listed above the knights, next above the baronets, next above the barons, and so on, and so on, climbing steadily, as my notoriety augmented, until I reached the highest altitude possible, and there I remained, taking precedence of all dukes not royal, and of all ecclesiastics except the primate of all England. But mind, this was not fame; as yet I had achieved only notoriety. Then came the climaxing stroke—the accolade, so to speak—which in a single instant transmuted the perishable dross of notoriety into the enduring gold of fame: *Punch* caricatured me! Yes, I was a made man now; my place was established. I might be joked about still, but reverently, not hilariously, not rudely; I could be smiled at, but not laughed at. The time for that had gone by. *Punch* pictured me all a-flutter with rags, dickering with a beef-eater for the Tower of London. Well, you can imagine how it was with a young fellow who had never been taken notice of before, and now all of a sudden couldn't say a thing that wasn't taken up and repeated everywhere; couldn't stir abroad without constantly overhearing the remark flying from lip to lip, "There he goes; that's him!" couldn't take his breakfast without a crowd to look on; couldn't appear in an operabox without concentrating there the fire of a thousand lorgnettes. Why, I just swam in glory all day long—that is the amount of it.

You know, I even kept my old suit of rags, and every now and then appeared in them, so as to have the old pleasure of buying trifles, and being insulted, and then shooting the scoffer dead with the million-pound bill. But I couldn't keep that up. The illustrated papers made the outfit so familiar that when I went out in it I was at once recognized and followed by a crowd, and if I attempted a purchase the man would offer me his whole shop on credit before I could pull my note on him.

About the tenth day of my fame I went to fulfil my duty to my flag by paying my respects to the American minister. He received me with the enthusiasm proper in my case, upbraided me for being so tardy in my duty, and said that there was only one way to get his forgiveness, and that was to take the

---

① I was the making of Harris: 我让哈里斯发财了。

seat at his dinner-party that night made vacant by the illness of one of his guests. I said I would, and we got to talking. It turned out that he and my father had been schoolmates in boyhood, Yale students together later, and always warm friends up to my father's death. So then he required me to put in at his house all the odd time I might have to spare, and I was very willing, of course.

In fact, I was more than willing; I was glad. When the crash should come, he might somehow be able to save me from total destruction; I didn't know how, but he might think of a way, maybe. I couldn't venture to unbosom myself to him at this late date, a thing which I would have been quick to do in the beginning of this awful career of mine in London. No, I couldn't venture it now; I was in too deep; that is, too deep for me to be risking revelations to so new a friend, though not clear beyond my depth, as I looked at it. Because, you see, with all my borrowing, I was carefully keeping within my means—I mean within my salary. Of course, I couldn't know what my salary was going to be, but I had a good enough basis for an estimate in the fact, that if I won the bet I was to have choice of any situation in that rich old gentleman's gift provided I was competent—and I should certainly prove competent; I hadn't any doubt about that. And as to the bet, I wasn't worrying about that; I had always been lucky. Now my estimate of the salary was six hundred to a thousand a year; say, six hundred for the first year, and so on up year by year, till I struck the upper figure by proved merit. At present I was only in debt for my first year's salary. Everybody had been trying to lend me money, but I had fought off the most of them on one pretext or another; so this indebtedness represented only £300 borrowed money, the other £300 represented my keep and my purchases. I believed my second year's salary would carry me through the rest of the month if I went on being cautious and economical, and I intended to look sharply out for that. My month ended, my employer back from his journey, I should be all right once more, for I should at once divide the two years' salary among my creditors by assignment, and get right down to my work.

It was a lovely dinner-party of fourteen. The Duke and Duchess of Shoreditch, and their daughter the Lady Anne-Grace-Eleanor-Celeste-and-so-forth-and-so-forth-de-Bohun, the Earl and Countess of Newgate, Viscount Cheapside, Lord and Lady Blatherskite, some untitled people of both sexes, the minister and his wife and daughter, and his daughter's visiting friend, an English girl of twenty-two, named Portia Langham, whom I fell in love with in two minutes, and she with me—I could see it without glasses. There was still another guest, an American—but I am a little ahead of my story. While the people were still in the drawing-room, whetting up for dinner, and coldly inspecting the late comers, the servant announced:

"Mr. Lloyd Hastings."

The moment the usual civilities were over, Hastings caught sight of me, and came straight with cordially outstretched hand; then stopped short when about to shake, and said, with an embarrassed look:

"I beg your pardon, sir, I thought I knew you."

"Why, you do know me, old fellow."

"No. Are you the—the—"

"Vest-pocket monster? I am, indeed. Don't be afraid to call me by my nickname; I'm used to it."

"Well, well, well, this is a surprise. Once or twice I've seen your own name coupled with the nickname, but it never occurred to me that you could be the Henry Adams referred to. Why, it isn't six months since you were clerking away for Blake Hopkins in Frisco on a salary, and sitting up nights on an extra allowance, helping me arrange and verify the Gould and Curry Extension papers and statistics. The idea of your being in London, and a vast millionaire, and a colossal celebrity! Why, it's the Arabian Nights come again. Man, I can't take it in at all; can't realize it; give me time to settle the whirl in my head."

"The fact is, Lloyd, you are no worse off than I am. I can't realize it myself."

"Dear me, it is stunning, now isn't it? Why, it's just three months today since we went to the Miners' restaurant—"

"No; the What Cheer."

"Right, it was the What Cheer; went there at two in the morning, and had a chop and coffee after a hard six-hours grind over those Extension papers, and I tried to persuade you to come to London with me, and offered to get leave of absence for you and pay all your expenses, and give you something over if I succeeded in making the sale; and you would not listen to me, said I wouldn't succeed, and you couldn't afford to lose the run of business and be no end of time getting the hang of things again when you got back home. And yet here you are. How odd it all is! How did you happen to come, and whatever did give you this incredible start?"

"Oh, just an accident. It's a long story—a romance, a body may say. I'll tell you all about it, but not now."

"When?"

"The end of this month."

"That's more than a fortnight yet. It's too much of a strain on a person's curiosity. Make it a week."

"I can't. You'll know why, by and by. But how's the trade getting along?"

His cheerfulness vanished like a breath, and he said with a sigh:

"You were a true prophet, Hal, a true prophet. I wish I hadn't come. I don't want to talk about it."

"But you must. You must come and stop with me to-night, when we leave here, and tell me all about it."

"Oh, may I? Are you in earnest?" and the water showed in his eyes.

"Yes; I want to hear the whole story, every word."

"I'm so grateful! Just to find a human interest once more, in some voice and in some eye, in me and affairs of mine, after what I've been through here—lord! I could go down on my knees for it!"

He gripped my hand hard, and braced up, and was all right and lively after that for the dinner—which didn't come off. No; the usual thing happened, the thing that is always happening under that vicious and aggravating English system—the matter of precedence couldn't be settled, and so there was no dinner. Englishmen always eat dinner before they go out to dinner, because they know the risks they are running; but nobody ever warns the stranger, and so he walks placidly into trap. Of course, nobody was hurt this time, because we had all been to dinner, none of us being novices excepting Hastings, and he having been informed by the minister at the time that he invited him that in deference to the English custom he had not provided any dinner. Everybody took a lady and processioned down to the dining-room, because it is usual to go through the motions; but there the dispute began. The Duke of Shoreditch wanted to take precedence, and sit at the head of the table, holding that he outranked a minister who represented merely a nation and not a monarch; but I stood for my rights, and refused to yield. In the gossip column I ranked all dukes not royal, and said so, and claimed precedence of this one. It couldn't be settled, of course, struggle as we might and did, he finally (and injudiciously) trying to play birth and antiquity, and I "seeing" his Conqueror and "raising" him with Adam, whose direct posterity I was, as shown by my name, while he was of a collateral branch, as shown by his, and by his recent Norman origin; so we all processioned back to the drawing-room again and had a perpendicular lunch—plate of sardines and a strawberry, and you group yourself and stand up and eat it. Here the religion of precedence is not so strenuous; the two persons of highest rank chuck up a shilling, the one that wins has first go at his strawberry, and the loser gets the shilling. The next two chuck up, then the next two, and so on. After refreshment, tables were brought, and we all played cribbage, sixpence a game. The English never play any game for amusement. If they can't make something or lose something—they don't care which—they won't play.

We had a lovely time; certainly two of us had, Miss Langham and I. I was so bewitched with her that I couldn't count my hands if they went above a double sequence; and when I struck home I never discovered it, and started up the outside row again, and would have lost the game every time, only the girl did the same, she being in just my condition, you see; and consequently neither of us ever got out, or cared to wonder why we didn't; we only just knew we were happy, and didn't wish to know anything else, and didn't want to be interrupted. And I told her—I did, indeed—told her I loved her; and she—well, she blushed till her hair turned red, but she liked it; she said she did. Oh, there was never such an evening! Every time I pegged I put on a postscript; every time she pegged she acknowledged receipt of it, counting the hands the same. Why, I couldn't even say "Two for his heels" without adding, "My, how sweet you do look!" and she would say, "Fifteen two, fifteen four, fifteen six, and a pair are eight, and eight are sixteen—do you think so?"—peeping out aslant from under her lashes, you know, so sweet and cunning. Oh, it was just too-too!

Well, I was perfectly honest and square with her; told her I hadn't a cent in the world but just the million-pound note she'd heard so much talk about, and it didn't belong to me, and that started her curiosity; and then I talked low, and told her the whole history right from the start, and it nearly killed her laughing. What in the nation she could find to laugh about I couldn't see, but there it was; every half-minute some new detail would fetch her, and I would have to stop as much as a minute and a half to give her a chance to settle down again. Why, she laughed herself lame—she did, indeed; I never saw anything like it. I mean I never saw a painful story—a story of a person's troubles and worries and fears—produce just that kind of effect before. So I loved her all the more, seeing she could be so cheerful when there wasn't anything to be cheerful about; for I might soon need that kind of wife, you know, the way things looked. Of course, I told her we should have to wait a couple of years, till I could catch up on my salary; but she didn't mind that, only she hoped I would be as careful as possible in the matter of expenses, and not let them run the least risk of trenching on our third year's pay. Then she began to get a little worried, and wondered if we were making any mistake, and starting the salary on a higher figure for the first year than I would get. This was good sense, and it made me feel a little less confident than I had been feeling before; but it gave me a good business idea, and I brought it frankly out.

"Portia, dear, would you mind going with me that day, when I confront those old gentlemen?"

She shrank a little, but said:

"N-o; if my being with you would help hearten you. But—would it be quite proper, do you think?"

"No, I don't know that it would—in fact, I'm afraid it wouldn't; but, you see, there's so much dependent upon it that—"

"Then I'll go anyway, proper or improper," she said, with a beautiful and generous enthusiasm. "Oh, I shall be so happy to think I'm helping!"

"Helping, dear? Why, you'll be doing it all. You're so beautiful and so lovely and so winning, that with you there I can pile our salary up till I break those good old fellows, and they'll never have the heart to struggle."

Sho! you should have seen the rich blood mount, and her happy eyes shine!

"You wicked flatterer! There isn't a word of truth in what you say, but still I'll go with you. Maybe it will teach you not to expect other people to look with your eyes."

Were my doubts dissipated? Was my confidence restored? You may judge by this fact: privately I raised my salary to twelve hundred the first year on the spot. But I didn't tell her; I saved it for a surprise.

All the way home I was in the clouds, Hastings talking, I not hearing a word. When he and I entered my parlor, he brought me to myself with his fervent appreciations of my manifold comforts and luxuries.

"Let me just stand here a little and look my fill. Dear me! it's a palace—it's just a palace! And in it everything a body could desire, including cosy coal fire and supper standing ready. Henry, it doesn't merely make me realize how rich you are; it makes me realize, to the bone, to the marrow, how poor I am—how poor I am, and how miserable, how defeated, routed, annihilated!"

Plague take it! this language gave me the cold shudders. It scared me broad awake, and made me comprehend that I was standing on a halfinch crust, with a crater underneath. I didn't know I had been dreaming—that is, I hadn't been allowing myself to know it for a while back; but now—oh, dear! Deep in debt, not a cent in the world, a lovely girl's happiness or woe in my hands, and nothing in front of me but a salary which might never—oh, would never—materialize! Oh, oh, oh! I am ruined past hope! nothing can save me!

"Henry, the mere unconsidered drippings of your daily income would—"

"Oh, my daily income! Here, down with this hot Scotch, and cheer up your soul. Here's with you! Or, no—you're hungry; sit down and—"

"Not a bite for me; I'm past it. I can't eat, these days; but I'll drink with you till I drop. Come!"

"Barrel for barrel, I'm with you! Ready? Here we go! Now, then, Lloyd, unreel your story while I brew."

"Unreel it? What, again?"

"Again? What do you mean by that?"

"Why, I mean do you want to hear it over again?"

"Do I want to hear it over again? This is a puzzler. Wait; don't take any more of that liquid. You don't need it."

"Look here, Henry, you alarm me. Didn't I tell you the whole story on the way here?"

"You?"

"Yes, I."

"I'll be hanged if I heard a word of it."

"Henry, this is a serious thing. It troubles me. What did you take up yonder at the minister's?"

Then it all flashed on me, and I owned up like a man.

"I took the dearest girl in this world—prisoner!"

So then he came with a rush, and we shook, and shook, and shook till our hands ached; and he didn't blame me for not having heard a word of a story which had lasted while we walked three miles. He just sat down then, like the patient, good fellow he was, and told it all over again. Synopsized, it amounted to this: He had come to England with what he thought was a grand opportunity; he had an "option" to sell the Gould and Curry Extension for the "locators" of it, and keep all he could get over a million dollars. He had worked hard, had pulled every wire he knew of, had left no honest expedient untried, had spent nearly all the money he had in the world, had not been able to get a solitary capitalist to listen to him, and his option would run out at the end of the month. In a word, he was ruined. Then he jumped up and cried out:

"Henry, you can save me! You can save me, and you're the only man in the universe that can. Will you do it? Won't you do it?"

"Tell me how. Speak out, my boy."

"Give me a million and my passage home for my 'option'! Don't, don't refuse!"

I was in a kind of agony. I was right on the point of coming out with the words, "Lloyd, I'm a pauper myself—absolutely penniless, and in debt!" But a white-hot idea came flaming through my head, and I gripped my jaws together, and calmed myself down till I was as cold as a capitalist. Then I said, in a commercial and self-possessed way:

"I will save you, Lloyd—"

"Then I'm already saved! God be merciful to you forever! If ever I—"

"Let me finish, Lloyd. I will save you, but not in that way; for that would not be fair to you, after your hard work, and the risks you've run. I don't need to buy mines; I can keep my capital moving, in a commercial center like London, without that; it's what I'm at, all the time; but here is what I'll do. I know all about that mine, of course; I know its immense value, and can swear to it if anybody wishes it. You shall sell out inside of the fortnight for three millions cash, using my name freely, and we'll divide, share and share alike."

Do you know, he would have danced the furniture to kindling-wood in his insane joy, and broken everything on the place, if I hadn't tripped him up and tied him.

Then he lay there, perfectly happy, saying:

"I may use your name! Your name—think of it! Man, they'll flock in droves, these rich Londoners; they'll fight for that stock! I'm a made man, I'm a made man forever, and I'll never forget you as long as I live!"

In less than twenty-four hours London was abuzz! I hadn't anything to do, day after day, but sit at home, and say to all comers:

"Yes; I told him to refer to me. I know the man, and I know the mine. His character is above reproach, and the mine is worth far more than he asks for it."

Meantime I spent all my evenings at the minister's with Portia. I didn't say a word to her about the mine; I saved it for a surprise. We talked salary; never anything but salary and love; sometimes love, sometimes salary, sometimes love and salary together. And my! the interest the minister's wife and daughter took in our little affair, and the endless ingenuities they invented to save us from interruption, and to keep the minister in the dark and unsuspicious—well, it was just lovely of them!

When the month was up at last, I had a million dollars to my credit in the London and County Bank, and Hastings was fixed in the same way. Dressed at my level best, I drove by the house in Portland Place, judged by the look of things that my birds were home again, went on towards the minister's and got my precious, and we started back, talking salary with all our might. She was so excited and anxious that it made her just intolerably beautiful. I said:

"Dearie, the way you're looking it's a crime to strike for a salary a single penny under three thousand a year."

"Henry, Henry, you'll ruin us!"

"Don't you be afraid. Just keep up those looks, and trust to me. It'll all come out right."

So, as it turned out, I had to keep bolstering up her courage all the way. She kept pleading with me, and saying:

"Oh, please remember that if we ask for too much we may get no salary at all; and then what will become of us, with no way in the world to earn our living?"

We were ushered in by that same servant, and there they were, the two old gentlemen. Of course, they were surprised to see that wonderful creature with me, but I said:

"It's all right, gentlemen; she is my future stay and helpmate."

And I introduced them to her, and called them by name. It didn't surprise them; they knew I would know enough to consult the directory. They seated us, and were very polite to me, and very solicitous to relieve her from embarrassment, and put her as much at her ease as they could. Then I said:

"Gentlemen, I am ready to report."

"We are glad to hear it," said my man, "for now we can decide the bet which my brother Abel and I made. If you have won for me, you shall have any situation in my gift. Have you the million-pound note?"

"Here it is, sir," and I handed it to him.

"I've won!" he shouted, and slapped Abel on the back. "Now what do you say, brother?"

"I say he did survive, and I've lost twenty thousand pounds. I never would have believed it."

"I've a further report to make," I said, "and a pretty long one. I want you to let me come soon, and detail my whole month's history; and I promise you it's worth hearing. Meantime, take a look at that."

"What, man! Certificate of deposit for £200,000. Is it yours?"

"Mine. I earned it by thirty days' judicious use of that little loan you let me have. And the only use I made of it was to buy trifles and offer the bill in change."

"Come, this is astonishing! It's incredible, man!"

"Never mind, I'll prove it. Don't take my word unsupported."

But now Portia's turn was come to be surprised. Her eyes were spread wide, and she said:

"Henry, is that really your money? Have you been fibbing to me?"

"I have, indeed, dearie. But you'll forgive me, I know."

She put up an arch pout, and said:

"Don't you be so sure. You are a naughty thing to deceive me so!"

"Oh, you'll get over it, sweetheart, you'll get over it; it was only fun, you know. Come, let's be going."

"But wait, wait! The situation, you know. I want to give you the situation," said my man.

"Well," I said, "I'm just as grateful as I can be, but really I don't want one."

"But you can have the very choicest one in my gift."

"Thanks again, with all my heart; but I don't even want that one."

"Henry, I'm ashamed of you. You don't half thank the good gentleman. May I do it for you?"

"Indeed, you shall, dear, if you can improve it. Let us see you try."

She walked to my man, got up in his lap, put her arm round his neck, and kissed him right on the mouth. Then the two old gentlemen shouted with laughter, but I was dumfounded, just petrified, as you may say. Portia said:

"Papa, he has said you haven't a situation in your gift that he'd take; and I feel just as hurt as—"

"My darling, is that your papa?"

"Yes; he's my step-papa, and the dearest one that ever was. You understand now, don't you, why I was able to laugh when you told me at the minister's, not knowing my relationships, what trouble and worry papa's and Uncle Abel's scheme was giving you?"

Of course, I spoke right up now, without any fooling, and went straight to the point.

"Oh, my dearest dear sir, I want to take back what I said. You have got a situation open that I want."

"Name it."

"Son-in-law."

"Well, well, well! But you know, if you haven't ever served in that capacity, you, of course, can't furnish recommendations of a sort to satisfy the conditions of the contract, and so—"

"Try me—oh, do, I beg of you! Only just try me thirty or forty years, and if—"

"Oh, well, all right; it's but a little thing to ask, take her along."

Happy, we two? There are not words enough in the unabridged to describe it. And when London got the whole history, a day or two later, of my month's adventures with that bank-note, and how they ended, did London talk, and have a good time? Yes.

My Portia's papa took that friendly and hospitable bill back to the Bank of England and cashed it; then the Bank canceled it and made him a present of it, and he gave it to us at our wedding, and it has always hung in its frame in the sacredest place in our home ever since. For it gave me my Portia. But for it I could not have remained in London, would not have appeared at the minister's, never should have met her. And so I always say, "Yes, it's a million-pounder, as you see; but it never made but one purchase in its life, and then got the article for only about a tenth part of its value."

短篇《百万英镑》("The £1,000,000 Bank-Note")被改编成电影(*The Man with a Million*, 1953)。小说以倒叙手法讲述了叙述者亨利·亚当斯与百万英镑的奇特经历。篇首简要交代叙述者以智慧和诚实为立身之本，这两种品质恰恰给他带来财富，接着展开叙述，层层递进，吸引读者进一步了解详情。叙述者是美国人，在旧金山海湾乘船闲游，不巧遇难，途遇去伦敦的船只，一路颠簸，竟来到伦敦，身无分文的他开始了英国历险记。

叙述者作为旁观者，揭示了英美两国人的诸多特征。譬如，英国上流社会喜好打赌解决问题，一对富家兄弟在叙述者身上押下2万英镑赌注，希望获知百万英镑落在叙述者这样一个落魄鬼手中会是怎样的结局，反映出英国上流社会阶层精神空虚的特点。马克·吐温擅长以细节刻画人物，尤其通过幽默和反讽手法揭示人物特征。上述兄弟在街上物色诚实聪颖的实验对象一事，便流露出作者对他们的嘲讽。叙述者被认为具备优秀品质，也很快具有反讽意味，因为当他发现信封里的百万英镑时，顿时对兄弟俩刮目相看。小说通过刻画典型人物批判了英国嫌贫爱富的社会现象，譬如，裁缝店老板看到叙述者手中的百万英镑后，其谄媚表现指向他以貌取人、趋炎附势的本性。这种势利行为在美国公使身上也表现得淋漓尽致，在得知叙述者的富翁身份后，公使立即邀他赴宴，并告知他两家交情源远流长。

马克·吐温熟谙叙述技巧，他没有安排叙述者提前告知读者波西娅的真实身份，其实波西娅是百万英镑主人的女儿，这让叙述者和读者喜出望外，喜剧效果由此产生。而使叙述者成为幸运儿的根本原因在于，他既诚实又智慧。诚然，叙述者也曾受到物质诱惑，但他力图保持清醒，也成功做到了这点。小说似乎提醒读者，真正珍贵的物品无须花费太多金钱，从而启发读者对物质与精神的关系作进一步思考。

 思考题

1. How do you evaluate the bet that the two brothers have on the narrator?
2. Why does the narrator feel "a tragic side" in the night after finding himself drifting "naturally into buying whatever I wanted, and asking for change"?
3. How is the "religion of precedence" typical of the English system satirized in the story?
4. The narrator's name is used to save his friend's mine business. What does this act suggest?
5. What does the narrator's refusal to ask for a position that is within Portia's father's gift imply about his character?

"The Man That Corrupted Hadleyburg" (1899)
"The Stolen White Elephant" (1882)
The Adventures of Huckleberry Finn (1883)
The Tragedy of Pudd'nhead Wilson (1894)
A Connecticut Yankee in King Arthur's Court (1889)

参考资料

Hutchinson, Stuart. Ed. *Mark Twain: Critical Assessments*. Mountfield, East Sussex: Helm Information, 1993.

Messent, Peter B. *The Cambridge Introduction to Mark Twain*. New York: Cambridge University Press, 2007.

Twain, Mark. *Autobiography of Mark Twain: The Complete and Authoritative Edition*. 2 vols. Ed. Harriet Elinor Smith. Berkeley, California: University of California Press, 2010-2013.

（李　晋）

第七单元

Henry James (1843—1916)
亨利·詹姆斯

 作者简介

　　亨利·詹姆斯,小说家,生于纽约市一个富裕的知识分子家庭,在五个孩子中排行老二,兄长是后来成为著名哲学家和心理学家的威廉·詹姆斯(1842—1910)。他小时候常随父母去英国、瑞士、法国、德国等欧洲国家旅游居住,在家教指导下学习这些国家的语言文化。19岁进入哈佛大学法学院,但因受豪威尔斯等作家的影响对文学产生兴趣,不久便终止了法律学习。1864年在久负盛名的《北美评论》上发表第一篇评论。次年又发表了第一篇短篇小说。随后十年,他旅居欧洲,潜心创作,结识了屠格涅夫、福楼拜、左拉、乔治·艾略特、拉斯金、丁尼生、布朗宁等著名作家。1875年,他发表短篇小说集《热衷游历的人》(*A Passionate Pilgrim*)和长篇小说《罗德里克·赫德森》(*Roderick Hudson*)后,开始定居欧洲,先是在巴黎,后又去了伦敦。去世前一年,由于不满美国参加第一次世界大战迟缓,放弃美国国籍,加入英国国籍。詹姆斯一生写下大量不同类型的作品,有长篇小说22部、短篇小说114篇、剧本15个、评论约10部、传记5部、游记7部、书信1万5千多封。他的纽约版《亨利·詹姆斯小说、故事集》(*The Novels and Tales of Henry James*, 1907—1917)共出了26卷。代表作有《一个美国人》(*The American*, 1877)、《黛西·密勒》(*Daisy Miller*, 1879)、《一位女士的画像》(*The Portrait of a Lady*, 1881)、《波士顿人》(*The Bostonians*, 1886)、《卡萨玛西玛公主》(*The Princess of Casamashima*, 1886)、《波音敦的珍藏品》(*The Spoils of Poynton*, 1897)、《螺丝在拧紧》(*The Turn of the Screw*, 1898)、《未成熟的少年时代》(*The Awkward Age*, 1899)、《鸽翼》(*The Wings of the Dove*, 1902)、《专使》(*The Ambassadors*, 1903)、《金碗》(*The Golden Bowl*, 1904)。詹姆斯作品的主题主要有单纯的美国人与世故的欧洲人之间的文化冲突、艺术家和作家的清高自得等。詹姆斯非常看重表现主题的手法,在《小说艺术》("The Art of Fiction", 1884)一文中要求读者依据技巧而不是主题来判断一个作家。他的常用技巧包括第三人称有限视角和心理现实主义。尽管他的艺术追求有违于当时的大众趣味,对人物复杂内心的描写有时显得晦涩难解,他在观察生活、讲述故事的技巧实验等方面的突出成就还是得到了高度肯定。哈佛大学和牛津大学先后于1911年和1912年授予他名誉博士学位。英王乔治五世1916年向他颁发了殊勋勋章。1916年,他病逝于伦敦。

The Real Thing

I

　　When the porter's wife, who used to answer the house-bell, announced "A gentleman and a lady, sir," I had, as I often had in those days—the wish being father to the thought—an immediate vision of sitters. Sitters my visitors in this case proved to be; but not in the sense I should have preferred. However, there was nothing at first to indicate that they mightn't have come for a portrait. The gentleman, a man of fifty, very high and very straight, with a moustache slightly grizzled and a dark grey walking-coat admirably fitted, both of which I noted professionally—I don't mean as a barber or yet as a tailor—would have struck me as a celebrity if celebrities often were striking. It was a truth of which I had for some time been conscious that a figure with a good deal of frontage① was, as one might say, almost never a public institution. A glance at the lady helped to remind me of this paradoxical law: she

---

① a good deal of frontage: 仪表堂堂。

also looked too distinguished to be a "personality." Moreover one would scarcely come across two variations together.

Neither of the pair spoke immediately—they only prolonged the preliminary gaze which suggested that each wished to give the other a chance. They were visibly shy; they stood there letting me take them in—which, as I afterwards perceived, was the most practical thing they could have done. In this way their embarrassment served their cause. I had seen people painfully reluctant to mention that they desired anything so gross as to be represented on canvas; but the scruples of my new friends appeared almost insurmountable. Yet the gentleman might have said "I should like a portrait of my wife," and the lady might have said "I should like a portrait of my husband." Perhaps they were not husband and wife—this naturally would make the matter more delicate. Perhaps they wished to be done together—in which case they ought to have brought a third person to break the news.

"We come from Mr. Rivet," the lady said at last, with a dim smile which had the effect of a moist sponge passed over a "sunk"① piece of painting, as well as of a vague allusion to vanished beauty. She was as tall and straight, in her degree, as her companion, and with ten years less to carry. She looked as sad as a woman could look whose face was not charged with expression; that is her tinted oval mask showed waste as an exposed surface shows friction. The hand of time had played over her freely, but to an effect of elimination. She was slim and stiff, and so well-dressed, in dark blue cloth, with lappets and pockets and buttons, that it was clear she employed the same tailor as her husband. The couple had an indefinable air of prosperous thrift—they evidently got a good deal of luxury for their money. If I was to be one of their luxuries it would behove me to consider my terms.

"Ah, Claude Rivet recommended me?" I echoed; and I added that it was very kind of him, though I could reflect that, as he only painted landscape, this wasn't a sacrifice.

The lady looked very hard at the gentleman, and the gentleman looked round the room. Then staring at the floor a moment and stroking his moustache, he rested his pleasant eyes on me with the remark: "He said you were the right one."

"I try to be, when people want to sit."

"Yes, we should like to," said the lady anxiously.

"Do you mean together?"

My visitors exchanged a glance. "If you could do anything with me, I suppose it would be double," the gentleman stammered.

"Oh yes, there's naturally a higher charge for two figures than for one."

"We should like to make it pay," the husband confessed.

"That's very good of you," I returned, appreciating so unwonted a sympathy—for I supposed he meant pay the artist.

A sense of strangeness seemed to dawn on the lady. "We mean for the illustrations—Mr. Rivet said you might put one in."

"Put one in—an illustration?" I was equally confused.

"Sketch her off, you know," said the gentleman, colouring.

It was only then that I understood the service Claude Rivet had rendered me; he had told them that I worked in black-and-white, for magazines, for story-books, for sketches of contemporary life, and consequently had copious employment for models. These things were true, but it was not less true—I may confess it now; whether because the aspiration was to lead to everything or to nothing I leave the reader to guess—that I couldn't get the honours, to say nothing of the emoluments②, of a great painter

---

① sunk: 已褪色的。
② emoluments: 收益。

of portraits out of my head. My "illustrations" were my pot-boilers; I looked to a different branch of art—far and away the most interesting it had always seemed to me—to perpetuate my fame. There was no shame in looking to it also to make my fortune; but that fortune was by so much further from being made from the moment my visitors wished to be "done" for nothing. I was disappointed; for in the pictorial sense I had immediately seen them. I had seized their type—I had already settled what I would do with it. Something that wouldn't absolutely have pleased them, I afterwards reflected.

"Ah, you're—you're—a—?" I began, as soon as I had mastered my surprise. I couldn't bring out the dingy word "models": it seemed to fit the case so little.

"We haven't had much practice," said the lady.

"We've got to *do* something, and we've thought that an artist in your line might perhaps make something of us," her husband threw off. He further mentioned that they didn't know many artists and that they had gone first, on the off-chance①—he painted views of course, but sometimes put in figures; perhaps I remembered—to Mr. Rivet, whom they had met a few years before at a place in Norfolk where he was sketching.

"We used to sketch a little ourselves," the lady hinted.

"It's very awkward, but we absolutely *must* do something," her husband went on.

"Of course, we're not so *very* young," she admitted, with a wan smile.

With the remark that I might as well know something more about them, the husband had handed me a card extracted from a neat new pocket-book—their appurtenances were all of the freshest—and inscribed with the words "Major Monarch." Impressive as these words were they didn't carry my knowledge much further; but my visitor presently added: "I've left the army, and we've had the misfortune to lose our money. In fact our means are dreadfully small."

"It's an awfully trying—a regular strain," said Mrs. Monarch.

They evidently wished to be discreet—to take care not to swagger because they were gentlefolks. I felt them willing to recognise this as something of a drawback, at the same time that I guessed at an underlying sense—their consolation in adversity—that they *had* their points. They certainly had; but these advantages struck me as preponderantly social; such for instance as would help to make a drawing-room look well. However, a drawing-room was always, or ought to be, a picture.

In consequence of his wife's allusion to their age Major Monarch observed: "Naturally, it's more for the figure that we thought of going in. We can still hold ourselves up." On the instant I saw that the figure was indeed their strong point. His "naturally" didn't sound vain, but it lighted up the question. "*She* has got the best," he continued, nodding at his wife with a pleasant after-dinner absence of circumlocution. I could only reply, as if we were in fact sitting over our wine, that this didn't prevent his own from being very good; which led him in turn to make answer: "We thought that if you ever have to do people like us, we might be something like it. *She*, particularly—for a lady in a book, you know."

I was so amused by them that, to get more of it, I did my best to take their point of view; and though it was an embarrassment to find myself appraising physically, as if they were animals on hire or useful blacks, a pair whom I should have expected to meet only in one of the relations in which criticism is tacit, I looked at Mrs. Monarch judicially enough to be able to exclaim after a moment with conviction: "Oh yes, a lady in a book!" She was singularly like a bad illustration.

"We'll stand up, if you like," said the Major; and he raised himself before me with a really grand air.

---

① on the off-chance: 带着侥幸心理。

I could take his measure at a glance—he was six feet two and a perfect gentleman. It would have paid any club in process of formation and in want of a stamp to engage him at a salary to stand in the principal window. What struck me immediately was that in coming to me they had rather missed their vocation; they could surely have been turned to better account for advertising purposes. I couldn't of course see the thing in detail, but I could see them make someone's fortune—I don't mean their own. There was something in them for a waistcoat-maker, an hotel-keeper or a soap-vendor. I could imagine "We always use it" pinned on their bosoms with the greatest effect; I had a vision of the brilliancy with which they would launch a table d'hôte①.

Mrs. Monarch sat still, not from pride but from shyness, and presently her husband said to her: "Get up, my dear, and show how smart you are." She obeyed, but she had no need to get up to show it. She walked to the end of the studio, and then she came back blushing, her fluttered eyes on the partner of her appeal. I was reminded of an incident I had accidentally had a glimpse of in Paris—being with a friend there, a dramatist about to produce a play—when an actress came to him to ask to be entrusted with a part. She went through her paces before him, walked up and down as Mrs. Monarch was doing. Mrs. Monarch did it quite as well, but I abstained from applauding. It was very odd to see such people apply for such poor pay. She looked as if she had ten thousand a year. Her husband had used the word that described her: she was in the London current jargon essentially and typically "smart." Her figure was, in the same order of ideas, conspicuously and irreproachably "good." For a woman of her age her waist was surprisingly small; her elbow moreover had the orthodox crook. She held her head at the conventional angle; but why did she come to *me*? She ought to have tried on jackets at a big shop. I feared my visitors were not only destitute, but "artistic"—which would be a great complication. When she sat down again I thanked her, observing that what a draughtsman most valued in his model was the faculty of keeping quiet.

"Oh, *she* can keep quiet," said Major Monarch. Then he added, jocosely: "I've always kept her quiet."

"I'm not a nasty fidget, am I?" It was going to wring tears from me, I felt, the way she hid her head, ostrich-like, in the other broad bosom.

The owner of this expanse addressed his answer to me. "Perhaps it isn't out of place to mention—because we ought to be quite business-like, oughtn't we?—that when I married her she was known as the Beautiful Statue."

"Oh dear!" said Mrs. Monarch ruefully.

"Of course I should want a certain amount of expression," I rejoined.

"Of *course*!" they both exclaimed.

"And then I suppose you know that you'll get awfully tired."

"Oh, we *never* get tired!" they eagerly cried.

"Have you had any kind of practice?"

They hesitated—they looked at each other. "We've been photographed—*immensely*," said Mrs. Monarch.

"She means the fellows have asked us themselves," added the Major.

"I see—because you're so good-looking."

"I don't know what they thought, but they were always after us."

"We always got our photographs for nothing," smiled Mrs. Monarch.

"We might have brought some, my dear," her husband remarked.

"I'm not sure we have any left. We've given quantities away," she explained to me.

---

① table d'hôte:(按规定价格和品种供应的)客饭。这里指饭馆。

"With our autographs and that sort of thing," said the Major.

"Are they to be got in the shops?" I enquired as a harmless pleasantry.

"Oh, yes; *hers*—they used to be."

"Not now," said Mrs. Monarch, with her eyes on the floor.

II

  I could fancy the "sort of thing" they put on the presentation copies of their photographs, and I was sure they wrote a beautiful hand. It was odd how quickly I was sure of everything that concerned them. If they were now so poor as to have to earn shillings and pence, they could never have had much of a margin. Their good looks had been their capital, and they had good-humouredly made the most of the career that this resource marked out for them. It was in their faces, the blankness, the deep intellectual repose of the twenty years of country-house[①] visiting which had given them pleasant intonations. I could see the sunny drawing-rooms, sprinkled with periodicals she didn't read, in which Mrs. Monarch had continuously sat; I could see the wet shrubberies in which she had walked, equipped to admiration for either exercise. I could see the rich covers[②] the Major had helped to shoot and the wonderful garments in which, late at night, he repaired to the smoking-room to talk about them. I could imagine their leggings and waterproofs, their knowing tweeds and rugs, their rolls of sticks and cases of tackle and neat umbrellas; and I could evoke the exact appearance of their servants and the compact variety of their luggage on the platforms of country stations.

  They gave small tips, but they were liked; they didn't do anything themselves, but they were welcome. They looked so well everywhere; they gratified the general relish for stature, complexion and "form." They knew it without fatuity or vulgarity, and they respected themselves in consequence. They were not superficial; they were thorough and kept themselves up—it had been their line. People with such a taste for activity had to have some line. I could feel how even in a dull house they could have been counted on for the joy of life. At present something had happened—it didn't matter what, their little income had grown less, it had grown least—and they had to do something for pocket-money. Their friends could like them, I made out, without liking to support them. There was something about them that represented credit—their clothes, their manners, their type; but if credit is a large empty pocket in which an occasional chink reverberates, the chink at least must be audible. What they wanted of me was to help to make it so. Fortunately they had no children—I soon divined that. They would also perhaps wish our relations to be kept secret: this was why it was "for the figure"—the reproduction of the face would betray them.

  I liked them—I felt, quite as their friends must have done—they were so simple; and I had no objection to them if they would suit. But somehow with all their perfections I didn't easily believe in them. After all they were amateurs, and the ruling passion of my life was the detestation of the amateur. Combined with this was another perversity—an innate preference for the represented subject over the real one: the defect of the real one was so apt to be a lack of representation. I liked things that appeared; then one was sure. Whether they *were* or not was a subordinate and almost always a profitless question. There were other considerations, the first of which was that I already had two or three recruits in use, notably a young person with big feet, in alpaca[③], from Kilburn, who for a couple of years had come to me regularly for my illustrations and with whom I was still—perhaps ignobly—satisfied. I frankly explained to my visitors how the case stood, but they had taken more precautions than I supposed. They

---

① country-house: 富人的乡村别墅。
② cover: 猎物藏身的树林或灌木丛。
③ in alpaca: 穿着羊驼呢衣服。

had reasoned out their opportunity, for Claude Rivet had told them of the projected *édition de luxe*① of one of the writers of our day—the rarest of the novelists—who, long neglected by the multitudinous vulgar and dearly prized by the attentive (need I mention Philip Vincent?) had had the happy fortune of seeing, late in life, the dawn and then the full light of a higher criticism; an estimate in which on the part of the public there was something really of expiation. The edition in question, planned by a publisher of taste, was practically an act of high reparation; the wood-cuts with which it was to be enriched were the homage of English art to one of the most independent representatives of English letters. Major and Mrs. Monarch confessed to me that they had hoped I might be able to work *them* into my share of the enterprise. They knew I was to do the first of the books, "Rutland Ramsay," but I had to make clear to them that my participation in the rest of the affair—this first book was to be a test—must depend on the satisfaction I should give. If this should be limited my employers would drop me with scarce common forms. It was therefore a crisis for me, and naturally I was making special preparations, looking about for new people, should they be necessary, and securing the best types. I admitted however that I should like to settle down to two or three good models who would do for everything.

"Should we have often to—a—put on special clothes?" Mrs. Monarch timidly demanded.

"Dear, yes—that's half the business."

"And should we be expected to supply our own costumes?"

"Oh, no; I've got a lot of things. A painter's models put on—or put off—anything he likes."

"And do you mean—a—the same?"

"The same?"

Mrs. Monarch looked at her husband again.

"Oh, she was just wondering," he explained, "if the costumes are in *general* use." I had to confess that they were, and I mentioned further that some of them—I had a lot of genuine, greasy last-century things—had served their time, a hundred years ago, on living world-stained men and women; on figures not perhaps so far removed, in that vanished world, from *their* type, the Monarchs', *quoi!*② of a breeched bewigged age. "We'll put on anything that *fits*," said the Major.

"Oh, I arrange that—they fit in the pictures."

"I'm afraid I should do better for the modern books. I'd come as you like," said Mrs. Monarch.

"She has got a lot of clothes at home: they might do for contemporary life," her husband continued.

"Oh, I can fancy scenes in which you'd be quite natural." And indeed I could see the slipshod rearrangements of stale properties—the stories I tried to produce pictures for without the exasperation of reading them—whose sandy tracts the good lady might help to people. But I had to return to the fact that for this sort of work—the daily mechanical grind—I was already equipped: the people I was working with were fully adequate.

"We only thought we might be more like *some* characters," said Mrs. Monarch mildly, getting up.

Her husband also rose; he stood looking at me with a dim wistfulness that was touching in so fine a man. "Wouldn't it be rather a pull sometimes to have—a—to have—?" He hung fire③; he wanted me to help him by phrasing what he meant. But I couldn't—I didn't know. So he brought it out, awkwardly: "The *real* thing; a gentleman, you know, or a lady." I was quite ready to give a general assent—I admitted that there was a great deal in that. This encouraged Major Monarch to say, following

---

① *édition de luxe*:(法语)精装本,豪华版。
② *quoi*:(法语)什么。
③ hang fire:(枪炮)不开火,(人)不说话。

up his appeal with an unacted gulp: "It's awfully hard—we've tried everything." The gulp was communicative; it proved too much for his wife. Before I knew it Mrs. Monarch had dropped again upon a divan and burst into tears. Her husband sat down beside her, holding one of her hands; whereupon she quickly dried her eyes with the other, while I felt embarrassed as she looked up at me. "There isn't a confounded job I haven't applied for—waited for—prayed for. You can fancy we'd be pretty bad first. Secretaryships and that sort of thing? You might as well ask for a peerage. I'd be *anything*—I'm strong; a messenger or a coalheaver. I'd put on a gold-laced cap and open carriage-doors in front of the haberdasher's; I'd hang about a station, to carry portmanteaus; I'd be a postman. But they won't *look* at you; there are thousands, as good as yourself, already on the ground. *Gentlemen*, poor beggars, who have drunk their wine, who have kept their hunters!"

I was as reassuring as I knew how to be, and my visitors were presently on their feet again while, for the experiment, we agreed on an hour. We were discussing it when the door opened and Miss Churm came in with a wet umbrella. Miss Churm had to take the omnibus to Maida Vale and then walk half a mile. She looked a trifle blowsy and slightly splashed. I scarcely ever saw her come in without thinking afresh how odd it was that, being so little in herself, she should yet be so much in others. She was a meagre little Miss Churm, but she was an ample heroine of romance. She was only a freckled cockney[①], but she could represent everything, from a fine lady to a shepherdess; she had the faculty as she might have had a fine voice or long hair. She couldn't spell and she loved beer, but she had two or three "points," and practice, and a knack, and mother-wit, and a kind of whimsical sensibility, and a love of the theatre, and seven sisters, and not an ounce of respect, especially for the *h*[②]. The first thing my visitors saw was that her umbrella was wet, and in their spotless perfection they visibly winced at it. The rain had come on since their arrival.

"I'm all in a soak; there was a mess of people in the bus. I wish you lived near a styion[③]," said Miss Churm. I requested her to get ready as quickly as possible, and she passed into the room in which she always changed her dress. But before going out she asked me what she was to get into this time.

"It's the Russian princess, don't you know?" I answered; "the one with the 'golden eyes,' in black velvet, for the long thing in the *Cheapside*[④]."

"Golden eyes? I *say*!" cried Miss Churm, while my companions watched her with intensity as she withdrew. She always arranged herself, when she was late, before I could turn round; and I kept my visitors a little, on purpose, so that they might get an idea, from seeing her, what would be expected of themselves. I mentioned that she was quite my notion of an excellent model—she was really very clever.

"Do you think she looks like a Russian princess?" Major Monarch asked, with lurking alarm.

"When I make her, yes."

"Oh, if you have to *make* he—!" he reasoned, acutely.

"That's the most you can ask. There are so many that are not makeable."

"Well now, *here's* a lady"—and with a persuasive smile he passed his arm into his wife's—"who's already made!"

"Oh, I'm not a Russian princess," Mrs. Monarch protested, a little coldly. I could see that she had known some and didn't like them. There, immediately, was a complication of a kind that I never had to fear with Miss Churm.

---

① cockney: 住在伦敦东区的人,通常属于社会下层。
② 伦敦东区人说话通常不发"h"音。
③ 这里 station 中的 a 被发成 y 音。后面的 tyke 和 reputytion 同此。
④ 以伦敦的一条商业街命名的虚构杂志。

This young lady came back in black velvet—the gown was rather rusty and very low on her lean shoulders—and with a Japanese fan in her red hands. I reminded her that in the scene I was doing she had to look over someone's head. "I forget whose it is; but it doesn't matter. Just look over a head."

"I'd rather look over a stove," said Miss Churm; and she took her station near the fire. She fell into position, settled herself into a tall attitude, gave a certain backward inclination to her head and a certain forward droop to her fan, and looked, at least to my prejudiced sense, distinguished and charming, foreign and dangerous. We left her looking so, while I went downstairs with Major and Mrs. Monarch.

"I think I could come about as near it as that," said Mrs. Monarch.

"Oh, you think she's shabby, but you must allow for the alchemy of art."

However, they went off with an evident increase of comfort founded on their demonstrable advantage in being the real thing. I could fancy them shuddering over Miss Churm. She was very droll about them when I went back, for I told her what they wanted.

"Well, if *she* can sit I'll tyke to bookkeeping," said my model.

"She's very lady-like," I replied as an innocent form of aggravation.

"So much the worse for *you*. That means she can't turn round."

"She'll do for the fashionable novels."

"Oh yes, she'll *do* for them!" my model humorously declared. "Ain't they bad enough without her?" I had often sociably denounced them to Miss Churm.

III

It was for the elucidation of a mystery in one of these works that I first tried Mrs. Monarch. Her husband came with her, to be useful if necessary—it was sufficiently clear that as a general thing he would prefer to come with her. At first I wondered if this were for "propriety's" sake—if he were going to be jealous and meddling. The idea was too tiresome, and if it had been confirmed it would speedily have brought our acquaintance to a close. But I soon saw there was nothing in it and that if he accompanied Mrs. Monarch it was—in addition to the chance of being wanted—simply because he had nothing else to do. When she was away from him his occupation was gone—she never *had* been away from him. I judged rightly that in their awkward situation their close union was their main comfort and that this union had no weak spot. It was a real marriage, an encouragement to the hesitating, a nut for pessimists to crack. Their address was humble—I remember afterwards thinking it had been the only thing about them that was really professional—and I could fancy the lamentable lodgings in which the Major would have been left alone. He could sit there more or less grimly with his wife—he couldn't sit there anyhow without her.

He had too much tact to try and make himself agreeable when he couldn't be useful; so when I was too absorbed in my work to talk he simply sat and waited. But I liked to make him talk—it made my work, when not interrupting it, less mechanical, less special. To listen to him was to combine the excitement of going out with the economy of staying at home. There was only one hindrance—that I seemed not to know any of the people this brilliant couple had known. I think he wondered extremely, during the term of our intercourse, whom the deuce I *did* know. He hadn't a stray sixpence of an idea to fumble for, so we didn't spin it very fine; we confined ourselves to questions of leather and even of liquor—saddlers and breeches-makers and how to get excellent claret cheap—and matters like "good trains" and the habits of small game. His lore on these last subjects was astonishing—he managed to interweave the station-master with the ornithologist. When he couldn't talk about greater things he could talk cheerfully about smaller, and since I couldn't accompany him into reminiscences of the fashionable world he could lower the conversation without a visible effort to my level.

So earnest a desire to please was touching in a man who could so easily have knocked one down. He looked after the fire and had an opinion on the draught of the stove without my asking him, and I could see that he thought many of my arrangements not half knowing. I remember telling him that if I were only rich I'd offer him a salary to come and teach me how to live. Sometimes he gave a random sigh of which the essence was: "Give me even such a bare old barrack as *this*, and I'd do something with it!" When I wanted to use him he came alone; which was an illustration of the superior courage of women. His wife could bear her solitary second floor, and she was in general more discreet; showing by various small reserves that she was alive to the propriety of keeping our relations markedly professional—not letting them slide into sociability. She wished it to remain clear that she and the Major were employed, not cultivated, and if she approved of me as a superior, who could be kept in his place, she never thought me quite good enough for an equal.

She sat with great intensity, giving the whole of her mind to it, and was capable of remaining for an hour almost as motionless as before a photographer's lens. I could see she had been photographed often, but somehow the very habit that made her good for that purpose unfitted her for mine. At first I was extremely pleased with her lady-like air, and it was a satisfaction, on coming to follow her lines, to see how good they were and how far they could lead the pencil. But after a few times I began to find her too insurmountably stiff; do what I would with it my drawing looked like a photograph or a copy of a photograph. Her figure had no variety of expression—she herself had no sense of variety. You may say that this was my business and was only a question of placing her. Yet I placed her in every conceivable position and she managed to obliterate their differences. She was always a lady certainly and into the bargain was always the same lady. She was the real thing, but always the same thing. There were moments when I rather writhed under the serenity of her confidence that she *was* the real thing. All her dealings with me and all her husband's were an implication that this was lucky for *me*. Meanwhile I found myself trying to invent types that approached her own, instead of making her own transform itself—in the clever way that was not impossible for instance to poor Miss Churm. Arrange as I would and take the precautions I would, she always came out, in my pictures, too tall—landing me in the dilemma of having represented a fascinating woman as seven feet high, which (out of respect perhaps to my own very much scantier inches) was far from my idea of such a personage.

The case was worse with the Major—nothing I could do would keep *him* down, so that he became useful only for the representation of brawny giants. I adored variety and range, I cherished human accidents, the illustrative note; I wanted to characterise closely, and the thing in the world I most hated was the danger of being ridden by a type. I had quarrelled with some of my friends about it; I had parted company with them for maintaining that one *had* to be, and that if the type was beautiful—witness Raphael and Leonardo[①]—the servitude was only a gain. I was neither Leonardo nor Raphael—I might only be a presumptuous young modern searcher, but I held that everything was to be sacrificed sooner than character. When they claimed that the obsessional form could easily *be* character I retorted, perhaps superficially, "Whose?" It couldn't be everybody's—it might end in being nobody's.

After I had drawn Mrs. Monarch a dozen times I perceived more clearly than before that the value of such a model as Miss Churm resided precisely in the fact that she had no positive stamp, combined of course with the other fact that what she did have was a curious and inexplicable talent for imitation. Her usual appearance was like a curtain which she could draw up at request for a capital performance. This performance was simply suggestive; but it was a word to the wise—it was vivid and pretty. Sometimes even I thought it, though she was plain herself, too insipidly pretty; I made it a reproach to

---

① Raphael and Leonardo: Raffaelo Sanzio (1483—1520)和 Leonardo da Vinci (1452—1519),意大利著名画家。

her that the figures drawn from her were monotonously (*bêtement*①, as we used to say) graceful. Nothing made her more angry: it was so much her pride to feel that she could sit for characters that had nothing in common with each other. She would accuse me at such moments of taking away her "reputytion."

It suffered a certain shrinkage, this queer quantity, from the repeated visits of my new friends. Miss Churm was greatly in demand, never in want of employment, so I had no scruple in putting her off occasionally, to try them more at my ease. It was certainly amusing at first to do the real thing—it was amusing to do Major Monarch's trousers. They *were* the real thing, even if he did come out colossal. It was amusing to do his wife's back hair—it was so mathematically neat—and the particular "smart" tension of her tight stays②. She lent herself especially to positions in which the face was somewhat averted or blurred; she abounded in ladylike back views and *profils perdus*③. When she stood erect she took naturally one of the attitudes in which court-painters represent queens and princesses; so that I found myself wondering whether, to draw out this accomplishment, I couldn't get the editor of the *Cheapside* to publish a really royal romance, "A Tale of Buckingham Palace." Sometimes however the real thing and the make-believe came into contact; by which I mean that Miss Churm, keeping an appointment or coming to make one on days when I had much work in hand, encountered her invidious rivals. The encounter was not on their part, for they noticed her no more than if she had been the housemaid; not from intentional loftiness, but simply because as yet, professionally, they didn't know how to fraternise, as I could guess that they would have liked—or at least that the Major would. They couldn't talk about the omnibus—they always walked; and they didn't know what else to try—she wasn't interested in good trains or cheap claret. Besides, they must have felt—in the air—that she was amused at them, secretly derisive of their ever knowing how. She wasn't a person to conceal the limits of her faith if she had had a chance to show them. On the other hand Mrs. Monarch didn't think her tidy; for why else did she take pains to say to me—it was going out of the way, for Mrs. Monarch—that she didn't like dirty women?

One day when my young lady happened to be present with my other sitters—and she even dropped in, when it was convenient, for a chat—I asked her to be so good as to lend a hand in getting tea, a service with which she was familiar and which was one of a class that, living as I did in a small way, with slender domestic resources, I often appealed to my models to render. They liked to lay hands on my property, to break the sitting, and sometimes the china—I made them feel Bohemian④. The next time I saw Miss Churm after this incident she surprised me greatly by making a scene about it—she accused me of having wished to humiliate her. She hadn't resented the outrage at the time, but had seemed obliging and amused, enjoying the comedy of asking Mrs. Monarch, who sat vague and silent, whether she would have cream and sugar, and putting an exaggerated simper into the question. She had tried intonations—as if she too wished to pass for the real thing—till I was afraid my other visitors would take offence.

Oh *they* were determined not to do this, and their touching patience was the measure of their great need. They would sit by the hour, uncomplaining, till I was ready to use them; they would come back on the chance of being wanted and would walk away cheerfully if it failed. I used to go to the door with them to see in what magnificent order they retreated. I tried to find other employment for them—I introduced them to several artists. But they didn't "take," for reasons I could appreciate, and I became

---

① *bêtement*:(法语)愚蠢地。
② stays: 胸衣里的支撑物。
③ *profils perdus*:(法语)显现头的背面而不是侧面的姿势。
④ Bohemian: 像艺术家一样,无拘无束。

rather anxiously aware that after such disappointments they fell back upon me with a heavier weight. They did me the honour to think me most *their* form. They weren't romantic enough for the painters, and in those days there were few serious workers in black-and-white. Besides, they had an eye to the great job I had mentioned to them—they had secretly set their hearts on supplying the right essence for my pictorial vindication of our fine novelist. They knew that for this undertaking I should want no costume-effects, none of the frippery① of past ages—that it was a case in which everything would be contemporary and satirical and presumably genteel. If I could work them into it their future would be assured, for the labour would of course be long and the occupation steady.

One day Mrs. Monarch came without her husband—she explained his absence by his having had to go to the City②. While she sat there in her usual relaxed majesty there came at the door a knock which I immediately recognised as the subdued appeal of a model out of work. It was followed by the entrance of a young man whom I at once saw to be a foreigner and who proved in fact an Italian acquainted with no English word but my name, which he uttered in a way that made it seem to include all others. I hadn't then visited his country, nor was I proficient in his tongue; but as he was not so meanly constituted—what Italian is?—as to depend only on that member for expression he conveyed to me, in familiar but graceful mimicry, that he was in search of exactly the employment in which the lady before me was engaged. I was not struck with him at first, and while I continued to draw I dropped few signs of interest and encouragement. He stood his ground however—not importunately, but with a dumb dog-like fidelity in his eyes which amounted to innocent impudence, the manner of a devoted servant—he might have been in the house for years—unjustly suspected. Suddenly it struck me that this very attitude and expression made a picture, whereupon I told him to sit down and wait till I should be free. There was another picture in the way he obeyed me, and I observed as I worked that there were others still in the way he looked wonderingly, with his head thrown back, about the high studio. He might have been crossing himself in St. Peter's③. Before I finished I said to myself: "The fellow's a bankrupt orange-monger, but a treasure."

When Mrs. Monarch withdrew he passed across the room like a flash to open the door for her, standing there with the rapt, pure gaze of the young Dante spellbound by the young Beatrice④. As I never insisted, in such situations, on the blankness of the British domestic, I reflected that he had the making of a servant—and I needed one, but couldn't pay him to be only that—as well as of a model; in short I resolved to adopt my bright adventurer if he would agree to officiate in the double capacity. He jumped at my offer, and in the event my rashness—for I had really known nothing about him—wasn't brought home to me. He proved a sympathetic though a desultory ministrant, and had in a wonderful degree the *sentiment de la pose*⑤. It was uncultivated, instinctive, a part of the happy instinct that had guided him to my door and helped him to spell out my name on the card nailed to it. He had had no other introduction to me than a guess, from the shape of my high north window, seen outside, that my place was a studio and that as a studio it would contain an artist. He had wandered to England in search of fortune, like other itinerants, and had embarked, with a partner and a small green handcart, on the sale of penny ices. The ices had melted away and the partner had dissolved in their train. My young man wore tight yellow trousers with reddish stripes and his name was Oronte. He was sallow but fair, and when I put him into some old clothes of my own he looked like an Englishman. He was as good as

---

① frippery: 廉价、俗丽的衣服。
② City: 伦敦的金融商业区。
③ St. Peter's: 梵蒂冈的圣彼得大教堂。
④ Beatrice: Beatrice Portinari (1266—1290),佛罗伦萨女子,意大利诗人但丁(Dante Alighieri, 1265—1321)的偶像,他的《神曲》中的人物。
⑤ *sentiment de la pose*:(法语)摆姿势的本能。

Miss Churm, who could look, when requested, like an Italian.

IV

I thought Mrs. Monarch's face slightly convulsed when, on her coming back with her husband, she found Oronte installed. It was strange to have to recognise in a scrap of a *lazzarone*① a competitor to her magnificent Major. It was she who scented danger first, for the Major was anecdotically unconscious. But Oronte gave us tea, with a hundred eager confusions—he had never seen such a queer process—and I think she thought better of me for having at last an "establishment." They saw a couple of drawings that I had made of the establishment, and Mrs. Monarch hinted that it never would have struck her he had sat for them. "Now the drawings you make from us, they look exactly like *us*," she reminded me, smiling in triumph; and I recognised that this was indeed just their defect. When I drew the Monarchs I couldn't anyhow get away from them—get into the character I wanted to represent; and I hadn't the least desire my model should be discoverable in my picture. Miss Churm never was, and Mrs. Monarch thought I hid her, very properly, because she was vulgar; whereas if she was lost it was only as the dead who go to heaven are lost—in the gain of an angel the more.

By this time I had got a certain start with "Rutland Ramsay," the first novel in the great projected series; that is I had produced a dozen drawings, several with the help of the Major and his wife, and I had sent them in for approval. My understanding with the publishers, as I have already hinted, had been that I was to be left to do my work, in this particular case, as I liked, with the whole book committed to me; but my connection with the rest of the series was only contingent. There were moments when, frankly, it *was* a comfort to have the real thing under one's hand; for there were characters in "Rutland Ramsay" that were very much like it. There were people presumably as erect as the Major and women of as good a fashion as Mrs. Monarch. There was a great deal of country-house life—treated, it is true, in a fine fanciful ironical generalized way—and there was a considerable implication of knickerbockers and kilts. There were certain things I had to settle at the outset; such things for instance as the exact appearance of the hero and the particular bloom and figure of the heroine. The author of course gave me a lead, but there was a margin for interpretation. I took the Monarchs into my confidence, I told them frankly what I was about, I mentioned my embarrassments and alternatives. "Oh, take *him*!" Mrs. Monarch murmured sweetly, looking at her husband; and "What could you want better than my wife?" the Major enquired with the comfortable candour that now prevailed between us.

I was not obliged to answer these remarks—I was only obliged to place my sitters. I wasn't easy in mind, and I postponed a little timidly perhaps the solution of the question. The book was a large canvas, the other figures were numerous, and I worked off at first some of the episodes in which the hero and the heroine were not concerned. When once I had set *them* up I should have to stick to them—I couldn't make my young man seven feet high in one place and five feet nine in another. I inclined on the whole to the latter measurement, though the Major more than once reminded me that *he* looked about as young as any one. It was indeed quite possible to arrange him, for the figure, so that it would have been difficult to detect his age. After the spontaneous Oronte had been with me a month, and after I had given him to understand several times over that his native exuberance would presently constitute an insurmountable barrier to our further intercourse, I waked to a sense of his heroic capacity. He was only five feet seven, but the remaining inches were latent. I tried him almost secretly at first, for I was really rather afraid of the judgment my other models would pass on such a choice. If they regarded Miss Churm as little better than a snare what would they think of the representation by a person so little

---

① *lazzarone*:(意大利语)乞丐。

the real thing as an Italian street-vendor of a protagonist formed by a public school?

If I went a little in fear of them it wasn't because they bullied me, because they had got an oppressive foothold, but because in their really pathetic decorum and mysteriously permanent newness they counted on me so intensely. I was therefore very glad when Jack Hawley came home: he was always of such good counsel. He painted badly himself, but there was no one like him for putting his finger on the place. He had been absent from England for a year; he had been somewhere—I don't remember where—to get a fresh eye. I was in a good deal of dread of any such organ, but we were old friends; he had been away for months and a sense of emptiness was creeping into my life. I hadn't dodged a missile for a year.

He came back with a fresh eye, but with the same old black velvet blouse, and the first evening he spent in my studio we smoked cigarettes till the small hours. He had done no work himself, he had only got the eye; so the field was clear for the production of my little things. He wanted to see what I had done for the *Cheapside*, but he was disappointed in the exhibition. That at least seemed the meaning of two or three comprehensive groans which, as he lounged on my big divan, his legs folded under him, looking at my latest drawings, issued from his lips with the smoke of the cigarette.

"What's the matter with you?" I asked.

"What's the matter with *you*?"

"Nothing save that I'm mystified."

"You are indeed. You're quite off the hinge. What's the meaning of this new fad?" And he tossed me, with visible irreverence, a drawing in which I happened to have depicted both my elegant models. I asked if he didn't think it good, and he replied that it struck him as execrable, given the sort of thing I had always represented myself to him as wishing to arrive at; but I let that pass—I was so anxious to see exactly what he meant. The two figures in the picture looked colossal, but I supposed this was *not* what he meant, inasmuch as, for aught he knew to the contrary, I might have been trying for some such effect. I maintained that I was working exactly in the same way as when he last had done me the honour to tell me I might do something some day. "Well, there's a screw loose somewhere," he answered; "wait a bit and I'll discover it." I depended upon him to do so: where else was the fresh eye? But he produced at last nothing more luminous than "I don't know—I don't like your types." This was lame for a critic who had never consented to discuss with me anything but the question of execution, the direction of strokes and the mystery of values.

"In the drawings you've been looking at I think my types are very handsome."

"Oh, they won't do!"

"I've been working with new models."

"I see you have. *They* won't do."

"Are you very sure of that?"

"Absolutely—they're stupid."

"You mean I am—for I ought to get round that."

"You *can't*—with such people. Who are they?"

I told him, so far as was necessary, and he concluded heartlessly: "Ce sont des gens qu'il faut mettre à la porte."①

"You've never seen them; they're awfully good"—I flew to their defence.

"Not seen them? Why, all this recent work of yours drops to pieces with them. It's all I want to see of them."

---

① Ce sont des gens qu'il faut mettre à la porte:(法语)这些人都应打发走。

"No one else has said anything against it—the *Cheapside* people are pleased."

"Everyone else is an ass, and the *Cheapside* people the biggest asses of all. Come, don't pretend at this time of day to have pretty illusions about the public, especially about publishers and editors. It's not for *such* animals you work—it's for those who know, *coloro che sanno*①; so keep straight for *me* if you can't keep straight for yourself. There's a certain sort of thing you used to try for—and a very good thing it is. But this twaddle isn't *in* it." When I talked with Hawley later about "Rutland Ramsay" and its possible successors he declared that I must get back into my boat again or I would go to the bottom. His voice in short was the voice of warning.

I noted the warning, but I didn't turn my friends out of doors. They bored me a good deal; but the very fact that they bored me admonished me not to sacrifice them—if there was anything to be done with them—simply to irritation. As I look back at this phase they seem to me to have pervaded my life not a little. I have a vision of them as most of the time in my studio, seated against the wall on an old velvet bench to be out of the way, and resembling the while a pair of patient courtiers in a royal ante-chamber. I'm convinced that during the coldest weeks of the winter they held their ground because it saved them fire. Their newness was losing its gloss, and it was impossible not to feel that they were objects of charity. Whenever Miss Churm arrived they went away, and after I was fairly launched in "Rutland Ramsay" Miss Churm arrived pretty often. They managed to express to me tacitly that they supposed I wanted her for the low life of the book, and I let them suppose it, since they had attempted to study the work—it was lying about the studio—without discovering that it dealt only with the highest circles. They had dipped into the most brilliant of our novelists without deciphering many passages. I still took an hour from them, now and again, in spite of Jack Hawley's warning: it would be time enough to dismiss them, if dismissal should be necessary, when the rigour of the season was over. Hawley had made their acquaintance—he had met them at my fireside—and thought them a ridiculous pair. Learning that he was a painter they tried to approach him, to show him too that they were the real thing; but he looked at them, across the big room, as if they were miles away: they were a compendium of everything that he most objected to in the social system of his country. Such people as that, all convention and patent-leather, with ejaculations that stopped conversation, had no business in a studio. A studio was a place to learn to see, and how could you see through a pair of feather-beds?

The main inconvenience I suffered at their hands was that at first I was shy of letting it break upon them that my artful little servant had begun to sit to me for "Rutland Ramsay." They knew that I had been odd enough—they were prepared by this time to allow oddity to artists—to pick a foreign vagabond out of the streets when I might have had a person with whiskers and credentials; but it was some time before they learned how high I rated his accomplishments. They found him in an attitude more than once, but they never doubted I was doing him as an organ-grinder. There were several things they never guessed, and one of them was that for a striking scene in the novel, in which a footman briefly figured, it occurred to me to make use of Major Monarch as the menial. I kept putting this off, I didn't like to ask him to don the livery—besides the difficulty of finding a livery to fit him. At last, one day late in the winter, when I was at work on the despised Oronte, who caught one's idea on the wing, and was in the glow of feeling myself go very straight, they came in, the Major and his wife, with their society laugh about nothing (there was less and less to laugh at); came in like country-callers—they always reminded me of that—who have walked across the park after church and are presently persuaded to stay to luncheon. Luncheon was over, but they could stay to tea—I knew they wanted it. The fit was on me, however, and I couldn't let my ardour cool and my work wait, with the fading

---

① *coloro che sanno*:(意大利语)那些知者,出自但丁《神曲·地狱》(IV, 131)。

daylight, while my model prepared it. So I asked Mrs. Monarch if she would mind laying it out—a request which for an instant brought all the blood to her face. Her eyes were on her husband's for a second, and some mute telegraphy passed between them. Their folly was over the next instant; his cheerful shrewdness put an end to it. So far from pitying their wounded pride, I must add, I was moved to give it as complete a lesson as I could. They bustled about together and got out the cups and saucers and made the kettle boil. I know they felt as if they were waiting on my servant, and when the tea was prepared I said: "He'll have a cup, please—he's tired." Mrs. Monarch brought him one where he stood, and he took it from her as if he had been a gentleman at a party squeezing a crush-hat with an elbow.

Then it came over me that she had made a great effort for me—made it with a kind of nobleness—and that I owed her a compensation. Each time I saw her after this I wondered what the compensation could be. I couldn't go on doing the wrong thing to oblige them. Oh it was the wrong thing, the stamp of the work for which they sat—Hawley was not the only person to say it now. I sent in a large number of the drawings I had made for "Rutland Ramsay," and I received a warning that was more to the point than Hawley's. The artistic adviser of the house for which I was working was of opinion that many of my illustrations were not what had been looked for. Most of these illustrations were the subjects in which the Monarchs had figured. Without going into the question of what *had* been looked for, I had to face the fact at this rate I shouldn't get the other books to do. I hurled myself in despair upon Miss Churm—I put her through all her paces. I not only adopted Oronte publicly as my hero, but one morning when the Major looked in to see if I didn't require him to finish a *Cheapside* figure for which he had begun to sit the week before, I told him that I had changed my mind—I would do the drawing from my man. At this my visitor turned pale and stood looking at me. "Is *he* your idea of an English gentleman?" he asked.

I was disappointed, I was nervous, I wanted to get on with my work; so I replied with irritation: "Oh, my dear Major—I can't be ruined for *you*!"

It was a horrid speech, but he stood another moment—after which, without a word, he quitted the studio. I drew a long breath, for I said to myself that I shouldn't see him again. I had not told him definitely that I was in danger of having my work rejected, but I was vexed at his not having felt the catastrophe in the air, read with me the moral of our fruitless collaboration, the lesson that in the deceptive atmosphere of art even the highest respectability may fail of being plastic①.

I didn't owe my friends money, but I did see them again. They reappeared together, three days later, and, given all the other facts, there was something tragic in that one. It was a clear proof that they could find nothing else in life to do. They had threshed the matter out in a dismal conference—they had digested the bad news that they were not in for the series. If they weren't useful to me even for the *Cheapside* their function seemed difficult to determine, and I could only judge at first that they had come, forgivingly, decorously, to take a last leave. This made me rejoice in secret that I had little leisure for a scene; for I had placed both my other models in position together and I was pegging away at a drawing from which I hoped to derive glory. It had been suggested by the passage in which Rutland Ramsay, drawing up a chair to Artemisia's piano-stool, says extraordinary things to her while she ostensibly fingers out a difficult piece of music. I had done Miss Churm at the piano before—it was an attitude in which she knew how to take on an absolutely poetic grace. I wished the two figures to "compose" together with intensity, and my little Italian had entered perfectly into my conception. The pair were vividly before me, the piano had been pulled out; it was a charming show of blended youth

---

① fail of being plastic: 太僵硬，不适于艺术表现。

and murmured love, which I had only to catch and keep. My visitors stood and looked at it, and I was friendly to them over my shoulder.

They made no response, but I was used to silent company and went on with my work, only a little disconcerted—even though exhilarated by the sense that *this* was at least the ideal thing—at not having got rid of them after all. Presently I heard Mrs. Monarch's sweet voice beside or rather above me: "I wish her hair was a little better done." I looked up and she was staring with a strange fixedness at Miss Churm, whose back was turned to her. "Do you mind my just touching it?" she went on—a question which made me spring up for an instant as with the instinctive fear that she might do the young lady a harm. But she quieted me with a glance I shall never forget—I confess I should like to have been able to paint *that*—and went for a moment to my model. She spoke to her softly, laying a hand upon her shoulder and bending over her; and as the girl, understanding, gratefully assented, she disposed her rough curls, with a few quick passes, in such a way as to make Miss Churm's head twice as charming. It was one of the most heroic personal services I have ever seen rendered. Then Mrs. Monarch turned away with a low sigh and, looking about her as if for something to do, stooped to the floor with a noble humility and picked up a dirty rag that had dropped out of my paint-box.

The Major meanwhile had also been looking for something to do, and, wandering to the other end of the studio, saw before him my breakfast-things neglected, unremoved. "I say, can't I be useful *here*?" he called out to me with an irrepressible quaver. I assented with a laugh that I fear was awkward, and for the next ten minutes, while I worked, I heard the light clatter of china and the tinkle of spoons and glass. Mrs. Monarch assisted her husband—they washed up my crockery, they put it away. They wandered off into my little scullery, and I afterwards found that they had cleaned my knives and that my slender stock of plate had an unprecedented surface. When it came over me, the latent eloquence of what they were doing, I confess that my drawing was blurred for a moment—the picture swam. They had accepted their failure, but they couldn't accept their fate. They had bowed their heads in bewilderment to the perverse and cruel law in virtue of which the real thing could be so much less precious than the unreal; but they didn't want to starve. If my servants were my models, then my models might be my servants. They would reverse the parts—the others would sit for the ladies and gentlemen, and *they* would do the work. They would still be in the studio—it was an intense dumb appeal to me not to turn them out. "Take us on," they wanted to say—"we'll do *anything*."

My pencil dropped from my hand; my sitting was spoiled and I got rid of my sitters, who were also evidently rather mystified and awestruck. Then, alone with the Major and his wife, I had a most uncomfortable moment. He put their prayer into a single sentence: "I say, you know—just let us do for you, can't you?" I couldn't—it was dreadful to see them emptying my slops; but I pretended I could, to oblige them, for about a week. Then I gave them a sum of money to go away, and I never saw them again. I obtained the remaining books, but my friend Hawley repeats that Major and Mrs. Monarch did me a permanent harm, got me into false ways. If it be true I am content to have paid the price—for the memory.

这篇1892年发表于英国周刊《黑与白》上的短篇小说《真品》,选用一个无姓名有抱负的插图画家作叙述者,讲述了破败贵族莫纳克夫妇作他模特儿期间的故事。这对夫妇是"真品",能够真实体现贵族气质,但他们不能改变形象满足画家的不同创作要求,致使画家不得不更多依靠另外两个变化自如的模特儿——意大利乞丐奥伦迪和英国平民切姆小姐。最后,画家听从同行的建议,解雇了给他的艺术造成损害的莫纳克夫妇。

《真品》是一个关于艺术的故事,涉及了绘画、摄影和小说等艺术门类,其中的主要人物和事件也都与艺术有关。作品关注的核心问题是艺术与生活的关系,具体表现为画家与模特儿尤其是莫纳克夫妇的关系。在莫纳克夫妇(他们名字在英语里是"君主"的意思)看来,艺术应该服从生活,画家应该服从模特儿。与另外两位模特儿不同,他们从不顾及画家的创作需要,所摆的始终是贵族的姿势,画家不久就感到自己的画越来越接近他们,越来越缺乏想象的自由与空间,越来越难以超越他们进入他想画的形象。朋友的建议和出版社的警告最终使他意识到这一问题的严重性。

《真品》也是一个关于生活的故事,作家在写以画家、切姆小姐和奥伦迪为一方,以莫纳克夫妇为另一方在艺术上的冲突的同时,也写了他们在生活上的冲突。画家对莫纳克夫妇一直持尊重和同情的态度,总是设法消除他们受雇者的感觉。切姆小姐对莫纳克夫妇作为模特儿的局限性有看法,但没有对他们的人格表现过不敬。相比之下,莫纳克夫妇则始终端着贵族的架子,不但不能平等待人,还处处歧视人。他们嫌切姆小姐和奥伦迪肮脏粗俗。即便在物质上依赖于画家,他们也能在精神上找到自己的优越之处。尽管他们接受失败但不接受命运的态度有几分悲壮,但作品似乎想说,思想保守、不善应变者并不能真正地代表生活,因为他们无论在哪里都不适合生存,无论是在不断创新的艺术中,还是不断发展的社会中。

在《小说艺术》一文中,为了争取小说的艺术地位,詹姆斯将小说与艺术地位稳固的绘画做了比较,指出小说在关注生活动机、过程和结局等方面与绘画是一致的,并提出小说是最宏伟的艺术形式。在《真品》中,詹姆斯就是用短篇小说形式艺术地表现了绘画艺术的方方面面,尤其是绘画与生活的复杂关系。对于这一关系,国画大师齐白石曾做过这样的归纳。他说,好画"妙在似与不似之间",因为"不似则欺世,太似则媚俗"。借用他的话来说,莫纳克夫妇的主要问题,就在于使画家的作品"太似"生活,排除了它们"不似"生活或艺术想象的可能,从而使它们丧失了艺术性,流于"媚俗"。或许可以说,这篇小说题目中的"真品"二字除了指莫纳克夫妇,也表达了作家想把这篇作品写成艺术真品的愿望。

  思考题

1. Why does the illustrator decide to employ the Monarchs in the beginning?
2. What are the illustrator's expectations of a good model?
3. How are the four models compared and contrasted?
4. Discuss the importance of eyes and seeing in the story.

The Portrait of a Lady (1881)
The Bostonians (1886)
The Ambassadors (1903)

Edel, Leon. *Henry James: A Life.* New York: Harper Collins, 1985.
James, Henry. *The Art of the Novel: Critical Prefaces.* Lincoln: University of Nebraska Press, 1984.
Jolly, Roslyn. *Henry James: History, Narrative, Fiction.* New York: Oxford University Press, 1993.
Kaplan, Fred. *Henry James: The Imagination of Genius.* New York: William Morrow, 1992.
Teahan, Sheila. *The Rhetorical Logic of Henry James.* Baton Rouge: Louisiana State University Press, 1995.

(刘建华)

Sherwood Anderson (1876—1941)

舍伍德·安德森

 作者简介

　　舍伍德·安德森是20世纪早期美国小说家，一生富有传奇色彩。他没有接受过多少正规教育，曾从事过多种职业：工人、广告的文字撰稿人、美国西部战争的士兵、油漆生产商和作家，等等。一个众所周知的说法是，为了全身心地投入严肃文学创作、表达工业文明对美国农业小镇生活的冲击，有一天他突然走出他的工厂就再也没有回去过。

　　安德森的创作受到斯泰因、德莱塞和D.H.劳伦斯的极大影响，是美国作家中描写心理活动和潜意识的先驱之一。他的短篇小说与欧·亨利及其模仿者们精心安排情节的作品有很大差异，强调形式而不看重情节，对第一次世界大战和第二次世界大战之间的美国文学，特别是对海明威、福克纳、菲茨杰拉德等作家产生了深远的影响。福克纳称他为"我们这一代作家的父亲"。他的语言基于日常对话，朴实自然。他力求描写美国生活的原貌，人称美国的"陀思妥耶夫斯基"。

　　安德森的经典作品是短篇小说，著有短篇小说集《小镇畸人》(*Winesburg, Ohio*, 1919)、《鸡蛋的胜利》(*The Triumph of the Egg*, 1921)、《马和人》(*Horses and Men*, 1923)和《林中之死》(*Death in the Woods*, 1931)。此外，他的自传性作品《讲故事者的故事》(*A Story Teller's Story*, 1924)和《塔尔：一个中西部人的童年》(*Tar:A Midwest Childhood*, 1926)也备受赞誉。

A Story Teller's Story

My Thoughts on Story-Telling (Note I, Book Four)

　　I walked about the city of New York looking at people. I was not too young any more and could not make myself over to fit a new city. No doubt certain characteristics of my own nature had become fixed. I was a man of the mid-western towns who had gone from his town to the mid-western cities and there had gone through the adventures common to such fellows as myself. Was there some salt in me? To the end of my life I would talk with the half slovenly drawl of the middle-westerner, would walk like such a middle-westerner, have the air of something between a laborer, a man of business, a gambler, a race horse owner, an actor. If I was, as I then fully intended, to spend the rest of my life trying to tell such tales as I could think and feel my way through, I would have to tell the tales of my own people. Would I gain new power and insight for telling by having come East, by consorting with other story-tellers? Would I understand better my own people and what had made the tragedies, the comedies and the wonders of their lives?

　　I was in New York as a guest, as an onlooker, wondering about the city and the men of the city and what they were thinking and feeling. There were certain men I wanted to see, who had written things I thought had given me new lights on own people, the subjects of my tales.

　　I dare say there was a good deal of a certain half-rural timidity in me.

　　There was Mr. Van Wyck Brooks[①], whose book "America's Coming-of-Age", had moved me

---

① Van Wyck Brooks: 布鲁克斯(1886—1963)，美国文学史家和评论家。

deeply. He with Mr. Waldo Frank, Paul Rosenfeld, James Oppenheim and others had just started a magazine, *The Seven Arts* (that after its death was to be replaced by *The Dial*, published by a quite different group), and the magazine had not only offered to publish some of my things but its editors had asked me to come to see them.

I wanted to go and was at the same time a little afraid. At that time there was a good deal of talk abroad as to a new artistic awakening in America. Mr. Waldo Frank's "Our America" must have been in preparation at just about that time and it could not have been much later that Mr. William Allen White[①] wrote in *The New Republic*, an article the import of which was that "The King is dead! Long live the King!" If there were new things in the land, I wanted to see and consort with them if I could.

As for *The Seven Arts* magazine, there had been rumors of its coming birth, even in Chicago. Miss Edna Kenton had come from New York to Chicago at about that time and a meeting was held. There was a large party in a large house and upstairs somewhere the new day was under discussion. We, downstairs, did not just know what was being discussed but there was a kind of tingling sensation in the air. Little groups of us gathered in the rooms below. "What's up?" It is to be remembered this was in Chicago and we were all young and no doubt naïve. "What they whispering about upstairs?" "Don't you know?" Not to know was, we all felt, a kind of cultural blight. I had run from one group to another trying to find out and at just that moment a young doctor, who in his spare moments wrote poetry, came into the house and went hurriedly upstairs. A rather ribald fellow among the guests—Ben Hecht perhaps—who like the rest of us was angry that he had not been let into the secret, made an announcement. "I know what it is. Someone's having a baby," he said.

What about the men of New York, the writers whose work I admired, the painters whose work I admired? I had always having sensations and seeing forms that could perhaps have been expressed in paint and in no other way but the materials of the painter's craft seemed to me to lie far outside my way of life. One had to know drawing, to know what green did to yellow and yellow to brown. When one talked to painters they spoke of things that lay far outside one's pathway. There had been one painter I have known quite well. He had lived in a room near my own in Chicago and painted landscapes. Rather he painted one landscape over and over. It was evening and two cows were coming home along a road, to a barn one fancied, but the barn could not be seen for the deep shadows that had gathered behind the house. Then there were some trees, the tops of which could be but faintly seen on the horizon. The last rays of the sun had splashed the sky with red. Often in the evening the painter, a large man with red hair, came into my room and spoke to me. He also had been touched with the new day and had read Paul Gauguin's[②] notebook and a work by Mr. Clive Bell[③]. "The new fellows have nothing on me," he declared and taking me into his room he showed me half a dozen of his canvases and how that in one the tops of the trees could just be seen above the roof of the house and in another that there were really no trees at all. "What you think is trees is only clouds," he declared, "and what you think is the sun going down is really the moon coming up."

Returning with me to my room he had talked so long and well of the effect of light on color, of form and its significance, of the new cubistic and post-impressionistic movements, the import and significance of which he declared scornfully he had measured and for the most part discarded, that I became frightened and did not for years afterwards try to paint. Once in Chicago I went into a store, intending to buy some colors with which to play at idle moments in my room but a certain air of the clerk had frightened me. My own father, when he was alive, had often received from manufacturers certain

---

① William Allen White: 怀特(1868—1944)，美国新闻工作者、作家，《恩波里亚日报》主编，以所写社论闻名，曾获1923年普利策奖。
② Paul Gauguin: 高更(1848—1903)，法国后期印象派画家，醉心于"原始主义"，作品有《黄色的基督》《两个塔希提女人》等。
③ Clive Bell: 贝尔(1881—1964)，英国美术和文学批评家，著有《19世纪绘画里程碑》《普鲁斯特》等。

cards on which the house-painter's colors were shown and the trade name of each color printed below and I had thought I might find such a card lying on a counter in the art store but saw none and was ashamed to ask. Perhaps I wanted the clerk to think me a painter who knew his craft. How glibly the red-haired man had reeled off the names of colors. I was like one who has wandered into a church where people are kneeling in prayer. I began walking on tiptoes. "I only wanted to buy a pencil eraser," I said.

And so now there I was in the city of New York and there were certain men in city to whom I would have liked to go, to talk with them of my craft, but when I thought of doing so I was afraid.

My own position was something like this: there were in my head certain tales I knew but could not yet tell and certain others I had told but felt I had told badly or haltingly. Was there a certain formula one could learn that might help one out of the difficulty? There was a sense in which I thought of myself as an ignorant man. The tales I had already put down on paper had been a sort of growth in me. There was *The little Review*, run by two Chicago women who had preceded me to New York. They had published tales of mine and might publish more. When I went to see them we had much fun together and Miss Anderson and myself had in common a fondness for rather striking clothes and for strutting a bit upon the stage of life that drew us closely together but being at bottom fellow Chicagoans we were bound not to take each other too seriously—at least not under the rose.

Did I want, above everything else, to be taken seriously? No doubt I did. That may have been the notion I had in coming to the city. And I suppose I wanted also to find superior craftsman at whose feet I could sit. I already had my own notions concerning American story-tellers in general.

I was walking in the street or sitting in a train and overheard a remark dropped from the lips of some man or woman. Out of a thousand such remarks, heard almost every day, one stayed in my head. I could not shake it out. And then people constantly told me tales and in the telling of them there was a sentence used that intoxicated. I was lying on my back on the porch and the street lamp shone on my mother's face. What was the use? I could not say to her what was in my mind. She would not have understood. There was a man lived next door who kept going past the house and smiling at me. I got it into my head that he knew all that I could not tell my mother.

A few such sentences in the midst of a conversation overheard or dropped into a tale someone told. These were the seeds of stories. How could one make them grow?

In telling tale of themselves people constantly spoiled the tale in telling. They has some notion of how a story should be told got from reading. Little lies crept in. They had done something mean and tried to justify some action that for the tale's sake did not need justification.

There was a notion that ran through all story-telling in America, that stories must be built about a plot and that absurd Anglo-Saxon notion that they must point a moral, uplift the people, make better citizens, etc. The magazines were filled with these plot stories and most of the plays on our stage were plot plays. "The Poison Plot," I called it in conversation with my friends as the plot notion did seem to me to poison all story-telling. What was wanted I thought was form, not plot, an altogether more elusive and difficult thing to come at.

The plots were frameworks about which the stories were to be constructed and editors were inordinately fond of them. One got "an idea for a story." What was met was that a new trick had been thought out. Nearly all the adventure stories and the well-known American western stories were so constructed. A man went into the redwood forests or into the deserts and took up land. He has been a rather mean, second-rate chap in civilization but in the new place a great change comes over him. Well, the writer had got him out where there was no one looking and could do as he pleased with the fellow. Never mind what he had been. The forests or the deserts had changed him completely. The writer could make a regular angel of him, have him rescue downtrodden women, catch horse thieves, exhibit any kind of bravery required to keep the reader excited and happy.

A word of good sense dropped in anywhere would have blown the whole thing to pieces but there was no danger. In all such writing all consideration for human beings was thrown aside. No one lived in such tales. Let such a writer begin to think of human beings, care a little for human beings, and his pasteboard world would melt before his eyes. The man in the desert or in the redwood forests was of course the same man he had been before he went there. He had the same problems to face. God knows we would all flee to the forests or the deserts at once if going there could so transform anyone. At least I know I should waste no time in getting there.

In the construction of these stories there was endless variation but in all of them human beings, the lives of human beings, were altogether disregarded. An Alabama Negro was given the shrewdness of a Connecticut Yankee, a trick that made some writer temporarily famous and brought him wealth. Having made his Negro think like a Yankee, having made him practice all the smart cute tricks of the Yankee, there was nothing to stop the writer producing a thousand tales with the hybrid Negro as the hero of them all. Only the giving out of the patience of the editors or of the public could stop him, and both seemed inexhaustible.

As to what the writer himself suffered under these circumstances, that was a different matter. One supposed that any man who attempted the writer's craft had, at the beginning, some real interest in the people about him but this was quickly lost. The imaginative life of the romancer must be lived entirely in a queer pasteboard world.

It was a peculiarity of the writer's craft that one must of necessity give oneself to the people about whom one wrote, must in a quite special way believe in the existence of these people, and a peculiar childlike credulousness must result to the writer who so completely separated himself from actual life. Having acquired sudden fame and wealth such a writer woke up some morning to find himself irrevocably dead. The actuality of life could not reach him. On all sides of him people suffered, were touched with moments of nameless joy, loved and died, and the manufacturer of society detectives, desert heroes and daring adventures by sea and land could no longer see life at all. With unseeing eyes, deaf ears and benumbed senses he must walk through life—a movie hero, a stage star or a rich and successful manufacturer of romances—no longer a human being at all. One had no notion of giving oneself to that kind of death in life but to find out what one did not want to do was but half the battle.

After all the tales themselves came quickly. In certain moods one became impregnated with the seeds if a hundred new tales in one day. The telling of the tales, to get them into form, to clothe them, find just the words and the arrangement of words that would clothe them—that was a quite different matter. I wanted to find, if I could, the men who would help me toward the solution of that problem.

For even an unknown and unsuccessful scribbler in America the situation is difficult enough. Even the very sweetness of our people in their attitude toward our writers is destructive. You have seen how I myself was allowed to play like a reckless child among advertising men, constantly forgiven for my impudence, often paid an absurd figure for writing an unimportant advertisement—that any one of forty men, not authors, would have gladly written with more care at half my price—simply because I was an author.

Well, I have published certain tales over my own name and my fate was sealed. That the tales were not liked by many of the critics did not matter too much. To be sure, my books did not sell, but I was discussed in the newspapers and literary magazines and my picture was occasionally printed and finally a very second-rate English writer of romances, very popular in our country, spoke well of me and Mr. Frank Harris[①] spoke ill of me.

[①] Frank Harris：哈里斯(1856—1931)，英国新闻记者、作家，早年侨居美国，返回英国后曾主编《星期六评论》等刊物，写过王尔德、莎士比亚等人传记，以自传《我的生活与爱情》闻名。

Ye gods, I was lost and must flee. The very grocer at the corner, with whom I was wont to sit on the steps by the back door of the store on summer evenings while he talked of his life as a young sailor on a lake steamer looked at me with new eyes. He began speaking like a very movie hero. His tales, that had been so naturally and humanly told, became grotesques of tales. The fellow had some idea I might make him the hero of some improbable romance of our inland seas, one always holding the helm in some desperate storm or jumping overboard to rescue some broker's daughter, and tried heroically to supply me with materials. He had in his youth read some novel of the seas and now he began to lie valiantly, telling me all the desperate escapades of which he had heard or read as having happened to himself. Shades of Defoe① and Melville, such a sea and such a sailor's life as he manufactured! I remembered almost with tears in my eyes the little homely real stories he had formerly been in the habit of telling of himself, and left him never to return. I was even vicious enough to rob him, for his defection, of my grocery trade.

How utterly all my life had been changed by a little public attention! Even some of my friends went the road of the grocer. I remember that I had, at just that time, done a deed affecting my personal life that had lost me the respect of some of my acquaintances. One of them saw my picture, printed I think in the *Literary Digest*, and immediately afterward wrote me a letter. "You are a great artist and may do anything you please. I forgive you everything," he wrote and as I read the letter my heart went sick within me. "At any rate why do they want to dehumanize us?" I asked myself. Violently then I cursed the romances. They were in reality at the bottom of it all. Not satisfied with the cowboys the sailors and the detectives they had descended upon their brothers of the pen and the brush. A poet was a certain kind of man with long hair and no food who went about muttering to himself. There was no escape for him. That he was and his fate was fixed. To be sure I had myself known some American poets and had found them in their everyday life much like all the other people I knew except that they were a trifle more sensitive to life and its beauties and, before they became widely known as poets, sometimes wrote beautiful bits describing their inner reaction to some flash of beauty that had come to them. They were that before they became widely known as poets and then later they were usually goners.

That was how it was with the poet. The painter usually starved in a garret and went about his small room pale and emaciated, with a palette stuck on his thumb, and then one day a lovely lady came along the street, saw how that he was a genius and married him. I'll say this for us scribblers and actors. We got off better. We usually, in the romances, sat on a park bench with the tramps and had a dirty newspaper blown to us by a cold wind. On the front page of the newspaper was a large picture of ourselves and an announcement that fame had come. Then we went and bought the tramps a breakfast with our last dollar before we went to live in a great house with servants. We scribblers and the actors got off the least shamefully in the romances but then, it is to be remembered, fellows of our own craft got up these yarns that had so stuck in the public mind and that they had for that reason perhaps a little pity for us.

All of this however concerned the materials for tales. One had to do one's own winnowing in any event. I was in New York and was after something other than stories. Would I find what I wanted? I was somewhat afraid of the writers, particularly of the ones whose work I most admired because I thought they must be a special kind of being, quite different from the men I had known. (No doubt I was myself the victim of the same romancers I have just been cursing.) There were certain men I thought had written of America and American writing with an understanding that had been a help to me. I was what I was, a rough and tumble participant in life. As yet there had been little time for study, for quiet thought.

As for these other men, the fellows of the East, what of them? I fancied in them an erudition the

---

① Defoe: 笛福（Daried Defoe, 1660—1731），英国小说家、报刊撰稿人，写过讽刺诗和大量政论小册子，代表作为《鲁滨孙漂流记》。

contemplation of which made me afraid. Now I understood how Mark Twain felt when he went up to Boston. Did he, like myself, want something without knowing just what he wanted?

For such men as myself you must understand there is always a great difficulty about telling the tale after the scent had been picked up. The tales that continually came to me in the way indicated above could of course not become tales until I had clothed them. Having, from a conversation overheard or in some other way, got the tone of a tale, I was like a woman who has just become impregnated. Something was growing inside me. At night when I lay in my bed I could feel the heels of the tale kicking against the walls of my body. Often as I lay thus every word of the tale came to me quite clearly but when I got out of bed to write it down the words would not come.

I had constantly to seek in roads new to me. Other men had felt what I had felt, had seen what I had seen—how had they met the difficulties I faced? My father when he told his tales walked up and down the room before his audience. He pushed out little experimental sentences and watched his audience narrowly. There was a dull-eyed farmer sitting in a corner of the room. Father had his eyes on the fellow. "I'll get him," he said to himself. He watched the farmer's eyes. When the experimental sentence he had tried did not get anywhere he tried another and kept trying. Beside words he had—to help the telling of his tales—the advantage of being able to act out those parts for which he could find no words. He could frown, shake his fists, smile, let a look of pain or annoyance drift over his face.

These were his advantages that I had to give up if I was to write my tales rather than tell them and how often I cursed my fate.

How significant words had become to me! At about this time an American woman living in Paris, Miss Gertrude Stein[①], had published a book called "Tender Buttons" and it had come into my hands. How it had excited me! Here was something purely experimental and dealing in words separated from sense—in the ordinary meaning of the word sense—an approach I was sure the poets must often be compelled to make. Was it an approach that would help me? I decided to try it.

A year of two before the time of which I am now writing an American painter, Mr. Felix Russman, had taken me one day into his workshop to show me his colors. He laid them out on a table before me and then his wife called him out the room and he stayed for half an hour. It had been one of the most exciting moments of my life. I shifted the little pans of color about, laid one color against another. I walked away and came near. Suddenly there had flashed into my consciousness, for perhaps the first time in my life, the secret inner world of the painters. Before that time I had wondered often enough why certain paintings, done by the old masters, and hung in our Chicago Art Institute, had so strange an effect upon me. Now I thought I know. The true painter revealed all of himself in every stroke of his brush. Titian[②] made one feel so utterly the splendor of himself; From Fra Angelico[③] and Sandro Botticelli[④] there came such a deep human tenderness that on some days it fairly brought tears to the eyes; in a most dreadful way and in spite of all his skill Bouguereau[⑤] gave away his own inner nastiness while Leonardo[⑥] made one feel all of the grandeur of his mind just as Balzac had made his readers feel the universality and wonder of his mind.

---

① Gertrude Stein：斯泰因(1874—1946)，美国女作家，移居巴黎，提倡先锋派艺术，运用重复、片段化、简单化手法写作，作品有小说《三个女人的一生》等。
② Titan：提香(1488—1576)，意大利文艺复兴盛期威尼斯画家，擅长肖像画、宗教和神话题材画，作品有《乌尔宾诺的维纳斯》《圣母升天》等。
③ Fra Angelico：安吉利科(1400—1455)，意大利文艺复兴早期佛罗伦萨画派的著名画家，作品主要为祭坛画和教堂壁画。
④ Sandro Botticelli：波提切利(1445—1510)，意大利文艺复兴时期画家，运用背离传统的新画派方法，创造出富于线条节奏且擅长表现情感的独特风格，代表作有《春》《维纳斯的诞生》等。
⑤ Bouguereau：布格罗(1825—1905)，法国学院派画家，维护正统艺术，排斥印象派，多画裸体、田园、宗教话题材，风格严谨细腻。
⑥ Leonardo：达·芬奇(Leonardo Da Vinci, 1452—1519)，意大利文艺复兴时期画家、雕塑家、建筑师和工程师，在艺术和科学方面均有创造性见解和成就，代表作有壁画《最后的晚餐》、祭坛画《岩下圣母》及肖像画《蒙娜丽莎》等。

Very well then, the words used by the tale-teller were as the colors used by the painter. Form was another matter. It grew out of the materials of the tale and the teller's reaction to them. It was the tale and the teller's reaction to them. It was the tale trying to take form that kicked about inside the taleteller at night when he wanted to sleep.

And words were something else. Words were surfaces, the clothes of the tale. I thought I had begun to get something a little clearer now. I had smiled to myself a little at the sudden realization of how little native American words had been used by American story-writers. When most American writers wanted to be very American they went in for slang. Surely we American scribblers had paid long and hard for the English blood in our veins. The English had got their books into our schools, their ideas of correct forms of expression were firmly fixed in our minds. Words as commonly used in our writing were in reality an army that marched in a certain array and the generals in command of the army were still English. One saw the words as marching, always just so—in books—and came to think of them so—in books.

But when one told a tale to a group of advertising men sitting in a barroom in Chicago or to a group of laborers by a factory door in Indiana one instinctively disbanded the army. There were moments then for what have always been called by our correct writers "unprintable words." One got now and then a certain effect by a bit of profanity. One dropped instinctively into the vocabulary of the men about, was compelled to do so to get the full effect sought for the tale. Was the tale he was telling not just the tale of a man named Smokey Pete① and how he caught his foot in the trap set by himself?—or perhaps one was giving them the Mama Geigans story. The devil. What had the words of such a tale to do with Thackeray or Fielding②? Did the men to whom one told the tale not know a dozen Smokey Petes and Mama Geigans? Has one ventured into the classic English models for tale-telling at that moment there would have been a roar? "What the devil! Don't you go high-toning us!"

And it was sure one did not always seek a laugh from his audience. Sometimes one wanted to move the audience, make them squirm with sympathy. Perhaps one wanted to throw an altogether new light on a tale the audience already knew.

Would the common words of our daily speech in shops and offices do the trick. Surely the Americans among whom one sat talking had felt everything the Greeks had felt, everything the English felt? Deaths came to them, the tricks of fate assailed their lives. I was certain none of them lived felt or talked as the average American novel made them live feel and talk and as for the plot short stories of the magazines—those bastard children of De Maupassant③, Poe④ and O.Henry⑤—it was certain there were no plot short stories ever lived in any life I had known anything about.

Did it come to this, that Americans worked, made love, settled new western states, arranged their personal affairs, drive their fords, using one language while they read books, wanted perhaps to read books, in quite another language?

I had come to Gertrude Stein's book about which everyone laughed but about which I did not laugh. It excited me as one might grow excited in going into a new and wonderful country where every-

---

① Smokey Pete：一个苦恼的胡子拉碴的人。
② Fielding：菲尔丁(Henry Fielding, 1707—1754)，英国小说家、剧作家，英国现实主义小说奠基人之一，代表作有《弃婴汤姆·琼斯的故事》《约瑟夫·安德鲁斯》。
③ Maupassant：莫泊桑(Guy de Maupassant, 1850—1893)，法国小说家，著有长篇小说《俊友》及短篇小说《羊脂球》《项链》等，尤以短篇小说著称。
④ Poe：爱伦·坡(Edgar Alan Poe, 1809—1849)，美国诗人、小说家、文艺评论家、现代侦探小说的创始人，主要作品有诗歌《乌鸦》、侦探小说《摩格街凶杀案》等。
⑤ O.Henry：欧·亨利(1862—1910)，美国短篇小说家，代表作有《麦琪的礼物》《警察和赞美诗》等。

thing is strange—a sort of Lewis[①] and Clark[②] expedition for me. Here were words laid before me as the painter had laid the color pans on the table in my presence. My mind did a kind of jerking flop and after Miss Stein's book had come into my hands I spent days going about with a tablet of paper in my pocket and making new and strange combinations of words. The result was I thought a new familiarity with the words of my own vocabulary. I became a little conscious where before I had been unconscious. Perhaps it was then I really fell in love with words, wanted to give each word I used every chance to show itself at its best.

It had then not occurred to me that the men I had really come to New York hoping to see and know, fellows of the schools, men who knew their Europe, knew the history of the arts, who knew a thousand things I could not know, it had never occurred to me that in the end I would find them as frankly puzzled as myself. When I found that out there was a new adjustment to make. It was then only the trick men, the men who worked from the little patent formula they had learned, the critics who could never get English literature out of their heads, who thought they were sure of their grounds? That knowledge was relief when I found it out but I was a long long time finding out. It takes a long time to find out one's limitations and perhaps a longer time to find out the limitations of one's critics.

Was there really something new in the air of America? I remember that about this time some told me that I was myself something new and how thankful I was to hear it. "Very well," I said to myself, "if there are certain men launching a new ship from the harbor of New York and if they are willing to take me aboard I'll sure go." I was just as willing to be a modern as anything else, was glad to be. It was very sure I was not going to be a successful author and well enough I knew that, not being a successful, there would be a great deal of consolation to me in being at least a modern.

What I at the moment felt toward all the more deeply cultured men whose acquaintanceship I sought and still in a sense feel toward them was something like what a young mechanic might feel when his boss comes into the shop accompanied by his daughter. The young mechanic is standing at his lathe and there is grease on his face and hands. The boss's daughter had never been shown over the shop before and is a little excited by the presence of so many strange men and as she and her father approach the lathe where the young workman stands he does not know whether to appear surly and uncommunicative or bold and a bit impudent. (In his place I, being an American, should probably have winked at the girl and been terribly embarrassed and ashamed later.)

There he stands fumbling about with his fingers and pretending to look out of the window and—the devil!—now the boss has stopped behind his lathe and is attempting to explain something to the daughter, "This is a sprocket post, is it not?" he says to the workman, who is compelled to turn around. "Yes, sir," he mutters, in embarrassment but his eyes, in just that fraction of a second, have taken a sweeping glance at the daughter.

And now she is gone and the workman is asking himself questions. "If I was a swell now I suppose maybe I'd be invited to their house." He imagines himself in a dress suit going up a long driveway to the front of a grand house. He is swinging a cane and there on the front steps is the boss's daughter waiting to receive him. What will he talk to her about? Dare a man speak in such company of the only things he knows? What does he know?

He knows that Jack Johnson[③] could probably have whipped Jess Willard[④] if he had really tried. There is a woman lives in his rooming house who is unfaithful to her husband. He knows who with.

---

① Lewis：刘易斯（Meriwether Lewis, 1774—1809），美国探险家。曾与克拉克率探险队对广大西北地区进行探险和勘察。
② Clark：克拉克（William Clark, 1770—1838），美国军人、探险家，曾与刘易斯率探险队对广大西北地区进行探险和勘察。
③ Jack Johnson：约翰逊（1878—1946），美国拳击运动员，获最重量级世界冠军的第一个黑人。
④ Jess Willard：威拉德（1881—1968），美国拳击运动员，世界最重量级冠军。

She is going to have a child but the chances are it is not her husband's child. Often he has asked himself how she will feel on the night when the child is born and when her husband is so excited and proud.

After all, the young workman knows a good many things of his own sort, but of how many of them can he, dare he, speak with the boss's daughter whose voice was so soft and whose skin looked so delicate that day when she came into the shop with her father? "Dare I ask her what she thinks the unfaithful wife will be thinking and feeling when the child is born?"

Young workmen have a kind of fear of the thing called culture. Most middle-westerners think of it—in spite of their protestations to the country—as in some vague way to be breathed in the air of New York. New Yorkers seem to think of it as to be found in London or Paris. Bankers and manufacturers of the Middle-West hope to get it for their sons by sending them to Yale or Harvard and as there are a good many bankers and manufacturers Yale and Harvard are inclined to be crowded. Mark Twain thought he would find it in Boston—a whole generation of Americans thought that.

To the young workman culture is somewhat like a new suit of clothes that does not fit too well. It binds under the arms when one first puts it on.

《讲故事者的故事》是安德森的自传性作品,讲述了他成为作家的心路历程。这是作者——一个美国中部人借助语言这一媒介表达出来的心灵声音。他讲述了人们想知道的讲故事者的一些事情——他与生俱来的讲故事的爱好,他因发表了几部小说而成为稿酬丰厚的广告文字撰稿人的故事,还有他作为油漆生产商,突然有一天发现他是"在出卖自己的灵魂而不是在卖商品"的故事。他很冷静地讲述这些事情,没有卖弄也没有矫情。在书中他用了很大的篇幅描写他的父亲,因为他父亲讲的故事对他有重大影响,同时也谈到了他对父亲的矛盾心理。生活的压力使他的父亲不堪重负,最终染上了酗酒的恶习,因此作者对父亲爱恨交织。安德森的讲述与其他作家相比更贴近他自己的世界。他试图解释"虚幻世界"和"梦想世界"本身毫无价值,而只有自己的"视界"才最有意义。

这里选了书中第四部第一章。首先是作者的内心独白,反思了自己作为讲故事者的定位:他只适合讲述他熟悉的美国中西部农业小镇的故事。作者讲述了他对讲故事以及对短篇小说创作的看法:讲的故事要真实,而不是夸大其词、胡编乱造;讲故事要讲究形式,而不注重情节;讲故事要表现生活表象下的真实、人们真正的想法,而不是用美丽辞藻堆砌的生活的浮光掠影。

安德森使用的是简短、口语化的美国英语。其口语化的特征之一是文中有许多动词短语。以第一段为例,有诸如"walk about""make myself over""go through""feel way through""consort with"等。口语化的特征之二是用了许多源于盎格鲁-撒克逊语的词汇,即口语用词,而源于拉丁语的正式词汇用得很少。作者的叙述娓娓道来,十分自然亲切。同时他注意选词,使得文字异常简约,就此形成了一种"既贴近生活又去掉了土味的韵律悠扬的美国口语"。文中作者多次使用设问手法,使段与段之间的衔接连贯自然。此外,作者还运用了比喻、类比等修辞手法。例如,作者在讲述自己读到斯泰因作品时的欣喜时,把她的作品比作绘画,把她的措辞比作画家用的颜料。他还运用类比手法描述了讲故事时自己的感受。

 思考题

1. What is the author's opinion on the plot of a story?
2. Why does he mention his experience in a painter's studio?
3. Why does the author mention the young workman and his boss's daughter?

推荐作品

"The Corn Planting" (1912)
"Hands" (1919)
"The Egg" (1921)
"Death in the Woods" (1933)

 参考资料

Bassett, John Earl. *Sherwood Anderson: An American Career*. Plainsboro, New Jersey: Susquehanna University Press, 2005.

Howe, Irving. *Sherwood Anderson*. New York: William Sloane Associates, 1951.

Schevill, James. *Sherwood Anderson: His Life and Work*. Denver, CO: University of Denver Press, 1951.

(崔鲜泉)

第八单元

Ezra Pound (1885—1972)

艾兹拉·庞德

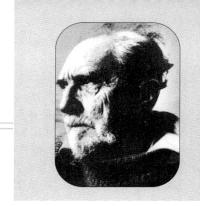

 作者简介

  艾兹拉·庞德,诗人、批评家、翻译家。生于爱达荷州海雷市。16岁就读于宾夕法尼亚州大学,1906年获硕士学位。大学时代,庞德与后来同样叱咤诗坛的W. C. 威廉斯为同窗好友,彼此影响至深,结为终生志同道合的朋友。在大学短暂执教两年后,庞德前往西班牙、意大利、英国和法国等欧洲国家考察,由此开始进行文学创作与出版活动,并对中国文学和日本文学产生了浓厚的兴趣。1914年结婚后,庞德更多地致力于诗歌创作和翻译等活动,1917年起担任颇有影响的刊物《诗歌》驻伦敦通信员,1924年移居意大利。第二次世界大战中,庞德为意大利法西斯政权效力,通过意大利电台广播攻击美国。战争结束时,他在比萨被美军抓获,囚禁在露天的笼子里,但他坚持写作,完成了《比萨诗章》(*Pisan Cantos*)。庞德1945年返回美国因叛国罪被捕入狱,后因众多知名作家呼吁,以其精神不正常为理由未判罪而送进精神病医院。其间,他因《比萨诗章》于1948年获国会博林根图书馆奖。1958年,由于作家们的呼吁,庞德被释放,再度移居意大利,隐居威尼斯,直至辞世。他的主要诗歌作品还包括:《向塞克斯图斯·佩罗提乌斯致敬》(*Homage to Sextus Propertius*, 1918)以及《休·塞尔温·莫伯利》(*Hugh Selwyn Mauberley*, 1920);他最重要的作品当推长诗《诗章》(*Cantos*, 1915—1970)。庞德在20世纪美国诗歌史上具有重要的地位,主要基于他在两个方面的贡献:一是他个人不同凡响的诗歌探索与创作,二是他鼎力提携新秀,在理论与诗歌创作实践两个方面引领美国诗歌的发展,包括20世纪初他与美国诗人休姆一起发起意象派诗歌运动,并帮助乔伊斯、T. S. 艾略特与弗罗斯特等人在创作初期发表作品。

 作品

A Girl

The tree has entered my hands,
The sap① has ascended my arms,
The tree has grown in my breast—
Downward,
The branches grow out of me, like arms.

Tree you are,
Moss② you are,
You are violets with wind above them.
A child—so high—you are,
And all this is folly③ to the world.

---

① sap: 树液;汁液;精力;活力。
② Moss: 苔藓;指任何一种苔藓植物。
③ folly: 荒唐事;蠢事;邪恶;危险或犯法的愚蠢行为。

 《少女》一诗是庞德的短诗代表作之一,与《地铁站里》("In a Station of Metro")和《画》("The Picture")一样典型地体现了诗人所倡导的意象派诗歌的主要特征与风范。意象派诗歌崇尚再现具有鲜明特色的、处于静态的意象,并着力渲染诗人瞬间捕捉到这些意象时的感官体验,但诗中并不铺陈任何解说或评论性的内容。换言之,意象派诗歌是刻意突出意象作为诗歌艺术本源的作用,注重通过视觉来捕捉那些有内涵的事物,回避或者淡化概念性的内容,试图借此匡正诗歌中理性成分过于浓重的倾向。上述特征都在《少女》一诗中得以展现。该诗是庞德根据李白的名诗《玉阶怨》改写而成,比较李白的原作:

玉阶生白露,夜久侵罗袜。
却下水晶帘,玲珑望秋月。

不难发现,庞德之所以改写此诗是因为此诗契合意象派诗歌的要旨,或者说他在此诗中寻找到了共鸣抑或启迪。李白虽以"怨"字作为诗的标题,但诗中字面不见"怨"字,反倒是夜色中冰凉的露水浸湿罗袜,水晶帘掩映孤独,秋月照射寒意,凡此种种,无一不淋漓尽致地再现了深深的"怨"情。《少女》也是要复原《玉阶怨》的上述特征,以意象衬托出意境和情怀。

 思考题

1. What stylistic features can you find in this poem?
2. Some critics think that the theme of this poem departs from that of the original text by Li Bai. What do you think of it?

 "In a Station of the Metro" (1913)
"A Pact" (1916)

 参考资料

Ackroyd, Peter. *Ezra Pound and His World*. London: Thames and Hudson, 1980.
Brooker, Peter. *A Student's Guide to the Selected Poems of Ezra Pound*. London: Faber and Faber, 1979.
Hamilton, Scott. *Ezra Pound and the Symbolist Inheritance*. Princeton: Princeton University Press, 1992.

(刘树森)

Wallace Stevens (1879—1955)

华莱士·史蒂文斯

 作者简介

    华莱士·史蒂文斯，诗人、律师。生于宾夕法尼亚州雷丁市，父亲是一位成功且在当地颇有影响的律师。曾就读哈佛大学三年，后转学纽约法学院，1904年获得学士学位，并成为律师。1909年结婚。在哈佛大学学习期间，史蒂文斯萌生诗歌创作的欲望，曾在校刊发表少量习作。毕业后他虽然以律师为业，但始终没有放弃诗歌创作，直至36岁正式发表第一首诗作，1923年出版第一部诗集《簧风琴》(*Harmonium*)，可谓大器晚成。《簧风琴》首版只售出一百余册，但是却赢得了文学批评界极高的赞誉，由此奠定了史蒂文斯在美国诗歌界乃至诗歌史上的地位。史蒂文斯的诗歌创作长达四十余年，曾经获得许多殊荣，包括门罗诗歌奖、博林根诗歌奖、美国国家图书奖和普利策奖等，被誉为20世纪最重要的美国诗人之一，但他一生为人低调，素为世人称道。他的主要诗集还包括《秩序的概念》(*Ideas of Order*, 1935)、《猫头鹰的三叶草》(*Owl's Clover*, 1937)、《带蓝吉他的人》(*The Man with the Blue Guitar*, 1937)、《世界的各个部分》(*Parts of a World*, 1942)以及《关于最高虚构的札记》(*Notes Toward a Supreme Fiction*, 1942)。学术界一般认为，史蒂文斯的诗歌深邃难解，因为他主张诗歌的任务是阐发诗人对人、社会以及自然的广泛而独特的抽象思考。因此，他的主要诗作都具有两个显著的特色：一是较为抽象的思考贯穿诗歌的字里行间，二是主题丰富多变，体现出他宽广的视野与胸襟。

The Snow Man

One must have a mind of winter
To regard the frost and the boughs
Of the pine-trees crusted① with snow;

And have been cold a long time
To behold the junipers② shagged③ with ice,
The spruces④ rough in the distant glitter

Of the January sun; and not to think
Of any misery in the sound of the wind,
In the sound of a few leaves,

Which is the sound of the land
Full of the same wind

---

① crusted：有外皮的；用外皮(壳)覆盖的。
② junipers：刺柏属丛木或树木；杜松。
③ shagged：筋疲力尽的；树的枝叶不整齐、毛茸茸的样子。此处可能有双重含义。
④ spruces：云杉，属于松柏科，四季常绿树，叶如针状，结球形果。

That is blowing in the same bare place

For the listener, who listens in the snow,
And, nothing himself, beholds
Nothing that is not there and the nothing that is.

　　　　作为史蒂文斯脍炙人口的名篇之一,《雪人》可以从多重角度进行解读与赏析。由于受到庞德等意象派诗人的影响,史蒂文斯在描写冬天的景色时,将他宽广、敏锐而深邃的目光所捕捉到的别有新意的意象以组合的方式呈现出来,例如诗歌开篇亭亭玉立的"雪人""白雪包裹的松树""在远方闪烁的粗糙的云杉"以及"残叶发出的声音"等,犹如画龙点睛之笔,旋即将大自然的妩媚、纯洁,以及春夏秋冬周而复始的力量跃然纸上,而且冰雪覆盖的冬天所展示的妩媚多姿也反衬出"雪人"的渺小,能够给人带来富有哲理的想象。如果把这首诗看作诗人对人与自然之间关系的思考,或者说是对人类如何认识自己的思考,那么他笔下似乎处于休眠状态的自然就是一种自我投射,是心灵与自然景色美妙的契合。由此着眼,可以将该诗分为两个段落,前7行是第一段落,着重以视觉意象投射出"冬天的心灵",第二段落是从第7行后半部分到结尾,转而以听觉的力量展示"冬天的心灵"的孤独和深邃。诗歌的结尾叙写了一个物我交融的瞬间,宛如格言,隽永精辟,使诗中的张力达到了极致。

 思考题

1. If the poem presents a picture of the harmony of nature and man, how does the poet attempt to inspire his readers in both visual and audio ways so that they may have access to perceiving that point?
2. What can you find if you look into the poem from the perspective of literary ecology?
3. What is your interpretation of the poem?

"Thirteen Ways of Looking at a Blackbird" (1917)
"Sunday Morning" (1915)
"The Emperor of Ice Cream" (1922)

 参考资料

Baird, James. *The Dome and the Rock: Structure in the Poetry of Wallace Stevens.* Baltimore: Johns Hopkins Press, 1968.
Benamou, Michel. *Wallace Stevens and the Symbolist Imagination.* Princeton, New Jersey: Princeton University Press, 1972.
Filreis, Alan. *Wallace Stevens and the Actual World.* Princeton, New Jersey: Princeton University Press, 1991.

（林　斌）

Robert Frost (1874—1963)

罗伯特·弗罗斯特

 作者简介

  罗伯特·弗罗斯特，诗人。生于加利福尼亚州旧金山市，父亲为记者，后从政，在儿子11岁时亡故。母亲为中学教师，收入微薄，加之外祖父多病，一家人勉强维持生计。弗罗斯特曾就读于达特茅斯学院和哈佛大学，但均中途辍学，在30岁之前的十余年间始终靠打零工谋生。1895年结婚，有6个子女。弗罗斯特自幼喜好文学，自学写诗，20岁时在《纽约独立报》发表第一首诗歌《我的蝴蝶》（"My Butterfly"）。20世纪初叶，赴欧洲进行创作和发展是当时美国作家的时尚，弗罗斯特为之所动，1912年举家迁居英国，开始了诗歌创作的一个辉煌时期。次年，他在庞德的帮助下出版了第一部诗集《少年的心愿》（*A Boy's Will*, 1913），1914年出版第二部诗集《波士顿之北》（*North of Boston*），其中包括许多脍炙人口的诗作，例如《修墙》（"Mending Wall"）和《雇工之死》（"The Death of the Hired Man"）。他由此获得国际声誉，随后于1915年返回美国，在密歇根州立大学等多家大学任教。弗罗斯特曾四次荣获普利策诗歌奖，获奖次数之多，至今无人企及。1961年1月20日，弗罗斯特应邀在美国总统约翰·F.肯尼迪总统的就职仪式上朗诵诗歌"The Gift Outright"，因此举世瞩目。他的其他主要诗集还包括《山间洼地》（*Mountain Interval*, 1916）等。弗罗斯特的诗风不是以新奇取胜，而是在传统的诗歌形式上有所创新，他称之为"以旧形式表达新内容"。他擅长以象征性的手法描写树木花草等植物以及司空见惯的场景与意象，进而通过它们投射出诗人推崇的价值观念。弗罗斯特始终是美国最受欢迎的诗人之一，不能不说与他的诗风密切相关。

Love and a Question

A Stranger came to the door at eve①,
  And he spoke the bridegroom fair.
He bore a green-white stick in his hand,
  And, for all burden, care.
He asked with the eyes more than the lips
  For a shelter for the night,
And he turned and looked at the road afar
  Without a window light.

The bridegroom came forth into the porch
  With, 'Let us look at the sky,
And question what of the night to be,
  Stranger, you and I.'
The woodbine② leaves littered the yard,
  The woodbine berries were blue,

---

① eve：常用于诗歌中，指黄昏；除夕；前夕；傍晚。
② woodbine：忍冬，一种微黄色的花，也指任何一种攀生藤蔓植物。

Autumn, yes, winter was in the wind;
    'Stranger, I wish I knew.'

Within, the bride in the dusk alone
    Bent over the open fire,
Her face rose-red with the glowing coal
    And the thought of the heart's desire.
The bridegroom looked at the weary road,
    Yet saw but her within,
And wished her heart in a case of gold
    And pinned with a silver pin.

The bridegroom thought it little to give
    A dole① of bread, a purse,
A heartfelt prayer for the poor of God,
    Or for the rich a curse;
But whether or not a man was asked
    To mar the love of two
By harboring② woe in the bridal house,
    The bridegroom wished he knew.

弗罗斯特的诗歌创作特征之一是他能够在貌似平凡的事物中发现不平凡的深刻内涵，或者说他善于将似乎司空见惯的场景和意象与寓意深邃的思想和情感交织在一起，物我相依，其诗情画意耐人寻味。如同他在几乎家喻户晓的《未选择的路》("The Road Not Taken")一诗中刻画了一种难以抉择的困惑，《爱与问题》惟妙惟肖地展示了一种内心的张力，或者说是渲染了面对某些未知因素的时候人与人之间内心难以言表的困窘与互动。在弗罗斯特的笔下，一对生活拮据的新婚夫妇和一个富有的男性"陌生人"在一个黑夜的短暂时刻戏剧化地再现了爱、猜疑、陌生、贫富差异、恐惧以及无奈等复杂因素所构成的矛盾，由表及里，三个人彼此影响和牵制，能够使人更深刻地品味到"爱"的内涵。在诗歌的结尾，诗人并没有向读者提供明确的答案，而是选择了带有悬念的开放性结局，这一点与《修墙》等名篇不同。诗中的许多意象和表达方式都体现了弗罗斯特细腻而独到的眼光与文字表现能力，例如：陌生人"用眼睛而不是用嘴唇询问"这句诗优美而活灵活现地将这位过路客的谨慎而高雅的修养、对新郎的揣测以及与新郎的差异全然呈现在读者面前。

 思考题

1. How does the poet dramatize the tension of love in this poem?
2. What devices does the poet use to depict the profundity of mind in the simplicity of verses?

 推荐作品
"Mending Wall" (1914)
"The Road Not Taken" (1916)
"Stopping by Woods on a Snowy Evening" (1922)

---

① dole：施舍；施舍品；悲哀。
② harboring：为……提供栖息地或者地点。

参考资料

Oster, Judith. *Toward Robert Frost: The Reader and the Poet.* Athens: University of Georgia Press, 1991.
Potter, James L. *Robert Frost Handbook.* U Park: Pennsylvania State University Press, 1980.
Thompson, Lawrance R. *Fire and Ice: The Art and Thought of Robert Frost.* New York: Russell & Russell, 1961.

（刘树森）

William Carlos Williams (1883—1963)

威廉·卡洛斯·威廉斯

 作者简介

　　威廉·卡洛斯·威廉斯,诗人、剧作家、散文家、儿科医生。生于新泽西州卢瑟福市,父亲经商,家境殷实。母亲喜爱绘画,并在威廉斯少年时代送其远赴日内瓦和巴黎学习。在宾夕法尼亚大学学习期间,威廉斯结识庞德,虽然专业有别,但因二人均钟情于诗歌创作,且志向与见解相投,成为终生莫逆之交。威廉斯虽然学医且终生以医生为业,但从中学时代开始写诗,并立志以行医谋生,以诗歌创作实现自己的理想。威廉斯是意象派诗人群体中的核心成员之一,诗歌创作与艺术观念的影响虽然不及T.S.艾略特等与其同时代的诗人,但对20世纪中叶的一些重要诗人,诸如艾伦·金斯堡与罗伯特·洛威尔等人产生了显见的影响。1913年在庞德的帮助下,他在伦敦出版了第一部诗集《性情》(The Tempers),试图在欧洲拓展创作的空间。他的其他重要诗集包括《地狱中的柯拉》(Kora in Hell, 1920)、《春天及其他》(Spring and All, 1923)以及煌煌五卷本的史诗《帕特森》(Paterson, 1963)。其他体裁的作品还包括小说《白骡》(White Mule, 1937)。1963年,他谢世之后因诗集《来自布鲁盖尔的画像及其他》(Pictures from Brueghel and Other Poems, 1962)而获得普利策诗歌奖。威廉斯虽然与庞德、T.S.艾略特等声名显赫的人物属于同一时代的美国诗人,而且在其四十余年的诗歌创作生涯中也创作出了完全能够与前者相媲美的作品,但是就其创作思想与风格而言,他与他们差别迥异,反倒是与19世纪的爱默生、惠特曼、狄金森等诗人一脉相承,始终自觉地与欧洲文化传统拉开距离,孜孜追求具有美国民族特色的诗歌艺术。

作品

The Uses of Poetry

I've fond anticipation of a day
O'erfilled[①] with pure diversion presently,
For I must read a lady poesy[②]
The while we glide by m0any a leafy bay,

Hid deep in rushes, where at random play
The glossy black winged May-flies, or whence flee
Hush-throated nestlings[③] in alarm,
Whom we have idly frighted with our boat's long sway.

For, lest o'ersaddened[④] by such woes as spring
To rural peace from our meek onward trend,
What else more fit? We'll draw the latch-string

And close the door of sense; then satiate wend,

---

① O'erfilled: 充满的,装得太满的。
② poesy: 诗歌,作诗法,诗歌艺术。
③ nestlings: 雏鸟,尤指因年幼不能离巢的雏鸟。
④ o'ersaddened: 过于忧愁,过于难过。

On poesy's transforming giant wing,
To worlds afar whose fruits all anguish mend.

就其创作思想而言,《诗歌的用途》一诗典型地反映出了威廉斯自觉摒弃欧洲诗歌传统,大胆探索,刻意追求具有美国民族特色的诗歌艺术风格。从形式特征来看,这首诗较为传统,诗句采用惠特曼之后的诗歌中常见的自由体,具有独白特征,如流水般自然而然地推心置腹,与威廉斯的名篇佳作《红色手推车》《在墙之间》和《麻雀》等显然不同,利用诗文不规则排列所产生的几何造型,从而营造一种别开生面的视觉效果。在内容方面,该诗在第一节以女人为意象说明诗人所青睐的诗歌的特征。实际上,女性也始终是威廉斯在诗歌创作中关注的主要对象之一。诗的最后一节说明诗歌能够抚平人的心灵,消除人的痛楚,即使是在动荡不安的社会背景下也有其特定的价值和意义。

 思考题

1. Can you summarize the main ideas the poet presents in the poem?
2. American literature is not devoid of poems that project principles or theories of poetry. Can you give other examples apart from this poem?

"The Red Wheelbarrow" (1923)
"This Is Just to Say" (1934)

参考资料

Morris, Daniel. *The Writings of William Carlos Williams: Publicity for the Self*. Columbia: University of Missouri Press, 1995.
Schmidt, Peter. *William Carlos Williams, the Arts, and Literary Tradition*. Baton Rouge: Louisiana State University Press, 1988.
Whitaker, Thomas R. *William Carlos Williams*. Rev. ed. Twayne's United States Authors Ser. 139. Boston: Twayne, 1989.

(刘树森)

Langston Hughes (1902—1967)
兰斯顿·休斯

 作者简介

　　兰斯顿·休斯，生于密苏里州乔普林镇，童年随外祖母在堪萨斯州生活。13岁那年，外祖母去世，方与母亲共同生活。休斯上高中时就在校办杂志上发表诗作。1921年秋，他进入哥伦比亚大学学习，一年后辍学。其间，他对哈莱姆地区产生浓厚兴趣，迅速成为哈莱姆文学艺术圈的活跃分子，并最终成为哈莱姆文艺复兴的代言人和记录者。其自传《大海》(The Big Sea, 1940)至今仍是研究那场运动的第一手资料。1923年，他作为水手随货船访问了三十余个非洲港口。回国前，曾先后在巴黎、威尼斯等地居住。1925年，休斯创作的《疲惫的布鲁斯》("The Weary Blues")一诗获得《机会》杂志举办的文学竞赛诗歌类一等奖，他从此步入文坛。1926年，休斯的第一本诗集以《疲惫的布鲁斯》为名出版。同年，他得到七十多岁的白人富婆梅森(Charlotte Osgood Mason)的资助，进入宾夕法尼亚州的林肯大学学习。1927年，休斯发表第二部诗集《好衣服拿给犹太人》(Fine Clothes to the Jew)，但未获成功。在梅森的说服下，休斯创作了长篇小说《并非无笑》(Not Without Laughter, 1930)。1930年两人发生争执，资助关系终止。这时，休斯在思想上转向左翼，开始在《新大众》(New Masses)杂志发表诗作，于1932年访问苏联，1933年访问上海。随后几年，休斯转向戏剧创作，他以美国南方黑白人通婚为题材的剧目《混血儿》(Mulatto)在百老汇上演并获得成功。1942年，休斯开始为美国黑人办的报纸《芝加哥卫士》(Chicago Defender)撰写专栏。1943年，幽默的贫民人物辛普尔(Jesse B. Semple或Simple)出现在这个专栏里，休斯借此讨论严肃的种族问题。因为辛普尔幽默可爱，专栏大获成功，故事连载了20年，被收入几部书出版发行。1947年，休斯用为百老汇音乐剧写歌词挣的钱实现了他在哈莱姆购房的梦想。1951年，他发表了著名的诗集《延迟的梦之蒙太奇》(Montage of a Dream Deferred)。其后，他又发表了20余部作品。休斯将美国黑人音乐明快的节奏运用到诗歌中，努力表现黑人的活力，被誉为"哈莱姆桂冠诗人""黑人民族桂冠诗人"。

The Weary Blues①

Droning a drowsy syncopated② tune,
Rocking back and forth to a mellow croon,
　　I heard a Negro play.③

---

① Blues：布鲁斯音乐，原为美国南方黑人民间的一种即兴演唱形式，常表现悲伤的主题(美国人认为蓝色为忧郁、悲哀的颜色)，速度舒缓，节拍常为四二拍、四四拍，旋律多含切分节奏，常于大调音阶上降半音，而且带有滑音、颤音，使歌唱听起来哀声怨语，悲恸凄楚。布鲁斯演唱风格自由，生活气息浓厚，假声、呻吟、哭泣、嘟囔、呼喊都可以用来渲染表达情绪，烘托气氛。布鲁斯的发展经历了乡村布鲁斯、古典布鲁斯和城市布鲁斯三个阶段。乡村布鲁斯采用上升或下降的自然滑音，一般三句构成一段，没有固定的段落，可以即兴演唱很多段，有时采用班卓琴和吉他进行伴奏。古典布鲁斯，常有作曲者参与，不完全靠歌手即兴演唱，曲式更加规整，经常有爵士乐队伴奏。城市布鲁斯主要反映城市生活的感受，结构固定，四四拍，12小节分成三句，每4小节为一句，第一、二句重复。伴奏可能是乐队，或者是钢琴，伴奏和声趋于规范。
② syncopated：被切分的；syncopation：切分音。
③ 诗的前三行为一个句子，从表面上看，出现了语法上的"无依者"现象，即前两行分词短语的逻辑主语和第三句子主语不一致。这里，诗人通过这一结构表现布鲁斯音乐使歌手(分词短语的逻辑主语)和听众(句子主语)合二为一的效果，暗示布鲁斯音乐表达的不仅仅是个人情感，而是黑人的民族情感。

Down on Lenox Avenue① the other night
By the pale dull pallor of an old gas light
   He did a lazy sway...
   He did a lazy sway...
To the tune o' those Weary Blues.
With his ebony hands on each ivory key②
He made that poor piano moan with melody.
   O Blues!
Swaying to and fro on his rickety stool
He played that sad raggy③ tune like a musical fool.
   Sweet Blues!
Coming from a black man's soul.
   O Blues!
In a deep song voice with a melancholy tone
I heard that Negro sing, that old piano moan—
   "Ain't got nobody in all this world,
   Ain't got nobody but ma self.
   I's gwine to quit ma frownin'
   And put ma troubles on the shelf."④

Thump, thump, thump, went his foot on the floor.
He played a few chords then he sang some more —
   "I got the Weary Blues
   And I can't be satisfied.
   Got the Weary Blues
   And can't be satisfied—
   I ain't happy no mo'
   And I wish that I had died."
And far into the night he crooned that tune.
The stars went out and so did the moon.
The singer stopped playing and went to bed
While the Weary Blues echoed through his head.
He slept like a rock or a man that's dead.

  《疲惫的布鲁斯》一诗于1923年发表在纽约的《阿姆斯特丹新闻》(*Amsterdam News*)上。休斯在自传《大海》里说这首诗包含着他幼年在堪萨斯州最早听到的布鲁斯歌曲。诗歌用第一人称描述了一天夜晚在哈莱姆街道上听布鲁斯歌手演唱的情景,通过选词、重复句子、引用布鲁斯歌词表达悲哀之情和布鲁斯歌曲舒缓的节奏,从而使读者感受到布鲁斯歌手的情绪。无名歌手扭动着身躯,手弹钢琴,脚踩地板,用"懒洋洋

---

① Lenox Avenue:纽约市哈莱姆区的一条主要街道。
② With his ebony hands on each ivory key:注意该行中黑(ebony hands)白(ivory key)之间的关系,以及黑人乐手用白人乐器创造出自己的艺术形式的寓意。歌手低沉的歌声表现了"黑人的灵魂"(a black man's soul),布鲁斯帮助黑人界定身份。乌黑的手敲击在乳白色的琴键上,使产生于西方文化的钢琴倾诉着黑人的悲伤,白人的音乐形式被黑人文化改变。
③ raggy:相当于ragged,一般指衣衫褴褛的,这里指乐声狂躁刺耳。
④ 没有受过正规教育的美国黑人使用的英语,有不符合语法规范的地方,如用双重否定表示否定 Ain't got nobody, ain't 为助动词的否定式形式;ma:my; I's gwine to:I'm going to; frownin':frowing。省音现象在美国黑人英语中常见。

的切分调"低沉哀婉地唱出自己的希望、孤独与失望。手脚上的活力同低沉的音调形成反差,揭示歌手内心的张力。诗歌引用了两段布鲁斯歌词,第一段为8小节,表现的是歌手决心忘却烦恼,面对生活的愿望。但是,相对第二段12小节,8小节显得短小,暗示实现这种愿望的渺茫,从而深化了歌手的孤独。第二段通过两句重复进一步强化歌手的疲惫、失落和绝望。忧伤的布鲁斯似乎成了歌手拥有的一切,既是他表达"黑人的灵魂"的途径,也是他得以展示自己生命活力的舞台。他用布鲁斯宣泄生活在白人主宰的社会里的孤独,让白人的钢琴发出黑人的呐喊。他通宵达旦地演唱,直到精疲力竭,内心的感受得到完全的释放,然后安然入睡。布鲁斯因此界定了他的身份,显然也打动了作为诗歌叙述人的听众,使他用另一种艺术形式表现出歌手孤独、疲惫的感情,以及歌手通过布鲁斯音乐拒绝接受现状,力图展示活力,维护尊严的复杂心理。

 思考题

1. What figure of speech is used in the first line, and what effect does it have?
2. What effect does the monosyllabic rhyme of "tune" and "croon" have at the end of the first two lines?
3. How does the poet create a "rocking" or "swaying" effect?
4. How does the poem express pride in African-American forms of expression?
5. What do you think of the poet's use of "Sweet Blues" in line 14, against the title of "The Weary Blues"?

"The Negro Speaks of Rivers"(1921)
"As I Grew Older"(1925)
"Dream Variations"(1926)
"I, Too"(1926)
"Madam and the Phone Bill"(1926)
"Let American be America Again"(1935)
"Harlem"(1951)

Emanuel, James A. *Langston Hughes*. New York: Twayne Publishers, 1997.
Tracy, Steven C. *Langston Hughes and the Blues*. Urbana: University of Illinois Press, 1988.

(陈法春)

第九单元

Eugene Gladstone O'Neill (1888—1953)

尤金·格拉斯通·奥尼尔

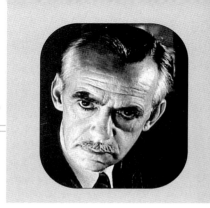

作者简介

　　尤金·格拉斯通·奥尼尔，美国现代戏剧的奠基人。在他之前，已有一批美国剧作家不满当时充斥着美国剧坛的伤感喜剧和情节悲剧，致力于创作既有艺术价值，又受大众欢迎的剧作。奥尼尔更是对艺术孜孜以求，取得了前人无法企及的成就，使严肃戏剧成为美国现代戏剧的主流。美国许多重要的剧作家都受到他的影响；他也使美国戏剧走向世界，影响到其他许多国家的剧作家，其中包括中国的曹禺和洪深。奥尼尔于1936年获得诺贝尔文学奖；他也四度获得普利策戏剧奖，获奖剧作为：《天边外》(Beyond the Horizon, 1920)、《安娜·克里斯蒂》(Anna Christle, 1921)、《奇异的插曲》(Strange Interlude, 1928)、《进入黑夜的漫长旅程》(Long Day's Journey into Night, 1956)。

　　奥尼尔的父亲是著名的戏剧演员，他年复一年地在各地巡演根据大仲马的小说改编的剧作《基度山伯爵》，而他们全家也随剧团四处漂泊。奥尼尔虽然有时也憎恨这种居无定所的生活，却也从小耳濡目染，血液中融进了对于戏剧的一手感觉。后来，奥尼尔在普林斯顿大学读过一年书，并在哈佛大学听过一年乔治·皮尔斯·贝克的著名的戏剧课；他十分喜欢尼采、叔本华、王尔德、波德莱尔、斯特林堡等作家。他也通过在世界各地的流浪和冒险经历，取得了丰富的生活体验。

　　奥尼尔从1913年开始创作，到1943年收笔，一共创作了50个剧本。他早期的剧作大多以大海为主题，真实地表现了海员的艰苦生活和他们对大海和陆地的复杂情感。他乐于尝试新的题材和表现手法：《琼斯皇帝》(The Emperor Jones, 1920)和《毛猿》(The Hairy Ape, 1922)运用了表现主义手法；《奇异的插曲》有大量的意识流成分；《上帝的儿女都有翅膀》(Au God's Chillun Got Wings, 1924)和《大神布朗》(The Great God Brown, 1926)则利用面具揭示出人物的双重性格和内心的挣扎。奥尼尔对不同的文化成分十分敏感：《马可百万》(Culture Decoding of Marco MIillions, 1928)对中国文化形象进行了美国式的塑造；《悲悼》(Mourning Becomes Electra, 1931)将古希腊题材移植到新英格兰加以本土化改造。他后期的作品《送冰的人来了》(The Iceman Cometh, 1939)和《进入黑夜的漫长旅程》是悲剧杰作。

　　奥尼尔剧作不断获得舞台重演，多部作品被改编成电影和电视作品。其中，被改编成电影的作品包括《安娜·克里斯蒂》(1923年的无声片；1930年由嘉宝主演的有声片)、《奇异的插曲》(1932)、《琼斯皇帝》(1933)、《啊，荒野！》(Ah, Wilderness!, 1935)、《漫长的返航》(The Long Voyage Home, 1940)、《毛猿》(1944)、《悲悼》(1947)、《榆树下的欲望》(1958)、《送冰的人来了》(1973)、《进入黑夜的漫长旅程》(1962; 1996)。

Long Day's Journey into Night
（第四幕选段）

TYRONE　(*Mechanically*) Drink hearty, lad. (*They drink. Tyrone again listens to sounds upstairs—with dread*) She's moving around a lot. I hope to God she doesn't come down.

EDMUND　(*Dully*)Yes. She'll be nothing but a ghost haunting the past by this time. (*He pauses—then miserably*) Back before I was born—

TYRONE　Doesn't she do the same with me? Back before she ever knew me.① You'd think the only happy days she's

---

① 詹姆斯·蒂龙和小儿子埃德蒙正在谈论玛丽，父子两人似乎很有默契。埃德蒙刚说"在我出生之前"，詹姆斯马上就明白他的意思：如果不是因为生他而被庸医染上毒瘾，玛丽现在还会很幸福。所以，詹姆斯忙说，"她在认识我之前"才过着幸福的生活。

ever known were in her father's home, or at the Convent, praying and playing the piano. (*Jealous resentment in his bitterness*) As I've told you before, you must take her memories with a grain of salt①. Her wonderful home was ordinary enough. Her father wasn't the great, generous, noble Irish gentleman she makes out. He was a nice enough man, good company and a good talker. I liked him and he liked me. He was prosperous enough, too, in his wholesale grocery business, an able man. But he had his weakness. She condemns my drinking but she forgets his. It's true he never touched a drop till he was forty, but after that he made up for lost time. He became a steady champagne drinker, the worst kind. That was his grand pose, to drink only champagne. Well, it finished him quick—that and the consumption②—(*He stops with a guilty glance at his son.*)

EDMUND (*Sardonically*) We don't seem able to avoid unpleasant topics, do we?

TYRONE (*Sighs sadly*) No. (*Then with a pathetic attempt at heartiness*) What do you say to a game or two of casino, lad?

EDMUND All right.

TYRONE (*Shuffling the cards clumsily*) We can't lock up and go to bed till Jamie comes on the last trolley—which I hope he won't—and I don't want to go upstairs, anyway, till she's asleep.

EDMUND Neither do I.

TYRONE (*Keeps shuffling the cards fumblingly, forgetting to deal them*) As I was saying, you must take her tales of the past with a grain of salt. The piano playing and her dream of becoming a concert pianist. That was put in her head by the nuns flattering her. She was their pet. They loved her for being so devout. They're innocent women, anyway, when it comes to the world.③ They don't know that not one in a million who shows promise ever rises to concert playing. Not that your mother didn't play well for a schoolgirl, but that's no reason to take it for granted she could have—

EDMUND (*Sharply*) Why don't you deal, if we're going to play.

TYRONE Eh? I am. (*Dealing with very uncertain judgment of distance*) And the idea she might have become a nun. That's the worst. Your mother was one of the most beautiful girls you could ever see. She knew it, too. She was a bit of a rogue and a coquette,④ God bless her, behind all her shyness and blushes. She was never made to renounce the world. She was bursting with health and high spirits and the love of loving.

EDMUND For God's sake, Papa! Why don't you pick up your hand?⑤

TYRONE (*Picks it up—dully*) Yes, let's see what I have here. (*They both stare at their cards unseeingly. Then they both start. Tyrone whispers.*) Listen!

EDMUND She's coming downstairs.

TYRONE (*Hurriedly*) We'll play our game. Pretend not to notice and she'll soon go up again.

EDMUND (*Staring through the front parlor—with relief*) I don't see her. She must have started down and then turned back.

TYRONE Thank God.

EDMUND Yes. It's pretty horrible to see her the way she must be now. (*With bitter misery*) The hardest thing to take is the blank wall she builds around her.⑥ Or it's more like a bank of fog in which she hides and loses herself. Deliberately, that's hell of it! You know something in her does it deliberately—to get beyond our reach, to be rid of us, to forget we're alive! It's as if, in spite of loving us, she hated us!

TYRONE (*Remonstrates gently*) Now, now, lad. It's not her. It's the damned poison⑦.

EDMUND (*Bitterly*) She takes it to get that effect. At least, I know she did this time! (*Abruptly*) My play, isn't it? Here. (*He plays a card.*)

TYRONE (*Plays mechanically—gently reproachful*) She's been terribly frightened about your illness, for all her pretending. Don't be too hard on her, lad. Remember she's not responsible. Once that cursed poison gets a

---

① with a grain / pinch of salt: with reservations, doubtfully, suspiciously, disbelievingly.
② consumption: 肺结核。埃德蒙也患有肺结核，詹姆斯无意中又提到这种当时的不治之症，所以感到内疚。
③ come to: to be a question of, "如果涉及人情世故，她们倒真是些不谙世事的女人"。
④ She was a bit of a rogue and a coquette.: 她有点调皮和调情。
⑤ Why don't you pick up your hand?: 你为什么不抓牌？
⑥ The hardest thing to take is the blank wall she builds around her.: 最难接受她在自己四周建起的无形墙壁。
⑦ poison: 指毒品。

hold on anyone—

EDMUND (*His face grows hard and he stares at his father with bitter accusation.*) It never should have gotten a hold on her! I know damned well she's not to blame! And I know who is! You are! Your damned stinginess! If you'd spent money for a decent doctor when she was so sick after I was born, she'd never have known morphine existed! Instead you put her in the hands of a hotel quack who wouldn't admit his ignorance and took the easiest way out, not giving a damn what happened to her afterwards! All because his fee was cheap! Another one of your bargains!

TYRONE (*Stung—angrily*) Be quiet! How dare you talk of something you know nothing about! (*Trying to control his temper*) You must try to see my side of it, too, lad. How was I to know he was that kind of a doctor? He had a good reputation—

EDMUND Among the souses in the hotel bar, I suppose!

TYRONE That's a lie! I asked the hotel proprietor to recommend the best—

EDMUND Yes! At the same time crying poorhouse and making it plain you wanted a cheap one! I know your system!① By God, I ought to after this afternoon!

TYRONE (*Guiltily defensive*) What about this afternoon?

EDMUND Never mind now. We're talking about Mama! I'm saying no matter how you excuse yourself you know damned well your stinginess is to blame—

TYRONE And I say you're a liar! Shut your mouth right now, or—

EDMUND (*Ignoring this*) After you found out she'd been made a morphine addict, why didn't you send her to a cure then, at the start, while she still had a chance? No, that would have meant spending some money! I'll bet you told her all she had to do was use a little will power! That's what you still believe in your heart, in spite of what doctors, who really know something about it, have told you!

TYRONE You lie again! I know better than that now! But how was I to know then? What did I know of morphine? It was years before I discovered what was wrong. I thought she'd never got over her sickness, that's all. Why didn't I send her to a cure, you say? (*Bitterly*) Haven't I? I've spent thousands upon thousands in cures! A waste. What good have they done her? She always started again.

EDMUND Because you've never given her anything that would help her want to stay off it! No home except this summer dump in a place she hates and you've refused even to spend money to make this look decent, while you keep buying more property, and playing sucker for every con man with a gold mine, or a silver mine, or any kind of get—rich—quick swindle! You've dragged her around on the road, season after season, on one—night stands, with no one she could talk to, waiting night after night in dirty hotel rooms for you to come back with a bun on② after the bars closed! Christ, is it any wonder she didn't want to be cured. Jesus, when I think of it I hate your guts③!

TYRONE (*Strickenly*) Edmund! (*Then in a rage*) How dare you talk to your father like that, you insolent young cub! After all I've done for you.

EDMUND We'll come to that, what you're doing for me!

TYRONE (*Looking guilty again—ignores this*) Will you stop repeating your mother's crazy accusations, which she never makes unless it's the poison talking? I never dragged her on the road against her will. Naturally, I wanted her with me. I loved her. And she came because she loved me and wanted to be with me. That's the truth, no matter what she says when she's not herself. And she needn't have been lonely. There was always the members of my company to talk to, if she'd wanted. She had her children, too, and I insisted, in spite of the expense, on having a nurse to travel with her.

EDMUND (*Bitterly*) Yes, your one generosity, and that because you were jealous of her paying too much attention to us, and wanted us out of your way! It was another mistake, too! If she'd had to take care of me all by herself, and had that to occupy her mind, maybe she'd have been able—

TYRONE (*Goaded into vindictiveness*) Or for that matter, if you insist on judging things by what she says when she's not in her right mind, if you hadn't been born she'd never—(*He stops ashamed.*)

---

① I know your system！：我知道你那一套！
② with a bun on：(俚)醉醺醺地。
③ hate one's guts：极端仇恨某人。

EDMUND (*Suddenly spent and miserable*) Sure. I know that's what she feels, Papa.
TYRONE (*Protests penitently*) She doesn't! She loves you as dearly as ever mother loved a son! I only said that because you put me in such a God-damned rage, raking up the past, and saying you hate me—
EDMUND (*Dully*) I didn't mean it, Papa. (*He suddenly smiles—kidding a bit drunkenly*) I'm like Mama, I can't help liking you, in spite of everything.
TYRONE (*Grins a bit drunkenly in return*) I might say the same of you. You're no great shakes① as a son. It's a case of "A poor thing but mine own."② (*They both chuckle with real, if alcoholic, affection. Tyrone changes the subject*) What's happened to our game? Whose play is it?
EDMUND Yours, I guess. (*Tyrone plays a card which Edmund takes and the game gets forgotten again.*)
TYRONE You mustn't let yourself be too downhearted, lad, by the bad news you had today. Both the doctors promised me, if you obey orders at this place you're going, you'll be cured in six months, or a year at most.
EDMUND (*His face hard again*) Don't kid me. You don't believe that.
TYRONE (*Too vehemently*) Of course I believe it! Why shouldn't I believe it when both Hardy and the specialist—?
EDMUND You think I'm going to die.
TYRONE That's a lie! You're crazy!
EDMUND —(*More bitterly*) So why waste money? That's why you're sending me to a state farm—
TYRONE (*In guilty confusion*) What state farm? It's the Hilltown Sanatorium, that's all I know, and both doctors said it was the best place for you.
EDMUND (*Scathingly*) For the money! That is, for nothing, or practically nothing. Don't lie, Papa! You know damned well Hilltown Sanatorium is a state institution! Jamie suspected you'd cry poorhouse to Hardy and he wormed the truth out of him.
TYRONE (*Furiously*) That drunken loafer! I'll kick him out in the gutter! He's poisoned your mind against me ever since you were old enough to listen!
EDMUND You can't deny it's the truth about the state farm, can you?
TYRONE It's not true the way you look at it! What if it is run by the state? That's nothing against it. The state has the money to make a better place than any private sanatorium. And why shouldn't I take advantage of it? It's my right—and yours. We're residents. I'm a property owner. I help to support it. I'm taxed to death—
EDMUND (*With bitter irony*) Yes, on property valued at a quarter of a million.
TYRONE Lies! It's all mortgaged!
EDMUND Hardy and the specialist know what you're worth. I wonder what they thought of you when they heard you moaning poorhouse and showing you wanted to wish me on charity!
TYRONE It's a lie! All I told them was I couldn't afford any millionaire's sanatorium because I was land poor③. That's the truth!
EDMUND And then you went to the Club to meet McGuire and let him stick you with another bum piece of property! (*As Tyrone starts to deny*) Don't lie about it! We met McGuire in the hotel bar after he left you. Jamie kidded him about hooking you, and he winked and laughed!
TYRONE (*Lying feebly*) He's a liar if he said—
EDMUND Don't lie about it! (*With gathering intensity*) God, Papa, ever since I went to sea and was on my own, and found out what hard work for little pay was, and what it felt like to be broke, and starve, and camp on park benches because I had no place to sleep. I've tried to be fair to you because I knew what you'd been up against as a kid. I've tried to make allowances. Christ, you have to make allowances in this damned family or go nuts! I have tried to make allowances for myself when I remember all the rotten stuff I've pulled! I've tried to feel like Mama that you can't help being what you are where money is concerned. But God Almighty, this last stunt of yours is too much! It makes me want to puke! Not because of the rotten way you're treating me. To hell with that! I've treated you rottenly, in my way, more than once. But to think when it's a question of your son having consumption, you can show yourself up before the whole town as such a stinking old tightwad! Don't you know Hardy will talk and the whole damned town will know! Jesus, Papa, haven't you

---

① no great shakes：没本事；不算重要。
② 莎士比亚剧作《皆大欢喜》(V.iv.57—58)中的台词。
③ land poor (一般为 land-poor)：土地多而收入少的；因支付高额土地税而导致经济困难的。

any pride or shame? (*Bursting with rage*) And don't think I'll let you get away with it! I won't go to any damned state farm just to save you a few lousy dollars to buy more bum property with! You stinking old miser—! (*He chokes huskily, his voice trembling with rage, and then is shaken by a fit of coughing.*)

TYRONE (*Has shrunk back in his chair under this attack, his guilty contrition greater than his anger. He stammers*) Be quiet! Don't say that to me! You're drunk! I won't mind you. Stop coughing, lad. You've got yourself worked up over nothing. Who said you had to go to this Hilltown place? You can go anywhere you like. I don't give a damn what it costs. All I care about is to have you get well. Don't call me a stinking miser, just because I don't want doctors to think I'm a millionaire they can swindle. (*Edmund has stopped coughing. He looks sick and weak. His father stares at him frightenedly*) You look weak, lad. You'd better take a bracer.

EDMUND (*Grabs the bottle and pours his glass brimful—weakly*) Thanks. (*He gulps down the whiskey.*)

TYRONE (*Pours himself a big drink, which empties the bottle, and drinks it. His head bows and he stares dully at the cards on the table— vaguely*) Whose play is it? (*He goes on dully, without resentment*) A stinking old miser. Well, maybe you're right. Maybe I can't help being, although all my life since I had anything I've thrown money over the bar to buy drinks for everyone in the house, or loaned money to sponges I knew would never pay it back—(*With a loose-mouthed sneer of self-contempt*) But, of course, that was in barrooms, when I was full of whiskey. I can't feel that way about it when I'm sober in my home. It was at home I first learned the value of a dollar and the fear of the poorhouse. I've never been able to believe in my luck since. I've always feared it would change and everything I had would be taken away. But still, the more property you own, the safer you think you are. That may not be logical, but it's the way I have to feel. Banks fail, and your money's gone, but you think you can keep land beneath your feet. (*Abruptly his tone becomes scornfully superior*) You said you realized what I'd been up against as a boy. The hell you do! How could you? You've had everything—nurses, schools, college, though you didn't stay there. You've had food, clothing. Oh I know you had a fling of hard work with your back and hands, a bit of being homeless and penniless in a foreign land, and I respect you for it. But it was a game of romance and adventure to you. It was play.

EDMUND (*Dully sarcastic*) Yes, particularly the time I tried to commit suicide at Jimmie the Priest's, and almost did.

TYRONE You weren't in your right mind. No son of mine would ever—You were drunk.

EDMUND I was stone cold sober. That was the trouble. I'd stopped to think too long.

TYRONE (*With drunken peevishness*) Don't start your damned atheist morbidness again! I don't care to listen. I was trying to make plain to you—(*Scornfully*) What do you know of the value of a dollar? When I was ten my father deserted my mother and went back to Ireland to die. Which he did soon enough, and deserved to, and I hope he's roasting in hell. He mistook rat poison for flour, or sugar, or something. There was gossip it wasn't by mistake but that's a lie. No one in my family ever—

EDMUND My bet is, it wasn't by mistake.

TYRONE More morbidness! Your brother put that in your head. The worst he can suspect is the only truth for him. But never mind. My mother was left, a stranger in a strange land, with four small children, me and a sister a little older and two younger than me. My two older brothers had moved to other parts. They couldn't help. They were hard put to it① to keep themselves alive. There was no damned romance in our poverty. Twice we were evicted from the miserable hovel we called home, with my mother's few sticks of furniture thrown out in the street, and my mother and sisters crying. I cried, too, though I tried hard not to, because I was the man of the family. At ten years old! There was no more school for me. I worked twelve hours a day in a machine shop, learning to make files. A dirty barn of a place where rain dripped through the roof, where you roasted in summer, and there was no stove in winter, and your hands got numb with cold, where the only light came through two small filthy windows, so on grey days I'd have to sit bent over with my eyes almost touching the files in order to see! You talk of work! And what do you think I got for it? Fifty cents a week! It's the truth! Fifty cents a week! And my poor mother washed and scrubbed for the Yanks by the day, and my older sister sewed, and my two younger stayed at home to keep the house. We never had clothes enough to wear, nor enough food to eat. Well I remember one Thanksgiving, or maybe it was Christmas, when some Yank in whose house mother had been scrubbing gave her a dollar extra for a present, and on the way home she spent

---

① hard put to it: 陷入困境;几乎无法。

it all on food. I can remember her hugging and kissing us and saying with tears of joy running down her tired face: "Glory be to God, for once in our lives we'll have enough for each of us!" (*He wipes tears from his eyes.*) A fine, brave, sweet woman. There never was a braver or finer.

EDMUND (*Moved.*) Yes, she must have been.

TYRONE Her one fear was she'd get old and sick and have to die in the poorhouse. (*He pauses—then adds with grim humor*) It was in those days I learned to be a miser. A dollar was worth so much then. And once you've learned a lesson, it's hard to unlearn it. You have to look for bargains. If I took this state farm sanatorium for a good bargain, you'll have to forgive me. The doctors did tell me it's a good place. You must believe that, Edmund. And I swear I never meant you to go there if you didn't want to. (*Vehemently*) You can choose any place you like! Never mind what it costs! Any place I can afford. Any place you like—within reason. (*At this qualification, a grin twitches Edmund's lips. His resentment has gone. His father goes on with an elaborately offhand, casual air.*) There was another sanatorium the specialist recommended. He said it had a record as good as any place in the country. It's endowed by a group of millionaire factory owners, for the benefit of their workers principally, but you're eligible to go there because you're a resident. There's such a pile of money behind it, they don't have to charge much. It's only seven dollars a week but you get ten times that value. (*Hastily*) I don't want to persuade you to anything, understand. I'm simply repeating what I was told.

EDMUND (*Concealing his smile—casually*) Oh, I know that. It sounds like a good bargain to me. I'd like to go there. So that settles that. (*Abruptly he is miserably desperate again—dully*) It doesn't matter a damn now, anyway. Let's forget it! (*Changing the subject*) How about our game? Whose play is it?

TYRONE (*Mechanically*) I don't know. Mine, I guess. No, it's yours. (*Edmund plays a card. His father takes it. Then about to play from his hand, he again forgets the game.*) Yes, maybe life overdid the lesson for me, and made a dollar worth too much and the time came when that mistake ruined my career as a fine actor. (*Sadly*) I've never admitted this to anyone before, lad, but tonight I'm so heartsick I feel at the end of everything, and what's the use of fake pride and pretense. That God—damned play I bought for a song[①] and made such a great success in—a great money success—it ruined me with its promise of an easy fortune. I didn't want to do anything else, and by the time I woke up to the fact I'd become a slave to the damned thing and did try other plays, it was too late. They had identified me with that one part, and didn't want me in anything else. They were right, too. I'd lost the great talent I once had through years of easy repetition, never learning a new part, never really working hard. Thirty-five to forty thousand dollars net profit a season like snapping your fingers! It was too great a temptation. Yet before I bought the damned thing I was considered one of the three or four young actors with the greatest artistic promise in America. I'd worked like hell. I'd left a good job as a machinist to take supers'[②] parts because I loved the theater. I was wild with ambition. I read all the plays ever written. I studied Shakespeare as you'd study the Bible. I educated myself. I got rid of an Irish brogue you could cut with a knife[③]. I loved Shakespeare. I would have acted in any of his plays for nothing, for the joy of being alive in his great poetry. And I acted well in him. I felt inspired by him. I could have been a great Shakespearean actor, if I'd kept on. I know that! In 1874 when Edwin Booth[④] came to the theater in Chicago where I was leading man, I played Cassius to his Brutus one night, Brutus to his Cassius the next, Othello to his Iago, and so on. The first night I played Othello, he said to our manager, "That young man is playing Othello better than I ever did!" (*Proudly*) That from Booth, the greatest actor of his day or any other! And it was true! And I was only twenty-seven years old! As I look back on it now, that night was the high spot in my career. I had life where I wanted it! And for a time after that I kept on upward with ambition high. Married your mother. Ask her what I was like in those days. Her love was an added incentive to ambition. But a few years later my good bad luck made me find the big money-maker. It wasn't that in my eyes at first. It was a great romantic part I knew I could play better than anyone. But it was a great box office success from

---

① for a song: 花很少钱。1883年，詹姆斯·奥尼尔买下了查尔斯·菲克纳改编的大仲马小说《基度山伯爵》的戏剧演出权，随后长期扮演该剧的男主人公，从而放弃了成为莎士比亚剧做演员的机会。
② super= supernumerary: 跑龙套的配角。
③ an Irish brogue you could cut with a knife: 浓重得都可以用刀割的爱尔兰口音。
④ Edwin Booth（1833—1893）：美国戏剧演员，被认为是当时最出色的哈姆莱特扮演者。

the start—and then life had me where it wanted me①—at from thirty-five to forty thousand net profit a season! A fortune in those days—or even in these. (*Bitterly*) What the hell was it I wanted to buy, I wonder, that was worth— Well, no matter. It's a late day for regrets. (*He glances vaguely at his cards.*) My play, isn't it?

EDMUND (*Moved, stares at his father with understanding—slowly*) I'm glad you've told me this, Papa. I know you a lot better now.

TYRONE (*With a loose, twisted smile*) Maybe I shouldn't have told you. Maybe you'll only feel more contempt for me. And it's a poor way to convince you of the value of a dollar. (*Then as if this phrase automatically aroused an habitual association in his mind, he glances up at the chandelier disapprovingly.*) The glare from those extra lights hurts my eyes. You don't mind if I turn them out, do you? We don't need them, and there's no use making the Electric Company rich.

EDMUND (*Controlling a wild impulse to laugh—agreeably*) No, sure not. Turn them out.

TYRONE (*Gets heavily and a bit waveringly to his feet and gropes uncertainly for the lights—his mind going back to its line of thought*) No, I don't know what the hell it was I wanted to buy. (*He clicks out one bulb.*) On my solemn oath, Edmund, I'd gladly face not having an acre of land to call my own, nor a penny in the bank—(*He clicks out another bulb.*) I'd be willing to have no home but the poorhouse in my old age if I could look back now on having been the fine artist I might have been. (*He turns out the third bulb, so only the reading lamp is on, and sits down again heavily. Edmund suddenly cannot hold back a burst of strained, ironical laughter. Tyrone is hurt.*) What the devil are you laughing at?

EDMUND Not at you, Papa. At life. It's so damned crazy.

TYRONE (*growls*) More of your morbidness! There's nothing wrong with life. It's we who—(*He quotes*) "The fault, dear Brutus, is not in our stars, but in ourselves that we are underlings."② (*He pauses—then sadly*) The praise Edwin Booth gave my Othello. I made the manager put down his exact words in writing. I kept it in my wallet for years. I used to read it every once in a while until finally it made me feel so bad I didn't want to face it any more. Where is it now, I wonder? Somewhere in this house. I remember I put it away carefully—

EDMUND (*With a wry ironical sadness*) It might be in an old trunk in the attic, along with Mama's wedding dress. (*Then as his father stares at him, he adds quickly*) For Pete's sake, if we're going to play cards, let's play. (*He takes the card his father had played and leads. For a moment, they play the game, like mechanical chess players. Then Tyrone stops, listening to a sound upstairs.*)

TYRONE She's still moving around. God knows when she'll go to sleep.

EDMUND (*Pleads tensely*) For Christ's sake, Papa, forget it! (*He reaches out and pours a drink. Tyrone starts to protest, then gives it up. Edmund drinks. He puts down the glass. His expression changes. When he speaks it is as if he were deliberately giving way to drunkenness and seeking to hide behind a maudlin manner.*) Yes, she moves above and beyond us, a ghost haunting the past, and here we sit pretending to forget, but straining our ears listening for the slightest sound, hearing the fog drip from the eaves like the uneven tick of a rundown, crazy clock—or like the dreary tears of a trollop spattering in a puddle of stale beer on a honky-tonk table top③! (*He laughs with maudlin appreciation.*) Not so bad, that last, eh? Original, not Baudelaire④. Give me credit! (*Then with alcoholic talkativeness*) You've just told me some high spots in your memories. Want to hear mine? They're all connected with the sea. Here's one. When I was on the Squarehead⑤ square rigger, bound for Buenos Aires. Full moon in the Trades⑥. The old hooker driving fourteen knots. I lay on the bowsprit, facing astern, with the water foaming into spume under me, the masts with every sail white in the moonlight, towering high above me. I became drunk with the beauty and singing rhythm of it, and for a moment I lost myself—actually lost my life. I was set free! I dissolved in the sea, became white sails and flying spray, became beauty and rhythm, became moonlight and the ship and the high dim-starred sky! I

---

① I had life where I wanted it... life had me where it wanted me：我想让生活怎样，生活就会怎样……生活想要我怎样，我就必须怎样。
② 见莎士比亚《裘力斯·凯撒》第一幕第二场。
③ or like the dreary tears of a trollop spattering in a puddle of stale beer on a honky-tonk table top：或者像下等夜总会里妓女潸然而下的泪水溅在桌上走了气的啤酒里(汪义群译文)。
④ Baudelaire：波德莱尔(1821—1867)：法国诗人和批评家，以诗集《恶之花》(1857)而闻名于世。
⑤ Squrehead：Squarehead号横帆船。
⑥ 贸易风；信风。

belonged, without past or future, within peace and unity and a wild joy, within some thing greater than my own life, or the life of Man, to Life itself! To God, if you want to put it that way. Then another time, on the American Line[①], when I was lookout on the crow's nest[②] in the dawn watch. A calm sea, that time. Only a lazy ground swell[③] and a slow drowsy roll of the ship. The passengers asleep and none of the crew in sight. No sound of man. Black smoke pouring from the funnels behind and beneath me. Dreaming, not keeping lookout, feeling alone, and above, and apart, watching the dawn creep like a painted dream over the sky and sea which slept together. Then the moment of ecstatic freedom came. The peace, the end of the quest, the last harbor, the joy of belonging to a fulfillment beyond men's lousy, pitiful, greedy fears and hopes and dreams! And several other times in my life, when I was swimming far out, or lying alone on a beach, I have had the same experience. Became the sun, the hot sand, green seaweed anchored to a rock, swaying in the tide. Like a saint's vision of beatitude. Like the veil of things as they seem drawn back by an unseen hand. For a second you see—and seeing the secret, are the secret.[④] For a second there is meaning! Then the hand lets the veil fall and you are alone, lost in the fog again, and you stumble on toward nowhere, for no good reason! (*He grins wryly.*) It was a great mistake, my being born a man, I would have been much more successful as a sea gull or a fish. As it is, I will always be a stranger who never feels at home, who does not really want and is not really wanted, who can never belong, who must always be a little in love with death!

TYRONE (*Stares at him—impressed.*) Yes, there's the makings of a poet in you all right. (*Then protesting uneasily.*) But that's morbid craziness about not being wanted and loving death.

EDMUND (*Sardonically.*) The makings of a poet. No, I'm afraid I'm like the guy who is always panhandling for a smoke. He hasn't even got the makings. He's got only the habit. I couldn't touch what I tried to tell you just now. I just stammered. That's the best I'll ever do, I mean, if I live. Well, it will be faithful realism, at least. Stammering is the native eloquence of us fog people. (*A pause. Then they both jump startledly as there is a noise from outside the house, as if someone had stumbled and fallen on the front steps. Edmund grins.*) Well, that sounds like the absent brother. He must have a peach[⑤] of a bun on.

TYRONE (*Scowling.*) That loafer! He caught the last car, bad luck to it. (*He gets to his feet.*) Get him to bed, Edmund. I'll go out on the porch. He has a tongue like an adder when he's drunk. I'd only lose my temper. (*He goes out the door to the side porch as the front door in the hall bangs shut behind Jamie. Edmund watches with amusement Jamie's wavering progress through the front parlor. Jamie comes in. He is very drunk and woozy on his legs. His eyes are glassy, his face bloated, his speech blurred, his mouth slack like his father's, a leer on his lips.*)

JAMIE (*Swaying and blinking in the doorway—in a loud voice.*) What ho! What ho!

EDMUND (*Sharply.*) Nix on the loud noise![⑥]

JAMIE (*Blinks at him.*) Oh, hello, Kid. (*With great seriousness.*) I'm as drunk as a fiddler's bitch[⑦].

EDMUND (*Dryly.*) Thanks for telling me your great secret.

JAMIE (*Grins foolishly.*) Yes. Unneshesary[⑧] information Number One, eh? (*He bends and slaps at the knees of his trousers.*) Had serious accident. The front steps tried to trample on me. Took advantage of fog to waylay me. Ought to be a lighthouse out there. Dark in here, too. (*Scowling.*) What the hell is this, the morgue? Lesh have some light on subjec.[⑨] (*He sways forward to the table, reciting Kipling[⑩].*)

"Ford, ford, ford o' Kabul river,
Ford o' Kabul river in the dark!

---

① the American Line：美国轮船公司。
② crow's nest：桅上瞭望台。
③ ground swell：涌浪。
④ For a second you see—and seeing the secret, are the secret.：瞬息之间，你具有了观察力——你看到秘密，也就成为秘密本身。
⑤ peach：十分出色的事物。"他一定醉得够呛"。
⑥ Nix on the loud noise！：别大声喧哗。
⑦ as drunk as a fiddler：酩酊大醉。Jamie 在这一惯用法后面加上了"bitch"这个不雅之词。
⑧ Jamie 因醉酒而口齿不清。Unneshesary=Unnecessary；Lesh=Let's；Thash=That's；lash=last；aw right=all right；shatisfied=satisfied；Egzactly=Exactly。
⑨ Lesh have some light on subjec.：让我们把话题挑明。
⑩ Rudyard Kipling（1865—1936），英国小说家、诗人。他的诗作 Ford o' Kabul River 描写了第二次英国—阿富汗战争（1878—1880）中，英军在渡过喀布尔河时发生的多人溺水身亡的惨剧。

Keep the crossing-stakes beside you, an' they will surely guide you
'Cross the ford o' Kabul river in the dark."
(*He fumbles at the chandelier and manages to turn on the three bulbs.*) Thash more like it. To hell with old Gaspard①. Where is the old tightwad?

EDMUND　Out on the porch.

JAMIE　Can't expect us to live in the Black Hole of Calcutta②. (*His eyes fix on the full bottle of whiskey.*) Say! Have I got the d.t.'s③? (*He reaches out fumblingly and grabs it.*) By God, it's real. What's matter with the Old Man tonight? Must be ossified to forget he left this out. Grab opportunity by the forelock.④ Key to my success. (*He slops a big drink into a glass.*)

EDMUND　You're stinking now. That will knock you stiff.

JAMIE　Wisdom from the mouth of babes. Can⑤ the wise stuff, Kid. You're still wet behind the ears.⑥ (*He lowers himself into a chair, holding the drink carefully aloft.*)

EDMUND　All right. Pass out if you want to.

JAMIE　Can't, that's trouble. Had enough to sink a ship, but can't sink. Well, here's hoping. (*He drinks.*)

EDMUND　Shove over the bottle. I'll have one, too.

JAMIE　(*With sudden, big-brotherly solicitude, grabbing the bottle.*) No, you don't. Not while I'm around. Remember doctor's orders. Maybe no one else gives a damn if you die, but I do. My kid brother. I love your guts⑦, Kid. Everything else is gone. You're all I've got left. (*Pulling bottle closer to him.*) So no booze for you, if I can help it. (*Beneath his drunken sentimentality there is a genuine sincerity.*)

EDMUND　(*Irritably.*) Oh, lay off it.

JAMIE　(*Is hurt and his face hardens.*) You don't believe I care, eh? Just drunken bull. (*He shoves the bottle over.*) All right. Go ahead and kill yourself.

EDMUND　(*Seeing he is hurt—affectionately.*) Sure I know you care, Jamie, and I'm going on the wagon⑧. But tonight doesn't count. Too many damned things have happened today. (*He pours a drink.*) Here's how. (*He drinks.*)

JAMIE　(*Sobers up momentarily and with a pitying look.*) I know, Kid. It's been a lousy day for you. (*Then with sneering cynicism.*) I'll bet old Gaspard hasn't tried to keep you off booze. Probably give you a case to take with you to the state farm for pauper patients. The sooner you kick the bucket, the less expense. (*With contemptuous hatred.*) What a bastard to have for a father! Christ, if you put him in a book, no one would believe it!

EDMUND　(*Defensively.*) Oh, Papa's all right, if you try to understand him—and keep your sense of humor.

JAMIE　(*Cynically.*) He's been putting on the old sob act for you, eh? He can always kid you. But not me. Never again. (*Then slowly.*) Although, in a way, I do feel sorry for him about one thing. But he has even that coming to him⑨. He's to blame. (*Hurriedly.*) But to hell with that. (*He grabs the bottle and pours another drink, appearing very drunk again.*) That lash drink's getting me. This one ought to put the lights out. Did you tell Gaspard I got it out of Doc Hardy this sanatorium is a charity dump?

EDMUND　(*Reluctantly.*) Yes. I told him I wouldn't go there. It's all settled now. He said I can go anywhere I want. (*He adds, smiling without resentment.*) Within reason, of course.

JAMIE　(*Drunkenly imitating his father.*) Of course, lad. Anything within reason. (*Sneering.*) That means another cheap dump. Old Gaspard, the miser in "The Bells," that's a part he can play without make-up.

EDMUND　(*Irritably.*) Oh, shut up, will you. I've heard that Gaspard stuff a million times.

---

① 法国作曲家简·罗伯特·普朗凯特（1850—1903）的歌剧《科尔内维尔的钟》（即下文中的 The Bells）一剧中的吝啬鬼。
② the Black Hole of Calcutta: 英国东印度公司在加尔各答的监狱的名称。这座监狱面积约20平方米，只有两个小窗户。1756年6月20日，孟加拉（当时为印度莫卧儿帝国的一个部分）的统治者从英国东印度公司手中夺取了加尔各答。据当时的英国守军将领说，146名守城的欧洲俘虏被关进这座监狱，其中幸存者只有23名。后来，也有人怀疑这一数据，认为监狱里只关押了64人，其中21人生还。在一些西方人眼里，这一监狱是非人待遇的象征。
③ d. t.=delirium tremens，(医)震颤性谵妄。
④ grab opportunity by the forelock: 不让机会溜走。类似的说法还有：take time by the forelock; take occasion by the forelock。
⑤ can: (俚)停止；放弃。"别玩聪明了"。
⑥ 你还乳臭未干。
⑦ Jamie将惯用法"hate one's guts"（恨死你了）改为"love one's guts"（爱死了），以开玩笑的方式表达他对弟弟的感情。
⑧ on the wagon: 发誓戒酒。
⑨ 不过连这件事也要算在他头上。

125

JAMIE   (*Shrugs his shoulders—thickly.*) Aw right, if you're satisfied—let him get away with it. It's your funeral—I mean, I hope it won't be.

EDMUND (*Changing the subject.*) What did you do uptown tonight? Go to Mamie Burns?

JAMIE   (*Very drunk, his head nodding.*) Sure thing. Where else could I find suitable feminine companionship? And love. Don't forget love. What is a man without a good woman's love? A God—damned hollow shell.

EDMUND (*Chuckles tipsily, letting himself go now and be drunk.*) You're a nut.

JAMIE   (*Quotes with gusto from Oscar Wilde's "The Harlot's House."*)①
"Then, turning to my love, I said,
'The dead are dancing with the dead,
The dust is whirring with the dust.'

But she—she heard the violin,
And left my side and entered in:
Love passed into the house of lust.
Then suddenly the tune went false,
The dancers wearied of the waltz..."
(*He breaks off, thickly.*) Not strictly accurate. If my love was with me, I didn't notice it. She must have been a ghost. (*He pauses.*) Guess which one of Mamie's charmers② I picked to bless me with her woman's love. It'll hand you a laugh, Kid. I picked Fat Violet.

EDMUND (*Laughs drunkenly.*) No, honest? Some pick! God, she weighs a ton. What the hell for, a joke?

JAMIE   No joke. Very serious. By the time I hit Mamie's dump I felt very sad about myself and all the other poor bums in the world. Ready for a weep on any old womanly bosom. You know how you get when John Barleycorn③ turns on the soft music inside you. Then, soon as I got in the door, Mamie began telling me all her troubles. Beefed④ how rotten business was, and she was going to give Fat Violet the gate. Customers didn't fall for Vi⑤. Only reason she'd kept her was she could play the piano. Lately Vi's gone on drunks and been too boiled⑥ to play, and was eating her out of house and home, and although Vi was a goodhearted dumbbell, and she felt sorry for her because she didn't know how the hell she'd make a living, still business was business, and she couldn't afford to run a home for fat tarts. Well, that made me feel sorry for Fat Violet, so I squandered two bucks of your dough to escort her upstairs. With no dishonorable intentions whatever. I like them fat, but not that fat. All I wanted was a little heart—to—heart talk concerning the infinite sorrow of life.

EDMUND (*Chuckles drunkenly.*) Poor Vi! I'll bet you recited Kipling and Swinburne⑦ and Dowson⑧ and gave her "I have been faithful to thee, Cynara, in my fashion."

JAMIE   (*Grins loosely.*) Sure—with the Old Master, John Barleycorn, playing soft music. She stood it for a while. Then she got good and⑨ sore. Got the idea I took her upstairs for a joke. Gave me a grand bawling out. Said she was better than a drunken bum who recited poetry. Then she began to cry. So I had to say I loved her because she was fat, and she wanted to believe that, and I stayed with her to prove it, and that cheered her up, and she kissed me when I left, and said she'd fallen hard for me, and we both cried a little more in the hallway, and everything was fine, except Mamie Burns thought I'd gone bughouse.

EDMUND (*Quotes derisively.*)

---

① Oscar Wilde (1854—1900)：爱尔兰小说家、诗人、剧作家。他的诗作"The Harlot's House"有12诗节，诗中"妓女之家"中幽灵般的居民随着斯特劳斯的华尔兹舞曲"真挚的爱心"翩翩起舞，但爱情已经为性欲所淹没。
② 迷人的女人。指Mamie Burns妓院的妓女。
③ John Barleycorn：大麦约翰（啤酒等含酒精饮料的拟人化名称）。
④ beef（俚）：抱怨。
⑤ Vi：即Violet。
⑥ boiled（俚）：醉酒。
⑦ Swinburne (1837—1909)，英国诗人和批评家。
⑧ Dowson (1867—1900)，英国颓废派抒情诗人。"I have been faithful to thee, Cynara, in my fashion"是他的一首诗作中的著名叠句。Cynara在她父亲的饭店里做服务员；Dowson爱上了她，但她却无法理解Dowson的爱，最后嫁给她父亲饭店里的一位男服务员。
⑨ good and：very；entirely。

"Harlots and

Hunted have pleasures of their own to give,

The vulgar herd can never understand."①

JAMIE (*Nods his head drunkenly.*) Exactly! Hell of a good time, at that.②You should have stuck around with me, Kid. Mamie Burns inquired after you. Sorry to hear you were sick. She meant it, too. (*He pauses—then with maudlin humor, in a ham-actor tone.*) This night has opened my eyes to a great career in store for me, my boy! I shall give the art of acting back to the performing seals, which are its most perfect expression. By applying my natural God-given talents in their proper sphere, I shall attain the pinnacle of success! I'll be the lover of the fat woman in Barnum and Bailey's circus③! (*Edmund laughs. Jamie's mood changes to arrogant disdain.*) Pah! Imagine me sunk to the fat girl in a hick town hooker shop! Me! Who have made some of the best-lookers on Broadway sit up and beg! (*He quotes from Kipling's "Sestina of the Tramp— Royal."*)

"Speakin' in general, I 'ave tried 'em all,

The 'appy roads that take you o'er the world."④

(*With sodden melancholy.*) Not so apt. Happy roads is bunk⑤. Weary roads is right. Get you nowhere fast. That's where I've got—nowhere. Where everyone lands in the end, even if most of the suckers won't admit it.

EDMUND (*Derisively.*) Can it! You'll be crying in a minute.

JAMIE (*Starts and stares at his brother for a second with bitter hostility—thickly.*) Don't get—too damned fresh. (*Then abruptly.*) But you're right. To hell with repining! Fat Violet's a good kid. Glad I stayed with her. Christian act. Cured her blues. Hell of a good time. You should have stuck with me, Kid. Taken your mind off your troubles. What's the use coming home to get the blues over what can't be helped. All over—finished now—not a hope! (*He stops, his head nodding drunkenly, his eyes closing—then suddenly he looks up, his face hard, and quotes jeeringly.*)

"If I were hanged on the highest hill,

Mother o' mine, O mother o' mine!

I know whose love would follow me still..."⑥

EDMUND (*Violently.*) Shut up!

JAMIE (*In a cruel, sneering tone with hatred in it.*) Where's the hophead? Gone to sleep? (*Edmund jerks as if he'd been struck. There is a tense silence. Edmund's face looks stricken and sick. Then in a burst of rage he springs from his chair.*)

EDMUND You dirty bastard! (*He punches his brother in the face, a blow that glances off the cheekbone. For a second Jamie reacts pugnaciously and half rises from his chair to do battle, but suddenly he seems to sober up to a shocked realization of what he has said and he sinks back limply.*)

JAMIE (*Miserably.*) Thanks, Kid. I certainly had that coming⑦. Don't know what made me—booze talking—You know me, Kid.

EDMUND (*His anger ebbing.*) I know you'd never say that unless—But God, Jamie, no matter how drunk you are, it's no excuse! (*He pauses—miserably.*) I'm sorry I hit you. You and I never scrap—that bad. (*He sinks back on his chair.*)

JAMIE (*Huskily.*) It's all right. Glad you did. My dirty tongue. Like to cut it out. (*He hides his face in his hands— dully.*) I suppose it's because I feel so damned sunk. Because this time Mama had me fooled. I really believed she had it licked. She thinks I always believe the worst, but this time I believed the best. (*His voice flutters.*) I suppose I can't forgive her—yet. It meant so much. I'd begun to hope, if she'd beaten the game, I could, too. (*He begins to sob, and the horrible part of his weeping is that it appears sober, not the maudlin*

---

① 波德莱尔《巴黎的忧郁》中的诗句,引自 Symons 的英译。
② Hell of a good time, at that.：也算是大大地开心一场。at that：regardless of what has been said or implied。
③ 由 Phineas Taylor 和 James Bailey 于 1881 年共同创建的著名的马戏团。
④ Kipling 的诗作"流浪皇族的六节诗"用伦敦方言写成,诗中的叙事者鼓吹四处漂泊、追求各种冒险和体验的生活。I'ave=I have; 'appy=happy。
⑤ bunk：废话；空话。
⑥ 这是 Kipling 为他自己的小说《湮灭之光》(*The Light That Failed*)所作的题诗的一部分。
⑦ have that / it coming：得到应得的东西。

tears of drunkenness.)

EDMUND (*Blinking back tears himself.*) God, don't I know how you feel! Stop it, Jamie!

JAMIE (*Trying to control his sobs.*) I've known about Mama so much longer than you. Never forget the first time I got wise. Caught her in the act with a hypo.① Christ, I'd never dreamed before that any women but whores took dope! (*He pauses.*) And then this stuff of you getting consumption. It's got me licked. We've been more than brothers. You're the only pal I've ever had. I love your guts. I'd do anything for you.

EDMUND (*Reaches out and pats his arm.*) I know that, Jamie.

JAMIE (*His crying over—drops his hands from his face—with a strange bitterness.*) Yet I'll bet you've heard Mama and old Gaspard spill so much bunk about my hoping for the worst, you suspect right now I'm thinking to myself that Papa is old and can't last much longer, and if you were to die, Mama and I would get all he's got, and so I'm probably hoping—

EDMUND (*Indignantly.*) Shut up, you damned fool! What the hell put that in your nut? (*He stares at his brother accusingly.*) Yes, that's what I'd like to know. What put that in your mind?

JAMIE (*Confusedly—appearing drunk again.*) Don't be a dumbbell! What I said! Always suspected of hoping for the worst. I've got so I can't help—(*Then drunkenly resentful.*) What are you trying to do, accuse me? Don't play the wise guy with me! I've learned more of life than you'll ever know! Just because you've read a lot of highbrow junk, don't think you can fool me! You're only an overgrown kid! Mama's baby and Papa's pet! The family White Hope②! You've been getting a swelled head lately. About nothing! About a few poems in a hick town newspaper! Hell, I used to write better stuff for the Lit③ magazine in college! You better wake up! You're setting no rivers on fire! You let hick town boobs flatter you with bunk about your future—(*Abruptly his tone changes to disgusted contrition. Edmund has looked away from him, trying to ignore this tirade.*) Hell, Kid, forget it. That goes for Sweeny④. You know I don't mean it. No one hopes more than I do you'll knock 'em all dead. No one is prouder you've started to make good. (*Drunkenly assertive.*) Why shouldn't I be proud? Hell, it's purely selfish. You reflect credit on me. I've had more to do with bringing you up than anyone. I wised you up about women, so you'd never be a fall guy⑤, or make any mistakes you didn't want to make! And who steered you on to reading poetry first? Swinburne, for example? I did! And because I once wanted to write, I planted it in your mind that someday you'd write! Hell, you're more than my brother. I made you! You're my Frankenstein⑥! (*He has risen to a note of drunken arrogance. Edmund is grinning with amusement now.*)

EDMUND All right, I'm your Frankenstein. So let's have a drink. (*He laughs.*) You crazy nut!

JAMIE (*Thickly.*) I'll have a drink. Not you. Got to take care of you. (*He reaches out with a foolish grin of doting affection and grabs his brother's hand.*) Don't be scared of this sanatorium business. Hell, you can beat that standing on your head. Six months and you'll be in the pink. Probably haven't got consumption at all. Doctors lot of fakers. Told me years ago to cut out booze or I'd soon be dead—and here I am. They're all con men. Anything to grab your dough. I'll bet this state farm stuff is political graft game. Doctors get a cut for every patient they send.

EDMUND (*Disgustedly amused.*) You're the limit!⑦ At the Last Judgment, you'll be around telling everyone it's in the bag.⑧

JAMIE And I'll be right. Slip a piece of change to the Judge and be saved, but if you're broke you can go to hell! (*He grins at this blasphemy and Edmund has to laugh. Jamie goes on.*) "Therefore put money in thy purse."⑨ That's the only dope⑩. (*Mockingly.*) The secret of my success! Look what it's got me! (*He lets Edmund's

---

① Caught her in the act with a hypo.：当场发现她皮下注射毒品。
② White Hope：人们寄予厚望的人或事。
③ Lit：literature.
④ That goes for Sweeny.：这只是骗骗小孩。Sweeny：什么都相信的天真家伙。
⑤ fall guy：容易受骗的人。
⑥ Frankenstein：玛丽·雪莱著名小说中的人物，他创造了一个最终毁灭了他自己的怪物。有时也指Frankenstein所创造的怪物。
⑦ You're the limit！：没有人比你更过分！
⑧ At the Last Judgment, you'll be around telling everyone it's in the bag.：在上帝的最后审判日，你也会在那儿告诉大家，一切都在掌握之中。
⑨ 这是莎士比亚的悲剧《奥赛罗》(I.iii.352)中的台词。剧中的反面人物伊阿古诱使迷恋苔丝德蒙娜的罗德利哥花钱来达到自己的目的。
⑩ dope：内部消息；内情。

hand go to pour a big drink, and gulps it down. He stares at his brother with bleary affection—takes his hand again and begins to talk thickly but with a strange, convincing sincerity.) Listen, Kid, you'll be going away. May not get another chance to talk. Or might not be drunk enough to tell you truth. So got to tell you now. Something I ought to have told you long ago—for your own good. (He pauses—struggling with himself. Edmund stares, impressed and uneasy. Jamie blurts out.) Not drunken bull①, but "in vino veritas"② stuff. You better take it seriously. Want to warn you—against me. Mama and Papa are right. I've been rotten bad influence. And worst of it is, I did it on purpose.

EDMUND (Uneasily.) Shut up! I don't want to hear—

JAMIE Nix, Kid! You listen! Did it on purpose to make a bum of you. Or part of me did. A big part. That part that's been dead so long. That hates life. My putting you wise so you'd learn from my mistakes. Believed that myself at times, but it's a fake. Made my mistakes look good. Made getting drunk romantic. Made whores fascinating vampires instead of poor, stupid, diseased slobs they really are. Made fun of work as sucker's game. Never wanted you succeed and make me look even worse by comparison. Wanted you to fail. Always jealous of you. Mama's baby, Papa's pet! (He stares at Edmund with increasing enmity.) And it was your being born that started Mama on dope. I know that's not your fault, but all the same, God damn you, I can't help hating your guts—!

EDMUND (Almost frightenedly.) Jamie! Cut it out! You're crazy!

JAMIE But don't get wrong idea, Kid. I love you more than I hate you. My saying what I'm telling you now proves it. I run the risk you'll hate me—and you're all I've got left. But I didn't mean to tell you that last stuff—go that far back③. Don't know what made me. What I wanted to say is, I'd like to see you become the greatest success in the world. But you'd better be on your guard. Because I'll do my damnedest to make you fail. Can't help it. I hate myself. Got to take revenge. On everyone else. Especially you. Oscar Wilde's "Reading Gaol" has the dope twisted.④ The man was dead and so he had to kill the thing he loved. That's what it ought to be. The dead part of me hopes you won't get well. Maybe he's even glad the game has got Mama again! He wants company, he doesn't want to be the only corpse around the house! (He gives a hard, tortured laugh.)

EDMUND Jesus, Jamie! You really have gone crazy!

JAMIE Think it over and you'll see I'm right. Think it over when you're away from me in the sanatorium. Make up your mind you've got to tie a can to⑤ me—get me out of your life—think of me as dead—tell people, "I had a brother, but he's dead." And when you come back, look out for me. I'll be waiting to welcome you with that "my old pal" stuff, and give you the glad hand, and at the first good chance I get stab you in the back.

EDMUND Shut up! I'll be God-damned if I'll listen to you any more—

JAMIE (As if he hadn't heard.) Only don't forget me. Remember I warned you—for your sake. Give me credit. Greater love hath no man than this, that he saveth his brother from himself.⑥ (Very drunkenly, his head bobbing.) That's all. Feel better now. Gone to confession. Know you absolve me, don't you, Kid? You understand. You're a damned fine kid. Ought to be. I made you. So go and get well. Don't die on me.⑦ You're all I've got left. God bless you, Kid. (His eyes close. He mumbles.) That last drink—the old K. O.⑧ (He falls into a drunken doze, not completely asleep. Edmund buries his face in his hands miserably. Tyrone comes in quietly through the screen door from the porch, his dressing gown wet with fog, the collar turned up around his throat. His face is stern and disgusted but at the same time pitying. Edmund does not notice his entrance.)

---

① bull: 蠢话;空话;废话。
② in vino veritas(拉): 酒醉吐真言。
③ go that far back: 说这么久之前的事。
④ Oscar Wilde's "Reading Gaol" has the dope twisted.: 奥斯卡·王尔德的《莱丁监狱》歪曲了真情。王尔德的诗作《莱丁监狱之歌》("The Ballad of Reading Goal")表达了对一位即将被绞死的犯人的同情。这位犯人杀害了自己的妻子,因此被判处死刑。"The man had killed the thing he loved, / And so he had to die"。但诗中的叙事者却表达了对他的同情: "Yet each man kills the thing he loves"。
⑤ tie a can to(俚): get rid of.
⑥ 这是对《圣经》的模仿。《圣经》的原文为: "Greater love hath no man than this, that a man lay down his life for his friends" (John, XV: 13)。
⑦ Don't die on me.: 不要死在我手上;不要死在我面前。
⑧ K. O.: 拳击比赛中击倒对手的一击。

TYRONE (*In a low voice.*) Thank God he's asleep. (*Edmund looks up with a start.*) I thought he'd never stop talking. (*He turns down the collar of his dressing gown.*) We'd better let him stay where he is and sleep it off. (*Edmund remains silent. Tyrone regards him—then goes on.*) I heard the last part of his talk. It's what I've warned you. I hope you'll heed the warning, now it comes from his own mouth. (*Edmund gives no sign of having heard. Tyrone adds pityingly.*) But don't take it too much to heart, lad. He loves to exaggerate the worst of himself when he's drunk. He's devoted to you. It's the one good thing left in him. (*He looks down on Jamie with a bitter sadness.*) A sweet spectacle for me! My first-born, who I hoped would bear my name in honor and dignity, who showed such brilliant promise!

EDMUND (*Miserably.*) Keep quiet, can't you, Papa?

TYRONE (*Pours a drink.*) A waste! A wreck, a drunken hulk, done with and finished! (*He drinks. Jamie has become restless, sensing his father's presence, struggling up from his stupor. Now he gets his eyes open to blink up at Tyrone. The latter moves back a step defensively, his face growing hard.*)

JAMIE (*Suddenly points a finger at him and recites with dramatic emphasis.*)
"Clarence is come, false, fleeting, perjured Clarence,
That stabbed me in the field by Tewksbury.
Seize on him, Furies, take him into torment."①
(*Then resentfully.*) What the hell are you staring at? (*He recites sardonically from Rossetti②.*)
"Look in my face. My name is Might-Have-Been;
I am also called No More, Too Late, Farewell."

TYRONE I'm well aware of that, and God knows I don't want to look at it.

EDMUND Papa! Quit it!

JAMIE (*Derisively.*) Got a great idea for you, Papa. Put on revival of "The Bells" this season. Great part in it you can play without make-up. Old Gaspard, the miser! (*Tyrone turns away, trying to control his temper.*)

EDMUND Shut up, Jamie!

JAMIE (*Jeeringly.*) I claim Edwin Booth never saw the day when he could give as good a performance as a trained seal. Seals are intelligent and honest. They don't put up any bluffs about the Art of Acting. They admit they're just hams earning their daily fish.

TYRONE (*Stung, turns on him in a rage.*) You loafer!

EDMUND Papa! Do you want to start a row that will bring Mama down? Jamie, go back to sleep! You've shot off your mouth too much already. (*Tyrone turns away.*)

JAMIE (*Thickly*) All right, Kid. Not looking for argument. Too damned sleepy. (*He closes his eyes, his head nodding. Tyrone comes to the table and sits down, turning his chair so he won't look at Jamie. At once he becomes sleepy, too.*)

TYRONE (*Heavily.*) I wish to God she'd go to bed so that I could, too. (*Drowsily.*) I'm dog tired. I can't stay up all night like I used to. Getting old—old and finished. (*With a bone-cracking yawn.*) Can't keep my eyes open. I think I'll catch a few winks. Why don't you do the same, Edmund? It'll pass the time until she— (*His voice trails off. His eyes close, his chin sags, and he begins to breathe heavily through his mouth. Edmund sits tensely. He hears something and jerks nervously forward in his chair, staring through the front parlor into the hall. He jumps up with a hunted, distracted expression. It seems for a second he is going to hide in the back parlor. Then he sits down again and waits, his eyes averted, his hands gripping the arms of his chair. Suddenly all five bulbs of the chandelier in the front parlor are turned on from a wall switch, and a moment later someone starts playing the piano in there—the opening of one of Chopin's simpler waltzes, done with a forgetful, stiff-fingered groping, as if an awkward schoolgirl were practicing it for the first time. Tyrone starts to wide-awakeness and sober dread, and Jamie's head jerks back and his eyes open. For a moment they listen frozenly. The playing stops as abruptly as it began, and Mary appears in the doorway. She wears a sky-blue dressing gown over her nightdress, dainty slippers with pompons on her bare feet. Her*

---

① 引自莎士比亚剧作《理查三世》(I. iv. 55—57)。为了得到王位，理查派凶手去杀害自己的哥哥克莱伦斯。在凶手到达之前，克莱伦斯正在讲述他做的噩梦。这段引文是噩梦中"一个天使般的阴影"对克莱伦斯所讲的话。
② Gabriel Charles Dante Rossetti (1828—1882)：英国画家、诗人。诗行引自"生活之屋：系列十四行诗"("The House of Life: a Sonnet-Sequence")。该诗表达了典型的失败感、负罪感、悔恨感。

face is paler than ever. Her eyes look enormous. They glisten like polished black jewels. The uncanny thing is that her face now appears so youthful. Experience seems ironed out of it. It is a marble mask of girlish innocence, the mouth caught in a shy smile. Her white hair is braided in two pigtails which hang over her breast. Over one arm, carried neglectfully, trailing on the floor, as if she had forgotten she held it, is an old-fashioned white satin wedding gown, trimmed with duchesse lace①. She hesitates in the doorway, glancing round the room, her forehead puckered puzzledly, like someone who has come to a room to get something but has become absent-minded on the way and forgotten what it was. They stare at her. She seems aware of them merely as she is aware of other objects in the room, the furniture, the windows, familiar things she accepts automatically as naturally belonging there but which she is too preoccupied to notice.)

JAMIE (*Breaks the cracking silence—bitterly, self-defensively sardonic.*) The Mad Scene. Enter Ophelia!② (*His father and brother both turn on him fiercely. Edmund is quicker. He slaps Jamie across the mouth with the back of his hand.*)

TYRONE (*His voice trembling with suppressed fury.*) Good boy, Edmund. The dirty blackguard! His own mother!

JAMIE (*Mumbles guiltily, without resentment.*) All right, Kid. Had it coming. But I told you how much I'd hoped— (*He puts his hands over his face and begins to sob.*)

TYRONE I'll kick you out in the gutter tomorrow, so help me God. (*But Jamie's sobbing breaks his anger, and he turns and shakes his shoulder, pleading.*) Jamie, for the love of God, stop it! (*Then Mary speaks, and they freeze into silence again, staring at her. She has paid no attention whatever to the incident. It is simply a part of the familiar atmosphere of the room, a background which does not touch her preoccupation; and she speaks aloud to herself, not to them.*)

MARY I play so badly now. I'm all out of practice. Sister Theresa will give me a dreadful scolding. She'll tell me it isn't fair to my father when he spends so much money for extra lessons. She's quite right, it isn't fair, when he's so good and generous, and so proud of me. I'll practice every day from now on. But something horrible has happened to my hands. The fingers have gotten so stiff—(*She lifts her hands to examine them with a frightened puzzlement.*) The knuckles are all swollen. They're so ugly. I'll have to go to the Infirmary and show Sister Martha. (*With a sweet smile of affectionate trust.*) She's old and a little cranky, but I love her just the same, and she has things in her medicine chest that'll cure anything. She'll give me something to rub on my hands, and tell me to pray to the Blessed Virgin, and they'll be well again in no time. (*She forgets her hands and comes into the room, the wedding gown trailing on the floor. She glances around vaguely, her forehead puckered again.*) Let me see. What did I come here to find? It's terrible, how absent-minded I've become. I'm always dreaming and forgetting.

TYRONE (*In a stifled voice.*) What's that she's carrying, Edmund?

EDMUND (*Dully.*) Her wedding gown, I suppose.

TYRONE Christ! (*He gets to his feet and stands directly in her path—in anguish.*) Mary! Isn't it bad enough—? (*Controlling himself—gently persuasive.*) Here, let me take it, dear. You'll only step on it and tear it and get it dirty dragging it on the floor. Then you'd be sorry afterwards. (*She lets him take it, regarding him from somewhere far away within herself, without recognition, without either affection or animosity.*)

MARY (*With the shy politeness of a well-bred young girl toward an elderly gentleman who relieves her of a bundle.*) Thank you. You are very kind. (*She regards the wedding gown with a puzzled interest.*) It's a wedding gown. It's very lovely, isn't it? (*A shadow crosses her face and she looks vaguely uneasy.*) I remember now. I found it in the attic hidden in a trunk. But I don't know what I wanted it for. I'm going to be a nun—that is, if I can only find—(*She looks around the room, her forehead puckered again.*) What is it I'm looking for? I know it's something I lost. (*She moves back from Tyrone, aware of him now only as some obstacle in her path.*)

TYRONE (*In hopeless appeal.*) Mary! (*But it cannot penetrate her preoccupation. She doesn't seem to hear him. He gives up helplessly, shrinking into himself, even his defensive drunkenness taken from him, leaving him sick and sober. He sinks back on his chair, holding the wedding gown in his arms with an unconscious clumsy,

---

① duchesse lace: 公爵夫人花边。从1840年前后到19世纪末，这种生产于布鲁塞尔的花边廉价而又畅销。其特点是用粗线织成的凸起的花卉和叶子图案。
② 在莎士比亚的悲剧《哈姆莱特》中，Ophelia因父亲被哈姆莱特杀害而变疯（Ⅳ. v.）。而哈姆莱特本人也装疯。

protective gentleness.)

JAMIE (*Drops his hand from his face, his eyes on the table top. He has suddenly sobered up, too—dully.*) It's no good, Papa. (*He recites from Swinburne's "A Leave-taking" and does it well, simply but with a bitter sadness.*)
"Let us rise up and part; she will not know.
Let us go seaward as the great winds go,
Full of blown sand and foam; what help is here?
There is no help, for all these things are so,
And all the world is bitter as a tear.
And how these things are, though ye strove to show,
She would not know."

MARY (*Looking around her.*) Something I miss terribly. It can't be altogether lost. (*She starts to move around in back of Jamie's chair.*)

JAMIE (*Turns to look up into her face—and cannot help appealing pleadingly in his turn.*) Mama! (*She does not seem to hear. He looks away hopelessly.*) Hell! What's the use? It's no good. (*He recites from "A Leave-taking" again with increased bitterness.*)
"Let us go hence, my songs; she will not hear.
Let us go hence together without fear;
Keep silence now, for singing-time is over,
And over all old things and all things dear.
She loves not you nor me as all we love her.
Yea, though we sang as angels in her ear,
She would not hear."

MARY (*Looking around her.*) Something I need terribly. I remember when I had it I was never lonely nor afraid. I can't have lost it forever, I would die if I thought that. Because then there would be no hope. (*She moves like a sleepwalker, around the back of Jamie's chair, then forward toward left front, passing behind Edmund.*)

EDMUND (*Turns impulsively and grabs her arm. As he pleads he has the quality of a bewilderedly hurt little boy.*) Mama! It isn't a summer cold! I've got consumption!

MARY (*For a second he seems to have broken through to her. She trembles and her expression becomes terrified. She calls distractedly, as if giving a command to herself.*) No! (*And instantly she is far away again. She murmurs gently but impersonally.*) You must not try to touch me. You must not try to hold me. It isn't right, when I am hoping to be a nun. (*He lets his hand drop from her arm. She moves left to the front end of the sofa beneath the windows and sits down, facing front, her hands folded in her lap, in a demure school girlish pose.*)

JAMIE (*Gives Edmund a strange look of mingled pity and jealous gloating.*) You damned fool. It's no good. (*He recites again from the Swinburne poem.*)
"Let us go hence, go hence; she will not see.
Sing all once more together; surely she,
She too, remembering days and words that were,
Will turn a little toward us, sighing; but we,
We are hence, we are gone, as though we had not been there.
Nay, and though all men seeing had pity on me,
She would not see."

TYRONE (*Trying to shake off his hopeless stupor.*) Oh, we're fools to pay any attention. It's the damned poison. But I've never known her to drown herself in it as deep as this. (*Gruffly.*) Pass me that bottle, Jamie. And stop reciting that damned morbid poetry. I won't have it in my house! (*Jamie pushes the bottle toward him. He pours a drink without disarranging the wedding gown he holds carefully over his other arm and on his lap, and shoves the bottle back. Jamie pours his and passes the bottle to Edmund, who, in turn, pours one. Tyrone lifts his glass and his sons follow suit mechanically, but before they can drink Mary speaks and they slowly lower their drinks to the table, forgetting them.*)

MARY (*Staring dreamily before her. Her face looks extraordinarily youthful and innocent. The shyly eager, trusting smile is on her lips as she talks aloud to herself.*) I had a talk with Mother Elizabeth. She is so sweet and good. A saint on earth. I love her dearly. It may be sinful of me but I love her better than my own mother. Because she always understands, even before you say a word. Her kind blue eyes look right into your heart. You can't keep any secrets from her. You couldn't deceive her, even if you were mean enough to want to. (*She gives a little rebellious toss of her head—with girlish pique.*) All the same, don't think she was so understanding this time. I told her I wanted to be a nun. I explained how sure I was of my vocation, that I had prayed to the Blessed Virgin to make me sure, and to find me worthy. I told Mother I had had a true vision when I was praying in the shrine of Our Lady of Lourdes, on the little island in the lake. I said I knew, as surely as I knew I was kneeling there, that the Blessed Virgin had smiled and blessed me with her consent. But Mother Elizabeth told me I must be more sure than that, even, that I must prove it wasn't simply my imagination. She said, if I was so sure, then I wouldn't mind putting myself to a test by going home after I graduated, and living as other girls lived, going out to parties and dances and enjoying myself; and then if after a year or two I still felt sure, I could come back to see her and we would talk it over again. (*She tosses her head—indignantly.*) I never dreamed Holy Mother would give me such advice! I was really shocked. I said, of course, I would do anything she suggested, but I knew it was simply a waste of time. After I left her, I felt all mixed up, so I went to the shrine and prayed to the Blessed Virgin and found peace again because I knew she heard my prayer and would always love me and see no harm ever came to me so long as I never lost my faith in her. (*She pauses and a look of growing uneasiness comes over her face. She passes a hand over her forehead as if brushing cobwebs from her brain—vaguely.*) That was in the winter of senior year. Then in the spring something happened to me. Yes, I remember. I fell in love with James Tyrone and was so happy for a time. (*She stares before her in a sad dream. Tyrone stirs in his chair. Edmund and Jamie remain motionless.*)

CURTAIN

作品赏析

《进入黑夜的漫长旅程》是奥尼尔创作生涯晚期的呕心沥血之作,是奥尼尔一家悲剧生活的真实写照,也是美国的悲剧杰作。奥尼尔在剧作的献辞中写道:这部剧作"以泪水和鲜血写成……对蒂龙一家受尽折磨的四个成员充满着深深的怜悯、谅解和宽恕之情"。根据奥尼尔的遗嘱,该剧不得上演,并只有在奥尼尔去世25年之后才可以出版。但奥尼尔的遗孀卡罗塔·蒙特利(Carlotta Monterey)并未遵从奥尼尔的遗愿,使该剧于1956年先后在斯德哥尔摩和纽约两地上演,引起极大轰动。

剧作通过蒂龙一家一天的生活,浓缩了全家人痛苦的一生。小儿子埃德蒙身患当时的不治之症肺结核,而母亲玛丽则染上毒瘾不能自拔。他们肉体上的痛苦逐渐引出了不堪回首的往事,辛酸的回忆带来了精神上的更大痛苦。原来,父亲詹姆斯·蒂龙本有可能成为著名的莎士比亚戏剧演员,但却为了丰厚的票房收入而四处巡演商业化的剧目《基度山伯爵》。他生性吝啬,在玛丽生产埃德蒙时请了庸医,使她染上毒瘾;为了省钱,即使埃德蒙身患绝症,他也只想把他送到廉价的公立疗养院。全家充满怨恨,男人们更是以酒浇愁,互相指责和谩骂。

剧中的大雾是重要的象征主义道具,与毒品和酒精一起,使现实消失在梦幻当中。剧终时,在酗酒后的三父子的注视下,玛丽在毒品的作用下,神情恍惚地拖着婚纱走了过来,仿佛实现了少女时的两个梦想:即成为修女和钢琴家。这是美国戏剧中最令人心碎的场面之一。

美丽的梦幻和丑陋的现实之间的冲突似乎也为这部悲剧带来理解和和解:玛丽随丈夫四处巡演,居无定所,举目无亲,使自己的理想化为泡影,也造成了她以后的悲剧;蒂龙是一位爱尔兰移民,他早年的艰辛使他对贫困充满恐惧,也造成了他病态般的吝啬。这一切最终得到了理解。

1962年,《进入黑夜的漫长旅程》被搬上电影银幕,并获得广泛好评。这部由西德尼·鲁麦特导演、凯瑟琳·赫本主演的电影影响了批评界对剧中人物的评价。此前,剧中谁是主要人物一直存有争议。在该片中,赫本扮演的女主人公的分量远远超过了男主人公,此后一般都认为玛丽·蒂龙,而不是詹姆斯·蒂龙,是剧中的主要人物。该剧还曾于1973年、1982年、1987年三次被改编为电视剧。1996年,加拿大又再次将该剧改编为电影。

本单元的课文选自《进入黑夜的漫长旅程》第四幕的结尾,也是全剧的结尾。本幕的时间为午夜,地点为蒂龙家的客厅。幕启时,喝醉的詹姆斯·蒂龙正在独自玩纸牌,而同样喝醉的埃德蒙从雾中散步归来,开始了父子间的交锋。生性吝啬的詹姆斯只开了一盏灯,跟跟跄跄、摸黑进屋的埃德蒙极为不满,指责父亲吝啬并且自以为是,居然将莎士比亚说成爱尔兰天主教徒。詹姆斯先是愤怒,后又想起埃德蒙所患的疾病,愧疚之中起身打开了所有的灯。埃德蒙背诵起波德莱尔颓废的诗篇,与父亲推崇的莎士比亚格格不入。正在这时,他们听到了楼上玛丽走路的声音。

思考题

1. What role does the past play in *Long Day's Journey into Night*?
2. What role do drugs and alcohol play within the play?
3. In what way is the "fog" important in the play?
4. What is the relationship between the two brothers?
5. What is the relationship between Tyrone and Mary?

Marco Millions (1924)
Strange Interlude (1928)
A Touch of the Poet (1939)
The Iceman Cometh (1939)
"Hughie" (1941)

参考资料

Manheim, Michael, ed. *The Cambridge Companion to Eugene O'Neill*. Shanghai: Shanghai Foreign Language Education Press, 2000.

Black, Stephen A. *Eugene O'Neill: Beyond Mourning and Tragedy*. New Haven: Yale University Press, 1999.

Houchin, John H. *The Critical Response to Eugene O'Neill*. Westport, Connecticut: Greenwood Press, 1993.

Berlin, Normand. *Eugene O'Neill*. New York: Macmillan, 1982.

(程朝翔)

第十单元
F. Scott Fitzgerald (1896—1940)
弗·斯科特·菲茨杰拉德

 作者简介

　　弗·斯科特·菲茨杰拉德,小说家,生于明尼苏达州一个破落士绅家庭。他曾就读于圣保罗学院和普林斯顿大学,但经济上主要依靠母亲娘家资助。1917年,美国宣布对德作战,他辍学参军。1918年夏,他在训练驻地与当地的富家女泽尔达·塞尔(Zelda Sayre)订婚。1919年他退役后,却和泽尔达解除了婚约,原因是他事业发展并不顺利。1920年3月,他出版了小说《人间天堂》(This Side of Paradise),因此一鸣惊人,名利双收。同年4月,他与泽尔达结婚。他们婚后的生活奢华,恰成美国战后享乐风潮的写照。这期间他发表了短篇小说集《姑娘们与哲学家们》(Flappers and Philosophers, 1920)和第二部小说《漂亮的冤家》(The Beautiful and Damned, 1922)和短篇小说集《爵士乐时代的故事》(Tales of the Jazz Age, 1922)。1924年,他来到巴黎,结识了斯泰因、庞德、海明威等一批"迷惘的一代"[①]旅欧美国作家并创作了《了不起的盖茨比》(The Great Gatsby, 1925)。1934年,他发表了另一部重要小说《夜色温柔》(Tender Is the Night),但小说并没有获得预期的成功。1940年他死于心脏病。他的好友、文学评论家威尔逊(Edmund Wilson)把他的散文结集出版,题名为《崩溃》(The Crack-Up, 1945)。菲茨杰拉德的创作活跃期间适值美国第一次世界大战后所谓"喧嚣的二十年代"和"爵士乐世代"。他深入刻画了注重金钱和享乐的时代潮流,一方面他自己随波逐流,沉湎于物质享乐,另一方面却又能客观审视自身的矛盾心态,以冷静批判的笔触反思社会现实和浮华表面下蕴藏的精神危机以及"美国梦"的追寻与幻灭,因而他的作品被看作时代风貌的真实写照。菲茨杰拉德曾给女儿写信谈到,"我想我骨子里是个道德家,总想以一种可以接受的方式向人们说教,而不是娱乐大众。"

　　菲茨杰拉德在20世纪50年代前已失去公众的关注,但在威尔逊和其他评论家的推动下,菲茨杰拉德的声誉重上新的台阶。一些调查结果显示,在美国,菲茨杰拉德作为经典文学作家和明星人物的魅力在20世纪末仍未衰减,人们普遍认为他是20世纪最重要的美国作家之一。菲茨杰拉德曾对电影的表现能力表示羡慕,而大概不会想到他的经典作品《了不起的盖茨比》被多次改编成影视作品(1926年默片电影版,1949年电影版,1974电影年版,2000年电视版,2013年电影版等),2002年的电影《G》(G)和2014年的电影《物欲病》(Affluenza)也是根据其主题改编摄制,而他的《夜色温柔》也被多次搬上影视屏幕。2001年摄制的"美国大师"系列纪录片《弗·斯科特·菲茨杰拉德·冬天的梦》再现了主人公的生活和创作经历。根据他的同名短篇小说改编的电影《本杰明·巴顿奇事》(又译《返老还童》)(The Curious Case of Benjamin Button)在2008年上映。

 作　品

Winter Dreams

I

　　Some of the caddies were poor as sin and lived in one-room houses with a neurasthenic cow in the front yard, but Dexter Green's father owned the second best grocery-store in Black Bear—the best one

---

[①] "迷惘的一代"(the Lost Generation)泛指第一次世界大战后的一代人,也特指一批美国作家,他们是第一次世界大战时的青年,20世纪20年代在文坛初露头角。作家斯泰因曾对海明威说:"你们都是迷惘的一代",这句话被海明威用作小说《太阳照样升起》的卷首语。这一代人的迷惘是因为他们的传统价值观与战后的现实格格不入。这些作家包括海明威、菲茨杰拉德、多斯·帕索斯等多人,不过他们并没有形成统一的文学流派,而是各自保留自己的独立风格。

was "The Hub," patronized by the wealthy people from Sherry Island—and Dexter caddied only for pocket-money.

In the fall when the days became crisp and gray, and the long Minnesota winter shut down like the white lid of a box, Dexter's skis moved over the snow that hid the fairways of the golf course. At these times the country gave him a feeling of profound melancholy—it offended him that the links should lie in enforced fallowness, haunted by ragged sparrows for the long season. It was dreary, too, that on the tees where the gay colors fluttered in summer there were now only the desolate sand-boxes knee-deep in crusted ice. When he crossed the hills the wind blew cold as misery, and if the sun was out he tramped with his eyes squinted up against the hard dimensionless glare.

In April the winter ceased abruptly. The snow ran down into Black Bear Lake scarcely tarrying for the early golfers to brave the season with red and black balls. Without elation, without an interval of moist glory, the cold was gone.

Dexter knew that there was something dismal about this Northern spring, just as he knew there was something gorgeous about the fall. Fall made him clinch his hands and tremble and repeat idiotic sentences to himself, and make brisk abrupt gestures of command to imaginary audiences and armies. October filled him with hope which November raised to a sort of ecstatic triumph, and in this mood the fleeting brilliant impressions of the summer at Sherry Island were ready grist to his mill.① He became a golf champion and defeated Mr. T. A. Hedrick in a marvellous match played a hundred times over the fairways of his imagination, a match each detail of which he changed about untiringly—sometimes he won with almost laughable ease, sometimes he came up magnificently from behind.② Again, stepping from a Pierce-Arrow③ automobile, like Mr. Mortimer Jones, he strolled frigidly into the lounge of the Sherry Island Golf Club④— or perhaps, surrounded by an admiring crowd, he gave an exhibition of fancy diving from the spring-board of the club raft.... Among those who watched him in open-mouthed wonder was Mr. Mortimer Jones.

And one day it came to pass that Mr. Jones—himself and not his ghost⑤ — came up to Dexter with tears in his eyes and said that Dexter was the—best caddy in the club, and wouldn't he decide not to quit if Mr. Jones made it worth his while, because every other caddy in the club lost one ball a hole for him— regularly—

"No, sir," said Dexter decisively, "I don't want to caddy any more." Then, after a pause: "I'm too old."

"You're not more than fourteen. Why the devil did you decide just this morning that you wanted to quit? You promised that next week you'd go over to the State tournament with me."

"I decided I was too old."

Dexter handed in his "A Class" badge, collected what money was due him from the caddy master, and walked home to Black Bear Village.

"The best—caddy I ever saw," shouted Mr. Mortimer Jones over a drink that afternoon. "Never lost a ball! Willing! Intelligent! Quiet! Honest! Grateful!"

The little girl who had done this⑥ was eleven—beautifully ugly as little girls are apt to be who are destined after a few years to be inexpressibly lovely and bring no end of misery to a great number of

---

① grist to his mill: 可供他想象发挥的素材。
② come up ... from behind: 从落后的局面反超。
③ Pierce-Arrow: 20 世纪初美国一款豪华车品牌。
④ Golf Club: 高尔夫球俱乐部往往是财富的象征,俱乐部会员一般都是社会名流和富人。
⑤ himself and not his ghost: 是他本人而不是梦中幻影。
⑥ The little girl who had done this: 促使他做出决定的小姑娘。

men. The spark, however, was perceptible. There was a general ungodliness in the way her lips twisted, down at the corners when she smiled, and in the—Heaven help us!—in the almost passionate quality of her eyes. Vitality is born early in such women. It was utterly in evidence now, shining through her thin frame in a sort of glow.

She had come eagerly out on to the course at nine o'clock with a white linen nurse and five small new golf-clubs in a white canvas bag which the nurse was carrying. When Dexter first saw her she was standing by the caddy house, rather ill at ease and trying to conceal the fact by engaging her nurse in an obviously unnatural conversation graced by startling and irrelevant grimaces from herself.

"Well, it's certainly a nice day, Hilda," Dexter heard her say. She drew down the corners of her mouth, smiled, and glanced furtively around, her eyes in transit falling for an instant on Dexter.

Then to the nurse:

"Well, I guess there aren't very many people out here this morning, are there?"

The smile again—radiant, blatantly artificial—convincing.

"I don't know what we're supposed to do now," said the nurse, looking nowhere in particular.

"Oh, that's all right. I'll fix it up."

Dexter stood perfectly still, his mouth slightly ajar. He knew that if he moved forward a step his stare would be in her line of vision—if he moved backward he would lose his full view of her face. For a moment he had not realized how young she was. Now he remembered having seen her several times the year before in bloomers.

Suddenly, involuntarily, he laughed, a short abrupt laugh— then, startled by himself, he turned and began to walk quickly away.

"Boy!"

Dexter stopped.

"Boy—"

Beyond question he was addressed. Not only that, but he was treated to that absurd smile, that preposterous smile—the memory of which at least a dozen men were to carry into middle age.

"Boy, do you know where the golf teacher is?"

"He's giving a lesson."

"Well, do you know where the caddy-master is?"

"He isn't here yet this morning."

"Oh." For a moment this baffled her. She stood alternately on her right and left foot.

"We'd like to get a caddy," said the nurse. "Mrs. Mortimer Jones sent us out to play golf, and we don't know how without we get a caddy①."

Here she was stopped by an ominous glance from Miss Jones, followed immediately by the smile.

"There aren't any caddies here except me," said Dexter to the nurse, "and I got to stay here in charge until the caddy-master gets here."

"Oh."

Miss Jones and her retinue now withdrew, and at a proper distance from Dexter became involved in a heated conversation, which was concluded by Miss Jones taking one of the clubs and hitting it on the ground with violence. For further emphasis she raised it again and was about to bring it down smartly upon the nurse's bosom, when the nurse seized the club and twisted it from her hands.

"You damn little mean old *thing*!" cried Miss Jones wildly.

Another argument ensued. Realizing that the elements of the comedy were implied in the scene,

---

① we don't know how without we get a caddy: 没有球童管理员,我们不知道怎么找到球童。

Dexter several times began to laugh, but each time restrained the laugh before it reached audibility. He could not resist the monstrous conviction that the little girl was justified in beating the nurse.

The situation was resolved by the fortuitous appearance of the caddymaster, who was appealed to immediately by the nurse.

"Miss Jones is to have a little caddy, and this one says he can't go."

"Mr. McKenna said I was to wait here till you came," said Dexter quickly.

"Well, he's here now." Miss Jones smiled cheerfully at the caddy-master. Then she dropped her bag and set off at a haughty mince toward the first tee.

"Well?" The caddy-master turned to Dexter. "What you standing there like a dummy for? Go pick up the young lady's clubs."

"I don't think I'll go out to-day," said Dexter.

"You don't—"

"I think I'll quit."

The enormity of his decision frightened him. He was a favorite caddy, and the thirty dollars a month he earned through the summer were not to be made elsewhere around the lake. But he had received a strong emotional shock, and his perturbation required a violent and immediate outlet.

It is not so simple as that, either. As so frequently would be the case in the future, Dexter was unconsciously dictated to by his winter dreams.

II

Now, of course, the quality and the seasonability of these winter dreams varied, but the stuff of them remained. They persuaded Dexter several years later to pass up a business course at the State university—his father, prospering now, would have paid his way—for the precarious advantage of attending an older and more famous university in the East, where he was bothered by his scanty funds. But do not get the impression, because his winter dreams happened to be concerned at first with musings on the rich, that there was anything merely snobbish in the boy. He wanted not association with glittering things and glittering people—he wanted the glittering things themselves. Often he reached out for the best without knowing why he wanted it—and sometimes he ran up against the mysterious denials and prohibitions in which life indulges. It is with one of those denials and not with his career as a whole that this story deals.

He made money. It was rather amazing. After college he went to the city from which Black Bear Lake draws its wealthy patrons. When he was only twenty-three and had been there not quite two years, there were already people who liked to say: "Now *there's* a boy—" All about him rich men's sons were peddling bonds precariously, or investing patrimonies precariously, or plodding through the two dozen volumes of the "George Washington Commercial Course," but Dexter borrowed a thousand dollars on his college degree and his confident mouth,[①] and bought a partnership in a laundry.

It was a small laundry when he went into it but Dexter made a specialty of learning how the English washed fine woollen golf-stockings without shrinking them, and within a year he was catering to the trade that wore knickerbockers. Men were insisting that their Shetland hose and sweaters go to his laundry just as they had insisted on a caddy who could find golfballs. A little later he was doing their wives' lingerie as well—and running five branches in different parts of the city. Before he was twenty-seven he owned the largest string of laundries in his section of the country. It was then that he sold out and went to New York. But the part of his story that concerns us goes back to the days when he

---

① on his college degree and his confident mouth: 指主人公以他的大学学历和他自信的口才使人相信他有能力偿还借款。

was making his first big success.

When he was twenty-three Mr. Hart—one of the gray-haired men who like to say "Now there's a boy"—gave him a guest card to the Sherry Island Golf Club for a week-end. So he signed his name one day on the register, and that afternoon played golf in a foursome with Mr. Hart and Mr. Sandwood and Mr. T. A. Hedrick. He did not consider it necessary to remark that he had once carried Mr. Hart's bag over this same links, and that he knew every trap and gully with his eyes shut—but he found himself glancing at the four caddies who trailed them, trying to catch a gleam or gesture that would remind him of himself, that would lessen the gap which lay between his present and his past.

It was a curious day, slashed abruptly with fleeting, familiar impressions. One minute he had the sense of being a trespasser—in the next he was impressed by the tremendous superiority he felt toward Mr. T. A. Hedrick, who was a bore and not even a good golfer any more.

Then, because of a ball Mr. Hart lost near the fifteenth green, an enormous thing happened. While they were searching the stiff grasses of the rough there was a clear call of "Fore!" from behind a hill in their rear. And as they all turned abruptly from their search a bright new ball sliced abruptly over the hill and caught Mr. T. A. Hedrick in the abdomen.

"By Gad!" cried Mr. T. A. Hedrick, "they ought to put some of these crazy women off the course. It's getting to be outrageous."

A head and a voice came up together over the hill:

"Do you mind if we go through?"

"You hit me in the stomach!" declared Mr. Hedrick wildly.

"Did I?" The girl approached the group of men. "I'm sorry. I yelled 'Fore!'"

Her glance fell casually on each of the men—then scanned the fairway for her ball.

"Did I bounce into the rough?"

It was impossible to determine whether this question was ingenuous or malicious. In a moment, however, she left no doubt, for as her partner came up over the hill she called cheerfully:

"Here I am! I'd have gone on the green except that I hit something."

As she took her stance for a short mashie shot, Dexter looked at her closely. She wore a blue gingham dress, rimmed at throat and shoulders with a white edging that accentuated her tan. The quality of exaggeration, of thinness, which had made her passionate eyes and down-turning mouth absurd at eleven, was gone now. She was arrestingly beautiful. The color in her cheeks was centered like the color in a picture—it was not a "high" color①, but a sort of fluctuating and feverish warmth, so shaded that it seemed at any moment it would recede and disappear. This color and the mobility of her mouth gave a continual impression of flux, of intense life, of passionate vitality—balanced only partially by the sad luxury of her eyes.

She swung her mashie impatiently and without interest, pitching the ball into a sand-pit on the other side of the green. With a quick, insincere smile and a careless "Thank you!" she went on after it.

"That Judy Jones!" remarked Mr. Hedrick on the next tee, as they waited—some moments—for her to play on ahead. "All she needs is to be turned up and spanked for six months and then to be married off to an oldfashioned cavalry captain."

"My God, she's good-looking!" said Mr. Sandwood, who was just over thirty.

"Good-looking!" cried Mr. Hedrick contemptuously, "she always looks as if she wanted to be kissed! Turning those big cow-eyes on every calf in town!"

It was doubtful if Mr. Hedrick intended a reference to the maternal instinct.

---

① "high" color: 较明显的红色。

"She'd play pretty good golf if she'd try," said Mr. Sandwood.

"She has no form," said Mr. Hedrick solemnly.

"She has a nice figure," said Mr. Sandwood.

"Better thank the Lord she doesn't drive a swifter ball," said Mr. Hart, winking at Dexter.

Later in the afternoon the sun went down with a riotous swirl of gold and varying blues and scarlets, and left the dry, rustling night of Western summer. Dexter watched from the veranda of the Golf Club, watched the even overlap of the waters in the little wind, silver molasses under the harvest-moon. Then the moon held a finger to her lips and the lake became a clear pool, pale and quiet. Dexter put on his bathing-suit and swam out to the farthest raft, where he stretched dripping on the wet canvas of the springboard.

There was a fish jumping and a star shining and the lights around the lake were gleaming. Over on a dark peninsula a piano was playing the songs of last summer and of summers before that—songs from "Chin-Chin" and "The Count of Luxemburg" and "The Chocolate Soldier"—and because the sound of a piano over a stretch of water had always seemed beautiful to Dexter he lay perfectly quiet and listened.

The tune the piano was playing at that moment had been gay and new five years before when Dexter was a sophomore at college. They had played it at a prom once when he could not afford the luxury of proms, and he had stood outside the gymnasium and listened. The sound of the tune precipitated in him a sort of ecstasy and it was with that ecstasy he viewed what happened to him now. It was a mood of intense appreciation, a sense that, for once, he was magnificently attune to life and that everything about him was radiating a brightness and a glamour he might never know again.

A low, pale oblong detached itself suddenly from the darkness of the Island, spitting forth the reverberate sound of a racing motor-boat. Two white streamers of cleft water rolled themselves out behind it and almost immediately the boat was beside him, drowning out the hot tinkle of the piano in the drone of its spray. Dexter raising himself on his arms was aware of a figure standing at the wheel, of two dark eyes regarding him over the lengthening space of water—then the boat had gone by and was sweeping in an immense and purposeless circle of spray round and round in the middle of the lake. With equal eccentricity one of the circles flattened out and headed back toward the raft.

"Who's that?" she called, shutting off her motor. She was so near now that Dexter could see her bathing-suit, which consisted apparently of pink rompers.

The nose of the boat bumped the raft, and as the latter tilted rakishly he was precipitated toward her. With different degrees of interest they recognized each other.

"Aren't you one of those men we played through this afternoon?" she demanded.

He was.

"Well, do you know how to drive a motor-boat? Because if you do I wish you'd drive this one so I can ride on the surf-board behind. My name is Judy Jones"—she favored him with an absurd smirk—rather, what tried to be a smirk, for, twist her mouth as she might, it was not grotesque, it was merely beautiful—"and I live in a house over there on the Island, and in that house there is a man waiting for me. When he drove up at the door I drove out of the dock because he says I'm his ideal."

There was a fish jumping and a star shining and the lights around the lake were gleaming. Dexter sat beside Judy Jones and she explained how her boat was driven. Then she was in the water, swimming to the floating surfboard with a sinuous crawl. Watching her was without effort to the eye, watching a branch waving or a sea-gull flying. Her arms, burned to butternut, moved sinuously among the dull platinum ripples, elbow appearing first, casting the forearm back with a cadence of falling water, then reaching out and down, stabbing a path ahead.

They moved out into the lake; turning, Dexter saw that she was kneeling on the low rear of the now uptilted surf-board.

"Go faster," she called, "fast as it'll go."

Obediently he jammed the lever forward and the white spray mounted at the bow. When he looked around again the girl was standing up on the rushing board, her arms spread wide, her eyes lifted toward the moon.

"It's awful cold," she shouted. "What's your name?"

He told her.

"Well, why don't you come to dinner to-morrow night?"

His heart turned over like the fly-wheel of the boat, and, for the second time, her casual whim gave a new direction to his life.

III

Next evening while he waited for her to come down-stairs, Dexter peopled the soft deep summer room and the sun-porch that opened from it with the men who had already loved Judy Jones. He knew the sort of men they were—the men who when he first went to college had entered from the great prep schools with graceful clothes and the deep tan of healthy summers. He had seen that, in one sense, he was better than these men. He was newer and stronger. Yet in acknowledging to himself that he wished his children to be like them he was admitting that he was but the rough, strong stuff from which they eternally sprang.

When the time had come for him to wear good clothes, he had known who were the best tailors in America, and the best tailors in America had made him the suit he wore this evening. He had acquired that particular reserve peculiar to his university, that set it off from other universities. He recognized the value to him of such a mannerism and he had adopted it; he knew that to be careless in dress and manner required more confidence than to be careful. But carelessness was for his children. His mother's name had been Krimslich. She was a Bohemian of the peasant class① and she had talked broken English to the end of her days. Her son must keep to the set patterns.

At a little after seven Judy Jones came down-stairs. She wore a blue silk afternoon dress, and he was disappointed at first that she had not put on something more elaborate. This feeling was accentuated when, after a brief greeting, she went to the door of a butler's pantry and pushing it open called: "You can serve dinner, Martha." He had rather expected that a butler would announce dinner, that there would be a cocktail. Then he put these thoughts behind him as they sat down side by side on a lounge and looked at each other.

"Father and mother won't be here," she said thoughtfully.

He remembered the last time he had seen her father, and he was glad the parents were not to be here to-night—they might wonder who he was. He had been born in Keeble, a Minnesota village fifty miles farther north, and he always gave Keeble as his home instead of Black Bear Village. Country towns were well enough to come from if they weren't inconveniently in sight and used as footstools by fashionable lakes.

They talked of his university, which she had visited frequently during the past two years, and of the near-by city which supplied Sherry Island with its patrons, and whither Dexter would return next day to his prospering laundries.

During dinner she slipped into a moody depression which gave Dexter a feeling of uneasiness. Whatever petulance she uttered in her throaty voice worried him. Whatever she smiled at—at him, at a

---

① a Bohemian of the peasant class: 作者在这里表明主人公的母亲是贫穷移民,来自中欧农民阶层。

chicken liver, at nothing—it disturbed him that her smile could have no root in mirth, or even in amusement. When the scarlet corners of her lips curved down, it was less a smile than an invitation to a kiss.

Then, after dinner, she led him out on the dark sun-porch and deliberately changed the atmosphere.

"Do you mind if I weep a little?" she said.

"I'm afraid I'm boring you," he responded quickly.

"You're not. I like you. But I've just had a terrible afternoon. There was a man I cared about, and this afternoon he told me out of a clear sky that he was poor as a church-mouse. He'd never even hinted it before. Does this sound horribly mundane?"

"Perhaps he was afraid to tell you."

"Suppose he was," she answered. "He didn't start right. You see, if I'd thought of him as poor—well, I've been mad about loads of poor men, and fully intended to marry them all. But in this case, I hadn't thought of him that way, and my interest in him wasn't strong enough to survive the shock. As if a girl calmly informed her fiancé that she was a widow. He might not object to widows, but—"

"Let's start right," she interrupted herself suddenly. "Who are you, anyhow?"

For a moment Dexter hesitated. Then:

"I'm nobody," he announced. "My career is largely a matter of futures."

"Are you poor?"

"No," he said frankly, "I'm probably making more money than any man my age in the Northwest. I know that's an obnoxious remark, but you advised me to start right."

There was a pause. Then she smiled and the corners of her mouth drooped and an almost imperceptible sway brought her closer to him, looking up into his eyes. A lump rose in Dexter's throat, and he waited breathless for the experiment, facing the unpredictable compound that would form mysteriously from the elements of their lips. Then he saw—she communicated her excitement to him, lavishly, deeply, with kisses that were not a promise but a fulfillment. They aroused in him not hunger demanding renewal but surfeit that would demand more surfeit ... kisses that were like charity, creating want by holding back nothing at all.

It did not take him many hours to decide that he had wanted Judy Jones ever since he was a proud, desirous little boy.

IV

It began like that—and continued, with varying shades of intensity, on such a note right up to the dénouement. Dexter surrendered a part of himself to the most direct and unprincipled personality with which he had ever come in contact. Whatever Judy wanted, she went after with the full pressure of her charm. There was no divergence of method, no jockeying for position or premeditation of effects—there was a very little mental side to any of her affairs. She simply made men conscious to the highest degree of her physical loveliness. Dexter had no desire to change her. Her deficiencies were knit up with a passionate energy that transcended and justified them.

When, as Judy's head lay against his shoulder that first night, she whispered, "I don't know what's the matter with me. Last night I thought I was in love with a man and to-night I think I'm in love with you—"—it seemed to him a beautiful and romantic thing to say. It was the exquisite excitability that for the moment he controlled and owned. But a week later he was compelled to view this same quality in a different light. She took him in her roadster to a picnic supper, and after supper she disappeared, likewise in her roadster, with another man. Dexter became enormously upset and was scarcely able to be decently civil to the other people present. When she assured him that she had not kissed the other man, he knew she was lying—yet he was glad that she had taken the trouble to lie to him.

He was, as he found before the summer ended, one of a varying dozen who circulated about her. Each of them had at one time been favored above all others—about half of them still basked in the solace of occasional sentimental revivals. Whenever one showed signs of dropping out through long neglect, she granted him a brief honeyed hour, which encouraged him to tag along for a year or so longer. Judy made these forays upon the helpless and defeated without malice, indeed half unconscious that there was anything mischievous in what she did.

When a new man came to town every one dropped out—dates were automatically cancelled.

The helpless part of trying to do anything about it was that she did it all herself. She was not a girl who could be "won" in the kinetic sense—she was proof against cleverness, she was proof against charm; if any of these assailed her too strongly she would immediately resolve the affair to a physical basis, and under the magic of her physical splendor the strong as well as the brilliant played her game and not their own. She was entertained only by the gratification of her desires and by the direct exercise of her own charm. Perhaps from so much youthful love, so many youthful lovers, she had come, in self-defense, to nourish herself wholly from within.

Succeeding Dexter's first exhilaration came restlessness and dissatisfaction. The helpless ecstasy of losing himself in her was opiate rather than tonic. It was fortunate for his work during the winter that those moments of ecstasy came infrequently. Early in their acquaintance it had seemed for a while that there was a deep and spontaneous mutual attraction that first August, for example—three days of long evenings on her dusky veranda, of strange wan kisses through the late afternoon, in shadowy alcoves or behind the protecting trellises of the garden arbors, of mornings when she was fresh as a dream and almost shy at meeting him in the clarity of the rising day. There was all the ecstasy of an engagement about it, sharpened by his realization that there was no engagement. It was during those three days that, for the first time, he had asked her to marry him. She said "maybe some day," she said "kiss me," she said "I'd like to marry you," she said "I love you"—she said—nothing.

The three days were interrupted by the arrival of a New York man who visited at her house for half September. To Dexter's agony, rumor engaged them. The man was the son of the president of a great trust company. But at the end of a month it was reported that Judy was yawning. At a dance one night she sat all evening in a motor-boat with a local beau, while the New Yorker searched the club for her frantically. She told the local beau that she was bored with her visitor, and two days later he left. She was seen with him at the station, and it was reported that he looked very mournful indeed.

On this note the summer ended. Dexter was twenty-four, and he found himself increasingly in a position to do as he wished. He joined two clubs in the city and lived at one of them. Though he was by no means an integral part of the stag-lines at these clubs, he managed to be on hand at dances where Judy Jones was likely to appear. He could have gone out socially as much as he liked—he was an eligible young man, now, and popular with down-town fathers. His confessed devotion to Judy Jones had rather solidified his position. But he had no social aspirations and rather despised the dancing men who were always on tap for the Thursday or Saturday parties and who filled in at dinners with the younger married set. Already he was playing with the idea of going East to New York. He wanted to take Judy Jones with him. No disillusion as to the world in which she had grown up could cure his illusion as to her desirability.

Remember that—for only in the light of it can what he did for her be understood.

Eighteen months after he first met Judy Jones he became engaged to another girl. Her name was Irene Scheerer, and her father was one of the men who had always believed in Dexter. Irene was light-haired and sweet and honorable, and a little stout, and she had two suitors whom she pleasantly relinquished when Dexter formally asked her to marry him.

Summer, fall, winter, spring, another summer, another fall—so much he had given of his active life to the incorrigible lips of Judy Jones. She had treated him with interest, with encouragement, with malice, with indifference, with contempt. She had inflicted on him the innumerable little slights and indignities possible in such a case—as if in revenge for having ever cared for him at all. She had beckoned him and yawned at him and beckoned him again and he had responded often with bitterness and narrowed eyes. She had brought him ecstatic happiness and intolerable agony of spirit. She had caused him untold inconvenience and not a little trouble. She had insulted him, and she had ridden over him, and she had played his interest in her against his interest in his work—for fun. She had done everything to him except to criticise him—this she had not done—it seemed to him only because it might have sullied the utter indifference she manifested and sincerely felt toward him.

When autumn had come and gone again it occurred to him that he could not have Judy Jones. He had to beat this into his mind but he convinced himself at last. He lay awake at night for a while and argued it over. He told himself the trouble and the pain she had caused him, he enumerated her glaring deficiencies as a wife. Then he said to himself that he loved her, and after a while he fell asleep. For a week, lest he imagined her husky voice over the telephone or her eyes opposite him at lunch, he worked hard and late, and at night he went to his office and plotted out his years.

At the end of a week he went to a dance and cut in on her once. For almost the first time since they had met he did not ask her to sit out with him or tell her that she was lovely. It hurt him that she did not miss these things—that was all. He was not jealous when he saw that there was a new man to-night. He had been hardened against jealousy long before.

He stayed late at the dance. He sat for an hour with Irene Scheerer and talked about books and about music. He knew very little about either. But he was beginning to be master of his own time now, and he had a rather priggish notion that he—the young and already fabulously successful Dexter Green—should know more about such things.

That was in October, when he was twenty-five. In January, Dexter and Irene became engaged. It was to be announced in June, and they were to be married three months later.

The Minnesota winter prolonged itself interminably, and it was almost May when the winds came soft and the snow ran down into Black Bear Lake at last. For the first time in over a year Dexter was enjoying a certain tranquility of spirit. Judy Jones had been in Florida, and afterward in Hot Springs, and somewhere she had been engaged, and somewhere she had broken it off. At first, when Dexter had definitely given her up, it had made him sad that people still linked them together and asked for news of her, but when he began to be placed at dinner next to Irene Scheerer people didn't ask him about her any more—they told him about her. He ceased to be an authority on her.

May at last. Dexter walked the streets at night when the darkness was damp as rain, wondering that so soon, with so little done, so much of ecstasy had gone from him. May one year back had been marked by Judy's poignant, unforgivable, yet forgiven turbulence—it had been one of those rare times when he fancied she had grown to care for him. That old penny's worth of happiness he had spent for this bushel of content. He knew that Irene would be no more than a curtain spread behind him, a hand moving among gleaming tea-cups, a voice calling to children...fire and loveliness were gone, the magic of nights and the wonder of the varying hours and seasons...slender lips, down-turning, dropping to his lips and bearing him up into a heaven of eyes.... The thing was deep in him. He was too strong and alive for it to die lightly.

In the middle of May when the weather balanced for a few days on the thin bridge that led to deep summer he turned in one night at Irene's house. Their engagement was to be announced in a week now—no one would be surprised at it. And to-night they would sit together on the lounge at the University Club and look on for an hour at the dancers. It gave him a sense of solidity to go with her—she was so sturdily popular, so intensely "great."

He mounted the steps of the brownstone house and stepped inside.

"Irene," he called.

Mrs. Scheerer came out of the living-room to meet him.

"Dexter," she said, "Irene's gone up-stairs with a splitting headache. She wanted to go with you but I made her go to bed."

"Nothing serious, I—"

"Oh, no. She's going to play golf with you in the morning. You can spare her for just one night, can't you, Dexter?"

Her smile was kind. She and Dexter liked each other. In the living-room he talked for a moment before he said good-night.

Returning to the University Club, where he had rooms, he stood in the doorway for a moment and watched the dancers. He leaned against the door-post, nodded at a man or two—yawned.

"Hello, darling."

The familiar voice at his elbow startled him. Judy Jones had left a man and crossed the room to him—Judy Jones, a slender enamelled doll in cloth of gold: gold in a band at her head, gold in two slipper points at her dress's hem. The fragile glow of her face seemed to blossom as she smiled at him. A breeze of warmth and light blew through the room. His hands in the pockets of his dinner-jacket tightened spasmodically. He was filled with a sudden excitement.

"When did you get back?" he asked casually.

"Come here and I'll tell you about it."

She turned and he followed her. She had been away—he could have wept at the wonder of her return. She had passed through enchanted streets, doing things that were like provocative music. All mysterious happenings, all fresh and quickening hopes, had gone away with her, come back with her now.

She turned in the doorway.

"Have you a car here? If you haven't, I have."

"I have a coup—."

In then, with a rustle of golden cloth. He slammed the door. Into so many cars she had stepped—like this—like that— her back against the leather, so—her elbow resting on the door—waiting. She would have been soiled long since had there been anything to soil her—except herself—but this was her own self outpouring.

With an effort he forced himself to start the car and back into the street. This was nothing, he must remember. She had done this before, and he had put her behind him, as he would have crossed a bad account from his books[①].

He drove slowly down-town and, affecting abstraction, traversed the deserted streets of the business section, peopled here and there where a movie was giving out its crowd or where consumptive or pugilistic youth lounged in front of pool halls. The clink of glasses and the slap of hands on the bars issued from saloons, cloisters of glazed glass and dirty yellow light.

She was watching him closely and the silence was embarrassing, yet in this crisis he could find no casual word with which to profane the hour. At a convenient turning he began to zigzag back toward the University Club.

"Have you missed me?" she asked suddenly.

"Everybody missed you."

He wondered if she knew of Irene Scheerer. She had been back only a day—her absence had been

---

① books: 指账簿。

almost contemporaneous with his engagement.

"What a remark!" Judy laughed sadly—without sadness. She looked at him searchingly. He became absorbed in the dashboard.

"You're handsomer than you used to be," she said thoughtfully. "Dexter, you have the most rememberable eyes."

He could have laughed at this, but he did not laugh. It was the sort of thing that was said to sophomores. Yet it stabbed at him.

"I'm awfully tired of everything, darling." She called every one darling, endowing the endearment with careless, individual comraderie. "I wish you'd marry me."

The directness of this confused him. He should have told her now that he was going to marry another girl, but he could not tell her. He could as easily have sworn that he had never loved her.

"I think we'd get along," she continued, on the same note, "unless probably you've forgotten me and fallen in love with another girl."

Her confidence was obviously enormous. She had said, in effect, that she found such a thing impossible to believe, that if it were true he had merely committed a childish indiscretion—and probably to show off. She would forgive him, because it was not a matter of any moment but rather something to be brushed aside lightly.

"Of course you could never love anybody but me," she continued. "I like the way you love me. Oh, Dexter, have you forgotten last year?"

"No, I haven't forgotten."

"Neither have I!"

Was she sincerely moved—or was she carried along by the wave of her own acting?

"I wish we could be like that again," she said, and he forced himself to answer:

"I don't think we can."

"I suppose not.... I hear you're giving Irene Scheerer a violent rush."

There was not the faintest emphasis on the name, yet Dexter was suddenly ashamed.

"Oh, take me home," cried Judy suddenly; "I don't want to go back to that idiotic dance—with those children."

Then, as he turned up the street that led to the residence district, Judy began to cry quietly to herself. He had never seen her cry before.

The dark street lightened, the dwellings of the rich loomed up around them, he stopped his coup in front of the great white bulk of the Mortimer Joneses house, somnolent, gorgeous, drenched with the splendor of the damp moonlight. Its solidity startled him. The strong walls, the steel of the girders, the breadth and beam and pomp of it were there only to bring out the contrast with the young beauty beside him. It was sturdy to accentuate her slightness—as if to show what a breeze could be generated by a butterfly's wing.

He sat perfectly quiet, his nerves in wild clamor, afraid that if he moved he would find her irresistibly in his arms. Two tears had rolled down her wet face and trembled on her upper lip.

"I'm more beautiful than anybody else," she said brokenly, "why can't I be happy?" Her moist eyes tore at his stability—her mouth turned slowly downward with an exquisite sadness: "I'd like to marry you if you'll have me, Dexter. I suppose you think I'm not worth having, but I'll be so beautiful for you, Dexter."

A million phrases of anger, pride, passion, hatred, tenderness fought on his lips. Then a perfect wave of emotion washed over him, carrying off with it a sediment of wisdom, of convention, of doubt, of honor. This was his girl who was speaking, his own, his beautiful, his pride.

"Won't you come in?" He heard her draw in her breath sharply.

Waiting.

"All right," his voice was trembling, "I'll come in."

V

It was strange that neither when it was over nor a long time afterward did he regret that night. Looking at it from the perspective of ten years, the fact that Judy's flare for him endured just one month seemed of little importance. Nor did it matter that by his yielding he subjected himself to a deeper agony in the end and gave serious hurt to Irene Scheerer and to Irene's parents, who had befriended him. There was nothing sufficiently pictorial about Irene's grief to stamp itself on his mind.

Dexter was at bottom hard-minded. The attitude of the city on his action was of no importance to him, not because he was going to leave the city, but because any outside attitude on the situation seemed superficial. He was completely indifferent to popular opinion. Nor, when he had seen that it was no use, that he did not possess in himself the power to move fundamentally or to hold Judy Jones, did he bear any malice toward her. He loved her, and he would love her until the day he was too old for loving—but he could not have her. So he tasted the deep pain that is reserved only for the strong, just as he had tasted for a little while the deep happiness.

Even the ultimate falsity of the grounds upon which Judy terminated the engagement that she did not want to "take him away" from Irene—Judy, who had wanted nothing else—did not revolt him. He was beyond any revulsion or any amusement.

He went East in February with the intention of selling out his laundries and settling in New York—but the war came to America in March and changed his plans. He returned to the West, handed over the management of the business to his partner, and went into the first officers' training-camp in late April. He was one of those young thousands who greeted the war with a certain amount of relief, welcoming the liberation from webs of tangled emotion.

VI

THIS STORY is not his biography, remember, although things creep into it which have nothing to do with those dreams he had when he was young. We are almost done with them and with him now. There is only one more incident to be related here, and it happens seven years farther on.

It took place in New York, where he had done well—so well that there were no barriers too high for him. He was thirty-two years old, and, except for one flying trip immediately after the war, he had not been West in seven years. A man named Devlin from Detroit came into his office to see him in a business way, and then and there this incident occurred, and closed out, so to speak, this particular side of his life.

"So you're from the Middle West," said the man Devlin with careless curiosity. "That's funny—I thought men like you were probably born and raised on Wall Street. You know—wife of one of my best friends in Detroit came from your city. I was an usher at the wedding."

Dexter waited with no apprehension of what was coming.

"Judy Simms," said Devlin with no particular interest; "Judy Jones she was once."

"Yes, I knew her." A dull impatience spread over him. He had heard, of course, that she was married—perhaps deliberately he had heard no more.

"Awfully nice girl," brooded Devlin meaninglessly, "I'm sort of sorry for her."

"Why?" Something in Dexter was alert, receptive, at once.

"Oh, Lud Simms has gone to pieces in a way. I don't mean he ill-uses her, but he drinks and runs around"

"Doesn't she run around?"

"No. Stays at home with her kids."

"Oh."

"She's a little too old for him," said Devlin.

"Too old!" cried Dexter. "Why, man, she's only twenty-seven."

He was possessed with a wild notion of rushing out into the streets and taking a train to Detroit. He rose to his feet spasmodically.

"I guess you're busy," Devlin apologized quickly. "I didn't realize—"

"No, I'm not busy," said Dexter, steadying his voice. "I'm not busy at all. Not busy at all. Did you say she was— twenty-seven? No, I said she was twenty-seven."

"Yes, you did," agreed Devlin dryly.

"Go on, then. Go on."

"What do you mean?"

"About Judy Jones."

Devlin looked at him helplessly.

"Well, that's, I told you all there is to it. He treats her like the devil. Oh, they're not going to get divorced or anything. When he's particularly outrageous she forgives him. In fact, I'm inclined to think she loves him. She was a pretty girl when she first came to Detroit."

A pretty girl! The phrase struck Dexter as ludicrous.

"Isn't she—a pretty girl, any more?"

"Oh, she's all right."

"Look here," said Dexter, sitting down suddenly, "I don't understand. You say she was a 'pretty girl' and now you say she's 'all right.' I don't understand what you mean—Judy Jones wasn't a pretty girl, at all. She was a great beauty. Why, I knew her, I knew her. She was—"

Devlin laughed pleasantly.

"I'm not trying to start a row," he said. "I think Judy's a nice girl and I like her. I can't understand how a man like Lud Simms could fall madly in love with her, but he did." Then he added: "Most of the women like her."

Dexter looked closely at Devlin, thinking wildly that there must be a reason for this, some insensitivity in the man or some private malice.

"Lots of women fade just like that," Devlin snapped his fingers. "You must have seen it happen. Perhaps I've forgotten how pretty she was at her wedding. I've seen her so much since then, you see. She has nice eyes."

A sort of dulness settled down upon Dexter. For the first time in his life he felt like getting very drunk. He knew that he was laughing loudly at something Devlin had said, but he did not know what it was or why it was funny. When, in a few minutes, Devlin went he lay down on his lounge and looked out the window at the New York sky-line into which the sun was sinking in dull lovely shades of pink and gold.

He had thought that having nothing else to lose he was invulnerable at last—but he knew that he had just lost something more, as surely as if he had married Judy Jones and seen her fade away before his eyes.

The dream was gone. Something had been taken from him. In a sort of panic he pushed the palms of his hands into his eyes and tried to bring up a picture of the waters lapping on Sherry Island and the moonlit veranda, and gingham on the golf-links and the dry sun and the gold color of her neck's soft down. And her mouth damp to his kisses and her eyes plaintive with melancholy and her freshness like new fine linen in the morning. Why, these things were no longer in the world! They had existed and they existed no longer.

For the first time in years the tears were streaming down his face. But they were for himself now. He did not care about mouth and eyes and moving hands. He wanted to care, and he could not care. For he had gone away and he could never go back any more. The gates were closed, the sun was gone down, and there was no beauty but the gray beauty of steel that withstands all time. Even the grief he could have borne was left behind in the country of illusion, of youth, of the richness of life, where his winter dreams had flourished.

"Long ago," he said, "long ago, there was something in me, but now that thing is gone. Now that thing is gone, that thing is gone. I cannot cry. I cannot care. That thing will come back no more."

《冬天的梦》(1922)是一个穷小子爱上富家小姐的故事,这是作者创作的一个主要题材。故事的主人公戴克斯特住在穷人区黑熊镇,在高尔夫球俱乐部作球童,为来自雪利岛的富人服务。在这样的贫富反差环境下,他小小年纪就被富家小姐裘德所吸引,开始了他的追梦之旅:他"要的不仅是接近五光十色的东西和人们,而是自己拥有五光十色的东西"。从美国建国时期开始的功利主义文化变革将幸福更多归结于外在利益(external goods),如财富、地位、名誉、权势等,能够拥有这些也意味着此生的成功,也表明上帝对自己的恩典。在作者所经历的"爵士乐时代",财富带来的享乐更加是人们孜孜以求的目的。在裘德身上,可以看到多重性格特点:她看重财富,但她选择男人的标准又不仅仅是金钱;她追求享乐,寻求情感刺激,但她又安守并不理想的婚姻;她我行我素,将男人玩弄于掌股,不愿按男人的"游戏"规则行事,但她又时时依附于男人的情感和金钱。这就是戴克斯特梦幻理想的矛盾混合体。而戴克斯特自身难道就没有这些特点吗?他同样崇尚财富,追求享乐和梦想;与艾琳的平淡比较,他更喜欢裘德带给他的情感刺激;在艾琳眼里,他的情感同样不可预测,没有原则。裘德身上的特质不仅代表了20世纪20年代的"新女性",而且是传统价值和功利个人主义时代价值的矛盾混合体。冬天的梦或所谓"美国梦"对个人来说可以幻灭,但它的魅力在这样的社会则永远难于消退。作者以巧妙的细节描写和色彩运用创造出丰富的象征寓意,细细读来,亦有相当解读空间。

 思考题

1. What are Dexter's first dreams?
2. Why does Dexter want to attend an older and more famous university in the East?
3. What does Sherry Island represent to Dexter?
4. What does Judy look for in a man?
5. Why is Dexter in tears after hearing about Judy's unhappy marriage?

The Great Gatsby (1925)
"Babylon Revisited" (1931)
Tender is the Night (1934)

参考资料

Bruccoli, Matthew J., ed. *New Essays on The Great Gatsby*. Beijing: Peking University Press, 2006.
Bryer, Jackson R., Allan Margolies, and Ruth Prigozy, eds. *F. Scott Fitzgerald: New Perspectives*. Athens: University of Georgia Press, 2000.
Pelzer, Linda C. *Student Companion to F. Scott Fitzgerald*. Westport: Greenwood Press, 2000.
Prigozy, Ruth, ed. *The Cambridge Companion to F. Scott Fitzgerald*. Cambridge: Cambridge University Press, 2002.

(张世耘)

第十一单元
William Faulkner (1897—1962)
威廉·福克纳

 作者简介

　　威廉·福克纳,小说家,生于密西西比州的新奥尔巴尼(New Albany)的一没落贵族家庭,后随家迁居奥克斯福(Oxford)。中学时代迷上诗歌,经常逃课,于最后一年辍学,在就读于耶鲁大学的好友斯东(Phil Stone)的指点下,广泛阅读文学名著。1918年,在女友奥昌(Estelle Oldham)与别人订婚后,参加英国皇家空军赴加拿大受训,因第一次世界大战结束而没能参战。退伍后,在密西西比大学学习一年,开始发表诗作。1924年,发表第一部诗集《大理石牧神》(*The Marble Faun*)后,动身去欧洲旅行,途经新奥尔良时结识了安德森(Sherwood Anderson, 1876—1941),在他的帮助下发表了第一部小说《士兵的报酬》(*Soldier's Pay*, 1926)。安德森建议他着力用小说体裁描写他熟悉的家乡,他便在发表了描写艺术家的《蚊群》(*Mosquitoes*, 1927)后,以家乡为原型虚构出约克纳帕塔法(Yoknapatawpha)县,开始创作反映美国内战后南方的物质与精神衰败的约克纳帕塔法系列小说,其中主要作品有《喧哗与骚动》(*The Sound and the Fury*, 1929)、《我弥留之际》(*As I Lay Dying*, 1930)、《八月之光》(*Light in August*, 1932)、《押沙龙,押沙龙!》(*Absalom, Absalom!*, 1936)等。这些作品创造性地运用了意识流与多视角等叙事手法,具有复杂的结构和史诗的风格。他名下共有19部长篇小说、100多个短篇、7个诗集。他还曾把自己或他人的作品改编成电影剧本。其中被拍成电影并署有他名字的共有6部电影及1个电视剧剧本。他获得的大奖有1949年度诺贝尔文学奖、1954年和1962年度普利策奖等。他去世之时,已被公认为同代人中最伟大的美国小说家。《纽约时报》头版刊登了他逝世的消息,并转引了肯尼迪总统对他的评价:"自亨利·詹姆斯以来,还没有哪位作家为繁荣的美国文学留下过这样一座不朽的丰碑。"如今,福克纳的名声有增无减。他的主要长篇小说和《献给爱米丽的一朵玫瑰花》《干旱的九月》《烧畜棚》《红叶》《夕阳》等短篇小说已经成为大学文学课上的必读作品。他也是最受研究者关注的美国作家。每年在他家乡召开的福克纳研讨会都会吸引数以百计的世界各地的学者。每年出版研究他的专著和论文有一二百种。冷战时期的读者把福克纳看作代表了个人主义和言论自由等美国价值的典范。如今的读者更重视他对美国价值的批判,包括他在揭露南方种族压迫过程中对美国的自由和平等理想的反思。

Barn Burning

　　The store in which the Justice of the Peace's court was sitting smelled of cheese. The boy, crouched on his nail keg at the back of the crowded room, knew he smelled cheese, and more: from where he sat he could see the ranked shelves close-packed with the solid, squat, dynamic shapes of tin cans whose labels his stomach read, not from the lettering which meant nothing to his mind but from the scarlet devils and the silver curve of fish—this, the cheese which he knew he smelled and the hermetic meat[①] which his intestines believed he smelled coming in intermittent gusts momentary and brief between the other constant one, the smell and sense just a little of fear because mostly of despair and grief, the old fierce pull of blood. He could not see the table where the Justice sat and before which

---

① hermetic meat: 罐装肉。

his father and his father's enemy (*our enemy he thought in that despair; ourn*① *!mine and hisn*② *both! He's my father!*) stood, but he could hear them, the two of them that is, because his father had said no word yet:

"But what proof have you, Mr. Harris?"

"I told you. The hog got into my corn. I caught it up and sent it back to him. The next time I put the hog in my pen. When he came to get it I gave him enough wire to patch up his pen. The next time I put the hog up and kept it. I rode down to his house and saw the wire I gave him still rolled on to the spool in his yard. I told him he could have the hog when he paid me a dollar pound fee. That evening a nigger came with the dollar and got the hog. He was a strange nigger. He said, 'He say to tell you wood and hay kin burn.' I said, 'What? That whut he say to tell you,' the nigger said. 'Wood and hay kin burn.' That night my barn burned. I got the stock out but I lost the barn."

"Where is the nigger? Have you got him?"

"It was a strange nigger, I tell you. I don't know what became of him."

"But that's not proof. Don't you see that's not proof?"

"Get that boy up here. He knows." For a moment the boy thought too that the man meant his older brother until Harris said, "Not him. The little one. The boy," and, crouching, small for his age, small and wiry like his father, in patched and faded jeans even too small for him, with straight, uncombed, brown hair and eyes gray and wild as storm scud, he saw the men between himself and the table part and become a lane of grim faces, at the end of which he saw the Justice, a shabby, collarless, graying man in spectacles, beckoning him. He felt no floor under his bare feet; he seemed to walk beneath the palpable weight of the grim turning faces. His father, stiff in his black Sunday coat donned not for the trial but for the moving, did not even look at him. He aims for me to lie, he thought, again with that frantic grief and despair. *And I will have to do hit*③.

"What's your name, boy?" the Justice said.

"Colonel Sartoris④ Snopes," the boy whispered.

"Hey?" the Justice said. "Talk louder. Colonel Sartoris? I reckon anybody named for Colonel Sartoris in this country can't help but tell the truth, can they?" The boy said nothing. *Enemy! Enemy!* He thought; for a moment he could not even see, could not see that the Justice's face was kindly nor discern that his voice was troubled when he spoke to the man named Harris: "Do you want me to question this boy?" But he could hear, and during those subsequent long seconds while there was absolutely no sound in the crowded little room save that of quiet and intent breathing it was as if he had swung outward at the end of a grape vine, over a ravine, and at the top of the swing had been caught in a prolonged instant of mesmerized gravity, weightless in time.

"No!" Harris said violently, explosively. "Damnation! Send him out of here!" Now time, the fluid world, rushed beneath him again, the voices coming to him again through the smell of cheese and sealed meat, the fear and despair and the old grief of blood:

"This case is closed. I can't find against you, Snopes, but I can give you advice. Leave this country and don't come back to it."

His father spoke for the first time, his voice cold and harsh, level, without emphasis: "I aim to. I don't figure to stay in a country among people who..." he said something unprintable and vile,

---

① ourn: ours.
② hisn: his.
③ hit: it.
④ Colonel Sartoris: 沙多里斯上校,福克纳所虚构的杰弗逊(Jefferson)镇上的名人,美国内战中的南军军官。穷白人斯诺普斯家族也住此镇。两个家族多次出现于福克纳的其他作品中。

addressed to no one.

"That'll do," the Justice said. "Take your wagon and get out of this country before dark. Case dismissed."

His father turned, and he followed the stiff black coat, the wiry figure walking a little stiffly from where a Confederate provost's man's musket ball had taken him in the heel① on a stolen horse thirty years ago, followed the two backs now, since his older brother had appeared from somewhere in the crowd, no taller than the father but thicker, chewing tobacco steadily, between the two lines of grim-faced men and out of the store and across the worn gallery and down the sagging steps and among the dogs and half-grown boys in the mild May dust, where as he passed a voice hissed:

"Barn burner!"

Again he could not see, whirling; there was a face in a red haze, moonlike, bigger than the full moon, the owner of it half again his size②, he leaping in the red haze toward the face, feeling no blow, feeling no shock when his head struck the earth, scrabbling up and leaping again, feeling no blow this time either and tasting no blood, scrabbling up to see the other boy in full flight and himself already leaping into pursuit as his father's hand jerked him back, the harsh, cold voice speaking above him: "Go get in the wagon."

It stood in a grove of locusts and mulberries across the road. His two hulking sisters in their Sunday dresses and his mother and her sister in calico and sunbonnets were already in it, sitting on and among the sorry residue of the dozen and more movings③ which even the boy could remember—the battered stove, the broken beds and chairs, the clock inlaid with mother-of-pearl, which would not run, stopped at some fourteen minutes past two o'clock of a dead and forgotten day and time, which had been his mother's dowry. She was crying, though when she saw him she drew her sleeve across her face and began to descend from the wagon. "Get back," the father said.

"He's hurt. I got to get some water and wash his..."

"Get back in the wagon," his father said. He got in too, over the tail-gate. His father mounted to the seat where the older brother already sat and struck the gaunt mules two savage blows with the peeled willow, but without heat. It was not even sadistic; it was exactly that same quality which in later years would cause his descendants to over-run the engine before putting a motor car into motion, striking and reining back in the same movement. The wagon went on, the store with its quiet crowd of grimly watching men dropped behind; a curve in the road hid it. *Forever* he thought. *Maybe he's done*④ *satisfied now, now that he has...* stopping himself, not to say it aloud even to himself. His mother's hand touched his shoulder.

"Does hit hurt?" she said.

"Naw," he said. "Hit don't hurt. Lemme be."

"Can't you wipe some of the blood off before it dries?"

"I'll wash to-night," he said. "Lemme be, I tell you."

The wagon went on. He did not know where they were going. None of them ever did or ever asked, because it was always somewhere, always a house of sorts waiting for them a day or two days or even three days away. Likely his father had already arranged to make a crop on another farm before he... Again he had to stop himself. He (the father) always did. There was something about his wolflike independence and even courage when the advantage was at least neutral which impressed strangers, as

---

① a Confederate provost's man's musket ball had taken him in the heel：一位南方军宪兵的滑膛枪子弹击中他的脚后跟。
② half again his size：个子比他高出一半。
③ the sorry residue of the dozen and more movings：因十多次搬迁而剩下的几样残破的家具。
④ done：已经。

if they got from his latent ravening ferocity not so much a sense of dependability as a feeling that his ferocious conviction in the rightness of his own actions would be of advantage to all whose interest lay with his.

That night they camped, in a grove of oaks and beeches where a spring ran. The nights were still cool and they had a fire against it, of a rail lifted from a nearby fence and cut into lengths—a small fire, neat, niggard almost, a shrewd fire; such fires were his father's habit and custom always, even in freezing weather. Older, the boy might have remarked this and wondered why not a big one; why should not a man who had not only seen the waste and extravagance of war, but who had in his blood an inherent voracious prodigality with material not his own, have burned everything in sight? Then he might have gone a step farther and thought that that was the reason: that niggard blaze was the living fruit of nights passed during those four years in the woods hiding from all men, blue or gray①, with his strings of horses (captured horses, he called them). And older still, he might have divined the true reason: that the element of fire spoke to some deep mainspring of his father's being, as the element of steel or of powder spoke to other men, as the one weapon for the preservation of integrity, else breath were not worth the breathing, and hence to be regarded with respect and used with discretion.

But he did not think this now and he had seen those same niggard blazes all his life. He merely ate his supper beside it and was already half asleep over his iron plate when his father called him, and once more he followed the stiff back, the stiff and ruthless limp, up the slope and on to the starlit road where, turning, he could see his father against the stars but without face or depth—a shape black, flat, and bloodless as though cut from tin in the iron folds of the frockcoat which had not been made for him, the voice harsh like tin and without heat like tin:

"You were fixing② to tell them. You would have told him." He didn't answer. His father struck him with the flat of his hand on the side of the head, hard but without heat, exactly as he had struck the two mules at the store, exactly as he would strike either of them with any stick in order to kill a horse fly, his voice still without heat or anger: "You're getting to be a man. You got to learn. You got to learn to stick to your own blood or you ain't going to have any blood to stick to you. Do you think either of them, any man there this morning, would? Don't you know all they wanted was a chance to get at me because they knew I had them beat? Eh?" Later, twenty years later, he was to tell himself, "If I had said they wanted only truth, justice, he would have hit me again." But now he said nothing. He was not crying. He just stood there. "Answer me," his father said.

"Yes," he whispered. His father turned.

"Get on to bed. We'll be there tomorrow."

To-morrow they were there. In the early afternoon the wagon stopped before a paintless two-room house identical almost with the dozen others it had stopped before even in the boy's ten years, and again, as on the other dozen occasions, his mother and aunt got down and began to unload the wagon, although his two sisters and his father and brother had not moved.

"Likely hit ain't fitten for hawgs,"③ one of the sisters said.

"Nevertheless, fit it will and you'll hog it and like it," his father said. "Get out of them chairs and help your Ma unload."

The two sisters got down, big, bovine, in a flutter of cheap ribbons; one of them drew from the jumbled wagon bed a battered lantern, the other a worn broom. His father handed the reins to the older son and began to climb stiffly over the wheel. "When they get unloaded, take the team to the barn and

---

① blue or gray: 蓝色和灰色分别是美国内战中北军和南军的军服颜色,这里指北军和南军。
② fixing: 打算,准备。
③ Likely hit ain't fitten for hawgs: Likely it isn't fit for hogs.

feed them." Then he said, and at first the boy thought he was still speaking to his brother:

"Come with me."

"Me?" he said.

"Yes," his father said. "You."

"Abner," his mother said. His father paused and looked back—the harsh level stare beneath the shaggy, graying, irascible brows.

"I reckon I'll have a word with the man that aims to begin to-morrow owning me body and soul for the next eight months."

They went back up the road. A week ago—or before last night, that is—he would have asked where they were going, but not now. His father had struck him before last night but never before had he paused afterward to explain why; it was as if the blow and the following calm, outrageous voice still rang, repercussed, divulging nothing to him save the terrible handicap of being young, the light weight of his few years, just heavy enough to prevent his soaring free of the world as it seemed to be ordered but not heavy enough to keep him footed solid in it, to resist it and try to change the course of its events.

Presently he could see the grove of oaks and cedars and the other flowering trees and shrubs and where the house would be, though not the house yet. They walked beside a fence massed with honeysuckle and Cherokee roses and came to a gate swinging open between two brick pillars, and now, beyond a sweep of drive, he saw the house for the first time and at that instant he forgot his father and the terror and despair both, and even when he remembered his father again (who had not stopped) the terror and despair did not return. Because, for all the twelve movings, they had sojourned until now in a poor country, a land of small farms and fields and houses, and he had never seen a house like this before. *Hit's big as a courthouse* he thought quietly, with a surge of peace and joy whose reason he could not have thought into words, being too young for that: *They are safe from him. People whose lives are a part of this peace and dignity are beyond his touch, he no more to them than a buzzing wasp: capable of stinging for a little moment but that's all; the spell of this peace and dignity rendering even the barns and stable and cribs which belong to it impervious to the puny flames he might contrive...*this, the peace and joy, ebbing for an instant as he looked again at the stiff black back, the stiff and implacable limp of the figure which was not dwarfed by the house, for the reason that it had never looked big anywhere and which now, against the serene columned backdrop, had more than ever that impervious quality of something cut ruthlessly from tin, depthless, as though, sidewise to the sun, it would cast no shadow. Watching him, the boy remarked the absolutely undeviating course which his father held and saw the stiff foot come squarely down in a pile of fresh droppings where a horse had stood in the drive and which his father could have avoided by a simple change of stride. But it ebbed only for a moment, though he could not have thought this into words either, walking on in the spell of the house, which he could even want but without envy, without sorrow, certainly never with that ravening and jealous rage which unknown to him walked in the ironlike black coat before him: *Maybe he will feel it too. Maybe it will even change him now from what maybe he couldn't help but be.*

They crossed the portico. Now he could hear his father's stiff foot as it came down on the boards with clocklike finality, a sound out of all proportion to the displacement of the body it bore and which was not dwarfed either by the white door before it, as though it had attained to a sort of vicious and ravening minimum not to be dwarfed by anything—the flat, wide, black hat, the formal coat of broadcloth which had once been black but which had now that friction-glazed greenish cast of the bodies of old house flies, the lifted sleeve which was too large, the lifted hand like a curled claw. The door opened so promptly that the boy knew the Negro must have been watching them all the time, an old man with neat grizzled hair, in a linen jacket, who stood barring the door with his body, saying,

"Wipe yo foots, white man, fo you come in here.① Major ain't home nohow."

"Get out of my way, nigger," his father said, without heat too, flinging the door back and the Negro also and entering, his hat still on his head. And now the boy saw the prints of the stiff foot on the doorjamb and saw them appear on the pale rug behind the machinelike deliberation of the foot which seemed to bear (or transmit) twice the weight which the body compassed. The Negro was shouting "Miss Lula! Miss Lula!" somewhere behind them, then the boy, deluged as though by a warm wave by a suave turn of carpeted stair and a pendant glitter of chandeliers and a mute gleam of gold frames, heard the swift feet and saw her too, a lady—perhaps he had never seen her like before either—in a gray, smooth gown with lace at the throat and an apron tied at the waist and the sleeves turned back, wiping cake or biscuit dough from her hands with a towel as she came up the hall, looking not at his father at all but at the tracks on the blond rug with an expression of incredulous amazement.

"I tried," the Negro cried. "I tole② him to..."

"Will you please go away?" she said in a shaking voice. "Major de Spain is not at home. Will you please go away?"

His father had not spoken again. He did not speak again. He did not even look at her. He just stood stiff in the center of the rug, in his hat, the shaggy iron-gray brows twitching slightly above the pebble-colored eyes as he appeared to examine the house with brief deliberation. Then with the same deliberation he turned; the boy watched him pivot on the good leg and saw the stiff foot drag round the arc of the turning, leaving a final long and fading smear. His father never looked at it, he never once looked down at the rug. The Negro held the door. It closed behind them, upon the hysteric and indistinguishable woman-wail. His father stopped at the top of the steps and scraped his boot clean on the edge of it. At the gate he stopped again. He stood for a moment, planted stiffly on the stiff foot, looking back at the house. "Pretty and white, ain't it?" he said. "That't sweat. Nigger sweat. Maybe it ain't white enough yet to suit him. Maybe he wants to mix some white sweat with it."

Two hours later the boy was chopping wood behind the house within which his mother and aunt and the two sisters (the mother and aunt, not the two girls, he knew that; even at this distance and muffled by walls the flat loud voices of the two girls emanated an incorrigible idle inertia) were setting up the stove to prepare a meal, when he heard the hooves and saw the linen-clad man on a fine sorrel mare, whom he recognized even before he saw the rolled rug in front of the Negro youth following on a fat bay carriage horse—a suffused, angry face vanishing, still at full gallop, beyond the corner of the house where his father and brother were sitting in the two tilted chairs; and a moment later, almost before he could have put the axe down, he heard the hooves again and watched the sorrel mare go back out of the yard, already galloping again. Then his father began to shout one of the sisters' names, who presently emerged backward from the kitchen door dragging the rolled rug along the ground by one end while the other sister walked behind it.

"If you ain't going to tote, go on and set up the wash pot," the first said.

"You, Sarty!" the second shouted. "Set up the wash pot!" His father appeared at the door, framed against that shabbiness, as he had been against that other bland perfection, impervious to either, the mother's anxious face at his shoulder.

"Go on," the father said. "Pick it up." The two sisters stooped, broad, lethargic; stooping, they presented an incredible expanse of pale cloth and a flutter of tawdry ribbons.

"If I thought enough of a rug to have to git hit③ all the way from France I wouldn't keep hit where

---

① Wipe yo foots, white man, fo you come in here.: Wipe your feet, white man, before you come in here.
② tole: told.
③ git hit: get it.

folks coming in would have to tromp on hit," the first said. They raised the rug.

"Abner," the mother said. "Let me do it."

"You go back and git dinner," his father said. "I'll tend to this."

From the woodpile through the rest of the afternoon the boy watched them, the rug spread flat in the dust beside the bubbling wash-pot, the two sisters stooping over it with that profound and lethargic reluctance, while the father stood over them in turn, implacable and grim, driving them though never raising his voice again. He could smell the harsh homemade lye they were using; he saw his mother come to the door once and look toward them with an expression not anxious now but very like despair; he saw his father turn, and he fell to with the axe and saw from the corner of his eye his father raise from the ground a flattish fragment of field stone and examine it and return to the pot, and this time his mother actually spoke: "Abner. Abner. Please don't. Please, Abner."

Then he was done too. It was dusk; the whippoorwills had already begun. He could smell coffee from the room where they would presently eat the cold food remaining from the mid-afternoon meal, though when he entered the house he realized they were having coffee again probably because there was a fire on the hearth, before which the rug now lay spread over the backs of the two chairs. The tracks of his father's foot were gone. Where they had been were now long, water-cloudy scoriations resembling the sporadic course of a lilliputian① mowing machine.

It still hung there while they ate the cold food and then went to bed, scattered without order or claim up and down the two rooms, his mother in one bed, where his father would later lie, the older brother in the other, himself, the aunt, and the two sisters on pallets on the floor. But his father was not in bed yet. The last thing the boy remembered was the depthless, harsh silhouette of the hat and coat bending over the rug and it seemed to him that he had not even closed his eyes when the silhouette was standing over him, the fire almost dead behind it, the stiff foot prodding him awake. "Catch up the mule," his father said.

When he returned with the mule his father was standing in the black door, the rolled rug over his shoulder. "Ain't you going to ride?" he said.

"No. Give me your foot."

He bent his knee into his father's hand, the wiry, surprising power flowed smoothly, rising, he rising with it, on to the mule's bare back (they had owned a saddle once; the boy could remember it though not when or where) and with the same effortlessness his father swung the rug up in front of him. Now in the starlight they retraced the afternoon's path, up the dusty road rife with honeysuckle, through the gate and up the black tunnel of the drive to the lightless house, where he sat on the mule and felt the rough warp of the rug drag across his thighs and vanish.

"Don't you want me to help?" he whispered. His father did not answer and now he heard again that stiff foot striking the hollow portico with that wooden and clocklike deliberation, that outrageous overstatement of the weight it carried. The rug, hunched, not flung (the boy could tell that even in the darkness) from his father's shoulder struck the angle of wall and floor with a sound unbelievably loud, thunderous, then the foot again, unhurried and enormous; a light came on in the house and the boy sat, tense, breathing steadily and quietly and just a little fast, though the foot itself did not increase its beat at all, descending the steps now; now the boy could see him.

"Don't you want to ride now?" he whispered. "We kin② both ride now," the light within the house altering now, flaring up and sinking. *He's coming down the stairs now,* he thought. He had already

---

① lilliputian: 小人国(人)的。源自英国作家斯威夫特(Jonathan Swift)所著小说《格列佛游记》(*Gulliver's Travels*, 1726)中的虚构岛国小人国(Lilliput)。此国的居民身高仅六英寸左右,他们的用品也都很小。

② kin: can.

ridden the mule up beside the horse block; presently his father was up behind him and he doubled the reins over and slashed the mule across the neck, but before the animal could begin to trot the hard, thin arm came round him, the hard, knotted hand jerking the mule back to a walk.

In the first red rays of the sun they were in the lot, putting plow gear on the mules. This time the sorrel mare was in the lot before he heard it at all, the rider collarless and even bareheaded, trembling, speaking in a shaking voice as the woman in the house had done, his father merely looking up once before stooping again to the hame he was buckling, so that the man on the mare spoke to his stooping back:

"You must realize you have ruined that rug. Wasn't there anybody here, any of your women..." he ceased, shaking, the boy watching him, the older brother leaning now in the stable door, chewing, blinking slowly and steadily at nothing apparently. "It cost a hundred dollars. But you never had a hundred dollars. You never will. So I'm going to charge you twenty bushels of corn against your crop. I'll add it in your contract and when you come to the commissary you can sign it. That won't keep Mrs. de Spain quiet but maybe it will teach you to wipe your feet off before you enter her house again."

Then he was gone. The boy looked at his father, who still had not spoken or even looked up again, who was now adjusting the logger-head① in the hame.

"Pap," he said. His father looked at him—the inscrutable face, the shaggy brows beneath which the gray eyes glinted coldly. Suddenly the boy went toward him, fast, stopping as suddenly. "You done the best you could!" he cried. "If he wanted hit done different why didn't he wait and tell you how? He won't git no twenty bushels! He won't git none!② We'll gether hit and hide hit! I kin watch..."

"Did you put the cutter back in that straight stock③ like I told you?"

"No, sir," he said.

"Then go do it."

That was Wednesday. During the rest of that week he worked steadily, at what was within his scope and some which was beyond it, with an industry that did not need to be driven nor even commanded twice; he had this from his mother, with the difference that some at least of what he did he liked to do, such as splitting wood with the half-size axe which his mother and aunt had earned, or saved money somehow, to present him with at Christmas. In company with the two older women (and on one afternoon, even one of the sisters), he built pens for the shoat and the cow which were a part of his father's contract with the landlord, and one afternoon, his father being absent, gone somewhere on one of the mules, he went to the field.

They were running a middle buster④ now, his brother holding the plow straight while he handled the reins, and walking beside the straining mule, the rich black soil shearing cool and damp against his bare ankles, he thought *Maybe this is the end of it. Maybe even that twenty bushels that seems hard to have to pay for just a rug will be a cheap price for him to stop forever and always from being what he used to be;* thinking, dreaming now, so that his brother had to speak sharply to him to mind the mule: *Maybe he even won't collect the twenty bushels. Maybe it will all add up and balance and vanish— corn, rug, fire; the terror and grief, the being pulled two ways like between two teams of horses—gone, done with for ever and ever.*

Then it was Saturday; he looked up from beneath the mule he was harnessing and saw his father in the black coat and hat. "Not that," his father said. "The wagon gear." And then, two hours later, sitting

---

① logger-head：马颈轭的一部分。
② He won't git no twenty bushels! He won't git none!：这里的双重否定仍表示否定的意思。两句中的 no 与 none 意为 any。
③ straight stock：犁。
④ middle buster：犁的一种。

in the wagon bed behind his father and brother on the seat, the wagon accomplished a final curve, and he saw the weathered paintless store with its tattered tobacco-and patent-medicine posters and the tethered wagons and saddle animals below the gallery. He mounted the gnawed steps behind his father and brother, and there again was the lane of quiet, watching faces for the three of them to walk through. He saw the man in spectacles sitting at the plank table and he did not need to be told this was a Justice of the Peace; he sent one glare of fierce, exultant, partisan defiance at the man in collar and cravat now, whom he had seen but twice before in his life, and that on a galloping horse, who now wore on his face an expression not of rage but of amazed unbelief which the boy could not have known was at the incredible circumstance of being sued by one of his own tenants, and came and stood against his father and cried at the Justice: "He ain't done it! He ain't burnt..."

"Go back to the wagon," his father said.

"Burnt?" the Justice said. "Do I understand this rug was burned too?"

"Does anybody here claim it was?" his father said. "Go back to the wagon." But he did not, he merely retreated to the rear of the room, crowded as that other had been, not to sit down this time, instead, to stand pressing among the motionless bodies, listening to the voices:

"And you claim twenty bushels of corn is too high for the damage you did to the rug?"

"He brought the rug to me and said he wanted the tracks washed out of it. I washed the tracks out and took the rug back to him."

"But you didn't carry the rug back to him in the same condition it was in before you made the tracks on it."

His father did not answer, and now for perhaps half a minute there was no sound at all save that of breathing, the faint, steady suspiration of complete and intent listening.

"You decline to answer that, Mr. Snopes?" Again his father did not answer. "I'm going to find against you, Mr. Snopes. I'm going to find that you were responsible for the injury to Major de Spain's rug and hold you liable for it. But twenty bushels of corn seems a little high for a man in your circumstances to have to pay. Major de Spain claims it cost a hundred dollars. October corn will be worth about fifty cents. I figure that if Major de Spain can stand a ninety-five-dollar loss on something he paid cash for, you can stand a five-dollar loss you haven't earned yet. I hold you in damages to Major de Spain to the amount of ten bushels of corn over and above your contract with him, to be paid to him out of your crop at gathering time. Court adjourned."

It had taken no time hardly, the morning was but half begun. He thought they would return home and perhaps back to the field, since they were late, far behind all other farmers. But instead his father passed on behind the wagon, merely indicating with his hand for the older brother to follow with it, and crossed the road toward the blacksmith shop opposite, pressing on after his father, overtaking him, speaking, whispering up at the harsh, calm face beneath the weathered hat: "He won't git no ten bushels neither. He won't git one. We'll..." until his father glanced for an instant down at him, the face absolutely calm, the grizzled eyebrows tangled above the cold eyes, the voice almost pleasant, almost gentle:

"You think so? Well, we'll wait till October anyway."

The matter of the wagon—the setting of a spoke or two and the tightening of the tires—did not take long either, the business of the tires accomplished by driving the wagon into the spring branch behind the shop and letting it stand there, the mules nuzzling into the water from time to time, and the boy on the seat with the idle reins, looking up the slope and through the sooty tunnel of the shed where the slow hammer rang and where his father sat on an upended cypress bolt, easily, either talking or listening, still sitting there when the boy brought the dripping wagon up out of the branch and halted it before the door.

"Take them on to the shade and hitch," his father said. He did so and returned. His father and the smith and a third man squatting on his heels inside the door were talking, about crops and animals; the boy, squatting too in the ammoniac dust and hoof-parings and scales of rust, heard his father tell a long and unhurried story out of the time before the birth of the older brother even when he had been a professional horsetrader. And then his father came up beside him where he stood before a tattered last year's circus poster on the other side of the store, gazing rapt and quiet at the scarlet horses, the incredible poisings and convolutions of tulle and tights and the painted leers of comedians, and said, "It's time to eat."

But not at home. Squatting beside his brother against the front wall, he watched his father emerge from the store and produce from a paper sack a segment of cheese and divide it carefully and deliberately into three with his pocket knife and produce crackers from the same sack. They all three squatted on the gallery and ate, slowly, without talking; then in the store again, they drank from a tin dipper tepid water smelling of the cedar bucket and of living beech trees. And still they did not go home. It was a horse lot this time, a tall rail fence upon and along which men stood and sat and out of which one by one horses were led, to be walked and trotted and then cantered back and forth along the road while the slow swapping and buying went on and the sun began to slant westward, they—the three of them—watching and listening, the older brother with his muddy eyes and his steady, inevitable tobacco, the father commenting now and then on certain of the animals, to no one in particular.

It was after sundown when they reached home. They ate supper by lamplight, then, sitting on the doorstep, the boy watched the night fully accomplish, listening to the whippoorwills and the frogs, when he heard his mother's voice: "Abner! No! No! Oh, God. Oh, God. Abner!" and he rose, whirled, and saw the altered light through the door where a candle stub now burned in a bottle neck on the table and his father, still in the hat and coat, at once formal and burlesque as though dressed carefully for some shabby and ceremonial violence, emptying the reservoir of the lamp back into the five-gallon kerosene can from which it had been filled, while the mother tugged at his arm until he shifted the lamp to the other hand and flung her back, not savagely or viciously, just hard, into the wall, her hands flung out against the wall for balance, her mouth open and in her face the same quality of hopeless despair as had been in her voice. Then his father saw him standing in the door.

"Go to the barn and get that can of oil we were oiling the wagon with," he said. The boy did not move. Then he could speak.

"What..." he cried. "What are you..."

"Go get that oil," his father said. "Go."

Then he was moving, running, outside the house, toward the stable: this the old habit, the old blood which he had not been permitted to choose for himself, which had been bequeathed him willy nilly and which had run for so long (and who knew where, battening on what of outrage and savagery and lust) before it came to him. *I could keep on, he thought, I could run on and on and never look back, never need to see his face again. Only I can't. I can't*, the rusted can in his hand now, the liquid sploshing in it as he ran back to the house and into it, into the sound of his mother's weeping in the next room, and handed the can to his father.

"Ain't you going to even send a nigger?" he cried. "At least you sent a nigger before!"

This time his father didn't strike him. The hand came even faster than the blow had, the same hand which had set the can on the table with almost excruciating care flashing from the can toward him too quick for him to follow it, gripping him by the back of his shirt and on to tiptoe before he had seen it quit the can, the face stooping at him in breathless and frozen ferocity, the cold, dead voice speaking over him to the older brother who leaned against the table, chewing with that steady, curious, sidewise motion of cows:

"Empty the can into the big one and go on. I'll catch up with you."

"Better tie him up to the bedpost," the brother said.

"Do like I told you," the father said. Then the boy was moving, his bunched shirt and the hard, bony hand between his shoulder-blades, his toes just touching the floor, across the room and into the other one, past the sisters sitting with spread heavy thighs in the two chairs over the cold hearth, and to where his mother and aunt sat side by side on the bed, the aunt's arms about his mother's shoulders.

"Hold him," the father said. The aunt made a startled movement. "Not you," the father said. "Lennie. Take hold of him. I want to see you do it." His mother took him by the wrist. "You'll hold him better than that. If he gets loose don't you know what he is going to do? He will go up yonder." He jerked his head toward the road. "Maybe I'd better tie him."

"I'll hold him," his mother whispered.

"See you do then." Then his father was gone, the stiff foot heavy and measured upon the boards, ceasing at last.

Then he began to struggle. His mother caught him in both arms, he jerking and wrenching at them. He would be stronger in the end, he knew that. But he had no time to wait for it. "Lemme go!" he cried. "I don't want to have to hit you!"

"Let him go!" the aunt said. "If he don't go, before God, I am going there myself!"

"Don't you see I can't!" his mother cried. "Sarty! Sarty! No! No! Help me, Lizzie!"

Then he was free. His aunt grasped at him but it was too late. He whirled, running, his mother stumbled forward on to her knees behind him, crying to the nearer sister: "Catch him, Net! Catch him!" But that was too late too, the sister (the sisters were twins, born at the same time, yet either of them now gave the impression of being, encompassing as much living meat and volume and weight as any other two of the family) not yet having begun to rise from the chair, her head, face, alone merely turned, presenting to him in the flying instant an astonishing expanse of young female features untroubled by any surprise even, wearing only an expression of bovine interest. Then he was out of the room, out of the house, in the mild dust of the starlit road and the heavy rifeness of honeysuckle, the pale ribbon unspooling with terrific slowness under his running feet, reaching the gate at last and turning in, running, his heart and lungs drumming, on up the drive toward the lighted house, the lighted door. He did not knock, he burst in, sobbing for breath, incapable for the moment of speech; he saw the astonished face of the Negro in the linen jacket without knowing when the Negro had appeared.

"De Spain!" he cried, panted. "Where's ..." then he saw the white man too emerging from a white door down the hall. "Barn!" he cried. "Barn!"

"What?" the white man said. "Barn?"

"Yes!" the boy cried. "Barn!"

"Catch him!" the white man shouted.

But it was too late this time too. The Negro grasped his shirt, but the entire sleeve, rotten with washing, carried away, and he was out that door too and in the drive again, and had actually never ceased to run even while he was screaming into the white man's face.

Behind him the white man was shouting, "My horse! Fetch my horse!" and he thought for an instant of cutting across the park and climbing the fence into the road, but he did not know the park nor how high the vine-massed fence might be and he dared not risk it. So he ran on down the drive, blood and breath roaring; presently he was in the road again though he could not see it. He could not hear either: the galloping mare was almost upon him before he heard her, and even then he held his course, as if the very urgency of his wild grief and need must in a moment more find him wings, waiting until the ultimate instant to hurl himself aside and into the weed-choked roadside ditch as the horse thundered past and on, for an instant in furious silhouette against the stars, the tranquil early summer night sky which, even before the shape of the horse and rider vanished, stained abruptly and violently upward: a long, swirling roar incredible and soundless, blotting the stars, and he springing up and into the road again, running again, knowing it was too late yet still running even after he heard the shot and, an instant later, two shots, pausing now without knowing he had ceased to run, crying "Pap! Pap!", running again before he knew he had begun to run, stumbling, tripping over something and scrabbling up again without ceasing to run, looking backward over his shoulder at the glare as he got up, running on among the invisible trees, panting, sobbing, "Father! Father!"

At midnight he was sitting on the crest of a hill. He did not know it was midnight and he did not know how far he had come. But there was no glare behind him now and he sat now, his back toward what he had called home for four days anyhow, his face toward the dark woods which he would enter when breath was strong again, small, shaking steadily in the chill darkness, hugging himself into the remainder of his thin, rotten shirt, the grief and despair now no longer terror and fear but just grief and despair. *Father. My father*, he thought. "He was brave!" he cried suddenly, aloud but not loud, no more than a whisper: "He was! He was in the war! He was in Colonel Sartoris' cav'ry①!" not knowing that his father had gone to that war a private in the fine old European sense, wearing no uniform, admitting the authority of and giving fidelity to no man or army or flag, going to war as Malbrouck② himself did: for booty—it meant nothing and less than nothing to him if it were enemy booty or his own.

The slow constellations wheeled on. It would be dawn and then sun-up after a while and he would be hungry. But that would be to-morrow and now he was only cold, and walking would cure that. His breathing was easier now and he decided to get up and go on, and then he found that he had been asleep because he knew it was almost dawn, the night almost over. He could tell that from the whippoorwills. They were everywhere now among the dark trees below him, constant and inflectioned and ceaseless, so that, as the instant for giving over to the day birds drew nearer and nearer, there was no interval at all between them. He got up. He was a little stiff, but walking would cure that too as it would the cold, and soon there would be the sun. He went on down the hill, toward the dark woods within which the liquid silver voices of the birds called unceasing—the rapid and urgent beating of the urgent and quiring heart of the late spring night. He did not look back.

《烧畜棚》(又译《烧马棚》)写于福克纳创作鼎盛期中的1938年,1939年作为该年度美国最佳短篇小说获得首届欧·亨利纪念奖,一直被视为福克纳最具代表性的短篇小说之一。

南方穷白人的生活是福克纳较为关注的题材。斯诺普斯(Snopes)这一穷白人家族的故事在福克纳后来写的《村子》(*The Hamlet*, 1940)、《小镇》(*The Town*, 1957)、《大宅》(*The Mansion*, 1959)等长篇小说中得到了更为详细的表现。《烧畜棚》主要是通过描写他们与庄园主的激烈冲突来表现穷白人的。阿伯纳(Abner)擅入德斯潘(de Spain)的大宅、糟蹋他的地毯、烧他的畜棚等行为,都明确表现了阿伯纳对于庄园主的仇恨,以及誓死维护自尊的意志。但小说强调使他众叛亲离、自取灭亡的偏执与暴烈,也传达出作者对他的责备。

处于痛苦的成长期的男孩也是福克纳所感兴趣的。在《烧畜棚》里,萨蒂(Sarty)的痛苦不仅在于他必须承受过去的罪孽所产生的后果,比如在哈里斯的畜棚被烧之后,他被骂作"畜棚纵火犯",并被打得头破血流;还在于他必须做出艰难的选择,必须决定是按父亲的要求忠实于自己的血统,继续生活在"恐惧与绝望"之中,还是背叛血统,去追求德斯潘"漂亮、雪白","像法院一般"的大宅所象征的"和平与

---

① cav'ry: cavalry.
② Malbrouck:马尔布鲁克,18世纪法国民谣《马尔布鲁克已赴战场》(*Malbrouck Has Gone to the War*)中的人物,常被看成约翰·丘吉尔(John Churchill),即第一代马尔伯勒(Marlborough)公爵。他靠非凡的军事才能从士兵升至中将,曾率英军战胜法王路易十四,是历史上的名将之一。但他也是一个有争议的人物,被指责为谋乱反上,唯利是图。

快乐"。萨蒂的最后选择无疑为他的追求创造了机会。但他天真,没有像阿伯纳那样认识到德斯潘的大宅建在黑人和白人的汗水之上,这又难免让人对他的未来感到担忧。萨蒂在福克纳的作品中没有再出现过。

萨蒂当时没有认识到的还有阿伯纳为什么只生小火取暖,阿伯纳在内战中的真实表现等。而读者则可从叙述者的有关叙述中了解到他的这种幼稚以及他所不了解的其他情况。小说叙述者具有传统的第三人称叙述的全知视角,但他的叙述具有高度的选择性,主要选择叙述萨蒂所能看到、感到、想到的东西,使得叙述客观而又简洁。叙述者有时也站出来表达年幼的主人公尚不具备的洞见,从而加强了他可悲处境的感染力和他成熟过程的戏剧性。

思考题

1. What is the nature of the story's conflict? How does each of the story's six scenes serve to reveal, clarify, and intensify the conflict?
2. What seems to motivate Abner's violent, antisocial behaviour? Why does he try to make Sarty an accomplice to the burning of Major de Spain's barn? Why does Sarty finally defy him and try to warn Major de Spain?
3. What comments does the story offer about the social, moral, and economic values of the old and the new South?

推荐作品

"A Rose for Emily" (1931)
The Sound and the Fury (1929)
Absalom, Absalom! (1936)

参考资料

Blotner, Joseph. *Faulkner: A Biography.* 2 vols. New York: Random House, 1974.
Brooks, Cleanth. *William Faulkner: The Yoknapatawpha Country.* New Haven: Yale University Press, 1963.
Polk, Noel, ed. *New Essays on The Sound and the Fury.* Beijing: Peking University Press, 2006.
Wagner-Martin, Linda, ed. *New Essays on Go Down, Moses.* Beijing: Peking University Press, 2006.
Weinstein, Philip M. *The Cambridge Companion to William Faulkner.* Cambridge: Cambridge University Press, 1995.

(刘建华)

第十二单元
Ernest Hemingway (1899—1961)
厄内斯特·海明威

 作者简介

厄内斯特·海明威，小说家，出生在伊利诺伊州一个医生家庭。他儿时常随父亲参加捕鱼狩猎活动，这些户外经历后来成为他文学创作中的重要题材。他中学毕业后成为报社记者。第一次世界大战期间，他因视力原因无法参军，但他参加了志愿救护车队来到前线作战。这段战争经历也成了他的小说题材。1925年，他发表了短篇小说集《在我们的时代里》(*In Our Time*)，其凝练、简朴的文笔，不动声色的叙述风格开始引起人们的注意。1926年，他发表了第一部长篇小说《太阳照样升起》(*The Sun Also Rises*)。故事描述了第一次世界大战后流落巴黎的青年，他们迷惘、空虚，靠酗酒、情爱的刺激寻求精神慰藉。主人公巴恩斯在战争中受伤，丧失了性爱能力后，仍然能够坦然面对生活。这部小说一举奠定了海明威的文坛重要地位，同时成为所谓"迷惘的一代"作家代表。三年后，他发表了另一部长篇小说《永别了，武器》(*A Farewell to Arms*, 1929)。小说主人公亨利在第一次世界大战中负伤，恋爱，然而爱人最终却因难产而死，对他而言，战争带来的只有心灵创伤。1940年，他发表了《丧钟为谁而鸣》(*For Whom the Bell Tolls*)。故事以西班牙内战为背景，描写主人公在残酷的战斗中勇敢面对死亡。他的最后一部小说《老人与海》(*The Old Man and the Sea*, 1952)体现了他的人生价值观和行为准则，为他赢得了诺贝尔文学奖。1961年，他终因病痛折磨而自杀。在他的许多作品中，男主人公们可以遭遇逆境、灾难、厄运或失败，他们也可能会迷惘、绝望，但他们却总能谈笑若定，保持优雅风度、勇气和尊严。正是因为这一点，评论家曾较多关注其作品中的男性中心地位或他对女性的偏见，但随着人们重新审视其作品中的女性视角，评论界的看法已有所改变①。海明威的文风承接马克·吐温的口语体传统，文字质朴无华，生动自然，叙述简约，却蕴涵丰富。借用他本人的比喻：冰山移动的尊严在于它仅有八分之一露出水面。

海明威独特的个人经历与其作品之间具有相当复杂的关联，这使得他的个人生活和作品同样受到公众的关注，也一直是评论家和传记作家所争论褒贬的焦点。海明威去世后陆续面世的手稿、通信和其他文献资料，甚至包括联邦调查局的档案使沉寂一时的海明威研究在20世纪80年代高潮重现。1939至1960年期间，海明威曾经住在古巴哈瓦那郊外他的"眺望农场"(Finca Vigia)。2002年，古巴政府和美国国会众议院议员詹姆斯·麦戈文(James McGovern)签署协议，同意共同修复、保管海明威这期间留在那里的大量文字材料，其中包括2000多封信件及作品草稿等。

 作品

Hills Like White Elephants

The hills across the valley of the Ebro② were long and white. On this side there was no shade and no trees and the station was between two lines of rails in the sun.③ Close against the side of the station there was the warm shadow of the building and a curtain, made of strings of bamboo beads, hung across the open door into the bar, to keep out flies. The American and the girl with him sat at a table in the shade, outside the building. It was very hot and the express from Barcelona would come in forty

---

① 参见本章节的作品赏析部分。
② the Ebro: the Ebro River.
③ 故事发生的地点是在巴塞罗那—马德里铁路线上一个车站。该地点在现实中位于埃布罗河附近的嘉塞塔镇(Caseta)，铁道由此经过，北面是白色的山峦和荒野，南面是郁郁葱葱的埃布罗河岸区和山峰。南面的勃勃生机与北面的荒芜恰与围绕堕胎产生的冲突形成对应。

minutes. It stopped at this junction for two minutes and went to Madrid.

"What should we drink?" the girl asked. She had taken off her hat and put it on the table.

"It's pretty hot," the man said.

"Let's drink beer."

"Dos cervezas①," the man said into the curtain.

"Big ones?" a woman asked from the doorway.

"Yes. Two big ones."

The woman brought two glasses of beer and two felt pads. She put the felt pads and the beer glass on the table and looked at the man and the girl. The girl was looking off at the line of hills. They were white in the sun and the country was brown and dry.

"They look like white elephants," she said.

"I've never seen one," the man drank his beer.

"No, you wouldn't have."

"I might have," the man said. "Just because you say I wouldn't have doesn't prove anything."

The girl looked at the bead curtain. "They've painted something on it," she said. "What does it say?"

"Anis del Toro. It's a drink."

"Could we try it?"

The man called "Listen" through the curtain. The woman came out from the bar.

"Four reales②."

"We want two Anis del Toro③."

"With water?"

"Do you want it with water?"

"I don't know," the girl said. "Is it good with water?"

"It's all right."

"You want them with water?" asked the woman.

"Yes, with water."

"It tastes like liquorice," the girl said and put the glass down.

"That's the way with everything."

"Yes," said the girl. "Everything tastes of liquorice. Especially all the things you've waited so long for, like absinthe④."

"Oh, cut it out."

"You started it," the girl said. "I was being amused. I was having a fine time."

"Well, let's try and have a fine time."

"All right. I was trying. I said the mountains looked like white elephants. Wasn't that bright?"

"That was bright."

"I wanted to try this new drink. That's all we do, isn't it—look at things and try new drinks?"

"I guess so."

The girl looked across at the hills.

"They're lovely hills," she said. "They don't really look like white elephants. I just meant the coloring of their skin through the trees."

---

① Dos cervezas：(西班牙语)two beers.
② reales：雷阿尔(旧时西班牙以及其属地使用的货币单位)。
③ Anis del Toro：(西班牙语)一种深色、甘草味的酒,西班牙语的意思是：Anis of the Bull。
④ absinthe：苦艾酒,在当时大多欧洲国家,苦艾酒因可能引起不良反应已被禁止。当时的看法认为苦艾会导致幻觉和不孕。

"Should we have another drink?"

"All right."

The warm wind blew the bead curtain against the table.

"The beer's nice and cool," the man said.

"It's lovely," the girl said.

"It's really an awfully simple operation, Jig," the man said. "It's not really an operation at all."

The girl looked at the ground the table legs rested on.

"I know you wouldn't mind it, Jig. It's really not anything. It's just to let the air in."①

The girl did not say anything.

"I'll go with you and I'll stay with you all the time. They just let the air in and then it's all perfectly natural."

"Then what will we do afterwards?"

"We'll be fine afterwards. Just like we were before."

"What makes you think so?"

"That's the only thing that bothers us. It's the only thing that's made us unhappy."

The girl looked at the bead curtain, put her hand out and took hold of two of the strings of beads.

"And you think then we'll be all right and be happy."

"I know we will. Yon don't have to be afraid. I've known lots of people that have done it."

"So have I," said the girl. "And afterwards they were all so happy."

"Well," the man said, "if you don't want to you don't have to. I wouldn't have you do it if you didn't want to. But I know it's perfectly simple."

"And you really want to?"

"I think it's the best thing to do. But I don't want you to do it if you don't really want to."

"And if I do it you'll be happy and things will be like they were and you'll love me?"

"I love you now. You know I love you."

"I know. But if I do it, then it will be nice again if I say things are like white elephants, and you'll like it?"

"I'll love it. I love it now but I just can't think about it. You know how I get when I worry."

"If I do it you won't ever worry?"

"I won't worry about that because it's perfectly simple."

"Then I'll do it. Because I don't care about me."

"What do you mean?"

"I don't care about me."

"Well, I care about you."

"Oh, yes. But I don't care about me. And I'll do it and then everything will be fine."

"I don't want you to do it if you feel that way."

The girl stood up and walked to the end of the station. Across, on the other side, were fields of grain and trees along the banks of the Ebro. Far away, beyond the river, were mountains. The shadow of a cloud moved across the field of grain and she saw the river through the trees.

"And we could have all this," she said. "And we could have everything and every day we make it more impossible."

"What did you say?"

"I said we could have everything."

---

① It's just to let the air in: 这里指"简单手术"的方法。

"We can have everything."

"No, we can't."

"We can have the whole world."

"No, we can't."

"We can go everywhere."

"No, we can't. It isn't ours any more."

"It's ours."

"No, it isn't. And once they take it away, you never get it back."

"But they haven't taken it away."

"We'll wait and see."

"Come on back in the shade," he said. "You mustn't feel that way."

"I don't feel any way," the girl said. "I just know things."

"I don't want you to do anything that you don't want to do—"

"Nor that isn't good for me," she said. "I know. Could we have another beer?"

"All right. But you've got to realize— "

"I realize," the girl said. "Can't we maybe stop talking?"

They sat down at the table and the girl looked across at the hills on the dry side of the valley and the man looked at her and at the table.

"You've got to realize," he said, "that I don't want you to do it if you don't want to. I'm perfectly willing to go through with it if it means anything to you."

"Doesn't it mean anything to you? We could get along."

"Of course it does. But I don't want anybody but you. I don't want anyone else. And I know it's perfectly simple."

"Yes, you know it's perfectly simple."

"It's all right for you to say that, but I do know it."

"Would you do something for me now?"

"I'd do anything for you."

"Would you please please please please please please please stop talking?"

He did not say anything but looked at the bags against the wall of the station. There were labels on them from all the hotels where they had spent nights.

"But I don't want you to," he said, "I don't care anything about it."

"I'll scream," the girl said.

The woman came out through the curtains with two glasses of beer and put them down on the damp felt pads. "The train comes in five minutes," she said.

"What did she say?" asked the girl.

"That the train is coming in five minutes."

The girl smiled brightly at the woman, to thank her.

"I'd better take the bags over to the other side of the station," the man said. She smiled at him.

"All right. Then come back and we'll finish the beer."

He picked up the two heavy bags and carried them around the station to the other tracks. He looked up the tracks but could not see the train. Coming back, he walked through the bar-room, where people waiting for the train were drinking. He drank an Anis at the bar and looked at the people. They were all waiting reasonably for the train. He went out through the bead curtain. She was sitting at the table and smiled at him.

"Do you feel better?" he asked.

"I feel fine," she said. "There's nothing wrong with me. I feel fine."

　　《白象似的群山》发表于1927年。故事发生在火车站，一对男女正在等车，他们之间的话题显然是关于一个"简单手术"。两人的谈话透露出两人相互冲突的看法和态度，而直至故事的结尾，冲突并没有真正解决。故事极为独特的场景以及两人对环境和事物的不同观察和反应与故事中心题材相互呼应，凸显故事冲突的含义。女主人公吉格将群山比喻成"白象"，评论家的解读不尽相同，但大多认为，"白象"的形象象征生育，但在男女主人公眼中，却含有截然不同的寓意，对一方这意味着自然中的罕物珍奇，盎然生机，对另一方却意味无用之物，荒芜死寂。故事中的对话自然、简洁，看似无意闲谈，然而其弦外之音才是水面下的"冰山"。男子实际、"理智"，情感麻木；吉格则想象丰富，感性。这里值得一提的是，传统上认为海明威作品主要突出表现了海明威式男性硬汉角色和相应的男性视角，而20世纪70年代兴起的女权主义文学批评对此自然多有关注。而有意思的是，新的批评视角却使海明威研究更加重视海明威作品的女性视角和女性情感体验，[①]从而也进一步扩展了海明威研究的视野。

　　另一方面，如果将故事中心题材置于具有深厚宗教传统的美国文化大背景之下，我们应该了解，堕胎问题至今仍然是美国社会一个重大公共议题，公众意见极端对立。反对堕胎一方（Pro-lifer）的一些人相信传统基督教义的胎儿自受孕即被赋予灵魂一说（ensoulment），一些人坚持胎儿有独立人格权，认为堕胎就是谋杀无辜生命；而支持堕胎一方（Pro-choicer）则强调女性自由选择的权利。当然，男主人公要求对方堕胎自有其目的。不难理解，有评论家从故事中帘子上的珠子和主人公们相关的行为细节上推断吉格的宗教信仰；[②]无疑，特定文化背景强化了该题材寓意中自然和生命与人为干预和死亡之间的对立。与传统故事结局不同，没有解决的故事冲突拓展了读者参与和思考的空间，而冲突本身也蕴涵了两性关系、权力结构、语言交流，不同性别对幸福、情爱和同一生活世界的不同理解等诸多层面的意义。

 思考题

1. Are the two characters in the story a married couple?
2. What is the nature of their relationship?
3. Why does Jig want to scream but then soften and smile at her companion?
4. Do they communicate their thoughts and feelings effectively? Why or why not?
5. Will Jig agree to the operation?

"Indian Camp" (1924)（短篇小说）
"A Clean, Well-lighted Place" (1932)（短篇小说）
"The Short Happy Life of Francis Macomber" (1936)（短篇小说）

 参考资料

Donaldson, Scott, ed. *The Cambridge Companion to Ernest Hemingway*. 上海：上海外语教育出版社，2000。
Smith, Paul, *A Reader's Guide to the Short Stories of Ernest Hemingway*. Boston: G. K. Hall & Co., 1989.
Smith, Paul, ed. *New Essays on Hemingway's Short Fiction*. Beijing: Peking University Press, 2006.
海明威，《海明威谈创作》，董衡巽编选，北京：三联书店，1985。

（张世耘）

---

① 海明威其他表现独特女性视角的作品包括："The Short Happy Life of Francis Macomber" "Up in Michigan" "Cat in the Rain" 等。
② 天主教有以念珠记数祈祷的做法。

第十三单元

Ralph(Waldo)Ellison (1914—1994)
拉尔夫·埃里森

 作者简介

拉尔夫·埃里森,黑人小说家、杂文家,生于俄克拉荷马市,自幼酷爱音乐,上高中期间开始演奏小号。1933年高中毕业时获得音乐奖学金,进入亚拉巴马州塔斯克基黑人学院(Tuskegee Institute)学习音乐。亚拉巴马州的种族隔离政策和学院视爵士乐为野蛮音乐的保守思想使他大为不快,1936年,他离开学院到纽约学习雕塑。在纽约,他结识了兰斯顿·休斯和理查德·赖特,受两人的影响,加上他在塔斯克基学院期间曾经被海明威、萧伯纳、艾略特等人的著作吸引的因素,他加入了美国联邦作家项目(Federal Writers' Project),开始写杂文、书评和短篇小说。1942年,埃里森退出联邦作家工程,担任《黑奴季刊》(Negro Quaterly)执行编辑。第二次世界大战结束后,他开始创作《看不见的人》(又译《无形人》,Invisible Man, 1952),该书出版前,埃里森共发表9个短篇小说和10多篇评论文章。《看不见的人》一鸣惊人,被誉为"划时代的小说""现代美国人生活的史诗",1953年获得美国国家图书奖,评审委员会赞扬作家的"文学冒险勇气"。此后,该书再版数十次,1982年和2002年分别发行了作品发表30周年和50周年纪念版。1965年,《看不见的人》被《图书周报》的民意测验列为"第二次世界大战后美国最卓越的小说";甚至到1982年,还连续16周高居最畅销作品排行榜;2000年,在美国现代书库(The Modern Library)所评选的20世纪100种最佳英语小说中列第19位。在这部以主人公寻求"自我"为主题的小说里,埃里森运用众多艺术手段,力图赋予无名主人公超越种族的感受,着力把黑人经受的种族压迫升华为人类经受的社会压迫。1960年,埃里森发表短篇小说《乡下佬来了》(And Hickman Arrives),这本是他计划中另一部反映美国黑人生活的长篇力作的一部分。不幸的是,1967年,已经写了368页的手稿被毁之一炬。但他继续辛勤耕耘,1994年去世时留下一部约2,000页手稿的未完成长篇小说,后经学者卡拉瀚(John F. Callahan)整理节选,于1999年以《六一九》(又译《六月庆典》,Juneteenth)为名出版。埃里森生前曾在哥伦比亚、耶鲁、芝加哥、纽约等大学讲学或任教,获得过"自由勋章"(1969)、"文学艺术骑士勋章"(1970)、"国家艺术勋章"(1985)等众多奖励和学术头衔,还发表了两部论文集:《影子与行动》(Shadow and Act, 1964)和《走向领地》(Going to the Territory, 1986)。

 作品

King of the Bingo Game[①]

The woman in front of him was eating roasted peanuts that smelled so good that he could barely contain his hunger. He could not even sleep and wished they'd hurry and begin the bingo game. There, on his right, two fellows were drinking wine out of a bottle wrapped in a paper bag, and he could hear soft gurgling in the dark. His stomach gave a low, gnawing growl. "If this was down South," he

---

① Bingo:一种赌博游戏,一般翻译为宾果(或宾戈),16世纪起源于意大利,18世纪流行欧洲,后经狂欢节商贩传到美国。1929年12月,在佐治亚州的亚特兰大狂欢节上,推销员爱德文·洛(Edwin S. Lowe)发现一个帐篷里人们正在兴奋地玩一种游戏,大家都热切地等待着叫号,当叫到的号同某人卡片上的相同时,那人便在数字上放一粒豆子(bean),当某人的豆子排成一排时,他就大喊一声"Beago!"爱德文·洛还发现玩游戏的人兴致甚浓,赶都赶不走,他意识到这种游戏有巨大的市场潜力。回到纽约后,爱德文·洛照葫芦画瓢,也邀请朋友玩起了这种游戏。情景正如他预料的那样,其中一女士眼看自己的一排豆子即将成行,激动不已,等到她赢得游戏时,舌头发紧,结巴了一阵子也没能喊出"Beago",而是说成了"B-b-bingo!"爱德文·洛也备感兴奋,决定推广这一游戏,并称之为"Bingo"。现在,美国的宾果游戏通常在游戏厅进行,游戏使用的卡片多分为5行5列,对应"Bingo"的5个字母,卡上有24个数字加一个空格。在75以内随机抽取数字,在1—15中选择B对应的数字,16—30中选择I对应的数字,31—45中选择N对应的数字,46—60中选择G对应的数字,61—75中选择O对应的数字。由专业人士叫号,游戏者根据叫号,迅速在自选的卡上找到这些数字,并做出标记。一人所做标记垂直、水平或对角线成行者获胜。

thought, "all I'd have to do is lean over and say, 'Lady, gimme a few of those peanuts, please ma'am,' and she'd pass me the bag and never think nothing of it." Or he could ask the fellows for a drink in the same way. Folks down South stuck together that way; they didn't even have to know you. But up here it was different. Ask somebody for something, and they'd think you were crazy. Well, I ain't crazy. I'm just broke, 'cause I got no birth certificate to get a job, and Laura 'bout to die 'cause we got no money for a doctor. But I ain't crazy①. And yet a pinpoint of doubt was focused in his mind as he glanced toward the screen and saw the hero stealthily entering a dark room and sending the beam of a flashlight② along a wall of bookcases. This is where he finds the trapdoor③, he remembered. The man would pass abruptly through the wall and find the girl tied to a bed, her legs and arms spread wide, and her clothing torn to rags. He laughed softly to himself. He had seen the picture three times, and this was one of the best scenes.

On his right the fellow whispered wide-eyed to his companion, "Man, look a-yonder!"

"Damn!"

"Wouldn't I like to have her tied up like that ..."

"Hey! That fool's letting her loose!"

"Aw, man, he loves her."④

"Love or no love!"

The man moved impatiently beside him, and he tried to involve himself in the scene. But Laura was on his mind. Tiring quickly of watching the picture he looked back to where the white beam⑤ filtered from the projection room above the balcony. It started small and grew large, specks of dust dancing in its whiteness as it reached the screen. It was strange how the beam always landed right on the screen and didn't mess up and fall somewhere else. But they had it all fixed. Everything was fixed. Now suppose when they showed that girl with her dress torn the girl started taking off the rest of her clothes, and when the guy came in he didn't untie her but kept her there and went to taking off his own clothes? That would be something to see. If a picture got out of hand like that those guys up there would go nuts⑥. Yeah, and there'd be so many folks in here you couldn't find a seat for nine months! A strange sensation played over his skin. He shuddered. Yesterday he'd seen a bedbug on a woman's neck as they walked out into the bright street. But exploring his thigh through a hole in his pocket he found only goose pimples and old scars.

The bottle gurgled again. He closed his eyes. Now a dreamy music was accompanying the film and train whistles were sounding in the distance, and he was a boy again walking along a railroad trestle⑦ down South, and seeing the train coming, and running back as fast as he could go, and hearing the whistle blowing, and getting off the trestle to solid ground just in time, with the earth trembling beneath his feet, and feeling relieved as he ran down the cinder-strewn embankment⑧ onto the highway,

---

① 故事开头部分描写一个来自南方的黑人痛苦孤独的心理。他客居他乡,身无分文,而且因为没有身份证而无法找工作,饥肠辘辘地在北方一家电影院里等待着电影结束,为的是从将在电影院举行的宾果游戏中得奖以为其重病在床的妻子罗拉(Laura)治病。如同理查德·赖特在《土生子》里表现的一样,电影院成为黑人产生美国梦、幻想实现美国梦的场所。故事里的主人公已经多次到过电影院,所以他从曾经奴役过黑人的南方来到象征自由的北方,而且相信自己可以通过工作或博彩获得成功。然而,事实上,饥饿、南北方文化差异以及妻子的疾病使他身心交瘁、无助无奈,甚至担心别人会把他当作疯子(这一点也为故事的发展埋下了伏笔)。自由与束缚、黑人与白人、南方与北方、疯狂与清醒、理想与现实等众多冲突开始显现。 故事中的主人公显然没有受过什么教育,使用的是黑人英语: ain't 为 be 动词的否定式形式;有很多吞音现象,'bout=about, 'cause=because。
② the beam of a flashlight: 手电光。黑暗中的白光具有象征意义。
③ trapdoor: 暗门,因为 trap 具有"陷阱"之意,可以将该词理解为双关,或象征。
④ 两个黑人男子(因为 man 是黑人之间打招呼的方式,相当于"老兄""哥儿们"。)对电影里被困在床上,衣服被撕烂的女孩不怀好意的调侃。一方面说明他们精神空虚,另一方面也说明他们没有认识到女孩也代表他们自己所处的境地,黑人和妇女都是白人男子霸权主义的受害者。
⑤ white beam: (电影放映机发出的)白光,象征白人控制的技术和权力(下文有"They had it all fixed.")。
⑥ nuts: 疯子。这里指这些观众会因此而疯狂。
⑦ railroad trestle: 铁路桥。下文中的也是此意。
⑧ the cinder-strewn embankment: 铺满炉渣的路堤。

and looking back and seeing with terror that the train had left the track and was following him right down the middle of the street, and all the white people laughing as he ran screaming...①

"Wake up there, buddy! What the hell do you mean hollering like that? Can't you see we trying to enjoy this here picture?"

He stared at the man with gratitude.

"I'm sorry, old man," he said. "I musta been dreaming."

"Well, here, have a drink. And don't be making no noise like that, damm!"

His hands trembled as he tilted his head. It was not wine, but whiskey. Cold rye whiskey. He took a deep swoller, decided it was better not to take another, and handed the bottle back to its owner.

"Thanks, old man," he said.

Now he felt the cold whskey breaking a warm path straight through the middle of him, growing hotter and sharper as it moved. He had not eaten all day, and it made him light-headed. The smell of the peanuts stabbed him like a knife, and he got up and found a seat in the middle aisle. But no sooner did he sit than he saw a row of intense-faced young girls, and got up again, thinking, "You chicks musta been Lindy-hopping somewhere."② He found a seat several rows ahead as the lights came on, and he saw the screen disappear behind a heavy red and gold curtain; then the curtain rising, and the man with the microphone and a uniformed attendant coming on the stage.

He felt for his bingo cards, smiling. The guy at the door wouldn't like it if he knew about his having *five* cards. Well, not everyone played the bingo game; and even with five cards he didn't have much of a chance. For Laura, though, he had to have faith. He studied the cards, each with its different numerals, punching the free center hole③ in each and spreading them neatly across his lap; and when the lights faded he sat slouched in his seat so that he could look from his cards to the bingo wheel with but a quick shifting of his eyes.

Ahead, at the end of the darkness, the man with the microphone was pressing a button attached to a long cord and spinning the bingo wheel and calling out the number each time the wheel came to rest. And each time the voice rang out his finger raced over the cards for the number. With five cards he had to move fast. He became nervous; there were too many cards, and the man went too fast with his grating voice. Perhaps he should just select one and throw the others away. But he was afraid. He became warm. Wonder how much Laura's doctor would cost? Damn that, watch the cards! And with despair he heard the man call three in a row which he missed on all five cards. This way he'd never win...

When he saw the row of holes punched across the third card, he sat paralyzed and heard the man call three more numbers before he stumbled forward, screaming.

"Bingo! Bingo!"

"Let that fool up there," someone called.

"Get up there, man!"

He stumbled down the aisle and up the steps to the stage into a light so sharp and bright that for a moment it blinded him, and he felt that he had moved into the spell of some strange, mysterious power④. Yet it was as familiar as the sun, and he knew it was the perfectly familiar bingo.

The man with the microphone was saying something to the audience as he held out his card. A

---

① 主人公睡着后做了一个噩梦。现实与梦幻的交织使故事具有超现实主义特征，梦中脱轨追赶他的火车是白人技术和权力的另一个象征物。
② You chicks musta been Lindy-hopping somewhere.: chick: (俚) 少妇; musta=must have。"你们这帮小娘儿们肯定是跑到哪里去跳爵士舞了。" Lindy Hop, 又称 Jitterbug, 一种随爵士乐节拍跳的快速舞, 名称来自1927年林德伯格首次飞越大西洋后的新闻报道标题："LINDY HOPS THE ATLANTIC"。主人公连续换座位是在寻找光亮之处, 为游戏做准备。
③ the free center hole: 游戏卡片中间没有数字号码的空格。主人公为了增加赢钱的机会, 拿了5张卡片, 属游戏中的欺诈行为。
④ 明亮刺眼的光让他感到像是被某种神秘的力量迷住了。象征意义极强, 注意主持人称呼主人公的词。

cold light flashed from the man's finger as the card left his hand. His knees trembled. The man stepped closer, checking the card against the numbers chalked on the board. Suppose he had made a mistake? The pomade on the man's hair made him feel faint, and he backed away. But the man was checking the card over the microphone now, and he had to stay. He stood tense, listening.

"Under the O, forty-four," the man chanted. "Under the I, seven. Under the G, three. Under the B, ninety-six. Under the N, thirteen!"

His breath came easier as the man smiled at the audience.

"Yes sir, ladies and gentlemen, he's one of the chosen people①!"

The audience rippled with laughter and applause.

"Step right up to the front of the stage."

He moved slowly forward, wishing that the light was not so bright.

"To win tonight's jackpot of $36.90 the wheel must stop between the double zero, understand?"②

He nodded, knowing the ritual from the many days and nights he had watched the winners march across the stage to press the button that controlled the spinning wheel and receive the prizes. And now he followed the instructions as though he'd crossed the slippery stage a million prize-winning times.

The man was making some kind of a joke, and he nodded vacantly. So tense had he become that he felt a sudden desire to cry and shook it away. He felt vaguely that his whole life was determined by the bingo wheel③; not only that which would happen now that he was at last before it, but all that had gone before, since his birth, and his mother's birth and the birth of his father. It had always been there, even though he had not been aware of it, handing out the unlucky cards and numbers of his days. The feeling persisted, and he started quickly away. I better get down from here before I make a fool of myself, he thought.

"Here, boy," the man called. "You haven't started yet."

Someone laughed as he went hesitantly back.

"Are you all reet?"④

He grinned at the man's jive talk, but no words would come, and he knew it was not a convincing grin. For suddenly he knew that he stood on the slippery brink of some terrible embarrassment.

"Where are you from, boy?" the man asked.

"Down South."

"He's from down South, ladies and gentlemen," the man said. "Where from? Speak right into the mike."

"Rocky Mont," he said, "Rock'Mont, North Car'lina."

"So you decided to come down off that mountain to the U.S.," the man laughed. He felt that the man was making a fool of him, but then something cold was placed in his hand, and the lights were no longer behind him.

Standing before the wheel he felt alone, but that was somehow right, and he remembered his plan. He would give the wheel a short quick twirl. Just a touch of the button. He had watched it many times, and always it came close to double zero when it was short and quick. He steeled himself; the fear had left, and he felt a profound sense of promise, as though he were about to be repaid for all the things he'd suffered all his life. Trembling, he pressed the button. There was a whirl of lights, and in a second

---

① the chosen people：上帝的选民，清教徒认为上帝要拯救其灵魂的那一少部分人。主持人这里的意思是"他是个幸运儿！"但是，把这个清教徒自以为是的词用在一个黑人身上颇具讽刺意味。
② jackpot：头奖，累计奖金。有人认为把奖金总数写成36.90美元是有意通过3的倍数消解三位一体的神学观念。两个零，即"00"，代表多层意义的缺失，甚至包括主人公和他妻子的死。
③ the bingo wheel：游戏盘，可理解为"幸运之盘""命运之盘"的含义。
④ Are you all reet?：Are you all right? 注意主持人居高临下的话语。

he realized with finality that though he wanted to, he could not stop. It was as though he held a high-powered line in his naked hand. His nerves tightened. As the wheel increased its speed it seemed to draw him more and more into his power, as though it held his fate; and with it came a deep need to submit, to whirl, to lose himself in its swirl of color. He could not stop it now, he knew. So let it be.

The button rested snugly in his palm where the man had placed it. And now he became aware of the man beside him, advising him through the microphone, while behind the shadowy audience hummed with noisy voices. He shifted his feet. There was still that feeling of helplessness within him, making part of him desire to turn back, even now that the jackpot was right in his hand. He squeezed the button until his fist ached. Then, like the sudden shriek of a subway whistle, a doubt tore through his head. Suppose he did not spin the wheel long enough? What could he do, and how could he tell? And then he knew, even as he wondered, that as long as he pressed the button, he could control the jackpot. He and only he could determine whether or not it was to be his. Not even the man with the microphone could do anything about it now. He felt drunk. Then, as though he had come down from a high hill into a valley of people, he heard the audience yelling.

"Come down from there, you jerk[①]!"

"Let somebody else have a chance...."

"Ole Jack thinks he done found the end of the rainbow..."[②]

The last voice was not unfriendly, and he turned and smiled dreamily into the yelling mouths. Then he turned his back squarely on them.

"Don't take too long, boy," a voice said.

He nodded. They were yelling behind him. Those folks did not understand what had happened to him. They had been playing the bingo game day in and night out for years, trying to win rent money or hamburger change. But not one of those wise guys had discovered this wonderful thing. He watched the wheel whirling past the numbers and experienced a burst of exaltation: This is God! This is the really truly God! He said it aloud, "This is God!"

He said it with such absolute conviction[③] that he feared he would fall fainting into the footlights. But the crowd yelled so loud that they could not hear. Those fools, he thought. I'm here trying to tell them the most wonderful secret in the world, and they're yelling like they gone crazy. A hand fell upon his shoulder.

"You'll have to make a choice now, boy. You've taken too long."

He brushed the hand violently away.

"Leave me alone, man. I know what I'm doing!"

The man looked surprised and held on to the microphone for support. And because he did not wish to hurt the man's feelings he smiled, realizing with a sudden pang that there was no way of explaining to the man just why he had to stand there pressing the button forever.

"Come here," he called tiredly.

The man approached, rolling the heavy microphone across the stage.

"Anybody can play this bingo game, right?" he said.

"Sure, but..."

He smiled, feeling inclined to be patient with this slick looking white man with his blue sport shirt

---

① jerk: (俚) 笨蛋。
② Ole Jack thinks he done found the end of the rainbow...: 那家伙以为他梦想成真了…… Ole: old; Jack 不是故事主人公的名字,相当于"那家伙""那个老兄"。the end of the rainbow 来自典故 the pot of gold at the end of the rainbow, 意为不可能实现的愿望。
③ absolute conviction: 深信无疑。

and his sharp gabardine① suit.

"That's what I thought," he said. "Anybody can win the jackpot as long as they get the lucky number, right?"

"That's the rule, but after all..."

"That's what I thought," he said. "And the big prize goes to the man who knows how to win it?"

The man nodded speechlessly.

"Well then, go on over there and watch me win like I want to. I ain't going to hurt nobody," he said, "and I'll show you how to win. I mean to show the whole world how it's got to be done."

And because he understood, he smiled again to let the man know that he held nothing against him for being white and impatient. Then he refused to see the man any longer and stood pressing the button, the voices of the crowd reaching him like sounds in distant streets. Let them yell. All the Negroes down there were just ashamed because he was black like them. He smiled inwardly, knowing how it was. Most of the time he was ashamed of what Negroes did himself. Well, let them be ashamed for something this time. Like him. He was like a long thin black wire that was being stretched and wound upon the bingo wheel; wound until he wanted to scream; wound, but this time himself controlling the winding and the sadness and the shame, and because he did, Laura would be all right. Suddenly the lights flickered. He staggered backwards. Had something gone wrong? All this noise. Didn't they know that although he controlled the wheel, it also controlled him, and unless he pressed the button forever and forever and ever it would stop, leaving him high and dry, dry and high on this hard high slippery hill and Laura dead? There was only one chance; he had to do whatever the wheel demanded. And gripping the button in despair, he discovered with surprise that it imparted a nervous energy. His spine tingled. He felt a certain power.

Now he faced the raging crowd with defiance, its screams penetrating his eardrums like trumpets shrieking from a juke-box②. The vague faces glowing in the bingo lights gave him a sense of himself that he had never known before. He was running the show, by God! They had to react to him, for he was their luck. This is *me*, he thought. Let the bastards yell. Then someone was laughing inside him, and he realized that somehow he had forgotten his own name. It was a sad, lost feeling to lose your name, and a crazy thing to do. That name had been given him by the white man who had owned his grandfather a long lost time ago down South. But maybe those wise guys knew his name.

"Who am I?" he screamed.

"Hurry up and bingo, you jerk!"

They didn't know either, he thought sadly. They didn't even know their own names, they were all poor nameless bastards. Well, he didn't need that old name; he was reborn. For as long as he pressed the button he was The-man-who- pressed-the-button-who-held-the-prize-who-was-the-King-of-Bingo. That was the way it was, and he'd have to press the button even if nobody understood, even though Laura did not understand.

"Live!" he shouted.

The audience quieted like the dying of a huge fan.

"Live, Laura, baby. I got holt of it now③, sugar. Live!"

He screamed it, tears streaming down his face. "I got nobody but YOU!"

The screams tore from his very guts. He felt as though the rush of blood to his head would burst out in baseball seams of small red droplets, like a head beaten by police clubs. Bending over he saw a

---

① sharp：(俚) 时髦的, 漂亮的; gabardine：华达呢。
② juke-box：(美口)投币唱片播放机。
③ I got holt of it now：I got hold of it now. 主人公以为自己控制住了一切, 反复用 control, power 等词。

trickle of blood splashing the toe of his shoe. With his free hand he searched his head. It was his nose. God, suppose something has gone wrong? He felt that the whole audience had somehow entered him and was stamping its feet in his stomach and he was unable to throw them out. They wanted the prize, that was it. They wanted the secret for themselves. But they'd never get it; he would keep the bingo wheel whirling forever, and Laura would be safe in the wheel. But would she? It had to be, because if she were not safe the wheel would cease to turn; it could not go on. He had to get away, vomit all, and his mind formed an image of himself running with Laura in his arms down the tracks of the subway just ahead of an A train, running desperately *vomit* with people screaming for him to come out but knowing no way of leaving the tracks because to stop would bring the train crushing down upon him and to attempt to leave across the other tracks would mean to run into a hot third rail as high as his waist which threw blue sparks that blinded his eyes until he could hardly see.

He heard singing and the audience was clapping its hands.

> *Shoot the liquor to him, Jim, boy!*
> *Clap-clap-clap*
> *Well a-calla the cop*[①]
> *He's blowing his top!*
> *Shoot the liquor to him, Jim, boy!*

Bitter anger grew within him at the singing. They think I'm crazy. Well let'em laugh. I'll do what I got to do.

He was standing in an attitude of intense listening when he saw that they were watching something on the stage behind him. He felt weak. But when he turned he saw no one. If only his thumb did not ache so. Now they were applauding. And for a moment he thought that the wheel had stopped. But that was impossible, his thumb still pressed the button. Then he saw them. Two men in uniform beckoned from the end of the stage. They were coming toward him, walking in step, slowly, like a tap-dance team returning for a third encore[②]. But their shoulders shot forward, and he backed away, looking wildly about. There was nothing to fight them with. He had only the long black cord which led to a plug somewhere back stage, and he couldn't use that because it operated the bingo wheel. He backed slowly, fixing the men with his eyes as his lips stretched over his teeth in a tight, fixed grin; moved toward the end of the stage and realizing that he couldn't go much further, for suddenly the cord became taut and he couldn't afford to break the cord. But he had to do something. The audience was howling. Suddenly he stopped dead, seeing the men halt, their legs lifted as in an interrupted step of a slow-motion dance. There was nothing to do but run in the other direction and he dashed forward, slipping and sliding. The men fell back, surprised. He struck out violently going past.

"Grab him!"

He ran, but all too quickly the cord tightened, resistingly, and he turned and ran back again. This time he slipped them, and discovered by running in a circle before the wheel he could keep the cord from tightening. But this way he had to flail his arms to keep the men away. Why couldn't they leave a man alone? He ran, circling.

"Ring down the curtain," someone yelled. But they couldn't do that. If they did the wheel flashing from the projection room would be cut off. But they had him before he could tell them so, trying to pry open his fist, and he was wrestling and trying to bring his knees into the fight and holding on to the button, for it was his life. And now he was down, seeing a foot coming down, crushing his wrist

---

① a-calla the cop: Call the police.
② like a tap-dance team returning for a third encore: tap-dance: 踢踏舞; encore: 应观众要求加演。像是应观众要求第三次还场演出的踢踏舞队。

cruelly, down, as he saw the wheel whirling serenely above.

"I can't give it up." he screamed. Then quietly, in a confidential tone, "Boys, I really can't give it up."

It landed hard against his head. And in the blank moment they had it away from him, completely now. He fought them trying to pull him up from the stage as he watched the wheel spin slowly to a stop. Without surprise he saw it rest at double-zero.

"You see," he pointed bitterly.

"Sure, boy, sure, it's O.K.," one of the men said smiling.

And seeing the man bow his head to someone he could not see, he felt very, very happy; he would receive what all the winners received.

But as he warmed in the justice of the man's tight smile he did not see the man's slow wink, nor see the bow-legged man behind him step clear of the swiftly descending curtain and set himself for a blow①. He only felt the dull pain exploding in his skull, and he knew even as it slipped out of him that his luck had run out on the stage.

《宾果游戏之王》最初于1944年发表,融现实主义情节和超现实主义手法于一体。无名黑人主人公试图通过宾果游戏筹取为妻子治病款项的叙事线索将黑人在美国被奴役的历史与孤立无援的现状交织在一起,解构了通过个人努力取得成功、北方是黑人获得自由平等的天堂等美国神话。故事还通过隐喻、象征、梦境、幻觉等手法创造了一个虚实共存的情景,显现了黑人在美国无助无望的残酷社会现实。一个身无分文的黑人,无名无姓、无依无靠,抱着改变命运的希望,从南方山区走进北方都市;然而,身份(证)的缺失制约着他(工作)的权利,妻子的重病既加重他的责任又增添了他的孤立。万般无奈之时,他走进电影院,饥肠辘辘地从电影人物的行为和自己的想象中获得虚幻的自由和权力。博彩中,他侥幸地握住了控制游戏转盘的按钮,于是自以为控制了命运的车轮,要与历史和命运抗争,试图改变游戏规则不让转盘停下,结果被砸死在制造幻想的电影院的舞台上。电影和游戏一样,都是主流社会通过幻觉奴役他者的文化霸权工具,"他们把一切都安排好了"。象征命运或社会力量的白色亮光和火车让他睁不开眼、喘不出气,北方工业文明同南方种植园经济一样压榨着黑人;象征机会的游戏转盘给予他力量,让他忘却过去的屈辱,成为西方文化(电影)中的英雄人物,然而他最终还是在一个警察向另一个警察挤眼的瞬间成为牺牲品,在赢得游戏的同时失去自身的存在。无名黑人的故事就像一则寓言揭示了生活在现代美国社会的人的困境:生活在自由的国度却受各种枷锁束缚,人与人(黑人与黑人、黑人与白人)之间隔阂重重,工作不像清教宣传的那样会得到报偿(有人没有工作权利,有人因工作失去理智),取胜却一无所获。

思考题

1. Where does the action of the story take place? What is the significance of this setting?
2. Why does the protagonist, an African American, miss the American South? What does that suggest about the alternatives open to such a person?
3. Is the protagonist's sense of power hallucination or insight?
4. What is the significance of the nameless protagonist's forgetting his own name?
5. What are the symbolic meanings of the bingo wheel?

---

① set himself for a blow: 跑开。

Invisible Man (1952)

Busby, Mark. *Ralph Ellison*. Boston: Twayne Publishers, 1991.
Graham, Maryemma and Amritjit Singh, eds. *Conversations with Ralph Ellison*. University Press of Mississippi, 1995.
Jackson, Lawrence. *Ralph Ellision: Emergence of Genius*. New York: John Wiley & Sons, 2002
O'Meally, Robert G. *The Craft of Ralph Ellison*. Cambridge, Mass.: Harvard University Press, 1980.
—, ed. *New Essays on Invisible Man*. Beijing: Peking University Press; Cambridge University Press, 2006.

(陈法春)

第十四单元
John Updike (1932—2009)
约翰·厄普代克

 作者简介

约翰·厄普代克，美国当代重要作家，出生于宾夕法尼亚州一个教师家庭。他在哈佛大学读书时就显露才华，经常为学生幽默杂志撰稿、作画。毕业后，他到英国学习美术一年，回国后曾在《纽约客》(The New Yorker)杂志任记者。厄普代克的作品体裁包括了小说、诗歌、散文、戏剧和文学评论。他创作了28部长篇小说，包括《贫民院集市》(The Poorhouse Fair, 1959)、《兔子，跑吧!》(Rabbit, Run, 1960)、《马人》(又译：《半人半马》)(The Centaur, 1963)、《夫妇们》(又译：《成双成对》)(Couples, 1968)、《兔子归来》(Rabbit Redux, 1971)、《都是星期天的一个月》(A Month of Sundays, 1975)、《嫁给我：一段浪漫史》(Marry Me: A Romance, 1976)、《政变》(The Coup, 1978)、《兔子富了》(Rabbit Is Rich, 1981)、《伊斯特威克的女巫们》(The Witches of Eastwick, 1984)、《罗杰教授的版本》(Roger's Version, 1986)、《S.》(S., 1988)、《兔子安息》(Rabbit at Rest, 1990)、《巴西》(Brazil, 1994)、《圣洁百合》(In the Beauty of the Lilies, 1996)、《末日来临》(Toward the End of the Time, 1997)、《葛特露和克劳迪斯》(Gertrude and Claudius, 2000)、《寻找我的面容》(Seek My Face, 2002)、《恐怖分子》(The Terrorist, 2006)等；短篇小说集包括：《同一道门》(The Same Door, 1959)、《鸽羽和其他故事》(Pigeon Feathers and Other Stories, 1962)、《音乐学校》(The Music School, 1966)、《爱的插曲：短篇及续集》(Licks of Love: Short Stories and a Sequel, 2000)，其中收有"兔子"系列的续集，中篇小说《兔子受到了怀念》(Rabbit Remembered)、《早期短篇小说集》(The Early Stories: 1953—1975, 2003)、《梅普尔短篇小说集》(The Maples Stories, 2009)等。厄普代克的作品多次获奖。其中，"兔子"系列小说中的《兔子富了》获得了美国国家图书奖、美国书评界奖和普利策奖。其后，该系列的另一部小说《兔子安息》又获得了美国书评界奖和普利策奖。厄普代克主要采用现实主义方法创作，同时他也关注欧洲、拉丁美洲作家的不同创作风格和实验，并在自己的创作中尝试不同方法，如《巴西》中的魔幻现实主义、《末日来临》中的科幻技巧等。厄普代克的主要作品以20世纪50年代以来社会现实为背景，细致入微地刻画了当代美国中产阶级的生存状态以及个人面对家庭、性爱、信仰危机等诸多问题时的心路历程和行为选择，用他自己的话说，他笔下关注焦点是"居住在美国小城镇、信仰新教的中产阶级群体"。

尽管按厄普代克的说法，写评论与小说和诗歌创作之间的差别如同"贴岸航行"与"远海航行"之间的差别，但他自己却不仅是著作等身的作家，同时也是多产的评论家。除了为《纽约客》《纽约时报书评》(The New York Times Book Review)、《纽约书评》(The New York Review of Books)等刊物撰写大量评论文章外，他已结集出版了多本散文评论，如《杂文集》(Assorted Prose, 1965)、《过往短文集》(Picked-Up Pieces, 1975)、《贴岸航行：评论文集》(Hugging the Shore: Essays and Criticism, 1983)、《观赏：美术评论集》(Just Looking: Essays on Art, 1989)、《零散之作：评论文集》(Odd Jobs: Essays and Criticism, 1991)、《高尔夫之梦》(Golf Dreams: Writings on Golf, 1996)、《多点儿实事儿：评论文集》(More Matter: Essays and Criticism, 1999)、《继续观赏：美国美术评论集》(Still Looking: Essays on American Art, 2005)、《细思：评论文集》(Due Considerations: Essays and Criticism, 2007)等，其中《贴岸航行：评论文集》更是获得了1983年美国书评界奖。

厄普代克著述颇多，生前发表作品有60部之多，在世时即受到公众和学界高度关注，这样的作家并不多。他两度成为《时代周刊》的封面人物，而受到同样待遇的小说家只有乔伊斯、海明威、福克纳和辛克莱·刘易斯。《现代小说研究》(Modern Fiction Studies)两次出版厄普代克专刊，而同享此殊荣的只有乔伊斯、詹姆斯、康拉德、沃尔夫、福克纳和海明威。然而，厄普代克的文学成就尚难盖棺定论，有人就认为其文体华丽有余，而思想和主题深度相对不足。文学评论家布鲁姆(Harold Bloom)就认为，对于读者来说，厄普代克长于令人愉悦，但相对而言，享受如此愉悦却无须太多费心劳神，尽管这样的愉悦绝非虚幻，但毕竟不足以挑战思考能力。不过大多评论者对厄普代克评价颇高，英国作家艾米斯(Martin

Amis)称其为天才,较之同行,若论活力,自劳伦斯(D.H. Lawrence)至今,尚无能出其右者;美国作家罗斯(Philip Roth)则将其成就与霍桑相提并论,并赞誉他"集卓越的文学评论家、散文家和小说家于一身,堪称我们时代最伟大的作者"。

Separating

The day was fair. Brilliant. All that June the weather had mocked the Maples internal misery with solid sunlight—golden shafts and cascades of green in which their conversations had wormed unseeing, their sad murmuring selves the only stain in Nature. Usually by this time of the year they had acquired tans; but when they met their elder daughter's plane on her return from a year in England they were almost as pale as she, though Judith was too dazzled by the sunny opulent jumble of her native land to notice. They did not spoil her homecoming by telling her immediately. Wait a few days, let her recover from jet lag, had been one of their formulations, in that string of gray dialogues—over coffee, over cocktails, over Cointreau①—that had shaped the strategy of their dissolution, while the earth performed its annual stunt of renewal unnoticed beyond their closed windows. Richard had thought to leave at Easter; Joan had insisted they wait until the four children were at last assembled, with all exams passed and ceremonies attended, and the bauble of summer to console them. So he had drudged away, in love, in dread, repairing screens, getting the mowers sharpened, rolling and patching their new tennis court.

The court, clay, had come through its first winter pitted and windswept bare of redcoat. Years ago the Maples had observed how often, among their friends, divorce followed a dramatic home improvement, as if the marriage were making one last twitchy effort to live; their own worst crisis had come amid the plaster dust and exposed plumbing of a kitchen renovation. Yet, a summer ago, as canary-yellow bulldozers gaily churned a grassy, daisy-dotted knoll into a muddy plateau, and a crew of pigtailed young men raked and tamped clay into a plane, this transformation did not strike them as ominous, but festive in its impudence; their marriage could rend the earth for fun.② The next spring, waking each day at dawn to a sliding sensation as if the bed were being tipped, Richard found the barren tennis court, its net and tapes still rolled in the barn, an environment congruous with his mood of purposeful desolation, and the crumbling of handfuls of clay into cracks and holes (dogs had frolicked on the court in a thaw; rivulets had evolved trenches) an activity suitably elemental and interminable. In his sealed heart he hoped the day would never come.

Now it was here. A Friday. Judith was reacclimated; all four children were assembled, before jobs and camps and visits again scattered them. Joan thought they should be told one by one. Richard was for making an announcement at the table. She said, "I think just making an announcement is a cop-out. They'll start quarrelling and playing to each other instead of focusing. They're each individuals, you know, not just some corporate obstacle to your freedom."

"O.K., O.K. I agree." Joan's plan was exact. That evening, they were giving Judith a belated welcome-home dinner, of lobster and champagne. Then, the party over, they the two of them, who nineteen years before would push her in a baby carriage along Tenth Street to Washington Square③, were to walk her out of the house, to the bridge across the salt creek, and tell her, swearing her to

---

① Cointreau: 一种甜酒。
② but festive in its impudence; their marriage could rend the earth for fun.: its impudence 指把原来遍布花草的小丘推成平地的冒失行为;rend the earth for fun 指前面所说的行为是为了取乐而破坏了大地原貌。
③ along Tenth Street to Washington Square: 该地点位于纽约市。

secrecy. Then Richard Jr., who was going directly from work to a rock concert in Boston, would be told, either late when he returned on the train or early Saturday morning before he went off to his jobs; he was seventeen and employed as one of a golf-course maintenance crew. Then the two younger children, John and Margaret, could, as the morning wore on, be informed.

"Mopped up, as it were," Richard said.

"Do you have any better plan?" That leaves you the rest of Saturday to answer any questions, pack, and make your wonderful departure.

"No," he said, meaning he had no better plan, and agreed to hers, though it had an edge of false order, a plea for control in the semblance of its achievement, like Joan's long chore lists and financial accountings and, in the days when he first knew her, her too copious lecture notes. Her plan turned one hurdle for him into four—four knife-sharp walls, each with a sheer blind drop① on the other side.

All spring he had been morbidly conscious of insides and outsides, of barriers and partitions. He and Joan stood as a thin barrier between the children and the truth. Each moment was a partition, with the past on one side and the future on the other, a future containing this unthinkable now. Beyond four knifelike walls a new life for him waited vaguely. His skull cupped a secret, a white face, a face both frightened and soothing, both strange and known, that he wanted to shield from tears, which he felt all about him, solid as the sunlight. So haunted, he had become obsessed with battening down the house against his absence, replacing screens and sash cords, hinges and latches—a Hoodini② making things snug before his escape.

The lock. He had still to replace a lock on one of the doors of the screened porch. The task, like most such, proved more difficult than he had imagined. The old lock, aluminum frozen by corrosion, had been deliberately rendered obsolete by manufacturers. Three hardware stores had nothing that even approximately matched the mortised hole its removal (surprisingly easy) left. Another hole had to be gouged, with bits too small and saws too big, and the old hole fitted with a block of wood—the chisels dull, the saw rusty, his fingers thick with lack of sleep. The sun poured down, beyond the porch, on a world of neglect. The bushes already needed pruning, the windward side of the house was shedding flakes of paint, rain would get in when he was gone, insects, rot, death. His family, all those he would lose, filtered through the edges of his awareness as he struggled with screw holes, splinters, opaque instructions, minutiae of metal.

Judith sat on the porch, a princess returned from exile. She regaled them with stories of fuel shortages, of bomb scares in the Underground, of Pakistani workmen loudly lusting after her as she walked past on her way to dance school. Joan came and went, in and out of the house, calmer than she should have been, praising his struggles with the lock as if this were one more and not the last of their chain of shared chores. The younger of his sons, John, now at fifteen suddenly, unwittingly handsome, for a few minutes held the rickety screen door while his father clumsily hammered and chiseled, each blow a kind of sob in Richard's ears. His younger daughter, having been at a slumber party, slept on the porch hammock through all the noise—heavy and pink, trusting and forsaken. Time, like the sunlight, continued relentlessly; the sunlight slowly slanted. Today was one of the longest days. The lock clicked, worked. He was through. He had a drink; he drank it on the porch, listening to his daughter. "It was so sweet," she was saying, "during the worst of it, how all the butcher's and bakery shops kept open by candlelight. They're all so plucky and cute. From the papers, things sounded so much worse here—people shooting people in gas lines③, everybody freezing."

---

① blind drop: 指障碍物另一面陡然下落的形态。
② Houdini: 胡迪尼(Harry Houdini, 1874—1926)美国魔术师和脱逃表演大师,常将自己锁在看似无法逃脱的牢笼中,在限定时间内挣脱出来。
③ in gas lines: 指排队为汽车加油。

Richard asked her, "Do you still want to live in England forever?" Forever: the concept, now a reality upon him, pressed and scratched at the back of his throat.

"No," Judith confessed, turning her oval face to him, its eyes still childishly far apart, but the lips set as over something succulent and satisfactory. "I was anxious to come home. I'm an American." She was a woman. They had raised her; he and Joan had endured together to raise her, alone of the four. The others had still some raising left in them. Yet it was the thought of telling Judith—the image of her, their first baby, walking between them arm in arm, to the bridge—that broke him. The partition between himself and the tears broke. Richard sat down to the celebratory meal with the back of his throat aching; the champagne, the lobster seemed phases of sunshine; he saw them and tasted them through tears. He blinked, swallowed, croakily joked about hay fever. The tears would not stop leaking through; they came not through a hole that could be plugged but through a permeable spot in a membrane, steadily, purely, endlessly, fruitfully. They became, his tears, a shield for himself against these others—their faces, the fact of their assembly, a last time as innocents, at a table where he sat the last time as head. Tears dropped from his nose as he broke the lobster's back; salt flavored his champagne as he sipped it; the raw clench at the back of his throat was delicious. He could not help himself.

His children tried to ignore his tears. Judith on his right, lit a cigarette, gazed upward in the direction of her too energetic, too sophisticated exhalation; on her other side, John earnestly bent his face to the extraction of the last morsels—legs, tail segments—from the scarlet corpse. Joan, at the opposite end of the table, glanced at him surprised, her reproach displaced by a quick grimace, of forgiveness, or of salute to his superior gift of strategy. Between them, Margaret, no longer called Bean, thirteen and large for her age, gazed from the other side of his pane of tears as if into a shop-window at something she coveted—at her father, a crystalline heap of splinters and memories. It was not she, however, but John who, in the kitchen, as they cleared the plates and carapaces away, asked Joan the question: "Why is Daddy crying?"

Richard heard the question but not the murmured answer. Then he heard Bean cry, "Oh, no-oh"— the faintly dramatized exclamation of one who had bong expected it.

John returned to the table carrying a bowl of salad. He nodded tersely at his father and his lips shaped the conspiratorial words "She told."

"Told what?" Richard asked aloud, insanely.

The boy sat down as if to rebuke his father's distraction with the example of his own good manners and said quietly, "The separation."

Joan and Margaret returned; the child, in Richard's twisted vision, seemed diminished in size, and relieved, relieved to have had the boogeyman① at last proved real. He called out to her—the distances at the table had grown immense—"You knew, you always knew," but the clenching at the back of his throat prevented him from making sense of it. From afar he heard Joan talking, levelly, sensibly, reciting what they had prepared: it was a separation for the summer, and experiment. She and Daddy both agreed it would be good for them; they needed space and time to think; they liked each other but did not make each other happy enough, somehow.

Judith, imitating her mother's factual tone, but in her youth off-key, too cool, said, "I think it's silly. You should either live together or get divorced."

Richard's crying, like a wave that has crested and crashed, had become tumultuous, but it was overtopped by another tumult, for John, who had been so reserved, now grew larger and larger at the

---

① boogeyman: bogeyman.

table. Perhaps his younger sister's being credited with knowing set him off. "Why didn't you tell us?" he asked, in a large round voice quite unlike his own. "You should have told us you weren't getting along."

Richard was startled into attempting to force words through his tears. "We do get along, that's the trouble, so it doesn't show even to us—"That we do not love each other" was the rest of the sentence; he couldn't finish it.

Joan finished for him, in her style. "And we've always, especially, loved our children."

John was not mollified. "What do you care about *us*?" he boomed. "We're just little things you *had*." His sister's laughing forced a laugh from him, which he turned hard and parodistic: "Ha ha ha." Richard and Joan realized simultaneously that the child was drunk, on Judith's homecoming champagne. Feeling bound to keep the center of the stage, John took a cigarette from Judith's pack, poked it into his mouth, let it hang from his lower lip, and squinted like a gangster.

"You're not little things we had," Richard called to him. "You're the whole point. But you're grown. Or almost."

The boy was lighting matches. Instead of holding them to his cigarette (for they had never seen him smoke; being "good" had been his way of setting himself apart), he held them to his mother's face, closer and closer, for her to blow out. Then he lit the whole folder—a hiss and then a torch, held against his mother's face. Prismed by tears, the flame filled Richard's vision; he didn't know how it was extinguished. He heard Margaret say, "Oh stop showing off," and saw John, in response, break the cigarette in two and put the halves entirely into his mouth and chew, sticking out his tongue to display the shreds to his sister.

Joan talked to him, reasoning—a fountain of reason, unintelligible. "Talked about it for year... our children must help us... Daddy and I both want..." As the boy listened, he carefully wadded a paper napkin into the leaves of his salad, fashioned a ball of paper and lettuce, and popped it into his mouth, looking around the table for the expected laughter. None came. Judith said, "Be mature," and dismissed a plume of smoke.

Richard got up from this stifling table and led the boy outside. Though the house was in twilight, the outdoors still brimmed with light, the long waste light of high summer. Both laughing, he supervised John's spitting out the lettuce and paper and tobacco into the pachysandra①. He took him by the hand—a square gritty hand, but for its softness a man's.② Yet, it held on. They ran together up into the field, past the tennis court. The raw banking left by the bulldozers was dotted with daisies. Past the court and a flat stretch where they used to play family baseball stood a soft green rise glorious in the sun, each weed and species of grass distinct as illumination on parchment. "I'm sorry, so sorry," Richard cried. "You were the only one who ever tried to help me with all the goddam jobs around this place."

Sobbing, safe within his tears and the champagne, John explained, "It's not just the separation, it's the whole crummy year, I hate that school, you can't make any friends, the history teacher's a scud③."

They sat on the crest of the rise, shaking and warm from their tears but easier in their voices, and Richard tried to focus on the child's sad year—the weekdays long with homework, the weekends spent in his room with model airplanes, while his parents murmured down below, nursing their separation. How selfish, how blind, Richard thought; his eyes felt scoured. He told his son, "We'll think about getting you transferred. Life's too short to be miserable."

---

① pachysandra: 草本植物,常用于草坪。
② but for its softness a man's: 要不是还得柔软,就会被当做成人的手了。
③ scud: 令人反感的人。

They had said what they could, but did not want the moment to heal, and talked on, about the tennis court, whether it would ever again be as good as it had been that first summer. They walked to inspect it and pressed a few more tapes more firmly down. A little stiltedly, perhaps trying to make too much of the moment, to prolong it, Richard led the boy to the spot in the field where the view was best, of the metallic blue river, the emerald marsh far away. "Wee," he said. "It goes on being beautiful. It'll be here tomorrow."

"I know," John answered, impatiently. The moment had closed.

Back in the house, the others had opened some white wine, the champagne being drunk, and still sat at the table, the three females, gossiping. Where Joan sat had become the head. She turned, showing him a tearless face, and asked, "All right?"

"We're fine," he said, resenting it, though relieved, that the party went on without him.

In bed she explained, "I couldn't cry I guess because I cried so much all spring. It really wasn't fair. It's your idea, and you made it look as though I was kicking you out."

"I'm sorry," he said. "I couldn't stop. I wanted to but couldn't."

"You didn't want to. You loved it. You were having your way, making a general announcement."

"I love having it over," he admitted. "God, those kids were great. So brave and funny." John, returned to the house, had settled to a model airplane in his room, and kept shouting down to them, "I'm O.K. No sweat." "And the way," Richard went on, cozy in his relief, "they never questioned the reasons we gave. Not thought of a third person. Not even Judith."

"That was touching," Joan said.

He gave her a hug. "You were great too. Thank you." Guiltily, he realized he did not feel separated.

"You still have Dickie to do," she told him. These words set before him a black mountain in the darkness, its cold breath, its near weight affected his chest. Of the four children Dickie was most nearly his conscience. Joan did not need to add, "That's one piece of your dirty work I won't do for you."

"I know. I'll do it. You go to sleep."

Within minutes, her breathing slowed, became oblivious and deep. It was quarter to midnight. Dickie's train from the concert would come in at one-fourteen. Richard set the alarm for one. He had slept atrociously for weeks. But whenever he closed his lids some glimpse of the last hours scorched them—Judith exhaling toward the ceiling in a kind of aversion, Bean's mute staring, the sunstruck growth of the field where he and John had rested. The mountain before him moved closer, moved within him; he was huge, momentous. The ache at the back of his throat felt stale. His wife slept as if slain beside him. When, exasperated by his hot lids, his crowded heart, he rose from the bed and dressed, she awoke enough to turn over. He told her then, "If I could undo it all, I would."

"Where would you begin?" she asked. There was no place. Giving him courage, she was always giving him courage. He put on shoes without socks in the dark. The children were breathing in their rooms, the downstairs was hollow. In their confusion they had left lights burning. He turned off all but one, the kitchen overhead. The car started. He had hoped it wouldn't. He met only moonlight on the roan; it seemed a diaphanous companion, flickering in the leaves along the roadside, haunting his rearview mirror like a pursuer, melting under his headlights. The center of town, not quite deserted, was eerie at this hour. A young cop in uniform kept company with a gang of T-shirted kids on the steps of the bank. Across from the railroad station, several bars kept open. Customers, mostly young, passed in and out of the warm night, savoring summer's novelty. Voices shouted from cars as they passed, an immense conversation seemed in progress. Richard parked and in his weariness put his head on the passenger seat, out of the commotion and wheeling lights. It was as when, in the movies, an assassin grimly carries his mission through the jostle of a carnival—except the movies cannot show the precipitous, palpable slope you cling to within. You cannot climb back down; you can only fall. The synthetic fabric of the car seat, warmed by his cheek, confided to him an ancient, distant scent of vanilla.

A train whistle caused him to lift his head. It was on time; he had hoped it would be late. The slender drawgates descended. The bell of approach tingled happily. The great metal body, horizontally fluted, rocked to a stop, and sleepy teen-agers disembarked, his son among them. Dickie did not show surprise that his father was meeting him at this terrible hour. He sauntered to the car with two friends, both taller than he. He said "Hi" to his father and took the passenger's seat with an exhausted promptness that expressed gratitude. The friends got into the back, and Richard was grateful; a few more minutes' postponement would be won by driving them home.

He asked, "How was the concert?"

"Groovy," one boy said from the back seat.

"It bit," the other said.

"It was O.K.," Dickie said, moderate by nature, so reasonable that in his childhood the unreason of the world had given him headaches, stomach aches, nausea. When the second friend had been dropped off at his dark house, the boy blurted, "Dad, my eyes are killing me with hay fever! I'm out there cutting that mothering grass all day!"

"Do we still have those drops?"

"They didn't do any good last summer."

"They might this." Richard swung a U-turn on the empty street. The drive home took a few minutes. The mountain was here, in his throat. "Richard," he said, and felt the boy, slumped and rubbing his eyes, go tense at his tone, "I didn't come to meet you just to make your life easier. I came because your mother and I have some news for you, and you're a hard man to get ahold of these days. It's sad news."

"That's O.K." The reassurance came out soft, but quick, as if released from the tip of a spring.

Richard had feared that his tears would return and choke him, but the boy's manliness set an example, and his voice issued forth steady and dry. "It's sad news, but it needn't be tragic news, at least for you. It should have no practical effect on your life, though it's bound to have an emotional effect. You'll work at your job, and go back to school in September. Your mother and I are really proud of what you're making of your life; we don't want that to change at all."

"Yeah," the boy said lightly, on the intake of his breath, holding himself up. They turned the corner, the church they went to loomed like a gutted fort. The home of the woman Richard hoped to marry stood across the green. Her bedroom light burned.

"Your mother and I," he said, "have decided to separate. For the summer. Nothing legal, no divorce yet. We want to see how it feels. For some years now, we haven't been doing enough for each other, making each other as happy as we should be. Have you sensed that?"

"No," the boy said. It was an honest, unemotional answer: true or false in a quiz.

Glad for the factual basis, Richard pursued, even garrulously, the details. His apartment across town, his utter accessibility, the split vacation arrangements, the advantages to the children, the added mobility and variety of the summer. Dickie listened, absorbing. "Do the others know?"

Richard described how they had been told.

"How did they take it?"

"The girls pretty calmly. John flipped out; he shouted and ate a cigarette and made a salad out of his napkin and told us how much he hated school."

His brother chuckled. "He did?"

"Yeah. The school issue was more upsetting for him than Mom and me. He seemed to feel better for having exploded."

"He did?" The repetition was the first sign that he was stunned.

"Yes. Dickie, I want to tell you something. This last hour, waiting for your train to get in, has been about the worst of my life. I hate this. Hate it. My father would have died before doing it to me." He felt immensely lighter, saying this. He had dumped the mountain on the boy. They were home. Moving swiftly as a shadow, Dickie was out of the car, through the bright kitchen. Richard called after him, "Want a glass of milk or anything?"

"No thanks."

"Want us to call the course tomorrow and say you're too sick to work?"

"No, that's all right." The answer was faint, delivered at the door to his room; Richard listened for the lam of a tantrum. The door closed normally. The sound was sickening.

Joan had sunk into the first deep trough of sleep and was slow to awake. Richard had to repeat, "I told him."

"What did he say?"

"Nothing much. Could you go say good night to him? Please."

She left their room, without putting on a bathrobe. He sluggishly changed back into his pajamas and walked down the hall. Dickie was already in bed, Joan was sitting beside him, and the boy's bedside clock radio was murmuring music. When she stood, an inexplicable light—the moon?—outlined her body through the nightie. Richard sat on the warm place she had indented on the child's mattress. He asked him, "Do you want the radio on like that?"

"It always is."

"Doesn't it keep you awake? It would me."

"Are you sleepy?"

"Yeah."

"Good. Sure you want to get up and go to work? You've had a big night."

"I want to."

Away at school this winter he had learned for the first time that you can go short of sleep and live. As an infant he had slept with an immobile, sweating intensity that had alarmed his babysitter. As the children aged, he became the first to go to bed, earlier for a time than his younger brother and sister. Even now, he would go slack in the middle of a television show, his sprawled legs hairy and brown. "O. K. Good boy, Dickie, listen. I love you so much, I never knew how much until now. No matter how this works out, I'll always be with you. Really."

Richard bent to kiss an averted face but his son, sinewy, turned and with wet cheeks embraced him and gave him a kiss, on the lips, passionate as a woman's. In his father's ear he moaned one word, the crucial, intelligent word: "Why?"

Why. It was a whistle of wind in a crack, a knife thrust, a window thrown open on emptiness. The white face was gone, the darkness was featureless. Richard had forgotten why.

《分居》(1975)是梅普尔夫妇系列故事中的一篇。作者自己的婚姻历程与故事主人公的婚姻经历有相当的对应。故事中,梅普尔夫妇像其他中产阶级家庭一样生活,物质上富足,行事也显得井井有条:他们承担培育子女成长的职责,扮演各自的家庭社会角色,他们遵循主流中产阶级的自由、平等、个人主义价值,梅普尔夫妇准备分居时,宣布决定的计划都象征性地具有"秩序"的意味。然而,这只是一种"虚假"的秩序感。主人公心理活动表明,无论他如何决断,都无法逃脱错综复杂的情感矛盾和迷茫。即便他愿意时光倒退,也根本"无处着落"。故事中不止一处描写他内心感受的"滑落",甚至"坠落",似乎他完全无法脚踏实地。分居究竟是"为什么?"他做出抉择,或者并非抉择,而是孤独中的应对,但他能够为此找到理由或依据吗? 或者这竟然是"打开窗户后所面对的虚空"。的确,在现代美国,以宗教为基础的道德秩序早已失去往昔的权威,让位于理性,虽然个人权利和功利主义构建了社会、经济秩序,个人能够自由追求并获取物欲满足,但是对作品主人公所代表的、具有深厚宗教传统的美国个人来说,人生意义难于建立在虚空之中,而最终还需要落实在道德和信仰之上,对此,"理性"本身则无能为力。而观念开放时代的家庭解体和情欲旋涡更是凸显出缺失的个人信念支点。作者将事物细节与心理描述有机地交织在一起:理查德对加固房屋的执著和内心关于屏障和禁锢的联想,子女对父母分居的反应和父爱与责任交织的歉疚感,对家庭的留恋以及寻求新爱的情感纠葛,而这些交错的细节是当代个人生存现状的现实主义写照。故事叙述采用第三人称视角中的有限全知视角:即读者只能看到男主人公的内心活动。

 思考题

1. What is the Maple family's socioeconomic status?
2. What age group is Richard in?
3. What secret does Richard keep in his mind?
4. What are the four hurdles to Richard?
5. How does John react to the news?
6. Is John more upset about school than about his parents' separation? Why or why not?
7. How does Dickie take the news?
8. How does Richard feel about his new life?
9. Why does Richard want this major change in life at this age?

 Rabbit, Run (1960)
"A & P" (1961)
Couples (1968)
In the Beauty of the Lilies (1996)

 参考资料

Boswell, Marshall. *John Updike's Rabbit Tetralogy: Mastered Irony in Motion*. Columbia: University of Missouri Press, 2001.

Greiner, Donald J. *John Updike's Novels*. Athens: Ohio University Press, 1984.

Olster, Stacey Michele. *The Cambridge Companion to John Updike*. Cambridge: Cambridge University Press, 2006.

Trachtenberg, Stanley, ed. *New Essays on Rabbit, Run*. Beijing: Peking Univeristy Press, 2007.

Updike, John. *Conversations with John Updike,* Ed. James Plath. Jackson: University Press of Mississippi, 1994.

(张世耘)

第十五单元
Saul Bellow (1915—2005)
索尔·贝娄

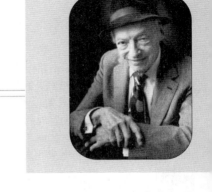

 作者简介

索尔·贝娄,犹太裔小说家,生于加拿大的魁北克,后移居芝加哥。贝娄先后就读于芝加哥大学和西北大学,1937年获社会学和人类学学士学位。同年在威斯康星大学做研究工作,第二次世界大战期间曾在商船运输部门服役。曾在普林斯顿大学、明尼苏达大学、芝加哥大学和波士顿大学任教,2005年4月去世。

早期作品包括《晃来晃去的人》(Dangling Man, 1944)、《受害者》(The Victim, 1947)、《只争朝夕》(Seize the Day, 1956)。有评论家认为,这些作品虽然出色,但在许多方面不如《奥吉·玛琪历险记》(The Adventures of Augie March, 1953, 获美国国家图书奖)、《雨王汉德逊》(Henderson The Rain King, 1959)、《赫尔索格》(Herzog, 1964, 获美国国家图书奖)、《赛姆勒先生的行星》(Mr. Sammler's Planet, 1964, 获美国国家图书奖)、《洪堡的礼物》(Humboldt's Gift, 1975, 获普利策奖)。1976年因其作品反映出"对人类的理解以及对当代文化的细致分析"而荣获诺贝尔文学奖。《院长的十二月》(The Dean's December, 1982)不同于之前作者的自嘲作品,是"真实而严肃的自画像"。评论家马尔科姆·布拉德伯里认为,该作品"代表贝娄对当代社会最有力的反抗"。《愁思伤情》(More Die of Heartbreak, 1987)深入细致地刻画出当代美国社会中欲望对个人的折磨。小说《拉维尔斯坦》(Ravelstein, 2000)以作者在芝加哥大学的好友艾伦·布卢姆(Alan Bloom)为原型。第一部非虚构作品《往返耶路撒冷:个人报道》(To Jerusalem and Back: A Personal Account)于1976问世,记录了他逗留以色列期间的个人生活和文学创作。贝娄还发表过《最后的分析》(The Last Analysis, 1965)以及三个短剧。出版的短篇故事集有《莫斯比的回忆及其他故事》(Mosby's Memoirs and Other Stories, 1968)和《出言不逊者及其他故事》(Him with His Foot in His Mouth and Other Stories, 1984)。贝娄的作品主要以他最为熟悉的芝加哥为背景,探索现代犹太人如何悲喜交加地在物欲横流的世界中寻找生活"更崇高的意义"。贝娄叙事技巧精湛,语言丰富多彩,善于捕捉生活场景,并赋以深刻寓意。他曾说:"最普通的犹太人对话中都会充满历史、神话、宗教典故。"

A Silver Dish

WHAT DO YOU DO ABOUT DEATH—IN THIS CASE, the death of an old father? If you're a modern person, sixty years of age, and a man who's been around, like Woody Selbst, what do you do? Take this matter of mourning, and take it against a contemporary background. How, against a contemporary background, do you mourn an octogenarian[①] father, nearly blind, his heart enlarged, his lungs filling with fluid, who creeps, stumbles, gives off the odors, the moldiness or gassiness, of old men. I mean! As Woody put it, be realistic. Think what times these are. The papers daily give it to you—the Lufthansa pilot in Aden is described by the hostages on his knees, begging the Palestinian terrorists not to execute him, but they shoot him through the head. Later they themselves are killed. And still others shoot others, or shoot themselves. That's what you read in the press, see on the tube, mention at dinner. We know now what goes daily through the whole of the human community, like a

---

① octogenarian: 80岁到90岁(的人)的。

global death-peristalsis①.

  Woody, a businessman in South Chicago, was not an ignorant person. He knew more such phrases than you would expect a tile contractor (offices, lobbies, lavatories) to know. The kind of knowledge he had was not the kind for which you get academic degrees. Although Woody had studied for two years in a seminary, preparing to be a minister. Two years of college during the Depression was more than most high-school graduates could afford. After that, in his own vital, picturesque, original way (Morris, his old man, was also, in his days of nature, vital and picturesque), Woody had read up on many subjects, subscribed to *Science* and other magazines that gave real information, and had taken night courses at De Paul and Northwestern in ecology, criminology, existentialism. Also he had traveled extensively in Japan, Mexico, and Africa, and there was an African experience that was especially relevant to mourning. It was this: on a launch near the Murchison Falls in Uganda, he had seen a buffalo calf seized by a crocodile from the bank of the White Nile. There were giraffes along the tropical river, and hippopotamuses, and baboons, and flamingos and other brilliant birds crossing the bright air in the heat of the morning, when the calf, stepping into the river to drink, was grabbed by the hoof and dragged down. The parent buffaloes couldn't figure it out. Under the water the calf still threshed, fought, churned the mud. Woody, the robust traveler, took this in as he sailed by, and to him it looked as if the parent cattle were asking each other dumbly what had happened. He chose to assume that there was pain in this, he read brute grief into it②. On the White Nile, Woody had the impression that he had gone back to the pre-Adamite③ past, and he brought reflections on this impression home to South Chicago. He brought also a bundle of hashish④ from Kampala. In this he took a chance with the customs inspectors, banking perhaps on his broad build, frank face, high color. He didn't look like a wrongdoer, a bad guy; he looked like a good guy. But he liked taking chances. Risk was a wonderful stimulus. He threw down his trenchcoat on the customs counter. If the inspectors searched the pockets, he was prepared to say that the coat wasn't his. But he got away with it, and the Thanksgiving turkey was stuffed with hashish. This was much enjoyed. That was practically the last feast at which Pop, who also relished risk or defiance, was present, The hashish Woody had tried to raise in his backyard from the Africa seeds didn't take. But behind his warehouse, where the Lincoln Continental was parked, he kept a patch of marijuana. There was no harm at all in Woody, but he didn't like being entirely within the law. It was simply a question of self-respect.

  After that Thanksgiving, Pop gradually sank as if he had a slow leak. This went on for some years. In and out of the hospital, he dwindled, his mind wandered, he couldn't even concentrate enough to complain, except in exceptional moments on the Sundays Woody regularly devoted to him. Morris, an amateur who once was taken seriously by Willie Hoppe, the great pro⑤ himself, couldn't execute the simplest billiard shots anymore. He could only conceive shots; he began to theorize about impossible three-cushion⑥ combinations. Halina, the Polish woman with whom Morris had lived for over forty years as man and wife, was too old herself now to run to the hospital. So Woody had to do it. There was Woody's mother, too—a Christian convert—needing care; she was over eighty and frequently hospitalized. Everybody had diabetes and pleurisy and arthritis and cataracts and cardiac pacemakers⑦. And everybody had lived by the body, but the body was giving out.

---

① peristalsis: (生理)蠕动。
② he read brute grief into it: 他看出野兽也有悲伤。
③ pre-Adamite: 人类出现前的。
④ hashish: 大麻。
⑤ pro: 专业人员。
⑥ three-cushion: (台)三边的(指每一击使球三次撞边的)。
⑦ pleurisy: 肋膜炎。arthritis: 关节炎。cataract: 白内障。cardiac pacemaker: 心脏电子起搏器。

There were Woody's two sisters as well, unmarried, in their fifties, very Christian, very straight, still living with Mama in an entirely Christian bungalow. Woody, who took full responsibility for them all, occasionally had to put one of the girls (they had become sick girls) in a mental institution. Nothing severe. The sisters were wonderful women, both of them gorgeous once, but neither of the poor things was playing with a full deck①. And all the factions had to be kept separate—Mama, the Christian convert; the fundamentalist② sisters; Pop, who read the Yiddish paper as long as he could still see print; Halina, a good Catholic. Woody, the seminary forty years behind him, described himself as an agnostic③. Pop had no more religion than you could find in the Yiddish paper, but he made Woody promise to bury him among Jews, and that was where he lay now, in the Hawaiian shirt Woody had bought for him at the tilers' convention in Honolulu. Woody would allow no undertaker's assistant to dress him, but came to the parlor and buttoned the stiff into the shirt himself, and the old man went down looking like Ben-Gurion④ in a simple wooden coffin, sure to rot fast. That was how Woody wanted it all. At the graveside, he had taken off and folded his jacket, rolled up his sleeves on thick freckled biceps, waved back the little tractor standing by, and shoveled the dirt himself. His big face, broad at the bottom, narrowed upward like a Dutch house. And, his small good lower teeth taking hold of the upper lip in his exertion, he performed the final duty of a son. He was very fit, so it must have been emotion, not the shoveling, that made him redden so. After the funeral, he went home with Halina and her son, a decent Polack like his mother, and talented, too—Mitosh played the organ at hockey and basketball games in the Stadium, which took a smart man because it was a rabble-rousing kind of occupation—and they had some drinks and comforted the old girl. Halina was true blue, always one hundred percent for Morris.

Then for the rest of the week Woody was busy, had jobs to run, office responsibilities, family responsibilities. He lived alone; as did his wife; as did his mistress: everybody in a separate establishment. Since his wife, after fifteen years of separation, had not learned to take care of herself, Woody did her shopping on Fridays, filled her freezer. He had to take her this week to buy shoes. Also, Friday night he always spent with Helen—Helen was his wife de facto⑤. Saturday he did his big weekly shopping. Saturday night he devoted to Mom and his sisters. So he was too busy to attend to his own feelings except, intermittently, to note to himself, "First Thursday in the grave." "First Friday, and fine weather." "First Saturday; he's got to be getting used to it." Under his breath he occasionally said, "Oh, Pop."

But it was Sunday that hit him, when the bells rang all over South Chicago—the Ukrainian, Roman Catholic, Greek, Russian, African Methodist churches⑥, sounding off one after another. Woody had his offices in his warehouse, and there had built an apartment for himself, very spacious and convenient, in the top story. Because he left every Sunday morning at seven to spend the day with Pop, he had forgotten by how many churches Selbst Tile Company was surrounded. He was still in bed when he heard the bells, and all at once he knew how heartbroken he was. This sudden big heartache in a man of sixty, a practical, physical, healthy-minded, and experienced man, was deeply unpleasant. When he had an unpleasant condition, he believed in taking something for it. So he thought: What shall I take? There were plenty of remedies available. His cellar was stocked with cases of Scotch whisky, Polish

---

① neither of the poor things was playing with a full deck：她俩脑子没一个够用的。
② fundamentalist：原教旨主义的。
③ agnostic：不可知论者。
④ Ben-Gurion：本·古里安（1886—1973），犹太复国主义运动领导人，1930年组成以色列工人党，自任领袖，是以色列国主要创建者和首任总理兼国防部长。
⑤ de facto：(拉)实际上的，事实上的。
⑥ African Methodist churches：非洲循道宗教堂。

vodka, Armagnac, Moselle, Burgundy①. There were also freezers with steaks and with game and with Alaskan king crab. He bought with a broad hand—by the crate and by the dozen. But in the end, when he got out of bed, he took nothing but a cup of coffee. While the kettle was heating, he put on his Japanese judo-style suit and sat down to reflect.

Woody was moved when things were honest. Bearing beams② were honest, undisguised concrete pillars inside highrise apartments were honest. It was bad to cover up anything. He hated faking. Stone was honest. Metal was honest. These Sunday bells were very straight. They broke loose, they wagged and rocked, and the vibrations and the banging did something for him—cleansed his insides, purified his blood. A bell was a one-way throat, had only one thing to tell you and simply told it. He listened.

He had had some connections with bells and churches. He was after all something of a Christian. Born a Jew, he was a Jew facially, with a hint of Iroquois or Cherokee③, but his mother had been converted more than fifty years ago by her brother-in-law, the Reverend Doctor Kovner. Kovner, a rabbinical④ student who had left the Hebrew Union College in Cincinnati to become a minister and establish a mission, had given Woody a partly Christian upbringing. Now, Pop was on the outs with these fundamentalists. He said that the Jews came to the mission to get coffee, bacon, canned pineapple, day-old bread, and dairy products. And if they had to listen to sermons, that was okay—this was the Depression and you couldn't be too particular—but he knew they sold the bacon.

The Gospels said it plainly: "Salvation is from the Jews."⑤

Backing the Reverend Doctor were wealthy fundamentalists, mainly Swedes, eager to speed up the Second Coming⑥ by converting all Jews. The foremost of Kovner's backers was Mrs. Skoglund, who had inherited a large dairy business from her late husband. Woody was under her special protection.

Woody was fourteen years of age when Pop took off with Halina, who worked in his shop, leaving his difficult Christian wife and his converted son and his small daughters. He came to Woody in the backyard one spring day and said, "From now on you're the man of the house." Woody was practicing with a golf club, knocking off the heads of dandelions. Pop came into the yard in his good suit, which was too hot for the weather, and when he took off his fedora⑦ the skin of his head was marked with a deep ring and the sweat was sprinkled over his scalp—more drops than hairs. He said, "I'm going to move out." Pop was anxious, but he was set to go—determined. "It's no use. I can't live a life like this." Envisioning the life Pop simply had to live, his free life, Woody was able to picture him in the billiard parlor, under the El tracks in a crap game, or playing poker at Brown and Koppel's upstairs. "You're going to be the man of the house," said Pop. "It's okay. I put you all on welfare.⑧ I just got back from Wabansia Avenue, from the relief station." Hence the suit and the hat. "They're sending out a caseworker." Then he said, "You got to lend me money to buy gasoline—the caddie money⑨ you saved."

Understanding that, couldn't get away without his help, Woody turned over to him all he had earned at the Sunset Ridge Country Club in Winnetka. Pop felt that the valuable life lesson he was

---

① Armagnac: 阿马尼亚克酒。Moselle: (德国)摩泽尔白葡萄酒。Burgundy: 勃艮第葡萄酒。
② bearing beams: 过梁。
③ Iroquois: 易洛魁人(北美印第安人)。Cherokee: 彻罗基人(北美印第安人)。
④ rabbinical: 拉比的; (尤指中世纪的)拉比著作(或学识、教海、语言等)的。
⑤ Salvation is from the Jews.: 拯救来自犹太人。
⑥ Second Coming: (宗)(世界末日前的)基督复临。
⑦ fedora: 浅顶软呢男帽。
⑧ I put you all on welfare.: 我给你们都办了接受政府福利救济。
⑨ caddie money: 当高尔夫球场服务员赚得的钱。

transmitting was worth far more than these dollars, and whenever he was conning his boy a sort of high-priest expression came down over his bent nose, his ruddy face. The children, who got their finest ideas at the movies, called him Richard Dix. Later, when the comic strip came out, they said he was Dick Tracy①.

As Woody now saw it, under the tumbling bells, he had bankrolled② his own desertion. Ha ha! He found this delightful; and especially Pop's attitude of "That'll teach you to trust your father." For this was a demonstration on behalf of real life and free instincts, against religion and hypocrisy. But mainly it was aimed against being a fool, the disgrace of foolishness. Pop had it in for the Reverend Doctor Kovner,③ not because he was an apostate④ (Pop couldn't have cared less); not because the mission was a racket (he admitted that the Reverend Doctor was personally honest), but because Doctor Kovner behaved foolishly, spoke like a fool, and acted like a fiddler. He tossed his hair like a Paganini (this was Woody's addition; Pop had never even heard of Paganini). Proof that he was not a spiritual leader was that he converted Jewish women by stealing their hearts. "He works up all those broads," said Pop. "He doesn't even know it himself, I swear he doesn't know how he gets them."

From the other side, Kovner often warned Woody, "Your father is a dangerous person. Of course, you love him; you should love him and forgive him, Voodrow, but you are old enough to understand he is leading a life of wice."

It was all petty stuff: Pop's sinning was on a boy level and therefore made a big impression on a boy. And on Mother. Are wives children, or what? Mother often said, "I hope you put that brute in your prayers. Look what he has done to us. But only pray for him, don't see him." But he saw him all the time. Woodrow was leading a double life, sacred and profane. He accepted Jesus Christ as his personal redeemer. Aunt Rebecca took advantage of this. She made him work. He had to work under Aunt Rebecca. He filled in for⑤ the janitor at the mission and settlement house⑥. In winter, he had to feed the coal furnace, and on some nights he slept near the furnace room, on the pool table. He also picked the lock of the storeroom. He took canned pineapple and cut bacon from the flitch⑦ with his pocketknife. He crammed himself with uncooked bacon. He had a big frame to fill out.⑧

Only now, sipping Melitta coffee, he asked himself: Had he been so hungry? No, he loved being reckless. He was fighting Aunt Rebecca Kovner when he took out his knife and got on a box to reach the bacon. She didn't know, she couldn't prove that Woody, such a frank, strong, positive boy, who looked you in the eye, so direct, was a thief also. But he was also a thief. Whenever she looked at him, he knew that she was seeing his father. In the curve of his nose, the movements of his eyes, the thickness of his body, in his healthy face, she saw that wicked savage Morris.

Morris, you see, had been a street boy in Liverpool—Woody's mother and her sister were British by birth. Morris's Polish family, on their way to America, abandoned him in Liverpool because he had an eye infection and they would all have been sent back from Ellis Island. They stopped awhile in England, but his eyes kept running and they ditched him. They slipped away, and he had to make out alone in Liverpool at the age of twelve. Mother came of better people. Pop, who slept in the cellar of her house; fell in love with her. At sixteen, scabbing⑨ during a seamen's strike, he shoveled his way

---

① Dick Tracy：1931年起在美国报刊上登载的连环画中的大侦探，后又在电台、电视、电影中出现。
② bankroll：为……提供资金。
③ Pop had it in for the Reverend Doctor Kovner.：(口)爸爸对Reverend Doctor Kovner有恶感；总是与Reverend Doctor Kovner过不去。
④ apostate：叛教者。
⑤ fill in for：临时补缺、替代。
⑥ settlement house：街坊文教馆(指为城市贫民区民提供教育、娱乐等社会服务的场所)。
⑦ flitch：烟熏猪肋条肉。
⑧ He had a big frame to fill out.：他的大骨架需要食物填充起来。
⑨ scab：(美口)顶替罢工工人去上工。

across the Atlantic and jumped ship in Brooklyn. He became an American, and America never knew it. He voted without papers, he drove without a license, he paid no taxes, he cut every corner①. Horses, cards, billiards, and women were his lifelong interests, in ascending order. Did he love anyone (he was so busy)? Yes, he loved Halina. He loved his son. To this day, Mother believed that he had loved her most and always wanted to come back. This gave her a chance to act the queen, with her plump wrists and faded Queen Victoria face. "The girls are instructed never to admit him," she said. The Empress of India speaking.

Bell-battered Woodrow's soul was whirling this Sunday morning, indoors and out, to the past, back to his upper corner of the warehouse, laid out with such originality—the bells coming and going, metal on naked metal, until the bell circle expanded over the whole of steel-making, oil-refining, power-producing mid-autumn South Chicago, and all its Croatians, Ukrainians, Greeks, Poles, and respectable blacks heading for their churches to hear Mass or to sing hymns.

Woody himself had been a good hymn singer. He still knew the hymns. He had testified, too. He was often sent by Aunt Rebecca to get up and tell a churchful of Scandihoovians that he, a Jewish lad, accepted Jesus Christ. For this she paid him fifty cents. She made the disbursement. She was the book-keeper, fiscal chief, general manager of the mission. The Reverend Doctor didn't know a thing about the operation. What the Doctor supplied was the fervor. He was genuine, a wonderful preacher. And what about Woody himself? He also had fervor. He was drawn to the Reverend Doctor. The Reverend Doctor taught him to lift up his eyes, gave him his higher life. Apart from this higher life, the rest was Chicago—the ways of Chicago, which came so natural that nobody thought to question them. So, for instance, in 1933(what ancient, ancient times!), at the Century of Progress World's Fair, when Woody was a coolie and pulled a rickshaw, wearing a peaked straw hat and trotting with powerful, thick legs, while the brawny red farmers—his boozing② passengers —were laughing their heads off and pestered him for whores, he, although a freshman at the seminary, saw nothing wrong, when girls asked him to steer a little business their way, in making dates and accepting tips from both sides. He necked in③ Grant Park with a powerful girl who had to go home quickly to nurse her baby. Smelling of milk, she rode beside him on the streetcar to the West Side, squeezing his rickshaw puller's thigh and wetting her blouse. This was the Roosevelt Road car. Then, in the apartment where she lived with her mother, he couldn't remember that there were any husbands around. What he did remember was the strong milk odor. Without inconsistency, next morning he did New Testament Greek: The light shineth in darkness—to fos en te skotia fainei—and the darkness comprehended it not.

And all the while he trotted between the shafts on the fairgrounds he had one idea, nothing to do with these horny giants having a big time in the city: that the goal, the project, the purpose was (and he couldn't explain why he thought so; all evidence was against it)—God's idea was that this world should be a love world, that it should eventually recover and be entirely a world of love. He wouldn't have said this to a soul, for he could see himself how stupid it was—personal and stupid. Nevertheless, there it was at the center of his feelings. And at the same time, Aunt Rebecca was right when she said to him, strictly private, close to his ear even, "You're a little crook, like your father."

The Reverend Doctor preached, Rebecca preached, rich Mrs. Skoglund preached from Evanston, Mother preached. Pop also was on a soapbox. Everyone was doing it. Up and down Division Street, under every lamp, almost, speakers were giving out: anarchists, Socialists, Stalinists, single-taxers,

---

① cut every corner: (不按常规而)用简便方法办事。
② boozing: 狂饮的。
③ neck in: (美口)亲吻, 拥抱。

Zionists, Tolstoyans①, vegetarians, and fundamentalist Christian preachers—you name it. A beef, a hope, a way of life or salvation, a protest. How was it that the accumulated gripes of all the ages took off so when transplanted to America?②

And that fine Swedish immigrant Aase (Osie, they pronounced it), who had been the Skoglunds' cook and married the eldest son, to become his rich, religious widow—she supported the Reverend Doctor. In her time she must have been built like a chorus girl. And women seem to have lost the secret of putting up their hair in the high basketry fence of braid she wore. Aase took Woody under her special protection and paid his tuition at the seminary. And Pop said... But on this Sunday, at peace as soon as the bells stopped banging, this velvet autumn day when the grass was finest and thickest, silky green: before the first frost, and the blood in your lungs is redder than summer air can make it and smarts with oxygen, as if the iron in your system was hungry for it, and the chill was sticking it to you in every breath... Pop, six feet under, would never feel this blissful sting gain. The last of the bells still had the bright air streaming with vibrations.

On weekends, the institutional vacancy of decades came back to the warehouse and crept under the door of Woody's apartment. It felt as empty on Sundays as churches were during the week. Before each business day, before the trucks and the crews got started, Woody jogged five miles in his Adidas suit. Not on this day still reserved for Pop, however. Although it was tempting to go out and run off the grief. Being alone hit Woody hard this morning. He thought: Me and the world; the world and me. Meaning that there always was some activity to interpose, an errand or a visit, a picture to paint (he was a creative amateur), a massage, a meal—a shield between himself and that troublesome solitude which used the world as its reservoir. But Pop! Last Tuesday, Woody had gotten into the hospital bed with Pop because he kept pulling out the intravenous needles③. Nurses stuck them back, and then Woody astonished them all by climbing into bed to hold the struggling old guy in his arms. "Easy, Morris, Morris, go easy." But Pop still groped feebly for the pipes.

When the tolling stopped, Woody didn't notice that a great lake of quiet had come over his kingdom, the Selbst Tile warehouse. What he heard and saw was an old red Chicago streetcar, one of those trams the color of a stockyard steer. Cars of this type went out before Pearl Harbor—clumsy, big-bellied, with tough rattan seats and brass grips for the standing passengers. Those cars used to make four stops to the mile, and ran with a wallowing motion. They stank of carbolic or ozone and throbbed when the air compressors were being charged. The conductor had his knotted signal cord to pull, and the motorman beat the foot gong with his mad heel.

Woody recognized himself on the Western Avenue line and riding through a blizzard with his father, both in sheepskins and with hands and faces raw, the snow blowing in from the rear platform when the doors opened and getting into the longitudinal cleats of the floor. There wasn't warmth enough inside to melt it. And Western Avenue was the longest car line in the world, the boosters said, as if it was a thing to brag about. Twenty-three miles long, made by a draftsman with a T square, lined with factories, storage buildings, machine shops, used-car lots, trolley barns, gas stations, funeral parlors, six-flats, utility buildings, and junkyards, on and on from the prairies on the south to Evanston on the north. Woodrow and his father were going north to Evanston, to Howard Street, and then some, to see Mrs. Skoglund. At the end of the line they would still have about five blocks to hike. The purpose of the trip? To raise money for Pop. Pop had talked him into this. When they found out, Mother

---

① single-taxers: 主张单一税制者。Zionists: 犹太复国主义者。Tolstoyans: 信奉托尔斯泰哲学者。
② How was it that the accumulated gripes of all the ages took off so when transplanted to America?: 各个时代积累的痛苦怎么一到美国就全部开始发作了呢？
③ intravenous needles: 静脉注射针。

and Aunt Rebecca would be furious, and Woody was afraid, but he couldn't help it.

Morris had come and said, "Son, I'm in trouble. It's bad."

"What's bad, Pop?"

"Halina took money from her husband for me and has to put it back before old Bujak misses it. He could kill her."

"What did she do it for?"

"Son, you know how the bookies[①] collect? They send a goon[②]. They'll break my head open."

"Pop! You know I can't take you to Mrs. Skoglund."

"Why not? You're my kid, aren't you? " The old broad wants to adopt you, doesn't she? Shouldn't I get something out of it for my trouble? What am I—outside? And what about Halina? She puts her life on the line, but my own kid says no.

"Oh, Bujak wouldn't hurt her."

"Woody, he'd beat her to death."

Bujak? Uniform in color with his dark-gray work clothes, short in the legs, his whole strength in his tool-and-die-maker's[③] forearms and black fingers; and beat-looking—there was Bujak for you. But, according to Pop, there was big, big violence in Bujak, a regular boiling Bessemer[④] inside his narrow chest. Woody could never see the violence in him. Bujak wanted no trouble. If anything, maybe he was afraid that Morris and Halina would gang up on him and kill him, screaming. But Pop was no desperado murderer. And Halina was a calm, serious woman. Bujak kept his savings in the cellar (banks were going out of business). The worst they did was to take some of his money, intending to put it back. As Woody saw him, Bujak was trying to be sensible. He accepted his sorrow. He set minimum requirements for Halina: cook the meals, clean the house, show respect. But at stealing Bujak might have drawn the line, for money was different, money was vital substance. If they stole his savings he might have had to take action, out of respect for the substance, for himself—self-respect. But you couldn't be sure that Pop hadn't invented the bookie, the goon, the theft—the whole thing. He was capable of it, and you'd be a fool not to suspect him. Morris knew that Mother and Aunt Rebecca had told Mrs. Skoglund how wicked he was. They had painted him for her in poster colors-purple for vice, black for his soul, red for Hell flames: a gambler, smoker, drinker, deserter, and atheist. So Pop was determined to reach her. It was risky for everybody. The Reverend Doctor's operating costs were met by Skoglund Dairies. The widow paid Woody's seminary tuition; she bought dresses for the little sisters.

Woody, now sixty, fleshy and big, like a figure for the victory of American materialism, sunk in his lounge chair, the leather of its armrests softer to his fingertips than a woman's skin, was puzzled and, in his depths, disturbed by certain blots within him, blots of light in his brain, a blot combining pain and amusement in his breast (how did that get there?). Intense thought puckered the skin between his eyes with a strain bordering on headache. Why had he let Pop have his way? Why did he agree to meet him that day, in the dim rear of the poolroom?

"But what will you tell Mrs. Skoglund?"

"The old broad? Don't worry, there's plenty to tell her, and it's all true. Ain't I trying to save my little laundry-and-cleaning shop? Isn't the bailiff coming for the fixtures next week?" And Pop rehearsed his pitch[⑤] on the Western Avenue car. He counted on Woody's health and his freshness. Such

---

① bookie：(口)赛马等赌注登记经纪人。
② goon：(俚)打手，受雇的流氓。
③ tool-and-die-maker：工具和模具制作者。
④ Bessemer：以发明家贝塞麦命名的转炉。
⑤ pitch：(美口)商品推销员的行话。

a straightforward-looking body was perfect for a con.

Did they still have such winter storms in Chicago as they used to have? Now they somehow seemed less fierce. Blizzards used to come straight down from Ontario, from the Arctic, and drop five feet of snow in an afternoon. Then the rusty green platform cars, with revolving brushes at both ends, came out of the barns to sweep the tracks. Ten or twelve streetcars followed in slow processions, or waited, block after block.

There was a long delay at the gates of Riverview Park, all the amusements covered for the winter, boarded up—the dragon's-back high-rides, the Bobs, the Chute, the Tilt-a-Whirl [1], all the fun machinery put together by mechanics and electricians, men like Bujak the tool-and-die-maker, good with engines. The blizzard was having it all its own way behind the gates, and you couldn't see far inside; only a few bulbs burned behind the palings. When Woody wiped the vapor from the glass, the wire mesh of the window guards was stuffed solid at eye level with snow. Looking higher, you saw mostly the streaked wind horizontally driving from the north. In the seat ahead, two black coal heavers, both in leather Lindbergh flying helmets, sat with shovels between their legs, returning from a job. They smelled of sweat, burlap sucking, and coal. Mostly dull with black dust, they also sparkled here and there.

There weren't many riders. People weren't leaving the house. This was a day to sit legs stuck out beside the stove, mummified by both the outdoor and the indoor forces. Only a fellow with an angle, like Pop, would go and buck such weather. A storm like this was out of the compass, and you kept the human scale by having a scheme to raise fifty bucks. Fifty soldiers! [2] Real money in 1933.

"That woman is crazy for you," said Pop.

"She's just a good woman, sweet to all of us."

"Who knows what she's got in mind. You're a husky kid. Not such a kid, either."

"She's a religious woman. She really has religion."

"Well, your mother isn't your only parent. She and Rebecca and Kovner aren't going to fill you up with their ideas. I know your mother wants to wipe me out of your life. Unless I take a hand, you won't even understand what life is. Because they don't know those silly Christers."

"Yes, Pop."

"The girls I can't help. They're too young. I'm sorry about them, but I can't do anything. With you it's different."

He wanted me like himself, an American.

They were stalled in the storm, while the cattle-colored car waited to have the trolley reset in the crazy wind, which boomed, tingled, blasted. At Howard Street they would have to walk straight into it, due north.

"You'll do the talking at first," said Pop.

Woody had the makings of a salesman, a pitchman. He was aware of this when he got to his feet in church to testify before fifty or sixty people. Even though Rebecca made it worth his while, he moved his own heart when he spoke up about his faith. But occasionally, without notice, his heart went away as he spoke religion and he couldn't find it anywhere. In its absence, sincere behavior got him through. He had to rely for delivery on his face, his voice—on behavior. Then his eyes came closer and closer together.

And in this approach of eye to eye he felt the strain of hypocrisy. The twisting of his face

---

[1] the Bobs, the Chute, the Tilt-a-Whirl：都指儿童娱乐项目。
[2] buck：顶着……前进。You kept the human scale by having a scheme to raise fifty bucks.：你想方设法筹五十块钱好维持人的生活标准。Fifty soldiers：五十块钱。

threatened to betray him. It took everything he had to keep looking honest. So, since he couldn't bear the cynicism of it, he fell back on mischievousness. Mischief was where Pop came in. Pop passed straight through all those divided fields, gap after gap, and arrived at his side, bent-nosed and broad-faced. In regard to Pop, you thought of neither sincerity nor insincerity. Pop was like the man in the song: he wanted what he wanted when he wanted it. Pop was physical; Pop was digestive, circulatory, sexual. If Pop got serious, he talked to you about washing under the arms or in the crotch or of drying between your toes or of cooking supper, of baked beans and fried onions, of draw poker① or of a certain horse in the fifth race at Arlington. Pop was elemental. That was why he gave such relief from religion and paradoxes, and things like that. Now, Mother *thought* she was spiritual, but Woody knew that she was kidding herself. Oh, yes, in the British accent she never gave up she was always talking to God or about Him—please God, God willing, praise God. But she was a big substantial bread-and-butter down-to-earth woman, with down-to-earth duties like feeding the girls, protecting, refining, keeping pure the girls. And those two protected doves grew up so overweight, heavy in the hips and thighs, that their poor heads looked long and slim. And mad. Sweet but cuckoo—Paula cheerfully cuckoo, Joanna depressed and having episodes.

"I'll do my best by you, but you have to promise, Pop, not to get me in Dutch with② Mrs. Skoglund."

"You worried because I speak bad English? Embarrassed? I have a mockie accent③?"

"It's not that. Kovner has a heavy accent, and she doesn't mind."

"Who the hell are those freaks to look down on me? You're practically a man and your dad has a right to expect help from you. He's in a fix. And you bring him to her house because she's bighearted, and you haven't got anybody else to go to."

"I got you, Pop."

The two coal trimmers stood up at Devon Avenue, One of them wore a woman's coat. Men wore women's clothing in those years, and women men's, when there was no choice. The fur collar was spiky with the wet, and sprinkled with soot. Heavy, they dragged their shovels and got off at the front. The slow car ground on, very slow. It was after four when they reached the end of the line, and somewhere between gray and black, with snow spouting and whirling under the street lamps. In Howard Street, autos were stalled at all angles and abandoned. The sidewalks were blocked. Woody led the way into Evanston, and Pop followed him up the middle of the street in the furrows made earlier by trucks. For four blocks they bucked the wind and then Woody broke through the drifts to the snowbound mansion, where they both had to push the wrought-iron gate because of the drift behind it. Twenty rooms or more in this dignified house and nobody in them but Mrs. Skoglund and her servant Hjordis, also religious.

As Woody and Pop waited, brushing the slush from their sheepskin collars and Pop wiping his big eyebrows with the ends of his scarf, sweating and freezing, the chains began to rattle and Hjordis uncovered the air holes of the glass storm door by turning a wooden bar. Woody called her "monk-faced." You no longer see women like that, who put no female touch on the face. She came plain, as God made her. She said, "Who is it and what do you want?"

"It's Woodrow Selbst. Hjordis? It's Woody."

"You're not expected."

"No, but we're here."

---

① draw poker: 抽彩(得奖)。
② get... in Dutch with: (俚)处于困境(或苦恼中); 失宠的; 受嫌疑的。
③ mockie accent: (美俚)犹太口音。

"What do you want?"

"We came to see Mrs. Skoglund."

"What for do you want to see her?"

"Just tell her we're here."

"I have to tell her what you came for, without calling up first."

"Why don't you say it's Woody with his father, and we wouldn't come in a snowstorm like this if it wasn't important."

The understandable caution of women who live alone. Respectable old-time women, too. There was no such respectability now in those Evanston houses, with their big verandas and deep yards and with a servant like Hjordis, who carried at her belt keys to the pantry and to every closet and every dresser drawer and every padlocked bin in the cellar. And in High Episcopal Christian Science Women's Temperance Evanston①, no tradespeople rang at the front door. Only invited guests. And here, after a ten-mile grind through the blizzard, came two tramps from the West Side. To this mansion where a Swedish immigrant lady, herself once a cook and now a philanthropic widow, dreamed, snowbound, while frozen lilac twigs clapped at her storm windows, of a new Jerusalem and a Second coming and a Resurrection and a Last Judgment. To hasten the Second Coming, and all the rest, you had to reach the hearts of these scheming bums arriving in a snowstorm.

Sure, they let us in.

Then in the heat that swam suddenly up to their muffled chins Pop and Woody felt the blizzard for what it was; their cheeks were frozen slabs. They stood beat, itching, trickling in the front hall that was a hall, with a carved newel post staircase and a big stained-glass window at the top. Picturing Jesus with the Samaritan woman. There was a kind of Gentile② closeness to the air. Perhaps when he was with Pop, Woody made more Jewish observations than he would otherwise. Although Pop's most Jewish characteristic was that Yiddish was the only language he could read a paper in. Pop was with Polish Halina, and Mother was with Jesus Christ, and Woody ate uncooked bacon from the flitch. Still, now and then he had a Jewish impression.

Mrs. Skoglund was the cleanest of women—her fingernails, her white neck, her ears—and Pop's sexual hints to Woody all went wrong because she was so intensely clean, and made Woody think of a waterfall, large as she was, and grandly built. Her bust was big. Woody's imagination had investigated this. He thought she kept things tied down tight, very tight. But she lifted both arms once to raise a window and there it was, her bust, beside him, the whole unbindable thing. Her hair was like the raffia③ you had to soak before you could weave with it in a basket class—pale, pale. Pop, as he took his sheepskin off, was in sweaters, no jacket. His darting looks made him seem crooked. Hardest of all for these Selbsts with their bent noses and big, apparently straightforward faces was to look honest. All the signs of dishonesty played over them. Woody had often puzzled about it. Did it go back to the muscles, was it fundamentally a jaw problem—the projecting angles of the jaws? Or was it the angling that went on in the heart? The girls called Pop Dick Tracy, but Dick Tracy was a good guy. Whom could Pop convince? Here Woody caught a possibility as it flitted by. Precisely because of the way Pop looked, a sensitive person might feel remorse for condemning unfairly or judging unkindly. Just because of a face? Some must have bent over backward. Then he had them. Not Hjordis. She would have put Pop into the street then and there, storm or no storm. Hjordis was religious, but she was wised up, too. She hadn't come over in steerage and worked forty years in Chicago for nothing.

---

① High Episcopal Christian Science Women's Temperance Evanston：埃文斯顿高级圣工会基督教科学派妇女戒酒协会。
② Samaritan：原指巴勒斯坦北部撒马利亚王国人，现泛指乐善好施者。Gentile：非犹太人的。
③ raffia：酒椰叶纤维。

Mrs. Skoglund, Awse (Osie), led the visitors into the front room. This, the biggest room in the house, needed supplementary heating. Because of fifteen-foot ceilings and high windows, Hjordis had kept the parlor stove burning. It was one of those elegant parlor stoves that wore a nickel crown, or miter, and this miter, when you moved it aside, automatically raised the hinge of an iron stove lid. That stove lid underneath the crown was all soot and rust, the same as any other stove lid. Into this hole you tipped the scuttle and the anthracite① chestnut rattled down. It made a cake or dome of fire visible through the small isinglass② frames. It was a pretty room, three-quarters paneled in wood. The stove was plugged into the flue of the marble fireplace, and there were parquet floors and Axminster carpets③ and cranberry-colored tufted Victorian upholstery, and a kind of Chinese étagère,④ inside a cabinet, lined with mirrors and containing silver pitchers, trophies won by Skoglund cows, fancy sugar tongs and cut-glass pitchers and goblets. There were Bibles and pictures of Jesus and the Holy Land and that faint Gentile odor, as if things had been rinsed in a weak vinegar solution.

"Mrs. Skoglund, I brought my dad to you. I don't think you ever met him," said Woody.

"Yes, Missus, that's me, Selbst."

Pop stood short but masterful in the sweaters, and his belly sticking out, not soft but hard. He was a man of the hard-bellied type. Nobody intimidated Pop. He never presented himself as a beggar. There wasn't a cringe in him anywhere. He let her see at once by the way he said "Missus" that he was independent and that he knew his way around. He communicated that he was able to handle himself with women. Handsome Mrs. Skoglund, carrying a basket woven out of her own hair, was in her fifties—eight, maybe ten years his senior.

"I asked my son to bring me because I know you do the kid a lot of good. It's natural you should know both of his parents."

"Mrs. Skoglund, my dad is in a tight corner and I don't know anybody else to ask for help."

This was all the preliminary Pop wanted. He took over and told the widow his story about the laundry-and-cleaning business and payments overdue, and explained about the fixtures and the attachment notice, and the bailiff's office and what they were going to do to him; and he said, "I'm a small man trying to make a living."

"You don't support your children," said Mrs. Skoglund.

"That's right," said Hjordis.

"I haven't got it. If I had it, wouldn't I give it? There's bread lines and soup lines all over town. Is it just me? What I have I divvy⑤ with. I give the kids. A bad father? You think my son would bring me if I was a bad father into your house? He loves his dad, he trusts his dad, he knows his dad is a good dad. Every time I start a little business going I get wiped out. This one is a good little business, if I could hold on to that little business. Three people work for me, I meet a payroll, and three people will be on the street, too, if I close down. Missus, I can sign a note and pay you in two months. I'm a common man, but I'm a hard worker and a fellow you can trust."

Woody was startled when Pop used the word "trust." It was as if from all four corners a Sousa band⑥ blew a blast to warn the entire world: "Crook! This is a crook!" But Mrs. Skoglund, on account of her religious preoccupations, was remote. She heard nothing. Although everybody in this part of the

---

① anthracite: 无烟煤。
② isinglass: 鱼胶。
③ parquet floor: 镶木地板。Axminster carpet: 阿克斯明斯特绒头地毯（取名来自原产地英国德文郡的阿克斯明斯特）。
④ étagère: （法）放置古玩及小摆设的陈列架。
⑤ divvy: （俚）分享，分配。
⑥ Sousa: 美国乐队指挥兼作曲家。Sousa band: 管乐队。

world, unless he was crazy, led a practical life, and you'd have nothing to say to anyone, your neighbors would have nothing to say to you, if communications were not of a practical sort, Mrs. Skoglund, with all her money, was unworldly—two-thirds out of this world.

"Give me a chance to show what's in me," said Pop, "and you'll see what I do for my kids."

So Mrs. Skoglund hesitated, and then she said she'd have to go upstairs, she'd have to go to her room and pray on it and ask for guidance—would they sit down and wait. There were two rocking chairs by the stove. Hjordis gave Pop a grim look (a dangerous person) and Woody a blaming one (he brought a dangerous stranger and disrupter to injure two kind Christian ladies). Then she went out with Mrs. Skoglund.

As soon as they left, Pop jumped up from the rocker and said in anger, "What's this with the praying? She has to ask God to lend me fifty bucks?"

Woody said, "It's not you, Pop, it's the way these religious people do."

"No," said Pop. "She'll come back and say that God wouldn't let her."

Woody didn't like that; he thought Pop was being gross and he said, "No, she's sincere. Pop, try to understand: she's emotional, nervous, and sincere, and tries to do right by everybody."

And Pop said, "That servant will talk her out of it. She's a toughie. It's all over her face that we're a couple of chiselers."

"What's the use of us arguing," said Woody. He drew the rocker closer to the stove. His shoes were wet through and would never dry. The blue flames fluttered like a school of fishes in the coal fire. But Pop went over to the Chinese-style cabinet or étagère and tried the handle, and then opened the blade of his penknife and in a second had forced the lock of the curved glass door. He took out a silver dish.

"Pop, what is this?" said Woody.

Pop, cool and level, knew exactly what this was. He relocked the étagère, crossed the carpet, listened. He stuffed the dish under his belt and pushed it down into his trousers. He put the side of his short thick finger to his mouth.

So Woody kept his voice down, but he was all shook up. He went to Pop and took him by the edge of his hand. As he looked into Pop's face, he felt his eyes growing smaller and smaller, as if something were contracting all the skin on his head. They call it hyperventilation when everything feels tight and light and close and dizzy. Hardly breathing, he said, "Put it back, Pop."

Pop said, "It's solid silver; it's worth dough."

"Pop, you said you wouldn't get me in Dutch."

"It's only insurance in case she comes back from praying and tells me no. If she says yes, I'll put it back."

"How?"

"It'll get back. If I don't put it back, you will."

"You picked the lock. I couldn't. I don't know how."

"There's nothing to it."

"We're going to put it back now. Give it here."

"Woody, it's under my fly, inside my underpants. Don't make such a noise about nothing."

"Pop, I can't believe this."

"For cry-ninety-nine,[①] shut your mouth. If I didn't trust you I wouldn't have let you watch me do it. You don't understand a thing. What's with you?"

---

① For cry-ninety-nine：够了，别说了。

"Before they come down, Pop, will you dig that dish out of your long johns."

Pop turned stiff on him. He became absolutely military. He said, "Look, I order you!"

Before he knew it, Woody had jumped his father and begun to wrestle with him. It was outrageous to clutch your own father, to put a heel behind him, to force him to the wall. Pop was taken by surprise and said loudly, "You want Halina killed? Kill her! Go on, you be responsible." He began to resist, angry, and they turned about several times, when Woody, with a trick he had learned in a Western movie and used once on the playground, tripped him and they fell to the ground. Woody, who already outweighed the old man by twenty pounds, was on top. They landed on the floor beside the stove, which stood on a tray of decorated tin to protect the carpet. In this position, pressing Pop's hard belly, Woody recognized that to have wrestled him to the floor counted for nothing. It was impossible to thrust his hand under Pop's belt to recover the dish. And now Pop had turned furious, as a father has every right to be when his son is violent with him, and he freed his hand and hit Woody in the face. He hit him three or four times in midface. Then Woody dug his head into Pop's shoulder and held tight only to keep from being struck and began to say in his ear, "Jesus, Pop, for Christ sake remember where you are. Those women will be back!" But Pop brought up his short knee and fought and butted him with his chin and rattled Woody's teeth. Woody thought the old man was about to bite him. And because he was a seminarian, he thought: Like an unclean spirit. And held tight. Gradually Pop stopped threshing and struggling. His eyes stuck out and his mouth was open, sullen. Like a stout fish. Woody released him and gave him a hand up. He was then overcome with many many bad feelings of a sort he knew the old man never suffered. Never, never. Pop never had these groveling emotions. There was his whole superiority. Pop had no such feelings. He was like a horseman from Central Asia. It was Mother, from Liverpool, who had the refinement, the English manners. It was the preaching Reverend Doctor in his black suit. You have refinements, and all they do is oppress you? The hell with that.

The long door opened and Mrs. Skoglund stepped in, saying, "Did I imagine, or did something shake the house?"

"I was lifting the scuttle to put coal on the fire and it fell out of my hand. I'm sorry I was so clumsy," said Woody.

Pop was too huffy to speak. With his eyes big and sore and the thin hair down over his forehead, you could see by the tightness of his belly how angrily he was fetching his breath, though his mouth was shut.

"I prayed," said Mrs. Skoglund.

"I hope it came out well," said Woody.

"Well, I don't do anything without guidance, but the answer was yes, and I feel right about it now. So if you'll wait, I'll go to my office and write a check. I asked Hjordis to bring you a cup of coffee. Coming in such a storm."

And Pop, consistently a terrible little man, as soon as she shut the door, said, "A check? Hell with a check. Get me the greenbacks."

"They don't keep money in the house. You can cash it in her bank tomorrow. But if they miss that dish, Pop, they'll stop the check, and then where are you?"

As Pop was reaching below the belt, Hjordis brought in the tray. She was very sharp with him. She said, "Is this a place to adjust clothing, Mister? A men's washroom?"

"Well, which way is the toilet, then?" said Pop.

She had served the coffee in the seamiest mugs in the pantry, and she bumped down the tray and led Pop down the corridor, standing guard at the bathroom door so that he shouldn't wander about the house.

Mrs. Skoglund called Woody to her office and after she had given him the folded check said that they should pray together for Morris. So once more he was on his knees, under rows and rows of musty marbled-cardboard files, by the glass lamp by the edge of the desk, the shade with flounced edges, like the candy dish. Mrs. Skoglund, in her Scandinavian accent—an emotional contralto—raising her voice to Jesus-uh Christ-uh, as the wind lashed the trees, kicked the side of the house, and drove the snow seething on the windowpanes, to send light-uh, give guidance-uh, put a new heart-uh in Pop's bosom. Woody asked God only to make Pop put the dish back. He kept Mrs. Skoglund on her knees as long as possible. Then he thanked her, shining with candor (as much as he knew how), for her Christian generosity and he said, "I know that Hjordis has a cousin who works at the Evanston YMCA. Could she please phone him and try to get us a room tonight so that we don't have to fight the blizzard all the way back? We're almost as close to the Y as to the car line. Maybe the cars have even stopped running."

Suspicious Hjordis, coming when Mrs. Skoglund called to her, was burning now. First they barged in, made themselves at home, asked for money, had to have coffee, probably left gonorrhea① on the toilet seat. Hjordis, Woody remembered, was a woman who wiped the doorknobs with rubbing alcohol after guests had left. Nevertheless, she telephoned the Y and got them a room with two cots for six bits.

Pop had plenty of time, therefore, to reopen the étagère, lined with reflecting glass or German silver (something exquisitely delicate and tricky), and as soon as the two Selbsts had said thank you and goodbye and were in midstreet again up to the knees in snow, Woody said, "Well, I covered for you. Is that thing back?"

"Of course it is," said Pop.

They fought their way to the small Y building, shut up in wire grille and resembling a police station—about the same dimensions. It was locked, but they made a racket on the grille, and a small black man let them in and shuffled them upstairs to a cement corridor with low doors. It was like the small-mammal house in Lincoln Park. He said there was nothing to eat, so they took off their wet pants, wrapped themselves tightly in the khaki army blankets, and passed out on their cots.

First thing in the morning, they went to the Evanston National Bank and got the fifty dollars. Not without difficulties. The teller went to call Mrs. Skoglund and was absent a long time from the wicket.

"Where the hell has he gone?" said Pop.

But when the fellow came back, he said, "How do you want it?"

Pop said, "Singles." He told Woody, "Bujak stashes② it in one-dollar bills."

But by now Woody no longer believed Halina had stolen the old man's money.

Then they went into the street, where the snow-removal crews were at work. The sun shone broad, broad, out of the morning blue, and all Chicago would be releasing itself from the temporary beauty of those vast drifts.

"You shouldn't have jumped me last night, Sonny."

"I know, Pop, but you promised you wouldn't get me in Dutch."

"Well, it's okay. We can forget it, seeing you stood by me."

Only, Pop had taken the silver dish. Of course he had, and in a few days Mrs. Skoglund and Hjordis knew it, and later in the week they were all waiting for Woody in Kovner's office at the settlement house. The group included the Reverend Doctor Crabbie, head of the seminary, and Woody, who had been flying along, level and smooth, was shot down in flames.③ He told them he was innocent. Even as he was falling, he warned that they were wronging him. He denied that he or Pop had touched

---

① gonorrhea: 淋病。
② stash: 藏起来。
③ who had been flying along, level and smooth, was shot down in flames.: 一直平稳顺利地飞翔, 却被击中坠入枪火中。

Mrs. Skoglund's property. The missing object—he didn't even know what it was—had probably been misplaced, and they would be very sorry on the day it turned up. After the others were done with him, Dr. Crabbie said that until he was able to tell the truth he would be suspended from the seminary, where his work had been unsatisfactory anyway. Aunt Rebecca took him aside and said to him, "You are a little crook, like your father. The door is closed to you here."

To this Pop's comment was "So what, kid?"

"Pop, you shouldn't have done it."

"No? Well, I don't give a care, if you want to know. You can have the dish if you want to go back and square yourself with all those hypocrites①."

"I didn't like doing Mrs. Skoglund in the eye, she was so kind to us."

"Kind?"

"Kind."

"Kind has a price tag."

Well, there was no winning such arguments with Pop. But they debated it in various moods and from various elevations and perspectives for forty years and more, as their intimacy changed, developed, matured.

"Why did you do it, Pop? For the money? What did you do with the fifty bucks?" Woody, decades later, asked him that.

"I settled with the bookie, and the rest I put in the business."

"You tried a few more horses."

"I maybe did. But it was a double, Woody. I didn't hurt myself, and at the same time did you a favor."

"It was for me?"

"It was too strange of a life. That life wasn't *you*, Woody. All those women... Kovner was no man, he was an in-between. Suppose they made you a minister? Some Christian minister! First of all, you wouldn't have been able to stand it, and second, they would throw you out sooner or later."

"Maybe so."

"And you wouldn't have converted the Jews, which was the main thing they wanted."

"And what a time to bother the Jews," Woody said. "At least *I* didn't bug②them."

Pop had carded him back to his side of the line, blood of his blood, the same thick body walls, the same coarse grain. Not cut out for a spiritual life. Simply not up to it.

Pop was no worse than Woody, and Woody was no better than Pop. Pop wanted no relation to theory, and yet he was always pointing Woody toward a position—a jolly, hearty, natural, likable, unprincipled position. If Woody had a weakness, it was to be unselfish. This worked to Pop's advantage, but he criticized Woody for it, nevertheless. "You take too much on yourself," Pop was always saying. And it's true that Woody gave Pop his heart because Pop was so selfish. It's usually the selfish people who are loved the most. They do what you deny yourself, and you love them for it. You give them your heart.

Remembering the pawn ticket for the silver dish, Woody startled himself with a laugh so sudden that it made him cough. Pop said to him after his expulsion from the seminary and banishment from the settlement house, "You want in again? Here's the ticket. I hocked that thing. It wasn't so valuable as I thought."

---

① square yourself with all those hypocrites: 要求所有那些伪善者宽恕你。
② bug: (俚)烦扰。

"What did they give?"

"Twelve-fifty was all I could get. But if you want it you'll have to raise the dough yourself, because l haven't got it anymore."

"You must have been sweating in the bank when the teller went to call Mrs. Skoglund about the check."

"I was a little nervous," said Pop. "But I didn't think they could miss the thing so soon."[①]

That theft was part of Pop's war with Mother. With Mother, and Aunt Rebecca, and the Reverend Doctor. Pop took his stand on realism. Mother represented the forces of religion and hypochondria. In four decades, the fighting never stopped. In the course of time, Mother and the girls turned into welfare personalities and lost their individual outlines. Ah, the poor things, they became dependents and cranks. In the meantime, Woody, the sinful man, was their dutiful and loving son and brother. He maintained the bungalow—this took in roofing, pointing[②], wiring, insulation, air-conditioning—and he paid for heat and light and food, and dressed them all out of Sears, Roebuck and Wieboldt's, and bought them a TV, which they watched as devoutly as they prayed. Paula took courses to learn skills like macramé[③]-making and needlepoint, and sometimes got a little job as recreational worker in a nursing home. But she wasn't steady enough to keep it. Wicked Pop spent most of his life removing stains from people's clothing. He and Halina in the last years ran a Cleanomat in West Rogers Park—a so-so business resembling a laundromat—which gave him leisure for billiards, the horses, rummy and pinochle. Every morning he went behind the partition to check out the filters of the cleaning equipment. He found amusing things that had been thrown into the vats with the clothing—sometimes, when he got lucky, a locket chain or a brooch. And when he had fortified the cleaning fluid, pouring all that blue and pink stuff in from plastic jugs, he read the *Forward* over a second cup of coffee, and went out, leaving Halina in charge. When they needed help with the rent, Woody gave it.

After the new Disney World was opened in Florida, Woody treated all his dependents to a holiday. He sent them down in separate batches, of course. Halina enjoyed this more than anybody else. She couldn't stop talking about the address given by an Abraham Lincoln automaton. "Wonderful, how he stood up and moved his hands, and his mouth. So real! And how beautiful he talked." Of them all, Halina was the soundest, the most human, the most honest. Now that Pop was gone, Woody and Halina's son, Mitosh, the organist at the Stadium, took care of her needs over and above Social Security, splitting expenses. In Pop's opinion, insurance was a racket. He left Halina nothing but some out-of-date equipment.

Woody treated himself, too. Once a year, and sometimes oftener, he left his business to run itself, arranged with the trust department at the bank to take care of his gang, and went off. He did that in style, imaginatively, expensively. In Japan, he wasted little time on Tokyo. He spent three weeks in Kyoto and stayed at the Tawaraya Inn, dating from the seventeenth century or so. There he slept on the floor, the Japanese way, and bathed in scalding water. He saw the dirtiest strip show on earth, as well as the holy places and the temple gardens. He visited also Istanbul, Jerusalem, Delphi, and went to Burma and Uganda and Kenya on safari[④], on democratic terms with drivers, Bedouins[⑤], bazaar merchants. Open, lavish, familiar, fleshier and fleshier but (he jogged, he lifted weights) still muscular—in his

---

① But I didn't think they could miss the thing so soon.：可我没想到她们那么快就发现丢了那样东西。
② pointing：(建)用水泥等勾嵌砖石墙等的砌缝。
③ macramé：(家具装饰用)流苏，花边。
④ safari：徒步旅游队。
⑤ Bedouins：贝都因人;游牧人。

naked person beginning to resemble a Renaissance courtier in full costume—becoming ruddier every year, an outdoor type with freckles on his back and spots across the flaming forehead and the honest nose. On the Nile, below Murchison Falls, those fever trees[①] rose huge from the mud, and hippos on the sandbars belched at the passing launch, hostile. One of them danced on his spit of sand, springing from the ground and coming down heavy, on all fours. There, Woody saw the buffalo calf disappear, snatched by the crocodile.

Mother, soon to follow Pop, was being lightheaded these days. In company, she spoke of Woody as her boy—"What do you think of my Sonny?"—as though he was ten years old. She was silly with him, her behavior was frivolous, almost flirtatious. She just didn't seem to know the facts. And behind her all the others, like kids at the playground, were waiting their turn to go down the slide: one on each step, and moving toward the top.

Over Woody's residence and place of business there had gathered a pool of silence of the same perimeter as the church bells while they were ringing, and he mourned under it, this melancholy morning of sun and autumn. Doing a life survey, taking a deliberate look at the gross side of his case—of the other side as well, what there was of it. But if this heartache continued, he'd go out and run it off. A three-mile jog—five, if necessary. And you'd think that this jogging was an entirely physical activity, wouldn't you? But there was something else in it. Because, when he was a seminarian, between the shafts of his World's Fair rickshaw, he used to receive, pulling along (capable and stable), his religious experiences while he trotted. Maybe it was all a single experience repeated. He felt truth coming to him from the sun. He received a communication that was also light and warmth. It made him very remote from his horny Wisconsin passengers, those farmers whose whoops and whore cries he could hardly hear when he was in one of his states. And again out of the flaming of the sun would come to him a secret certainty that the goal set for this earth was that it should be filled with good, saturated with it. After everything preposterous, after dog had eaten dog, after the crocodile death had pulled everyone into his mud. It wouldn't conclude as Mrs. Skoglund, bribing him to round up the Jews and hasten the Second Coming, imagined it, but in another way. This was his clumsy intuition. It went no further. Subsequently, he proceeded through life as life seemed to want him to do it.

There remained one thing more this morning, which was explicitly physical, occurring first as a sensation in his arms and against his breast and, from the pressure, passing into him and going into his breast.

It was like this: When he came into the hospital room and saw Pop with the sides of his bed raised, like a crib, and Pop, so very feeble, and writhing, and toothless, like a baby, and the dirt already cast into his face, into the wrinkles—Pop wanted to pluck out the intravenous needles and he was piping his weak death noise. The gauze patches taped over the needles were soiled with dark blood. Then Woody took off his shoes, lowered the side of the bed, and climbed in and held him in his arms to soothe and still him. As if he were Pop's father, he said to him, "Now, Pop. Pop." Then it was like the wrestle in Mrs. Skoglund's parlor, when Pop turned angry like an unclean spirit and Woody tried to appease him, and warn him, saying, "Those women will be back!" Beside the coal stove, when Pop hit Woody in the teeth with his head and then became sullen, like a stout fish. But this struggle in the hospital was weak—so weak! In his great pity, Woody held Pop, who was fluttering and shivering. From those people, Pop had told him, you'll never find out what life is, because they don't know what it is. Yes, Pop—well, what is it, Pop? Hard to comprehend that Pop, who was dug in for eighty-three years and had done all he could to stay, should now want nothing but to free himself. How could Woody allow the

---

① fever tree: 蓝桉树。

old man to pull the intravenous needles out? Willful Pop, he wanted what he wanted when he wanted it. But what he wanted at the very last Woody failed to follow, it was such a switch①.

After a time, Pop's resistance ended. He subsided and subsided. He rested against his son, his small body curled there. Nurses came and looked. They disapproved, but Woody, who couldn't spare a hand to wave them out, motioned with his head toward the door. Pop, whom Woody thought he had stilled, only had found a better way to get around him. Loss of heat was the way he did it. His heat was leaving him. As can happen with small animals while you hold them in your hand, Woody presently felt him cooling. Then, as Woody did his best to restrain him, and thought he was succeeding, Pop divided himself. And when he was separated from his warmth, he slipped into death. And there was his elderly, large, muscular son, still holding and pressing him when there was nothing anymore to press. You could never pin down that self-willed man. When he was ready to make his move, he made it—always on his own terms. And always, always, something up his sleeve②. That was how he was.

《银盘子》选自1984年出版的《出言不逊者及其他故事》。通过讲述有犹太血统的主人公伍迪(Woody)在美国经济大萧条时期的成长故事,用讽刺辛辣的笔触揭示出犹太人的宗教信仰以及个人道德危机。大萧条时期美国的移民生活对犹太人产生隔离影响,造成犹太人信仰危机,使犹太人在迫切需要接受功利性基督教会提供的生活援助的同时,又对基督教是否真正具备拯救灵魂这一神圣功效产生怀疑。青年时代的伍迪徘徊在艰辛的物质生活与岌岌可危的宗教信仰之间;而当中年时代的伍迪享受着实现美国梦所带来的物质成功之时,也咀嚼着美国的犹太移民特有的酸涩;耳顺之年的伍迪在百感交集的回忆中,似乎要通过回忆父亲笃信犹太教来解除自己的信仰困惑,而父亲的话语背后时刻交织着不同宗教教堂鸣响的钟声。伍迪的这种两难境地恐怕正是贝娄向犹太人以及其他读者提出的问题。

《银盘子》展示了贝娄独特的叙事技巧,故事开端采用第二人称直截了当的问句,让读者设身处地体验主人公伍迪的丧父之痛以及他魂牵梦绕的精神困惑。故事展开后,采用由意象引发的意识流手法,例如,伍迪对他从非洲带回大麻并塞入感恩节火鸡腹内的这段回忆,通过火鸡这一意象,自然过渡到对父亲最后一次在家吃火鸡这一令人心酸场景的描写,之后笔锋一转,又回到伍迪对父亲的回忆,突出了伍迪对父亲的理解不断深化的过程。故事的叙述往返于以伍迪为内聚焦与全知视角之间,通过不断切换主观与客观的认知视角,读者的认识不断丰富,叙述的可信性也不断增强。贯穿全文的教堂钟声这一象征高度深化了故事的主旨,既烘托出笃信犹太教的父亲的孤独,又折射出伍迪对包括自己在内的新一代美国犹太人的迷茫和反思。此外,圣经中的银杯典故(Genesis 44:4 "A Silver Cup in a Sack")是深入理解本文宗教内涵的重要线索。

 思考题

1. What kind of person is Morris?
2. How do you characterize Mrs. Skoglund?
3. How does Woody revise his idea about Morris throughout the story?
4. Why do you think Morris says "Kind has a price tag"?
5. How is Woody's wrestle with his father at the hospital similar to and different from that in Mrs. Skoglund's parlor?
6. What narrative techniques are used to enhance the theme?

---

① switch:(口)调换,交换;(欺骗性的)调包。
② something up his sleeve:总有锦囊妙计;留有……一招。

推荐作品

Herzog (1964)
Humboldt's Gift (1975)
The Dean's December (1982)
"Looking for Mr. Green" (1968)

参考资料

Atalas, James. *Bellow: A Biography*. Rpt. ed. New York: Modern Library, 2002.
Bach, Gerhard, et al., eds. *Small Planets: Saul Bellow and the Art of Short Fiction*. East Lansing: Michigan State University Press, 2000.
Cronin, Gloria L. and B. Siegel, eds. *Conversations with Saul Bellow*. Jackson: University Press of Mississippi, 1994.
Kramer, Mincheal P., ed. *New Essays on Seize the Day*. Beijing: Peking University Press, 2006.
Bellow, Saul. *Saul Bellow: Letters*. Ed. Benjamin Taylor. London: Penguin Books, 2012.
—. *There Is Simply Too Much to Think About: Collected Nonfiction*. Ed. Benjamin Taylor. New York: Viking, 2015.

(李　晋)

第十六单元
Robert Hayden (1913—1980)
罗伯特·海登

 作者简介

  罗伯特·海登，美国国会图书馆第一个黑人"诗歌顾问"（后改称为"美国桂冠诗人"），生于底特律的贫民区，亲生父母在他出生后不久即离异，被邻居海登家收养。养父母不休的争吵和打骂，以及自身的近视和矮小，使少年罗伯特郁郁寡欢，只好从书籍中寻找慰藉。海登就读于芝加哥城市学院（后改名为韦恩州立大学），主修西班牙语，1936年以一学分之差辍学，加入美国联邦作家项目，开始研究美国黑人历史和民间文化，为后来的诗歌创作积累了素材。1940年，海登发表第一部诗集《尘土中的心形》(*Heart-Shape in the Dust*)。1941年，他进入密歇根大学攻读英语硕士学位，1942年师从奥登(W. H. Auden)，在诗歌创作上取得很大进步。从1946年起，他到南方的菲斯克大学(Fisk University)任教23年，陆续发表《狮子与弓箭手》(*The Lion and the Archer*, 1948)、《时间的数字：诗集》(*Figures of Time: Poems*, 1955)、《记忆的歌谣》(*A Ballad of Remembrance*, 1962)和《诗选》(*Selected Poems*, 1966)。1969年重返密歇根大学，舌笔同耕，发表了《哀悼时的言语》(*Words in the Mourning Time*, 1970)、《夜间绽开的尾须》(*The Night-Blooming Cereus*, 1972)和《上飘的天使》(*Angle of Ascent*, 1975)，成为重要的美国诗人。1975年，因为"对诗歌杰出的贡献"被美国诗院奖励每年一万美元的创作奖金。次年，被任命为国会图书馆的诗歌顾问。1980年1月，应卡特总统之邀到白宫参加诗人庆祝活动，同年2月去世，遗著《美国日志》于1982年出版。海登是巴哈伊教徒，信奉世界大同、民族友爱，认为诗人不应该是民族的代言人，政治和种族标准不应该用在对"好诗"与"坏诗"的判断上。然而，他的很多诗歌反映的仍是黑人的情感和体验。海登善于运用诗歌细节性技巧，通过压缩、委婉陈述、并列组合、蒙太奇等手法提升诗歌的象征浓度，诗作洗练优美，受到越来越多的读者的喜爱。

Those Winter Sundays①

Sundays too my father got up early
and put his clothes on in the blueblack cold②,
then with cracked hands that ached
from labor in the weekday weather made
banked fires③ blaze. No one ever thanked him.

I'd wake and hear the cold splintering④, breaking.
When the rooms were warm, he'd call,
and slowly I would rise and dress,

---

① 《冬天的早晨》用清晰、准确的语言描绘了一位父亲在冬天的早晨任劳任怨地为孩子生火驱寒的往事，最后又通过成熟的"我"对童年的反思，抒发父子间复杂的感情和"我"对爱的深刻理解。全诗十四行，有人因此称之为"十四行诗"。虽然本诗在最后两行点明主题，但是全诗的分阕方法、音步和韵式都不同于彼得拉克体、莎士比亚体和斯宾塞体三种传统的十四行诗。
② in the blueblack cold：在冻得人发青的黑暗的寒冷中。blue可以指人的肤色发青、发紫、发灰；black指天还未亮，一片漆黑。
③ banked fires：封炉的火，用火灰掩盖的火。
④ splinter：撕裂，刺穿。这里splintering和breaking两个词一起生动地展示了"我"听到寒冷被火驱散的情景。

fearing the chronic angers① of that house,
Speaking indifferently to him,
who had driven out the cold
and polished my good shoes② as well.
What did I know, what did I know
of love's austere and lonely offices③?

《冬天的早晨》于1962年发表在《记忆的歌谣》(A Ballad of Remembrance)里。诗歌展示了诗人卓越的文字能力和对复杂情感的细腻表现能力,通过"我"对父爱的缓慢认识过程揭示了"我"对儿时不知感恩(比如:"No one ever thanked him","Speaking indifferently to him")的复杂心理。诗歌开头两句通过"too"一词说明父亲终年累月含辛茹苦,没有休息日,又通过父亲在黑暗中起床穿衣暗示了他默默无闻的奉献。3—5行,通过对父亲用粗糙疼痛的手为家人生火的具体描写表现了父亲的自我牺牲精神,然而这一切却没有人领情,第5行后半句"没谁感谢他",突兀地衬托了父亲的孤独。第一阕中[k]音的反复出现不仅让全阕诗有一气呵成、浑然一体之势,而且也让人联想到火烧劈柴的声音。第二阕写"我"的感受和行为,将无形的寒冷描绘成可以撕裂、可以破碎的有形之物,通过黑暗和寒冷的破碎引出光明和温暖的到来,"我"在温暖的房间慢腾腾地穿着衣服。然而一幅温馨的图画突然又被家庭内部的"慢性愤怒"所破坏,[k]音(在chronic中)的出现似乎将这一愤怒同父亲变形的手(cracked hands)和炉火(banked fire)联系到一起,愤怒主体和原因的含混更加准确地揭示了家庭关系的复杂性。第三阕从父子心存隔阂、疏于交流、缺乏热情的过去,到长大成人后的儿子认识到父亲生火驱寒、擦亮皮鞋的关爱之后的现在,表现了觉醒后的"我"黯然神伤的心理。父爱朴实无华,甚至带有几分酸苦,显得严厉,不被理解,然而,它真真切切地存在,给家庭以温暖,等到"我"意识到这些时,已经没有机会再向父亲道谢或者回报父亲了,可谓"子欲养,而亲不待也",只得借助诗歌这种情感的载体聊表思念了。

思考题

1. Who is the speaker (narrator or persona)? What's the story of this poem?
2. What do you know about the father?
3. What are the emotions of the speaker to his father?
4. What do you think the word "offices" mean in the last line?
5. What's the significance of the word "Sundays" in the title? Will it make any difference if it is changed to "mornings"?

"Night, Death, Mississippi"(1962)
"Middle Passage"(1962)
"Runagate, Runagate"(1962)
"The Whipping"(1970)

---

① the chronic angers: 慢性愤怒。一说指父子间的敌对情绪;另一说指诗人的养母(Sue Ellen Hayden),因其婚姻不幸福,常发脾气,亦可理解为贫困家庭因生活所迫而滋生的不满情绪。
② good shoes: 星期天是上教堂的日子,人们一般都穿最好的衣服,所以父亲为孩子擦亮了那双好鞋。
③ office: 一词多义,既可以指父亲艰辛劳作的实质和单词的复数形式,把它理解为"照料、帮助",也可以根据上文中孩子对父亲淡漠的态度,理解为"职责",甚至还可以理解为"礼仪"。前者表示成年的"我"感受到父亲对自己的爱怜之情,后者则表示儿时的"我"认为父亲所做的一切都是他应尽的职责。

参考资料

Fetrow, Fred M. *Robert Hayden*. Boston: Twayne, 1984.
Hatcher, John. *From the Auroral Darkness: The Life and Poetry of Robert Hayden*. Oxford: George Ronald, 1984.
Williams, Pontheolla T. *Robert Hayden: A Critical Analysis of His Poetry*. Urbana: University of Illinois Press, 1987.

(陈法春)

Robert Lowell (1917—1977)

罗伯特·洛威尔

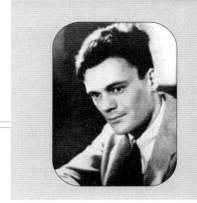

 作者简介

    罗伯特·洛威尔,诗人,"自白派"诗歌的代表人物之一。生于马萨诸塞州波士顿市,父亲为海军军官。他的父母及前辈中不乏颇有建树的文学家,如19世纪赫赫有名的诗人詹姆斯·拉塞尔·洛威尔(James Russell Lowell)以及20世纪的知名意象派诗人艾米·洛威尔(Amy Lowell)。在哈佛大学期间,洛威尔开始对诗歌创作感兴趣,两年后追随"逃亡派"诗人艾伦·塔特(Allen Tate)到田纳西并入肯庸学院受塔特和约翰·兰塞姆(John Crowe Ransom)等诗人的栽培。大学毕业后,他前往路易斯安那州立大学进一步深造,师从当时走红的新批评派核心人物罗伯特·潘·沃伦(Robert Penn Warren)与克林斯·布鲁克斯(Cleanth Brooks)。1940年,他首次结婚,配偶是小说家简恩·斯塔福德(Jean Stafford),但很快离异;此后又两度结婚,但均不美满,后因与第三位夫人发生口角而猝死在出租汽车上。第二次世界大战期间,他参军在德国服役,目睹战争的血腥与残酷,萌生反战思想,拒绝执行军务,因此被捕入狱。战后,洛威尔专注于诗歌创作,成就非凡。他的第一部诗集《威利爵爷的城堡》(*Lord Weary's Castle*, 1947),取材于苏格兰民谣,荣获普利策诗歌奖。1959年出版的诗集《人生研究》(*Life Studies*)获得美国国家图书奖。其他作品还包括获得普利策奖的诗集《海豚》(*The Dolphin*, 1973)。

Man and Wife

Tamed by *Miltown*①, we lie on Mother's bed;
the rising sun in war paint dyes us red;
in broad daylight her gilded bed-posts② shine,
abandoned, almost Dionysian③.
At last the trees are green on Marlborough④ Street,
blossoms on our magnolia ignite
the morning with their murderous five day's white.
All night I've held your hand,
as if you had
a fourth time faced the kingdom of the mad—
its hackneyed⑤ speech, its homicidal⑥ eye—
and dragged me home alive... Oh my *Petite*,
clearest of all God's creatures, still all air and nerve:
you were in your twenties, and I,

---

① Miltown: 眠尔通(甲丙氨酯),药名:即一种安眠药;安宁。
② bed-posts: 床柱,床角的垂直柱子。
③ Dionysian: 酒神节的;放荡的;源于古希腊神话中的酒神狄俄尼索斯(Dionysus),指与狄俄尼索斯有关的。
④ Marlborough: 也称Marlboro,指美国马萨诸塞州中东部一城市,位于伍斯特市东北偏东方向,1657年开始有人定居。此处为街名。(美国很多街道往往取名于他处的地名或名人之名)
⑤ hackneyed: 陈词滥调的,老生常谈的,不新奇的。
⑥ homicidal: 杀人的,可导致杀人的。

once hand on glass
and heart in mouth,
outdrank the Rahvs① in the heat
of Greenwich Village②, fainting at your feet—
too boiled and shy
and poker-faced③ to make a pass,
while the shrill verve
of your invective④ scorched the traditional South.

Now twelve years later, you turn your back.
Sleepless, you hold
your pillow to your hollows like a child,
your old-fashioned tirade⑤—
loving, rapid, merciless—
breaks like the Atlantic Ocean on my head.

洛威尔的诗歌题材和主题都非常广泛,从思考现实问题到改写古代的民谣,展示了他宽阔的视野和胸怀。他与同时代的许多诗人一样,诸如金斯堡和西尔维娅·普拉斯,在很大程度上动用"自白"手法,即毫无顾忌地叙说自身非同一般、刻骨铭心的经历和感受,强烈关注个人的生活境遇以及内心世界的感受,而并非像古希腊的诗人荷马那样凭借想象与传说就能够写就事关人类命运和国家社稷的史诗。在《夫与妻》一诗中,作为主人公的叙事者讲述了他与妻子在服用"眠尔通"之后进入似睡非睡的幻觉状态,由此无拘无束地倾诉了心灵中痛苦不安的感受。位于诗歌之首的"被眠尔通制服以后",提示读者主人公与妻子在服用安眠药之前的苦楚与疯狂。在诗的结尾,"妻子"的愤懑再一次像"大西洋一样"倾泻而出,"丈夫"也再一次领略到了"司空见惯的长篇唠叨"。虽然这一幕仅仅是主人公在幻觉中的感受,但在"自白派"诗人看来,只有在解除意识束缚的状况下的"自白"才能展示最真实的内心世界。

 思考题

 What do you think the poet means when he refers to Dionysus in the poem?
 How does the poet represent the habitual but gnawing tension between the husband and his wife?

 "Skunk Hour" (1959)
"To Speak of Woe That Is in Marriage" (1959)
"Walking in the Blue" (1959)

---

① the Rahvs:一种酒精饮料。
② Greenwich Village:格林威治村,位于美国纽约市曼哈顿的一个居民区,1910年后成为艺术家和作家的聚居地。
③ poker-faced:没有表情的,神情木然的,一本正经的。
④ invective:非难的,漫骂的,恶言的。
⑤ tirade:抨击;激烈演说;愤怒的或激烈的长篇言辞,通常为挑剔或谴责性质。

参考资料

Perloff, Marjorie. *The Poetic Art of Robert Lowell*. Ithaca: Cornell University Press, 1973.
Rudman, Mark. *Robert Lowell: An Introduction to the Poetry*. New York: Columbia University Press, 1983.
Tillinghast, Richard. *Robert Lowell' Life and Work: Damaged Grandeur*. Ann Arbor: University of Michigan Press, 1995.

（刘树森）

Allen Ginsberg (1926—1997)
艾伦·金斯堡

 作者简介

  艾伦·金斯堡(1926—1997),诗人。生于新泽西州首府纽瓦克市,父亲为中学英语教师,为人厚道谨慎,母亲为犹太移民,因在俄国曾遭受迫害而患有精神疾病。金斯堡曾就读于哥伦比亚大学,主修经济,但热衷于诗歌创作,并开始发表作品。其间,他结识了威廉·巴勒斯与杰克·凯鲁亚克等后来投身文学创作的同学,志同道合,后来形成一个颇有特色的文学创作群体,史称"垮掉的一代"。后因生活放荡不羁、吸食毒品、破坏学校秩序等原因,金斯堡被开除学籍。1956年,他发表了诗集《嚎叫及其他》(*Howl and Other Poems*),以其反传统的主题内容和效仿惠特曼的诗歌风格震撼了美国诗坛,其中包括他最负盛名的一些诗篇,诸如《嚎叫》("Howl")与《加利福尼亚的超级市场》("A Supermarket in California")。金斯堡前半生缺乏稳定的生活,长期周游各州,靠打零工谋生,并曾因窝赃而被捕入狱,但始终致力于诗歌创作。此外,他还积极参与反战游行、民权运动、吸毒和同性恋等活动,与其诗歌创作主题相互呼应。他的社会活动与个人生活经历实际上也成为其诗歌的主要内容。金斯堡总共出版了11部诗集,主要包括《卡迪西及其他》(*Kaddish and Other Poems*, 1961),《现实三明治》(*Reality Sandwiches*, 1963),《星球消息》(*Planet News: 1961—1967*),以及荣获美国全国图书奖的《美国的堕落》(*The Fall of America: Poems of These States*)。金斯堡1984年曾随美国作家代表团访问中国,与多位中国作家进行交流,在北京大学举办有关英语诗歌节奏与音乐性的讲座,后在河北大学讲授英美文学一个月。在访问中国期间,金斯堡创作了《北京即兴》("Improvisation of Beijing")与《一天清晨,我在中国漫步》("One Morning I Took a Walk in China")等诗歌。金斯堡晚年除写诗之外,还举办讲习班扶掖年轻诗人,研究佛教,并从1986年开始受聘为布鲁克林学院杰出英语教授,讲授英语诗歌,直至辞世。

Howl
For Carl Solomon[①]

I saw the best minds of my generation destroyed by madness, starving hysterical[②] naked,
dragging themselves through the negro[③] streets at dawn looking for an angry fix[④],
angelheaded[⑤] hipsters[⑥] burning for the ancient heavenly connection to the starry dynamo[⑦] in the machinery of night,

---

① Carl Solomon: 卡尔·所罗门(1928—1993),美国作家,20世纪40末在精神病院邂逅艾伦·金斯堡,二人情趣相投,随后一同从事文学创作与出版等活动;其代表作为《来自精神病院的报告:一位休克病人的反思》(*Report from the Asylum: Afterthoughts of a Shock Patient*)。金斯堡将倾注两年的时光创作的代表作《嚎叫》献给所罗门,其中还包括有关二人情谊的抒情内容。
② hysterical: 歇斯底里的;情绪异常激动的。
③ negro: 黑人(带有歧视含义)。
④ fix: (毒品)一剂;一次用量,一个剂量。
⑤ angelheaded: 头脑如天使一般的,寓意为圣洁。
⑥ hipster: 嬉皮士;赶时髦的人。
⑦ dynamo: 发电机;精力充沛的人。

who poverty and tatters① and hollow-eyed and high sat up smoking in the supernatural darkness of cold-water flats floating across the tops of cities contemplating jazz,

who bared their brains to Heaven under the El② and saw Mohammedan③ angels staggering on tenement roofs illuminated,

who passed through universities with radiant cool eyes hallucinating④ Arkansas⑤ and Blake-light⑥ tragedy among the scholars of war,

who were expelled from the academies for crazy & publishing obscene⑦ odes on the windows of the skull⑧,

who cowered⑨ in unshaven rooms in underwear, burning their money in wastebaskets and listening to the Terror through the wall,

who got busted⑩ in their pubic beards⑪ returning through Laredo⑫ with a belt of marijuana⑬ for New York,

who ate fire in paint hotels⑭ or drank turpentine⑮ in Paradise Alley⑯, death, or purgatoried⑰ their torsos⑱ night after night

with dreams, with drugs, with waking nightmares, alcohol and cock⑲ and endless balls⑳,

incomparable blind streets of shuddering cloud and lightning in the mind leaping toward poles of Canada & Paterson㉑, illuminating all the motionless world of Time㉒ between,

Peyote㉓ solidities of halls, backyard green tree cemetery dawns, wine drunkenness over the rooftops, storefront boroughs of teahead㉔ joyride㉕ neon blinking traffic light, sun and moon and tree vibrations in the roaring winter dusks of Brooklyn㉖, ashcan㉗ rantings㉘ and kind king light㉙ of mind,

---

① tatters: 破衣烂衫。
② the El: 纽约市高架铁道(the Elevated Railway)的简称,现已大多拆除。
③ Mohammedan: (伊斯兰教创立人)穆罕默德的;伊斯兰教的。
④ hallucinating: 产生迷幻感觉的。
⑤ Arkansas: 阿肯色州,位于美国南部,农牧业发达,首府为小石城。
⑥ Blake-light: 布莱克的影响;威廉·布莱克(William Blake, 1757—1827),英国诗人、作家、版画家,多才多艺,但在世时长期怀才不遇,去世后被公认为欧洲浪漫主义的奠基人之一。
⑦ obscene: 猥亵的;淫秽的。金斯堡在哥伦比亚大学就读时曾因多次在校内建筑物的窗户上张贴淫秽诗作而被捕,并被强制送入该校精神病院治疗。
⑧ skull: 骷髅;颅骨。
⑨ cowered: 畏缩;退缩。
⑩ busted: 被逮捕的;被打碎的。
⑪ pubic beards: 耻毛;阴毛。
⑫ Laredo: 拉雷多市,位于美国德克萨斯州南部,比邻美国与墨西哥的边境,是各种形形色色跨境贸易的重要枢纽。
⑬ marijuana: 大麻(毒品);大麻(桑科植物)。
⑭ paint hotels: 指生活拮据的艺术家或者吸毒者经常光顾的廉价旅馆,住宿条件简陋,但艺术家可用画作等作品冲抵房租。
⑮ turpentine: 松节油,常用作油画颜料调制过程中的稀释剂,并具有一定的医药作用,外用可减轻肌肉痛、关节痛、神经痛以及扭伤疼痛等。
⑯ Paradise Alley: 20世纪中叶垮掉派文化的标志性地点之一,位于旧金山市内的一个高档住宅区,垮掉派艺术家将其称为"天堂幽径",在此举办创作活动或者居住。
⑰ purgatoried: 使备受折磨的;源于"炼狱"(purgatory)。
⑱ torsos: (人体的)躯干;躯体。
⑲ cock: 粗俗的俚语,指阴茎。
⑳ balls: 睾丸。
㉑ Paterson: 帕特森市,位于美国新泽西州东北部,历来以制造业发达闻名。
㉒ Time: 时代广场(Time Square),素以"世界的十字路口"闻名,是位于美国纽约市曼哈顿区的著名繁华街区,因《纽约时报》总部大楼在此而命名。
㉓ Peyote: 仙人掌;佩奥特(一种致幻药),因其原料为仙人掌而得名。
㉔ teahead: (俚语)习惯于吸食大麻的人;瘾君子。
㉕ joyride: 驾车兜风,尤其指偷车并高速驾车兜风的犯罪行为。
㉖ Brooklyn: 布鲁克林区,位于美国纽约市西南部,素以典型地体现美国作为移民国家的文化而闻名。
㉗ ashcan: 垃圾箱;垃圾桶。
㉘ rantings: 厉声呵斥;咆哮;夸夸其谈。
㉙ kind king light: 亲切而至关重要之光。

who chained themselves to subways for the endless ride from Battery① to holy Bronx② on benzedrine③ until the noise of wheels and children brought them down shuddering mouth-wracked and battered bleak of brain all drained of brilliance in the drear light of Zoo,

who sank all night in submarine light of Bickford's④ floated out and sat through the stale beer afternoon in desolate Fugazzi's⑤, listening to the crack of doom on the hydrogen jukebox⑥,

who talked continuously seventy hours from park to pad to bar to Bellevue⑦ to museum to the Brooklyn Bridge⑧,

a lost battalion of platonic conversationalists jumping down the stoops off fire escapes off windowsills off Empire State⑨ out of the moon,

yacketayakking⑩ screaming vomiting whispering facts and memories and anecdotes and eyeball kicks and shocks of hospitals and jails and wars,

whole intellects disgorged in total recall for seven days and nights with brilliant eyes, meat for the Synagogue⑪ cast on the pavement,

who vanished into nowhere Zen⑫ New Jersey⑬ leaving a trail of ambiguous picture postcards of Atlantic City⑭ Hall,

suffering Eastern sweats and Tangerian⑮ bone-grindings and migraines⑯ of China under junk-withdrawal in Newark's⑰ bleak furnished room,

who wandered around and around at midnight in the railroad yard wondering where to go, and went, leaving no broken hearts,

......

《嚎叫》是诗人金斯堡的代表作,也是美国文学流派"垮掉的一代"最负盛名的代表作之一。20世纪50年代中期,金斯堡被哥伦比亚大学取消学籍之后,没有固定的职业,在冷战时期动荡不安的社会背景下仍与"垮掉的一代"的其他成员一道狂热地致力于诗歌创作,以反传统而具有争议的玩世不恭的诗歌内容与形式表达青年一代对美国经济萧条、政治迫害与社会暴力横行、贫富差距悬殊、民权有名无实等社会问题的极度失望与愤怒。《嚎叫》便是这一时期的代表作品,主题与核心内容如同诗作的标题画龙点睛的提示,是对诗人社会的沉沦与堕落所发出的歇斯底里的嚎叫,以此表达难以忍受的挫败感、失望与愤懑,希望能够以此唤起社会的醒悟,摆脱堕落与颓废的状况。

"垮掉的一代"诗人创作的一个显著特征,是将诗歌回归到口头艺术,即首先在公共场所朗诵诗歌,使得听众能够在现场感受诗人的朗诵与表演艺术,以此强化诗人及其诗歌所能够产生的社会效应,其

---

① Battery:巴特尼市,位于纽约曼哈顿西侧,比邻哈德逊河。
② Bronx:布朗克斯区,位于美国纽约市北部,居民以拉丁美洲后裔为主。
③ benzedrine:苯齐巨林(苯丙胺,一种合成的兴奋剂毒品),别名为安非他明。
④ Bickford's:指20世纪20年代以后在纽约市发展起来的比克福德连锁餐厅,尤其以其自助餐闻名。
⑤ Fugazzi's:指福加齐连锁餐厅。
⑥ jukebox:半自动唱片点唱机,可按照存入唱片的号码点播。
⑦ Bellevue:指纽约的贝尔雅综合医院。
⑧ Brooklyn Bridge:布鲁克林大桥,纽约市标志性建筑之一,也是工业革命的代表性成就之一,建成于1883年,全长1834米,是世界上第一座用钢材建造的桥梁,也是当时世界上最长的悬索桥。
⑨ Empire State:指位于纽约市曼哈顿区的帝国大厦(The Empire State Building),纽约市标志性建筑之一,建成于1931年,高443米,一直到20世纪70年代都是世界上最高的建筑物。
⑩ yacketayakking:拟声词,指喋喋不休、语无伦次的说话。
⑪ Synagogue:犹太教堂;犹太教徒的集会。
⑫ Zen:禅,禅宗,中国佛教宗派之一。
⑬ New Jersey:新泽西州,位于美国东北部。
⑭ Atlantic City:大西洋城,位于新泽西州,著名的旅游、疗养以及博彩业胜地。
⑮ Tangerian:丹吉尔的;丹吉尔(Tangier,或Tanger)为历史名城,位于摩洛哥西北部。
⑯ migraines:偏头疼。
⑰ Newark's:纽瓦克市,新泽西州首府,也是金斯堡的故乡。

次才是以现代出版方式将诗歌呈现给读者。《嚎叫》的创作与出版也不例外，在初稿创作完成之后，1955年10月13日晚，在位于旧金山一个废弃汽车修理厂的"垮掉的一代"诗人的活动场所"六画廊"(Six Gallery)，金斯堡激情澎湃，向在场的150余位听众，包括杰克·克鲁亚克与肯尼斯·雷克斯罗斯等"垮掉的一代"核心作家在内，朗诵了这首惊世骇俗并具有史诗般原始风格与艺术能量的长诗，大获成功。此后，该诗旋即出版发行，巨大的社会反响使得金斯堡一举成名。

该诗1955年首次出版时由三节构成，金斯堡同年又创作了短诗《〈嚎叫〉的脚注》("Footnote to Howl")，作为附加内容收入《嚎叫》。《嚎叫》的第一节约为全诗三分之二的篇幅，叙事者以第一人称咆哮般的节奏与气势对社会的衰败与堕落以及由此对青年一代而带来的毁灭性的恶果进行了控诉："我这一代最杰出的人才被疯狂毁灭"，无所适从，只能如行尸走肉一般堕落、吸毒、酗酒、乱性、醉生梦死。第二节、第三节与《脚注》的内容与节奏风格则明显有别于第一节，内容空灵抽象，在劫难之后期盼拯救，强调"世界是神圣的！灵魂是神圣的！"，"每个人都是天使！"。上文选自《嚎叫》第一节开篇的部分。

就该诗的风格而言，金斯堡师法19世纪美国诗人惠特曼，并推崇其同时代与惠特曼风格类似的威廉·卡洛斯·威廉斯等诗人，《嚎叫》采用了自由诗的诗行结构，与传统的英语韵体诗不同。诗句多为散文体的长句，犹如江河之水汪洋肆意，气势磅礴，但因节奏缺乏规律，可能在一定程度上削弱了诗篇的音乐性。

  思考题

1. If you take the selected passage of "Howl" as an example for a comparative study, in which way do you think that Allen Ginsberg was influenced by Walt Whitman?
2. When you look into the narrative traits of "Howl", whom do you think Allen Ginsberg intends to denote in his use of "we"?

 推荐作品

"A Supermarket in California" (1956)
"On the Conduct of the World Seeking Beauty against Government" (1956)

 参考资料

Graham, Caveney. *Screaming with Joy: The Life of Allen Ginsberg*. New York: Broadway Books, 1999.
Hyde, Lewis.ed. *On the Poetry of Allen Ginsberg*. Ann Arbor: University of Michigan Press, 1998.
Portuguese, Paul Cornel. *The Visionary Poetics of Allen Ginsberg*. Santa Barbara, California: Ross-Erickson, 1978.

（刘树森）

Robert Creeley (1926—2005)
罗伯特·克里莱

 **作者简介**

  罗伯特·克里莱,诗人、小说家、编辑。生于马萨诸塞州阿林顿市,父亲为医生,在克里莱幼年时亡故。在哈佛大学学习期间,他开始写诗并在校刊上发表;后转学至黑山学院,获得学士学位,并担任《黑山评论》的编辑。黑山学院是"黑山派"诗歌的发祥地,克里莱在此与查尔斯·奥森(Charles Olsen)以及罗伯特·邓肯(Robert Duncan)等诗人结识,并以其创作和理论使该学院成为20世纪50年代和60年代美国诗歌的一个中心。他们主张,诗歌创作应当采用与当时主流的格律诗体和广征博引的学院派诗风不同风格的"放射体",强调口语性和自然的音乐性,将诗人的"能"传递给自己的读者。克里莱曾周游北美、欧洲和亚洲的许多国家,并几度作为富布莱特专家在芬兰和尼泊尔等国家任教。1978年以后担任纽约州立大学诗歌教授。他的诗歌以风格清新、情真意切、文字简洁明快见长,在国内外出版60部诗集,可谓当代最高产的美国诗人。他的主要作品包括《诗选》(*Selected Poems*, 1976)、《记忆花园》(*Memory Gardens*, 1986)、《生与死》(*Life & Death*, 1998),以及《准时》(*Just in Time*, 2001)。其他作品还包括小说《岛》(*The Island*, 1963)。他曾荣获许多奖项,包括美国诗歌协会奖以及波林根奖。

 作品

Water Music

The words are a beautiful music
The words bounce like in water.

Water music,
loud in the clearing

off the boats,
birds, leaves.

They look for a place
To sit and eat—

no meaning,
no point.

作品赏析 克里莱的诗歌素来以高度聚焦的题材、短小精悍的诗篇、简洁清新的风格与崇尚诗歌的音乐性而见长,在美国诗坛独树一帜。他几乎从不使用恢宏的背景和完整的叙事结构,完全不同于惠特曼、T. S.艾略特、金斯堡,甚至弗罗斯特等各种流派的经典诗人的风格,尽管他也受到了金斯堡和威廉斯的影响。可以说,《水音乐》实际上是以浓缩而优美的方式体现了克里莱的诗歌创作原则。如该诗所示,克里莱可谓惜字如金,许多诗篇只有十几个字,但是着意追求意象的清新与诗句的音乐美感。他将他理想中的诗称为"水音乐",自然而然地使人感受到这一形象的比喻所昭示的诗的特性:在形式上,应当具有自然的音乐性,清澈如泉,舒展如云,追求内心与外在现实的和谐,不事雕琢,但沁人心脾;在内涵方面,诗文字面上"没有意义",也不追求表层的意义,而是期盼读者在诗人创造的美妙语境中感悟到诗的主旨。

思考题

1. What lyrical and musical qualities can you find in this poem?
2. Some people hold the idea that imagery plays a more important role in the poems whose narrative structure is loose. Do you agree or not? Why?

"The World" (1962)
"Time" (1957)
"The Whip" (1957)

参考资料

Foster, Edward Halsey. "Robert Creeley, Poetics of Solitude." *Understanding the Black Mountain Poets*. Columbia: University of South Carolina Press, 1994.

Mandel, Ann. *Measures: Robert Creeley's Poetry*. Toronto: The Coach House Press, 1974.

Wilson, John, ed. *Robert Creeley's Life and Work: A Sense of Increment*. Ann Arbor: University of Michigan Press, 1988.

(刘树森)

Sylvia Plath (1932—1963)

西尔维娅·普拉斯

 作者简介

  西尔维娅·普拉斯,诗人、小说家。生于马萨诸塞州波士顿市,父亲是大学教师,因病在普拉斯8岁时亡故。父亲之死对年幼的普拉斯影响巨大,使她对人生与死亡产生了复杂的想法,如同她后来在一首题为《爸爸》("Daddy", 1966)的诗中所描述的那样,爱、怀念、恐惧、失望、孤独、猜疑等形形色色的感受与概念交织在一起,充斥了她幼稚的心灵。这种复杂的心理特征始终与她形影不离,并导致其悲剧性的早逝。她在1950年获史密斯学院的奖学金前往该校学习,学业优异,但因没能入选参加哈佛大学的写作班而自杀未遂。后来在剑桥大学学习期间,她与英国诗人泰德·休斯(Ted Hughes)相爱并结婚,7年后先患产后忧郁症,随后发现丈夫婚后有私情,与之分居,由于贫困无法生活而产生绝望,自杀身亡。

  她生前出版的两部诗集是:《冬天的船》(*A Winter Ship*, 1960)、《巨人的石像及其他》(*The Colossus and Other Poems*, 1960)。她生命中的最后6个月是她的创作高峰期,平均每天写2—3首诗篇,由此将"自白派"诗歌推向其成就的巅峰。她去世以后出版的诗集包括《爱丽尔》(*Ariel*, 1965)和《渡湖》(*Crossing the Water*, 1971)。1982年,她的诗歌汇集出版,获得了普利策奖。普拉斯创作的唯一一部小说是《钟罩》(*The Bell Jar*, 1963),其中许多内容与她曾经自杀的生活经历相吻合,自传色彩充斥字里行间。在当今文学批评界,由于女权主义批评理论的发展,加上普拉斯独特的个性与命运,她正在获得越来越多的关注。

Last Words

I do not want a plain box, I want a sarcophagus①
With tigery② stripes, and a face on it
Round as the moon, to stare up.
I want to be looking at them when they come
Picking among the dumb minerals, the roots.
I see them already—the pale, star-distance faces.
Now they are nothing, they are not even babies.
I imagine them without fathers or mothers, like the first gods.
They will wonder if I was important.
I should sugar③ and preserve my days like fruit!
My mirror is clouding over—
A few more breaths, and it will reflect nothing at all.
The flowers and the faces whiten to a sheet.

I do not trust the spirit. It escapes like steam

---

① sarcophagus: 石棺;源于希腊语,常指古埃及、古希腊、古罗马雕刻精美的石制棺椁。
② tigery: 斑驳的;有花斑的。
③ sugar: 粉饰;美化;用甜言蜜语描述。

In dreams, through mouth-hole or eye-hole. I can't stop it.
One day it won't come back. Things aren't like that.
They stay, their little particular lusters
Warmed by much handling. They almost purr①
When the soles of my feet grow cold,
The blue eye of my tortoise② will comfort me.
Let me have my copper cooking pots, let my rouge pots
Bloom about me like night flowers, with a good smell.
They will roll me up in bandages, they will store my heart
Under my feet in a neat parcel.
I shall hardly know myself. It will be dark,
And the shine of these small things sweeter than the face of Ishtar③.

由于其特殊的生活经历，普拉斯创作的许多诗歌都以讨论死亡或者描述死亡的感受为主题，《遗言》可以说是一个范例。惠特曼、狄金森以及梭罗等19世纪美国诗人也热衷于在诗歌中思考死亡，但他们描写死亡的诗歌一般都不会给读者带来恐惧，因为他们的思考与描述主要是侧重于理性的探索，是一种空灵的想象。对他们来说，探索死亡就如同探索社会现实中其他需要探索的事物一样。相比之下，就主题而言，普拉斯则是侧重描述死亡对她作为一个活生生的人的意义，描绘她在"死亡"之后的感受。她对死亡的认识，甚至向往，在一定程度上是将其视为一种生命的力量，明显带有病态的特征，例如在《女拿撒勒》("Lady Lazarus"，1962)中将死亡称为"美妙的""艺术"，并描述自己死亡的过程。20世纪50年代和60年代的美国诗人乃至其他文学体裁的作家都或多或少具有这一特有的共性，如金斯堡、罗伯特·克里莱等作家以吸毒或者同性恋来表达对社会的不满和抗争。从技巧的角度来看，诗的张力主要是借助于诗中叙事者"我"跨越生死界限的对话，以及诗人巧妙地使用"石棺""沉默的物质""最原始的神明""夜色中的花朵"以及古巴比伦女神"伊师塔"等意象。这些代表死亡的意象也使得读者能够窥视普拉斯复杂而充满矛盾的内心世界以及她对生活和艺术所做的痛苦的探索。

 思考题

1. How and why does the poet attempt to universalize a depressing and even hopeless mood in the poem?
2. If you do not have to relate the subject-matter of the poem to the tragic life of Sylvia Plath, what thematic significance can you find in this poem?

"Daddy" (1962)
"Lady Lazarus" (1962)
"Ariel" (1965)
The Bell Jar: A Novel (1963)

---

① purr: 发出一种轻柔且颤动的声音。
② tortoise: 龟；常指在陆地生存的乌龟。
③ Ishtar: 伊师塔，古巴比伦和亚述神话中专司爱情、生育及战争的女神。

参考资料

Bloom, Harold, ed. *Sylvia Plath: Comprehensive Research and Study Guide.* Chelsea House Publishers, 2001.
Hughes, Ted. "On Sylvia Plath." *A Quarterly Review* 14.2 (1994): 1–10.
Newman, Charles. *The Art of Sylvia Plath.* Bloomington: Indiana University Press, 1970.

(林　斌)

第十七单元
Edward Franklin Albee (1928—2016)
爱德华·富兰克林·阿尔比

 作者简介

爱德华·阿尔比,20世纪美国最重要的剧作家之一。他幼年被富裕的养父母收养,但与他们(尤其是养母)的关系紧张。由于他的经历,他最成功的剧作也大多描写家庭关系。他在纽约及附近的西切斯特县(Westchester County)长大,中学时曾多次转学,后上过一年大学。他早年写过诗歌和一部未发表的长篇小说,而在50年代后期开始进行戏剧创作。阿尔比早期的独幕剧,包括《动物园故事》(*The Zoo Story*, 1959)、《贝茜·斯密斯之死》(*The Death of Bessle Smith*, 1960)、《沙盒》(*The Sand Box*, 1960)、《美国梦》(*The American Dream*, 1961)等,精辟地批评了所谓美国的价值观,奠定了他作为一位重要剧作家的地位。而他的第一部多幕剧《谁害怕弗吉尼亚·沃尔夫?》(*Who's Afraid of Virginia Woolf?* 1962;电影1966)是他最主要的作品之一。他以后的剧作包括《伤心咖啡馆之歌》(*The Ballad of the Sad Cafe*, 1963;电影1991;改编自卡森·麦卡勒斯的长篇小说)、《小爱丽斯》(*Tiny Alice*, 1964)、《微妙的平衡》(*A Delicate Balance*, 1966;电影1973年)、《盒子》与《毛泽东主席语录》(*Box and Quotations from Chairman Mao Tse-Tung*,"两部互相关联的剧作";1968)、《海景》(*Seascape*, 1975)、《三臂男人》(*The Man Who Had Three Arms*, 1983)、《一部关于婴儿的剧》(*The Play About the Baby*, 1998)、《三位高个女人》(*Three Tall Women*, 1999)、《山羊,或谁是西尔维亚》(*The Goat or Who Is Sylvia*, 2002)等。他的剧作大多具有荒诞戏剧的典型特征,剧中人物无法或不愿意与他人交流;他们内心孤独,得不到同情也并不同情他人。

阿尔比是一位严肃、博学的主流剧作家;与尤金·奥尼尔、田纳西·威廉斯、阿瑟·米勒一起,他能够跻身于美国一流的主流剧作家之列。但是,他也是一位具有高度反叛精神的剧作家,不断颠覆现行的社会价值观念。在他2002年的剧作《山羊,或谁是西尔维亚》中,他描写了建筑师马丁生活中的两天。马丁的事业如日中天;他与妻子斯蒂薇情投意合;他们夫妻得体地接受了儿子是同性恋的消息。后来,事情却急转直下:原来马丁一直在与一只他称为西尔维亚的山羊恋爱和做爱。剧终时,斯蒂薇拖着被她杀戮的山羊血淋淋地走上了舞台。像他以往的多部剧作一样,该剧也描写了家庭生活;但该剧对人兽恋的宽容,似乎预示着同性恋之类的关系已成为常态。对山羊的杀戮似乎也是祭祀的典礼:在古希腊,悲剧的原意是"山羊歌";这种类似似乎点明了该剧的当代悲剧意义。

阿尔比在当代的影响持久不衰。他的重要剧目不断重演,而他的剧作《家庭生活》(*Homelife*, 2004)也受到评论界的重视。这部剧作是45年前的《动物园故事》的前传,描写彼得在到动物园的前一天,与妻子安妮之间的故事。这部剧作也许是对阿尔比所有"家庭生活"戏剧的回归和总结。

Who's Afraid of Virginia Woolf?

GEORGE ... Now, take our son ...
HONEY   Who?
GEORGE Our son ... Martha's and my little joy!
NICK (*Moving toward the bar*)   Do you mind if I ...?
GEORGE No, no; you go right ahead.
MARTHA George ...
GEORGE (*Too kindly*) Yes, Martha?
MARTHA Just what are you doing?

GEORGE　Why, Love, I was talking about our son.

MARTHA　Don't.

GEORGE　Isn't Martha something? Here we are, on the eve of our boy's homecoming, the eve of his twenty-first birthday, the eve of his majority... and Martha says don't talk about him.

MARTHA　Just... don't.

GEORGE　But I want to, Martha! It's very important we talk about him. Now bunny① and the... houseboy or stud here, whichever he is... don't know much about junior, and I think they should.

MARTHA　Just... don't.

GEORGE　(*Snapping his fingers at* NICK) You. Hey, you! You want to play bringing up baby, don't you!

NICK　(*Hardly civil*)　Were you snapping at me?

GEORGE　That's right. (*Instructing him*) You want to hear about our bouncy boy.

NICK　(*Pause; then, shortly*) Yeah; sure.

GEORGE　(*To* HONEY) And you, my dear? You want to hear about him, too, don't you.

HONEY　Whom?

GEORGE　Martha's and my son.

HONEY　Oh, you have a child? (MARTHA *and* NICK *laugh uncomfortably*)

GEORGE　Oh, indeed; do we ever! Do you want to talk about him, Martha, or shall I? Hunh?

MARTHA　(*A smile that is a sneer*) Don't, George.

GEORGE　All rightie. Well, now; let's see. He's a nice kid, really, in spite of his home life; I mean, most kids'd grow up neurotic, what with② Martha here carrying on the way she does: sleeping 'til four in the P.M., climbing all over the poor bastard, trying to break the bathroom door down to wash him in the tub when he's sixteen, dragging strangers into the house at all hours...

MARTHA　(*Rising*) O. K. YOU!

GEORGE　(*Mock concern*) Martha!

MARTHA　That's enough!

GEORGE　Well, do you want to take over?

HONEY　(*To* NICK) Why would anybody want to wash somebody who's sixteen years old?

NICK　(*Slamming his drink down*)　Oh, for Christ's sake, Honey!

HONEY　(*Stage whisper*) Well, why?!

GEORGE　Because it's her baby-poo③.

MARTHA　ALL RIGHT!! (*By rote; a kind of almost-tearful recitation*) Our son. You want our son? You'll have it.

GEORGE　You want a drink, Martha?

MARTHA　(*Pathetically*) Yes.

NICK　(*To* MARTHA *kindly*) We don't have to hear about it ... if you don't want to.

GEORGE　Who says so? You in a position to set the rules around here?

NICK　(*Pause; tight-lipped*) No.

GEORGE　Good boy; you'll go far. All right, Martha; your recitation, please.

MARTHA　(*From far away*④) What, George?

GEORGE　(*Prompting*) "Our son..."

MARTHA　All right. Our son. Our son was born in a September night, a night not unlike tonight, though tomorrow, and twenty... one... years ago.

GEORGE　(*Beginning of quiet asides*) You see? I told you.

MARTHA　It was an easy birth...

GEORGE　Oh, Martha; no. You labored... how you labored.

---

① bunny: 小兔子，可爱的女郎；指 Honey。她26岁，长相平平，继承了父亲的一大笔遗产。Nick 因她怀孕才与他结婚，但她却对怀孕极为恐惧。在剧中，她因醉酒而一直在呕吐，对身边发生的事情不闻不问，是剧中最无心计的人物。最后，她克服了自己的恐惧，决心生育孩子，以承担起生活的责任。

② what with: 由于，因为。

③ poo: 表示轻蔑或者弱小的单词后缀。

④ From far away: 心不在焉。

MARTHA It was an easy birth ... once it had been ... accepted, relaxed into.
GEORGE Ah ... yes. Better.
MARTHA It was an easy birth, once it had been accepted, and I was young.
GEORGE And I was younger ... (*Laughs quietly to himself*)
MARTHA And I was young, and he was a healthy child, a red, bawling child, with slippery firm limbs ...
GEORGE ...Martha thinks she saw him at delivery...
MARTHA ...with slippery, firm limbs, and a full head of black, fine, fine hair which, oh, later, later, became blond as the sun, our son①.
GEORGE He was a healthy child.
MARTHA And I had wanted a child ... oh, I had wanted a child.
GEORGE (*Prodding her*) A son? A daughter?
MARTHA A child! (*Quieter*) A child. And I had my child.
GEORGE Our child.
MARTHA (*With great sadness*) Our child. And we raised him ...(*Laughs, briefly, bitterly*) yes, we did; we raised him...
GEORGE With teddy bears and an antique bassinet from Austria ... and *no nurse*.
MARTHA ... with teddy bears and transparent floating goldfish, and a pale blue bed with cane at the headboard when he was older, cane which he wore through... finally... with his little hands ... in his ... sleep ...
GEORGE ... nightmares...
MARTHA ... *sleep*... He was a restless child...
GEORGE ... (*Soft chuckle, head-shaking of disbelief*)... Oh Lord...
MARTHA ... sleep... and a croup tent... a pale green croup tent, and the shining kettle hissing in the one light of the room that time he was sick②... those four days... and animal crackers, and the bow and arrow he kept under his bed ...
GEORGE ... the arrows with rubber cups at their tip ...
MARTHA ... at their tip, which he kept beneath his bed ...
GEORGE Why? Why, Martha?
MARTHA ... for fear ... for fear of ...
GEORGE For fear. Just that: for fear.
MARTHA (*Vaguely waving him off; going on*) ...and ...and sandwiches on Sunday night, and Saturdays ... (*Pleased recollection*) ... and Saturdays the banana boat, the whole peeled banana, scooped out on top, with green grapes for the crew, a double line of green grapes, and along the sides, stuck to the boat with toothpicks, orange slices ... SHIELDS.
GEORGE And for the oar?
MARTHA (*Uncertainly*) A ... carrot?
GEORGE Or a swizzle stick③, whatever was easier.
MARTHA No. A carrot. And his eyes were green ... green with ... if you peered so deep into them ... so deep ... bronze ... bronze parentheses around the irises ... such green eyes!
GEORGE ... blue, green, brown ...
MARTHA ... and he loved the sun! ... He was tan before and after everyone ... and in the sun his hair ... became ... fleece.
GEORGE (*Echoing her*) ... fleece ...
MARTHA ... beautiful, beautiful boy.
GEORGE Absolve, Domine, animas omnium fidelium defunctorum ab omni vinculo delictorum.④
MARTHA ... and school ... and summer camp ... and sledding ... and swimming ...
GEORGE Et gratia tua illis succurrente, mereantur evadere judicium ultionis.⑤

---

① sun和son发音一样，构成双关语。在莎士比亚的剧作《哈姆莱特》中，也有类似的双关。
② croup：儿童哮喘；croup tent：治疗哮喘的氧气帐。烧一壶开水也是为了增加湿度，缓解哮喘症状。
③ swizzle stick：调酒棒。
④ Absolve, Domine, animas omnium fidelium defunctorum ab omni vinculo delictorum.：（拉）天主，求你赦免所有虔诚者的一切罪行（杨敦惠译，下同）。出自"安魂曲"中的"联唱曲"（Tractus）。拉丁语的"安魂曲"在西方极为流行，很多著名作曲家都为之谱曲，其中包括莫扎特、柏辽兹、凯鲁比尼、德沃夏克、威尔第、布鲁克纳、佛瑞、迪律弗莱等。
⑤ 本句出处同上：（拉）借着你的慈悲之助，希望他们能够逃脱惩罚式的判决。

MARTHA (*Laughing, to herself*) ...and how he broke his arm ... how funny it was ... oh, no, it hurt him! ...but, oh, it was funny ... in a field, his very first cow, the first he'd ever seen ... and he went into the field, to the cow, where the cow was grazing, head down, busy ... and he moo'd at it! (*Laughs ibid*①) He moo'd at it and the beast, oh, surprised, swung its head up and moo'd at him, all three years of him, and he ran, startled, and he stumbled ... fell ... and broke his poor arm. (*Laughs, ibid*) Poor lamb.

GEORGE Et lucis aeternae beatitudine perfrui.②

MARTHA George cried! Helpless ...George ... cried. I carried the poor lamb. George snuffling beside me, I carried the child, having fashioned a sling ... and across the great fields.

GEORGE In Paradisum deducant te Angeli.③

MARTHA And as he grew ... and as he grew ... oh! so wise! ...he walked evenly between us ... (*She spreads her hands*) ... a hand out to each of us for what we could offer by way of support, affection, teaching, even love ... and these hands, still, to hold us off a bit, for mutual protection, to protect us all from George's ... weakness ... and my necessary greater strength ... to protect himself ... and *us*.

GEORGE In memoria aeterna erit justus: ab auditione mala non timebit.④

MARTHA So wise; so wise.

NICK (*To* GEORGE) What is this? What are you doing?

GEORGE Shhhhh.

HONEY Shhhhh.

NICK (*Shrugging*) O.K.

MARTHA So beautiful; so wise.

GEORGE (*Laughs quietly*) All truth being relative.

MARTHA It was true! Beautiful; wise; perfect.

GEORGE There's a real mother talking.

HONEY (*Suddenly; almost tearfully*) I want a child.

NICK Honey ...

HONEY (*More forcefully*) I want a child!

GEORGE On principle?

HONEY (*in tears*) I want a child. I want a baby.

MARTHA (*Waiting out the interruption, not really paying it any mind*) Of course, this state, this perfection ... couldn't last. Not with George ...not with George around.

GEORGE (*To the others*) There; you see? I knew she'd shift.

HONEY Be still!

GEORGE (*Mock awe*) Sorry ... mother.

NICK Can't you be still?

GEORGE (*Making a sign at* NICK) Dominus vobiscum.⑤

MARTHA Not with George around. A drowning man takes down those nearest. George tried, but, oh, God, how I fought him. God, how I fought him.

GEORGE (*A satisfied laugh*)   Ahhhhhhhh.

MARTHA Lesser states can't stand those above them. Weakness, imperfection cries out against strength, goodness and innocence. And George tried.

GEORGE How did I try, Martha? How did I try?

MARTHA How did you ... what? ... No! No ... he grew ... our son grew ... up; he is grown up; he is away at school, college. He is fine, everything is fine.

GEORGE (*Mocking*) Oh, come on, Martha!

---

① ibid: 同前。指同前一条舞台说明一样，"自己发笑"。
② Et lucis aeternae beatitudine perfrui.：（拉）并享有永生的快乐。
③ In Paradisum deducant te Angeli.：（拉）愿天使引导你进入天堂。出自"安魂曲"中的"在天堂"（In Paradisum）。
④ In memoria aeterna erit justus: ab auditione mala non timebit.：（拉）正直的人将留存于不朽的回忆中；他将不畏邪恶的审讯（杨敦惠译）。出自"安魂曲"中的"阶台经"（Graduale）。
⑤ Dominus vobiscum.：（拉）愿主与你们同在。

MARTHA No. That's all.
GEORGE Just a minute! You can't cut a story off like that, sweetheart. You started to say something ... now you say it!
MARTHA No!
GEORGE Well, I will.
MARTHA No!
GEORGE You see, Martha, here, stops just when the going gets good ... just when things start getting a little rough. Now, Martha, here, is a misunderstood little girl; she really is. Not only does she have a husband who is a bog ... a younger-than-she-is bog albeit ... not only does she have a husband who is a bog, she has as well a tiny problem with spiritous liquors—like she can't get enough ...
MARTHA (*Without energy*) No more, George.
GEORGE ... and on top of all that, poor weighed-down girl, PLUS a father who really doesn't give a damn whether she lives or dies, who couldn't care less *what* happens to his only daughter ... on top of all that she has a *son*. She has a son who fought her every inch of the way, who didn't want to be turned into a weapon against his father, who didn't want to be used as a goddamn club whenever Martha didn't get things like she wanted them!
MARTHA (*Rising to it*) Lies! Lies!!
GEORGE Lies? All right. A son who would *not* disown his father, who came to him for advice, for information, for love that wasn't mixed with sickness—and you know what I mean, Martha!—who could not tolerate the slashing, braying residue that called itself his MOTHER. MOTHER? HAH!!
MARTHA (*Cold*): All right, you. A son who was so ashamed of his father he asked me once if it—possibly—wasn't true, as he had heard, from some cruel boys, maybe, that he was not our child; who could not tolerate the shabby failure his father had become....
GEORGE Lies!
MARTHA Lies? Who would not bring his girl friends to the house ...
GEORGE ... in shame of his mother ...
MARTHA ... of his father! Who writes letters only to me!
GEORGE Oh, so you think! To me! At my office!
MARTHA Liar!
GEORGE I have a stack of them!
MARTHA YOU HAVE NO LETTERS!
GEORGE And you have?
MARTHA He has no letters. A son... a son who spends his summers away... away from his family... ON ANY PRETEXT ... because he can't stand the shadow of a man flickering around the edges of a house...
GEORGE ... who spends his summers away... and he does! Who spends his summers away because there isn't room for him in a house full of empty bottles, lies, strange men, and a harridan who ...
MARTHA Liar!!
GEORGE Liar?
MARTHA ...A son who I have raised as best I can against ... vicious odds, against the corruption of weakness and petty revenges...
GEORGE ... A son who is, deep in his gut, sorry, to have been born ...

(BOTH TOGETHER)

MARTHA	GEORGE
I have tried, oh God I have tried; the one thing ... the one thing I've tried to carry pure and unscathed through the sewer of this marriage; through the sick nights, and the pathetic, stupid days, through the derision and the laughter ... *God*, the laughter, through one failure after another, one failure	Libera me, Domine, de morte aeterna, in die illa trelnenda: Quando caeli movendi sunt et terra: Dum veneris judicare saeculum per ignem. Tremens factus sum ego, et timeo, dum discussio venerit, atque ventura ira. Quando caeli movendi sunt et terra. Dies illa, dies irae, calamitatis et miseri-

compounding another failure, each attempt more sickening, more numbing than the one before; the one thing, the one *person* I have tried to protect, to raise above the mire of this vile, crushing marriage; the one light in all this hopeless ... *darkness* ... our SON.

ae; dies magna et amara valde. Dum veneris judicare saeculum per ignem. Requiem aeternam dona eis, Domine: et lux perpetua luceat eis. Libera me Domine de morte aeterna in die illa tremenda quando caeli mo vendi sunt et terra: Dum veneris judicare saeculum per ignem.①

(*End together*)

HONEY (*Her hands to her ears*)   STOP IT!! STOP IT!!

GEORGE (*With a hand sign*) Kyrie, eleison. Christe, eleison. Kyrie, eleison.②

HONEY   JUST STOP IT!!

GEORGE   Why, baby? Don't you like it?

HONEY (*Quite hysterical*) You ... can't ... do ... this!

GEORGE (*Triumphant*) Who says!

HONEY   I! Say!

NICK   Is this game over?

HONEY   Yes! Yes, it is.

GEORGE   Ho-ho! Not by a long shot. (*To* MARTHA) I've got a little surprise for you, baby. It's about sunny-Jim.

MARTHA   No more, George.

GEORGE   YES!

NICK   Leave her be!

GEORGE   I'M RUNNING THIS SHOW! (*To* MARTHA) Sweetheart, I'm afraid I've got some bad news for you ... for us, of course. Some rather sad news.

(HONEY *begins weeping, head in hands*)

MARTHA (*Afraid, suspicious*) What is this?

GEORGE (*Oh, so patiently*) Well, Martha, while you were out of the room, while the ... two of you were out of the room ... I mean, I don't know where, hell, you both must have been somewhere (*Little laugh*) ... While you were out of the room, for a while ... well, the doorbell chimed ... and ... well, it's hard to tell you, Martha ...

MARTHA (*A strange throaty voice*) Tell me.

GEORGE   ... and ... what it was ... it was good old Western Union③, some little boy about seventy.

MARTHA (*Involved*) Crazy Billy?

GEORGE   Yes, Martha, that's right ... crazy Billy ... and he had a telegram, and it was for us, and I have to tell you about it.

MARTHA (*As if from a distance*) Why didn't they phone it? Why did they bring it; why didn't they telephone it?

GEORGE   Some telegrams you have to deliver, Martha; some telegrams you can't phone.

MARTHA (*Rising*) What do you mean?

GEORGE   Martha ... I can hardly bring myself to say it. (*Sighing heavily*) Well, Martha ... I'm afraid our boy isn't coming home for his birthday.

MARTHA   Of course he is.

GEORGE   No, Martha.

MARTHA   Of course he is. I say he is!

GEORGE   He ... can't.

---

① 本段的拉丁语出自"安魂曲"中的"答唱曲"(Responsorium)，其中有叠句。译文为："天主，在那可怕的一天里，请从永恒的死亡中将我拯救出来：届时天地都将震撼，而你将以地狱之火来审判人世。惊惧与颤抖遍布我身，我极度害怕即将来临的审判与神怒。届时天地都将震撼。那一天，神怒之日，充满深刻的绝望与无限的悲惨，那将会是伟大而极其痛苦的一天。届时你将以地狱之火来审判人世。 天主，赐予他们永恒的安息吧，也让永续的光芒照耀他们"(杨敦惠译)。

② Kyrie, eleison. Christe, eleison. Kyrie, eleison.：(拉)主，怜悯我们吧。基督，怜悯我们吧。主，怜悯我们吧(译者不详)。出自"安魂曲"中的"慈悲经"(Kyrie，又译"垂怜经")。

③ Western Union：西联汇款。美国的特快汇款机构，现已遍布全球。

MARTHA He is! I say so!
GEORGE Martha ... (*Long pause*) ...our son is ... dead. (*Silence*) He was ... killed ... late in the afternoon ... (*Silence*) (*A tiny chuckle*) on a country road, with his learner's permit in his pocket, he swerved, to avoid a porcupine, and drove straight into a ...
MARTHA (*Rigid fury*) YOU ... CAN'T ... DO ... THAT!
GEORGE ...large tree.
MARTHA YOU CANNOT DO THAT!
NICK (*Softly*) Oh my God. (HONEY *is weeping louder*)
GEORGE (*Quietly, dispassionately*) I thought you should know.
NICK Oh my God; no.
MARTHA (*Quivering with rage and loss*) NO! NO! YOU CANNOT DO THAT! YOU CAN'T DECIDE THAT FOR YOURSELF! I WILL NOT LET YOU DO THAT!
GEORGE We'll have to leave around noon, I suppose ...
MARTHA I WILL NOT LET YOU DECIDE THESE THINGS!
GEORGE ... because there are matters of identification, naturally, and arrangements to be made ...
MARTHA (*Leaping at* GEORGE, *but ineffectual*) YOU CAN'T DO THIS! (NICK *rises, grabs hold of* MARTHA, *pins her arms behind her back*) I WON'T LET YOU DO THIS, GET YOUR HANDS OFF ME!
GEORGE (*As* NICK *holds on; right in* MARTHA'S *face*) You don't seem to understand, Martha; I haven't done anything. Now, pull yourself together. Our son is DEAD! Can you get that into your head?
MARTHA YOU CAN'T DECIDE THESE THINGS.
NICK Lady, please.
MARTHA LET ME GO!
GEORGE Now listen, Martha; listen carefully. We got a telegram; there was a car accident, and he's dead. POUF! Just like that! Now, how do you like it?
MARTHA (*A howl which weakens into a moan*) NOOOOOOOooooo.
GEORGE (*To* NICK) Let her go. (MARTHA *slumps to the floor in a sitting position*) She'll be all right now.
MARTHA (*Pathetic*) No; no, he is not dead; he is not dead.
GEORGE He is dead. Kyrie, eleison. Christe, eleison. Kyrie, eleison.
MARTHA You can*not*. You may not decide these things.
NICK (*Leaning over her; tenderly*) He hasn't decided anything, lady. It's not his doing. He doesn't have the power ...
GEORGE That's right, Martha; I'm not a god. I don't have the power over life and death, do I?
MARTHA YOU CAN'T KILL HIM! YOU CAN'T HAVE HIM DIE!
NICK Lady ... please ...
MARTHA YOU CAN'T!
GEORGE There was a telegram, Martha.
MARTHA (*Up; facing him*) Show it to me! Show me the telegram!
GEORGE (*Long pause; then, with a straight face*) I ate it.
MARTHA (*A pause; then with the greatest disbelief possible, tinged with hysteria*) What did you just say to me?
GEORGE (*Barely able to stop exploding with laughter*) I ... ate ... it. (MARTHA *stares at him for a long moment, then spits in his face*)
GEORGE (*With a smile*) Good for you, Martha.
NICK (*To* GEORGE) Do you think that's the way to treat her at a time like this? Making an ugly goddamn joke like that? Hunh?
MARTHA (*To* GEORGE, *coldly*) You're not going to get away with this.
GEORGE (*With disgust*) YOU KNOW THE RULES, MARTHA! FOR CHRIST'S SAKE, YOU KNOW THE RULES!!
MARTHA NO!
NICK (*With the beginnings of a knowledge he cannot face*) What are you two talking about?
GEORGE I can kill him, Martha, if I want to.
MARTHA HE IS OUR CHILD!
GEORGE Oh yes, and you bore him, and it was a good delivery ...
MARTHA HE IS OUR CHILD!

GEORGE　AND I HAVE KILLED HIM!

MARTHA　NO!

GEORGE　YES! (*Long silence*)

NICK (*Very quietly*)　I think I understand this.

GEORGE (*Ibid*) Do you?

NICK (*Ibid*) Jesus Christ, I think I understand this.

GEORGE (*Ibid*) Good for you, buster.

NICK (*Violently*) JESUS CHRIST I THINK I UNDERSTAND THIS!

MARTHA (*Great sadness and loss*) You have no right ... you have no right at all ...

GEORGE (*Tenderly*) I have the right, Martha. We never spoke of it; that's all. I could kill him any time I wanted to.

MARTHA　But why? Why?

GEORGE　You broke our rule, baby. You mentioned him ...you mentioned him to someone else.

MARTHA (*Tearfully*) I did not. I never did.

GEORGE　Yes, you did.

MARTHA　Who? WHO?!

HONEY (*Crying*) To me, You mentioned him to me.

MARTHA (*Crying*) I FORGET! Sometimes ... sometimes when it's night, when it's late, and ... and everybody else is ... talking ... I forget and I ... want to mention him ... but I ... HOLD ON ... I hold on ... but I've wanted to ... so often ... oh, George, you've *pushed* it ... there was no need ... there Was no need for *this*. I *men*tioned him ... all right ... but you didn't have to push it over the EDGE. You didn't have to ... kill him.

GEORGE　Requiescat in pace.①

HONEY　Amen.

MARTHA　You didn't have to have him die, George.

GEORGE　Requiem aeternam dona eis, Domine.

HONEY　Et lux perpetua luceat eis.②

MARTHA　That wasn't ...needed. (*A long silence*)

GEORGE (*Softly*) It will be dawn soon. I think the party's over.

NICK (*To* GEORGE; *quietly*) You couldn't have ... any?

GEORGE　We couldn't.

MARTHA (*A hint of communion in this*) We couldn't.

GEORGE (*To* NICK *and* HONEY) Home to bed, children; it's way past your bedtime.

NICK (*His hand out to* HONEY)　Honey?

HONEY (*Rising, moving to him*) Yes.

GEORGE (MARTHA *is sitting on the floor by a chair now*) You two go now.

NICK　　Yes.

HONEY　Yes.

NICK　　I'd like to ...

GEORGE　Good night.

NICK (*Pause*) Good night.

(NICK *and* HONEY *exit;* GEORGE *closes the door after them; looks around the room; sighs, picks up a glass or two, takes it to the bar*) (*This whole last section very softly, very slowly*)

GEORGE　Do you want anything, Martha?

MARTHA (*Still looking away*): No ... nothing.

GEORGE　All right. (*Pause*) Time for bed.

MARTHA　Yes.

GEORGE　Are you tired?

MARTHA　Yes.

---

① Requiescat in pace.：(拉)愿他灵魂安眠。

② Requiem aeternam dona eis, Domine. Et lux perpetua luceat eis.：(拉)天主，赐予他们永恒的安息吧，也让永续之光芒照耀他们（杨敦惠译）。出自"安魂曲"中的"领主曲"（Communio）。

GEORGE I am.
MARTHA Yes.
GEORGE Sunday tomorrow; all day.
MARTHA Yes. (*A long silence between them*) Did you ... did you ... have to?
GEORGE (*Pause*) Yes.
MARTHA It was ...? You had to?
GEORGE (*Pause*) Yes.
MARTHA I don't know.
GEORGE It was ... time.
MARTHA Was it?
GEORGE Yes.
MARTHA (*Pause*) I'm cold.
GEORGE It's late.
MARTHA Yes.
GEORGE (*Long silence*)   It will be better.
MARTHA (*Long silence*)   I don't ... know.
GEORGE It will be ... maybe.
MARTHA I'm ... not ... sure.
GEORGE No.
MARTHA Just ... us?
GEORGE Yes.
MARTHA I don't suppose, maybe, we could ...
GEORGE No, Martha.
MARTHA Yes. No.
GEORGE Are you all right?
MARTHA Yes. No.
GEORGE (*Puts his hand gently on her shoulder; she puts her head back, and sings to her, very softly*) Who's afraid of Virginia Woolf

                Virginia Woolf

                Virginia Woolf,

MARTHA I ... am ... George ...
GEORGE Who's afraid of Virginia Woolf ...
MARTHA I ... am ... George ... I ... am ...
(GEORGE *nods, slowly*)
(*Silence; tableau*)

CURTAIN

    《谁害怕弗吉尼亚·伍尔夫?》描写了一对知识夫妻的婚姻关系。46岁的乔治是某大学历史系的副教授,而他52岁的妻子玛莎则是该校校长的女儿。他们的婚姻生活虽有默契,但也时有摩擦。在某一周末晚上,他们之间的摩擦终于爆发。当天晚上,他们参加在玛莎父亲家举办的晚会归来,两人都有几分醉意。这时,玛莎告诉乔治,她已邀请尼克夫妇于凌晨二时来家中小酌。尼克年仅30岁,刚到该校生物系任教。他们到乔治家后,即成为主人夫妇吵架的听众,后来又参与了他们的争斗。玛莎一直认为乔治没有进取心,没有利用校长女婿的有利条件谋求升职。在酒精的作用下,她公开羞辱乔治。而乔治则利用自己能言善辩,与她反唇相讥。为了激怒乔治,玛莎故意与年轻且有魅力的尼克调情;而乔治的报复则是宣称他们的儿子死了:原来,他们一直想象自己有一个儿子,以作为自己失败的生活的安慰。剧作结束时,尼克夫妇离去,乔治和玛莎又只能单独面对对方。我们不知道在这场风波之后,他们会更好地珍惜对方,还是再也无法医治留下的创伤。

    本剧的剧名来自当天晚会上被加工过的一首童谣。童谣原名为"谁害怕大坏狼?"(Who's Afraid of the Big Bad Wolf?)"Wolf"与"Woolf"同音,所以就被这些知识界人士唱成了他们圈子内的人物:英国著名女作家弗吉尼亚·伍尔夫(1882—1941)。伍尔夫的作品描写人类的异化和生活的空虚,而她自己也有诸多心理问题,最后溺水自杀。原本的童谣其实也表现了生活中的恐惧和灾难:在童谣的三只小猪中,有两只因为未加防备而落入狼口。这首加工过的童谣似乎也是剧作的"主旋律",被剧中人物用来表达自己的情感。

阿尔比认为戏剧不仅是文学作品,而且也是音乐和雕塑作品。所以,他的剧作虽然以对话来推动情节的发展,但却具有很好的音乐感和节奏感。由于讲究雕塑的造型,阿尔比对于舞台道具也运用到了极致。在本剧中,主人公家中的家具就像他们的生活一样杂乱无章、拥挤不堪。

1966年,本剧被改编为一部十分成功的影片。著名影星理查德·伯顿和伊丽莎白·泰勒分别扮演男女主人公——35岁的泰勒扮演52岁的玛莎。影片未采用当时已经流行的"染印法彩色"(Technicolor),而摄制成纪录片风格的黑白片;在大多封闭的空间,以写实、不加修饰的风格,表现出主人公迷惘的内心世界。该片保留了原剧中大部分亵渎不敬和谈论性爱的语言,对当时的电影审查制度提出挑战。在发行时,华纳兄弟电影公司规定18岁以下人士只能在家长指导下观看,开了所谓"家长指导级影片"的先河,也促成了电影分级制度的实施。

本单元的课文选自《谁害怕弗吉尼亚·沃尔夫?》第三幕的结尾,也是全剧的结尾。本幕的题目为"驱魔"(Exorcism),也就是要驱除一切虚幻。幕启时,玛莎与尼克在一起,但显然他们之间的浪漫并不成功。乔治上场后,与玛莎一起揶揄尼克,称他为男仆。接着,他们玩起了"养孩子"的游戏。如选段所示,游戏逐渐变味,乔治与玛莎之间战火再起,而尼克也终于明白他们的儿子原来子虚乌有。最后,全剧在玛莎的"我害怕"声中结束。

思考题

1. Nick says: "I think I understand this." What does he understand?
2. What game is being played? Why do the characters play a game?
3. How are reality and illusion mixed up in the play?
4. Why do Martha and George keep fighting each other in front of Honey and Nick?
5. What human relationships does the play reflect?

The Zoo Story (1959)
The Ballad of a Sad Café (1963)
A Delicate Balance (1966)

🌹 **参考资料**

Bottoms, Stephen, ed. *The Cambridge Companion to Edward Albee.* Cambridge, UK; New York: Cambridge University Press, 2005.
—, ed. *Who's Afraid of Virginia Woolf?* Cambridge; New York: Cambridge University Press, 2000.

(程朝翔)

第十八单元
Toni Morrison (1931—   )
托妮·莫里森

 作者简介

托妮·莫里森,当代黑人女作家,生于俄亥俄州洛里恩(Lorain, Ohio)的工人家庭。1955年从康奈尔大学获得文学硕士学位后开始在大学任教。1958年和哈罗德·莫里森(Harold Morrison)结婚,1964年离婚。她带着两个儿子,一边进行文学创作,一边在兰登书屋担任编辑。1970年,莫里森的处女作《最蓝的眼睛》(The Bluest Eye)发表,大受评论界赞扬,成为其最有影响的作品之一。此后,莫里森集编辑、教授、作家于一身。作为编辑,她力推青年黑人作家的作品,所主编的《黑人之书》(The Black Book, 1974)被称为美国黑人史百科全书;作为教授,她先后在纽约州立大学、耶鲁大学和巴尔德学院教授英语,1989—2006年,她在普林斯顿大学讲授文学创作,创办了著名的普林斯顿工作室(Princeton Atelier),为有才华的学生同世界知名艺术家合作交流搭建平台;作为作家,她已发表11部小说:《秀拉》(Sula, 1974)、《所罗门之歌》(Song of Solomon, 1977)和《柏油娃》(Tar Baby, 1981),从不同的角度揭示了美国黑人的生活体验,《所罗门之歌》荣获美国图书评论家协会大奖。《娇女》(Beloved, 1987, 又译《宠儿》《爱娃》等),用魔幻现实主义和意识流的手法,通过黑人母亲宁肯亲手杀死亲生女儿也不愿让她回到奴隶制,以及被杀的女儿阴魂不散,18年后重返人间的故事,深刻揭露了奴隶制的残暴及其对美国黑人的影响,获得极大的成功,1988年获得普利策文学奖,也是作家1993年获得诺贝尔文学奖的主要作品。《娇女》、《爵士乐》(Jazz, 1992)和《天堂》(Paradise, 1998)被莫里森称为"爱的三部曲",同时也勾勒出美国黑人从奴隶制到20世纪下半叶的历史脉络。《爱》(Love, 2003)将过去与现在、爱与背叛交织在一起。《恩惠》(A Mercy, 2008)从不同人物的视角讲述北美殖民地时期不同肤色、不同身份的人的经历。耄耋之年的莫里森仍笔耕不辍,2012年,在她痛失爱子司雷德(Slade)一年半后,发表《家》(Home),关注朝鲜战争对黑人退伍军人造成的精神创伤;2015年,发表《上帝救救孩子》(God Help the Child),关注童年心理创伤对成长的影响。莫里森的作品构思独特,具有史诗般的震撼力;语言诗化,具有丰富的表现力;叙事诡秘,具有浓厚的感染力;心理揭示深刻,具有锐利的穿透力,深受评论界和普通读者的青睐。1993年,莫里森"以其富于洞察力和诗情画意的小说把美国现实的一个重要方面写活了",而荣获诺贝尔文学奖,成为获此殊荣的第一位黑人女性。1996年,她荣获美国图书基金会杰出贡献奖。

莫里森的文学成就不限于小说。在剧作方面,她创作了话剧《做梦的艾美特》(Dreaming Emmett, 1986)、歌剧《玛格丽特·加纳》(Margaret Garner, 2007)和《黛丝德蒙娜》(Desdemona, 2012)。她涉足儿童文学,同其小儿子司雷德合著《大盒子》(The Big Box, 1999)、《小人之书》(The Book of Mean People, 2002)、《蚂蚁还是蚱蜢?》(The Ant or the Grasshopper? 2003)、《小云儿与风姑娘》(Little Cloud and Lady Wind, 2010)。莫里森还发表过几部非虚构文集。

Beloved[①]

A FULLY DRESSED woman[②] walked out of the water. She barely gained the dry bank of the

---

[①]《娇女》第五章,原书共分三部分十八章,作家为三个部分编了1、2、3的序号,对各章却既不写标题,也不加序号。因为作家把本书献给了"六千万甚至更多"死于贩奴途中的黑人同胞,这种做法似乎暗指屈死的黑人无名无姓的状况。
[②] A fully dressed woman:《娇女》的主人公瑟丝不堪忍受奴隶主的污辱,克服重重困难,九死一生逃到了俄亥俄河北岸,同婆婆和先期到达的三个孩子相聚。28天后,奴隶主追来抓人。情急之下,瑟丝锯断刚刚会爬的女儿的喉咙,以免亲生骨肉再受奴役之苦。瑟丝从监狱出来后,以自己的身体作为代价,换来石匠为冤死的女儿刻"Beloved"一词墓碑。本章出现的这个女孩,一般认为就是瑟丝女儿的阴魂还阳,因为她名叫"Beloved",正好19—20岁,肤色光滑细嫩,语言能力低下,喜爱甜食,从(羊)水中来。然而,也有人认为她是那个被白人关在一间小屋当作泄欲工具的非洲女奴。

stream before she sat down and leaned against a mulberry tree. All day and all night she sat there, her head resting on the trunk in a position abandoned① enough to crack the brim in her straw hat. Everything hurt but her lungs most of all. Sopping wet and breathing shallow she spent those hours trying to negotiate the weight of her eyelids②. The day breeze blew her dress dry; the night wind wrinkled it. Nobody saw her emerge or came accidentally by. If they had, chances are③ they would have hesitated before approaching her. Not because she was wet, or dozing or had what sounded like asthma, but because amid all that she was smiling. It took her the whole of the next morning to lift herself from the ground and make her way through the woods past a giant temple of boxwood to the field and then the yard of the slate-gray house. Exhausted again, she sat down on the first handy place— a stump not far from the steps of 124④. By then keeping her eyes open was less of an effort. She could manage it for a full two minutes or more. Her neck, its circumference no wider than a parlor-service saucer, kept bending and her chin brushed the bit of lace edging her dress.

Women who drink champagne when there is nothing to celebrate can look like that: their straw hats with broken brims are often askew; they nod in public places; their shoes are undone. But their skin is not like that of the woman breathing near the steps of 124. She had new skin, lineless and smooth, including the knuckles of her hands⑤.

By late afternoon when the carnival was over, and the Negroes were hitching rides⑥ home if they were lucky—walking if they were not—the woman had fallen asleep again. The rays of the sun struck her full in the face, so that when Sethe, Denver and Paul D⑦ rounded the curve in the road all they saw was a black dress, two unlaced shoes below it, and Here Boy⑧ nowhere in sight.

"Look," said Denver. "What is that?"

And, for some reason she could not immediately account for, the moment she got close enough to see the face, Sethe's bladder filled to capacity⑨. She said, "Oh, excuse me," and ran around to the back of 124. Not since she was a baby girl, being cared for by the eight-year-old girl who pointed out her mother to her, had she had an emergency that unmanageable. She never made the outhouse. Right in front of its door she had to lift her skirts, and the water she voided was endless. Like a horse, she thought, but as it went on and on she thought, No, more like flooding the boat when Denver was born. So much water Amy⑩ said, "Hold on, Lu. You going to sink us you keep that up." But there was no stopping water breaking form a breaking womb and there was no stopping now. She hoped Paul D wouldn't take it upon himself to come looking for her and be obliged to see her squatting in front of her own privy making a mudhole too deep to be witnessed without shame. Just about the time she started wondering if the carnival would accept another freak, it stopped. She tidied herself and ran around to the porch. No one was there. All three were inside—Paul D and Denver standing before the stranger, watching her drink cup after cup of water.

"She said she was thirsty," said Paul D. He took off his cap. "Mighty thirsty look like."

---

① abandoned: 放任的，无拘无束的。
② trying to negotiate the weight of her eyelids: 试图解决眼皮的重量问题（想努力睁开眼）。
③ chances are: 后面跟一个完整的从句，指从句的情况很有可能出现。
④ 124: 瑟丝住房的门牌号，小说现在层面和部分往事的背景，小说的三个部分都从这座房子写起。有评论说，房子象征着贩运黑人的船，成倍数递增的门牌号码映射贩奴途中堆积如山的死尸。
⑤ 女孩耷拉脑袋(Her neck... kept bending...)，皮肤光滑细嫩，都表明她还是个婴儿。
⑥ hitch rides: hitchhike, 搭免费便车。
⑦ Sethe, Denver and Paul D: 小说中的三个主要人物。Sethe 18年前为了避免亲生骨肉受奴役之苦亲手杀死了女儿；Denver是Sethe在逃往北方的路上生的另一个女儿；Paul D原和Sethe及其丈夫在同一个种植园当奴隶，现在124号院和Sethe同居。这里，Paul D带Sethe母女参加狂欢节归来。
⑧ Here Boy: 瑟丝家养的狗。一说狗的失踪源于鬼魂的出现。
⑨ Sethe's bladder filled to capacity: 瑟丝膀胱充盈。瑟丝见到这个女孩时突然感到内急，还没到到厕所(She never made the outhouse.)就狂泻不止，让她不禁想起生孩子的情景。整个情景就是在暗示外来的女孩是瑟丝破羊水后生下的孩子。
⑩ Amy: 瑟丝向北方逃跑途中遇到的离家出走的善良穷白人女孩，帮助瑟丝治伤并为丹芙接生。她想当然地把瑟丝称为Lu。

The woman gulped water from a speckled tin cup and held it out for more. Four times Denver filled it, and four times the woman drank as though she had crossed a desert. When she was finished a little water was on her chin, but she did not wipe it away. Instead she gazed at Sethe with sleepy eyes. Poorly fed, thought Sethe, and younger than her clothes suggested—good lace at the throat, and a rich woman's hat. Her skin was flawless except for three vertical scratches① on her forehead so fine and thin they seemed at first like hair, baby hair before it bloomed and roped into the masses of black yarn under her hat.

"You from around here?" Sethe asked her.

She shook her head no and reached down to take off her shoes. She pulled her dress up to the knees and rolled down her stockings. When the hosiery was tucked into the shoes, Sethe saw that her feet were like her hands, soft and new. She must have hitched a wagon ride, thought Sethe. Probably one of those West Virginia girls looking for something to beat a life of tobacco and sorghum. Sethe bent to pick up the shoes.

"What might your name be?" asked Paul D.

"Beloved," she said, and her voice was so low and rough each one looked at the other two. They heard the voice first—later the name.

"Beloved. You use a last name, Beloved?" Paul D asked her.

"Last?" She seemed puzzled. Then "No," and she spelled it for them, slowly as though the letters were being formed as she spoke them.

Sethe dropped the shoes; Denver sat down and Paul D smiled. He recognized the careful enunciation of letters by those, like himself, who could not read but had memorized the letters of their name. He was about to ask who her people were but thought better of it. A young coloredwoman drifting was drifting from ruin.② He had been in Rochester four years ago and seen five women arriving with fourteen female children. All their men—brothers, uncles, fathers, husbands, sons—had been picked off one by one by one. They had a single piece of paper directing them to a preacher on DeVore Street. The War had been over four or five years then, but nobody white or black seemed to know it. Odd clusters and strays of Negroes wandered the back roads and cowpaths from Schenectady to Jackson. Dazed but insistent, they searched each other out for word of a cousin, an aunt, a friend who once said, "Call on me. Anytime you get near Chicago, just call on me." Some of them were running from family that could not support them, some to family; some were running from dead crops, dead kin, life threats, and took-over land. Boys younger than Buglar and Howard③, configurations and blends of families of women and children④, while elsewhere, solitary, hunted and hunting for, were men, men, men. Forbidden public transportation, chased by debt and filthy "talking sheets,"⑤ they followed secondary routes, scanned the horizon for signs and counted heavily on each other. Silent, except for social courtesies, when they met one another they neither described nor asked about the sorrow that drove them from one place to another. The whites didn't bear speaking on. Everybody knew.

So he did not press the young woman with the broken hat about where from or how come. If she wanted them to know and was strong enough to get through the telling, she would. What occupied them at the moment was what it might be that she needed. Underneath the major question, each harbored an-

---

① three vertical scratches：暗示瑟丝锯杀女儿时留下的伤口。
② A young coloredwoman... ruin.：一个年轻的黑人女孩外出流浪肯定是在逃避灾难。
③ Buglar and Howard：瑟丝的两个儿子，因为不堪忍受家里闹鬼，13岁时双双离家出走。
④ configurations and blends of families of women and children：由妇女和儿童构建组合的家庭。
⑤ talking sheets：指三K党成员，他们用白布裹身掩盖身份。

other. Paul D wondered at the newness of her shoes. Sethe was deeply touched by her sweet name; the remembrance of glittering headstone① made her feel especially kindly toward her. Denver, however, was shaking. She looked at this sleepy beauty and wanted more.

　　Sethe hung her hat on a peg and turned graciously toward the girl. "That's a pretty name, Beloved. Take off your hat, why don't you, and I'll made us something. We just got back from the carnival over near Cincinnati. Everything in there is something to see."

　　Bolt upright in the chair, in the middle of Sethe's welcome, Beloved had fallen asleep again.

　　"Miss. Miss." Paul D shook her gently. "You want to lay down a spell?"②

　　She opened her eyes to slits and stood up on her soft new feet which, barely capable of their job, slowly bore her to the keeping room. Once there, she collapsed on Baby Suggs'③ bed. Deven removed her hat and put the quilt with two squares of color over her feet. She was breathing like a steam engine.

　　"Sounds like croup④," said Paul D, closing the door.

　　"Is she feverish? Denver, could you tell?"

　　"No. She's cold."

　　"Then she is. Fever goes form hot to cold."

　　"Could have the cholera," said Paul D.

　　"Reckon?"

　　"All that water. Sure sign."

　　"Poor thing. And nothing in this house to give her for it. She'll just have to ride it out. That's a hateful sickness if ever there was one."

　　"She's not sick!" said Denver, and the passion in her voice made them smile.

　　Four days she slept, waking and sitting up only for water. Denver tended her, watched her sound sleep, listened to her labored breathing and, out of love and a breakneck possessiveness that charged her, hid like a personal blemish Beloved's incontinence⑤. She rinsed the sheets secretly, after Sethe went to the restaurant and Paul D went scrounging for barges to help unload.⑥ She boiled the underwear and soaked it in bluing, praying the fever would pass without damage. So intent was her nursing, she forgot to eat or visit the emerald closet.

　　"Beloved?" Denver would whisper. "Beloved?" and when the black eyes opened a slice all she could say was "I'm here. I'm still here."

　　Sometimes, when Beloved lay dreamy-eyed for a very long time, saying nothing, licking her lips and heaving deep sighs, Denver panicked. "What is it?" she would ask.

　　"Heavy," murmured Beloved. "This place is heavy."

　　"Would you like to sit up?"

　　"No," said the raspy voice.

　　It took three days for Beloved to notice the orange patches in the darkness of the quilt. Denver was pleased because it kept her patient awake longer. She seemed totally taken with those faded scraps of orange, even made the effort to lean on her elbow and stroke them. An effort that quickly exhausted her, so Denver rearranged the quilt so its cheeriest part was in the sick girl's sight line.

　　Patience, something Denver had never known, overtook her. As long as her mother did not

---

① glittering headstone：指瑟丝以身体作交换，为冤死的女儿买了一块墓石并让石匠在上刻下 Beloved 7 个字母，并漆成红色。
② You want to lay down a spell?：你想躺一会儿吗？ spell：一段时间。
③ Baby Suggs：瑟丝已故的婆婆。
④ croup：喉头炎。
⑤ (Denver) hid like a personal blemish Beloved's incontinence.：丹芙掩盖 Beloved 小便失禁之事，好像那是她自己的什么瑕疵似的。Beloved's incontinence 作动词 hid 的宾语。
⑥ Sethe 在一家餐馆工作，Paul D 靠打短工挣钱。

interfere, she was a model of compassion, turning waspish, though, when Sethe tried to help.

"Did she take a spoonful of anything today?" Sethe inquired.

"She shouldn't eat with cholera."

"You sure that's it? Was just a hunch① of Paul D's."

"I don't know, but she shouldn't eat anyway just yet."

"I think cholera people puke all the time."

"That's even more reason, ain't it?"

"Well she shouldn't starve to death either, Denver."

"Leave us alone, Ma'am. I'm taking care of her."

"She say anything?"

"I'd let you know if she did."

Sethe looked at her daughter and thought, Yes, she has been lonesome. Very lonesome.

"Wonder where Here Boy got off to?" Sethe thought a change of subject was needed.

"He won't be back," said Denver.

"How you know?"

"I just know." Denver took a square of sweet bread off the plate.

Back in the keeping room, Denver was about to sit down when Beloved's eyes flew wide open. Denver felt her heart race. It wasn't that she was looking at that face for the first time with no trace of sleep in it, or that the eyes were big and black. Nor was it that the whites of them were much too white—blue-white. It was that deep down in those big black eyes there was no expression at all.

"Can I get you something?"

Beloved looked at the sweet bread in Denver's hands and Denver held it out to her. She smiled then and Denver's heart stopped bouncing and sat down—relieved and easeful like a traveler who had made it home.

From that moment and through everything that followed, sugar could always be counted on to please her. It was as though sweet things were what she was born for. Honey as well as the wax it came in, sugar sandwiches, the sludgy molasses gone hard and brutal in the can, lemonade, taffy and any type of dessert Sethe brought home from the restaurant. She gnawed a cane stick to flax and kept the strings in her mouth long after the syrup had been sucked away. Denver laughed, Sethe smiled and Paul D said it made him sick to his stomach.

Sethe believed it was a recovering body's need—after an illness—for quick strength. But it was a need that went on and on into glowing health because Beloved didn't go anywhere. There didn't seem anyplace for her to go. She didn't mention one, or have much of an idea of what she was doing in that part of the country or where she had been. They believed the fever had caused her memory to fail just as it kept her slow-moving. A young woman, about nineteen or twenty, and slender, she moved like a heavier one or an older one, holding on to furniture, resting her head in the palm of her hand as though it was too heavy for a neck alone.

"You just gonna feed her? From now on?" Paul D, feeling ungenerous, and surprised by it, heard the irritability in his voice.

"Denver likes her. She's no real trouble. I thought we'd wait till her breath was better. She still sounds a little lumbar to me."

"Something funny 'bout that gal,"② Paul D said, mostly to himself.

---

① hunch：(口)预感。
② Something funny 'bout that gal.：There is something funny about that girl. 保罗·D原为奴隶，文盲，所以说话不合乎语法规范。

"Funny how?"

"Acts sick, sounds sick, but she don't look sick. Good skin, bright eyes and strong as a bull."

"She's not strong. She can hardly walk without holding on to something."

"That's what I mean. Can't walk, but I seen her pick up the rocker① with one hand."

"You didn't."

"Don't tell *me*. Ask Denver. She was right there with her."

"Denver! Come in here a minute."

Denver stopped rinsing the porch and stuck her head in the window.

"Paul D says you and him saw Beloved pick up the rocking chair single-headed. That so?"

Long, heavy lashes made Denver's eyes seem busier than they were; deceptive, even when she held a steady gaze as she did now on Paul D. "No," she said. "I didn't see no such thing."

Paul D frowned but said nothing. If there had been an open latch between them, it would have closed.

《娇女》根据真实的历史故事,用断断续续的叙述碎片,零散地将1873年辛辛那提城郊蓝石路124号的现实和1855年肯塔基州"甜蜜之家"种植园的过去交织在一起。在过去层面,黑人在奴隶制下遭受着非人的待遇:白人奴隶主教育白人少年列出黑人的"人的属性"和"动物属性",拿尺子测量黑人的身子。白人少年不仅把瑟丝(Sethe)毒打得皮开肉绽,甚至还残暴地践踏了她的母性权利,把她按倒在地,吸取她育婴的奶水。瑟丝历经千难万险,九死一生成功逃到北方。为了不让亲生骨肉再受奴役之苦,她亲手锯断自己刚刚会爬,还没有名字的女儿的喉咙。从监狱出来后,瑟丝用自己的身体换取石匠为冤死的女儿刻"娇女"(Beloved)墓碑。在现实层面,往事挥之不去,"娇女"冤魂不散,闹得奶奶因精神崩溃而死亡,两个哥哥离家出走,妈妈和妹妹备受孤立,郁郁寡欢。保罗·D(Paul D)到来,驱散鬼魂,和瑟丝同居,准备开始新生活。但是,"娇女"又以19—20岁少女的肉身还阳,回来索取母爱,使瑟丝几乎崩溃。最后,黑人集体赶走"娇女",帮助瑟丝迎接新生活。小说旨在揭示奴隶制无穷的贻害,所以着力表现过去对现实的影响。第五章讲述的是"娇女"的冤魂在瑟丝的住所徘徊18年后以肉身还阳的情景。这个女孩的出现打破了瑟丝、保罗·D和丹芙(Denver)三人间刚刚建立起的和谐,使得瑟丝不得不面对她一直努力忘却的过去,给予丹芙摆脱孤独的希望,疏远了保罗·D同瑟丝母女的关系。丹芙对女孩的同情、依恋和保护既是她孤独的表现,又是她对过去好奇的流露。但这个19岁左右的女孩既有血有肉,又缥缈恍惚,既天真无邪,又魔力无边,虽然有18年前那个冤死的女孩的一些特征,其身份并不确定。她也可能是死在贩奴船上被扔到大西洋的某个黑人少女的亡灵,抑或是现实中某个刚刚逃离白人虎口的姑娘,这个形象因此模糊了历史和现时,具有更为普遍的象征意义。

 思考题

1. What notable features of style have you noticed from this chapter?
2. What symbolic circumstances attend Beloved's return to Bluestone 124?
3. What characteristics or behaviors indicate that Beloved is like an infant?
4. Who does each of the other characters think Beloved is?
5. Why does Denver deny seeing Beloved pick up the rocker with one hand?

---

① rocker: 摇椅。Beloved表面弱不禁风,实际上却力大如牛,说明她是鬼魂。

The Bluest Eye (1970)
Song of Solomon (1977)
Sula (1974)

David, Ron. *Toni Morrison Explained: A Reader's Map to the Novels*. New York: Random House, 2000.
Grewal, Gurleen. *Circles of Sorrow, Lines of Struggle: The Novels of Toni Morrison*. Baton Rouge: Louisiana State University Press, 1999.
Peach, Linden. *Toni Morrison*. 2nd ed. New York: Macmillan, 2000.
Smith, Valerie, ed. *New Essays on Song of Solomon*. Beijing: Peking University Press, 2006.

（陈法春）

第十九单元
Maxine Hong Kingston (1940—)
汤亭亭

 作者简介

  汤亭亭,华裔女作家,出生于美国加利福尼亚,祖籍广东新会。儿时,她从母亲那里听到了许多有关中国的神话和传说,中国风俗习惯,以及祖先漂洋过海、寻找美国梦的传奇经历。她后来对这些故事题材进行了大胆改写,以丰富的文学想象力,创作了三部传记性长篇小说。虽然她对中国神话和传说的改写引起了不小的争议,但她蜚声美国文坛却是一个不争的事实。她的第一部长篇小说《女勇士》(*The Woman Warrior: Memoirs of a Girlhood Among Ghosts*,又译《女战士》),自1976年出版后,在美国多次获奖。该作品以独特的叙述视角和手法、丰富的文化形象和奇特的故事内容震撼了美国文坛,被翻译成二十多种文字。1995年,根据该作品改编的电视剧被评为该年度的美国最佳电视剧。她的第二部长篇小说《中国佬》(*China Men*,1980,又译《金山勇士》)、第三部长篇小说《孙行者》(*Tripmaster Monkey: His Fake Book*,1989),也都获得评论界的高度赞扬。这些作品的出版奠定了汤亭亭在当代亚裔作家群中的领先地位,也使她成为进入美国主流的亚裔女作家。她的小说被各种文选收录,也被当代美国文学、女性研究、族裔研究等课程列为必读书目,成为美国大学讲授最多、阅读最多的作品之一。

  2004年,汤亭亭又推出了第四部长篇小说《第五和平书》(*The Fifth Book of Peace*)。该作品以反战为主题,历时多年完成,出版后在文坛引起巨大反响。除了以上几部长篇小说,汤亭亭还创作了不少令人瞩目的散文、随笔和诗歌,例如散文集《夏威夷之夏》(*Hawaii One Summer*,1987)、随笔《穿过黑幕》(*Through the Black Curtain*,1988)、诗集《当诗人》(*To Be the Poet*,2002)、《我爱给生命留有宽广的余地》(*I Love the Broad Margin to My Life*,2011)。此外,她主编的反战文集《战争的老兵,和平的老兵》(*Veterans of War, Veterans of Peace*,2006),也同样引起广泛关注。她是目前美国最有影响的作家之一,先后获得"亚裔美国作家终身成就奖"(2006)、"美国文学杰出贡献奖"(2008),以及由美国总统颁发的"国家文学艺术勋章"(2013)等重大奖项和荣誉。

The Woman Warrior[①]

...

  Maybe that's why my mother cut my tongue. She pushed my tongue up and sliced the frenum. Or maybe she snipped it with a pair of nail scissors. I don't remember her doing it, only her telling me about it, but all during childhood I felt sorry for the baby whose mother waited with scissors or knife in hand for it to cry—and then, when its mouth was wide open like a baby bird's, cut. The Chinese say "a ready tongue is an evil."

  I used to curl up my tongue in front of the mirror and tauten my frenum into a white line, itself as thin as a razor blade. I saw no scars in my mouth. I thought perhaps I had had two frena, and she had cut one. I made other children open their mouths so I could compare theirs to mine. I saw perfect pink membranes stretching into precise edges that looked easy enough to cut. Sometimes I felt very proud that my mother committed such a powerful act upon me. At other times I was terrified—the first thing my mother did when she saw me was to cut my tongue.

---

① 本篇选自汤亭亭《女勇士》的第五章"羌笛之歌"(A Song for a Barbarian Reed Pipe)的前半部分。

"Why did you do that to me, Mother?"

"I told you."

"Tell me again."

"I cut it so that you would not be tongue-tied. Your tongue would be able to move in any language. You'll be able to speak languages that are completely different from one another. You'll be able to pronounce anything. Your frenum looked too tight to do those things, so I cut it."

"But isn't 'a ready tongue an evil'?"

"Things are different in this ghost[①] country."

"Did it hurt me? Did I cry and bleed?"

"I don't remember. Probably."

She didn't cut the other children's. When I asked cousins and other Chinese children whether their mothers had cut their tongues loose, they said, "What?"

"Why didn't you cut my brothers' and sisters' tongues?"

"They didn't need it."

"Why not? Were theirs longer than mine?"

"Why don't you quit blabbering and get to work?"

If my mother was not lying she should have cut more, scraped away the rest of the frenum skin, because I have a terrible time talking. Or she should not have cut at all, tampering with my speech. When I went to kindergarten and had to speak English for the first time, I became silent. A dumbness—a shame—still cracks my voice in two, even when I want to say "hello" casually, or ask an easy question in front of the check-out counter, or ask directions of a bus driver. I stand frozen, or I hold up the line with the complete, grammatical sentence that comes squeaking out at impossible length. "What did you say?" says the cab driver, or "Speak up," so I have to perform again, only weaker the second time. A telephone call makes my throat bleed and takes up that day's courage. It spoils my day with self-disgust when I hear my broken voice come skittering out into the open. It makes people wince to hear it. I'm getting better, though. Recently I asked the postman for special issue stamps; I've waited since childhood for postmen to give me some of their own accord. I am making progress, a little every day.

My silence was thickest—total—during the three years that I covered my school paintings with black paint. I painted layers of black over houses and flowers and suns, and when I drew on the blackboard, I put a layer of chalk on top. I was making a stage curtain, and it was the moment before the curtain parted or rose. The teachers called my parents to school, and I saw they had been saving my pictures, curling and cracking, all alike and black. The teachers pointed to the pictures and looked serious, talked seriously too, but my parents did not understand English. ("The parents and teachers of criminals were executed," said my father.) My parents took the pictures home. I spread them out (so black and full of possibilities) and pretended the curtains were swinging open, flying up, one after another, sunlight underneath, mighty operas.

During the first silent year I spoke to no one at school, did not ask before going to the lavatory, and flunked kindergarten. My sister also said nothing for three years, silent in the playground and silent at lunch. There were other quiet Chinese girls not of our family, but most of them got over it sooner than we did. I enjoyed the silence. At first it did not occur to me I was supposed to talk or to pass kindergarten. I talked at home and to one or two of the Chinese kids in class. I made motions and even made some jokes. I drank out of a toy saucer when the water spilled out of the cup, and everybody

---

① ghost: 这里指"洋鬼子"。

laughed, pointing at me, so I did it some more. I didn't know that Americans don't drink out of saucers.

    I liked the Negro students (Black Ghosts) best because they laughed the loudest and talked to me as if I were a daring talker too. One of the Negro girls had her mother coil braids over her ears Shanghai-style like mine; we were Shanghai twins except that she was covered with black like my paintings. Two Negro kids enrolled in Chinese school, and the teachers gave them Chinese names. Some Negro kids walked me to school and home, protecting me from the Japanese kids, who hit me and chased me and stuck gum in my ears. The Japanese kids were noisy and tough. They appeared one day in kindergarten, released from concentration camp, which was a tic-tac-toe mark, like barbed wire, on the map.

    It was when I found out I had to talk that school became a misery, that the silence became a misery. I did not speak and felt bad each time that I did not speak. I read aloud in first grade, though, and heard the barest whisper with little squeaks come out of my throat. "Louder," said the teacher, who scared the voice away again. The other Chinese girls did not talk either, so I knew the silence had to do with being a Chinese girl.

    Reading out loud was easier than speaking because we did not have to make up what to say, but I stopped often, and the teacher would think I'd gone quiet again. I could not understand "I." The Chinese "I" has seven strokes, intricacies. How could the American "I," assuredly wearing a hat like the Chinese, have only three strokes, the middle so straight? Was it out of politeness that this writer left off strokes the way a Chinese has to write her own name small and crooked? No, it was not politeness; "I" is a capital and "you" is lower-case. I stared at that middle line and waited so long for its black center to resolve into tight strokes and dots that I forgot to pronounce it. The other troublesome word was "here," no strong consonant to hang on to, and so flat, when "here" is two mountainous ideographs. The teacher, who had already told me every day how to read "I" and "here," put me in the low corner under the stairs again, where the noisy boys usually sat.

    When my second grade class did a play, the whole class went to the auditorium except the Chinese girls. The teacher, lovely and Hawaiian, should have understood about us, but instead left us behind in the classroom. Our voices were too soft or nonexistent, and our parents never signed the permission slips anyway. They never signed anything unnecessary. We opened the door a crack and peeked out, but closed it again quickly. One of us (not me) won every spelling bee, though.

    I remember telling the Hawaiian teacher, "We Chinese can't sing 'land where our fathers died.'" She argued with me about politics, while I meant because of curses. But how can I have that memory when I couldn't talk? My mother says that we, like the ghosts, have no memories.

    After American school, we picked up our cigar boxes, in which we had arranged books, brushes, and an inkbox neatly, and went to Chinese school, from 5:00 to 7:30 p.m. There we chanted together, voices rising and falling, loud and soft, some boys shouting, everybody reading together, reciting together and not alone with one voice. When we had a memorization test, the teacher let each of us come to his desk and say the lesson to him privately, while the rest of the class practiced copying or tracing. Most of the teachers were men. The boys who were so well behaved in the American school played tricks on them and talked back to them. The girls were not mute. They screamed and yelled during recess, when there were no rules; they had fist-fights. Nobody was afraid of children hurting themselves or of children hurting school property. The glass doors to the red and green balconies with the gold joy symbols were left wide open so that we could run out and climb the fire escapes. We played capture-the-flag in the auditorium, where Sun Yat-sen[①] and Chiang Kai-shek's[②] pictures hung

---

[①] Sun Yat-sen：孙逸仙，孙中山的字。
[②] Chiang Kai-shek：蒋介石。

at the back of the stage, the Chinese flag on their left and the American flag on their right. We climbed the teak ceremonial chairs and made flying leaps off the stage. One flag headquarters was behind the glass door and the other on stage right. Our feet drummed on the hollow stage. During recess the teachers locked themselves up in their office with the shelves of books, copybooks, inks from China. They drank tea and warmed their hands at a stove. There was no play supervision. At recess we had the school to ourselves, and also we could roam as far as we could go—downtown, Chinatown stores, home—as long as we returned before the bell rang.

At exactly 7:30 the teacher again picked up the brass bell that sat on his desk and swung it over our heads, while we charged down the stairs, our cheering magnified in the stairwell. Nobody had to line up.

Not all of the children who were silent at American school found voice at Chinese school. One new teacher said each of us had to get up and recite in front of the class, who was to listen. My sister and I had memorized the lesson perfectly. We said it to each other at home, one chanting, one listening. The teacher called on my sister to recite first. It was the first time a teacher had called on the second-born to go first. My sister was scared. She glanced at me and looked away; I looked down at my desk. I hoped that she could do it because if she could, then I would have to. She opened her mouth and a voice came out that wasn't a whisper, but it wasn't a proper voice either. I hoped that she would not cry, fear breaking up her voice like twigs underfoot. She sounded as if she were trying to sing though weeping and strangling. She did not pause or stop to end the embarrassment. She kept going until she said the last word, and then she sat down. When it was my turn, the same voice came out, a crippled animal running on broken legs. You could hear splinters in my voice, bones rubbing jagged against one another. I was loud, though. I was glad I didn't whisper. There was one little girl who whispered.

You can't entrust your voice to the Chinese, either; they want to capture your voice for their own use. They want to fix up your tongue to speak for them. "How much less can you sell it for?" we have to say. Talk the Sales Ghosts down. Make them take a loss.

We were working at the laundry when a delivery boy came from the Rexall drugstore around the corner. He had a pale blue box of pills, but nobody was sick. Reading the label we saw that it belonged to another Chinese family, Crazy Mary's family. "Not ours," said my father. He pointed out the name to the Delivery Ghost, who took the pills back. My mother muttered for an hour, and then her anger boiled over. "That ghost! That dead ghost! How dare he come to the wrong house?" She could not concentrate on her marking and pressing. "A mistake! Huh!" I was getting angry myself. She fumed. She made her press crash and hiss. "Revenge. We've got to avenge this wrong on our future, on our health, and on our lives. Nobody's going to sicken my children and get away with it." We brothers and sisters did not look at one another. She would do something awful, something embarrassing. She'd already been hinting that during the next eclipse we slam pot lids together to scare the frog from swallowing the moon. (The word for "eclipse" is *frog-swallowing-the-moon*.)① When we had not banged lids at the last eclipse and the shadow kept receding anyway, she'd said, "The villagers must be banging and clanging very loudly back home in China."

("On the other side of the world, they aren't having an eclipse, Mama. That's just a shadow the earth makes when it comes between the moon and the sun."

"You're always believing what those Ghost Teachers tell you. Look at the size of the jaws!")

"Aha!" she yelled. "You! The biggest." She was pointing at me. "You go to the drugstore."

"What do you want me to buy, Mother?" I said.

---

① The word for "eclipse" is *frog-swallowing-the-moon*.：汉语称"月食"为"蟾蜍吞月"。

"Buy nothing. Don't bring one cent. Go and make them stop the curse."

"I don't want to go. I don't know how to do that. There are no such things as curses. They'll think I'm crazy."

"If you don't go, I'm holding you responsible for bringing a plague on this family."

"What am I supposed to do when I get there?" I said, sullen, trapped. "Do I say, 'Your delivery boy made a wrong delivery'?"

"They know he made a wrong delivery. I want you to make them rectify their crime."

I felt sick already. She'd make me swing stinky censers around the counter, at the druggist, at the customers. Throw dog blood on the druggist. I couldn't stand her plans.

"You get reparation candy," she said. "You say, 'You have tainted my house with sick medicine and must remove the curse with sweetness.' He'll understand."

"He didn't do it on purpose. And no, he won't, Mother. They don't understand stuff like that. I won't be able to say it right. He'll call us beggars."

"You just translate." She searched me to make sure I wasn't hiding any money. I was sneaky and bad enough to buy the candy and come back pretending it was a free gift.

"Mymotherseztagimmesomecandy," I said to the druggist. Be cute and small. No one hurts the cute and small.

"What? Speak up. Speak English," he said, big in his white druggist coat.

"Tatatagimme somecandy."

The druggist leaned way over the counter and frowned. "Some free candy," I said. "Sample candy."

"We don't give sample candy, young lady," he said.

"My mother said you have to give us candy. She said that is the way the Chinese do it."

"What?"

"That is the way the Chinese do it."

"Do what?"

"Do things." I felt the weight and immensity of things impossible to explain to the druggist.

"Can I give you some money?" he asked.

"No, we want candy."

He reached into a jar and gave me a handful of lollipops. He gave us candy all year round, year after year, every time we went into the drugstore. When different druggists or clerks waited on us, they also gave us candy. They had talked us over. They gave us Halloween candy in December, Christmas candy around Valentine's day, candy hearts at Easter, and Easter eggs at Halloween. "See?" said our mother. "They understand. You kids just aren't very brave." But I knew they did not understand. They thought we were beggars without a home who lived in back of the laundry. They felt sorry for us. I did not eat their candy. I did not go inside the drugstore or walk past it unless my parents forced me to. Whenever we had a prescription filled, the druggist put candy in the medicine bag. This is what Chinese druggists normally do, except they give raisins. My mother thought she taught the Druggist Ghosts a lesson in good manners (which is the same word as "traditions").

My mouth went permanently crooked with effort, turned down on the left side and straight on the right. How strange that the emigrant villagers are shouters, hollering face to face. My father asks, "Why is it I can hear Chinese from blocks away? Is it that I understand the language? Or is it they talk loud?" They turn the radio up full blast to hear the operas, which do not seem to hurt their ears. And they yell over the singers that wail over the drums, everybody talking at once, big arm gestures, spit flying. You can see the disgust on American faces looking at women like that. It isn't just the loudness. It is the way Chinese sounds, chingchong ugly, to American ears, not beautiful like Japanese sayonara words with the consonants and vowels as regular as Italian. We make guttural peasant noise and have Ton Duc Thang names you can't remember. And the Chinese can't hear Americans at all; the language is too soft and western music unhearable. I've watched a Chinese audience laugh, visit, talk-story, and holler during a piano recital, as if the musician could not hear them. A Chinese-American, somebody's son, was playing Chopin①, which has no punctuation, no cymbals, no gongs. Chinese piano music is five black keys. Normal Chinese women's voices are strong and bossy. We American-Chinese girls had to whisper to make ourselves American-feminine. Apparently we whispered even more softly than the Americans. Once a year the teachers referred my sister and me to speech therapy, but our voices would straighten out, unpredictably normal, for the therapists. Some of us gave up, shook our heads, and said nothing, not one word. Some of us could not even shake our heads. At times shaking my head no is more self-assertion than I can manage. Most of us eventually found some voice, however faltering. We invented an American-feminine speaking personality, except for that one girl who could not speak up even in Chinese school.

She was a year older than I and was in my class for twelve years. During all those years she read aloud but would not talk. Her older sister was usually beside her; their parents kept the older daughter back to protect the younger one. They were six and seven years old when they began school. Although I had flunked kindergarten, I was the same age as most other students in our class; my parents had probably lied about my age, so I had had a head start and came out even. My younger sister was in the class below me; we were normal ages and normally separated. The parents of the quiet girl, on the other hand, protected both daughters. When it sprinkled, they kept them home from school. The girls did not work for a living the way we did. But in other ways we were the same.

We were similar in sports. We held the bat on our shoulders until we walked to first base. (You got a strike only when you actually struck at the ball.) Sometimes the pitcher wouldn't bother to throw to us. "Automatic walk," the other children would call, sending us on our way. By fourth or fifth grade, though, some of us would try to hit the ball. "Easy out," the other kids would say. I hit the ball a couple of times. Baseball was nice in that there was a definite spot to run to after hitting the ball. Basketball confused me because when I caught the ball I didn't know whom to throw it to. "Me. Me," the kids would be yelling. "Over here." Suddenly it would occur to me I hadn't memorized which ghosts were on my team and which were on the other. When the kids said, "Automatic walk," the girl who was quieter than I kneeled with one end of the bat in each hand and placed it carefully on the plate. Then she dusted her hands as she walked to first base, where she rubbed her hands softly, fingers spread. She always got tagged out before second base. She would whisper-read but not talk. Her whisper was as soft as if she had no muscles. She seemed to be breathing from a distance. I heard no anger or tension.

I joined in at lunchtime when the other students, the Chinese too, talked about whether or not she was mute, although obviously she was not if she could read aloud. People told how *they* had tried *their* best to be friendly. *They* said hello, but if she refused to answer, well, they didn't see why they had to say hello anymore. She had no friends of her own but followed her sister everywhere, although people and she herself probably thought I was her friend. I also followed her sister about, who was fairly normal. She was almost two years older and read more than anyone else.

I hated the younger sister, the quiet one. I hated her when she was the last chosen for her team and I, the last chosen for my team. I hated her for her China doll hair cut. I hated her at music time for the wheezes that came out of her plastic flute.

One afternoon in the sixth grade (that year I was arrogant with talk, not knowing there were going

---

① Chopin：肖邦，波兰作曲家、钢琴家。

to be high school dances and college seminars to set me back), I and my little sister and the quiet girl and her big sister stayed late after school for some reason. The cement was cooling, and the tetherball poles made shadows across the gravel. The hooks at the rope ends were clinking against the poles. We shouldn't have been so late; there was laundry work to do and Chinese school to get to by 5:00. The last time we had stayed late, my mother had phoned the police and told them we had been kidnapped by bandits. The radio stations broadcast our descriptions. I had to get home before she did that again. But sometimes if you loitered long enough in the schoolyard, the other children would have gone home and you could play with the equipment before the office took it away. We were chasing one another through the playground and in and out of the basement, where the playroom and lavatory were. During air raid drills (it was during the Korean War, which you knew about because every day the front page of the newspaper printed a map of Korea with the top part red and going up and down like a window shade), we curled up in this basement. Now everyone was gone. The playroom was army green and had nothing in it but a long trough with drinking spigots in rows. Pipes across the ceiling led to the drinking fountains and to the toilets in the next room. When someone flushed you could hear the water and other matter, which the children named, running inside the big pipe above the drinking spigots. There was one playroom for girls next to the girls' lavatory and one playroom for boys next to the boys' lavatory. The stalls were open and the toilets had no lids, by which we knew that ghosts have no sense of shame or privacy.

 Inside the playroom the lightbulbs in cages had already been turned off. Daylight came in x-patterns through the caging at the windows. I looked out and, seeing no one in the schoolyard, ran outside to climb the fire escape upside down, hanging on to the metal stairs with fingers and toes.

 I did a flip off the fire escape and ran across the school-yard. The day was a great eye, and it was not paying much attention to me now. I could disappear with the sun; I could turn quickly sideways and slip into a different world. It seemed I could run faster at this time, and by evening I would be able to fly. As the afternoon wore on we could run into the forbidden places—the boys' big yard, the boys' playroom. We could go into the boys' lavatory and look at the urinals. The only time during school hours I had crossed the boys' yard was when a flatbed truck with a giant thing covered with canvas and tied down with ropes had parked across the street. The children had told one another that it was a gorilla in captivity; we couldn't decide whether the sign said "Trail of the Gorilla" or "Trial of the Gorilla." The thing was as big as a house. The teachers couldn't stop us from hysterically rushing to the fence and clinging to the wire mesh. Now I ran across the boys' yard clear to the Cyclone fence and thought about the hair that I had seen sticking out of the canvas. It was going to be summer soon, so you could feel that freedom coming on too.

 I ran back into the girls' yard, and there was the quiet sister all by herself. I ran past her, and she followed me into the girls' lavatory. My footsteps rang hard against cement and tile because of the taps I had nailed into my shoes. Her footsteps were soft, padding after me. There was no one in the lavatory but the two of us. I ran all around the rows of twenty-five open stalls to make sure of that. No sisters. I think we must have been playing hide-and-go-seek. She was not good at hiding by herself and usually followed her sister; they'd hide in the same place. They must have gotten separated. In this growing twilight, a child could hide and never be found.

 I stopped abruptly in front of the sinks, and she came running toward me before she could stop herself, so that she almost collided with me. I walked closer. She backed away, puzzlement, then alarm in her eyes.

 "You're going to talk," I said, my voice steady and normal, as it is talking to the familiar, the weak, and the small. "I am going to make you talk, you sissy-girl." She stopped backing away and stood fixed.

I looked into her face so I could hate it close up. She wore black bangs, and her cheeks were pink and white. She was baby soft. I thought that I could put my thumb on her nose and push it bonelessly in, indent her face. I could poke dimples into her cheeks. I could work her face around like dough. She stood still, and I did not want to look at her face anymore; I hated fragility. I walked around her, looked her up and down the way the Mexican and Negro girls did when they fought, so tough. I hated her weak neck, the way it did not support her head but let it droop; her head would fall backward. I stared at the curve of her nape. I wished I was able to see what my own neck looked like from the back and sides. I hoped it did not look like hers; I wanted a stout neck. I grew my hair long to hide it in case it was a flower-stem neck. I walked around to the front of her to hate her face some more.

I reached up and took the fatty part of her cheek, not dough, but meat, between my thumb and finger. This close, and I saw no pores. "Talk," I said. "Are you going to talk?" Her skin was fleshy, like squid out of which the glassy blades of bones had been pulled. I wanted tough skin, hard brown skin. I had callused my hands; I had scratched dirt to blacken the nails, which I cut straight across to make stubby fingers. I gave her face a squeeze. "Talk." When I let go, the pink rushed back into my white thumbprint on her skin. I walked around to her side. "Talk!" I shouted into the side of her head. Her straight hair hung, the same all these years, no ringlets or braids or permanents. I squeezed her other cheek. "Are you? Huh? Are you going to talk?" She tried to shake her head, but I had hold of her face. She had no muscles to jerk away. Her skin seemed to stretch. I let go in horror. What if it came away in my hand? "No, huh?" I said, rubbing the touch of her off my fingers. "Say 'No.' then," I said. I gave her another pinch and a twist. "Say 'No.'" She shook her head, her straight hair turning with her head, not swinging side to side like the pretty girls'. She was so neat. Her neatness bothered me. I hated the way she folded the wax paper from her lunch; she did not wad her brown paper bag and her school papers. I hated her clothes—the blue pastel cardigan, the white blouse with the collar that lay flat over the cardigan, the homemade flat, cotton skirt she wore when everybody else was wearing flared skirts. I hated pastels; I would wear black always. I squeezed again, harder, even though her cheek had a weak rubbery feeling I did not like. I squeezed one cheek, then the other, back and forth until the tears ran out of her eyes as if I had pulled them out. "Stop crying," I said, but although she habitually followed me around, she did not obey. Her eyes dripped; her nose dripped. She wiped her eyes with her papery fingers. The skin on her hands and arms seemed powdery-dry, like tracing paper, onion skin. I hated her fingers. I could snap them like breadsticks. I pushed her hands down. "Say 'Hi,'" I said. "'Hi.' Like that. Say your name. Go ahead. Say it. Or are you stupid? You're so stupid, you don't know your own name, is that it? When I say, 'What's your name?' you just blurt it out, o.k.? What's your name?" Last year the whole class had laughed at a boy who couldn't fill out a form because he didn't know his father's name. The teacher sighed, exasperated, and was very sarcastic, "Don't you notice things? What does your mother call him?" she said. The class laughed at how dumb he was not to notice things. "She calls him father of me," he said. Even we laughed, although we knew that his mother did not call his father by name, and a son does not know his father's name. We laughed and were relieved that our parents had had the foresight to tell us some names we could give the teachers. "If you're not stupid," I said to the quiet girl, "what's your name?" She shook her head, and some hair caught in the tears; wet black hair stuck to the side of the pink and white face. I reached up (she was taller than I) and took a strand of hair. I pulled it. "Well, then, let's honk your hair," I said. "Honk. Honk." Then I pulled the other side—"ho-o-n-nk"—a long pull; "ho-o-n-n-nk"—a longer pull. I could see her little white ears, like white cutworms curled underneath the hair. "Talk!" I yelled into each cutworm.

I looked right at her. "I know you talk," I said. "I've heard you." Her eyebrows flew up. Something in those black eyes was startled, and I pursued it. "I was walking past your house when you didn't know I was there. I heard you yell in English and in Chinese. You weren't just talking. You were shouting. I heard you shout. You were saying, 'Where are you?' Say that again. Go ahead, just the way you did at home." I yanked harder on the hair, but steadily, not jerking. I did not want to pull it out. "Go ahead. Say, 'Where are you?' Say it loud enough for your sister to come. Call her. Make her come help you. Call her name. I'll stop if she comes. So call. Go ahead."

She shook her head, her mouth curved down, crying. I could see her tiny white teeth, baby teeth. I wanted to grow big strong yellow teeth. "You do have a tongue," I said. "So use it." I pulled the hair at her temples, pulled the tears out of her eyes. "Say, 'Ow,'" I said. "Just 'Ow.' Say, 'Let go.' Go ahead. Say it. I'll honk you again if you don't say, 'Let me alone.' Say, 'Leave me alone,' and I'll let you go. I will. I'll let go if you say it. You can stop this anytime you want to, you know. All you have to do is tell me to stop. Just say, 'Stop.' You're just asking for it, aren't you? You're just asking for another honk. Well then, I'll have to give you another honk. Say, 'Stop.'" But she didn't. I had to pull again and again.

Sounds did come out of her mouth, sobs, chokes, noises that were almost words. Snot ran out of her nose. She tried to wipe it on her hands, but there was too much of it. She used her sleeve. "You're disgusting," I told her. "Look at you, snot streaming down your nose, and you won't say a word to stop it. You're such a nothing." I moved behind her and pulled the hair growing out of her weak neck. I let go. I stood silent for a long time. Then I screamed, "Talk!" I would scare the words out of her. If she had had little bound feet, the toes twisted under the balls, I would have jumped up and landed on them—crunch!—stomped on them with my iron shoes. She cried hard, sobbing aloud. "Cry, 'Mama,'" I said. "Come on. Cry, 'Mama.' Say, 'Stop it.'"

I put my finger on her pointed chin. "I don't like you. I don't like the weak little toots you make on your flute. Wheeze. Wheeze. I don't like the way you don't swing at the ball. I don't like the way you're the last one chosen. I don't like the way you can't make a fist for tetherball. Why don't you make a fist? Come on. Get tough. Come on. Throw fists." I pushed at her long hands; they swung limply at her sides. Her fingers were so long, I thought maybe they had an extra joint. They couldn't possibly make fists like other people's. "Make a fist," I said. "Come on. Just fold those fingers up; fingers on the inside, thumbs on the outside. Say something. Honk me back. You're so tall, and you let me pick on you."

"Would you like a hanky? I can't get you one with embroidery on it or crocheting along the edges, but I'll get you some toilet paper if you tell me to. Go ahead. Ask me. I'll get it for you if you ask." She did not stop crying. "Why don't you scream, 'Help'?" I suggested. "Say, 'Help.' Go ahead." She cried on. "O.K. O.K. Don't talk. Just scream, and I'll let you go. Won't that feel good? Go ahead. Like this." I screamed, not too loudly. My voice hit the tile and rang it as if I had thrown a rock at it. The stalls opened wider and the toilets wider and darker. Shadows leaned at angles I had not seen before. It was very late. Maybe a janitor had locked me in with this girl for the night. Her black eyes blinked and stared, blinked and stared. I felt dizzy from hunger. We had been in this lavatory together forever. My mother would call the police again if I didn't bring my sister home soon. "I'll let you go if you say just one word," I said. "You can even say, 'a' or 'the,' and I'll let you go. Come on. Please." She didn't shake her head anymore, only cried steadily, so much water coming out of her. I could see the two duct holes where the tears welled out. Quarts of tears but no words. I grabbed her by the shoulder. I could feel bones. The light was coming in queerly through the frosted glass with the chicken wire embedded in it. Her crying was like an animal's—a seal's—and it echoed around the basement. "Do you want to stay here all night?" I asked. "Your mother is wondering what happened to her baby. You wouldn't want to have her mad at you. You'd better say something." I shook her shoulder. I pulled her hair again. I squeezed her face. "Come on! Talk! Talk! Talk!" She didn't seem to feel it anymore when I pulled her hair. "There's nobody here but you and me. This isn't a classroom or a playground or a crowd. I'm just one person. You can talk in front of one person. Don't make me pull harder and harder until you talk." But her hair seemed to stretch; she did not say a word. "I'm going to pull harder. Don't make me pull anymore, or your hair will come out and you're going to be bald. Do you want to be bald? You don't want to be bald, do you?"

Far away, coming from the edge of town, I heard whistles blow. The cannery was changing shifts, letting out the afternoon people, and still we were here at school. It was a sad sound—work done. The air was lonelier after the sound died.

"Why won't you talk?" I started to cry. What if I couldn't stop, and everyone would want to know what happened? "Now look what you've done," I scolded. "You're going to pay for this. I want to know why. And you're going to tell me why. You don't see I'm trying to help you out, do you? Do you want to be like this, dumb (do you know what dumb means?), your whole life? Don't you ever want to be a cheerleader①? Or a pompon girl②? What are you going to do for a living? Yeah, you're going to have to work because you can't be a housewife. Somebody has to marry you before you can be a housewife. And you, you are a plant. Do you know that? That's all you are if you don't talk. If you don't talk, you can't have a personality. You'll have no personality and no hair. You've got to let people know you have a personality and a brain. You think somebody is going to take care of you all your stupid life? You think you'll always have your big sister? You think somebody's going to marry you, is that it? Well, you're not the type that gets dates, let alone gets married. Nobody's going to notice you. And you have to talk for interviews, speak right up in front of the boss. Don't you know that? You're so dumb. Why do I waste my time on you?" Sniffling and snorting, I couldn't stop crying and talking at the same time. I kept wiping my nose on my arm, my sweater lost somewhere (probably not worn because my mother said to wear a sweater). It seemed as if I had spent my life in that basement, doing the worst thing I had yet done to another person. "I'm doing this for your own good," I said. "Don't you dare tell anyone I've been bad to you. Talk. Please talk."

I was getting dizzy from the air I was gulping. Her sobs and my sobs were bouncing wildly off the tile, sometimes together, sometimes alternating. "I don't understand why you won't say just one word," I cried, clenching my teeth. My knees were shaking, and I hung on to her hair to stand up. Another time I'd stayed too late, I had had to walk around two Negro kids who were bonking each other's head on the concrete. I went back later to see if the concrete had cracks in it. "Look. I'll give you something if you talk. I'll give you my pencil box. I'll buy you some candy. O.K.? What do you want? Tell me. Just say it, and I'll give it to you. Just say, 'yes,' or, 'O.K.,' or, 'Baby Ruth.'" But she didn't want anything.

I had stopped pinching her cheek because I did not like the feel of her skin. I would go crazy if it came away in my hands. "I skinned her," I would have to confess.

Suddenly I heard footsteps hurrying through the basement, and her sister ran into the lavatory calling her name. "Oh, there you are," I said. "We've been waiting for you. I was only trying to teach her to talk. She wouldn't cooperate, though." Her sister went into one of the stalls and got handfuls of toilet paper and wiped her off. Then we found my sister, and we walked home together. "Your family really ought to force her to speak," I advised all the way home. "You mustn't pamper her."

The world is sometimes just, and I spent the next eighteen months sick in bed with a mysterious illness. There was no pain and no symptoms, though the middle line in my left palm broke in two.

---

① cheerleader：(体育比赛时的)啦啦队队长。
② pompon girl：擅长交际的女孩。

Instead of starting junior high school, I lived like the Victorian recluses I read about. I had a rented hospital bed in the living room, where I watched soap operas on t.v., and my family cranked me up and down. I saw no one but my family, who took good care of me. I could have no visitors, no other relatives, no villagers. My bed was against the west window, and I watched the seasons change the peach tree. I had a bell to ring for help. I used a bedpan. It was the best year and a half of my life. Nothing happened.

But one day my mother, the doctor, said, "You're ready to get up today. It's time to get up and go to school." I walked about outside to get my legs working, leaning on a staff I cut from the peach tree. The sky and trees, the sun were immense—no longer framed by a window, no longer grayed with a fly screen. I sat down on the sidewalk in amazement—the night, the stars. But at school I had to figure out again how to talk. I met again the poor girl I had tormented. She had not changed. She wore the same clothes, hair cut, and manner as when we were in elementary school, no make-up on the pink and white face, while the other Asian girls were starting to tape their eyelids. She continued to be able to read aloud. But there was hardly any reading aloud anymore, less and less as we got into high school.

I was wrong about nobody taking care of her. Her sister became a clerk-typist and stayed unmarried. They lived with their mother and father. She did not have to leave the house except to go to the movies. She was supported. She was protected by her family, as they would normally have done in China if they could have afforded it, not sent off to school with strangers, ghosts, boys.

We have so many secrets to hold in. Our sixth grade teacher, who liked to explain things to children, let us read our files. My record shows that I flunked kindergarten and in first grade had no IQ—a zero IQ①. I did remember the first grade teacher calling out during a test, while students marked X's on a girl or a boy or a dog, which I covered with black. First grade was when I discovered eye control; with my seeing I could shrink the teacher down to a height of one inch, gesticulating and mouthing on the horizon. I lost this power in sixth grade for lack of practice, the teacher a generous man. "Look at your family's old addresses and think about how you've moved," he said. I looked at my parents' aliases and their birthdays, which variants I knew. But when I saw Father's occupations I exclaimed, "Hey, he wasn't a farmer, he was a ..." He had been a gambler. My throat cut off the word—silence in front of the most understanding teacher. There were secrets never to be said in front of the ghosts, immigration secrets whose telling could get us sent back to China.

...

　　《女勇士》是一部回忆录式的成长小说。全书分五个部分："无名女人""白虎山峰""巫医""西宫门外""羌笛之歌"。每个部分都有一位女主角，都与叙述者的成长有关。在前三部分中，叙述者"我"记述了儿时从妈妈那里听到的几个故事：在中国老家，她的姑姑因为"私通"，分娩的当天被村里人抄了家，抱着婴儿跳进家中的水井，从此，她的名字成为家族中的忌讳；作者想象自己成为故事中的花木兰，进白虎山修炼15年，然后带兵打仗报了国仇家恨，回到故乡成了英雄；母亲英兰年轻时是一个勇敢而独立的女性，她在旧中国有过学医和行医的经历，而且还有过捉鬼和招魂的大胆之举。第四、第五部分是叙述者本人的讲述。第四部分讲的是英兰得知妹妹月兰的丈夫在美国又结了婚，便把在香港的月兰"偷渡"到美国讨回她的权利；但软弱的月兰没有胆量面对丈夫，也不能适应美国的生活环境，最后病死在疯人院。第五部分，追述了叙述者童年的生活经历。叙述者的童年是在压抑和困惑中度过的。不过，她现在终于打破了沉默，像在异国他乡生活13年的女诗人蔡琰那样，用文学形式表达了自己的心声。全书以蔡琰的故事结尾，寓意深长。

　　该作品以"讲故事"的形式，通过充满想象力的虚构与简洁的白描，集中表现一个生活在美国唐人街华人圈中的小女孩在两种相互矛盾的文化影响下，从内心混乱、不知所措到怀疑和反抗，再到寻求自

---

① IQ: intelligence quotient.

我和定位的成长过程,反映了华裔美国人在东西文化冲突中的困境和痛苦,以及在双重文化背景下努力构建新的自我与文化认同的艰难历程。该作品侧重描写了女性在权力不平等社会中的失落和挣扎、沉默和反抗,抒发了她对旧中国男权压迫的愤恨。该小说具有较强的可读性和艺术性。题材涉及文化冲突、移民处境、女性经验、母女关系、个人成长与历史叙述等诸多方面,可从不同角度阅读它。作者打破了传说与现实、虚构与历史的界限,将多种风格相结合,采用多元的叙述视角,灵活转换的时空,使作品充满了传奇色彩和异国情调。其创作思想、主题和手法对其他华裔作家产生了重要的影响。

　　需要指出的是,《女勇士》是一本主要面向西方读者的书。作为一个在美国文化氛围中长大的华裔,汤亭亭对中国文化有着与我们不同的视角,而且也难免受到美国主流文化认知范式的影响。汤亭亭在一次采访中强调了其美国属性。她说:"实际上,我作品中的美国味儿要比中国味儿多得多。我觉得不论是写我自己还是写其他华人,我都是在写美国人。……虽然我写的人物有着让人感到陌生的中国记忆,但他们是美国人。再说我的创作是美国文学的一部分……评论家们还不了解我的文学创作其实是美国文学的另一个传统。"对于指责她歪曲中国神话的批评,她说:"把神话带到大洋彼岸的人成了美国人,同样,神话也成了美国神话。我写的神话是新的、美国的神话。"的确,她笔下的花木兰、关公等已不是中国传统文化中的人物形象了,而是有独特个性的华裔美国版的人物形象。

思考题

1. What do you think about the image of the barbarian used in the narrative?
2. Are there any similarities and differences between the narrator and the character, Ts'ai Yen?
3. Why does Kingston describe the Chinese children as silent at the American school but loud at the Chinese school?
4. What is the importance of the figure of the silent character in the narrative? Can you relate this figure to the dual themes of keeping silence and breaking silence?
5. In what ways does the young narrator attempt to reconcile Chinese and American cultural pressures within her developing sense of personal identity?

China Men (1980)
Tripmaster Monkey: His Fake Book (1989)
The Fifth Book of Peace (2003)

Bruccoli, Matthew J. and Layman Richard, eds. *The Woman Warrior and China Men*. Farmington Hills: The Gale Group, 2001.
Lim, Shirley Geok-lin, ed. *Approaches to Teaching Kingston's The Woman Warrior*. New York: Modern Language Association of America, 1991.
Wong, Sau-ling Cynthia, ed. *Maxine Hong Kingston's The Woman Warrior: A Casebook*. New York and Oxford: Oxford University Press, 1999.

（沈建青）

第二十单元
Leslie Marmon Silko (1948—)

莱丝莉·摩门·西尔柯

 作者简介

  莱丝莉·摩门·西尔柯，美国印第安女作家，出生于新墨西哥北部拉古那地区一个印第安部落的保留地，具有白人、墨西哥人、印第安人混合血统。1969年毕业于新墨西哥大学英语系并开始攻读法学，1971年"弃法从文"，开始写作生涯。1977年，第一部长篇小说《仪式》(Ceremony)出版，获得评论界的高度评价，被公认为美国当代最优秀的小说之一。作品将诗歌和叙事相结合，描写一个混血的土著印第安人在经历第二次世界大战的恐惧和绝望后返回保留地，在寻归印第安历史和传统的过程中获得新生的故事。该作品是迄今所发现的由土著美国女作家发表的第一部长篇小说。1981年，短篇小说和诗集《讲故事的人》(Storyteller)的出版进一步奠定了西尔柯在美国文学史上的重要地位。该作品将自传、历史、神话、摄影与诗歌和小说融合为一体，突出表现了作者对各种文学体裁的大胆探索和实验。

  西尔柯其他主要作品包括诗集《拉古那地区的女人》(Laguna Pueblo Woman, 1974)、短篇小说集《西部故事》(Western Stories, 1980)、书信集《蕾丝的纤巧和力量》(Delicacy and Strength of Lace, 1985)、叙事和摄影作品集《圣水》(Sacred Water: Narratives and Pictures, 1993)、《雨》(Rain, 1996)、散文集《黄女》(Yellow Woman and a Beauty of the Spirit, 1996)、长篇小说《死者的历书》(Almanac of the Dead: A Novel, 1991)、《沙丘里的庭院》(Gardens in the Dunes, 1999)，以及回忆录《绿松石矿脉：一部回忆录》(The Turquoise Ledge: A Memoir, 2010)等。其中，《死者的历书》尤其引人注意。这是一部历经十年完成的巨著，揭示了几百年以来美洲殖民主义所造成的各种后果，具有很强的批判性。

  西尔柯成功地将西方文学传统与美国印第安口头文学的传统结合在一起，再现了当代印第安人生活的方方面面：保护民族传统的重要性、语言和文学在民族文化遗产中的重要地位、人与土地的密切联系、民族权益及文化归属、印第安人遭受贫困与不公的生活现状及其顽强的生存精神、不同文化的相互影响和相互融合等，对当代美国文坛产生了很大影响。她因此获得多项文学奖(其中包括美国土著作家终身成就奖)，并且荣获"活的文化遗产"称号。

Lullaby

  The sun had gone down but the snow in the wind gave off its own light. It came in thick tufts like new wool—washed before the weaver spins it. Ayah reached out for it like her own babies had, and she smiled when she remembered how she had laughed at them. She was an old woman now, and her life had become memories. She sat down with her back against the wide cottonwood tree, feeling the rough bark on her back bones; she faced east and listened to the wind and snow sing a high-pitched Yeibechei① song. Out of the wind she felt warmer, and she could watch the wide fluffy snow fill in her tracks, steadily, until the direction she had come form was gone. By the light of the snow she could see the dark outline of the big arroyo a few feet away. She was sitting on the edge of Cebolleta Creek, where in the springtime the thin cows would graze on grass already chewed flat to the ground. In the wide deep creek bed where only a trickle of water flowed in the summer, the skinny cows would wander, looking for new grass along winding paths splashed with manure.

---

① Yeibechei：印第安纳瓦霍人用于驱除病魔的一首夜曲。

Ayah pulled the old Army blanket over her head like a shawl. Jimmie's blanket—the one he had sent to her. That was a long time ago and the green wool was faded, and it was unraveling on the edges. She did not want to think about Jimmie. So she thought about the weaving and the way her mother had done it. On the tall wooden loom set into the sand under a tamarack① tree for shade. She could see it clearly. She had been only a little girl when her grandma gave her the wooden combs to pull the twigs and burrs from the raw, freshly washed wool. And while she combed the wool, her grandma sat beside her, spinning a silvery strand of yarn around the smooth cedar spindle. Her mother worked at the loom with yarns dyed bright yellow and red and gold. She watched them dye the yarn in boiling black pots full of beeweed petals, juniper berries, and sage. The blankets her mother made were soft and woven so tight that rain rolled off them like birds' feathers. Ayah remembered sleeping warm on cold windy nights, wrapped in her mother's blankets on the hogan's② sandy floor.

The snow drifted now, with the northwest wind hurling it in gusts. It drifted up around her black overshoes—old ones with little metal buckles③. She smiled at the snow which was trying to cover her little by little. She could remember when they had no black rubber overshoes; only the high buckskin leggings④ that they wrapped over their elkhide moccasins⑤. If the show was dry or frozen, a person could walk all day and not get wet; and in the evenings the beams of the ceiling would hang with lengths of pale buckskin leggings, drying out slowly.

She felt peaceful remembering. She didn't feel cold any more. Jimmie's blanket seemed warmer than it had ever been. And she could remember the morning he was born. She could remember whispering to her mother, who was sleeping on the other side of the hogan, to tell her it was time now. She did not want to wake the others. The second time she called to her, her mother stood up and pulled on her shoes; she knew. They walked to the old stone hogan together, Ayah walking a step behind her mother. She waited alone, learning the rhythms of the pains while her mother went to call the old woman to help them. The morning was already warm even before dawn and Ayah smelled the bee flowers blooming and the young willow growing at the springs. She could remember that so clearly, but his birth merged into the births of the other children and to her it became all the same birth. They named him for the summer morning and in English they called him Jimmie.

It wasn't like Jimmie died. He just never came back, and one day a dark blue sedan with white writing on its doors pulled up in front of the boxcar shack where the rancher let the Indians live. A man in a khaki uniform trimmed in gold gave them a yellow piece of paper and told them that Jimmie was dead. He said the Army would try to get the body back and then it would be shipped to them; but it wasn't likely because the helicopter had burned after it crashed. All of this was told to Chato because he could understand English. She stood inside the doorway holding the baby while Chato listened. Chato spoke English like a white man and he spoke Spanish too. He was taller than the white man and he stood straighter too. Chato didn't explain why; he just told the military man they could keep the body if they found it. The white man looked bewildered; he nodded his head and he left. Then Chato looked at her and shook his head, and then he told her, "Jimmie isn't coming home anymore," and when he spoke, he used the words to speak of the dead. She didn't cry then, but she hurt inside with anger. And she mourned him as the years passed, when a horse fell with Chato and broke his leg, and the white rancher told them he wouldn't pay Chato until he could work again. She mourned Jimmie because

---

① tamarack: 美洲落叶松。
② hogan: 北美西南部印第安人(尤其是纳瓦霍族人)用圆木垒成上覆泥土的六边形泥屋,户门朝东。
③ buckle: 鞋上的扣形饰物。
④ buckskin leggings: 用鹿皮做成的绑腿。
⑤ elkhide moccasins: 北美印第安人穿的用鹿皮制的无后跟软底鞋。

he would have worked for his father then; he would have saddled the big bay horse and ridden the fence lines each day, with wire cutters and heavy gloves, fixing the breaks in the barbed wire and putting the stray cattle back inside again.

She mourned him after the white doctors came to take Danny and Ella away. She was at the shack alone that day they came. It was back in the days before they hired Navajo women to go with them as interpreters. She recognized one of the doctors. She had seen him at the children's clinic at Cañoncito about a month ago. They were wearing khaki uniforms and they waved papers at her and a black ball-point pen, trying to make her understand their English words. She was frightened by the way they looked at the children, like the lizard watches the fly. Danny was swinging on the tire swing on the elm tree behind the rancher's house, and Ella was toddling around the front door, dragging the broomstick horse Chato made for her. Ayah could see they wanted her to sign the papers, and Chato had taught her to sign her name. It was something she was proud of. She only wanted them to go, and to take their eyes away from her children.

She took the pen from the man without looking at his face and she signed the papers in three different places he pointed to. She stared at the ground by their feet and waited for them to leave. But they stood there and began to point and gesture at the children. Danny stopped swinging. Ayah could see his fear. She moved suddenly and grabbed Ella into her arms; the child squirmed, trying to get back to her toys. Ayah ran with the baby toward Danny; she screamed for him to run and then she grabbed him around his chest and carried him too. She ran south into the foothills of juniper trees and black lava rock. Behind her she heard the doctors running, but they had been taken by surprise, and as the hills became steeper and the cholla cactus① were thicker; they stopped. When she reached the top of the hill, she stopped to listen in case they were circling around her. But in a few minutes she heard a car engine start and they drove away. The children had been too surprised to cry while she ran with them. Danny was shaking and Ella's little fingers were gripping Ayah's blouse.

She stayed up in the hills for the rest of the day, sitting on a black lava boulder in the sunshine where she could see for miles all around her. The sky was light blue and cloudless, and it was warm for late April. The sun warmth relaxed her and took the fear and anger away. She lay back on the rock and watched the sky. It seemed to her that she could walk into the sky, stepping through clouds endlessly. Danny played with little pebbles and stones, pretending they were birds eggs and then little rabbits. Ella sat at her feet and dropped fistfuls of dirt into the breeze, watching the dust and particles of sand intently. Ayah watched a hawk soar high above them, dark wings gliding; hunting or only watching, she did not know. The hawk was patient and he circled all afternoon before he disappeared around the high volcanic peak the Mexicans called Guadalupe.

Late in the afternoon, Ayah looked down at the gray boxcar shack with the paint all peeled from the wood; the stove pipe on the roof was rusted and crooked. The fire she had built that morning in the oil drum stove had burned out. Ella was asleep in her lap now and Danny sat close to her, complaining that he was hungry; he asked when they would go to the house. "We will stay up here until your father comes," she told him, "because those white men were chasing us." The boy remembered then and he nodded at her silently.

If Jimmie had been there he could have read those papers and explained to her what they said. Ayah would have known then, never to sign them. The doctors came back the next day and they brought a BIA② policeman with them. They told Chato they had her signature and that was all they

---

① cholla cactus: 仙人掌。
② BIA: U. S. Bureau of Indian Affairs: 美国印第安人事务局。

needed. Except for the kids. She listened to Chato sullenly; she hated him when he told her it was the old woman who died in the winter, spitting blood; it was her old grandma who had given the children this disease. "They don't spit blood," she said coldly. "The whites lie." She held Ella and Danny close to her, ready to run to the hills again. "I want a medicine man first," she said to Chato, not looking at him. He shook his head. "It's too late now. The policeman is with them. You signed the paper." His voice was gentle.

It was worse than if they had died: to lose the children and to know that somewhere, in a place called Colorado, in a place full of sick and dying strangers, her children were without her. There had been babies that died soon after they were born, and one that died before he could walk. She had carried them herself, up to the boulders and great pieces of the cliff that long ago crashed down from Long Mesa; she laid them in the crevices of sandstone and buried them in fine brown sand with round quartz pebbles that washed down the hills in the rain. She had endured it because they had been with her. But she could not bear this pain. She did not sleep for a long time after they took her children. She stayed on the hill where they had fled the first time, and she slept rolled up in the blanket Jimmie had sent her. She carried the pain in her belly and it was fed by everything she saw: the blue sky of their last day together and the dust and pebbles they played with; the swing in the elm tree and broomstick horse choked life from her. The pain filled her stomach and there was no room for food or for her lungs to fill with air. The air and the food would have been theirs.

She hated Chato, not because he let the policeman and doctors put the screaming children in the government car, but because he had taught her to sign her name. Because it was like the old ones always told her about learning their language or any of their ways: it endangered you. She slept alone on the hill until the middle of November when the first snows came. Then she made a bed for herself where the children had slept. She did not lie down beside Chato again until many years later, when he was sick and shivering and only her body could keep him warm. The illness came after the white rancher told Chato he was too old to work for him anymore, and Chato and his old woman should be out of the shack by the next afternoon because the rancher had hired new people to work there. That had satisfied her. To see how the white man repaid Chato's years of loyalty and work. All of Chato's fine-sounding English talk didn't change things.

It snowed steadily and the luminous light from the snow gradually diminished into the darkness. Somewhere in Cebolleta a dog barked and other village dogs joined with it. Ayah looked in the direction she had come, from the bar where Chato was buying the wine. Sometimes he told her to go on ahead and wait; and then he never came. And when she finally went back looking for him, she would find him passed out at the bottom of the wooden steps to Azzie's Bar. All the wine would be gone and most of the money too, from the pale blue check that came to them once a month in a government envelope. It was then that she would look at his face and his hands, scarred by ropes and the barbed wire of all those years, and she would think, this man is a stranger; for forty years she had smiled at him and cooked his food, but he remained a stranger. She stood up again, with the snow almost to her knees, and she walked back to find Chato.

It was hard to walk in the deep snow and she felt the air burn in her lungs. She stopped a short distance from the bar to rest and readjust the blanket. But this time he wasn't waiting for her on the bottom step with his old Stetson hat pulled down and his shoulders hunched up in his long wool overcoat.

She was careful not to slip on the wooden steps. When she pushed the door open, warm air and cigarette smoke hit her face. She looked around slowly and deliberately, in every corner, in every dark place that the old man might find to sleep. The bar owner didn't like Indians in there, especially Navajos, but he let Chato come in because he could talk Spanish like he was one of them. The men at the bar stared at her, and the bartender saw that she left the door open wide. Snowflakes were flying inside like moths and melting into a puddle on the oiled wood floor. He motioned to her to close the door, but she did not see him. She held herself straight and walked across the room slowly, searching the room with every step. The snow in her hair melted and she could feel it on her forehead. At the far corner of the room, she saw red flames at the mica window of the old stove door; she looked behind the stove just to make sure. The bar got quiet except for the Spanish polka music playing on the jukebox. She stood by the stove and shook the snow from her blanket and held it near the stove to dry. The wet wool smell reminded her of new-born goats in early March, brought inside to warm near the fire. She felt calm.

In past years they would have told her to get out. But her hair was white now and her face was wrinkled. They looked at her like she was a spider crawling slowly across the room. They were afraid; she could feel the fear. She looked at their faces steadily. They reminded her of the first time the white people brought her children back to her that winter. Danny had been shy and hid behind the thin white woman who brought them. And the baby had not known her until Ayah took her into her arms, and then Ella had nuzzled close to her as she had when she was nursing. The blonde woman was nervous and kept looking at a dainty gold watch on her wrist. She sat on the bench near the small window and watched the dark snow clouds gather around the mountains; she was worrying about the unpaved road. She was frightened by what she saw inside too: the strips of venison drying on a rope across the ceiling and the children jabbering excitedly in a language she did not know. So they stayed for only a few hours. Ayah watched the government car disappear down the road and she knew they were already being weaned from these lava hills and from this sky. The last time they came was in early June, and Ella stared at her the way the men in the bar were now staring. Ayah did not try to pick her up; she smiled at her instead and spoke cheerfully to Danny. When he tried to answer her, he could not seem to remember and he spoke English words with the Navajo[①]. But he gave her a scrap of paper that he had found somewhere and carried in his pocket; it was folded in half, and he shyly looked up at her and said it was a bird. She asked Chato if they were home for good this time. He spoke to the white woman and she shook her head. "How much longer?" he asked, and she said she didn't know; but Chato saw how she stared at the boxcar shack. Ayah turned away then. She did not say good-bye.

She felt satisfied that the men in the bar feared her. Maybe it was her face and the way she held her mouth with teeth clenched tight, like there was nothing anyone could do to her now. She walked north down the road, searching for the old man. She did this because she had the blanket, and there would be no place for him except with her and the blanket in the old adobe barn near the arroyo. They always slept there when they came to Cebolleta. If the money and the wine were gone, she would be relieved because then they could go home again; back to the old hogan with a dirt roof and rock walls where she herself had been born. And the next day the old man could go back to the few sheep they still had, to follow along behind them, guiding them, into dry sandy arroyos where sparse grass grew. She knew he did not like walking behind old ewes when for so many years he rode big quarter horses[②] and worked with cattle. But she wasn't sorry for him; he should have known all along what would happen.

There had not been enough rain for their garden in five years; and that was when Chato finally hitched a ride into the town and brought back brown boxes of rice and sugar and big tin cans of welfare peaches. After that, at the first of the month they went to Cebolleta to ask the postmaster for the check; and then Chato would go to the bar and cash it. They did this as they planted the garden every May, not

---

① Navajo:纳瓦霍人,美国最大的印第安部落。现散居在美国新墨西哥州、亚利桑那州、犹他州。
② quarter horse:夸特马,善于短距离冲刺,原用于1/4英里比赛。

because anything would survive the summer dust, but because it was time to do this. The journey passed the days that smelled silent and dry like the caves above the canyon with yellow painted buffaloes on their walls.

He was walking along the pavement when she found him. He did not stop or turn around when he heard her behind him. She walked beside him and she noticed how slowly he moved now. He smelled strong of woodsmoke and urine. Lately he had been forgetting. Sometimes he called her by his sister's name and she had been gone for a long time. Once she had found him wandering on the road to the white man's ranch, and she asked him why he was going that way; he laughed at her and said, "You know they can't run that ranch without me," and he walked on determined, limping on the leg that had been crushed many years before. Now he looked at her curiously, as if for the first time, but he kept shuffling along, moving slowly along the side of the highway. His gray hair had grown long and spread out on the shoulders of the long overcoat. He wore the old felt hat pulled down over his ears. His boots were worn out at the toes and he had stuffed pieces of an old red shirt in the holes. The rags made his feet look like little animals up to their ears in snow. She laughed at his feet; the snow muffled the sound of her laugh. He stopped and looked at her again. The wind had quit blowing and the snow was falling straight down; the southeast sky was beginning to clear and Ayah could see a star.

"Let's rest awhile," she said to him. They walked away from the road and up the slope to the giant boulders that had tumbled down from the red sandrock mesa throughout the centuries of rainstorms and earth tremors. In a place where the boulders shut out the wind, they sat down with their backs against the rock. She offered half of the blanket to him and they sat wrapped together.

The storm passed swiftly. The clouds moved east. They were massive and full, crowding together across the sky. She watched them with the feeling of horses—steely blue-gray horses startled across the sky. The powerful haunches pushed into the distances and the tail hairs streamed white mist behind them. The sky cleared. Ayah saw that there was nothing between her and the stars. The light was crystalline. There was no shimmer, no distortion through earth haze. She breathed the clarity of the night sky; she smelled the purity of the half moon and the stars. He was lying on his side with his knees pulled up near his belly for warmth. His eyes were closed now, and in the light from the stars and the moon, he looked young again.

She could see it descend out of the night sky: an icy stillness from the edge of the thin moon. She recognized the freezing. It came gradually, sinking snowflake by snowflake until the crust was heavy and deep. It had the strength of the stars in Orion, and its journey was endless. Ayah knew that with the wine he would sleep. He would not feel it. She tucked the blanket around him, remembering how it was when Ella had been with her; and she felt the rush so big inside her heart for the babies. And she sang the only song she knew to sing for babies. She could not remember if she had ever sung it to her children, but she knew that her grandmother had sung it and her mother had sung it:

> *The earth is your mother,*
> > *she holds you.*
> *The sky is your father,*
> > *he protects you.*
> *Sleep,*
> *Sleep.*
> *Rainbow is your sister,*
> > *she loves you.*
> *The winds are your brothers,*
> > *they sing to you.*
> *Sleep,*

Sleep.
We are together always
We are together always
There never was a time
when this
was not so.

　　《摇篮曲》是西尔柯短篇小说集《讲故事的人》中的一个名篇,1974年发表于《芝加哥书评》并获奖,1975年被选入《美国最佳短篇小说选》。故事发生在一个冬天的晚上,一个叫阿雅的印第安老妇人一边到酒吧去寻找丈夫,一边回忆自己一生的经历:大儿子在为政府军队服役时死了,剩下的两个未成年孩子也被白人带走了——虽然他们后来回来看过她两次,但他们和她越来越疏远。失去孩子后,丈夫又被白人农场主榨干油水后解雇。失业后的丈夫变得颓废绝望,经常用酒精来麻痹自己。他们现在又老又穷,靠政府一点可怜的救济生活。失去两个孩子使她对白人的态度由害怕变成了愤怒,也使她对丈夫产生怨恨和隔膜,因为是他教她用英文签名,使她在白人的欺骗下签了让白人带走孩子的文件。当阿雅回忆一生的不幸遭遇时,让她悲伤的不仅是因为她失去了自己的孩子,而且还因为她的民族正在失去自己的传统和语言。不过,她的回忆并不都是痛苦的。她在回忆往事时,也会想起自己儿时与祖母和母亲的亲密关系,想起当年祖母和母亲编织毯子的美好时光,这一甜蜜回忆给予她极大的慰藉和力量。像西尔柯笔下的许多女性人物一样,阿雅坚强而沉着,具有大地母亲一般的胸怀。她后来宽恕了丈夫并陪伴他走完人生的最后路程。故事以一首摇篮曲结束,表达了她对孩子的思念、对祖母和母亲的怀念,也反映了印第安文化对人与大自然和谐关系的强调。作品采用第三人称叙述视角,故事情节主要由老妇人对往事的回忆和感受组成,再现了印第安人文化与白人文化的冲突、印第安人遭受歧视和压迫的历史,以及他们顽强生存的勇气和尊严,而这也是西尔柯创作中的一贯主题。作品语言通俗易懂,描写细致生动,体现了作家将传统和现代、叙事和诗歌融为一体的创作风格。

思考题

1. Discuss the structure of "Lullaby". Is it linear or cyclic?
2. How does the story impress you?
3. What criticisms of the American society are implied in the story?
4. What Navajo cultural values are evident in the story?

Ceremony (1977)
"Storyteller" (1981)
"Yellow Woman" (1996)

参考资料

Bernett, Louise K. and James L. Thorsen, eds. *Leslie Marmon Silko: A Collection of Critical Essays*. Albuquerque: University of New Mexico Press, 1999.

Porter, Joy and Kenneth M. Roemer, eds. *The Cambridge Companion to Native American Literature*. Cambridge: Cambridge University Press, 2005.

Salyer, Gregory. *Leslie Marmon Silko*. New York: Twayne Publishers, 1997.

(沈建青)

第二十一单元
Robert Bly (1926—)
罗伯特·布莱

 作者简介

  罗伯特·布莱生于明尼苏达州,祖籍挪威。1944年加入海军并服役两年,1947年在明尼苏达圣奥拉夫学院学习一年后转至哈佛大学,在哈佛大学期间经常参加文学创作讨论。1956年在挪威从事诗歌翻译期间,发现众多诸如智利诗人聂鲁达(Pablo Neruda)等杰出诗人并不为美国读者所熟悉,于是经过努力创办了诗歌翻译的文学杂志,如《五十年代》(The Fifties)、《六十年代》(The Sixties)和《七十年代》(The Seventies),翻译并介绍了许多著名诗歌作品。1966年与人合建美国作家反对越南战争组织,并多次领导反越战活动。诗歌《人体之光》(The Light Around the Body, 1967)获美国国家图书奖。该诗集反映了布莱反越战的坚定立场,他通过借鉴17世纪德国哲学家雅各布·贝姆的"内在"和"外在"思想,指出完整和谐的人生不应有战争,对越南战争是如何源自美国人内心进行了探索。布莱认为,人体之光只有在征服战争、治愈心灵之后才会出现。《黑衣男子回头》(The Man in the Black Coat Turns, 1981)和《在两个世界爱一个女人》(Loving a Woman in Two Worlds, 1985)分别体现出布莱的"男性意识"和"女性意识",前者主要探索父子关系,后者试图阐释男女两性间复杂关系的发展过程。布莱不仅创作诗歌,而且研究人,尤其是男性的心理。评论家指出,布莱是"席卷美国文化革新运动的催化剂"。《铁约翰:一本有关男人的书》(Iron John: A Book About Men, 1990)中,布莱根据格林童话同名故事追溯男性英雄的成长历程,深入探究当代美国男性的困惑,出版后畅销全球。《同胞社会》(The Sibling Society, 1996)是继《铁约翰:一本有关男人的书》之后的又一本探索男性意识的书,布莱认为当代美国男性处于"青少年"时期,在失去父辈指导后无法承担社会责任。罗伯特·布莱是美国诗歌深层意象运动的代表诗人,他认为,"意象与图画的区别在于,意象是想象力的自然表达,无法来自现实世界,也无法返回现实世界。它是一种源于想象力的动物。"布莱主张发挥想象力,借助深层意象,在"心理跳跃"("psychic leaps")中通过大脑中有意识和无意识两部分来完成诗歌创作。深层意象运动将弗洛伊德和荣格的精神分析理论引入诗歌创作,极大地推动了美国诗歌的发展。

The Buried Train

Tell me about the train that people say got buried
By the avalanche① —was it snow? —It was
In Colorado, and no one saw it happen.
There was smoke from the engine curling up
Lightly through fir tops, and the engine sounds.
There were all those people reading—some
From Thoreau②, some from Henry Ward Beecher③.
And the engineer smoking and putting his head out.
I wonder when that happened. Was it after
High School, or was it the year we were two?

---

① avalanche: 雪崩。
② Thoreau: 梭罗(1817—1862),美国作家,超验主义运动的代表人物,主张回归自然,反对蓄奴制和美国对墨西哥的战争。代表作为《沃尔登湖》。
③ Henry Ward Beecher: 比彻(1813—1887),美国基督教公理会自由派牧师、废奴运动领袖,主张妇女参政,赞成进化论。

We entered this narrow place, and we heard the sound
Above us—the train couldn't move fast enough.
It isn't clear what happened next. Are you and I
Still sitting there in the train, waiting for the lights
To go on? Or did the real train get really buried;
So at night a ghost train comes out and keeps going...

  该诗出自《黑衣男子回头》，通过深层意象"被埋的火车"揭示出现代美国生活的世态炎凉。"被埋的火车"这一深层意象本应让人们对这场灾难产生恐惧，对受难者产生同情，然而第一节中事无巨细、不含任何感情色彩的客观描述——There was smoke from the engine curling up / Lightly through fir tops, and the engine sounds. / There were all those people reading——直接反映出描述者的袖手旁观，更强化了遇难者的孤独无助，这种反讽效果不仅折射出诗人的洞察力，而且烘托出诗人的愤懑。第二节，诗人通过让"我们"介入（"We entered this narrow place, and we heard the sound"），进一步缩短"我们"与灾难之间的距离。令诗人痛心的是，这种亲密接触非但没有加强人与人之间的联系，反而更加突出人与人之间的隔离。"被埋的火车"俨然是现代人的心灵荒原，人类心中膨胀着自我，对同类的灾难视而不见，听而不闻，宛如被埋的火车。诗人采用"被埋的火车"这一深层意象，分别从想象中的旁观者与想象中的亲历者这两个角度对"你和我"漠不关心以及由此产生的隔离感进行细致披露。诗人采用问句邀请读者对个人的行为进行思考，从中可窥见诗人诚恳希望大家从自身做起，互相关心，共同创造和谐生活。至此，该诗实现了"心理飞跃"。这首诗由表及里，用忧郁的笔触传达了诗人对美国文化的忧虑。

 思考题

1. Dash is used four times in this poem. What are its effects?
2. What do the allusions to Thoreau and Henry Ward Beecher imply?
3. Why do you think the engineer is seen "smoking and putting his head out"?
4. To whom do you think "I" pose the question of "Was it after High School, or was it the year we were two"?
5. What does "the ghost train" suggest?
6. Describe the similarities and differences between Imagist poems and Deep Image poems.

Iron John: A Book about Men (1990)
The Light Around the Body (1991)
Loving a Woman in Two Worlds (1985)

参考资料

Davis, William V., ed. *Critical Essays on Robert Bly.* New York: Maxwell Macmillan International, 1992.

Wadden, Paul. *The Rhetoric of Self in Robert Bly and Adrienne Rich: Doubling and the Holotropic Urge.* New York: P. Lang, Publishers, 2003.

White, Terry, ed. *The Sibling Society: Papers Presented at the Robert Bly Colloquium.* Lanham, Md.: University Press of America, 2000.

（李　晋）

John Ashbery (1927—)

约翰·阿什贝利

 作者简介

  约翰·阿什贝利,美国后现代诗歌代表人物之一。生于纽约州罗切斯特。1949年毕业于哈佛大学,1951年获哥伦比亚大学硕士学位,1953年出版第一部诗集《图兰朵及其他诗歌》(*Turandot and Other Poems*),1955年作为富布莱特访问学者赴法国,逗留期间为《先驱论坛报》和《艺术新闻》撰稿,1965年回到纽约,1974年起在大学任教。

  阿什贝利与弗兰克·奥哈拉(Frank O'Hara)、肯尼思·柯克(Kenneth Koch)同为纽约派(New York Poets)核心人物。该派是一个以地域为基础的松散组合,其成员风格各有不同;总体来说,被归于超现实主义流派,通常以诗作中的大众意象、超现实主义思维方式和积极向上的幽默感著称。阿什贝利的诗歌被评论家称作"诗歌的诗歌",主题多是关于诗歌本身的;关注的焦点不是经验本身,而是经验渗透意识的方式,旨在揭示甚至颠覆意义建构的人为性。阿什贝利一度深受美国现代派诗人华莱士·史蒂文斯(Wallace Stevens, 1879—1955)诗风的影响,其诗歌充满了哲性思考。尽管作品经常取材于浪漫主义传统题材,其视角和处理手法却往往前卫,常常与抽象表现主义绘画有异曲同工之处。

  阿什贝利既受实验派艺术家推崇,又能得到学院派批评家认可,这在现当代诗人中是不多见的。其诗集《凸面镜中的自画像》(*Self-Portrait in a Convex Mirror*, 1975)获得美国国家图书奖、普利策奖和全美批评界奖。著名批评家布鲁姆夸赞诗人"把包括惠特曼、迪金森、史蒂文斯、哈特·克兰的美国的严肃性连接起来,从而实现了爱默生对于美国文学自治的幻想的预言"(王家新等编:《二十世纪外国诗人如是说》,河南人民出版社,1992年,第559页)。以下诗歌选自另一部重要诗集《休闲日》(又译《船屋的日子》,*Houseboat Days*, 1977)。

And Ut Pictura Poesis① Is Her Name

You can't say it way anymore.
Bothered about beauty you have to
Come out into the open, into a clearing②,
And rest. Certainly whatever funny happens to you
Is OK. To demand more than this would be strange
Of you, you who have so many lovers,
People who look up to you and are willing
To do things for you, but you think
It's not right, that if they really knew you...
So much for self-analysis③. Now,
About what to put in your poem-painting:

---

① Ut Pictura Poesis:(拉)u.p.p., "as is painting so is poetry"(Horace, Ars Poetica)。公元前1世纪罗马著名诗人贺拉斯在《诗论》中提出的"诗歌绘画性"概念。
② clearing:空地,相当于前面的open一词。
③ self-analysis:自我分析,这里指的是诗中称呼的"你",应为带给诗人创作灵感的缪斯女神。

259

Flowers are always nice, particularly delphinium①.
Names of boys you once knew and their sleds,
Skyrockets② are good—do they still exist?
There are a lot of other things of the same quality
As those I've mentioned. Now one must
Find a few important words, and a lot of low-keyed③,
Dull-sounding ones. She approached me
About buying her desk. Suddenly the street was
Bananas and the clangor④ of Japanese instruments.
Humdrum testaments⑤ were scattered around. His head
Locked into mine. We were a seesaw⑥. Something
Ought to be written about how this⑦ affects
You when you write poetry:
The extreme austerity⑧ of an almost empty mind
Colliding with the lush, Rousseau-like foliage⑨ of its desire to communicate
Something between breaths, if only for the sake
Of others and their desire to understand you and desert you
For other centers of communication⑩, so that understanding
May begin, and in doing so be undone⑪.

　　这里所选的诗作集中体现了诗人对诗歌创作原则的反思。本诗开篇提出的问题是：在现代语境下，"诗歌绘画性"的古典主义诗歌理念已变得不再适用。首先，在题材上，诗歌需要开诚布公地讲述日常发生的趣事，一贯受人仰视的缪斯女神不得不走下神坛，其凡性得到强化。其次，作为传统诗歌要素的浪漫意象遭到质疑，日常生活的平凡事件和琐碎细节被纳入诗歌创作中。另外，在语言上，低调、沉闷的词语多于华丽的辞藻，诗歌风格变得朴素平实。但是，极其空洞平淡的头脑与内涵丰富的交流欲望之间产生了强烈的反差。最后四行诗句表达了诗人在当下语境中的尴尬处境：诗人具有强烈的倾诉欲望，以便得到他人的理解并且让他人了解自己的愿望；可是，一旦理解，对方就会弃之而去。在这个互动过程中，理解与消解几乎同时发生，其中暗含了对当时盛行的解构主义思潮的应和。

　　宇宙的多变性（mutability）以及人类自我意识的多元流动性作为英国文艺复兴和美国超验主义时期的中心主题，也是阿什贝利在诗歌创作中反复思考的一个问题。对他来说，现实是充满变数的意识碎片之组合，而非切实固定的整体，因此，其诗作也就相应地折射出关于这种现实的记忆、印象、欲望碎片及其流动多变性。有评论说"在阅读阿什贝利的作品时，你偶然在这里那里抓住一些清晰的意义，但它们很快就转变成别的陌生的东西，或者迅速消失、融化。"线性时间模式的破坏、传统认知秩序的颠

---

① delphinium：飞燕草，翠雀花，在这里取其读音，并无特别意义。
② skyrocket：流星焰火。
③ low-keyed：低调的，有节制的。
④ clangor：连续的铿锵声，叮当声。
⑤ Humdrum testaments：平淡乏味的遗嘱。
⑥ seesaw：跷跷板。该意象在这里暗示现实的纷纭多变性对个体意识造成的冲击。
⑦ 这里this一词指的是上述所有这些日常生活的琐碎细节，诗人在此提出的问题是：它们是如何影响诗歌创作的。
⑧ austerity：严格，朴素。
⑨ lush：繁茂的，郁郁葱葱的；foliage：树叶。该意象在此与空虚乏味的头脑形成对照，用来比喻强烈的交流欲望。Rousseau：皮埃尔·卢梭（1812—1867），法国风景画家，巴比松画派主要人物之一，该画派诞生于巴黎南郊约50公里处紧挨着枫丹白露森林的一个村落，活跃于19世纪30—40年代，主张描绘具有民族特色的法国农村自然风景。
⑩ other centers of communication：其他交流中心，指具有不同特性的其他意识主体。
⑪ undone：未完成，消解。

覆、意义的随机性、反讽语气等特点都是造成阿什贝利的诗歌晦涩难懂的原因,这些特点可在本诗中窥见一斑,值得深刻探讨。

 思考题

1. The poet sets in contrast two kinds of artistic ideals in this poem. What are they?
2. In illustrating the contemporary poetic practices, who is the speaker addressing? What kind of tone is conveyed, didactic or ironic or whatsoever?
3. What do you make of the last four lines?

"The Painter" (1956)
"Self-Portrait in a Convex Mirror" (1975)
"Chinese Whispers: Poems" (2002)

 参考资料

Herd, David. *John Ashbery & American Poetry*. New York: Farrar, Straus, and Giroux, 2001.
Lehman, D. *Beyond Amazsement: New Essays on John Ashbery*. Ithaca, New York: Cornell University Press, 1980.
Shapiro, D. *John Ashbery: An Introduction to the Poetry*. New York: Columbia University Press, 1979.

(林 斌)

Adrienne Rich (1929—2012)

艾德里安娜·里奇

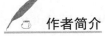 作者简介

  艾德里安娜·里奇生于美国马里兰州巴尔的摩的一个中上层家庭,出生在一家黑人区的医院;父亲有犹太人血统,等待多年也得不到约翰霍普金斯大学的教授职位;祖父留下的遗物包括一支象牙长笛、一只金怀表和一本希伯来语的祷告书。这些都在里奇追溯个人历史的诗歌里有所反映。1951年,里奇毕业于拉德克利夫学院,同年凭诗集《世事一沧桑》(*A Change of World*)获得耶鲁年轻诗人奖。作为评委之一的"现代派"诗人W.H.奥顿(W. H. Auden)在为其诗集所写的序言中评论道:"呈现在读者面前的这些诗有着整洁谦逊的衣着,言说从容平静而不含混,尊重长辈而不畏缩,并且没有谎言:这对于第一部诗集来说,已经相当不俗了。"字里行间多少暴露了男性轻视女性的文化沙文主义心态。

  1953年不顾家人的反对与哈佛大学经济学教授、德系东正教教徒阿尔弗雷德·康拉德结婚,随后生了三个儿子,完全沦为家庭主妇。经过八年之久的沉默,里奇于1963年出版了诗集《儿媳妇的快照》(*Snapshots of a Daughter-in-Law*),倾诉了具有创造力的女性受到压抑的愤懑。1969年和1971年分别出版诗集《传单》(*Leaflets: Poems 1965—1968*)和《改变的意志》(*The Will to Change: Poems 1968—1970*)。里奇在诗歌和散文创作中反映了女性以及女同性恋者在父权社会的成长经历和自我意识觉醒过程,并且将艺术创作与政治行动有效地结合起来,成了20世纪美国激进女权主义的艺术代言人。她写于1971年的著名论文《当我们死人醒来时:作为再修正的写作》(*When We Dead Awaken: Writing as Re-Vision*)和1978年的《强制的异性恋与同性恋的经验》(*Compulsory Heterosexuality and Lesbian Existence*)可谓当代女性主义思想的代表作。1974—1976年间创作的组诗《二十一首恋歌》(*Twenty-One Love Poems*)以她与米雪儿·克利芙(*Michelle Cliff*)之间从隐秘走向公开的同性恋情为主题,是她从女性主义诗人转向女性主义/同性恋诗人的标志性作品。

  里奇的诗歌作品曾多次获奖,曾凭借1973年出版的诗集《潜入沉船》(*Diving into the Wreck*)与金斯堡(Allen Ginsberg, 1926—1997)分享1974年的美国国家图书奖。作品中表现了她在这个阶段把"雌雄同体(androgyny)"看作父权制社会中两性关系调和的理想状态的女性主义思想。以下作品就是出自这个诗集。

Diving into the Wreck

First having read the book of myths,
and loaded the camera,
and checked the edge of the knife-blade,
I put on
the body-armor of black rubber
the absurd flippers
the grave and awkward mask[①].
I am having to do this

---

① the body-armor of black rubber / the absurd flippers / the grave and awkward mask: 黑橡胶的盔甲、脚蹼和面罩构成了全套的潜水用品。

not like Cousteau① with his
assiduous team
aboard the sun-flooded schooner②
but here alone.

There is a ladder.
The ladder is always there
hanging innocently
close to the side of the schooner.
We know what it is for,
we who have used it.
Otherwise
it's a piece of maritime floss③
some sundry④ equipment.

I go down.
Rung after rung⑤ and still
the oxygen immerses me
the blue light
the clear atoms
of our human air.
I go down.
My flippers cripple⑥ me,
I crawl like an insect down the ladder
and there is no one
to tell me when the ocean
will begin.
First the air is blue and then
it is bluer and then green and then
black I am blacking out⑦ and yet
my mask is powerful
it pumps my blood with power
the sea is another story
the sea is not a question of power
I have to learn alone
to turn my body without force
in the deep element⑧.

---

① Cousteau: 科斯特,指雅克·科斯特(1910—1997),法国水下探险家、作家。
② schooner: 斯库纳纵帆船,两桅纵帆船。
③ maritime floss: 海上漂浮物,絮状浮渣。
④ sundry: 各式各样的。
⑤ rung: 梯子的横档,梯级。
⑥ cripple: 使行动不便。
⑦ black out: 昏过去。
⑧ element: 自然环境,此处指海洋。

And now: it is easy to forget
what I came for
among so many who have always
lived here
swaying their crenellated① fans
between the reefs②
and besides
you breathe differently down here.

I came to explore the wreck.
The words are purposes.
The words are maps.
I came to see the damage that was done
and the treasures that prevail③.
I stroke the beam of my lamp
slowly along the flank④
of something more permanent
than fish or weed

the thing I came for:
the wreck and not the story of the wreck
the thing itself and not the myth
the drowned face always staring
toward the sun
the evidence of damage
worn by salt and sway into this threadbare⑤ beauty
the ribs of the disaster
curving their assertion
among the tentative haunters⑥.

This is the place.
And I am here, the mermaid whose dark hair
streams black, the merman in his armored body⑦
We circle silently
about the wreck
we dive into the hold⑧.
I am she: I am he

---

① crenellated: 锯齿状的。
② reef: 暗礁,珊瑚礁。
③ prevail: 盛行,占优势,这里指到处都是。
④ beam: 横梁；flank: 侧翼,侧面。
⑤ threadbare: 磨破了的,陈旧的,陈腐的。
⑥ the ribs of the disaster / curving their assertion / among the tentative haunters: 灾难的肋骨 / 在暂时的逗留者中 / 弯曲地倾诉着。
⑦ mermaid、merman: 美人鱼、雄人鱼,此指男女遇难者的尸体,前者长发飘扬,后者遍身盔甲。
⑧ hold: 船舱。

whose drowned face sleeps with open eyes
whose breasts still bear the stress
whose silver, copper, vermeil① cargo lies
obscurely② inside barrels
half-wedged③ and left to rot
we are the half-destroyed instruments
that once held to a course④
the water-eaten log
the fouled compass

We are, I am, you are
by cowardice or courage
the one who find our way
back to this scene
carrying a knife, a camera
a book of myths
in which
our names do not appear.

这首诗是里奇20世纪70年代诗歌的代表作,表达了诗人对女性命运的关注。首先,如玛格丽特·阿特伍德所说,"沉船"意象象征着"为世人遗忘的神话,特别是关于男女两性的神话"的残骸。诗歌开篇,"我"有备而来,带着一本神话书,而在诗歌结尾处,诗人指出,这是"一本没有我们名字的神话书"。值得注意的是,与男性探险家科斯特不同,"我"没有群体的协助,而是独自一人踏上这段充满未知的旅程:"那里无人告诉我 / 海洋何时 / 开始";"我必须独自学习 / 在深沉的海洋中 / 不费力地转身"。同时,"我"也是抱着特定目标而来,即:亲自搜集证据,以期发现事情的真相——尽管"词语是我的目标 / 词语是地图","我"却并不迷信文字,因为"我为它而来: / 是沉船而非沉船的故事 / 是事物本身而非神话"。结果,"我"看到了死去的同类,与他们相融合,从而获得了跨越时空的群体归属感和历史观。

从诗人特有的女性主义立场出发,"沉船"的意象承载了父权社会中被埋没的女性史。相应地,"潜入沉船"是一个象征性行动,集中体现了整个诗集的"探寻"(quest)主题。在一定程度上,潜水的过程正是女性个体发掘历史,唤醒沉睡的自我的过程。里奇信奉诗歌改变生活乃至带来社会变革的功用,而该诗恰好代表了20世纪六七十年代女权主义者发掘湮没的妇女史、女性文学史的积极行动倡议和艺术创作理念。

 思考题

1. What does the wreck symbolize? And what about the act of diving?
2. What message does the lines "the thing I came for: / the wreck and not the story of the wreck / the thing itself and not the myth" communicate?
3. Why do "I" identify with the mermaid and the merman at once? Who do you think "we" are toward the end of the poem?

---

① vermeil: 朱砂红。
② obscurely: 隐现地,朦胧地。
③ half-wedged: 半楔入的。
④ course: 航线,特定的行程。

"Aunt Jennifer's Tigers" (1951)
"When We Dead Awaken: Writing as Re-Vision" (1971)
"Compulsory Heterosexuality and Lesbian Existence" (1980)

Cooper, Jane R. *Reading Adrienne Rich: Reviews and Re-Visions, 1951—1981*. Ann Arbor: University of Michigan Press, 1984.

Gelpi, Barbara Charlesworth, and Albert Gelpi, eds. *Adrienne Rich's Poetry: A Norton Critical Edition*. New York: WW Norton, 1975.

—. *Adrienne Rich's Poetry and Prose*. New York: WW Norton, 1993.

(林 斌)

Robert Pinsky (1940—)

罗伯特·平斯基

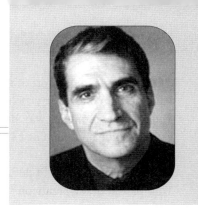

 作者简介

  罗伯特·平斯基生于美国新泽西州,在斯坦福大学获硕士、博士学位。诗歌《悲伤与欢愉》(*Sadness and Happiness*, 1975)用节奏明快的语言勾勒出美国寻常百姓生活的各个侧面,象征"美国诗歌步入充满信心的新时代"。长诗《对美国的一种解释》(*An Explanation of America*, 1980)一反传统诗歌创作手法,回顾美国的历史进程,在诗歌末尾借用12岁女孩的视角揭示商业文化使童趣消失殆尽的残酷现实。《我的心史》(*History of My Heart*, 1985)以诗人回忆其家庭庆祝圣诞节为开端,用冷峻的目光审视这个家庭所经历的酸甜苦辣,并融入他对政治、社会与哲学等问题的思考。该诗获美国诗歌学会设立的威廉·卡洛斯·威廉斯奖。1996年出版的《想象中的车轮:新旧诗选》(*The Figured Wheel: New and Collected Poems 1966—1996*,又译《花车巨轮》),用丰富的想象力展现遍及美国城乡、贫富阶层、男女老少、各色人种的"车轮",再次深刻体现出平斯基作为诗人兼评论家的创新和深邃。该诗集1997年获普里策诗歌奖提名。1997年至2000年,平斯基成为美国历史上第一位连任三届的桂冠诗人。在任桂冠诗人期间,平斯基与人合编《美国最受欢迎的诗歌:最受欢迎的诗歌项目选集》(*Americans' Favorite Poems: The Favorite Poem Project Anthology*, 1999),通过摄像和录音为美国人喜爱的诗歌留下宝贵资料,平斯基认为这种记录具有重要价值,"记录了我们的现在,为未来的教育树立了典范,并见证了或许忽略现有文化的这一事实。"2000年出版的诗集《泽西雨》(*Jersey Rain*)汇集平斯基对各种科技发明的感悟与思考。平斯基的译作《但丁的地狱》(*The Inferno of Dante*)荣获美国诗歌学会的诗歌翻译奖。平斯基现担任网络周刊《石板色》(*Slate*)的诗歌编辑,并在波士顿大学讲授文学创作课程。平斯基诗歌的特点主要表现在:一、关注现代技术与诗歌创作的联系;二、对平凡人生的辩证思考;三、使用丰富多彩的典故;四、在继承诗歌传统的基础上有所创新。

To Television

Not a "window on the world"
But as we call you,
A box a tube①

Terrarium② of dreams and wonders.
Coffer of shades, ordained
Cotillion of phosphors
Or liquid crystal

Raster dance,③
Quick one, little thief, escort

---

① tube:(美俚)电视。
② Terrarium: 陆栖小动物饲养箱。
③ Coffer: 保险箱。ordain: 注定。 Cotillion: 法国花式舞;早期法国交谊舞。phosphor: 磷光体。Raster: (电)光栅。

267

Of the dying and comfort of the sick, In a blue glow my father and little sister sat
Snuggled① in one chair watching you
Their wife and mother was sick in the head
I scorned you and them as I scorned so much
Homey miracle, tub
Of acquiescence, vein of defiance.
Your patron in the pantheon② would be Hermes

Now I like you best in a hotel room,
Maybe minutes
Before I have to face an audience: behind
The doors of the armoire, box
Within a box—Tom & Jerry, or also brilliant
And reassuring, Oprah Winfrey.③

Thank you, for I watched, I watched
Sid Caesar④ speaking French and Japanese not
Through knowledge but imagination,
His quickness, and Thank You, I watched live
Jackie Robinson⑤ stealing
Home, the image—O strung shell—enduring
Fleeter than light like these words we
Remember in, they too winged
At the helmet and ankles.

  《致电视》选自《泽西雨》,是诗人关注科技发明与诗歌创作之间关系的一个例证。诗人对电视的态度似难以捉摸:富有哲理的话语让读者领略到电视具有白衣天使的功效,"陪伴垂危的人,安抚卧榻的病人"("escort of the dying and comfort of the sick")。然而,诗人对电视的态度并非完全赞赏,电视作为大众媒体固然已成为人类生活不可或缺的一部分并且能改善人类生活,但它是否展示生活的真谛,诗人对此表示怀疑。诗人随即将电视与古希腊神话人物联系起来,一方面使读者认识到高科技发展如此迅猛以至于想象中的神话人物特征已成为现实,另一方面又暗示大众对电视到了顶礼膜拜的地步。电视传播速度之快,范围之广,堪称古罗马神话中的信神赫尔墨斯。电视为广大观众提供各种层次的娱乐节目,男女老少都成为电视的俘虏。诗人巧妙地将电视媒体切换到文字媒介,画龙点睛地突出了本诗的核心:诗的语言犹如头盔和双脚都长有双翼、科学与发明的象征的信神赫尔墨斯;与转瞬即逝的电视节目相比,诗歌将流芳千古,会真正深入人心。正如平斯基1999年在斯坦福大学毕业典礼上所讲,"诗歌的媒介就是人的声音。根据这种媒介的本质,诗歌就要与大众艺术保持平衡。"《致电视》借助电视这一娱乐媒介抒发诗人力图普及诗歌这一美好愿望,恰恰印证了诗人借助网络技术让诗歌进入百姓人家这一事实。

---

① Snuggle:偎依。
② pantheon:罗马万神殿。 Hermes:(希腊神话)赫尔墨斯(众神的使者,并为掌管疆界、道路、商业以及科学发明、辩才、幸运、灵巧之神,也是盗贼、赌徒的保护神)。
③ armoire:大型衣橱。 Tom & Jerry:美国《猫和老鼠》动画片。 Oprah Winfrey:美国著名黑人脱口秀女主持人。
④ Sid Caesar:美国著名喜剧家,擅长模仿外国语言。
⑤ Jackie Robinson:美国著名黑人棒球明星。

思考题

1. What does "a window on the world" suggest about television?
2. How can television be the "escort of the dying and comfort of the sick"?
3. For what reason do you think the speaker scorns the father and the little sister?
4. What relevance does television bear to Hermes?
5. Is there any purpose in the speaker's listing of so many celebrities?
6. Describe the poet's attitude toward television.

An Explanation of America (1980)
The Figured Wheel: New and Collected Poems 1966—1996 (1996)
History of My Heart (1985)

Matthias, John. *Five American Poets: Robert Hass, John Matthias, James McMichael, John Peck, Robert Pinsky*. New York: Persea Books, 1981.
Pinsky, Robert. *Democracy, Culture and the Voice of Poetry*. Princeton, New Jersey: Princeton University Press, 2002.

(李 晋)

Rita Dove (1952—　)

丽塔·达夫

 作者简介

　　丽塔·达夫,美国黑人女诗人,生于俄亥俄州,艾奥瓦大学获美术硕士学位。出版的诗集有《街角的黄房子》(*The Yellow House on the Corner*, 1980),《博物馆》(*Museum*, 1983),《托马斯和比尤拉》(*Thomas and Beulah*, 1986),其中《托马斯和比尤拉》于1987年获普利策诗歌奖,是继格温德琳·布鲁克斯(Gwendolyn Brooks)1950年获普利策诗歌奖后第二个获此殊荣的美国黑人诗人。1993年,达夫成为美国历史上最年轻的桂冠诗人,也是第一位黑人桂冠诗人,并连任两届。不过,达夫并不情愿被贴上美国黑人诗人的标签,她将自己首先定位为诗人,认为诗歌创作与种族无关。在担任桂冠诗人期间,达夫积极组织各种与诗歌相关的活动,倡导儿童阅读诗歌,为普及诗歌教育做出了贡献;此外,达夫还组织作家们从艺术角度研究非洲移民社群。达夫的诗歌语言质朴无华,将抒情与叙事有机结合起来,主题涵盖微观的生活事件与宏观的历史事件,以个人情感、家庭关系、历史事件、古代神话等相互交融为特点。正如达夫曾说过的,"个人的与历史的同样重要。"《托马斯和比尤拉》通过描写诗人外祖父母的生活历程生动呈现出南方农村黑人移居北方城市的历史画卷。《母爱》(*Mother Love*, 1995)是诗人对希腊神话人物得墨忒耳(Demeter)、珀尔塞弗涅(Persephone)以及冥王(Hades)的现代阐释,诗人根据这一神话框架用十四行诗传达出母爱的局限性以及母女之间相互依赖又相互独立的复杂关系。《与罗莎·帕克斯乘坐公共汽车》(*On the Bus with Rosa Parks*, 1999)诗集中的诗歌巧妙地将现代人纳入历史时空,既有对历史的体验,又有对人生的思考。最近出版的诗集有《美式平滑》(*American Smooth*, 2004)。达夫认为"诗歌是最精炼和最有力的语言"。因此,她的诗歌简洁明快,语颇隽永,耐人寻味。

My Mother Enters the Work Force

The path to ABC Business School
was paid for by a lucky sign:
Alterations①, Qualified Seamstress Inquire Within②.
Tested on Sleeves, hers
never puckered — puffed or sleek,③
Leg o' or Raglan —④
they barely needed the damp cloth
to steam them perfect.

Those were the afternoons. Evenings
she took in piecework, the treadle machine⑤
with its locomotive whir

---

① Alterations: 对衣服做的改动。
② Qualified Seamstress Inquire Within: 优秀女裁缝,欢迎咨询。
③ puckered: 折成褶的。puffed: 泡泡袖。sleek: 平整的。
④ Leg o': Leg-of-mutton 一头宽一头窄的,近似三角形的。Raglan: 套袖的,插肩袖的。
⑤ piecework: 计件工作。treadle machine: 脚踏缝纫机。

traveling the lit path of the needle
through quicksand taffeta①
or velvet deep as a forest.
And now and now sang the treadle,
I know, I know...

And then it was day again, all morning
at the office machines, their clack and chatter
another journey—rougher,
that would go on forever
until she could break a hundred words
with no errors—ah, and then
no more postponed groceries,
and that blue pair of shoes!

  《我母亲加入劳动大军》是首叙事兼抒情诗,该诗通过简练的叙事引出"我"对母亲的敬仰和同情。第一节中的"幸运招牌"("lucky sign")可谓一举三得:首先,流露出母亲的自豪("Qualified Seamstress");其次,表达出"我"对母亲自力更生精神的敬意;最后,却悄无声息地将注意力从这块令人陶醉的"幸运招牌"转移到母亲自己的穿戴上。这一颇具反讽意义的转折将贫富不均的阶级差异前景化。第二节用丰富的感官意象和拟人手法再现母亲挑灯夜战的情景:脚踏缝纫机喻喻作响暗喻"流沙塔夫绸"("quicksand taffeta")与明喻"天鹅绒深似森林"("velvet deep as a forest")比喻这些布料将母亲吞没,从而呈现母亲不堪重负的情形。诗人还通过拟人法进一步强化读者对"我"母亲的同情:踏板缝纫机的声音犹如雇主不容置疑的催促:"马上,马上"("And now and now"),"我"母亲疲惫不堪的应答,"我明白,我明白"("I know, I know")。第三节中的听觉与视觉意象巧妙结合,深刻再现母亲作为工人阶级一员含辛茹苦、单调乏味的现实生活。譬如,母亲敲打字机的嗒嗒声("clack and chatter")与上一节缝纫机发出的喻喻声遥相呼应,母亲的生命似乎注定在机器轰鸣声中日渐消耗。然而,诗人笔锋突转,随之出现的"那双蓝鞋子!"("that blue pair of shoes!")饱含母亲的期盼和乐观心态。全诗从细处着手,用精炼而有力的语言和丰富多彩的意象婉转表达出"我"对母亲的敬佩之情。正如诗人所说,"我情愿探索最亲密的时刻,那些和我们生活紧密相连的更微小、更晶莹剔透的细节。"

思考题

1. How do you understand "lucky sign"?
2. Why do you think "Those were the afternoons" is followed by "Evenings..."?
3. In what ways are "traveling" (in the second stanza) and "another journey" (in the third stanza) significant?
4. Describe the differences between "my" mother's sewing work and typing work. Why is the latter a "rougher" journey?
5. Explain the function of "ah, and then" in the last stanza.
6. State the reason why the poet entitles the poem "My Mother Enters the Work Force."

---

① quicksand taffeta:如流沙般的塔夫绸。

American Smooth (2004)
On the Bus with Rosa Parks (1999)
Grace Notes (1987)

Ingersoll, Earl G., ed. *Conversations with Rita Dove.* Jackson: University Press of Mississippi, 2003.
Therese, Steffen. *Crossing Color: Transcultural Space and Place in Rita Dove's Poetry, Fiction, and Drama.* New York: Oxford University Press, 2001.

(李　晋)

Gary Soto (1952—)

加里·索托

 作者简介

  加里·索托，美籍墨西哥人后裔，出生在富饶的加利福尼亚州圣约魁谷弗雷斯诺市的一个工人阶级家庭，早年受过良好的教育，受到普利策奖诗人菲利普·莱文(Philip Levine)的影响对文学产生兴趣，1973年在《爱荷华评论》(*Iowa Review*)上发表首篇诗作，1977年出版首部诗集《圣约魁谷要素》(*The Elements of San Joaquin*)，同年开始任教于加州大学伯克利分校，至今获得过包括古根海姆奖和美国诗人协会奖在内的多个重要诗歌奖项，是入选《诺顿现代诗选》的诗人中最年轻的一位。1995年，索托凭诗集《新诗精选》(*New and Selected Poems*)获得洛杉矶时报图书奖和美国国家图书奖两项提名奖。

  索托诗风平易朴实，创作中往往以童年时代所熟悉的场所和少数族裔的生活经历为素材，加州弗雷斯诺的街道和他自己的家庭成员经常出现在作品中。"失去"(loss)被看作记忆的一个必不可少的成分。虽然索托笔下的墨西哥裔美国家庭多半经济拮据窘迫，面临诸多生活难题，但是，他仅仅着眼于问题及其解决方法，并非表达怨天尤人的消极情绪。其作品集中反映丰富多彩的民族文化，强调以家庭为核心的价值观，有助于美国社会消除历史上墨西哥人懒惰的负面形象，树立健康积极的少数族裔形象，并且为后殖民主义研究提供了颇为有效的文本参照。

Mexicans Begin Jogging

At the factory I worked
In the fleck of rubber①, under the press②
Of an oven yellow with flame,
Until the border patrol③ opened
Their vans and my boss waved for us to run.
"Over the fence④, Soto," he shouted,
And I shouted that I was American.
"No time for lies," he said, and pressed
A dollar in my palm, hurrying me
Through the back door.
Since I was on his time⑤, I ran
And became the wag to a short tail of Mexicans—⑥
Ran past the amazed crowds that lined
The street and blurred like photographs, in rain.

---

① fleck of rubber：橡胶颗粒。
② press：熨烫。
③ border patrol：边境巡逻队，专门负责追查遣返非法越界人员。
④ Over the fence：跳过栅栏。
⑤ Since I was on his time：在他的工作时间里。由于"我"是受雇于老板，所以只好奉命开始奔跑。
⑥ the wag to a short tail of Mexicans：在美国的白人主流社会中，作为少数族裔的墨西哥移民(合法或非法)被边缘化。诗人在这里将其比作动物躯干以外的一条短短的尾巴，"我"这个个体则在奔跑中引起了这条短尾的摆动。

I ran from that industrial road to the soft
Houses where people paled at the turn of an autumn sky①.
What could I do but yell *vivas*②
To baseball, milkshakes, and those sociologists
Who would clock me③
As I jog into the next century
On the power of a great, silly grin④.

How Things Work

Today it's going to cost us twenty dollars
To live. Five for a softball⑤. Four for a book,
A handful of ones for coffee and two sweet rolls⑥,
Bus fare, rosin⑦ for your mother's violin.
We're completing our task. The tip I left
For the waitress filters down⑧
Like rain, wetting the new roots of a child⑨,
Perhaps, a belligerent cat⑩ that won't let go
Of a balled sock⑪ until there's chicken to eat.
As far as I can tell, daughter, it works like this:
You buy bread from a grocery, a bag of apples
From a fruit stand, and what coins
Are passed on helps others buy pencils, glue,
Tickets to a movie in which laughter
Is thrown into their faces.⑫
If we buy goldfish, someone tries on a hat.
If we buy crayons, someone walks home with a broom.
A tip, a small purchase⑬ here and there,
And things just keep going. I guess.

---

① the soft / Houses where people paled at the turn of an autumn sky：这里指贫民住宅区。按照字面的意思，房屋在雨中变得松软，人们在秋凉的天气中变得面色苍白。诗人通过这两个意象暗示了少数族裔贫民居住条件的恶劣和生活的窘迫。
② viva：意大利、西班牙语中"万岁"的欢呼，欢呼声。
③ baseball, milkshakes, and those sociologists / Who would clock me：棒球和奶昔都是美国中产阶级大众文化的代表；更具讽刺意味的是，那些社会学家理应对少数族裔的现状了如指掌，却无力改变，只能一味用计时等方法采集数据。
④ On the power of a great, silly grin：傻乎乎地咧嘴大笑，表示一种处事态度。意思是，促使"我"继续奔跑前行的力量唯有装傻充愣，自欺欺人。
⑤ softball：垒球。这里指一场垒球比赛。
⑥ sweet rolls：甜面包卷。
⑦ rosin：松香。
⑧ filter down：逐渐渗透。此处采用"陌生化"技巧，将付小费与细雨的意象联系起来，表示尽管微不足道，却由于连绵不断而产生累积效应，达到"润物细无声"的效果。对于付费者来说，累计起来，这会是一笔不小的开支。
⑨ wetting the new roots of a child：打湿一个孩子新生的毛发。暗指小费的去向：一方付出的小费很可能会帮助对方养育一个孩子。
⑩ a belligerent cat：执拗的猫。
⑪ a balled sock：卷成一团的袜子。
⑫ Tickets to a movie in which laughter / Is thrown into their faces：在电影中，人们享受到难得的欢笑。这里的动词"抛撒"代表了诗人对商业化社会娱乐活动的一种讽刺态度，花钱买到的快乐被轻率而粗暴地掷到人们的脸上去。
⑬ a small purchase：购物的小笔开支。

作品赏析

与其家庭背景和成长经历相对应,索托的诗歌创作有两个主要特征:

其一是鲜明的自传体特性,尤其是他的种族和群体意识。诗人的工人阶级出身和少数族裔身份赋予了他独特的文化视角以及对边缘群体所处困境的敏锐感知力和为受压迫人群代言的强烈责任感。他曾这样明确表述过自己的政治立场:"我信奉穷人的文化。"

可以说,这个特征在前一首诗里得以集中体现。开篇三行诗句交代了"我"身处的恶劣工作环境:空气中悬浮着橡胶颗粒,炉火烧得正旺,热浪逼人。随后,边境巡逻人员的到来打断了单调的工作,老板招呼工人们赶快逃跑,以免这些人被作为非法移民抓获而给自身带来麻烦。"我"也在其中,老板不理会"我"是合法公民的辩解,硬塞给"我"一美元,命令"我"跑。在雨中,"我"从工业区一直穿越少数族裔贫民窟,心中苦楚,却只能依靠傻乎乎咧嘴大笑的力量活下去。

其二则是生动的日常生活题材和朴素的生活口语。诗人擅长从熟悉的日常生活场景中提炼素材,具有将司空见惯的庸常事件化入诗歌语境的高超技巧。这里所选的两首短诗分别集中体现了上述特征。特别值得注意的是,与美国诗歌传统相符,诗中的主要意象多半取自于自然;然而,与经典主流诗风相异,自然意象并非旨在营造超脱尘世的美感,而是为了强化生活艰辛的主题。

后一首短诗借助于日常生活场景,采用了口语体语言,读来通俗平实,朗朗上口。开篇所直接称呼的"我们"以及第四行所指的"你"到第十行才得到具体化处理:该诗是一名父亲对女儿所讲的心里话。随之,语境也得以具体化,即父亲带年幼的女儿一起出发去逛街购物,前五行相当于列举了当天的开销预算清单(看球赛、买书、喝咖啡、吃甜点、乘坐公共汽车、买母亲拉小提琴用的松香,总共20美元),从中可以推知这是一个普通的美国中产阶级家庭。诗句通过可以为孩童所接受的一连串具体而浅显的实例解释了消费社会人类生存链条的运作方式,这其中体现了人际间紧密的相互依存关系,颇具朴素的哲理性。

思考题

1. What is the Mexican immigrants' situation in the American context? How is ethnic identity constructed in the first poem?
2. What kind of attitude toward life does "a great, silly grin" indicate? What does the first poem imply about the illegal immigrants' pursuit of the American dream?
3. Describe the specific view of human life and relationship the father imparts to his daughter in the second poem.

推荐作品

Living Up the Street: Narrative Recollections (1985)
New and Selected Poems (1995)
"Like Mexicans" (2000)

参考资料

Orr, Tamra. *Gary Soto*. New York: Rosen Publishing Group, 2005.

(林　斌)

第二十二单元
David Alan Mamet (1947—   )
大卫·艾伦·马麦特

 作者简介

大卫·马麦特，美国剧作家、电影剧本作家和导演。他出生于芝加哥，到佛蒙特州的戈达德学院读完大学后又回到芝加哥。他在好几家工厂和一家房地产经纪公司工作过，也做过出租车司机，这些经历都反映在他的剧作中。20世纪70年代，他最早的几部剧作《鸭子变奏曲》(*The Duck Variations*, 1972)、《芝加哥的性错乱》(*Sexual Perversity in Chicago*, 1974；电影1986，改名为《关于昨夜》)、《美国水牛》(*American Baffalo*, 1976；电影1996)等在"外百老汇"上演，使他成为美国当代最有影响的剧作家之一。他以后的剧作包括：《剧院里的生活》(*A Life in the Theatre*, 1977)、《埃德蒙》(*Edmond*, 1982；电影2005)、《快点耕耘》(*Speed-the-Plow*, 1987)、《格林格里·葛兰·罗斯》(*Glengarry Glen Ross*, 1983；电影1992)、《奥利安娜》(*Oleanna*, 1993；电影1994)、《密码》(*The Cryptogram*, 1995)、《老街区》(*The Old Neighborhood*, 1997)、《波士顿婚姻》(*Boston Marriage*, 1999)等。

马麦特擅长描写社会下层(包括中产阶级下层)孤单无助的人物，他们拙于表达，时有暴力或者欺诈行为。他笔下的人物包括推销员、无业游民和街头无赖；他们以不同的方式追寻着"美国梦"，但大多以失败告终。他们生活在一个世风日下的社会，而他们自己也是造成这一道德荒原的罪魁祸首。马麦特的戏剧语言具有极为独特的风格，被称为"马麦特式的语言"(Mametspeak)。这种语言具有生活和街头语言的节奏和风格，既粗俗猥亵，又简洁明快，富有诗意；马麦特的剧作甚至简洁到没有任何舞台说明。

在美国，以百老汇为基地、以少数"严肃艺术家"为代表的主流戏剧时代似乎已经完结；取而代之的是外百老汇(Off Broadway)、外外百老汇(Off Off Broadway)、地区剧院(regional theaters)，以及剧作家、电影剧本作家、导演、演员等各显身手的"后现代"戏剧。在这样一个时代，马麦特是一位将以上诸种成分、诸多角色集于一身的重要人物。作为电影编剧，马麦特不仅将自己的剧作《美国水牛》《埃德蒙》《格林格里·葛兰·罗斯》《奥里安娜》等改编为电影剧本，而且还改编了多部小说，其中包括：《邮差总按两次铃》(*The Postman Always Rings Twice*, 1981)、《判决》(*The Verdict*, 1982)、《摇尾狗》(*Wag the Dog*, 1997)、《汉尼拔》(*Hannibal*, 2001)等。他还创作了多部电影剧本，其中又有数部由他自己亲自执导，搬上电影屏幕，例如《赌场》(*House of Games*, 1987)、《杀人拼图》(*Homicide*, 1991)、《西班牙囚犯》(*The Spanish Prisoners*, 1998)、《欲望小镇》(*State and Main*, 2000)等。马麦特也曾在影片中担任角色。将戏剧与电影结合起来，将创作与改编结合起来，这也许正是"后戏剧"时代和数码时代的典型特点。

 作品

Oleanna
ACT ONE

JOHN *is talking on the phone*. CAROL *is seated across the desk from him*.

JOHN (*on phone*) And what about the land. (*Pause*) The land. And what about the land? (*Pause*) What about it? (*Pause*) No. I don't understand. Well, yes, I'm I'm... no, I'm *sure* it's signif ... I'm sure it's significant. (*Pause*) Because it's significant to mmmmmm... did you call Jerry? (*Pause*) Because ... no, no, no, no, no. What did they say...? Did you speak to the *real* estate... where *is* she ...? Well, well, all right. Where are her notes? Where are the notes we took with her? (*Pause*) I thought you were? No. No, I'm sorry, I didn't mean that, I just thought that I saw you, when we were there... what ...? I thought I saw you with a *pencil*. WHY NOW? Is what I'm say...well, that's why I say "call Jerry." Well, I can't right now, be ... no, I didn't schedule any ... Grace: *I didn't* ... I'm well aware ... Look: Look. Did you call Jerry? Will you call Jerry ...? Because I can't now. I'll be there, I'm sure I'll be there in fifteen, in twenty. I intend to. No, we aren't *going* to lose the, we aren't *going* to lose the house. Look: look, I'm not minimizing it. The "easement." Did she say "easement"? (*Pause*) What did she *say*; *is* it a "term of art," are we *bound* by it ... I'm sorry ... (*Pause*) are: we: yes. *Bound* by ... Look: (*He checks his watch.*) before the other side *goes home*, all right? "a term of art①." Because: that's right (*Pause*) The yard for the boy. Well, that's the whole ... Look: I'm going to meet you there ... (*He checks his watch.*) Is the realtor there? All right, tell her to show you the basement again. Look at the *this* because ... Bec ... I'm leaving in, I'm leaving in ten or fifteen ... Yes. No, no, I'll meet you at the new ... That's a good. If he thinks it's necc ... you tell Jerry to meet ... All right? We *aren't* going to lose the deposit. All right? I'm sure it's going to be ... (*Pause*) I hope so. (*Pause*) I love you, too. (*Pause*) I love you, too. As soon as ... I will.

(He hangs up.) (*He bends over the desk and makes a note.*) (*He looks up.*) (*To* CAROL:) I'm sorry ...

CAROL	(*Pause*) What is a "term of art"?
JOHN	(*Pause*) I'm sorry ...?
CAROL	(*Pause*) What is a "term of art"?
JOHN	Is that what you want to talk about?
CAROL	... to talk about ...?
JOHN	Let's take the mysticism out of it, shall we? Carol? (*Pause*) Don't you think? I'll tell you: when you have some "thing." Which must be broached. (*Pause*) Don't you think ...? (*Pause*)
CAROL	... don't I think ...?
JOHN	Mmm?
CAROL	... did I ...?
JOHN	... what?
CAROL	Did ... did I ... did I say something wr ...
JOHN	(*Pause*) No. I'm sorry. No. You're right. I'm very sorry. I'm somewhat rushed. As you see. I'm sorry. You're right. (*Pause*) What is a "term of art"? It seems to mean a *term*, which has come, through its use, to mean something *more specific* than the words would, to someone *not acquainted* with them ... indicate. That, I believe, is what a "term of art," would mean. (*Pause*)
CAROL	You don't know what it means ...?
JOHN	I'm not sure that I know what it means. It's one of those things, perhaps you've had them, that, you look them up, or have someone explain them to you, and you say "aha," and, you immediately *forget* what ...
CAROL	You don't do that.
JOHN	... I ...?
CAROL	You don't do ...
JOHN	... I don't, what ...?
CAROL	... for ...
JOHN	... I don't for ...
CAROL	... no ...
JOHN	... forget things? Everybody does that.
CAROL	No, they don't.
JOHN	They don't ...
CAROL	No.
JOHN	(*Pause*) No. Everybody does that.
CAROL	Why would they do that ...?
JOHN	Because. I don't know. Because it doesn't interest them.
CAROL	No.

---

① a term of art: 专门术语。在电话里，约翰提到房地产经纪人（realtor）使用了一些"专门术语"，其中包括"easement"（地役权；在他人土地上的通行权）。卡罗尔对此甚为好奇，询问"专门术语"是什么意思。但约翰并不想回答这一与她的功课无关的问题，所以居高临下地反问："这就是你想谈的事情么?"随后，他感到自己的态度有些生硬，所以又词不达意地进行了解释。剧中，"专门术语"是"话语权"的最重要内容：卡罗尔先是被学术的"专门术语"拒之门外，后来又因为女权的话语而掌控了权力。

JOHN   I think so, though. (*Pause*) I'm sorry that I was distracted.
CAROL   You don't have to say that to me.
JOHN   You paid me the compliment, or the "obeisance" —all right—of coming in here... All right. *Carol*. I find that I am at a *standstill*. I find that I ...
CAROL   ... what ...
JOHN   ... one moment. In regard to your ... to your ...
CAROL   Oh, oh. You're buying a new house!
JOHN   No, let's get on with it.
CAROL   "get on"? (*Pause*)
JOHN   I know how ... *believe* me. I know how ... potentially *humiliating* these ... I have no desire to ... I have no desire other than to help you. But: (*He picks up some papers on his desk.*) I won't even say "but." I'll say that as I go back over the ...
CAROL   I'm just, I'm just trying to ...
JOHN   ... no, it will not do.
CAROL   ... what? What will ...?
JOHN   No. I see, I see what you, it ... (*He gestures to the papers.*) but your work ...
CAROL   I'm just: I sit in class I ... (*She holds up her notebook.*) I take notes ...
JOHN (*simultaneously with "notes"*) Yes, I understand. What I am trying to *tell* you is that some, some basic ...
CAROL   ... I ...
JOHN   ... one moment: some basic missed communi ...
CAROL   I'm doing what I'm told. I bought your book, I read your ...
JOHN   No, I'm sure you ...
CAROL   No, no, no. I'm doing what I'm told. It's *difficult* for me. It's *difficult* ...
JOHN   ... but ...
CAROL   I don't ... lots of the *language* ...
JOHN   ... please ...
CAROL   The *language*, the "things" that you say ...
JOHN   I'm sorry. No. I don't think that that's true.
CAROL   It *is* true. I ...
JOHN   I think ...
CAROL   It *is* true.
JOHN   ... I ...
CAROL   Why would I ...?
JOHN   I'll tell you why: you're an incredibly bright girl.
CAROL   ... I ...
JOHN   You're an incredibly... you have no problem with the ... Who's kidding who?
CAROL   ... I ...
JOHN   No. No. I'll tell you why. I'll tell ... I think you're *angry*, I ...
CAROL   ... why would I ...
JOHN   ... wait one moment. I ...
CAROL   It *is* true. I have *problems* ...
JOHN   ... every ...
CAROL   ... I come from a different *social* ...
JOHN   ... ev ...
CAROL   a different economic ...
JOHN   ... Look:
CAROL   No. I: when I *came* to this school:
JOHN   Yes. Quite ... (*Pause*)
CAROL   ... does that mean nothing ...?
JOHN   ... but look: look ...
CAROL   ... I ...

JOHN	(*Picks up paper.*) Here: Please: Sit down. (*Pause*) Sit down. (*Reads from her paper.*) "I think that the ideas contained in this work express the author's feelings in a way that he intended, based on his results." What can that mean? Do you see? What ...
CAROL	I, the best that I ...
JOHN	I'm saying, that perhaps this course ...
CAROL	No, no, no, you can't, you can't ... I have to ...
JOHN	... how ...
CAROL	... I have to pass it ...
JOHN	Carol, I:
CAROL	I *have* to pass this course, I ...
JOHN	Well.
CAROL	... don't you ...
JOHN	Either the ...
CAROL	... I ...
JOHN	... either the, I ... either the *criteria* for judging progress in the class are ...
CAROL	No, no, no, no, I have to pass it.
JOHN	Now, look: I'm a human being, I ...
CAROL	I did what you told me. I did, I did everything that, I read your *book*, you told me to buy your book and read it. Everything you *say* I ... (*She gestures to her notebook.*) (*The phone rings.*) I do. ...Ev ...
JOHN	... look:
CAROL	... everything I'm told ...
JOHN	Look. Look. I'm not your *father*. (*Pause*)
CAROL	What?
JOHN	I'm.
CAROL	Did I say you were my father?
JOHN	... no ...
CAROL	Why did you say that ...?
JOHN	I ...
CAROL	... why ...?
JOHN	... in class I ... (*He picks up the phone.*) (*Into phone:*) Hello. I can't talk now. Jerry? Yes? I underst ... I can't talk now. I know ... I know ... Jerry. I can't *talk* now. Yes, I. Call me back in ... Thank you. (*He hangs up.*) (*To* CAROL:) What do you want me to do? We are two people, all right? Both of whom have subscribed to ...
CAROL	No, no ...
JOHN	... certain arbitrary ...
CAROL	No. You have to help me.
JOHN	Certain institutional ... you tell me what you want me to do ... You tell me what you want me to ...
CAROL	How can I go back and tell them the *grades* that I ...
JOHN	... what can I do ...?
CAROL	Teach me. Teach me.
JOHN	... I'm trying to teach you.
CAROL	I read your book. I read it. I don't under ...
JOHN	... you don't understand it.
CAROL	No.
JOHN	Well, perhaps it's not well *written* ...
CAROL	(*simultaneously with* "written") No. No. No. I want to *understand* it.
JOHN	What don't you understand? (*Pause*)
CAROL	*Any* of it. What you're trying to say. When you talk about ...
JOHN	... yes ...? (*She consults her notes.*)
CAROL	"Virtual warehousing of the young" ...

JOHN	"Virtual warehousing of the young." If we artificially prolong adolescence ...①
CAROL	... and about "The Curse of Modern Education."
JOHN	... well ...
CAROL	I don't ...
JOHN	Look. It's just a *course*, it's just a *book*, it's just a ...
CAROL	No. No. There are *people* out there. People who came *here*. To know something they didn't *know*. Who *came* here. To be helped. To be *helped*. So someone would *help* them. To *do* something. To *know* something. To get, what do they say? "To get on in the world." How can I do that if I don't, if I fail? But I don't *understand*. I don't *understand*. I don't understand what anything means... and I walk around. From morning 'til night: with this one thought in my head. I'm *stupid*.
JOHN	No one thinks you're stupid.
CAROL	No? What am I ...?
JOHN	I ...
CAROL	... what am I, then?
JOHN	I think you're angry. Many people are. I have a *telephone* call that I have to make. And an *appointment*, which is rather *pressing*; though I sympathize with your concerns, and though I wish I had the time, this was not a previously scheduled meeting and I ...
CAROL	... you think I'm nothing ...
JOHN	... have an appointment with a *realtor*, and with my wife and ...
CAROL	You think that I'm stupid.
JOHN	No. I certainly don't.
CAROL	You said it.
JOHN	No. I did not.
CAROL	You did.
JOHN	When?
CAROL	... you ...
JOHN	No. I never did, or never would say that to a student, and ...
CAROL	You said, "What can that mean?" (*Pause*) "What can that mean?" ... (*Pause*)
JOHN	... and what did that mean to you ...?
CAROL	That meant I'm stupid. And I'll never learn. That's what that meant. And you're right.
JOHN	... I ...
CAROL	But then. But then, what am I doing here...?
JOHN	... if you thought that I ...
CAROL	... when nobody wants me, and ...
JOHN	... if you interpreted ...
CAROL	Nobody *tells* me anything. And I *sit* there ... in the *corner*. In the *back*. And everybody's talking about "this" all the time. And "concepts," and "precepts" and, and, and, and, and, WHAT IN THE WORLD ARE YOU *TALKING* ABOUT? And I read your book. And they said, "Fine, go in that class." Because you talked about responsibility to the young. I DON'T KNOW WHAT IT MEANS AND I'M *FAILING* ...
JOHN	May ...
CAROL	No, you're right. "Oh, hell." I failed. Flunk me out of it. It's garbage. Everything I do. "The ideas contained in this work express the author's feelings." That's right. That's right. I know I'm stupid. I know what I am. (*Pause*) I know what I am, Professor. You don't have to tell me. (*Pause*) It's pathetic. Isn't it?
JOHN	... Aha ... (*Pause*) Sit down. Sit down. Please. (*Pause*) Please sit down.
CAROL	Why?
JOHN	I want to talk to you.
CAROL	Why?
JOHN	Just sit down. (*Pause*) Please. Sit down. Will you, please ...? (*Pause. She does so.*) Thank you.

---

① 约翰试图解释卡罗尔无法理解的书中内容和术语:"Virtual warehousing of the young"的意思就是"人为延长青春期"。

CAROL   What?
JOHN   I want to tell you something.
CAROL   (*Pause*) What?
JOHN   Well, I know what you're talking about.
CAROL   No. You don't.
JOHN   I think I do. (*Pause*)
CAROL   How can you?
JOHN   I'll tell you a story about myself. (*Pause*) Do you mind? (*Pause*) I was raised to think myself stupid. That's what I want to tell you. (*Pause*)
CAROL   What do you mean?
JOHN   Just what I said. I was brought up, and my earliest, and most persistent memories are of being told that I was stupid. "You have such *intelligence*. Why must you behave so *stupidly*?" Or, "Can't you *understand*? Can't you *understand*?" And I could *not* understand. I could *not* understand.
CAROL   What?
JOHN   The simplest problem. Was beyond me. It was a mystery.
CAROL   What was a mystery?
JOHN   How people learn. How *I* could learn. Which is what I've been speaking of in class. And of *course* you can't hear it. Carol. Of *course* you can't. (*Pause*) I used to speak of "real people," and wonder what the *real* people did. The *real* people. Who were they? *They* were the people other than myself. The *good* people. The *capable* people. The people who could do the things, I *could* not do: learn, study, retain ... all that *garbage*— which is what I have been talking of in class, and that's *exactly* what I have been talking of—If you are told... Listen to this. If the young child is told he cannot understand. Then he takes it as a *description* of himself. What am I? I am *that which can not understand*. And I saw you out there, when we were speaking of the concepts of ...
CAROL   I can't understand any of them.
JOHN   Well, then, that's *my* fault. That's not your fault. And that is not verbiage. That's what I firmly hold to be the truth. And I am sorry, and I owe you an apology.
CAROL   Why?
JOHN   And I suppose that I have had some *things* on my mind .... We're buying a *house*, and ...
CAROL   People said that you were stupid ...?
JOHN   Yes.
CAROL   When?
JOHN   I'll tell you when. Through my life. In my childhood; and, perhaps, they stopped. But I heard them continue.
CAROL   And what did they say?
JOHN   They said I was incompetent. Do you see? And when I'm tested the, the, the *feelings* of my youth about the *very subject of learning* come up. And I ... I become, I feel "unworthy," and "unprepared." ...
CAROL   ... yes.
JOHN   ... eh?
CAROL   ... yes.
JOHN   And I feel that I must fail. (*Pause*)
CAROL   ... but then you *do* fail. (*Pause*) You have to. (*Pause*) Don't you?
JOHN   A *pilot*. Flying a plane. The pilot is flying the plane. He thinks: Oh, my God, my mind's been drifting! Oh, my God! What kind of a cursed imbecile am I, that I, with this so precious cargo of *Life* in my charge, would allow my attention to wander. Why was I born? How deluded are those who put their trust in me, ... et cetera, so on, and he crashes the plane.
CAROL   (*Pause*) He could just ...
JOHN   That's right.
CAROL   He could say:
JOHN   My attention *wandered* for a moment ...
CAROL   ... uh huh ...
JOHN   I had a *thought* I did not like ... but now:

CAROL	... but now it's ...
JOHN	That's what I'm telling you. It's time to put my attention ... see: it is not: this is what I learned. It is Not Magic. Yes. Yes. *You*. You are going to be frightened. When faced with what may or may not be but which you are going to perceive as a test. You will become frightened. And you will say: "I am incapable of ..." and everything *in* you will think these two things. "I must. But I can't." And you will think: Why was I born to be the laughingstock of a world in which everyone is better than I? In which I am entitled to nothing. Where I can not learn. (*Pause*)
CAROL	Is that ... (*Pause*) Is that what I have ...?
JOHN	Well. I don't know if I'd put it that way. Listen: I'm talking to you as I'd talk to my son. Because that's what I'd like him to have that I never had. I'm talking to you the way I wish that someone had talked to me. I don't know how to do it, other than to be *personal*, ...but ...
CAROL	Why would you want to be personal with me?
JOHN	Well, you see? That's what I'm saying. We can only interpret the behavior of others through the screen we ... (*The phone rings.*) Through ... (*To phone:*) Hello ...? (*To CAROL:*) Through the screen we create. (*To phone:*) Hello. (*To CAROL:*) Excuse me a moment. (*To phone:*) Hello? No, I can't talk nnn ... I know I did. In a few ... I'm ... is he coming to the ... yes. I talked to him. We'll meet you at the No, because I'm with a *student*. It's going to be fff ... This is important, too. I'm with a *student*, Jerry's going to ... Listen: the sooner I get off, the sooner I'll be down, all right. I love you. Listen, listen, I said "I love you," it's going to work *out* with the, because I feel that it is, I'll be right down. All right? Well, then it's going to take as long as it takes. (*He hangs up.*) (*To CAROL:*) I'm sorry.
CAROL	What was that?
JOHN	There are some problems, as there usually are, about the final agreements for the new house.
CAROL	You're buying a new house.
JOHN	That's right.
CAROL	Because of your promotion.
JOHN	Well, I suppose that that's right.
CAROL	Why did you stay here with me?
JOHN	Stay here.
CAROL	Yes. When you should have gone.
JOHN	Because I like you.
CAROL	You like me.
JOHN	Yes.
CAROL	Why?
JOHN	Why? Well? Perhaps we're similar. (*Pause*) Yes. (*Pause*)
CAROL	You said "everyone has problems."
JOHN	Everyone has problems.
CAROL	Do they?
JOHN	Certainly.
CAROL	You do?
JOHN	Yes.
CAROL	What are they?
JOHN	Well. (*Pause*) Well, you're perfectly right. (*Pause*) If we're going to take off the Artificial *Stricture*, of "Teacher," and "Student,"[①] why should *my* own problems be any more a mystery than your own? Of *course* I have problems. As you saw.
CAROL	... with what?
JOHN	With my *wife* ... with work ...
CAROL	With work?
JOHN	Yes. And, and, perhaps my problems are, do you see? *Similar* to yours.

---

① the Artificial Stricture, of "Teacher," and "Student": "教师"和"学生"之间的人为限制。

CAROL Would you tell me?
JOHN All right. (*Pause*) I came *late* to teaching. And I found it Artificial. The notion of "I know and you do not"; and I saw an *exploitation* in the education process. I told you. I hated school, I hated teachers. I hated everyone who was in the position of a "boss" because I *knew*— I didn't *think*, mind you, I *knew* I was going to fail. Because I was a fuckup. I was just no goddamned good. When I ... late in life ... (*Pause*) When I *got out from under* ... when I worked my way out of the need to fail. When I ...[①]
CAROL How do you do that? (*Pause*)
JOHN You have to look at what you are, and what you feel, and how you act. And, finally, you have to look at how you act. And say: If that's what I *did*, that must be how I think of myself.
CAROL I don't understand.
JOHN If I fail all the time, it must be that I think of myself as a failure. If I do not want to think of myself as a failure, perhaps I should begin by *succeeding* now and again. Look. The tests, you see, which you encounter, in school, in college, in life, were designed, in the most part, for idiots. By *idiots*. There is no need to fail at them. They are not a test of your worth. They are a test of your ability to retain and spout back misinformation. Of *course* you fail them. They're *nonsense*. And I ...
CAROL ... no ...
JOHN Yes. They're *garbage*. They're a *joke*. Look at me. Look at me. The Tenure Committee. The Tenure Committee. Come to judge me. The Bad Tenure Committee. The "Test." Do you see? They put me to the test. Why, they had people voting on me I wouldn't employ to wax my car. And yet, I go before the Great Tenure Committee, and I have an urge, to *vomit*, to, to, to puke my *badness* on the table, to show them: "I'm not good. Why would you pick *me*?"
CAROL They granted you tenure.
JOHN Oh no, they announced it, but they haven't *signed*. Do you see? "At any moment ..."
CAROL ... mmm ...
JOHN "They might not *sign*" ... I might not ... the *house* might not go through ... Eh? Eh? They'll find out my "dark secret." (*Pause*)
CAROL ... what is it ...?
JOHN There *isn't* one. But *they* will find an index of my badness ...
CAROL Index?
JOHN A "... pointer." A "Pointer." You see? Do you see? I *understand* you. I. Know. That. Feeling. Am I entitled to my job, and my nice *home*, and my *wife*, and my *family*, and so on. This is what I'm saying: That theory of education which, that *theory*:
CAROL I ... I ... (*Pause*)
JOHN What?
CAROL I ...
JOHN What?
CAROL I want to know about my grade. (*Long pause*)
JOHN Of course you do.
CAROL Is that bad?
JOHN No.
CAROL Is it bad that I asked you that?
JOHN No.
CAROL Did I upset you?
JOHN No. And I apologize. Of *course* you want to know about your grade. And, of course, you can't concentrate on anyth ... (*The telephone starts to ring.*) Wait a moment.
CAROL I should go.
JOHN I'll make you a deal.

[①] 为了帮助卡罗尔,约翰试图表现得与她完全平等。所以,他不仅告诉卡罗尔他过去遭受过歧视,现在正在遭受现行制度的折磨,而且为了套近乎,他还使用了本剧中少见的脏字。但这其实表现了他的自我中心主义:他没有直接讨论卡罗尔的问题,而是变成了倾诉和抱怨的一方,希望以此与对方沟通。

CAROL   No, you have to ...
JOHN   Let it ring. I'll make you a deal. You stay here. We'll start the whole course over. I'm going to say it was not you, it was I who was not paying attention. We'll start the whole course over. Your grade is an "A." Your final grade is an "A." (*The phone stops ringing.*)
CAROL   But the class is only half over ...
JOHN   (*simultaneously with* "over") Your grade for the whole term is an "A." If you will come back and meet with me. A few more times. Your grade's an "A." Forget about the paper. You didn't like it, you didn't like writing it. It's not important. What's important is that I awake your interest, if I can, and that I answer your questions. Let's start over.[①] (*Pause*)
CAROL   Over. With what?
JOHN   Say this is the beginning.
CAROL   The beginning.
JOHN   Yes.
CAROL   Of what?
JOHN   Of the class.
CAROL   But we can't start over.
JOHN   I say we can. (*Pause*) I say we can.
CAROL   But I don't believe it.
JOHN   Yes, I know that. But it's true. What is The Class but you and me? (*Pause*)
CAROL   There are rules.
JOHN   Well. We'll break them.
CAROL   How can we?
JOHN   We won't tell anybody.
CAROL   Is that all right?
JOHN   I say that it's fine.
CAROL   Why would you do this for me?
JOHN   I like you. Is that so difficult for you to ...
CAROL   Um ...
JOHN   There's no one here but you and me. (*Pause*)
CAROL   All right. I did not understand. When you referred ...
JOHN   All right, yes?
CAROL   When you referred to hazing.
JOHN   Hazing.
CAROL   You wrote, in your book. About the comparative ... in the comparative ... (*She checks her notes.*)
JOHN   Are you checking your notes ...?
CAROL   Yes.
JOHN   Tell me in your own ...
CAROL   I want to make sure that I have it right.
JOHN   No. Of course. You want to be exact.
CAROL   I want to know everything that went on.
JOHN   ... that's good.
CAROL   ... so I ...
JOHN   That's very good. But I was suggesting, many times, that that which we wish to retain is retained oftentimes, I think, *better* with less expenditure of effort.
CAROL   (*Of notes*) Here it is: you wrote of *hazing*.
JOHN   ... that's correct. Now: I said "hazing." It means ritualized annoyance.[②] We shove this book at you, we say read it. Now, you say you've read it? I think that you're *lying*. I'll *grill* you, and when I find you've lied, you'll be

---

① 约翰决定完全抛开学校的规则,这表现出他对于自己权力的自信。但约翰的"权力"恰恰是"规则"赋予的;破坏了规则,约翰便丧失了他"控制"卡罗尔的权力。
② 约翰解释"hazing"的意思是"仪式化的难为"。按他下面举的例子,教育正是这种对于学生的"仪式化的难为"。

disgraced, and your life will be ruined. It's a sick game. Why do we do it? Does it educate? In no sense. Well, then, what is higher education? It is something-other-than-useful.

CAROL   What is "something-other-than-useful?"
JOHN   It has become a ritual, it has become an article of faith[①]. That all must be subjected to, or to put it differently, that all are entitled to Higher Education. And my point...
CAROL   You disagree with that?
JOHN   Well, let's address that. What do you think?
CAROL   I don't know.
JOHN   What do you think, though? (*Pause*)
CAROL   I don't know.
JOHN   I spoke of it in class. Do you remember my example?
CAROL   Justice.
JOHN   Yes. Can you repeat it to me? (*She looks down at her notebook.*) Without your notes? I ask you as a favor to me, so that I can see if my idea was interesting.
CAROL   You said "justice" ...
JOHN   Yes?
CAROL   ... that all are entitled ... (*Pause*) I ... I ... I ...
JOHN   Yes. To a speedy trial. To a fair trial. But they needn't be given a trial *at all* unless they stand accused. Eh? Justice is their right, should they choose to avail themselves of it, they should have a fair trial. It does not follow, of necessity, a person's life is incomplete without a trial in it. Do you see? My point is a confusion between equity and *utility* arose.[②] So we confound the usefulness of higher education with our, granted, right to equal access to the same. We, in effect, create a *prejudice* toward it, completely independent of ...
CAROL   ...that it is prejudice that we should go to school?
JOHN   Exactly. (*Pause*)
CAROL   How can you say that? How ...
JOHN   Good. Good. *Good.* That's right! Speak up! What is a prejudice? An unreasoned belief. We are all subject to it. None of us is not. When it is threatened, or opposed, we feel anger, and feel, do we not? As you do now. Do you not? Good.
CAROL   ... but how can you ...
JOHN   ... let us examine. Good.
CAROL   How ...
JOHN   Good. Good. When ...
CAROL   I'M SPEAKING ... (*Pause*)
JOHN   I'm sorry.
CAROL   How can you ...
JOHN   ... I beg your pardon.
CAROL   That's all right.
JOHN   I beg your pardon.
CAROL   That's all right.
JOHN   I'm sorry I interrupted you.
CAROL   That's all right.
JOHN   You were saying?
CAROL   I was saying ... I was saying ... (*She checks her notes.*) How can you say in a class. Say in a college class, that college education is prejudice?
JOHN   I said that our predilection for it ...

---

① an article of faith: 一种信仰；一个信条。
② My point is a confusion between equity and *utility* arose.: 我的观点是出现了将平等与应用混为一谈的情况。他在下一句解释说:"我们将高等教育的用途与我们被赋予的平等享受高等教育的权利混为一谈。"联系到他前面举的"正义"的例子，说"这并不必然意味着未经历过审判，一个人的一生就会不完整"。他的意思是:虽然人人都有受高等教育的权利，但这并不意味着高等教育有用，也并不意味着每一个人都必须接受"审讯"(Grill)似的考试和"仪式化的为难"。

CAROL	Predilection ...
JOHN	... you know what that means.
CAROL	Does it mean "liking"?
JOHN	Yes.
CAROL	But how can you say that? That College ...
JOHN	... that's my *job*, don't you know.
CAROL	What is?
JOHN	To provoke you.
CAROL	No.
JOHN	Oh. Yes, though.
CAROL	To provoke me?
JOHN	That's right.
CAROL	To make me mad?
JOHN	That's right. To force you ...
CAROL	... to make me mad is your job?
JOHN	To force you to ... listen: (*Pause*) Ah. (*Pause*) When I was young somebody told me, —are you ready?—the rich copulate less often than the poor. But when they do, they take more of their clothes off. Years. Years, mind you, I would compare experiences of my own to this dictum, saying, aha, that fits the norm, or ah, this is a variation from it. What did it mean? Nothing. It was some jerk thing, some school kid told me that took up room inside my head. (*Pause*)
	Somebody told *you*, and you hold it as an article of faith, that higher education is an unassailable good. This notion is so dear to you that when I question it you become angry. Good. Good, I say. Are not those the very things which we should question? I say college education, since the war, has become so a matter of course, and such a fashionable necessity, for those either of or aspiring *to* to[①] the new vast middle class, that we *espouse* it, as a matter of right, and have ceased to ask, "What is it good for?" (*Pause*)
	What might be some reasons for pursuit of higher education?
	One: A love of learning.
	Two: The wish for mastery of a skill.
	Three: For economic betterment. (*Stops. Makes a note.*)
CAROL	I'm keeping you.
JOHN	One moment. I have to make a note ...
CAROL	It's something that I said?
JOHN	No, we're buying a house.
CAROL	You're buying the new house.
JOHN	To go with the tenure. That's right. Nice *house*, close to the *private school* ... (*He continues making his note.*) ... We were talking of eco- nomic *betterment* (CAROL *writes in her notebook.*) ... I was thinking of the School Tax. (*He continues writing.*) (*To himself:*) ... where is it written that I have to send my child to public school .... Is it a law that I have to improve the City Schools at the expense of my own interest? And, is this not simply *The White Man's Burden*[②]? Good. And (*Looks up to* CAROL) ... does this interest you?
CAROL	No. I'm taking notes ...
JOHN	You don't have to take notes, you know, you can just listen.
CAROL	I want to make sure I remember it. (*Pause*)
JOHN	I'm not lecturing you, I'm just trying to tell you some things I think.
CAROL	What do you think?

---

① 因为这是两个人的对话,有停顿、重复的地方。在此,约翰重复了"to",以示强调。

② *The White Man's Burden*:原出处为英国小说家和诗人卢迪亚·吉卜林(Rudyard Kipling)在1899年写的一首诗。他在诗中敦促美国像英国和欧洲其他老牌帝国主义国家一样,担负起"帝国"的责任。"白人的负担"已被认为是种族主义和帝国主义的辞藻。约翰后来受到性别歧视和精英主义的指控;他在此无意地或者是玩世不恭地使用这一说法,颇具讽刺意味。

JOHN	Should all kids go to college? *Why* ...
CAROL	(*Pause*) To learn.
JOHN	But if he does not learn.
CAROL	If the child does not learn?
JOHN	Then why is he in college? Because he was told it was his "right"?
CAROL	Some might find college instructive.
JOHN	I would hope so.
CAROL	But how do they feel? Being told they are wasting their time?
JOHN	I don't think I'm telling them that.
CAROL	You said that education was "prolonged and systematic hazing."
JOHN	Yes. It can be so.
CAROL	... if education is so bad, why do you do it?
JOHN	I do it because I love it. (*Pause*) Let's ... I suggest you look at the demographics, wage-earning capacity, college- and non-college- educated men and women, 1855 to 1980, and let's see if we can wring some worth from the statistics. Eh? And ...
CAROL	No.
JOHN	What?
CAROL	I can't understand them.
JOHN	... you ...?
CAROL	... the "charts." The *Concepts*, the ...
JOHN	"Charts" are simply ...
CAROL	When I leave here ...
JOHN	Charts, do you see ...
CAROL	No, I can't ...
JOHN	You can, though.
CAROL	NO, NO—I DON'T UNDERSTAND. DO YOU SEE??? I DON'T *UNDERSTAND* ...
JOHN	What?
CAROL	*Any* of it. *Any* of it. I'm *smiling* in class, I'm *smiling*, the whole time. What are you *talking* about? What is everyone *talking* about? I don't *understand*. I don't know what it *means*. I don't know what it means to *be* here ... you tell me I'm intelligent, and then you tell me I should not be *here*, what do you *want* with me? What does it *mean*? Who should I *listen* to ... I ...
	(*He goes over to her and puts his arm around her shoulder.*)
	NO! (*She walks away from him.*)
JOHN	Sshhhh.
CAROL	No, I don't under ...
JOHN	Sshhhhh.
CAROL	I don't know what you're *saying* ...
JOHN	Sshhhhh. It's all right.
CAROL	...I have no ...
JOHN	Sshhhhh. Sshhhhh. Let it go a moment. (*Pause*) Sshhhh ... let it go. (*Pause*) Just let it go. (*Pause*) Just let it go. It's all right. (*Pause*) Sshhhhh. (*Pause*) I understand ... (*Pause*) What do you feel?
CAROL	I feel bad.
JOHN	I know. It's all right.
CAROL	I ... (*Pause*)
JOHN	What?
CAROL	I ...
JOHN	What? Tell me.
CAROL	I don't understand you.
JOHN	I know. It's all right.
CAROL	I ...
JOHN	What? (*Pause*) What? *Tell* me.

CAROL	I can't tell you.
JOHN	No, you must.
CAROL	I can't.
JOHN	No. Tell me. (*Pause*)
CAROL	I'm bad. (*Pause*) Oh, God. (*Pause*)
JOHN	It's all right.
CAROL	I'm ...
JOHN	It's all right.
CAROL	I can't talk about this.
JOHN	It's all right. Tell me.
CAROL	Why do you want to know this?
JOHN	I don't want to know. I want to know whatever you ...
CAROL	I always ...
JOHN	... good ...
CAROL	I always ... all my life ... I have never told anyone this ...
JOHN	Yes. Go on. (*Pause*) Go on.
CAROL	All of my life ... (*The phone rings.*) (*Pause. JOHN goes to the phone and picks it up.*)
JOHN	(*into phone*) I can't talk now. (*Pause*) What? (*Pause*) Hmm. (*Pause*) All right, I ... I. Can't. Talk. Now. No, no, no, I *Know* I did, but ... What? Hello. What? She *what*? She *can't*, she said the agreement is void? How, how is the agreement *void*? *That's Our House.* I have the *paper*; when we come down, next week, with the payment, and the paper, that house is ... wait, wait, wait, wait, wait, wait, wait: Did Jerry ... is Jerry there? (*Pause*) Is *she* there ...? Does she have a *lawyer* ...? How the *hell*, how the *Hell*. That is ... it's a question, you said, of the *easement*. I don't underst ... it's not the *whole agreement*. It's just the *easement*, why would she? Put, put, put, *Jerry* on. (*Pause*) Jer, *Jerry*: What the *Hell* ... that's my *house*. That's ... Well, I'm, no, no, no, I'm *not* coming ddd ... List, *Listen, screw* her. You *tell* her. You, listen: I want you to take *Grace*, you take Grace, and get out of that house. You *leave* her there. Her and her lawyer, and you *tell* them, we'll see them in court next ... no. No. Leave her there, leave her to *stew* in it: You tell her, we're *getting* that house, and we are going to ... No. I'm *not* coming down. I'll be damned if I'll sit in the same rrr ... the next, you tell her the next time I *see* her is in court ... I ... (*Pause*) What? (*Pause*) What? I don't understand. (*Pause*) Well, what about the house? (*Pause*) There isn't any problem with the hhh ... (*Pause*) No, no, no, that's all right. All ri ... All right ... (*Pause*) Of course. Tha ... Thank you. No, I will. Right away. (*He hangs up.*) (*Pause*)
CAROL	What is it? (*Pause*)
JOHN	It's a surprise party.
CAROL	It is.
JOHN	Yes.
CAROL	A party for you.
JOHN	Yes.
CAROL	Is it your birthday?
JOHN	No.
CAROL	What is it?
JOHN	The tenure announcement.
CAROL	The tenure announcement.
JOHN	They're throwing a party for us in our new house.
CAROL	Your new house.
JOHN	The house that we're buying.
CAROL	You have to go.
JOHN	It seems that I do.
CAROL	(*Pause*) They're proud of you.
JOHN	Well, there are those who would say it's a form of aggression.
CAROL	What is?
JOHN	A surprise.

作品赏析

《奥利安娜》涉及"政治正确""性骚扰""女权立场"等美国社会的敏感话题,所以曾引起很大争议。该剧开始时,大学教师约翰正在办公室与女学生卡罗尔谈话。卡罗尔性格忧郁、缺乏自信、拙于交流;她学习吃力,显然无法理解很多专业术语,也无法了解约翰的想法。约翰认为卡罗尔很聪明,但并未发挥出潜能,所以学习成绩很差。在谈话中,约翰不断接到妻子 Grace 和朋友 Jerry 的电话,谈论购买房屋和他本人申请终身教职(tenure)的事情。他对终身教职审批委员会的做法颇有微词,对整个高等教育也持批评态度。所以,他对卡罗尔的处境极为同情,并提出要帮助她。他说只要不告诉别人,他们两人就可以抛开规则,两人私下上课,据此重新给出成绩。约翰居高临下,完全掌控着学术权力,卡罗尔对此极为不满,而且她也对约翰用肢体语言表示亲近做出了她自己的判断。在女权组织的支持下,她控告约翰性骚扰、性别歧视、精英主义。在这之后,约翰与她又在办公室见面,要求她撤销指控。在沟通失败之后,卡罗尔拒绝了约翰的要求并要离去。约翰试图阻止她离去,进而发生了肢体上的冲突。卡罗尔这时已通过女权话语掌控了权力,而约翰则反而处于弱势。她还威胁要对约翰提出殴打和强奸未遂的刑事指控;面对着这一切,约翰举起一把椅子,真的要砸向卡罗尔。但我们不知道这是惶恐之举,还是孤注一掷。

该剧上演前,恰逢劳伦斯·托马斯大法官任命听证会的风波。时任美国总统乔治·布什提名保守的非洲裔美国人劳伦斯·托马斯担任美国最高法院大法官;但在国会听证时,他以前的下属、俄克拉荷马大学法学女教授安妮塔·希尔却对他提出了性骚扰的指控。这使工作场合的性骚扰问题成为全美国关注的热点。马麦特否认因为该事件而创作《奥利安娜》,但又承认在事件之后才将搁置已久的该剧最终完成。该剧反映了美国社会的热点问题,反映了"权力"和"支配话语"在"强势"和"弱势"群体之间的转移。但在更深的层面,该剧也反映了人与人之间的隔阂;尤其反映了在"权力""性别政治""政治正确"等话语的侵蚀下,人类生存中的异化状态。

因为该剧以大学教育为背景,剧中人物大多有良好的教养,所以马麦特其他剧作中的粗鲁猥亵的语言在该剧中出现较少,这使该剧有异于剧作家的惯常风格。该剧的剧名也有象征意义:这是一位19世纪的挪威歌唱家试图在西宾夕法尼亚州建立的一个理想化的、井然有序的住宅区,但其计划以失败告终。所以,"《奥利安娜》是一部关于失败了的乌托邦的剧作;是一个失败了的学术乌托邦的个案。"(马麦特语)

本剧共分为三幕,而本单元的课文为第一幕,主要表现约翰尚处于优势地位时对卡罗尔居高临下的指导、关怀和套近乎。

思考题

1. How does the telephone conversation interact with the conversation between John and Carol?
2. How does John deal with Carol's problem? What are his strategies?
3. Can any of John's language and gestures be interpreted as sexual harassment? Are they all proper?

Sexual Perversity in Chicago (1974)
American Buffalo (1976)
Glengarry Glen Ross (1983)

 参考资料

Bigsby, Christopher, ed. *The Cambridge Companion to David Mamet*. Cambridge: Cambridge University Press, 2004.
SparkNotes: Oleanna. From http:// www.sparknotes.com/drama/ oleanna/.

(程朝翔)